PLATO AND HEIDEGGER

FRANCISCO J. GONZALEZ

PLATO AND HEIDEGGER

A QUESTION OF DIALOGUE

THE PENNSYLVANIA STATE UNIVERSITY PRESS
UNIVERSITY PARK, PENNSYLVANIA

Library of Congress Cataloging-in-Publication Data

Gonzalez, Francisco J., 1963–
Plato and Heidegger : a question of dialogue/
Francisco J. Gonzalez.
    p.   cm.
Includes bibliographical references and index.
Summary: "A study of Martin Heidegger's engagement
with the philosophy of Plato. Examines how Heidegger's
understanding—and misunderstanding—of Plato
can help in assessing Heidegger's own philosophical
program"—Provided by publisher.
ISBN 978-0-271-03558-1 (cloth : alk. paper)
ISBN 978-0-271-03559-8 (pbk : alk. paper)
1. Heidegger, Martin, 1889–1976.
2. Plato.
I. Title.

B3279.H49G588 2009
193—dc22
2009009914

Copyright © 2009 The Pennsylvania State University
All rights reserved
Printed in the United States of America
Published by The Pennsylvania State University Press,
University Park, PA 16802-1003

The Pennsylvania State University Press is a
member of the Association of American University Presses.

It is the policy of The Pennsylvania State University Press
to use acid-free paper. Publications on uncoated stock satisfy
the minimum requirements of American National Standard
for Information Sciences—Permanence of Paper for
Printed Library Material, ANSI Z39.48–1992.

FOR SHIVANI

and the birds of the Black Forest
whose music always accompanied me
along *der Heideggerweg*

Nur das Alte veraltet nie. Doch bis wir das
Alte finden, werden wir selber alt.
—Heidegger (GA 81, 245)

CONTENTS

Acknowledgments ix
List of Abbreviations xi
Introduction: What Is to Be Gained from a
Confrontation Between Plato and Heidegger? 1

PART ONE
HEIDEGGER'S CRITICAL READING OF PLATO IN THE 1920S

1
Dialectic, Ethics, and Dialogue 8

Heidegger's Critique of Dialectic in the 1920s 8
Ethics and Ontology 29
Ethics in Plato's *Sophist* 50
Heidegger and Dialogue 63
Conclusion 69

2
Logos and Being 70

The Tensions in Heidegger's Critique 71
The Guiding Perspective of Λόγος as Undermining
the Ontic/Ontological Distinction 72
Heidegger on Plato's Forms 81
Being as Δύναμις 87
Conclusion: The Relation Between Being and Λόγος 98

PART TWO
HEIDEGGER ON PLATO'S TRUTH AND UNTRUTH IN THE 1930S AND 1940S

3
From the 1931–32 and 1933–34 Courses on the Essence
of Truth to "Plato's Doctrine of Truth":
Heidegger's Transformation of Plato into Platonism Through the
Interpretation of the Sun and Cave Analogies of the *Republic* 107

The Courses on the Essence of Truth from WS 1931/32 and WS 1933/34 107
Plato's Truth in the *Beiträge* of 1936–38 136
Plato's Doctrine of Truth in 1940 147
The End of Truth: The 1964 Retraction 161
Conclusion: The End of Truth? 167

4
The Dialogue That Could Have Been: Heidegger on the *Theaetetus*   173

The *Theaetetus* Interpretation in *Die Grundbegriffe der antiken Philosophie* (SS 1926)   173
The Interpretation of the *Theaetetus* in the *Vom Wesen der Wahrheit* Course of 1931–32 and 1933–34   182
Conclusion: Heidegger's Orthodoxy   221

5
The 1942 Interpretation of Λήθη in the Myth of Er (*Republic* Book 10)   225

The Roman Versus the Greek Conception of Truth   225
Saying Λήθη in the Myth of Er   232
Purging the Myth of Er: The Ontologizing of Ethics and Politics   247
The Greek Experience of the Open: A Saying That Points and Hints Versus the "Leap"   251
Conclusion: Leaping Beyond Plato   254

PART THREE
OPPORTUNITIES FOR A DIALOGUE WITH PLATO IN THE LATE HEIDEGGER

6
Calculative Thinking, Meditative Thinking, and the Practice of Dialogue   260

Heidegger's Critique of Logos in the 1930s   260
Dialogue as Bringing to Speech the Unsaid   263
Plato's Dialectic or Hegel's?   264
A Saying Beyond Assertion   267
Plato's Dialogues and Heidegger's Leap   269
Heidegger and the Dialogue Form   273
Redefining Hermeneutics   281
Back to the Beginning with Dialectic and Dialogue   288
Conclusion: Dialectic Versus Sophia Again   292

7
Dialectic and Phenomenology in "Zeit und Sein": A Pivotal Chapter in Heidegger's Confrontation with Plato   293

From Dialectic and Hermeneutics to Phenomenology   294
The *Auseinandersetzung* with Plato   308
Conclusion   342

Works Cited   347
Index   353

ACKNOWLEDGMENTS

This book has been many years in the making, often set aside in favor of other projects. During this time it has benefited from considerable assistance, both institutional and personal. Initial research for the book, as well as much of the writing of a first draft, were made possible by a year-long grant from the National Endowment for the Humanities as well as a research fellowship from the Humboldt Foundation, which enabled my very productive stay in Freiburg, Germany. This last opportunity would not have come about without the invitation of Günter Figal, whose own work has from the beginning been an inspiration for this project. Completion of the book was made possible by another grant, this time a Major Project Completion Grant offered by my home institution, Skidmore College.

It would be impossible for me to list here all of the people from whose work and conversation I have profited in the present task. One person I must single out for mention is Michael Gelven, who as my teacher when I was an undergraduate first introduced me to both Plato and Heidegger and predisposed me to seeing an affinity between the two. I must also mention my colleagues during the last seventeen years in the Department of Philosophy and Religion at Skidmore College for providing me with an ideal working environment. Then there are all of those colleagues at other institutions whom I may see only once or twice a year but whose philosophical friendship is an indispensable stimulus to my work and a source of joy: they know who they are. I have also received both encouragement and critical feedback from the many audiences to which I have presented different aspects of my work, starting many years ago with my first paper on Heidegger's *Sophist* lectures presented at the 1995 Collegium Phaenomenologicum in Perugia, Italy. Since then I have benefitted from presentations of my work at meetings of the Ancient Philosophy Society (Chicago), the Boston Area Colloquium in Ancient Philosophy (Boston College), the Society of Ancient Greek Philosophy (Binghamton, New York,) the Society for Phenomenology and Existential Philosophy (Georgetown University), and the Societat Catalana de Filosofia (Barcelona); as well as at the University of New Mexico, Siena College, Trinity College, the Università de Pavia, and, most recently, the Université de Nice Sophia Antipolis as part of a most congenial and productive *colloque* on Heidegger and Plato. Finally, I wish to thank two anonymous readers for Penn State Press whose comments on the manuscript certainly helped make this a stronger book.

Work on a major project such as this one always requires the support of family and friends. I wish especially to acknowledge my daughter, Shivani, who was so surrounded by this project when she was first learning how to spell that she asked that "Heidegger" be put on the list of words she needed to work on. I am very proud of her for now having learned to spell "Heidegger," and she is the faithful companion without whom I would probably be too unmoored to persist and succeed in my work. Explicit gratitude is also owed my parents, who are always my final safety net.

As can be expected from a project in development for many years, some of the material in this book has been previously published in different form and is reused here with permission: "History of an Embarrassment: Heidegger's Critique of Platonic Dialectic," *Journal of the History of Philosophy* 40, no. 3 (2002): 361–89, used in the first half of chapter 1; "On the Way to *Sophia*: Heidegger on Plato's Dialectic, Ethics, and *Sophist*," *Research in Phenomenology* 27 (1997): 16–60, used in the second half of chapter 1; "Confronting Heidegger on Logos and Being in Plato's *Sophist*," in *Platon und Aristoteles—sub ratione veritatis: Festschrift für Wolfgang Wieland zum 70. Geburtstag*, ed. Gregor Damschen, Rainer Enskat, and Alejandro G. Vigo (Göttingen: Vandenhoeck and Ruprecht, 2003), 102–33, used in chapter 2; "Plato's Question of Truth (Versus Heidegger's Doctrines)," in *Proceedings of the Boston Area Colloquium in Ancient Philosophy*, vol. 23, ed. John J. Cleary and Gary M. Gurtler (Leiden: Brill, 2008), 83–111, used in chapters 3 and 5; "Heidegger on a Few Pages of Plato's *Theaetetus*," *Epoché* 11, no. 2 (2007): 371–92, used in chapter 4.

ABBREVIATIONS

The following abbreviations mostly refer to works by Heidegger in the original German as cited throughout the book, with references to published translations. Unless otherwise indicated, translations in the book are my own, but the reader who wishes to investigate the sources in English can consult the translations cited below, which in most cases include the page numbers to the German edition.

GA 6.2   *Nietzsche II (1939–1946)*. Gesamtausgabe 6, no. 2. Frankfurt am Main: Vittorio Klostermann, 1997.

GA 7   *Vorträge und Aufsätze*. Gesamtausgabe 7. Frankfurt am Main: Vittorio Klostermann, 2000.

GA 9   *Wegmarken*. Gesamtausgabe 9. Frankfurt am Main: Vittorio Klostermann, 2004.

GA 12   *Unterwegs zur Sprache*. Gesamtausgabe 12. Frankfurt am Main: Vittorio Klostermann, 1985.

GA 13   *Aus der Erfahrung des Denkens (1910–1976)*. Gesamtausgabe 13. Frankfurt am Main: Vittorio Klostermann, 1983.

GA 16   *Reden und andere Zeugnisse eines Lebensweges (1910–1976)*. Gesamtausgabe 16. Frankfurt am Main: Vittorio Klostermann, 2000.

GA 17   *Einführung in die Phänomenologische Forschung*. *Gesamtausgabe* 17 (Frankfurt am Main: Vittorio Klostermann, 1994). Translated by Daniel O. Dahlstrom as *Introduction to Phenomenological Research*. Bloomington: Indiana University Press, 2005.

GA 18   *Grundbegriffe der aristotelischen Philosophie*. Gesamtausgabe 18. Frankfurt am Main: Vittorio Klostermann, 2002.

GA 19   *Platon: Sophistes*. Gesamtausgabe 19. Frankfurt am Main: Vittorio Klostermann, 1992. Translations have been taken from Martin Heidegger, *Plato's "Sophist,"* trans. Richard Rojcewicz and André Schuwer, except where otherwise indicated. All references, however, are to the Gesamtausgabe since these pages are also indicated in the translation. The Rojcewicz/Schuwer translation tends to leave out italics found in the German text, and I have restored these.

GA 20   *Prolegomena zur Geschichte des Zeitbegriffs*. Gesamtausgabe 20. Frankfurt am Main: Vittorio Klostermann, 1979. Translated by Theodore Kisiel as *History of the Concept of Time: Prolegomena*. Bloomington: Indiana University Press, 1985.

GA 21	*Logik: Die Frage nach der Wahreheit.* Gesamtausgabe 21. Frankfurt am Main: Vittorio Klostermann, 1976.
GA 22	*Grundbegriffe der antiken Philosophie.* Gesamtausgabe 22. Frankfurt am Main: Vittorio Klostermann, 1993. Translated by Richard Rojcewicz as *Basic Concepts of Ancient Philosophy.* Bloomington: Indiana University Press, 2007.
GA 24	*Grundprobleme der Phänomenologie.* Gesamtausgabe 24. Frankfurt am Main: Vittorio Klostermann, 1975. Translated by Albert Hofstadter as *The Basic Problems of Phenomenology.* Bloomington: Indiana University Press, 1982.
GA 26	*Metaphysische Anfangsgründe der Logik im Ausgang von Leibniz.* Gesamtausgabe 26. Frankfurt am Main: Vittorio Klostermann, 1978. Translated by Michael Heim as *The Metaphysical Foundations of Logic.* Bloomington: Indiana University Press, 1984.
GA 27	*Einleitung in die Philosophie.* Gesamtausgabe 27. Frankfurt am Main: Vittorio Klostermann, 1996.
GA 28	*Der deutsche Idealismus (Fichte, Schelling, Hegel) und die philosophische Problemlage der Gegenwart.* Gesamtausgabe 28. Frankfurt am Main: Vittorio Klostermann, 1997.
GA 29/30	*Die Grundbegriffe der Metaphysik: Welt, Endlichkeit, Einsamkeit.* Gesamtausgabe 29/30. Frankfurt am Main: Vittorio Klostermann, 1983. Translated by William McNeill and Nicholas Walker as *The Fundamental Concepts of Metaphysics.* Bloomington: Indiana University Press, 1995.
GA 31	*Vom Wesen der menschlichen Freiheit.* Gesamtausgabe 31. Frankfurt am Main: Vittorio Klostermann, 1982. Translated by Ted Sadler as *The Essence of Human Freedom.* London: Continuum, 2005.
GA 32	*Hegels Phänomenologie des Geistes.* Gesamtasugabe 32. Frankfurt am Main: Vittorio Klostermann, 1980. Translated by Parvis Emad and Kenneth Maly as *Hegel's Phenomenology of Spirit.* Bloomington: Indiana University Press, 1988.
GA 33	*Aristoteles, Metaphysik A 1–3: Von Wesen und Wirklichkeit der Kraft.* 2nd ed. Gesamtausgabe 33. Frankfurt am Main: Vittorio Klostermann, 1990. Translated by Walter Borgan as *Aristotle's "Metaphysics" Theta 1–3: On the Essence of and Actuality of Force.* Bloomington: Indiana University Press, 1995.
GA 34	*Vom Wesen der Wahrheit: Zu Platons Höhlengleichnis und Theätet.* Gesamtausgabe 34. Frankfurt am Main: Klostermann, 1988. Translated by Ted Sadler as *The Essence of Truth: On Plato's Cave Allegory and "Theaetetus."* London: Continuum, 2002.

GA 36/37   *Sein und Wahrheit*. Gesamtausgabe 36/37. Frankfurt am Main: Vittorio Klostermann, 2001.
GA 38   *Logik als die Frage nach dem Wesen der Sprache*. Gesamtausgabe 38. Frankfurt am Main: Vittorio Klostermann, 1998.
GA 45   *Grundfragen der Philosophie: Ausgewählte "Probleme" der "Logik."* 2nd ed. Gesamtausgabe 45. Frankfurt am Main: Vittorio Klostermann, 1992. Translated by Richard Rojcewicz and André Schuwer as *Basic Questions of Philosophy*. Bloomington: Indiana University Press, 2004.
GA 54   *Parmenides*. Gesamtausgabe 54. Frankfurt am Main: Vittorio Klostermann, 1982. Translated by André Schuwer and Richard Rojcewicz as *Parmenides*. Bloomington: Indiana University Press, 1992.
GA 56/57   *Zur Bestimmung der Philosophie, 1: Die Idee der Philosophie und das Weltanschauungsproblem*. 2nd ed. Gesamtausgabe 56/57. Frankfurt am Main: Vittorio Klostermann, 1999. Translated by Ted Sadler as *Towards the Definition of Philosophy*. London: Continuum, 2003.
GA 58   *Grundprobleme der Phänomenologie (WS 1919/20)*. Gesamtausgabe 58. Frankfurt am Main: Vittorio Klostermann, 1992.
GA 62   *Phänomenologische Interpretationen ausgewählter Abhandlungen des Aristoteles zur Ontologie und Logik*. Gesamtausgabe 62. Frankfurt am Main: Vittorio Klostermann, 2005.
GA 64   *Der Begriff der Zeit*. Gesamtausgabe 64. Frankfurt am Main: Vittorio Klostermann, 2004.
GA 65   *Beiträge zur Philosophie (Vom Ereignis)*. 2nd ed. Gesamtausgabe 65. Frankfurt am Main: Vittorio Klostermann, 1994. Translated by Parvis Emad and Kenneth Maly as *Contributions to Philosophy (From Enowning)*. Bloomington: Indiana University Press, 1999.
GA 66   *Besinnung*. Gesamtausgabe 66. Frankfurt am Main: Vittorio Klostermann, 1997.
GA 67   *Metaphysik und Nihilismus*. Gesamtausgabe 67. Frankfurt am Main: Vittorio Klostermann, 1999.
GA 77   *Feldweg-Gespräche*. Gesamtausgabe 77. Frankfurt am Main: Vittorio Klostermann, 1995.
GA 79   *Bremer und Freiburger Vorträge*. Gesamtausgabe 79. Frankfurt am Main: Vittorio Klostermann, 1994.
GA 81   *Gedachtes*. Gesamtausgabe 81. Frankfurt am Main: Vittorio Klostermann, 2007.
GA 87   *Nietzsche Seminare, 1937 und 1944*. Gesamtausgabe 87. Frankfurt am Main: Vittorio Klostermann, 2004.

AHB	Arendt, Hannah, and Martin Heidegger. *Briefe, 1925–1975.* Edited by Ursula Ludz. Frankfurt am Main: Vittorio Klostermann, 1998. Translated by Andrew Shields as *Letters, 1925–1975.* New York: Harcourt, 2004.
BH	*Brief über den "Humanismus.* In *Wegmarken*, 2nd ed., 311–60. Frankfurt am Main: Vittorio Klostermann, 1978. Translated as "Letter on 'Humanism,'" in *Pathmarks*, edited by William McNeill, 239–76. Cambridge: Cambridge University Press, 1998.
BT	*Being and Time.* Translated by Joan Stambaugh. Albany: State University of New York Press, 1996.
CD	"Colloquium über Dialektik." *Hegel Studien* 25 (1990): 9–40.
DE	*Denkerfahrungen, 1910–1976.* Frankfurt am Main: Vittorio Klostermann, 1983.
ED	*Aus der Erfahrung des Denkens.* Pfullingen: Günther Neske, 1976.
EM	*Einführung in die Metaphysik.* Tübingen: Max Neimeyer, 1976.
G	*Gelassenheit.* Pfullingen: Günther Neske, 1959.
HPD	Partenie, Catalin, and Tom Rockmore, eds. *Heidegger and Plato: Toward Dialogue.* Evanston: Northwestern University Press, 2005.
JHBW	Jaspers, Karl, and Martin Heidegger. *Briefwechsel: 1920–1963.* Edited by Walter Biemel and Hans Saner. Frankfurt am Main: Vittorio Klostermann; Munich: Piper, 1990. Translated by Gary E. Aylesworth as *The Heidegger-Jaspers Correspondence (1920–1963).* Amherst, N.Y.: Humanity Books, 2003.
N1	*Nietzsche.* Vol. 1. 4th ed. Pfullingen: Günther Neske, 1961.
N2	*Nietzsche.* Vol. 2. 4th ed. Pfullingen: Günther Neske, 1961.
PIA	*Phänomenologische Interpretationen zu Aristoteles.* Edited by Günther Neumann. Stuttgart: Reklam, 2002. Originally published in *Dilthey-Jahrbuch für Philosophie und Geschichte der Geisteswissenschaften* 6 (1989): 228–74; that text translated by Michael Baur as "Phenomenological Interpretations with Respect to Aristotle: Indication of the Hermeneutical Situation." *Man and World* 25 (1992): 358–93.
PLW	"Platons Lehre von der Wahrheit." In *Wegmarken*, 2nd ed., 201–36. Frankfurt am Main: Vittorio Klostermann, 1978. Translated as "Plato's Doctrine of Truth," in *Pathmarks*, edited by William McNeill, 155–82. Cambridge: Cambridge University Press, 1998.
SDU	*Die Selbstbehauptung der Deutschen Universität.* Frankfurt am Main: Vittorio Klostermann, 1983.
SZ	*Sein und Zeit.* 15th ed. Tübingen: Max Niemeyer, 1984.

VS   *Vier Seminare.* Frankfurt am Main: Vittorio Klostermann, 1977. Translated by Andrew Mitchell and François Raffoul as *Four Seminars.* Bloomington: Indiana University Press, 2003.
WG   "Vom Wesen des Grundes." In *Wegmarken,* 2nd ed. Frankfurt am Main: Vittorio Klostermann, 1978. Translated as "On the Essence of Ground," in *Pathmarks,* edited by William McNeill, 97–135. Cambridge: Cambridge University Press, 1998.
WHD   *Was Heisst Denken?* 4th ed. Tübingen: Max Niemeyer, 1984. Translated by J. Glenn Gray as *What Is Called Thinking.* New York: Harper and Row, 1976.
WM   *Wegmarken.* 2nd ed. Frankfurt am Main: Vittorio Klostermann, 1978.
WP   *Was ist da—die Philosophie?* 3rd ed. Pfullingen: Günther Neske, 1963.
ZS   *Zollikoner Seminare.* Edited by Medard Boss. Frankfurt am Main: Vittorio Klostermann, 1987. This text has been translated by Richard Askay and Franz Mayr as *Zollikon Seminars.* Evanston: Northwestern University Press, 2001.
ZSD   *Zur Sache des Denkens.* Tübingen: Niemeyer, 1969.

INTRODUCTION: WHAT IS TO BE GAINED FROM A CONFRONTATION BETWEEN PLATO AND HEIDEGGER?

Japanese: To us, at a distance, it had always seemed amazing that people never tired of imputing to you a negative attitude toward the history of previous thinking, while in fact you strive only for an original appropriation.
Inquirer: Whose success can and should be disputed.
—Heidegger, "A Dialogue on Language: Between a Japanese and an Inquirer," trans. Peter D. Hertz

On est pris entre deux feux. Je suis aussi allergique aux dévots de Heidegger qu'aux anti-heideggériens de service. J'essaie de trouver une voie, une ligne, un lieu où l'on puisse continuer à lire Heidegger sérieusement, à le questionner sans céder, ni à l'heideggérianisme politique ni au contraire.
—Jacques Derrida, "Entretien avec Dominique Janicaud"

The present book could be characterized as a critique of Heidegger's interpretation of Plato. But such a characterization would say both too little and too much. Too much, because the aim here is not to demonstrate that Heidegger's reading of Plato was "wrong." The present study will indeed show at a number of points that Heidegger misinterprets and distorts a text, that he ignores evidence against his interpretation, that he mistranslates, etc. In other words, his reading of Plato will often be criticized on purely philological grounds. However, though such a critique is both appropriate and necessary, it cannot be seen as a complete refutation of Heidegger's interpretation, for the simple reason that he never offers this interpretation as an objective, scholarly, and historical exegesis of what Plato said. The avowed goal of his interpretation is not accurately to represent and thereby retrieve the past, but to reawaken future possibilities for thought that remain unsaid in the texts of the past. In this way Heidegger's reflection on Plato, and on the Greeks in general, is inseparable from his own future-directed thinking; or, in Heidegger's own words, his reflection on the "first beginning" of Western philosophy is inseparable from, is indeed the same as, his attempt to think "another beginning." In short, one cannot distinguish between Heidegger the interpreter of ancient texts and Heidegger the contemporary thinker.

But in this case the characterization of the present book as a critique of Heidegger's interpretation of Plato also says too little, for such a critique must also necessarily be a critique of Heidegger's own thought. To confront and take issue with Heidegger's reading of Plato is necessarily to confront and take issue with Heidegger's own thinking. Any critique that evades the latter task, either by dismissing Heidegger's thought without any understanding of it[1] or by failing to challenge it, cannot fully succeed in the former. If Heidegger failed to understand Plato, this was due not to some peculiar psychological quirk or ignorance of the texts, but rather to the fact that, despite all the affinities between the two thinkers, there was something genuinely foreign to Heidegger's thought in Plato's texts, something that Heidegger could not appropriate without fundamentally changing the direction of his own thinking. If the confrontation between Heidegger and Plato proves fruitful for a critical assessment of Heidegger's own thought, that is because Plato is Heidegger's "other," though not the "other" Heidegger made him into. By identifying Plato with Platonism and the metaphysics of presence, Heidegger was able to make Plato a chapter in his history of being and transform Plato into his mere opposite, against which he could define himself. Only when we can see that Plato is not the mere opposite of Heidegger and that there is instead a very close affinity between the two can we see just how radically "other" Plato is, that is, the extent to which he represents a genuine alternative to Heidegger's way of thinking.

The present book can claim to confront Heidegger on his own terms because it shares two of the fundamental convictions that guided Heidegger's reading of the Greeks: (1) that unlike the questioning in the sciences, philosophical questioning can be genuinely original and radical only through constant reflection on its past; and (2) that such reflection must take the form, not of an exposition of the opinions and teachings of past philosophers, but rather of a reawakening of those directions and possibilities of thinking that, though grounding the subsequent tradition and history of philosophy, are also obstructed and flattened by this tradition and history.

The present critique of Heidegger can therefore be characterized as a Heideggerian critique: the aim is precisely to show that Heidegger failed to recognize and confront in Plato's dialogues a possibility of thinking that was obstructed by the subsequent tradition of Platonism (to which Heidegger, especially in later texts, too quickly assimilates Plato) and that could have fundamentally changed the direction of Heidegger's own thinking. The aim is not to show that Plato was "right" and Heidegger was "wrong." This critique

---

1. Jonathan Barnes's critique of *Platons Lehre von der Wahrheit* is a good example of this problem: "Heidegger spéléologue," *Revue de Métaphysique et de Morale* 95 (1990): 173–95.

of Heidegger follows, and is indebted to, Heidegger's own provocation to thinking and historical reflection. But in opening up in Plato's dialogues what Heidegger's reading tends to close off under the label of "the history of metaphysics," this critique aims to think beyond and even against Heidegger's overcoming of metaphysics. The departure from Heidegger's path attempted here may indeed be the only meaningful and philosophically respectable way of remaining faithful to Heidegger's path. Neither Heideggerianism nor anti-Heideggerianism is worthy of the task of thinking.

These observations explain the plan of the present book. The first two parts focus on Heidegger's most explicit and detailed readings of Plato as found in his courses of the 1920s and 1930s. The two most important texts here are the 1924–25 course on Plato's *Sophist* and the course *On the Essence of Truth*, devoted to a reading of the Cave Analogy and the *Theaetetus* and delivered first in 1931 and again, in a revised form, in 1933–34. Without question the most widely read of Heidegger's texts on Plato, because the only one Heidegger chose to publish during his lifetime and therefore for a long time the only one available, is the 1940 essay "Plato's Doctrine of Truth." But now that two versions of the *On the Essence of Truth* course from which the essay supposedly derived are available, it is essential to see the extent to which the essay grossly simplifies and sometimes even contradicts the much richer and conflicted reading in the courses: a reading that suggests certain affinities between Heidegger and Plato that are suppressed by the essay. Though the focus in these two parts of the book will be on Heidegger's interpretation of Plato's texts, an effort will be made to situate this interpretation within, and show it to be motivated by, Heidegger's thought at the time.

Part 3 turns to Heidegger's later work: a period after his identification of Plato with a Platonism to be "twisted out of" and during which he therefore devoted no time to a detailed reading of Plato's texts. The texts to be considered in this part therefore make only passing and often cryptic reference to Plato. That might seem to put them outside the aim of the present book. However, the goal of this part will be to show where Heidegger's turn away from Plato, and thus from dialectic and dialogue, leads his later thought and to start developing a Platonic critique of this thought. There are also in these later texts indications of surprising affinities between Plato and Heidegger, which, if pursued, could have led Heidegger in a very different direction. Heidegger himself, as will be seen, expressed during the 1950s a desire to read Plato anew and to rework in particular his course on the *Sophist*. Heidegger never followed through on this desire, and the general goal of part 3 is to show what was thereby lost.

A detailed critical examination of Heidegger's reading of Plato is long overdue. Because key texts have not been published until fairly recently, such an examination was for a long time impossible. The books by H. G. Wolz,[2] A. Boutot,[3] and even S. Rosen[4] (which has such an assessment as at least part of its aim) fall far short for the simple reason that the most important Heideggerian texts were not yet published at the time they were written. The mentioned *Sophist* course, the only text in which Heidegger interprets a Platonic dialogue at length, was not published until 1992 (GA 19). The nearest thing to this available before that time was, first, the *Parmenides* course (GA 54), published in 1982, which, as chapter 5 will show, contains a very important reading of the Myth of Er in the *Republic* that seriously qualifies, if not undermines, the "doctrine of truth" Heidegger attributed to Plato in the published essay. Yet surprisingly, this reading has been mostly neglected by those who have written on Heidegger's reading of Plato. The other text is the 1931–32 *Vom Wesen der Wahrheit* course, published in 1988 (GA 34), in which Heidegger interprets small parts of the *Republic* and *Theaetetus*. If this important course has itself been largely neglected in the literature, that is in part because it was not translated into English until 2002 (ET). The other reason is that many scholars, judging from their exclusive focus on "Plato's Doctrine of Truth," appear to assume that the essay contains everything worth knowing about the course; the truth, as chapters 3 and 4 will show, is that the essay departs radically from the course in key respects and, in contrast to the course, can hardly be considered a "reading" of Plato. Furthermore, the course contains an extraordinary reading of the *Theaetetus* that Heidegger completely drops from the essay and that all subsequent scholars, following suit, have simply ignored. Finally, as already noted above, there exists a significantly different version of the course delivered by Heidegger in 1933 and published only in 2001 (GA 36/37).

But there are also other texts that, while not focused exclusively on Plato, still make an essential contribution to our understanding of Heidegger's critique of Plato. The critique carried out in the *Sophist* course cannot be fully understood without the context of other courses from the 1920s, also published only recently. One very important course on Aristotle that immediately preceded the *Sophist* course and was billed by Heidegger as preparation for it was published as recently as 2002 (GA 18). Other recently published courses from the 1920s are essential for understanding the philosophical agenda and assumptions of Heidegger's critique of Plato during this period. Finally, there are some texts from the later Heidegger that address dialectic and display a new sensitivity to Plato's dialogues, such as the 1957 Freiburg lecture series, *Grundsätze des Denkens*, published in its entirety in 1994 (GA 79).

2. *Plato and Heidegger: In Search of Selfhood* (Lewisburg: Bucknell University Press, 1981).
3. *Platon et Heidegger: Le problème du nihilisme* (Paris: Presses Universitaires de France, 1987).
4. *The Question of Being: A Reversal of Heidegger* (New Haven: Yale University Press, 1993).

There are, of course, some recent discussions of Heidegger's reading of Plato that take into account some of the recently published materials. M. J. Brach's book on Plato and Heidegger focuses on showing the role played by the 1924–25 course on Plato's *Sophist* in Heidegger's philosophical development, particularly within the context of his response to Neo-Kantianism.[5] Yet, having this limited scope, Brach's book is not concerned with providing a critical assessment of the philosophical relationship between Plato and Heidegger throughout the latter's career. A recent collection of essays edited by Catalin Partenie and Tom Rockmore, *Heidegger and Plato: Toward Dialogue* (HPD), makes some useful contributions that will be cited in the course of this book. However, such a collection cannot be expected to offer a systematic and consistent assessment of Heidegger's reading of Plato. Furthermore, the collection still neglects important aspects of Heidegger's reading (his interpretations of the *Theaetetus* and the Myth of Er, for example), with the usual overemphasis on the published essay, "Plato's Doctrine of Truth." Drew A. Hyland's assessment of Heidegger's reading of Plato in his recent book, *Questioning Platonism*, is both broader in scope than Brach's and more systematic than HPD, but, taking up only sixty-six pages of the book, it also gives scant attention to key texts and excludes from its aim any critique of Heidegger's own thought: "Even less do I mean to infer from their readings of Plato [i.e., that of certain continental philosophers, including Heidegger] larger flaws in their philosophic standpoints as a whole, standpoints with which I am often very sympathetic."[6] With regard to Heidegger in particular, he at one point writes: "It is important to emphasize that my critical evaluation of Heidegger's reading of Plato is largely directed toward his way of reading the dialogues more than the technical analyses of this or that passage in the *Sophist*. My problems with Heidegger have largely to do with his hermeneutical principles" (51). There is nothing wrong with a critique that focuses exclusively on hermeneutical principles: Hyland's is without question very useful and illuminating. The point is only that it cannot go far enough. The one crucial question that Hyland's approach cannot answer is *why* Heidegger misread Plato in the way he did when, as Hyland argues and as certainly the example of Gadamer shows, there are resources in Heidegger's thought for a much more sensitive and faithful reading of Plato's dialogues. Though he does not explicitly assert this, Hyland must apparently assume that the reason is a purely contingent one: that a certain complacency, laziness, and preoccupation with other matters prevented Heidegger from being a better reader of Plato. At the end of his chapter on Heidegger, Hyland

---

5. *Heidegger—Platon: Vom Neukantianismus zur existentiellen Interpretation des "Sophistes"* (Würzburg: Königshausen and Neumann, 1996).

6. *Questioning Platonism: Continental Interpretations of Plato* (Albany: State University of New York Press, 2004), 14.

describes Heidegger's failure to reconsider his reading of Plato as "more puzzling" and "more disappointing" given the movement of his later thought and concludes: "Everything points to a rich dialogue between Heidegger and the Platonic dialogues; it is a loss to us all that Heidegger never apparently allowed that dialogue genuinely to take place" (83). But *why* did he not "allow" this? This question can be left unanswered only if we assume that the answer lies in some peculiar and unknowable fact about Heidegger's personal psychology. The present book will show that, on the contrary, Heidegger's thought itself requires this misreading of Plato, that a genuine dialogue with Plato would have forced him to go in certain directions where he did not want to go and could not go without his own thinking undergoing a radical transformation. A critique of this misreading of Plato therefore cannot avoid being a critique of the thought that needs this misreading.

In the ways indicated, then, the present book covers new ground and therefore asks to be excused for adding to the already huge literature devoted to either Heidegger or Plato. With what success the book traverses this often perilous ground is left to the reader to decide. Yet success should be measured according to the book's ability to make the confrontation between Plato and Heidegger philosophically fruitful. And since what is ultimately at stake in this confrontation is nothing less than the nature and aim of that activity we call "philosophy," the greatest reward it can promise is nothing less than a better understanding of the philosophical enterprise as such.

PART 1

HEIDEGGER'S CRITICAL READING OF PLATO IN THE 1920S

Heidegger's reading of Plato in the 1920s culminates in the 1924–25 course on the *Sophist* (GA 19), which for the first and last time in Heidegger's work provides a detailed, often line-by-line interpretation of a whole Platonic dialogue (though the course ends before Heidegger gets to the concluding part of the dialogue). This course will therefore be the focus of the present chapter and the next. However, it will also be seen that the assumptions and motivations of Heidegger's reading of Plato in this course cannot be understood outside the context of other courses from the 1920s in which Plato is barely mentioned, if at all. Specifically, Heidegger's engagement during this period with both Aristotle and Husserlian phenomenology, indeed, with working out a phenomenological reading of Aristotle, forms an indispensable backdrop. Separating for convenience issues that cannot strictly be separated, the first chapter will focus on Heidegger's *Auseinandersetzung* with Plato on the question of the methodological and ethical dimension of philosophy, while the second chapter will focus on this *Auseinandersetzung* as it concerns the question of being and of the proper approach to being (thus the methodological question again). Though the aim here is not to provide a page-by-page exegesis of Heidegger's course, the above division of topics roughly follows a natural division between two parts of Heidegger's course: the first part dedicated to the intellectual virtues as defined in Aristotle's ethics and as present more implicitly and confusedly in Plato's dialogues; the second part dedicated to the account of being and not-being, as well as of the five great kinds, in the *Sophist*.

1

DIALECTIC, ETHICS, AND DIALOGUE

A. HEIDEGGER'S CRITIQUE OF DIALECTIC IN THE 1920S

1. Dialectic Versus Intuition

One theme that is central to Heidegger's reading of the *Sophist* and is a major target of his critique of Plato is *dialectic*. Heidegger's account of dialectic in the *Sophist* course begins significantly with a description of the pervasiveness and potential obstructiveness of λόγος. Though λόγος ordinarily and most immediately pervades all forms of disclosing (GA 19, 196), "according to its original sense and original facticity, λόγος is not at all disclosing [*aufdeckend*], but is, if one may speak in an extreme way, precisely *concealing* [*verdeckend*]" (197). In other words, λόγος is initially and for the most part "idle talk" (*Gerede*), the kind of speech that is bandied about concerning anything whatsoever and that "has the facticity of not allowing the things themselves to be seen, but producing instead a self-satisfaction in resting content with what 'one says'" (197). Thus, speech at first presents itself as self-sufficient and autonomous; one hangs onto what is said without being directed beyond it to the things themselves.

This tendency of λόγος to conceal is a theme to which Heidegger returns repeatedly in the courses of the 1920s. In a course from WS 1923/24 he argues that deception has its origin in the very facticity of language (GA 17, 35–40). In the SS 1924 course (*Grundbegriffe der aristotelischen Philosophie*), the one that immediately preceded the *Sophist* course, Heidegger characterizes language as the proper domain of "Das Man" (GA 18, 64) and describes the dominance of λόγος as leading to *Gerede* (108). Heidegger therefore claims that because the Greeks lived in speech they were also *imprisoned by it*, with the result that a tremendous effort was needed for them to overcome their imprisonment and thus make science possible (109, 262–63).

In the *Sophist* lectures, Heidegger assigns to dialectic an important role in this effort. Given both the pervasiveness and the concealing character of λόγος, philosophy, in its attempt to disclose the things themselves, must both begin with λόγος and *break through* it by means of a "speaking for and against" ("Für- und Gegensprechen") that destroys the autonomy and self-sufficiency that λόγος has in *Gerede* and in this way "leads more and more to what is at issue and lets that be seen" (GA 19, 197). What is needed, in short, is *dia*-lectic: a speaking that passes *through* speech.

Already, however, one can see the tension that characterizes dialectic on Heidegger's account. Though dialectic is a λέγεσθαι, a speaking, it seeks to be more. Its aim is to disclose the things themselves of which it speaks, to *see* these things in a "pure seeing" uncontaminated by the distorting and concealing tendencies of λόγος. The Greek word for this "pure seeing" without λόγος is νοεῖν.[1] Thus, Heidegger writes, "διαλέγεσθαι therefore possesses imminently a tendency toward νοεῖν, seeing" (197).

Having characterized its goal in this way, Heidegger claims that dialectic can never attain it. As a "talking-through" (*Durchsprechen*), dialectic must still consider things in the medium of speech and therefore can never transcend λόγος. Heidegger at one point identifies dialectic with a "*confinement* to beings as addressed in speech" (206; my emphasis and translation). This confinement places the "pure seeing" of νοεῖν beyond dialectic's reach. While as a "talking-through" it can indeed transcend (*verlassen*) idle talk (*Gerede*), it "cannot do more than *make the attempt* [*Versuch*] to press on to the things themselves" (197; see also the SS 1924 course [GA 18, 7]). Heidegger therefore repeatedly characterizes dialectic as being *unterwegs* (see, e.g., 214).

This characterization of dialectic as "on the way" is itself faithful to Plato's thought. In the *Symposium*, philosophy is described as being *between* (ἐν μέσῳ) wisdom and ignorance (204b4–5) and therefore as not an activity of the immortal gods whose prerogative is wisdom itself (σοφία, 204a1–2). Though philosophy has an immanent tendency toward wisdom—a tendency which Plato calls ἔρως—it can never reach this aim. Heidegger, however, uses Aristotle's conception of philosophy as σοφία and θεωρα to show that philosophy can in fact be more than the kind of "erotic" dialectic to which Plato confines it. Aristotle, Heidegger argues, was able to attain a level of philosophizing higher than dialectic from which he then could, unlike Plato, put dialectic in its proper place, a place *beneath* philosophy, "a legitimate *preliminary stage of philosophizing*" (165). "Aristotle did deprive dialectic of its dignity, but not because he

---

1. Heidegger equates pure νοεῖν with "reines Vernehmen" (GA 19, 145), with "eine Aufdeckungsart, die über den λόγος hinausgeht" (145). See also the 1925–26 course, GA 21, 110 and 174–85.

did not understand it. On the contrary, it was because he understood it more radically, because he saw Plato himself as being underway toward θεωρεῖν in his dialectic, because he succeeded in making real what Plato was striving for" (199; see also 216, 351). Therefore, in seeing dialectic as purely "tentative,"[2] Aristotle does not demote it, but instead recognizes its inherently inferior position (621; see also 215, 624–26). It is in the *Sophist* course, therefore, that we find an explanation of Heidegger's claim in *Being and Time*, unexplained and unjustified there, that with the progress of ontology "'Dialectic,' which was a genuine philosophical embarrassment, becomes superfluous. Aristotle 'no longer has any understanding' of it, for *this* reason, that he places it on a more radical foundation and transcends it [*aufhob*]" (ZS, 25).[3]

Related to his critique of dialectic is Heidegger's frequently repeated charge that Plato's thought is confused and unclear (e.g., GA 19, 198). With regard to the different kinds of "unconcealing" (ἀληθεύειν, i.e., τέχνη, ἐπιστήμη, φρόνησις, and σοφία), for example, Heidegger finds nothing but "Konfusion" in Plato and contrasts the "complete clarity" with which Aristotle saw these phenomena (65–66).[4] Indeed, Heidegger finds Plato "confused" about practically every major philosophical issue addressed in the *Sophist*.[5] Aristotle was in the clear about the phenomena, he saw them directly and without distortion, while Plato, on account of his dialectic, remained mired in the ambiguities and deceptions of λόγος. This is why Heidegger must preface his interpretation of the *Sophist* with a lengthy examination of Aristotle's account of the different kinds of "unconcealing" (188 out of the 610 pages of the *Gesamtausgabe* text): invoking the hermeneutical principle that we should always proceed from what is clear back to what is obscure, Heidegger maintains that

---

2. Πειραστικὴ περὶ ὧν ἡ φιλοσοφία γνωριστική, *Metaph.* 1004b25–26.

3. Unless otherwise indicated, all quotations from *Sein und Zeit* will follow Stambaugh's translation in BT. Oddly and perplexingly, Catalin Partenie's discussion of the *Sophist* course treats Heidegger's critique of Platonic dialectic as an attempt to provide a faithful interpretation of Plato's own position: "Imprint: Heidegger's Interpretation of Platonic Dialectic in the *Sophist* Lectures (1924–25)," in HPD; see especially 45 and 56.

4. See also GA 19, 191. The same point is to be found in the 1926 course, GA 22, 207.

5. See GA 19, 124, 190, 198, 201, 222, 453, 523, 543, 546–47, 572, 591–92, 597. Heidegger insists that the characterization of Plato's thought as "verworren" is not an "abschätzige Bewertung," since the confusion stems from the difficulty of the problems (190). But Heidegger never charges Aristotle with *Verworrenheit*, even while drawing attention to the ambiguity of Aristotle's account of the different ways of ἀληθεύειν (GA 19, 129). In the SS 1924 course Heidegger distinguishes between three kinds of ambiguity (*Vieldeutigkeit*): (1) confusion (*Verwirrung*): the different meanings of a word are confused through lack of *Sachkenntnis*; (2) one that results from a lack of receptivity to specific differences; and (3) one that comes from a genuine understanding of the things themselves (GA 18, 22–23, 343). It is clearly the first, or at best second, type of ambiguity that Heidegger finds in Plato, while it is the third type that he finds in Aristotle, to whom he attributes the *Instinkt der Sachlichkeit*. However, even Aristotle is criticized for saying nothing about the origin and necessity of the different meanings (343–44); therefore, in his case the ambiguity "gerade aus dem *Umgang mit den Sachen* erwächst, der *ihrer dabei nur nicht Herr wird*" (343).

Plato must be interpreted by way of Aristotle (11–12, 189–90). Indeed, the course of SS 1924 that immediately preceded the *Sophist* course, and that was entirely devoted to the "basic concepts of Aristotelian philosophy," was billed by Heidegger as necessary preparation for the interpretation of Plato's *Sophist* to be undertaken the next semester (GA 18, 126). Furthermore, Heidegger in the SS 1924 course not only asserts the mentioned hermeneutical principle of interpreting the more obscure Plato by way of the clearer Aristotle (54), but even goes so far as to say that Aristotle has the answers to what are in Plato only questions (126).

But is the pure seeing to which Plato's dialectic is here contrasted really possible? Can the ambiguities and concealing tendencies of λόγος really be overcome? Is not the greater clarity of an Aristotle obtained at the cost of restricting one's view and confining it to the surface? In his introduction to *Plato's Dialectical Ethics,* Gadamer surprisingly agrees that Aristotle's thought has greater conceptual clarity than Plato's and that therefore Plato is to be read through Aristotle (Gadamer does not refer to Heidegger's *Sophist* course, but the echoes are unmistakable).[6] Unlike Heidegger, however, Gadamer recognizes that much is lost in turning from the ambiguities of Plato's dialectic to the greater clarity of Aristotelian θεωρία. "The gain in unambiguous comprehensibility and repeatable certainty is matched by a loss in stimulating multiplicity of meaning" (7; *Platos dialektische Ethik*, 9).

2. The Phenomenological Background of Heidegger's Critique of Plato's Dialectic

We get some idea of what is behind Heidegger's critique of Plato if we consider the scattered comments about dialectic in an earlier course, *Grundprobleme der Phänomenologie* (WS 1919–20) (GA 58). The general point that runs through these comments is that a distinction must be maintained between

---

6. *Plato's Dialectical Ethics: Phenomenological Interpretations Relating to the "Philebus,"* trans. Robert M. Wallace (New Haven: Yale University Press, 1991), 8; *Platos dialektische Ethik* (Hamburg: Felix Meiner, 2000), 9–10. For the ways in which Gadamer's interpretation of Plato departs from that of Heidegger, see Robert J. Dostal, "Gadamer's Continuous Challenge: Heidegger's Plato Interpretation," in *The Philosophy of Hans-Georg Gadamer,* ed. Lewis Edwin Hahn (Chicago: Open Court, 1997), 289–307; Manfred Riedel, "Hermeneutik und Gesprächsdialektik: Gadamers Auseinandersetzung mit Heidegger," in *Hören auf die Sprache* (Frankfurt am Main: Suhrkamp, 1990), 96–130; Catherine Zuckert, *Postmodern Platos* (University of Chicago Press, 1996), 70–103, especially 71–73; Otto Pöggeler, "Ein Streit um Platon: Heidegger und Gadamer," in *Platon in der Abendländischen Geistesgeschichte: Neue Forschungen zum Platonismus,* ed. T. Kobusch and T. Mojsisch (Darmstadt: Wissenschaftliche Buchgesellschaft, 1997), 241–54; François Renaud, *Die Resokratisierung Platons: Die Platonische Hermeneutik Hans-Georg Gadamers* (Sankt Augustin: Academia, 1999), 22–42; and, best of all, Brice R. Wachterhauser, *Beyond Being: Gadamer's Post-Platonic Hermeneutical Ontology* (Evanston: Northwestern University Press, 1999), 166–99.

Anschauung,[7] through which a phenomenon is first given, and *Ausdruck*, through which it is subsequently expressed in concepts. The mistake of dialectic is to confuse these two things (GA 58, 133), to believe that through its concepts it determines the phenomenon, and thus to recognize nothing as *given* (225–26). Phenomenology avoids this mistake by confining dialectic to *Ausdruck*, or expression (138, 161, 184). In another passage, Heidegger also grants dialectic a more important role: it performs a *critical destruction* of those objectifications that are always ready to settle on the phenomena (148, 240, 255). However, whether expressing the phenomena or destroying what obstructs them, dialectic is subordinate to a pure seeing (*Anschauung*) of the phenomena and therefore plays a subordinate role in, and cannot be identified with, philosophy.[8] This is, of course, precisely the critique of dialectic developed five years later in the *Sophist* lectures. This critique also points back to the KS 1919 course, in the latter part of which Heidegger, against the Marburg School's revival of dialectic and Paul Natorp's insistence that "there is no immediate grasping of experiences" ("kein unmittelbares Erfassen der Erlebnisse," GA 56/57, 101), defends Husserl's "principle of principles": "Everything that originally ... offers itself in intuition [is] simply to be taken ... as what it presents itself as" (109). Heidegger there interprets this principle as the fundamental demand of phenomenology to *look away from all standpoints* (109). Phenomenology is the philosophy of having no standpoint (*Standpunktlosigkeit*, 209). Dialectic, in contrast, is never free from standpoints because all it can do is play one received standpoint against another.

Some of the same assumptions provoke an especially vehement, and even shrill, attack on dialectic in the SS 1923 course *Ontologie (Hermeneutik und Faktizität)* (GA 63). Here Heidegger asserts that phenomenology and dialectic are as little capable of being mixed together as are fire and water (42). The basic objection is again that dialectic "steps into an already constructed context" (43) and "always lives from the tables of others" (45), lacking "the radical fundamental looking in the direction of and at the *object of philosophy* from out of which and on the basis of which even the how of what is understood emerges in its 'unity'" (43–44), and thus also lacking the direction that it could

---

7. On *Anschauung*, see also GA 21, 103ff. For the identification of *Anschauung* with νοῦς in contrast to λόγος, see GA 21, 110.

8. Yet a detailed reading of this course, which is not possible here, would show that Heidegger's account there of the relation between dialectic and phenomenology is fraught with ambiguity and tension, not to say contradiction. I offer such a reading in "Why Heidegger's Hermeneutics Is not a 'Diahermeneutics,'" *Philosophy Today* 45 (SPEP Supplement 2001): 138–52. All that needs to be noted here is that the oppositions upon which a distinction between phenomenology and dialectic would appear to rest, namely, oppositions between immediacy and mediation, intuition and expression, constructive insight and critical destruction, are all radically brought into question, and perhaps even undermined, as Heidegger grapples throughout the course with the nature of phenomenology as the *Urwissenschaft* of life.

receive only from "a fundamental looking in the direction of the *subject matter,* a fundamental rationality which constantly tests itself and proves itself by looking at the subject matter and not by means of dialectic as such" (45).[9] Heidegger's main target both in this course and in the earlier course of WS 1919/20 is the modern dialectic of the Hegelians, which Heidegger in the later course classifies under the "Platonism of barbarians": "'barbarian' because the authentic roots of Plato's thought are missing" (43; trans. van Buren). However, Heidegger does not at all limit his critique to one type of dialectic and does not so much as hint that another type, that is, Plato's, might be exempted. Furthermore, it is evident that the terms in which Heidegger critiques dialectic in these two courses are very similar to the terms in which he critiques Plato's dialectic in the *Sophist* lectures. The parallel with the SS 1924 course is even clearer: there Heidegger makes of Platonic philosophy exactly the same critique he makes of modern dialectic in the two earlier courses: that rather than beginning with what is phenomenologically given, it instead begins with concepts and theories (GA 18, 14, 37). Finally, the only difference Heidegger appears to recognize between the modern dialectic and Plato's dialectic, as is clear from certain comments in the *Sophist* lectures (see GA 19, 199, 262, 449), is that the latter is humbler than the former and therefore at least attempts to be phenomenological (i.e., to see the things themselves). Yet because Plato's dialectic does not thereby succeed in being phenomenology, Heidegger can still judge it inadequate in generally the same ways that modern dialectic is. In defending phenomenology against dialectic, he clearly feels that he can ignore the differences between the ancient and modern versions of the latter.

That it is a commitment to phenomenology that leads Heidegger to dismiss dialectic is especially evident in another, more indirect critique found in the course of WS 1925–26 (*Logik: Die Frage nach der Wahrheit*). Heidegger here argues that by relating the different colors to one another "in the most extreme dialectic imaginable" one will never be able to grasp any of them: "I grasp it [i.e., a color] only when I set out to see it itself, no help is provided by all relations to other colors; it is a kind of being that is grasped only in so far as it is taken purely in itself; the same is true of essence, motion, time, and the like" (GA 21, 184–85). Here we see most clearly what is behind

9. The translations of this text are those of John van Buren, *Ontology: The Hermeneutics of Facticity* (Bloomington: Indiana University Press, 1999). In the KS 1919 course, Heidegger makes a similar point about the "uncreative" character of dialectic, there with reference to Fichte: "Dialektik im Sinne der Auflösung immer neu zu setzender Widersprüche *ist sachlich unschöpferisch,* die Widerspruchssetzung selbst nur möglich durch ein verstecktes nicht dialektisches Prinzip, das ob seiner eigenen Verstecktheit und Ungeklärtheit außerstande ist, die Art und Geltung der deduzierten Formen und Normen als echte zu begründen" (GA 56/57, 40). In the SS 1924 course, Hegel's dialectic is similarly charged with being "uncreative" (GA 18, 10).

Heidegger's critique of dialectic: the belief in the possibility of a pure seeing that transcends λόγος. Earlier in the course Heidegger argues that "propositional truth" (*Satzwahrheit* or λόγος-*Wahrheit*) is derived from the more primordial phenomenon of "intuitional truth" (*Anschauungswahrheit*), which Heidegger also calls νοῦς-*Wahrheit* (110–12). He thus claims, following Husserl, that "the origin of all research in general and all knowledge is intuition as the first source of legitimacy [*Rechtsquelle*]" (114). Heidegger then traces the important role that *Anschauung* has played in the traditional conception of knowledge, going back to the Greek θεωρεῖν: "Genuine knowing is θεωρεῖν, the pure, seeing relation to the being itself" (123).

Yet does not Heidegger subject this traditional conception of knowledge to a radical critique? And is it not a well-known fact that Heidegger did not remain a faithful pupil of Husserl, departing in particular from his teacher's prioritizing of theoretical intuition? Heidegger's lengthiest critique of Husserlian phenomenology is to be found in the SS 1925 course *Prolegomena zur Geschichte des Zeitbegriffes* (GA 20, 140–82). Theodore Kisiel, along with others, has found in this critique a radical break with Husserl on two main points: Heidegger (1) rejects the primacy of perception and (2) displaces intuition by a more fundamental understanding.[10] While Kisiel sees the break as here only "virtually complete,"[11] he finds its completion in the following passage from *Sein und Zeit*: "By showing how all sight is primarily based on understanding [*Verstehen*]—the circumspection of taking care of things is understanding as *common sense* [*Verständigkeit*]—we have taken away from pure intuition its priority which noetically corresponds to the traditional ontological priority of objective presence. 'Intuition' and 'thought' are both already remote derivatives of understanding. Even the phenomenological 'intuition of essences' is based on existential understanding" (147). While one cannot rule out some shift in Heidegger's understanding of the priority of noetic intuition between the courses preceding (and including) the *Sophist* lectures of WS 1924–25 and those immediately following it, two observations are necessary to avoid exaggerating the shift: (1) the claim that noetic intuition is derivative of the circumspection that characterizes everyday being-in-the-world is perfectly compatible with the view that such intuition is the *goal* of phenomenology, as long as one recognizes that getting along circumspectly in the world and doing a phenomenological

---

10. Theodore Kisiel, *The Genesis of Heidegger's "Being and Time"* (Berkeley and Los Angeles: University of California Press, 1993), 373 (hereafter GH); and "From Intuition to Understanding: On Heidegger's Transposition of Husserlian Phenomenology," *Études Phénoménologiques* 22 (1995): 31–50. See also John van Buren, *The Young Heidegger: Rumor of the Hidden King* (Bloomington: Indiana University Press, 1994), 203–19, specifically, 209–15, on Heidegger's critique of the priority of the theoretical, and 216, on Heidegger's claim that interpretation, rather than perception, is primary.

11. And he sees the same criticisms of Husserl pursued in the WS 1925–26 course: see GH, especially 400, and "From Intuition to Understanding," 44–46.

analysis of being-in-the-world are two different things.[12] (2) Even if the knowledge sought by phenomenology is characterized by projection (understanding) and interpretation (*Auslegung*), it still retains for Heidegger the character of *Anschauung* (whether or not this is in the end consistent).[13]

These two claims receive some support from the fact that between the SS 1925 course and *Sein und Zeit* we have the WS 1925–26 course, where, as we have seen, Heidegger in his critique of dialectic seems as committed as ever to the priority of *Anschauung*. Yet it is also possible to find support in the SS 1925 course and *Sein und Zeit* themselves. In the SS 1925 course Heidegger characterizes the method of phenomenology as *descriptive*, where description is characterized as "a directly seeing apprehension and accentuation" ("Eine solche direkt sehende Erfassung und Hebung"), or more specifically, "an accentuating articulation of what is in itself intuited" ("ein heraushebendes

12. Of course, from early on Heidegger struggles to overcome this difference between phenomenology and life, but it is questionable whether it can ever be overcome. Even if we characterize phenomenology as simply the repetition and intensification of that familiarity that life already has with itself (see, e.g., GA 56/57, 110), this "intensification" still involves an explicit and direct awareness, and in this sense an "intuition," that transcends the everyday familiarity. As Heidegger himself states the objection: "Aber wenn das phänomenologische Forschen überhaupt ein 'Verhalten zu etwas' ist, dann liegt darin die unentrinnbare Vergegenständlichung, ein schlechterdings nicht zu beseitigendes Moment der Theoretisierung" (112). Heidegger's reply to this objection is complex and obscure, but its gist appears to be the following: any stage in the process of *Entlebung* can be seen as a "mere something" ("bloßes Etwas"); therefore, the formal theorizing of the "mere something" is not a stage in the *Entlebungsprozeß*, much less the highest stage, but rather something essentially different with a different motivation (114). The "something" as "Erlebbares überhaupt" signifies the *Vorweltliche*, that which is experienced in the movement from one *Erlebnissituation* to another (115). Far from being, therefore, the highest stage of *Entleben*, "Es ist vielmehr der Index für die höchste Potentialität des Lebens" (115). In short, "In dem Etwas als dem Erlebbaren überhaupt haben wir nicht ein radikal Theoretisiertes und Entlebtes, als vielmehr ein Wesensmoment des Lebens an und für sich zu sehen, das in einem engen Zusammenhang steht mit dem Ereignischarakter der Erlebnisse als solcher" (116). What we appear to have here is an opposition between the "theoretical" in the traditional sense and a new sense of the "theoretical" as an intensification of life. Heidegger can also in this way claim that the "etwas" given to phenomenological intuition is not an *object* (see 217). But even if the "something" of phenomenological intuition is not a theoretized "object" abstracted from life and stands in a close relation with the event-character of life, there is still a relation here rather than an identity and the above objection can return in a different formulation.

13. In addition to the specific points made below, it is also important to note that *Verstehen* and *Anschauung* are by no means incompatible opposites for Heidegger. In the WS 1919/20 course Heidegger often closely associates, if not identifies, the two terms (see, e.g., GA 58, 138, 146, 163, 185, 240, and 262), and even in *Sein und Zeit* itself, shortly before the passage cited above, Heidegger asserts: "In its character of project, understanding constitutes existentially what we call the *sight* [*Sicht*] of Da-sein" (146). As Heidegger proceeds to point out, this "sight" can of course be identified neither with sensible perception nor with nonsensory perception of what is objectively present (147). But it is still "sight" in the sense that "it lets the beings accessible to it be encountered in themselves without being concealed" (147). Many years later, in the 1968 seminar in Le Thor, Heidegger is reported to have said the following: "Zum Verstehen, sagt Heidegger, ist es nötig, phänomenologisch zu sehen" (VS, 26). See also the observations of Jacques Taminiaux (*Sillages Phénoménologiques: Auditeurs et lecteurs de Heidegger* [Brussels: OUSIA, 2002], 159–60), who concludes that "le concept heideggerien de l'herméneutique est ici de nature intuitionniste" (160).

Gliedern des an ihm selbst Angeschauten," GA 20, 107).[14] He thus still recognizes the "demand for an ultimate direct givenness of the phenomena," even if he immediately denies that this is a comfortable and immediate seeing, given that it requires a constant struggle against concealment (GA 20, 120).[15] Accordingly, Heidegger's major objection against Husserl is that Husserl is *unphenomenological* in the sense of remaining blinded by the traditional conceptions (179; see also 159). In this same course Heidegger appears to question the distinction between *Anschauung* and *Ausdruck* when he claims that even the simplest perceptions are always already *expressed* (*ausgedrückte*) and *interpreted*, so that "primarily and originally [*primär und ursprünglich*] we do not so much see the objects and things, but rather we most immediately [*zunächst*] talk about them; put more precisely, we do not say what we see but, on the contrary, we see what one says about the thing [*was man über die Sache spricht*]" (GA 20, 75; my trans.). But Heidegger is here describing the idle talk in which we primarily and at first find ourselves: certainly this description leaves open the possibility of saying what we first genuinely see instead of seeing only what has already been spoken. If *Ausdruck* at first determines *Anschauung*, it is the task of phenomenology to reverse this.

As for *Being and Time*, it must first be recalled that Heidegger's own characterization of phenomenology there appeals to the Greek conception of truth as residing most originally not in λόγος but in "pure *noein*, straightforwardly observant apprehension of the simplest determination of the being of beings as such" (33).[16] This appeal is certainly odd if Heidegger's intent is to disassociate his phenomenology from noetic intuition. Secondly, after asserting the derivative character of the phenomenological *Wesensschau* in the passage cited above, Heidegger proceeds, not to reject the idea of such a *Wesensschau*,

---

14. Quotations from GA 20 use Theodore Kisiel's translation (*History of the Concept of Time: Prolegomena* [Bloomington: Indiana University Press, 1985]), unless otherwise noted. Kisiel argues (GH, 368) that this characterization of phenomenology is superceded by Heidegger's later claim that "expository interpretation" (*Auslegung*) is "die Grundform alles Erkennens" (GA 20, 359). But these two characterizations of knowledge seem both here and in *Sein und Zeit* to exist side by side, rather than it being the case that one supercedes the other.

15. Kisiel describes Heidegger in the WS 1925–26 course as attempting "to get at a deeper structure of presence, immediacy, and givenness than the structure of immediacy offered by intuition" (GH, 400; see also "From Intuition to Understanding," 49). Kisiel's summary of the course also sees Heidegger as committed to the possibility of a "simple apprehension of things," though one more primary than direct intuition (GH, 402). That Heidegger rejects the priority of intuition narrowly conceived as "object-intuition" cannot be denied (though his characterization of phenomenology at one point as the "objectification of being" makes even this hard to assert without qualification: see note below). What concerns me here, because it is what lies at the basis of Heidegger's critique of dialectic, is his continued commitment to the priority of intuition conceived as the direct apprehension of what is immediately given.

16. See also the appeal to Aristotelian νόησις at 226 in the context of Heidegger's own account of truth as not lying essentially in judgment. When he refers to the priority granted seeing by the Greeks and the corresponding idea that "primordial and genuine truth lies in pure intuition" (SZ, 171), he does

but rather to leave its nature an open question: "We can decide about this kind of seeing only when we have gained the explicit concept of being and the structure of being" (147). Since this explicit concept will never be gained, the seeing in question will remain indeterminate; however, Heidegger can still consider phenomenology as aiming at some kind of seeing, however indeterminate and problematic.

Finally, and most importantly, there is Heidegger's discussion in section 69(b) of "The Temporal Meaning of the Way in Which Circumspect Taking Care Becomes Modified into the Theoretical Discovery of Things Objectively Present in the World." Heidegger here appears to be describing the genesis not only of the theoretical sciences, but also of his own phenomenological ontology (which he at this point considers to be a science). After again observing that "the idea of the *intuitus* has guided all interpretation of knowledge ever since the beginnings of Greek ontology up to today, whether that intuition is actually attainable or not" (358), Heidegger makes this the guideline for his following account of the existential genesis of science: "In accordance with the priority of 'seeing,' the demonstration of the existential genesis of science will have to start out by characterizing the circumspection that guides 'practical' taking care of things" (358). While Heidegger's account of the genesis of science will thus show theoretical intuition to be derivative of practical circumspection, it will thereby also ground and support the central role played by this intuition in science. Therefore, Heidegger concludes his account with the following description of the scientific project: "The articulation of the understanding of being, the definition of the subject-matter defined by that understanding, and the prefiguration of the concepts suitable to these beings, all belong to the totality of this projecting that we call *thematization*. It aims at freeing beings encountered within the world in such a way that they can 'project' themselves back upon pure discovery, that is, they can become objects. Thematization objectifies" (363). Note that what is projected here is projected for a "pure discovery" ("einem puren Entdecken").

It might be objected that this description of science cannot apply to phenomenology since the latter does not objectify. However, in the course that

---

so without any explicit criticism, though he does link the idea to the phenomenon of *curiosity*. This link by itself does not bring into question the role of pure intuition in genuine knowledge since in the article "The Concept of Time" of 1924 Heidegger described both curiosity and scientific investigation as arising when the "as-what" is detached from its "in-order-to," so that how the world appears to curiosity can provide the basis for scientific investigation: "Insofar, however, as curiosity always discloses the world within certain limits, the look [*Aussehen*] of the world that thereby becomes accessible can be seized upon as the ground for an *investigative* looking-at [*Hinsehen*]. In such going-after-the-things-themselves [*solchem den-Sachen-Nachgehen*] lies the possibility of forming an investigation [*Forschung*]" (GA 64, 38).

immediately followed *Sein und Zeit,* Heidegger indeed describes phenomenology as objectifying: he there claims that while the positive sciences constitute themselves in the objectification of beings (GA 24, 456),[17] "Our question aims at the objectification of being as such, at the second essential possibility of objectification, in which philosophy is supposed to constitute itself as a science" (GA 24, 458). There is no question that even in Heidegger's own eyes at the time, this characterization of philosophy is problematic. Immediately following the passage from *Sein und Zeit* cited above, Heidegger points out that objectification has the character of "making present" and then adds in a note the following remark: "The thesis that all cognition aims at 'intuition' has the temporal meaning that all cognition is a making present. Whether every science or even philosophical cognition aims at a making present must remain undecided here" (363n22).[18] There is a crisis in the making here that will eventually lead Heidegger to abandon the characterization of philosophy as a science (as will be documented below). However, the fact that despite all the problems Heidegger still cannot free himself from the idea of the priority of "pure seeing" in philosophy (though not in everyday life) only shows how committed he is to this priority. By *Sein und Zeit* there is in Heidegger a high level of discomfort with Husserl's conception of phenomenology and in some important respects even a radical break, but not with regard to the priority of some sort of noetic intuition. Furthermore, we will see that even after he abandons the characterization of philosophy as a science, Heidegger still does not give up on the noetic character of philosophical, and even postphilosophical, thinking.

Against Kisiel and others, then, we must conclude with Taminiaux[19] that Heidegger subscribes to Husserl's "clear-cut demarcation between the intuitive

17. The translation used is that of Albert Hofstadter, *The Basic Problems of Phenomenology* (Bloomington: Indiana University Press, 1982).

18. Kisiel considers this note, which he describes as entertaining "an entirely new thought," to be "no idle speculation" since "already in BT, it is clear what the ontological upshot of this destruction of *intuitus, Vernehmen* (ergo *Vernunft* = 'reason'!) will be: the light of eternal νοεῖν is to be replaced by the more understanding 'lighting' of a temporal 'clearing'" (GH, 413). Some such shift is indeed coming, but whether this will mean an abandonment of the very notion of "intuition" or a transformation of it still remains to be seen. In any case, the fact that Heidegger proceeds in the SS 1927 course to characterize philosophy as aiming at an objectification of being certainly brings into question Kisiel's contention that Heidegger succeeds in "replacing objectifying intuition with nonobjectifying understanding" within phenomenology (GH, 376).

19. *The Thracian Maid and the Professional Thinker: Arendt and Heidegger,* trans. Michael Gendre (Albany: State University of New York Press, 1997), 56–79; see also Taminiaux, "The Husserlian Heritage in Heidegger's Notion of the Self," in *Reading Heidegger from the Start: Essays in His Earliest Thought,* ed. Theodore Kisiel and John van Buren (Albany: State University of New York Press, 1994), 269–90. The crucial point to be made in response to Kisiel's reading is most clearly stated by Taminiaux in another text: "Rejeter la presence de l'*Anschauung* c'est seulement prendre ses distances à l'égard de ce qui, d'Aristote à Husserl, correspondait, à titre de correlate noétique, au 'privilège ontologique traditionnel du *Vorhanden*.' . . . Mais il ne resulte pas de cette prise de distance que l'être a

register and a merely symbolic one" (58) or, specifically, that "the phenomenon in the sense of Heideggerian phenomenology is defined as 'what shows itself within itself' and is at the outset delineated from the register of mediateness and the symbolic in general" (59), and that Heidegger subordinates λόγος, even *apophantic* λόγος, to noetic vision (61). This Husserlian legacy that Taminiaux finds in Heidegger and that is evident in the texts discussed above is certainly a central factor in explaining Heidegger's rejection of dialectic.[20] Indeed, this is the explanation Heidegger himself offered in 1952 during a colloquium on dialectic held in Muggenbrunn. Asked to explain the dismissal of dialectic as a "philosophical embarrassment" in *Being and Time*, Heidegger said the following: "The observation in question against dialectic is to be understood from the phenomenological position; it is a resistance against the blind conceptual [*begriffliche*] discussion of the themes of philosophy; what is at issue here is the opposition between conceptual [*begrifflicher*] dialectic and intuitive receiving [*anschauendem Entgegennehmen*] (seeing, immediate demonstration [*unmittelbare Aufweisung*])" (CD, 9).

---

dessein duquel le Dasein est tel qu'il est ne se livre pas à une vue" (*Sillages*, 45–46). Stanley Rosen also attributes to Heidegger "an inability to rid himself of the influence of the Husserlian orientation by perception" (*The Question of Being: A Reversal of Heidegger* [New Haven: Yale University Press, 1993], 294), while recognizing the important differences between the two thinkers: see 294–309. Taminiaux's basic critique of Heidegger, which he has defended in a number of places, is that Heidegger sees himself as having achieved "the status of an ultimate seer *aneu logou*." "Nothingness and the Professional Thinker: Arendt Versus Heidegger," in *The Ancients and the Moderns*, ed. Reginald Lilly (Bloomington: Indiana University Press, 1996), 209; see also *Thracian Maid*, 20 and especially 188; also *Sillages*, 31, 50–63, 82–84, 194). It is highly ironic, however, that Taminiaux sees Heidegger as here agreeing with Plato. Even in his discussions of the *Sophist* course (in *Heidegger and the Project of Fundamental Ontology*, trans. Michale Gendre [Albany: SUNY Press, 1991], 139–43, and "Nothingness and the Professional Thinker") Taminiaux makes no mention of the fact that Heidegger there sides with Aristotle against Plato, but instead continues to insist that Heidegger sides with Plato against Aristotle; see also "Plato's Legacy in Heidegger's Two Readings of *Antigone*," in HPD, where Taminiaux describes Heidegger in the *Sophist* course as siding with "Plato's deliberate dedication to the *bios theôrêtikos*" (34). Taminiaux, at least until recently, appears committed to a caricature of Plato derived exclusively from a naively literal, one-sided, and selective reading of the *Republic*. How else is one to explain Taminiaux's assertion that Plato, the great poet of dramatic dialogues and myths, believed that "an end should be brought to plots, or *mythoi*" (*Thracian Maid*, 78) and exhibited "disdain for human affairs" in favor of the solitary *bios theoretikos* (*Heidegger and the Project of Fundamental Ontology*, 130)? Yet the above qualification is necessary since in the 2005 essay cited above Taminiaux, in sharp contrast to earlier essays, repeatedly characterizes Plato's argument in the *Republic* as ironic (24, 26, 30), though without examining the implications of this irony for Plato's true position.

20. I therefore do not believe, as does Figal, that "there is nothing, absolutely nothing to prevent him [Heidegger] from understanding dialectic in this sense as hermeneutic, or conversely, there is nothing to prevent him from taking his bearings on the Platonic dialectic for the purpose of conceptually articulating a 'hermeneutics of facticity.'" "Refraining from Dialectic: Heidegger's Interpretation of Plato in the *Sophist* Lectures (1924/25)," in *Interrogating the Tradition: Hermeneutics and the History of Philosophy*, ed. Charles E. Scott and John Sallis (Albany: State University of New York Press, 2000), 104. What prevents him from doing this is a commitment, albeit qualified, to Husserlian phenomenology.

3. The Inconsistency and Untenableness of Heidegger's Critique

The dispute, in short, is this: for Plato, philosophy is identical with dialectic; for Heidegger the phenomenologist, as for Aristotle, philosophy is above dialectic. Is Heidegger's position sustainable? Here it will be useful to begin with a passage in the SS 1924 course that is perhaps the most extreme expression of the critique of Plato's dialectic that will be carried out in the subsequent *Sophist* course. In the context of discussing Aristotle's claim that we must proceed from what is better known to us to what is better known in itself, Heidegger comments (according to a *Nachschrift*): "These statements are programmatic, the genuine *countermovement* [*Gegenstoß*] *to Platonic philosophy*. Aristotle says: I must have some *ground* under my feet, a ground that is there in an initial self-evidence, in order to concern myself with being. I cannot fantastically cling to a determinate concept of being and then speculate" (GA 18, 37). The implication here that Plato, in contrast to Aristotle, merely starts with assumed abstract concepts and speculates "fantastically" is explicit in Heidegger's *Handschrift* for the course: "*Plato*, with a side glance at what is there, fantastically imprisons himself [*verfängt*] within λόγος and thereby, in Greek fashion, proceeds consistently" (352).[21] In contrast, "Aristotle decides this question [that of the unique ergon of man] not fantastically, but in such a way that he opens his eyes. The object here is to *see* the ἴδιον" (98). Here we have the germ of the critique that will be developed within the *Sophist* course: Plato, in contrast to Aristotle the phenomenologist, is trapped within λόγος. But can any reader of the dialogues believe that Plato does *not* always begin with everyday experience, that his inquires are not grounded in, and continually refer back to, such experience, that he only casts a "side glance" at what is there? And can any reader of the dialogues doubt that λόγος in the form of dialogue is not only rooted in the ground of ordinary experience but always continually points beyond itself to a reality that transcends it?

In the *Sophist* course, Heidegger himself must acknowledge that Plato's critique of writing in the *Phaedrus* shows him to have some awareness of the following limitation and danger of λόγος: "It has become clear that λόγος *is referred to* ὁρᾶν and therefore has a *derivative character*, that, on the other hand, insofar as it is carried out *in isolation*, insofar as it is the way in which humans merely speak, that is, chatter about things, it is precisely what in human existence can *obstruct* [*verstellt*] the possibility of seeing things. Thus in itself, insofar as it is *free-floating* [*freischwebend*], λόγος has the peculiar character of disseminating through repetition a presumed knowledge that

---

21. At one point Heidegger even uses the adverb *platonisch* in the sense of "explaining in terms of concepts or theories that already lie at hand" (GA 18, 14).

bears no relation to the things themselves" (GA 19, 339–40; my trans.). Central to Plato's critique of writing is the myth of Thamus and Theuth (274c–275b). Discussing Thamus's objection that Theuth's invention of writing would produce not wisdom, but only the conceit of wisdom (σοφίας δόξα, 275a6–7), not μνήμη, but only ὑπομνησις (275a5), Heidegger interprets this distinction as one between "a return to, recovery and appropriation of the things themselves" and "a mere recalling that clings to the spoken word" (GA 19, 342; my trans.). As Heidegger recognizes, λόγος, and not writing per se, is the main target here. Plato's point is that the kind of "clinging to λόγος" encouraged by, but not confined to, writing will not bring us into contact with the things themselves, but will only produce a superficial "learnedness" that can recall what has been said. Λόγος can indeed play a positive role in gaining wisdom, but only as long as its role is recognized to be completely secondary. As Heidegger observes, for Plato the written and spoken word can be a provocation to return to the things themselves, but nothing more. "What is said and written—this is essential—can by itself deliver nothing" (GA 19, 343). In contrast, the "living logos" of dialectic existing in the soul is one that "takes its life from a relation to the matters themselves" ("der aus dem *Sachverhältnis* lebt," 345). While λόγος can and should be guided by such a relation, it cannot itself provide this relation.

The *Seventh Letter* takes the critique of λόγος even further, though in passages unfortunately overlooked by Heidegger's brief discussion (GA 19, 346–47). Plato there speaks of "the weakness inherent in λόγοι" (τὸ τῶν λόγων ἀσθενές): the weakness being that λόγοι express how a thing is *qualified* (τὸ ποῖόν τι), that is, that *x* is *y*, rather than what it *is* in itself (τὸ ὄν, 342e2–343a1; see also 343b7–c5).[22] This appears to be the limitation of λόγος which Heidegger thought only Aristotle had seen: "Insofar as λόγος addresses something as something, it is in principle unfit to grasp that which by its very sense cannot be addressed as something else but can only be grasped for itself" (GA 19, 206).

The *Phaedrus* and the *Seventh Letter* thus show that we do not need Aristotle to recognize the secondary character of λόγος, since Plato himself already makes this perfectly clear.[23] The point of Heidegger's criticism, however, may

22. For further discussion of the argument of the *Seventh Letter*, see my *Dialectic and Dialogue: Plato's Practice of Philosophical Inquiry* (Evanston: Northwestern University Press, 1998), chap. 9; and "Nonpropositional Knowledge in Plato," *Apeiron* 31 (1998): 243–53.

23. Therefore, when Heidegger asserts that Plato, "obzwar er *in gewissem Sinne* die sekundäre Bedeutung des logos versteht, doch nicht dazu übergeht, den logos selbst in dieser seiner sekundären Stellung zum Thema zu machen und in seine eigentliche Struktur positive einzudringen" (GA 19, 338, my emphasis; see also the qualification "gewissermaßen" at 340), one must ask what more Plato could have done to make "thematic" the secondary position of λόγος. David Webb ("Continuity and Difference in Heidegger's *Sophist*," *Southern Journal of Philosophy* 38 [2000]: 153–54) completely overlooks Plato's critique of λόγος, claiming that Plato allowed "the predominant form of disclosure specific to

be that, while dialectic exposes the limits of λόγος and thereby destroys its pretensions, it provides us with no means of transcending λόγος. Yet Heidegger's own words contradict this charge. In the context of discussing the characterization of thinking (διανοεῖσθαι) in the *Theaetetus* (189e) as a λόγος that the soul goes through (διεξέρχεται) with itself, Heidegger points to the parallel with the characterization of dialectic in the *Sophist* as a διαπορεύεσθαι διὰ τῶν λόγων and rightly emphasizes the διά (GA 19, 409). This διάλογος which "takes apart" and distinguishes (Heidegger characterizes the διά as "Auseinandernehmen") is oriented toward what Heidegger here calls "the appropriation of what is seen in its unconcealedness" ("die Aneignung des Gesehenen in seiner Unverborgenheit," 409). Heidegger therefore draws the following conclusion: "If the discernment proper, διανοεῖν, is characterized as διάλογος, and specifically as a speaking of the soul with and to itself, then this indicates that λέγειν, as it is determined in διαλεκτική, is actually nothing else than a νοεῖν. Thus, the διαλέγεσθαι is a νοεῖν in an emphatic sense"[24] (GA 19, 410). And yet in criticizing dialectic Heidegger speaks as if νοεῖν were something completely *outside* it and therefore unattainable by it. As seen above, he characterizes dialectic as a "*confinement* to beings as addressed in speech."

Heidegger's ambivalence concerning the extent to which dialectic does or does not see the things themselves is strikingly apparent in another passage. Recognizing the danger that, by characterizing dialectic as having an inherent tendency toward a "pure seeing" that it can never attain, he might appear to make it a futile endeavour as well as to collapse any distinction between it and the "Unsachlichkeit" of sophistry (on which see GA 19, 215), Heidegger is forced to provide a more positive characterization of what dialectic *does* accomplish: "Although διαλέγεσθαι does not reach its goal and *does not purely and simply disclose beings*, as long as it still remains in λέγειν, it need not be a mere game but has a proper function insofar as it cuts through the idle talk, checks the prattle, and in a certain sense *lays its finger* on that which speaking intends. In this way διαλέγεσθαι presents the things spoken of in a *first indication* and in their *immediate outward look* [*in einer ersten Anzeige erstmalig und in ihrem nächsten Aussehen*]" (GA 19, 197, trans. modified and my

---

the *logos* to have overtaken the possibilities of disclosure inherent within *nous*. The *logos* is allowed to foist its own impoverished ontological attitude upon *nous*" (154). Accordingly, Webb also ignores the negative, refutative dimension of Plato's dialectic that distinguishes it from ordinary discourse (except perhaps at 169n32), treating this dialectic instead as nothing but a series of thematic statements about its object (and thus failing to see in it what he finds in Heidegger's conception of errancy, i.e., "the logos itself encountering its limit," 162).

24. Heidegger also emphasizes the inseparability of dialectic from a certain kind of "seeing" at 349–50, and in a note from the manuscript writes: "Denken ist nur gerade dialektisch, sofern es anschauend ist" (626). As Figal observes, "Heidegger concedes much more to the Platonic conception of dialectic than his introductory comments on this topic indicate" ("Refraining from Dialectic," 105).

emphases).²⁵ But if dialectic "does not *purely and simply* [*schlechthin*] disclose beings," then in what way and to what extent does it disclose them? The talk of "a first indication" and an "outward look" is not very helpful. Furthermore, is the "pure seeing" or νοεῖν that dialectic fails to achieve even possible? Heidegger himself elsewhere clearly questions, if not denies altogether, this possibility. In the SS 1924 course Heidegger similarly characterizes the limitations of dialectic: "διαλεκτική has indeed [as opposed to sophistry] the seriousness [*Ernst*], but it is only the seriousness of a tentative looking at [*des versuchenden Nachsehens*] what in the end could be meant [*was am End gemeint sein könnte*]" (GA 18, 7). But Heidegger then immediately proceeds to describe the "philology" he himself is practicing in the course in exactly the same terms with which he describes dialectic: "In this sense we are dealing with philosophy, *in the form of a looking at what in the end could be meant* [*in der Weise des Nachsehens, was am Ende gemeint sein könnte*]" (7).

If Heidegger in the 1924 course is a self-described "philologist," this is because for him, as for Plato and Aristotle on his interpretation, λόγος is not simply a means of expression that can be dispensed with: it is a fundamental characteristic of human existence (GA 19, 319, 577–78); because humans are the ζῷον λόγον ἔχον, the world is necessarily disclosed to them through λόγος. Even if we can to some extent attain a νοεῖν understood as *reines Hinsehen*, we can do so only through the medium of speech. In other words, νοεῖν can be achieved only in the form of a διανοεῖν, of a discursive "thinking through," which as such is also a διαλέγεσθαι. The consequence, in Heidegger's own words, is "that νοῦς as such is not a possibility of the being of man. Yet insofar as 'intending' and perceiving [*ein 'Vermeinen' und Vernehmen*] are characteristic of human *Dasein*, νοῦς can still be found in man. . . . This νοῦς in the human soul is not a νοεῖν, a straightforward seeing [*eine schlechthinniges Sehen*], but a διανοεῖν, because the human soul is determined by λόγος"²⁶ (GA 19, 59). This point is pursued at much greater length and depth in the SS 1924 course. There Heidegger, after asserting that "the νοῦς of man is not a pure one [*kein reines*]" (202), offers the following explanation: "So is νοῦς, with regard to the disclosedness of being-in, more than man can be, because

---

25. Heidegger calls this the "Grundsinn" of Plato's dialectic (GA 19, 197). The meaning and tendency of dialectic is "durch das nur Besprochene hindurch die echte ursprüngliche *Anschauung* vorzubereiten und auszubilden" (198). Note that according to this last description, dialectic not only *prepares*, but also *forms* the *Anschauung*.

26. Heidegger in this context points out that Aristotle did not say much about νοῦς, since this phenomenon presented him with great difficulties (58), something that Heidegger does not mention when he is intent on showing Aristotle's superiority over Plato. Figal sees in these passages a critique of Aristotle ("Refraining from Dialectic," 102–3), while Webb sees Heidegger here as following Aristotle ("Continuity and Difference," 161). Even if we have here a critique of Aristotle, it is a critique that strangely undermines Heidegger's critique of Plato.

the manner in which man seizes this possibility, νοῦς, is διανοεῖσθαι. Insofar as νοῦς constitutes the disclosedness of man, it is a διά, insofar as life is determined through λύπη and ἡδονή. Νοῦς is the fundamental condition of the possibility of being-in-the-world, which as such towers over the temporally particular concrete being of an individual human being" (201). Here νοῦς is identified with that disclosedness that characterizes being-in-the-world: that disclosedness within which we encounter beings in their being as well as our own being. But this disclosedness within which we stand is greater than us and can be actualized by us only in the form of διανοεῖσθαι. Though beings may stand disclosed to us in our being-in-the-world, so that we exist in truth and in νοῦς, we can disclose them, and thus realize this truth, only through a discursive thinking (διανοεῖσθαι). But why? In the passage cited above we are given a very strange answer: because our life is determined through λύπη and ἡδονή, pain and pleasure. It is not until much later in the course that Heidegger explains the cryptic connection between the inescapability of λόγος and the inescapability of pain and pleasure: because the disposition (*Befindlichkeit*) of pleasure and pain is characterized by the two possibilities of δίωξις and φυγή (pursuing and fleeing), and because the latter are necessarily the pursuing or fleeing of something *as* something, a life ruled by pain and pleasure is also a life ruled by λόγος in the form of a λέγειν τι κατά τινος, saying something *of* something (279–80, 364–65).²⁷

But if these claims are valid, how can any form of seeing be available to humans beyond that mediation between λόγος and νοῦς achieved by dialectic? Dialectic is indeed always only on the way toward a "pure seeing," but human nature is itself only on the way, as Heidegger himself points out in a passage in which the critique of Plato appears to be momentarily forgotten: "Human existence, insofar as it is oriented towards knowledge, is as such *on the way*

---

27. One could of course argue that for Aristotle himself the νοῦς in us is more than human and transcends our embodied state. At one point in the course Heidegger asks whether νοῦς "im Sein des Menschen aufgeht" or "von außen her in den Menschen hineinkommt" (GA 18, 200). Heidegger's comments on the preceding page suggest the former to be the case. The obstacle to such a view, however, is Aristotle's claim in *De Anima* III, 5, that one type of νοῦς is separable and immortal. Strangely, however, Heidegger's discussion of this chapter (201) makes no reference to this claim, does not distinguish between two types of νοῦς, and appears to treat all νοῦς as having the character of a δυνατόν, thereby ignoring Aristotle's identification of one kind of νοῦς with pure *energeia*. It is not until much later in the course that he finally mentions the distinction, interpreting it as one between the encountering of something as disclosed and the disclosing that makes such an encounter possible: "Dieses νοεῖν hat den Seinscharakter des Angegangenwerdens vom Entdeckten, was seinerseits nur so möglich ist, daß dieses Angegangenwerden von dem Entdeckten gründet in einem *Überhaupt-Entdeckthaben* und *Entdecktsein*, d. h. einem Entdecken, Sichtgeben *als solchen*. Der νοῦς τῆς ψυχῆς ist παθητικός (wie man später gesagt hat; Aristoteles hat diesen Terminus nicht) und er ist das als seiender νοῦς auf dem Grunde des ποιητικός, der überhaupt Vernehmbarkeit, Entdecktheit ermöglicht, d. h. Entdecktes *sehen läßt*, sehen macht—νοῦς ποιητικός" (391; see also 326). But again there is no consideration of the possibility that the νοῦς ποιητικός, as purely actual and immortal, transcends human being.

[*unterwegs*]. It is not and never will be finished with the disclosing of beings, that is, with ἐπίστασθαι" (GA 19, 389; see also 368, and GA 22, 312–13).

Yet what Heidegger says in the above passages stands in tension with his assertions in the same texts that the mediation of λόγος can be transcended. In the SS 1924 course, Heidegger asserts that "our being with regard to its uncoveredness is *immediately and for the most part [zunächst und zumeist]* διάνοια" (361), which suggests that it is possible to transcend διάνοια and achieve an uncoveredness that is pure νοῦς. In the WS 1925–26 course, Heidegger similarly claims only that νοῦς is "immediately and for the most part" ("zunächst und zumeist") διανοεῖν. Furthermore, he argues that ignorance has its source in this predominance of νοῦς as διανοεῖν, that is, in the tendency to take something to be perceived only when it is determined as something else in a sentence, and in the view that something has been revealed only when λέγειν is διαλέγεσθαι rather than mere φάναι (GA 21, 185). What Heidegger says here again appears to allow for the possibility of both a saying and a seeing that transcend διανοεῖν and διαλέγεσθαι. Especially revealing, however, is a passage in the *Sophist* course itself, a passage that is otherwise very similar to the passage from page 59 cited above: "λόγος, addressing something in speech, is our most immediate mode of carrying out ἀληθεύειν, whereas νοῦς, pure perception [*das reine Vernehmen*], is as such not possible for man, the ζῷον λόγον ἔχον. For us νοεῖν is initially and for the most part διανοεῖν, because our dealing with things is dominated by λόγος" (GA 19, 196). This passage exhibits in itself the tension, if not contradiction, in Heidegger's view: if νοῦς is simply not a possibility for human beings, then, as the cited passage from page 59 suggests, our νοεῖν should be *always* a διανοεῖν and not, as the present passage suggests, only *initially and for the most part* a διανοεῖν.[28] The same tension is evident in the SS 1924 course. Contrast with the passage on page 361 cited above the following: "This νοῦς [the νοῦς that characterizes the disclosedness of human being-in-the-world] is *always [immer]* a νοῦς τῆς ψυχῆς, a διανοεῖσθαι, thinking of something as something" (GA 18, 326; my emphasis). What, then, explains this puzzling oscillation in Heidegger's views within the *Sophist* course itself? It is probably not an accident that the passage on page 196 occurs in the context of a critique of Plato's dialectic, while the passage on page 59 does not: while in discussing the role of language in human existence Heidegger denies the possibility of a pure seeing that completely transcends the δια of διαλέγεσθαι, he can criticize Plato's dialectic only by affirming this possibility.

The exact nature of this possibility beyond dialectic that Heidegger wishes to maintain is explained most fully in the SS 1924 course. There Heidegger

---

28. Likewise, at 180 (GA 19) Heidegger asserts that human νοῦς "ist *immer* vollzogen in der Weise des Sprechens" (my emphasis) *and* that in order to grasp the ἀρχή or the ἔσχατον it must leave λόγος behind and be, not a διανοεῖν, but a "reines Hinsehen."

asserts that the philosopher must decide *against* the everyday interpretation of *Dasein*, in which "what is experienced and seen is for the most part [*zumeist*] there as *what is expressed in speech* [*Ausgesprochenes*]" (276). But what is the philosopher thereby deciding *for*? The answer is stated succinctly in Heidegger's *Handschrift*: "This task: in relation to the ruling as-what, this itself no longer in something else" (365); or a little more explicitly: "Leading the way only to it itself: τὶ καθ'αὐτο, not κατά τινος—no perspective [*keine Hinsicht*] and none under others" (364). Thus, the goal is the overcoming of the as-structure of λόγος altogether in some pure, direct vision of what a thing is in and by itself. Recall the characterization of phenomenology in the same course as the freedom from standpoints. But given the extent to which λόγος determines our being, is it possible to see something without seeing it *as* something, without seeing it from a certain perspective and standpoint? Another passage in which Heidegger articulates in more detail the possibility he sees as defining the philosophical life will help focus this question: "The average way of speaking and grasping is διανοεῖσθαι. Only against this average speaking (λέγειν τι κατά τινος) can ἕξις as ἀληθεύειν assert itself. The λόγος καθ'αὐτό addresses a being 'in itself.' It does not place the being in a foreign perspective [*Hinsicht*] but derives the perspectives in which it is to be examined from the being itself. *This λόγος that addresses the being in its being from out of itself is the* ὁρισμός" (283). Here we see that what Heidegger opposes to both dialectic and logic is not only a *seeing* of the thing itself, but also a saying that corresponds to this seeing by not addressing a being as something else, but rather addressing it only in and as itself. The only perspective or standpoint admitted here is one dictated by the thing itself rather than brought to it from outside of itself. But here two questions are unavoidable: (1) Is such a direct, unmediated access to the thing itself (Husserl's "principle of principles") a genuine human possibility? (2) If such "intuition" is possible, what kind of saying could possibly remain faithful to it? In response to the second question, Heidegger identifies this saying with ὁρισμός because a ὁρισμός (definition) says what something is according to its essence and thus in itself. But does not even such a ὁρισμός, if it is not to be a mere tautology, say something *of* something? Even if the perspective from which it defines a thing is not foreign to the thing, it is still *different* from it. Can there be here, in short, a clear demarcation between determining something *in itself and from itself* and determining it in terms of something distinct from itself? Why believe that the "in itself" is accessible in any way other than indirectly and mediately, that is, dialectically?

These are questions to which later chapters will repeatedly return. What must be noted now is the way in which Plato's description of dialectic overcomes Heidegger's either/or: either a λόγος that says something of something else or a seeing/saying of something in and of itself. The main problem with Heidegger's critique of dialectic is indeed that it assumes this either/or that it is precisely the task of dialectic to bring into question. In a passage from the *Seventh Letter*, unfortunately skipped by Heidegger's brief discussion of this work, Plato provides a characterization of dialectic that is consistent with Heidegger's own, but that also shows why a higher level of philosophizing is neither needed nor possible. Plato describes dialectic as a mediation between λέγειν and νοεῖν that not only *prepares*, but *provides* a partial vision of the things themselves precisely *in*, and not subsequent to, the destruction or refutation of concealing and distorting λόγοι: "When the three, i.e., names, propositions [λόγοι], as well as appearances and perceptions, are rubbed against each other, each of them being refuted through well-meaning refutations in a process of questioning and answering without envy, then will φρόνησις along with νοῦς barely [μόγις] commence to cast its light as the human mind exerts itself as much as is humanly possible" (344b3–c1). Recall that the "weakness of λόγος" that enables it to be refuted is that it only "qualifies" a thing, that is, asserts something *of* it rather than expressing directly its being. Though the cited passage describes the attainment of a νοῦς that transcends λόγος and its inherent weakness, this νοῦς is attained only in the discursive process of "rubbing" λόγοι against each other or *Für- und Gegensprechen*, that is, only in the context of διαλέγεσθαι. It is only in and through exposing the limits and contradictions of statements that say something of x that we can "barely" see x itself. In short, νοῦς is attainable, not *against* the average speaking of something *as* something, but only in and through this speaking.[29] Heidegger's phenomenological conviction that philosophical insight is attainable only *in opposition to* everyday discourse is precisely what Plato's dialectic rejects and what should therefore not be assumed in its critique.

How this assumption is operative in Heidegger's critique is made especially evident in some notes (*Beilagen*) included in the *Gesamtausgabe* edition of the SS 1924 course. In one passage Heidegger writes: "Not only ἄνευ . . .

---

29. In presenting Plato with the dilemma "either subsume the truth as given in *nous* within the structure of the *logos* (whereupon it loses its specifically ontological character), or allow it an independence that then threatens to be inarticulable and undemonstrable" ("Continuity and Difference," 149), Webb fails to see that Plato intends his dialectic to solve precisely this dilemma. Furthermore, though he observes that "Once *nous* is implicated in the *logos*, the moment of disclosure or truth it effects must itself be carried out through the very movement of dialectic itself" (161), he oddly asserts that Plato's dialectic could not do this because of its "inadequate conceptualization of movement" (161). But how do the practice and indirect disclosure of the movement between νοῦς and λόγος in dialectic depend on an adequate conceptualization and thematization of movement (something Plato could have considered impossible)? Specifically, Plato's "solution" to the problem of participation cited by Webb (169n29) is to avoid any thematic account of participation (since all accounts are necessarily inadequate, as the *Parmenides* shows), instead allowing participation to manifest itself in the very practice of dialectic.

[i.e., without λόγος], but to extricate oneself [*sich herausdrehen*] completely from this usual λόγος! ἐν οὐδεμιᾷ καταφάσει [in no saying something of something]—αὐτὸ καθ'αὑτό [itself by itself]. Here we have already the most genuine and sharpest opposition against all Platonic 'ontology' and 'logic'" (GA 18, 400). Plato's reply would of course be that it is delusional to think that one can "completely extricate oneself" from the usual λόγος, and Heidegger's critique only assumes that this is possible. In another note we read: "Plato and those who came before him did not see the λέγειν τι κατά τινος in its distinction from καθ'αὑτό λέγειν nor this itself in its fundamental structure" (402). As the *Seventh Letter* shows, Plato certainly did see the distinction between predicating something of something and expressing the being of a thing, that is, what it is in itself. But what he insisted on as constituting the weakness of λόγος was that any λόγος could not escape taking the form of predicating something of something and that therefore the true being of a thing could be seen and said only indirectly, that is, through the cracks exposed in λόγοι by well-meaning refutation. To critique Plato's dialectic for failing to attain a seeing/saying that grasps the being of a thing directly without the mediation expressed by the διά is therefore to beg the question.

It is in large part as a result of this question-begging that Heidegger's rejection of dialectic does not appear either consistent or coherent. If Heidegger's criticism is that dialectic does not attain νοεῖν at all, that νοεῖν remains completely outside of its λέγειν, then he is contradicted by his own statements. If, on the other hand, he means that dialectic can never attain a completely pure seeing beyond λόγος, then he is requiring of dialectic something that he himself sometimes recognizes to be impossible.[30] Plato would therefore see in Heidegger's belief that philosophy can and should be purer and clearer than dialectic nothing but self-delusion, the self-delusion of those who presume to write treatises on philosophy.

We have seen that what makes Heidegger side with Aristotelian σοφία and θεωρεῖν against Platonic dialectic is a commitment to phenomenology. But how is this compatible with the antitheoretical emphasis on πρᾶξις in Heidegger's thought? How can he assume that Aristotle's conceptual clarity does not miss something essential in the lived reality of dialectic as depicted in Plato's

---

30. See also GA 19, 624–25, where Heidegger describes dialectic as "Durchsprechen, mehr und mehr zur Sache hinführen." Can Heidegger claim that we are capable of more than this? Riedel draws attention to the nondialectical character of the language of *Being and Time*, which describes questioning as reaching its goal in the meaning of being, rather than recognizing that every answer will itself pose another question ("Hermeneutik," 105–6). Yet as Walter Brogan has pointed out, Heidegger in the *Beiträge* "ironically," given his critique of Plato, "also uses the word 'attempt' to describe his own efforts at thinking *Ereignis* and the truth of being." "Plato's Dialectical Soul: Heidegger on Plato's Ambiguous Relationship to Rhetoric," *Research in Phenomenology* 27 (1997): 15n4. Rosen observes that "Heidegger is never more Platonic than when he emphasizes that he is *unterwegs*" (*Question of Being*, 291).

dialogues, in this way falling *beneath* this dialectic? Does Heidegger believe that philosophy can entirely transcend the practical context of λόγος and δόξα concerning life and its meaning, a context embodied in the Platonic dialogue? In what follows I show that the distance between Heidegger and Plato is due not only to Heidegger's critique of dialectic in favor of phenomenology, but also to his related and radical appropriation of Aristotelian σοφία, an appropriation that has extremely important consequences for his own thought: in particular, the eclipsing of the practical and ethical dimension of φρόνησις and πρᾶξις in favor of the ontological, and the overestimation of philosophy's capacity to be *Wissenschaft*.

B. ETHICS AND ONTOLOGY

1. Σοφία Versus φρόνησις: Ontological Versus Practical Conception of the ἀγαθόν

As noted above, before Heidegger even turns to Plato he devotes a very large part of the *Sophist* course to Aristotle. Most of this discussion is devoted to the relation between two forms of unconcealing (ἀληθεύειν), φρόνησις and σοφία. According to Heidegger, one important difference between Aristotle and Plato is that Plato sees "the highest kind of unconcealing and the highest disposition overall, the highest existential possibility of man" in φρόνησις, while Aristotle sees it in σοφία (124). A consequence of this difference is that for Plato political science (πολιτικὴ ἐπιστήμη) is genuine wisdom (σοφία) and the statesman (πολιτικός) is the true philosopher (φιλόσοφος, 136), while for Aristotle they are not the same (*Nicomachean Ethics*, 1141a28-29). Heidegger apparently sees this difference as due to Aristotle's discovery of a higher level of ἀληθεύειν that Plato failed to see. Yet this is the kind of distortion that occurs in reading Plato through Aristotle. If we start with Aristotle's distinctions, it seems that Plato only recognizes the possibility of what Aristotle calls φρόνησις and thus does not attain the level of what Aristotle calls σοφία. If we read Aristotle through Plato, on the other hand, we see that Aristotle is simply separating what Plato considers inseparable and that Plato understands by his word φρόνησις *both* φρόνησις and σοφία as Aristotle understands them. Here we need only cite Heidegger against himself or, more specifically, the later Heidegger, who, as will be seen below, departs significantly in his interpretation of Plato on this issue from the Heidegger of the *Sophist* lectures: "Φρόνησις is for Plato *the* title for knowledge as a whole, that is, for the apprehension of what is true, for prudence and discernment, in relation to the world *and* the self, both in their unity. I emphasize this, because with Aristotle the concept of φρόνησις comes to be understood completely differently and, above all, *narrowly [verengt]*" (GA 34, 36; the last emphasis is my own).[31] The question in dispute is therefore not: is there a "theoretical" knowledge higher than the practical knowledge that Aristotle calls φρόνησις? The question is instead: should practical knowledge, that is, the knowledge that guides the human pursuit of the good, be separated from σοφία to the extent of being named and conceptualized differently? Does this "narrowing" represent an advance? Can the theoretical truly be divorced from the practical without thereby losing its relation to human life? To characterize Plato as "confused" or as failing to recognize anything higher than φρόνησις is to assume a positive answer to these questions.[32]

But what is to prevent a sharp distinction between σοφία and φρόνησις? Heidegger in the *Sophist* course recognizes that such a distinction involves separating the good (ἀγαθόν) from πρᾶξις so that it becomes an object of pure θεωρία. It is impossible to be in a purely theoretical stance towards the highest good or τέλος unless this good is not practical, that is, not a goal of any kind of acting or doing. Therefore, the reason why Aristotle, unlike Plato, was able to maintain the possibility of a σοφία distinguishable from, and ranked higher than, φρόνησις is that "he was able for the first time to show that the good is nothing other than an ontological determination of beings as defined by a *telos*."[33] Only on the basis of such an ontological understanding of the good can I relate myself to it in an attitude of pure contemplation; if the good were understood only as an object of πρᾶξις, I could relate myself to it only by *acting* and thus I would be capable of nothing higher than the practical knowledge with which Aristotle identifies φρόνησις (GA 19, 124). But now the questions raised above simply reappear in a different guise. Can the good as the "teleological"

---

31. Heidegger also recognizes that ἐπιστήμη undergoes a parallel narrowing (*Verengung*), with the result that for Aristotle, unlike Plato, it becomes in part synonymous with what we today call *Wissenschaft* (153–54).

32. For a helpful comparison between the Platonic and the Aristotelian conceptions of φρόνησις, see Monique Dixsaut, *Platon et la question de la pensée: Étude Platoniciennes* (Paris: J. Vrin, 2000), 109–19. I do not, however, agree with Dixsaut that the differences she cites arise from Plato's modeling of human action on τέχνη. There is indeed in Plato a dependence of virtuous action on knowledge of the forms, but this does not mean that acting virtuously is like following a blueprint in building a house. To interpret in that way the relation between knowledge and *praxis* in Plato is already to adopt the Aristotelian perspective.

33. "Ihm gelang es, zum ersten Mal zu zeigen, daß das ἀγαθόν nichts anderes ist als eine *Seinsbestimmung des Seienden*, das durch das τέλος bestimmt ist" (GA 19, 123). Heidegger makes the same point by claiming that Aristotle "gewinnt zum ersten Mal ein *ontologisches Grundverständnis* des ἀγαθόν" (123). This ontological understanding of the good is described by Heidegger as follows: "Das ἀγαθόν hat zunächst keinen Bezug auf die πρᾶξις, sondern es ist eine Bestimmung des Seienden, sofern es *fertig, voll-ständig* ist. Dasjenige Seiende, das immer ist, braucht gar nicht erst hergestellt zu werden; es ist immer schon ständig fertig da" (123). Heidegger bases his attribution to Aristotle of an ontological conception of the good on the statement in *Metaphysics* A that one of the four causes to be known by σοφία is τὸ οὗ ἕνεκα καὶ τἀγαθόν (τέλος γὰρ γενέσεως καὶ κινήσεως πάσης τοῦτ'ἐστίν) (983a31–32).

character of beings be completely sundered from the practical?[34] Can the good be given a *purely* ontological meaning? If Aristotle was the first to do this, then Plato clearly did not separate the ἀγαθόν from πρᾶξις. And indeed the practical and ontological functions of the idea of the good in the *Republic* do not appear to be sharply distinguished. Is this again due to Plato's "confusion"?

In order to discover what Heidegger during this period thought about Plato's own characterization of the ἀγαθόν, we must go outside the *Sophist* lectures to another nearly contemporaneous course, *Die Grundbegriffe der antiken Philosophie* (summer 1926). Heidegger in his manuscript for the course significantly prefaces his discussion of the idea of the good with the following question: "How does one get from the fundamental principles and determinations of beings, from ideas as structures of being to the idea of the ἀγαθόν, from the logical to the ethical, from being to 'ought'? οὐσία and ἀγαθόν" (GA 22, 140). Heidegger then proceeds to characterize the ἀγαθόν in Plato as simply an end (*Worumwillen*) for knowledge understood as a πρᾶξις (*Handeln*). Thus, as we are led to expect from the *Sophist* course, Heidegger does not think that Plato did what Aristotle was later able to do: separate the ἀγαθόν from πρᾶξις. But as a result, the ἀγαθόν in Plato does not characterize being as such. "Insofar as knowledge is taken to be a doing, being must be characterized as ἀγαθόν.... But this is no longer a characteristic of being as such, but is relative to knowledge. The ἀγαθόν is not a pure ontological determination [*nicht eine rein ontologische Bestimmung*]."[35] In this case Plato's characterization of being in terms of the ἀγαθόν is a mistake, a profound confusion, a failure to keep πρᾶξις and ontology distinct: "As long as one's subject is the analysis of the ὄν, one must avoid taking any step towards an ἀγαθόν. To address being as ἀγαθόν is to *misunderstand* being."[36] Heidegger can partially save Plato from this misunderstanding only by maintaining that Plato had the good sense to abandon the idea of the ἀγαθόν in his later dialogues, beginning with the *Theaetetus*: Heidegger characterizes this change, which he asserts to be a *fact*, as a "severing of the problem of being from the idea of the

---

34. A necessary assumption here is articulated by Heidegger in the SS 1924 course: "Τέλος heißt 'Ende' im Sinne der Fertigkeit, nicht 'Ziel' oder gar 'Zweck'" (GA 18, 39). This interpretation is defended at 82–88. For discussion and critique, see my "Beyond or Beneath Good and Evil? Heidegger's Purification of Aristotle's Ethics," in *Heidegger and the Greeks: Interpretative Essays*, ed. Drew A. Hyland and John Panteleimon Manoussakis (Bloomington: Indiana University Press, 2006), 129–38.

35. GA 22, 283. This is taken from the transcript of Hermann Mörchen, but appears to represent accurately what is stated much less clearly in Heidegger's own manuscript (140–41).

36. GA 22, 284. This is again from Mörchen's transcript, but an explanation of the way in which Being is misunderstood when addressed as ἀγαθόν can be found in Heidegger's own manuscript. The main objection is that Being (*Sein*) is thereby turned into *a being* (*ein Seiendes*): "Zum ἀγαθόν kommt es dadurch, daß Sein verstanden wird als Seiendes, eine seiende Eigenschaft, das Gute" (141). Furthermore, the view that the ἀγαθόν needs to be added to Being as its *value* (*Wert*) or *purpose* (*worumwillen, wozu*) arises from an inadequate interpretation of Being as *"puren Bestand,* nackte Dinganwesenheit" (141).

good" as well as from the fundamentally ethical orientation of Socrates.[37] We thus learn something that we cannot learn from the *Sophist* course itself, that is, Heidegger's view that the idea of the ἀγαθόν plays no role in the *Sophist*. The significance of this for his interpretation will be seen below.

Heidegger must acknowledge that the ἀγαθόν reappears in one later dialogue: the *Timaeus*. However, Heidegger explains this reappearance (according to Mörchen's transcript) by claiming that in the *Timaeus* "beings with respect to their being are explained in terms of making (in terms of a demiurge)" (GA 22, 284; see also 283). Thus, the ἀγαθόν reappears because Plato once again interprets, or rather misinterprets, being in terms of a πρᾶξις, in this case, the creation of the world by a creator. One year later, in the *Grundprobleme der Phänomenologie*, Heidegger goes so far as to suggest, very cryptically, that even in the *Republic* "the ἰδέα ἀγαθοῦ is nothing other than the δημιουργός, the pure maker" (GA 24, 405). What needs to be noted here is the assumption behind both Heidegger's commendation of Aristotle for distinguishing σοφία from φρόνησις and his critique of Plato: that we must avoid at all costs contaminating ontology by introducing into it a practical conception of the good.

It is important to note here both that this interpretation of the idea of the good during the 1920s undergoes several transformations in later years and that the central assumption nevertheless remains constant. To show this it is necessary to look forward to texts that will be discussed in detail in later chapters. In the lecture course *Vom Wesen der Wahrheit: Zu Platons Höhlengleichnis und Theätet* (1931–32), Heidegger performs a complete about-face. An indication of the change is that Heidegger now emphatically rejects the view that Plato gave up the idea of the good after the *Republic*, without acknowledging that this was *his own view* only a few years earlier! Heidegger now goes so far as to say that to give up the idea of the good, Plato would have had to give up the idea of philosophy altogether (GA 34, 110). The most striking specific change, however, is that Heidegger now identifies the idea of the good with the notion of δύναμις that defines being in the *Sophist* (110), whereas Heidegger earlier not only saw no connection between the two but even considered them incompatible (thus the theory that Plato in the *Sophist* abandoned the

---

37. This thesis is stated clearly in Heidegger's own manuscript: "Mit 'Theätet' beginnt in gewissem Sinne *die Ablösung des Seinsproblem von der Idee des Guten*. Stenzel hat das mit Recht als Kriterium der *Ablösung der Platonischen Philosophie von Sokrates und der spezifisch ethischen Grundorientierung* betrachtet. Zwei Perioden: Abschluß der ersten bildet der 'Staat.' . . . Neuer Ansatz im 'Theätet.' Ablösung des Seinsproblem von der Idee des Guten ist ein Faktum" (GA 22, 114, my emphases). It is also found in Mörchen's transcript, 265, 283–84. The only defense Heidegger offers, apart from the argument *ex silentio*, is the observation, found in Mörchen's transcript, that at one point in the *Theaetetus* (186a) the ἀγαθόν is mentioned as simply one characteristic among others and thus is given no prominence (271). As the above passage suggests, a corollary of the thesis is that starting with the *Theaetetus* Plato abandoned the Socratic conception of dialectic in favor of a new conception: for more on this see below.

idea of the good). What is the reason for these startling changes? Has Heidegger seen some way of reconciling Plato's practical conception of the good with ontology? Not at all. The difference is that Heidegger now does for Plato what he did for Aristotle: he gives the idea of the good a purely ontological interpretation.[38] The idea of the good, as that which is beyond being (ἐπέκεινα τῆς οὐσίας), is what renders possible and "warrants" the "giving" of being and the happening of unconcealment.[39] Its philosophical importance for Heidegger lies in the direction it gives to our questioning. How can we bring being and unconcealment into question if there is nothing *beyond* them toward which we can direct our questions?[40] What needs to be emphasized here, however, is what has *not* changed in Heidegger's later account: the view that the ἀγαθόν must be given ontological *or* practical significance *but not both*. He thus asserts that the idea of the good is nothing ethical or moral ("Ethisches oder Moralisches," 100), that the Greek word ἀγαθόν has nothing to do with morality: "The genuine and original meaning of ἀγαθόν is: that which is useful and makes other things useful, that with which one can do something; 'good!' means: it's done! it's decided! It does not at all mean *moral [sittlich]* good; *ethics has destroyed [verdorben] the fundamental meaning of this word*"

38. As noted above, in the *Grundbegriffe* course Heidegger understands Plato's ἀγαθόν as an end of action and therefore *a being*: "selbst als *Seiendes, Gutes*" (GA 22, 140–41; see also Mörchen's transcript, 283). In the *Vom Wesen der Wahrheit* course of 1931/32 Heidegger rejects this view: the ἀγαθόν is "*Ermächtigung* von Sein; nicht ein seiendes 'Gut' (ein 'Wert') sondern das, *worum es* vor allem Sein und für alles Sein und jede Wahrheit *geht*" (GA 34, 34, 109). In the earlier course Heidegger appears to treat Plato's idea of the good as a "Wert" (most explicitly at GA 22, 141), even though, according to Mörchen's notes, he claimed that "Die Ansetzung von Werten ist ein Mißverständnis der griechischen Fragestellung" (284). In the *Sophist* course itself Heidegger asserts: "Wenn man das ἀγαθόν als 'Wert' faßt, so ist das ein Widersinn" (GA 19, 123). Yet the only alternative Heidegger sees to understanding the good as a value is an ontological understanding. Therefore, if Heidegger in the *Sophist* course and the *Grundbegriffe* course cannot attribute this understanding to Plato, he has no choice but to identify Plato's good with a mere ontic value.

39. The good, as the highest idea, is characterized as "die Ermächtigung für das *Sein*, daß es sich als solches *gibt*, und in eins damit die Ermächtigung der *Unverborgenheit*, daß sie als solches *geschieht*" (GA 34, 99). As Adriaan T. Peperzak has shown, in *Basic Problems of Phenomenology* (summer 1927), *Metaphysical Foundations of Logic* (summer 1928), and *On the Essence of Ground* (1929), Heidegger, by emphasizing the transcendence of the good (ἐπέκεινα), seeks to identify it with *world* as a transcendental condition for *Dasein*'s understanding of Being ("Heidegger and Plato's Idea of the Good," in *Reading Heidegger: Commemorations*, ed. John Sallis [Bloomington: Indiana University Press, 1993], 259–62; in *Basic Problems*, however, as I have noted above, Heidegger's association of the idea of the good with the demiurge, an association not made in the later texts, shows that he there still sees Plato as failing to disassociate the good from the practical). An important consequence of such an identification is, in the words of Peperzak, that "the good is understood as τέλος without content, i.e., as a future which grants us the possibility of existing as worldly Dasein" (262). In Heidegger's own words, "Nicht zufällig ist das ἀγαθόν unbestimmt" (WG, 158), since it is "die Quelle von Möglichkeit als solcher" (159). Thus, on Heidegger's interpretation, the good ceases to be any kind of goal with a determinate content and therefore, apparently, ceases to have any specifically ethical significance.

40. See the excellent comments on 109–10 and the following characterization of the function of the good: "das, worauf es beim *Fragen* nach Sein und Unverborgenheit ankommt, ist die Ermächtigung dieser *zu* ihrem Wesen" (GA 34, 111).

(106; my emphasis). While there is truth in Heidegger's claim, it surely is not true in its extreme form, at least and especially if we are speaking of Plato's understanding of the word ἀγαθόν. While Paul Shorey's attempt to give the idea of the good a purely ethical interpretation must be reckoned a failure,[41] it is equally wrong to deny that the idea of the good has very strong moral connotations. The purpose of the study of the good, we are told (504d), is to fill in the account of the virtues (justice, courage, moderation, wisdom). The ontological discussion of the middle books of the *Republic* cannot be divorced from the ethical discussion that makes up the rest of the dialogue. It is therefore significant that Heidegger not only restricts his interpretation to the Cave Analogy (with some references to the Sun Analogy and the divided line), but even insists that it can be understood completely on its own, in separation from the rest of the dialogue (GA 34, 18). Is Heidegger again trying to avoid contamination of σοφία with φρόνησις?

In the *Beiträge zur Philosophie (Vom Ereignis)* of 1936–38, Heidegger performs another about-face. He now claims that, in the absence of the question of being (*Seyn*), the ἐπέκεινα τῆς οὐσίας can transcend the "beingness" (*Seiendheit*, οὐσία) of beings only *by relating it back to us*. The ἐπέκεινα is therefore characterized as ἀγαθόν, that is, as what makes οὐσία a condition for our life and happiness by giving it value and meaning. "The ἐπέκεινα can therefore be defined only as something that characterizes beingness as such in its relation to man (εὐδαιμονία), as the ἀγαθόν, the useful, as the ground of all usefullness, therefore as the condition of 'life,' of the soul and accordingly of the soul's very essence. In this way the step is taken towards 'value,' 'meaning,' 'ideal'" (GA 65, 210).[42] With the idea of the good, Heidegger continues, the question concerning beings as such reaches the point where it no longer *understands* (*begreift*) beingness in an original way, but only *values* (*bewertet*) it (210). Therefore, while in the 1931–32 course Heidegger characterized the ἀγαθόν as what makes possible the questioning of being and unconcealment, in the *Beiträge* he identifies it with "the *fundamental denial* [*grundsätzliche Verleugnung*] of any further and more original questioning with respect to beings as such, i.e., being" (211). With the idea of the good, being starts to become a value and therefore

---

41. Shorey identifies the good with "a rational, consistent conception of the greatest possible attainable human happiness, of the ultimate laws of God, nature or man that sanction conduct, and of the consistent application of these laws in legislation, government and education." "The Idea of the Good in Plato's *Republic*: A Study in the Logic of Speculative Ethics," in *Selected Papers*, vol. 2 (New York: Garland, 1980), 79. The good described by the Sun Analogy as causing knowledge and being is thus nothing but the "idea of what is best" existing in the minds of the rulers (67). Yet this is clearly a trivialization of the analogy and receives no support from the text. A more recent attempt to identify the form of the good with happiness can be found in Peter Stemmer, *Platons Dialektik: Die Früheren und Mittleren Dialoge* (Berlin: Walter de Gruyter, 1992); see especially 158–67, 183–84.

42. Heidegger accordingly calls Nietzsche's question concerning the worth (*Wert*) of truth "eine echt *platonisierende* [!] Frage" (216). In listing the heirs of Platonism, Heidegger includes "alle Lehren, die auf 'Werte,' auf 'Sinn,' auf 'Ideen' und 'Ideale' abzielen" (218).

ceases to be brought into question. Heidegger thus makes a startling return to his interpretation in the *Grundbegriffe* course: to characterize being as ἀγαθόν is to relate it to human πρᾶξις and desire (ἔρως, 210) and thus to distort and conceal it. "To address being as ἀγαθόν is to *misunderstand* being."[43]

These about-faces betray Heidegger's failure genuinely to encounter Plato's thought and at the same time reveal the cause of this failure: the insistence on a sharp distinction between being and any distinctly practical conception of the good, and thus between the comportments of σοφία and φρόνησις. Throughout the dramatic turns in Heidegger's interpretation, one thing remains constant: the assumption that the characterization of being as ἀγαθόν must either rid the ἀγαθόν of all ethical content, understanding it purely ontologically, or misunderstand being by reducing it to an ontic value. In other words, for Heidegger an ontology with ethical content is always bad ontology, unless ethics can be reduced to ontology.[44] This assumption represents a failure to encounter Plato's thought because the idea of the good cannot be adequately characterized as either purely ontological or an ontic value, as Heidegger's own indecision shows. More importantly, this assumption appears to render impossible any answer to the question which Heidegger himself asked in the *Grundbegriffe* course: to paraphrase, how do we get from the ontological to the ethical?[45] The insistence on a radical distinction between the two appears to preclude a priori any bridge between them.[46] Perhaps Plato's thought provides this bridge. Heidegger's reading of Plato refuses even to consider such a possibility.

2. Σοφία as a Way of Life; the "Ontologization" of φρόνησις and πρᾶξις

Heidegger's attempted *Auseinandersetzung* with Plato, as documented in the *Sophist* lectures and the other texts considered above, requires us to conclude

---

43. There is yet another chapter to the story that can only be mentioned here but that will receive detailed discussion in chapter 3. In *Platons Lehre von der Wahrheit* (written 1940), Heidegger notoriously does not so much as mention the ἐπέκεινα and reduces the ἀγαθόν to simply the most perfect of the ideas. See Peperzak, "Heidegger and Plato's Idea of the Good," 275–82. Heidegger here also denies that the ἀγαθόν means "ethical good" (*sittliche Gute*), though he claims that Plato's interpretation of the ἀγαθόν as *idea* will provide the impetus (*Anlaß*) for understanding the good morally and in the end reckoning it to be a value (PLW, 224–25). When thus deprived of both ontological transcendence and ethical content—Heidegger as usual makes no distinction between ethics and value-thinking—what remains of the ἀγαθόν? The eclipse now seems total.

44. This qualification is necessary to explain Heidegger's ontological politics in the early 1930s: see my "Heidegger's 1933 Misappropriation of Plato's *Republic*," Προβλήματα: *Quaderni di filosofia* 3 (2003): 39–80.

45. Heidegger in the *Sophist* course recognizes that one of the things at stake in the relation between φρόνησις and σοφία is an understanding of "in welchem Sinn es hinsichtlich des menschlichen Lebens so etwas wie eine Wissenschaft geben kann wie die Ethik, sofern die Ethik sich mit dem ἦθος, dem Sein des Menschen, beschäftigt, die auch anders sein kann" (GA 19, 130–31).

46. In the lecture course of the summer of 1928, *Metaphysische Anfangsgründe der Logik im Ausgang von Leibniz*, Heidegger reserves the question of ethics to what he calls *metontology*, the "overturning"

that (1) Heidegger in some sense shares Aristotle's ranking of σοφία above φρόνησις (thus the criticism of Plato for recognizing nothing higher than φρόνησις)[47] and (2) Heidegger seeks to divorce ontology from ethical πρᾶξις and the φρόνησις that guides such πρᾶξις (thus the criticism of Plato for making a practical conception of the good central to his ontology). These conclusions will startle and appear patently false to many readers. Two main objections can be anticipated: the first conclusion contradicts Heidegger's frequent criticisms in the 1920s of the theoretical stance privileged by the philosophical tradition and his corresponding defense of a "phronetic" conception of philosophy; both conclusions are contradicted by the centrality of πρᾶξις in Heidegger's ontology, especially evident in sections 15–18 of *Being and Time*.[48] The first point to be made in response is that these two conclusions are required to make sense of Heidegger's critique of Plato; therefore, if they are inconsistent with the general direction of Heidegger's philosophizing, this critique turns out to be profoundly schizophrenic. We then have the very strange spectacle of Heidegger the critic of σοφία criticizing Plato's dialectic for its failure to attain σοφία and Heidegger the "pragmatist" criticizing Plato for having only a practical, rather than an ontological, conception of the good. It is these apparent contradictions that make Heidegger's relation to Plato incomprehensible to many, including some of Heidegger's own students who, under the inspiration of his thought, have naturally turned to Plato as to an ally and found in his dialectic a paradigm for their own philosophizing. The contradictions begin to disappear, and the relation between Heidegger and Plato is illuminated, when we recognize that (1) Heidegger's critique of the tradition's theoretical stance is perfectly compatible with the ranking of a *reinterpreted* θεωρεῖν or σοφία above φρόνησις and (2) the πρᾶξις and φρόνησις central to Heidegger's ontology have, like the good, been assimilated to σοφία, that is, have been "ontologized," that is, have been abstracted from their specifically ethical dimension. This is what now needs to be shown.

Already in the KS 1919 course *Die Idee der Philosophie und das Weltanschauungsproblem*, Heidegger engages in a thorough and forceful critique of "the general dominance of the *theoretical*" (GA 56/57, 87), a critique frequently

---

(*Umschlag*) of fundamental ontology, a turning-around (*Kehre*) to *existentiell-ontic* questioning (GA 26, 199–202). Dostal correctly notes "the systematic difficulty of moving from fundamental ontology to the proposed metontology, for the doctrine of Being is not developed by Heidegger with the conceptual rigor that he himself demands" ("Gadamer's Continuous Challenge," 77).

47. Contrary to Günter Figal's claim that "Heidegger is no mere Aristotelian since by upgrading φρόνησις he placed himself at odds with Aristotle" ("Refraining from Dialectic," 100).

48. According to Robert Bernasconi, the view that σοφία is the highest possibility of human existence runs "counter to the tendency of *Being and Time*, or at least to the dominant reading of *Being and Time*." "Heidegger's Destruction of φρόνησις," in "Spindel Conference 1989: Heidegger and Praxis," ed. Thomas J. Nenon, *Southern Journal of Philosophy* 28, supp. (1989): 142.

echoed in subsequent years. Theory is here seen as an "Ent-lebung," a draining away of life, a negation of the lived experience in which we primarily exist and in which things have meaning for us. Theory "objectifies" our *Umwelt* and thereby drains it of the significance it has *as lived*, as *Umwelterlebnis*; it transforms what meaningfully encounters us in our lived world into a mere *thing* or *object*. Near the very end of the course Heidegger observes: "In theoretical acts I myself leave my lived experience [*Theoretisch komme ich selbst aus dem Erleben her*]; I bring something from this experience along with me, but no one knows what to do with this and so they invent the convenient label of the 'irrational'" (117). Theory takes one out of life and therefore out of the only context in which the world can be experienced *as world*.

Does this critique of the theoretical turn Heidegger into a "pragmatist"? Does it result in the identification of philosophy with the practical knowledge needed to get along in the world? Is philosophizing reduced to deciding how to act and how to live? In Aristotelian terms, can philosophy be no more than φρόνησις? To prevent such a conclusion, Heidegger in this course at one point clarifies that the predominance of the theoretical "must be broken, not indeed by proclaiming the primacy of the practical, nor in order now to bring for one time something else into the picture that clarifies the problems from a new angle, but because the theoretical itself and as such points back to the pre-theoretical" (59). But what exactly does this mean?

As already noted, Heidegger's critique of Plato assumes that philosophy can be σοφία and that this σοφία must be ranked higher than φρόνησις. But how can Heidegger share Aristotle's estimation of σοφία and θεωρία while at the same time criticizing the theoretical stance in favor of *Erlebnis*? The answer is simple: Aristotle's θεωρία is for Heidegger nothing "theoretical," that is, is not a draining away of life, an *Ent-lebnis*, but exactly the opposite: the highest and most authentic form of *living* of which human *Dasein* is capable and as such something *pre*-theoretical.[49]

In the *Sophist* course this view emerges in response to the following problem Heidegger notes in Aristotle's characterization of σοφία: because removed from πρᾶξις and concerned solely with the eternal, σοφία appears completely

---

49. In a handwritten marginal note on his copy of the 1922 *Phänomenologische Interpretationen zu Aristoteles* (see full reference below), Heidegger writes: "Und zwar hat ἀληθεύειν sowenig wie der νοῦς ursprünglich und eigentlich 'theoretischen' Charakter—im Gegenteil. . . . Doch! Nur das θεωρεῖν bzw. 'nicht theoretisch' verschieden vom modernen 'theoretisch'; es liegt nicht am 'Theoretischen' (modernen) des νοῦς, sondern am νοῦς-haften des Theoretischen" (PIA, 47). Bernasconi rightly notes that instead of rejecting the priority traditionally granted to the theoretical, Heidegger reinterprets the theoretical: "Heidegger does not reverse the traditional subjection of the practical to the theoretical, he simply insists on the fact that the theoretical life is, as a life to be lived, itself a practical life. In saying this he does not depart from Aristotle" (Bernasconi, "Heidegger's Destruction of φρόνησις," 143). As will be seen below, Heidegger even considers the theoretical life the most authentic practical life.

unrelated to human existence. As Aristotle acknowledges, σοφία "does not contemplate any of the things through which a human being will become happy [ἐξ ὧν ἔσται εὐδαίμων ἄνθρωπος], since it does not concern itself with any form of becoming" (*Nicomachean Ethics*, 1143b19–20). As Heidegger adds, "What philosophy considers according to its very meaning, settles nothing for *human existence*" (GA 19, 167–68). In this case, how can σοφία be the highest possibility of *human* existence? Aristotle's solution, according to Heidegger, is that θεωρεῖν can itself be a way of being for man, that it is comparable not to the art of medicine that produces health (and thus is concerned with γένεσις), but to the state of *being* healthy. Σοφία indeed does not contemplate the means of making us happy (as the doctor considers the means of making us healthy), but it itself *is* our happiness. Θεωρεῖν is not simply a means by which I come to be what I am; *I live in this* θεωρεῖν ("*ich in diesem* θεωρεῖν *lebe*," 169). This last claim contrasts sharply with the assertion in the 1919 course: "Theoretisch komme ich selbst aus dem Erleben her." What prevents this contrast from being a contradiction is that Aristotle's θεωρεῖν is not "theoretical" in the modern sense of the word, that is, is not divorced from life, but is itself a way of life.

Yet θεωρεῖν is not simply *a* way of living for *Dasein*, but the highest and most authentic: "Θεωρεῖν is a mode of being in which man attains his highest mode of being: his proper spiritual health [*sein eigentliches geistiges Gesundsein*]" (170). In a *Zusatz*, Heidegger goes so far as to suggest that σοφία is not incidental to *Dasein* but "in itself it is *the being of Dasein*" (613) and explains that it "is founded in an originally proper mode of being of human *Dasein*" (613). Likewise, at the beginning of the discussion of the different ways of ἀληθεύειν, Heidegger anticipates the conclusion "that it [σοφία] has a priority over φρόνησις, such that this ἀληθεύειν constitutes *a proper possibility, and the genuine* [*eine eigene und die eigentliche*] possibility, of Dasein" (61; my emphasis). But why is σοφία, rather than φρόνησις or any of the other ways of ἀληθεύειν, the way of being that is most *Dasein's* own? Heidegger's interpretation of *Metaphysics* A provides the answer: *Dasein* is characterized by a fundamental tendency to see and to know that emerges to varying degrees in the lower forms of ἀληθεύειν, but is fully realized only in σοφία. *Dasein* therefore comes *into its own* only in σοφία. This point is made most clearly in the *Zusatz* already referred to: "Whether or not it [σοφία] precisely liberates itself only slowly from the ἐπιστῆμαι ποιητικαί, it is *not* simply a *transformation* of this but is at the very outset sustained by the tendency merely to see and know" (613). In other words, σοφία does not add anything to the lower forms of ἀληθεύειν, but only realizes a tendency already to be found in them. In freeing ourselves from the practical forms of unconcealing, we are not leaving them behind in favor of something else, we are not leaving life behind in favor of something beyond life: instead, we are allowing to come into its own a tendency that has always been there, though only partially realized, in our πρᾶξις and our living. We not only live, but live most fully, in θεωρεῖν.⁵⁰

In *Die Grundbegriffe der antiken Philosophie* Heidegger accordingly describes the θεωρητικος βίος as the way of being "in which man to the highest degree fulfills his very own possibility to be, in which man authentically *is*" (GA 22, 312). Heidegger then adds that this is the life *that Aristotle himself lived* (313), the life of "philosophy" understood as "reine wissenschaftliche Forschung" (143). Likewise, in the *Sophist* lectures, Heidegger locates *Dasein's* proper and authentic possibility in "the βίος θεωρητικός, *the existence of scientific man [die Existenz des wissenschaftlichen Menschen]*" (GA 19, 61). These passages show why Heidegger is not simply paraphrasing⁵¹ Aristotle's characterization of σοφία, but appropriating it: what Heidegger finds in Aristotle is a characterization of philosophical, *scientific* existence as the highest and "authentic" possibility of human *Dasein*.⁵²

This appropriation is most evident in the 1922 introduction and program for the book on Aristotle Heidegger would never write (PIA). In reading this text for the first time many years later, Gadamer expressed surprise: "In my

---

50. Theodore Kisiel reads the *Sophist* course completely differently. In reference to the discussion of the *Nicomachean Ethics*, Kisiel comments: "But in his detailed gloss, Heidegger will time and again look for ways, both in and out of the Aristotelian opus, in which phronetic insight asserts its potential superiority over contemplative wisdom. For does not the human being find its own being to be the most important being, so that its discovery would be the highest and most crucial? And Plato himself made no distinction between these two highest virtues" (GH, 303–4). With the last point Kisiel undermines his interpretation: Plato indeed does not distinguish between σοφία and φρόνησις, but Heidegger repeatedly criticizes Plato's dialectic precisely for failing to attain the level of σοφία. Furthermore, as I hope the present reading shows, Heidegger's "gloss" supports the superiorty of σοφία. When one adds the evidence of other texts, it becomes impossible to see in the *Sophist* course a critique of σοφία as such (which is not to say that certain elements of Aristotle's characterization of σοφία, especially the inadequate conception of Being, are not criticized). On this point, Robert Bernasconi and Walter Brogan understand the text correctly (see other notes).

51. The possibility of mere paraphrase must of course always be kept in mind in reading these texts. In recalling Heidegger's lectures on Aristotle, Hans-Georg Gadamer writes: "In Heidegger's lectures we were often so personally touched that we no longer knew whether he was speaking of his own concern or that of Aristotle." *Philosophical Apprenticeships*, trans. Robert R. Sullivan (Cambridge, Mass.: MIT Press, 1985), 49.

52. In a *Zusatz* to the *Sophist* course (GA 19, 612), Heidegger even claims that the reason why the interpretation of the *Sophist* must be preceded by a preliminary characterization of σοφία is this dialogue's objective of revealing what the philosopher is. At the very beginning of the course he characterizes this objective as follows: "Im 'Sophistes' betrachtet Plato das menschliche Dasein in einer seiner extremsten Möglichkeiten, nämlich in der philosophischen Existenz" (12). Most important, however, for understanding Heidegger's motivation in discussing σοφία is his own objective in the course: to give his auditors "ein inneres Verständnis wissenschaftlicher Fragen," since "Nur auf diesem Wege wird die Frage: Wissenschaft und Leben, zur Entscheidung gebracht, nämlich, daß wir erst wieder lernen, die Bewegungsart wissenschaftlichen Arbeitens und damit den inneren Sinn wissenschaftlicher Existenz bei uns wahr zu machen" (10). It is precisely the question of "Wissenschaft und Leben" that Heidegger sees Aristotelian σοφία as addressing.

reading of the rediscovered program, I was startled to find that φρόνησις is not at all as prominent in Heidegger's manuscript as is instead the virtue of theoretical life, σοφία."[53] When Gadamer later read the *Sophist* course upon its publication, he found the same thing: that Heidegger, against Aristotle's own intention, was interested only in the understanding of being that lay at the foundation of Aristotle's theoretical philosophy.[54] In the 1922 text we indeed already find the major claims made about σοφία in the later lecture courses. Though σοφία does not have human life as its object, we must recognize in it the *being* of life ("das Sein des Lebens"), the *movement* of life (PIA, 57–59). Aristotle secures the meaning of σοφία or philosophy "through the interpretation of a factical movement of care with respect to its ultimate tendency" (61), namely, the tendency toward more seeing or knowing. That Heidegger here, as in the later lecture courses, is appropriating, and not simply paraphrasing, Aristotle's characterization of σοφία is evident not only in Heidegger's interpretation of σοφία as that toward which *Dasein*'s *care* ultimately tends,[55] but also in the claim, made without explicit reference to Aristotle in the introductory *Anzeige der hermeneutischen Situation*, that "philosophical inquiry is the explicit fulfilment of a fundamental movement of factical life and continually maintains itself within this life" (13; see also 32). This view that Heidegger presents as his own is what he finds and appropriates in Aristotle's characterization of σοφία as the highest realization possible of that tendency toward seeing and knowing that is the fundamental movement of human life.[56] It is also the view that years later, and after important transformations, finds expression in *Being and Time* in the claim that the *Seinsfrage* is "nothing other

---

53. "Heideggers 'theologische' Jugendschrift," in PIA, 81; originally published in *Dilthey-Jahrbuch für Philosophie und Geschichte der Geisteswissenschaften* 6 (1989); hereafter HTJ; my translation.

54. *Aristoteles: Nikomachische Ethik VI* (Frankfurt am Main: Vittorio Klostermann, 1998), 67. See Taminiaux, *Sillages*, 157–58.

55. In *Being and Time* Heidegger asserts emphatically that the phenomenon of care in no way expresses "einen Vorrang des 'praktischen' Verhaltens vor dem theoretischen.... Das nur anschauende Bestimmen eines Vorhandenen hat nicht weniger den Charakter der Sorge als eine 'politische Aktion' oder das ausruhende Sichvergnügen. 'Theorie' und 'Praxis' sind Seinsmöglichkeiten eines Seienden, dessen Sein als Sorge bestimmt werden muß" (193). As Heidegger suggests in the 1922 introduction, philosophical inquiry can even be a greater and more authentic realization of this care than the busiest political activity.

56. John van Buren sees this text as identifying σοφία with "ocular-aesthetic quietism" and claims that "What Heidegger thought was needed was a quasi-Lutheran destruction, unmasking, and demythologizing" of this, and that "Heidegger played the practical Aristotle off against the metaphysical Aristotle" (*Young Heidegger,* 225). Thus Van Buren, unlike Gadamer, finds in the text a critique and destruction of σοφία in favor of φρόνησις. This interpretation is also advanced by Kisiel, GH, 269–70. However, it cannot stand. Though there may be some elements of "ocular-aesthetic quietism" in Aristotelian σοφία that Heidegger wishes to "destruct," he finds at the heart of σοφία not quietism but "eine eigene Besorgnis" (PIA, 61), "die reinste Bewegtheit" (62), the highest actualization of the movement of care. Furthermore, rather than using the practical Aristotle against the metaphysical Aristotle, Heidegger's project, as Gadamer recognizes and as is shown below, completely subordinates the Aristotle of the *Ethics* to the Aristotle of the *Physics*.

than a radicalization of an essential tendency of being that belongs to *Dasein* itself, of a pre-ontological understanding of being" (SZ, 15). Finally, this view is the dominant theme of the *Rektoratsrede* of 1933, in which Heidegger insists that by θεωρία the Greeks meant not disinterested contemplation but "theory as itself the highest realization of genuine practice."[57] The Greeks are thus the model for Heidegger's attempt to locate the destiny of the German people in a will to science ("Wille zur Wissenschaft," 10). In this way, the *Rektoratsrede* grows out of Heidegger's study of Aristotelian σοφία.

Heidegger's appropriation of Aristotelian σοφία no doubt transforms it. Most importantly, given Heidegger's critique of the Greek conception of being, σοφία cannot be for him an abiding relation to eternal presence.[58] But if Aristotle's distinction between what always is and what changes is undermined, is not σοφία necessarily collapsed into φρόνησις? Such a collapse appears to take place when Heidegger in the 1922 introduction identifies the object of philosophy with human existence ("das menschliche Dasein"). Yet philosophy studies human existence only as questioned with regard to its kind of being ("befragt auf seinen Seinscharakter," PIA, 10). This is why the same text identifies philosophy with ontology (246). Φρόνησις, on the other hand, reveals human existence only in the specificity of its *Umgang* or πρᾶξις (259). In the words of the *Sophist* course, both φρόνησις and σοφία are concerned with the good or τέλος, but φρόνησις is concerned with a practical, ontic good, while σοφία is concerned with a purely ontological conception of the good. "Φρόνησις is nothing as long as it is not realized in πρᾶξις, which as such is determined by ἀρετή, by the πρακτόν as ἀγαθόν" (GA 19, 167). Furthermore, it is on account of its confinement to πρᾶξις that φρόνησις cannot be a science: "Φρόνησις is not any kind of speculation about the ἀρχή and the τέλος of action as such: it is no kind of ethics or science, no ἕξις μετὰ λόγου μόνον (*Eth. Nic.* VI, 5; 1140b28), but rather it is what it can be, according to its most proper meaning, when it is the seeing of a concrete action and decision" (57–58).[59] The life of φρόνησις is *not* "the existence of the scientific man" (61).[60]

---

57. "Die Theorie selbst als die höchste Verwirklichung echter Praxis" (SDU, 11–12).

58. For the Greek conception of Being as eternal being-present, see, for example, GA 19, 34 and 398; for the identification of Being with *Her-gestelltsein*, see 270. Heidegger claims that the Greeks failed to question the meaning of Being (466). This charge will be the focus of the next chapter.

59. In the *Parmenides* course Heidegger does identify philosophy with φρόνησις. In discussing lines 62127–8 of the concluding myth of the *Republic*, he characterizes φρόνησις as "die Einsicht jenes Einsehens, das den Einblick nimmt in das, was das eigentliche Erblickbare und Unverborgene ist" (GA 54, 178). He then asserts: "Φρόνησις meint hier dasselbe wie 'Philosophie,' und dieser Titel besagt: den Blick haben für das Wesenhafte" (178). Yet φρόνησις is here completely indistinguishable from σοφία and has no ethical or practical content. It has been "ontologized" in the way further described below.

60. Van Buren has attempted to attribute a "phronetic" conception of philosophy to the young Heidegger of 1919 and the early 1920s. Van Buren goes so far as to claim that "the young Heidegger of the early Freiburg period was more a negative Socratic, Pyrrhonian, and Kierkegaardian thinker than

It is already possible to see how a ranking of σοφία above φρόνησις is not only compatible with, but presupposed by the project of *Being and Time*. Walter Brogan has already seen and clearly expressed this connection: "If we were, like Plato, to stop with φρόνησις and subject all knowing to self-knowledge, then the ecstatic outside-itself character of *Dasein*'s being would be missed. Thus, Heidegger retrieves the Aristotelian insight that σοφία as a way of knowing is higher than the self-knowing of φρόνησις. In terms of *Being and Time*, I take this to mean that the analysis of *Dasein*'s way of being itself is preparatory for a further, higher consideration of *Dasein*'s understanding of being in general."[61] If *Being and Time* ended with sections 15–18,[62] if the analysis of *Dasein*'s being were not purely "preliminary" to the addressing of the question of being in general, then we perhaps could find in Heidegger a complete reversal of Aristotle's ranking of σοφία above φρόνησις. As it is, *Dasein*'s understanding of its own being is preparatory for *Dasein*'s understanding of being or σοφία. What is common to both the Aristotelian and Heideggerian conceptions of σοφία is that the highest possibility of human existence

---

a positive thinker, more a deconstructive than a constructive philosopher" (*Young Heidegger*, 360). Yet much of Van Buren's argument appears to depend on equating Heidegger's critique of the theoretical during this period with a rejection of σοφία in favor of φρόνησις. As I have tried to show, such an equation is erroneous. Consider one piece of evidence Van Buren cites: in the 1923–24 course *Einführung in die phänomenologische Forschung*, Heidegger apparently urged his students to adopt a more "phronetic" and less "theoretical" approach to their chosen science (234; Kisiel also cites this course to make the same point: Kisiel, 277). Understood in the context of the kind of critique of the theoretical that we find in the 1919 course, Heidegger's advice is clearly that his students should avoid divorcing their chosen science from their own lives, that they should *live* their chosen science. What Heidegger is therefore recommending is the *life* of σοφία understood as the *scientific way of living*. Already in the 1919 course, philosophy is for him a *Wissenschaft*, even if one more original and radical than other sciences. This is hardly a conception of philosophy that one would expect "a negative Socratic, Pyrrhonian, and Kierkegaardian thinker" to have. As for Heidegger's use of the word φρόνησις here, it will be seen below that for him σοφία is a kind of φρόνησις, namely, the highest and most authentic kind.

61. "A Response to Robert Bernasconi's 'Heidegger's Destruction of φρόνησις,'" in "Spindel Conference 1989: Heidegger and Praxis," ed. Thomas J. Nenon, *Southern Journal of Philosophy* 28, supp. (1989): 152. Franco Volpi also recognizes that the practical connotation of the ontological structure of *Dasein* is only preparatory: "One knows that, later, when *Dasein* is no longer understood in itself but out of the horizon in which it is always already constituted, Heidegger will systematically eliminate all traces of this practical connotation and will determine the 'open' character of existence no longer as having-to-be, but as ek-sistence in the opening of being." "Dasein as *Praxis*: the Heideggerian Assimilation and the Radicalization of the Practical Philosophy of Aristotle," in *Martin Heidegger: Critical Assessments*, vol. 2, ed. Christopher Macann (New York: Routledge, 1992), 107.

62. This appears to be the wish of some: "One can imagine a possible Heidegger who, after formulating the Dewey-like social-practice pragmatism of the early sections of *Being and Time*, would have felt that his job was pretty well done." Richard Rorty, "The Reification of Language," in *The Cambridge Companion to Heidegger*, ed. Charles Guignon (Cambridge: Cambridge University Press, 1993), 348. Incidentally, I cannot imagine this, since Heidegger's approach is thoroughly ontological from the very start; not a page of *Being and Time* contains a trace of "Dewey-like social-practice pragmatism" (unless one absurdly maintains that a recognition of the primacy of readiness-to-hand in everyday comportment commits one to pragmatism).

is sought in its relation to something "outside" itself, specifically, to being, whether understood as eternal presence or otherwise.[63] A lingering debt to Aristotelian σοφία is therefore still perceptible in Heidegger's later claim that the essence of humans, as consisting in a relation to being, is *nothing human*.[64] This means that even the essence or being of humans, as distinct from their concrete actions and decisions, cannot be an object of mere φρόνησις. To return to *Being and Time*, the goal there is not a "pragmatic" conception of *Dasein*'s being, but the development of a science (*Wissenschaft*) of being. Such a science can be nothing other than σοφία.

Yet Heideggger, unlike the philosophical tradition he criticizes, seeks to discover some unity between σοφία and φρόνησις, a unity that enables φρόνησις along with σοφία to transcend the narrowly practical. In the 1922 lecture course, *Phänomenologische Interpretationen ausgewählter Abhandlungen des Aristoteles zur Ontologie und Logik*, Heidegger maintains, in the context of a reading of *Metaphysics* A, that "The authentic form of comportment [*das eigentliche Umgehen*] is θεωρία, the authentic βίος πρακτικός is the βίος θεωρητικός" (GA 62, 309). This conclusion of course rejects any strong opposition between the theoretical and the practical; Heidegger in the course indeed aims to show that both are *movements of life*, that is, forms of *caring* (see, e.g., 116; though the former is caring in the form of not-caring, 112n3); and in doing so explicitly challenges the epistemological tradition, i.e., the tradition criticized in the 1919 course for divorcing theory from life (see, e.g., 119). But what needs to be emphasized in the present context is that here the practical is assimilated to the theoretical and not vice versa. Heidegger's suggestion is not that the βίος πρακτικός is the authentic βίος θεωρητικός, i.e., that the theoretical life fulfills itself and comes into its own in the practical

63. In the summer 1928 course, *Metaphysische Anfangsgründe der Logik im Ausgang von Leibniz*, Heidegger maintains that *Dasein*'s transcendence must be identified with *neither* θεωρεῖν *nor* πρᾶξις, but rather with the common root of both (GA 26, 235–36). But θεωρεῖν is limited in this context to the intuiting of Platonic ideas. Heidegger proceeds to characterize *Dasein*'s transcendence as transcending toward the idea of the good understood as beyond the ideas (ἐπέκεινα) and as *the-for-the-sake-of-which* (*Umwillen*) = world (237–38). Yet it is precisely this relation to a good understood ontologically, and not the intuiting of ideas, that Heidegger equates with σοφία in the *Sophist* lectures.

64. "Die Seinsgeschichtliche Bestimmung des Nihilismus," in N2, 377. After maintaining that "Das ekstatische Innestehen im Offenen der Ortschaft des Seins ist als das Verhältnis zum Sein, sei es zu Seiendem als solchem, sei es zum Sein selbst, das Wesen des Denken" (358), Heidegger indeed explains that this thinking should not be understood in opposition to willing and feeling, nor should "als das nur theoretische Verhalten gegen das praktische abgesetzt und in seiner Wesentragweite für das Wesen des Menschen eingeschränkt werden" (358). However, this restricted sense of theoretical comportment does not correspond to θεωρεῖν as understood in the courses of the 1920s, a θεωρεῖν that, far from being opposed to willing and feeling or the practical, is a way of life capable of fulfilling their innermost tendency. On the other hand, the description of the essence of thinking in this passage reads like a translation of the Aristotelian conception of σοφία, one that remains in large part faithful to the original.

life, but rather that the βίος θεωρητικός is the authentic βίος πράκτικος, that is, that the practical life fulfills itself and comes into its own in the theoretical life. Why the latter rather than the former must be the case is seen in a characteristic of σοφία that has already been noted: σοφία is the full realization of a fundamental tendency of human life to see and to know, a tendency that φρόνησις fulfills only partially and imperfectly. The theoretical life is what the practical life seeks to be, indeed, is what the practical life *is* in its fundamental movement. Φρόνησις and σοφία are not, strictly speaking, two separate ways of being, but rather different degrees of the same way of being, different stages of the same movement, different intensities of one life. In the 1922 lecture, Heidegger expressed forcefully the views we have already encountered in other texts: that θεωρία is "the highest and authentic how [*Wie*] of human existence" (116), and because "θεωρεῖν, as the most authentic meaning of pure movement [*Bewegtheit*], is thereby the way of living, the being of living, in which life enters its fully achieved state" (110). Θεωρία is not imposed from without upon a life that is in itself nontheoretical; instead, it frees life from what is extrinsic to it—including, presumably, the practical—and thus frees it to be entirely its own.

This characterization of the unity of the practical and the theoretical is also to be found in the *Sophist* course. Heidegger lays much stress on a text from *Metaphysics* A, in which σοφία is characterized as τοιαύτη φρόνησις (982b24).[65] Heidegger comments: "It is not φρόνησις as we know it in relation to beings that can be otherwise, in relation to the objects of our action; it is a φρόνησις which indeed is directed to an ἀγαθόν, but an ἀγαθόν that is not πρακτόν" (GA 19, 124). Σοφία is therefore a kind of φρόνησις for which the good has been freed from its practical dimension and ontologized. As such, it is the highest form of φρόνησις since, as Heidegger proceeds to remark, the theoretical comportment made possible by an ontological understanding of the good "*as theoretical*, presents the *correct* relation to the ἀγαθόν" (124).[66] This is an astonishing claim: it suggests that the φρόνησις that guides πρᾶξις is an *imperfect* φρόνησις since its comportment towards the good is not yet the right one. It is this view, however, that is behind Heidegger's critique of Plato's supposedly practical idea of the good.

But now we see what is lost in assimilating φρόνησις to σοφία, in characterizing it as simply a preliminary, imperfect step toward scientific ontology:

---

65. Heidegger's reading of this passage should be contrasted with that of W. D. Ross: "Φρόνησις is used here not in the strict sense defended in *E.N.* vi. 5, but in the wide sense in which it is not distinguished from σοφία or ἐπιστήμη. This is the regular usage in Plato and is not uncommon in Aristotle." *Aristotle's Metaphysics*, vol. 1 (Oxford: Clarendon Press, 1958), 123. Ross sees only two distinct meanings where Heidegger seeks to uncover a unity.

66. The converse of this claim is Heidegger's assertion that the ἀγαθόν can be a philosophical term only to the extent to which it is understood ontologically (GA 19, 124).

precisely its ethical dimension, its relation to a practical good. The claim that the authentic practical life is simply the theoretical life renders this ethical dimension accidental and extrinsic to being human. The ethical and practical good lies outside of the movement that finds its fulfilment in θεωρία. This movement that defines human existence for Heidegger is fundamentally an ontological movement, a movement toward being. Φρόνησις can be a preliminary stage in this movement, a way station on the road to a science of being, only to the extent that its determinate ethical or practical content is taken to be accidental to it. Φρόνησις fulfills its innermost tendency when it leaves the ethical and the practical behind and becomes σοφία. What emerges from Heidegger's reading is therefore something more complex than the mere ranking of σοφία above φρόνησις (or vice versa). The present analysis of Heidegger's reading has shown what Taminiaux has suggested such an analysis would show: that the "destruction" carried out by Heidegger's reading "results not in siding with *phronèsis* against *sophia* nor in siding with the latter against the former, but rather in retaining from the one as from the other, as each is played off against the other, what is susceptible of being reappropriated by the ontology of *Dasein*. It results, furthermore, in amalgamating *phronèsis* and *sophia* with regard to this ontology" (*Sillages*, 195; my trans.). It could still be argued that it is φρόνησις and πρᾶξις that are most transformed by this amalgamation since, as both Taminiaux (see 198) and others have recognized, they remain central to Heidegger's characterization of *Dasein* only to the extent to which they have been "ontologized."[67]

67. See Bernasconi, "Heidegger's Destruction of φρόνησις," 133–34, 142. A very helpful article on this issue is the one by Franco Volpi already referred to above. While seeking to show "a general correspondence between the practico-moral understanding of human life with Aristotle and the Heideggerian existential analysis [i.e., in *Being and Time*]" (120), Volpi recognizes the following transformation that the terms πρᾶξις, ποίησις and θεωρία undergo in Heidegger's appropriation of them: "The most perceptive transformation seems to me to be the accentuation, better the absolutization, of the ontological character which, to a certain extent, they also possess with Aristotle, but which, with him, is not the only character. Let me explain: Heidegger explains the Aristotelian determinations of *praxis, poiesis* and *theoria* as if they were only modalities of being, thereby rigorously excluding any understanding of their ontic significance" (104), and therefore, we might add, of their *ethical* significance. In the light of texts such as the *Sophist* course, the introduction to the planned book on Aristotle, and the SS 1924 course on Aristotle—texts not available when Volpi wrote his article—we must deny the occurrence of another transformation Volpi claims to find: "It is not *theoria* which is considered [by Heidegger] to be the supreme attitude, as the highest and preferred activity for man," but rather *praxis* (105). It is precisely because he considers θεωρία to be the highest and most genuine πρᾶξις that Heidegger sees the determinate actions in which πρᾶξις results and the determinate goals (practical goods) it pursues, in short, its ontic and ethical dimension, as incidental and extrinsic, as something from which πρᾶξις can be abstracted. Volpi correctly sees this "ontologization" of πρᾶξις as resulting "in the evaporation of its specific weight as an activity and in the loss of certain characteristics which, with Aristotle, belong to it constitutively; above all, its inter-personality and its rootedness in a *koinonia*. With Heidegger, 'ontologization' drives *praxis* into a sort of heroic solipsism which deforms its very appearance" (114). In the 1929 essay "Vom Wesen des Grundes," Heidegger identifies the understanding of Being ("Verstehen des Seins") with "die *Urhandlung* menschlicher Existenz" (VWG, 158).

This ontologization is already evident in the 1922 introduction and program for the unwritten Aristotle book. Gadamer rightly draws our attention to "the preponderance of ontological interest" in this text's account of φρόνησις and the corresponding silence regarding *ethos* ("Heideggers 'theologische' Jugendschrift" [HTJ], 233). The very order in which Heidegger intended to deal with the Aristotelian texts in his book, an order largely followed in the SS 1924 course, betrays this ontological interest (I indicate in brackets the topic Heidegger focuses on in connection with each text) :

Part 1: *Nicomachean Ethics* Z (φρόνησις)
Part 2: *Metaphysics* A 1 and 2 (the transition to σοφία)
Part 3: *Physics* A, B, Γ 1–3 (ontology)

As Gadamer notes (HTJ, 231), the *Ethics* appears in this plan as an introduction to the *Physics*. But in order for the discussion of the dianoetic virtues to serve as an introduction to ontology, their ethical dimension must be ignored. Heidegger acknowledges this: he admits that his interpretation of *Nicomachean Ethics* Z deals with the dianoetic virtues "with preliminary disregard [*vorläufigem Absehen*] for the specifically ethical problematic" (PIA, 45).[68] This approach raises some serious questions. Can one abstract these virtues from their ethical problematic without profoundly distorting them? And once one has given a purely ontological account of these virtues, how can one then regain their ethical dimension? Φρόνησις is here assimilated to σοφία to such an extent that its relation to the ethical is left completely obscure. The unity that Heidegger sees between φρόνησις and σοφία is therefore no unity at all since it excludes an important dimension of the former. And in thus divorcing ontology from ethics, does Heidegger leave any bridge between the two? As we have already seen, these are the issues at stake in the confrontation between Heidegger and Plato. Heidegger's principle is: ontology first, ethics later. He therefore criticizes Plato for mixing up the two. Yet might not Plato have seen a relation here that Heidegger's approach altogether misses, a relation between the *ethical* dimension of φρόνησις and the ontological dimension of σοφία? Whatever the answer, it is Heidegger's failure even to consider this possibility that prevents him from genuinely coming to terms with Plato's thought.

This shows to what extent πρᾶξις has ceased to be "practical" in the normal sense of the word and has become ontological. For an account of how Heidegger "ontologizes" Aristotle's ethics in the 1924 course, see my "Beyond or Beneath Good and Evil?"

68. Heidegger at some point added on the margin the cryptic comment: "Nachklang *alter* Einstellung!" (PIA, 45). Perhaps this comment is meant to question the implied distinction between the ethical problematic and the ontological problematic. If so, this is only at the cost of suppressing anything that would distinguish the ethical from the ontological.

This suppression of the ethical in Heidegger's planned book on Aristotle also characterizes the book that Heidegger would write instead: *Being and Time*. Heidegger there repeatedly resists any attempt to find an ethics in his analysis of *Dasein*. The reason is that this analysis is meant to serve a purely ontological purpose, the raising of the question of being. The analysis of *Dasein*'s being is no more self-contained than the discussion of *Nicomachean Ethics* Z was meant to be in the Aristotle book: both are simply preliminary, both are *introductions* to ontology. And in such an introduction ethics has no place.

Now we can understand in part why for Heidegger Plato's dialectic is itself only an introduction, only "on the way" to Aristotelian σοφία. Plato's dialectic fails to free itself from a practical conception of the good; it remains rooted in the ethical context of φρόνησις.[69] It therefore fails to reach the higher level of σοφία, of truly scientific inquiry. The life of dialectic is a practical life that has not yet become authentic, i.e., that has not yet fully realized in θεωρία its tendency towards seeing and knowing. It is led astray by a practical conception of the good that is incidental and extrinsic to the fundamental movement of human life, a movement that, as tending toward the understanding of being, is fundamentally ontological in character. This movement is fulfilled only in scientific existence, and dialectic, on account of its practical dimension, can never attain the level of science. We can now see more clearly what Heidegger commits himself to in parting ways with Plato: the identification of philosophy with a σοφία beyond φρόνησις, that is, with science, and the "ontologizing" of φρόνησις, that is, the divorcing of its ontological from its

---

69. Though significantly Heidegger in the SS 1924 course purifies dialectic itself by sharply distinguishing it from rhetoric in a way that even Plato, who clearly wishes to make some distinction, would not recognize: in dialectic as opposed to rhetoric "λόγος is released from the πρακτόν, λόγος itself has become the πρᾶξις. λόγος as a dealing [*Verhandeln*] here realizes its pure function of showing [*Aufzeigen*], with regard to what is being dealt with, how it is and what it is" (GA 18, 158). In Plato's dialogues dialectic is rarely a pure "showing" but is rather inextricably tied to the question of what is to be done. Even more questionable is the other difference Heidegger sees between dialectic and rhetoric: while in the everyday speaking with which rhetoric is concerned *who* is speaking (that person's ἦθος) and *to whom* he is speaking (that person's πάθος) are of central importance, "in contrast in the case of διαλέγεσθαι it is to a certain degree indifferent [*gleichgültig*] to whom one is speaking and it is also indifferent who I am and how I comport myself [*wie ich mich dabei bewege*]" (161). Heidegger's own qualification, "to a certain degree," suggests some awareness of the extent to which the mentioned "indifference" is not a characteristic of the διαλέγεσθαι practiced in Plato's dialogues. In the *Sophist* course Heidegger comments on "Platos zwiespältige Stellung zur Rhetorik," i.e., the negative assessment in the *Gorgias* versus the more positive assessment in the *Phaedrus* (GA 19, 308–10). What Heidegger insists on, however, is that unlike Aristotle Plato was never able to account for rhetoric as a techne because he either identified rhetoric with sophistry and thereby condemned both (219) or he absorbed rhetoric, along with everything else, into dialectic (338). What Heidegger does not at all consider is the rhetorical dimension of Plato's dialogues and therefore the genuinely rhetorical dimension of his dialectic.

ethical dimension. In deciding, against Plato, to pursue ontology while "disregarding" ethics, Heidegger is confronted with a completely un-Platonic problem: how do we get back from the ontological to the ethical?

3. Σοφία as a Genuine Possibility of Human *Dasein*: Ontological Hubris?

Heidegger's critique of Plato presupposes more than the characterization of a σοφία and scientific existence divorced from the ethical and practical: it also presupposes that such σοφία is a possible achievement for human beings. This possibility is brought into question by Heidegger himself when in the *Sophist* course he discusses Aristotle's characterization of σοφία as an enduring relation to that which is eternal, unchanging, and disassociated from πρᾶξις, γένεσις, and κίνησις of any kind. As Heidegger recognizes, such a relation is denied human beings: "Yet insofar as man is mortal, insofar as he needs recreation and relaxation [*Erholung und Abspannung*] in the widest sense, the constant tarrying with what is everlasting, the ultimately appropriate comportment to what always is, is denied him" (GA 19, 171; see also 130 and 134). To what extent, then, can σοφία be a genuine possibility of human existence? In drawing our attention to the limitations of human nature, Heidegger is simply following Aristotle's own recognition that σοφία might with justice (δικαίως) be thought not to be a possible possession of human beings (οὐκ ἀνθρωπίνη ἡ κτῆσις) since human nature is in many ways "enslaved" (πολλαχῇ γὰρ ἡ φύσις δούλη τῶν ἀνθρώπων ἐστίν, *Metaphysics* A, 982b29–30). Yet Aristotle's reply to this suggestion, that the poets lie when they say that the gods begrudge humans their success, does not go very far in addressing the serious concern it raises. Even if we can briefly, occasionally, and sporadically enter into such a pure relation to the eternal, can we ever be said to *exist* in such a relation, a relation that completely transcends and denies our enslaved condition? Is not σοφία, rather than a genuine possibility of human existence, instead an aberration, a kind of mystical state that briefly transports us beyond anything we could meaningfully call human existence?

But the fact is, as Heidegger recognizes, that Aristotle is not basing his characterization of σοφία on a consideration of the possibilities of human existence per se. Aristotle's ranking of σοφία above φρόνησις is based on a purely ontological consideration ("rein ontologische Betrachtung," 168; "rein theoretische Betrachtung," 169), that is, on the consideration that the kind of being to which σοφία is related, as that which always is and cannot be otherwise, must be ranked higher ontologically than the kind of being to which φρόνησις is related, that is, that which changes. "The decision in favor of the priority of σοφία is in the end derived from the being itself to which it relates itself" (171, my trans.; see also 137).

But to what extent can this "ontological consideration" be said to be Heidegger's own? To answer this question, we must consider Heidegger's general conclusion: "For the Greeks the consideration of human existence was oriented purely toward the meaning of being itself [*am Sinn des Seins selbst*], i.e., toward the extent to which it is possible for human Dasein to be everlasting" (178). The general kind of examination of human existence that Heidegger here attributes to the Greeks, if we put aside its specific application as described after the "i.e.," is echoed by his claim in *Being and Time* that "the possibility of carrying out the analytic of *Dasein* depends on a prior working-out of the question about the meaning of being in general" (SZ, 13). The important differences should not be ignored. The meaning of being as absolute presencing is derived by the Greeks from the being of the *world* ("am Sein der Welt abgelesen") and then subsequently applied to *Dasein* (GA 19, 178). Heidegger considers this approach completely mistaken: he insists that the raising of the question about the meaning of being must begin with an analysis of *Dasein's* being. However, what Heidegger sees himself as sharing with the Greeks, what he sees as distinguishing both of their approaches from those of modern philosophy, is an explicit orientation toward the meaning of being in the interpretation of human existence. This is why Heidegger considers the Greek conception of human existence to be as much outside the purview of modern ethics (see GA 19, 178) as is his own analytic of *Dasein*. Heidegger finds in the Greeks, though with less explicitness, his own view that "the ontic distinction of Dasein lies in the fact that it *is* ontological" (SZ, 12), that is, that its own being is defined by a relationship to, and understanding of, being in general.

But can an understanding of the ultimate existential possibilities of human existence be based on a purely ontological, purely theoretical consideration? This question takes us full circle back to where we began: can σοφία be separated from φρόνησις, can the τέλος for humans be abstracted from πρᾶξις and given a purely ontological characterization? Can the problem of being be completely severed from the ethical and made the object of a science? According to Heidegger's own critique, at least during 1924–26 and with respect to the "middle Plato" of the *Republic*, Plato's answers were negative. But should not affirmative answers to these questions be charged with a kind of ontological hubris? The most striking example of precisely this hubris is the Promethean *Rektoratsrede*, in which Heidegger braves the storm by defiantly willing *Wissenschaft* in full recognition of its weakness (11).

While seeking something higher, while attempting to see true being, Plato's dialectic remains firmly rooted in the practical, ethical, and discursive context of human existence. It is thus, as Heidegger says, essentially and always *on the way*. It mediates between πρᾶξις-oriented φρόνησις and being-oriented σοφία, between the ethical good and the ontological good. As Heidegger's general characterization of dialectic indicates, it also mediates between the discourse (λέγειν) that is the medium of ethical human existence and the "seeing" (νοεῖν) that transcends this discourse. Now we see the consequence of Heidegger's dismissal of dialectic as confused, tentative, and confined to φρόνησις: the identification of philosophy with an ethically neutral *Wissenschaft* transcending in its clarity the concealing and distorting tendencies of λόγος. This conception of philosophy as *Wissenschaft* would of course eventually run aground with the failure to complete the project of *Being and Time*.[70] The disassociation of philosophy from the ethical and the practical, on the other hand, seems to become, if anything, only more pronounced in the later Heidegger.[71] In the *Sophist* course Heidegger has left Plato's dialectic behind once and for all.

C. ETHICS IN PLATO'S *SOPHIST*

Plato's *Sophist* exposes the danger of disassociating philosophy from questions of *worth*. Ironically, one of the features of this dialogue that appealed to Heidegger is, as we have seen, precisely the absence of the good, the complete silence concerning ethics. Here he saw philosophical science finally freed from the practical conception of the good and the ethical import of Socratic questioning found in earlier dialogues. Yet what Heidegger's interpretation predictably fails to note are the many indications in the dialogue that this disassociation of philosophy from ethics is a problem. Most importantly, he does

---

70. See Heidegger's emphatic denial that philosophy is a *Wissenschaft* already (GA 34, 83). Only a few years earlier in the *Grundbegriffe* course he was arguing that philosophy is a *Wissenschaft*, though a *critical, radical Wissenschaft* (see GA 22, 1–11). For a detailed account of the history of this shift, see my "Dialectic as 'Philosophical Embarrassment': Heidegger's Critique of Plato's Method," *Journal of the History of Philosophy* 40, no. 3 (2002): 378–81.

71. In the *Brief über den "Humanismus"* Heidegger indeed explicitly rejects the identification of thinking with θεωρία, seeing it as a mere reaction to the characterization of thinking as a τέχνη (BH, 312). And later in the text, in response to the question, is the thinking of the truth of Being "nur ein theoretisches Vorstellen vom Sein und vom Menschen, oder lassen sich aus solcher Erkenntnis zugleich Anweisungen für das tätige Leben entnehmen und diesem an die Hand geben?" (354), he asserts that "dieses Denken ist weder theoretisch noch praktisch. Es ereignet vor dieser Unterscheidung" (354). Yet the description Heidegger proceeds to give of this thinking brings it much nearer to σοφία than to φρόνησις: "Solches Denken hat kein Ergebnis. Es hat keine Wirkung. Es genügt seinem Wesen, indem es ist. Aber es ist, indem es seine Sache sagt" (354). Likewise, Heidegger may appear to overcome the earlier opposition in his thought between ethics and ontology when he claims that the thinking of the truth of Being is the original ethics (353). "However," he immediately adds, "this thinking is not in the first instance ethics, because it is ontology" (353). As Joanna Hodge remarks, "The puzzle is why Heidegger presumes that ontology is not ethics." *Heidegger and Ethics* (New York: Routledge, 1995), 24. This puzzle seems to be the constant in Heidegger's thought that explains its unvarying disaccord with Plato's thought.

not see that this disassociation results in the Stranger's failure to distinguish the philosopher from the sophist.

The first indication that something important is indeed overlooked by Heidegger's interpretation is a feature that might initially appear harmless: Heidegger equates Plato with Socrates at the beginning of the *Sophist* (and in other dialogues),[72] but then equates Plato with the Stranger throughout the rest of the dialogue.[73] Not only is this identification of Plato with two different characters in the same dialogue at least puzzling, but it also prevents Heidegger from explicitly recognizing and coming to terms with a distinction between Socratic dialectic and the Stranger's dialectic.

1. Heidegger's Own Implied Distinction Between Socratic Dialectic and the Stranger's Dialectic

It is important to note that Heidegger's own interpretation of the *Sophist* implies, without being able to explain, this distinction. One of its major theses is that this dialogue aims at revealing the nature of the philosopher as well as that of the sophist. Heidegger at every opportunity argues against the suggestion of some scholars that Plato intended to write another dialogue on the philosopher, something that, on Heidegger's interpretation, would have been superfluous.[74] Yet clearly a definition of the philosopher is *not* a result of the Stranger's divisions. In what way, then, or by what method, is the nature of the philosopher revealed? Heidegger's reponse is that it is revealed Socratically, by which he evidently means indirectly, negatively, and "reflexively" (i.e., through the process of philosophizing itself).[75] He appeals here to "the Socratic bearing of Platonic philosophy, which offers what is positive only in performance and not by strictly making it a subject of reflection" (532; the nature of the

---

72. Heidegger is not ambiguous on this point: in interpreting Socrates' comment that the Stranger is perhaps a god come to judge men, Heidegger asserts that "Sokrates = Plato" (GA 19, 238) and therefore sees in Socrates' comment Plato's "ungeheure Schätzung" for Parmenides (238–39). In the context of discussing the *Phaedrus* Heidegger refers to "Sokrates-Plato" (322) and to "Sokrates bzw. Plato" (324). The same equation persists in the later lecture courses *Vom Wesen der Wahrheit* (GA 34, 250, 287) and *Parmenides* (GA 54, 186).

73. The fact that Heidegger in describing how two types of τέχνη are distinguished uses the phrase "daß Plato so verfährt" (GA 19, 272) shows that he is simply identifying Plato with the Stranger. In discussing the further division of τέχνη κτητική, Heidegger begins: "Plato macht einen doppelten Unterschied" (279). This identification of Plato with the Stranger is evident throughout the rest of Heidegger's discussion. The assumption that Plato can simply be identified with whomever happens to be the main speaker in a dialogue, while still fairly widespread in Platonic scholarship, is being increasingly challenged; see *Who Speaks for Plato? Studies in Platonic Anonymity*, ed. Gerald A. Press (Lanham, Md.: Rowman and Littlefield, 2000).

74. See GA 19, 245, 532, 574, 577, and 610.

75. "Vielmehr leistet die Aufgabe, zu klären, was der Philosoph sei, gerade der Dialog über den *Sophisten*, und zwar nicht in der primitiven Weise, daß einem erzählt wird, was er sei, sondern eben

"performance" or *Durchführung* must be nothing other than διαλέγεσθαι). But then what exactly is the relation between this Socratic method and the Stranger's method of division? And how is the difference between the two to be explained if both Socrates and the Stranger are mouthpieces of Plato? And why is the Stranger's method itself incapable of revealing the nature of the philosopher? Why can only Socrates' indirect, negative method accomplish this? And why in this case is Socrates kept silent throughout almost the entire dialogue? Heidegger appears oblivious to these questions.

2. The Distinction Between Socrates' Method of "Purification" and the Stranger's Value-Neutral Method

But there is a clear indication in the text, not noted by Heidegger as such, of the nature of the difference between the methods of Socrates and the Stranger. The definition of the "noble sophist," generally recognized to refer to Socrates (as the description at 230a5–d4 suggests), involves a distinction between two kinds of discrimination, that of like from like and that of better from worse. The latter is called "purification" (καθαρμός τις). The type of purification that casts out of the soul the κακία of ignorance (ἄγνοια) is described by Heidegger, following the Stranger, as one that, through questioning (*Durchfragen*; ἔλεγχος is what it is called in the text), shows inconsistencies in the beliefs of the ignorant person: "it has to be shown to him that he presents the matter at issue sometimes in one way and then again in another way: i.e., that he *does not have any relation at all to the matters themselves*" (GA 19, 377). According to Heidegger, this kind of purification "first opens up Dasein for a possible encounter with the world and with itself" (379). When the Stranger calls this teaching art of purification "noble-born sophistry" (ἡ γένει γενναία σοφιστική), Heidegger takes this phrase to refer to someone who "actually is what the factual sophist simply pretends to be" (380), that is, the philosopher. Thus, Heidegger clearly equates this form of purifying discrimination with the genuine philosophy to which the sophist only pretends. Later, in the context of discussing not-being, Heidegger further clarifies the nature of this purification by describing a type of negation that is productive: "negation, understood in this way, as possessing *a disclosive character* [*Erschließungscharakter*], can have, within the concrete uncovering

---

sokratisch" (GA 19, 245). The "reflexive" character of the disclosing of the nature of the philosopher is evident in Heidegger's claims that "*der Philosoph klärt sich von selbst auf,* und das einzig nur in der philosophischen Arbeit selbst" (532, immediately before Heidegger describes this way of revealing things as "Socratic") and that with the understanding of the sophist at the end of the dialogue "ist— und das ist das Entscheidende—der *Philosoph* in sich selbst durchsichtig geworden, und das einzig auf dem Wege des konkreten Philosophierens selbst, und nicht an beliebigen Sachen" (610; see also 12). Heidegger even suggests that "Plato" names the art of purification "noble sophistic," even though it is clearly philosophy, in order to *avoid* a direct and positive characterization of the philosopher (380).

of beings, a *purifying* function, so that negation itself acquires a *productive character*" (560). This purification that discloses by negating can apparently be identified with the negative, indirect method that Heidegger calls "Socratic."

But is the Stranger's method itself characterized by this kind of "purification"? In other words, do the Stranger's divisions discriminate better from worse? Plato does not leave us in doubt for long. In the very context of discussing purification, the Stranger, in what is ostensibly a methodological aside, claims that the rank or worth of an object is irrelevant to his method, since it is one that honors (τιμᾷ) all things alike (227b2–6). In the *Statesman*, the Stranger repeats this point when his divisions have the result of making humans and swine nearest of kin, thereby also undermining the ethical superiority of the statesman over the easygoing swineherd: "Things that possess greater dignity are of no more concern to this method of definition than things that do not. It does not dishonor what is petty in favor of what is greater, but always abiding by its own procedure it attains what is most true" (266d7–9). Thus, the Stranger's divisions discriminate only like from like, and therefore his method cannot be classified under the process of purification with which Heidegger himself (along with others!) has identified genuine philosophy.

3. The Distinction Between Socratic Elenctic Dialogue and the Stranger's Monological Method

There is further indication of the Stranger's inability to "purify." As already noted, the method of "purification" is identified with the type of *elenchos* practiced by Socrates. The dialogue makes abundantly clear how alien this *elenchos* is to the Stranger. At the beginning of the dialogue, Socrates attempts to see in the Stranger a kindred spirit by suggesting to Theodorus that "perhaps this man who accompanies you is one of the higher powers, come to look down on us and refute us for making such a poor showing in argument—some kind of god of refutation" (τάχ' οὖν ἂν καὶ σοί τις οὗτος τῶν κρειττόνων συνέποιτο, φαύλους ἡμᾶς ὄντας ἐν τοῖς λόγοις ἐποψόμενός τε καὶ ἐλέγξων, θεὸς ὤν τις ἐλεγκτικός, 216b3–6). However, Theodorus immediately denies this (with no protest from the Stranger): "That is not the stranger's way, Socrates, but he is more moderate than those who devote themselves to disputations" (μετριώτερος τῶν περὶ τὰς ἔριδας ἐσπουδακότων, 216b7–8). Two things are to be noted in this reply. First, Theodorus fails to make any distinction between *elenchos* and eristic.[76] The Stranger betrays a similar failure in the dialogue, as shown by the passage discussed above in which he equates

---

76. While in general the word ἔρις need not refer specifically to "eristic," Plato does use it in this way, thus opposing it to genuine dialectic: ἔριδι, οὐ διαλέκτῳ πρὸς ἀλλήλους χρώμενοι (*Republic* V, 454a8). Thus there is justification for Jacob Klein's claim that "Theodorus does not see the difference between a disputatious man, who disputes for the sake of disputing, and a man who cross-examines

elenctic purification with "noble-born sophistry."⁷⁷ Secondly, the characterization of the Stranger as μετριώτερος shows him to be unsuited to the elenctic method, which he himself later describes as "rough" or "harsh" (τραχυτέρα than admonition or νουθετητική, 229e1–2). The Stranger's lack of identification with the Socratic *elenchos* is thus betrayed by his ignorance of its nature and his aversion to its harshness.

This is only further betrayed when Socrates gives the Stranger the choice between two ways of presenting his views on the sophist, the statesman and the philosopher: either by giving a long, uninterrupted speech alone (μακρῷ λόγῳ διεξιέναι) or by asking questions of an interlocutor (δι' ἐρωτήσεων, 217c2–4). The Stranger clearly prefers the former method,⁷⁸ but agrees to proceed according to the latter (1) only because he is ashamed not to (αἰδώς τίς μ' ἔχει, 217d8) and (2) only on the condition that his interlocutor be untroublesome and tractable (ἀλύπως τε καὶ εὐηνίως προσδιαλεγομένῳ, 217d1–2). Thus, what the Stranger wants is a discussion that approximates as much as possible a monological (αὐτὸς ἐπὶ σαυτοῦ, Socrates' words at 217c3, or τὸ καθ' αὑτὸν, the Stranger's words at 217d2–3), uninterrupted speech.

Yet this is clearly not the kind of discussion that Socrates wants. The example he presents for the Stranger to follow is an earlier discussion that took place between himself as a young man and the old Parmenides, a clear reference to the dialogue *Parmenides*. There the young Socrates is far from being untroublesome and tractable: he begins the discussion by attacking no less a figure than Zeno and puts up a strong fight when he is in turn attacked

---

in order to refute what is untrue." *Plato's Trilogy: Theaetetus, the Sophist and the Statesman* (Chicago: University of Chicago Press, 1977), 7. Heidegger's interpretation of the phrase θεός τις ἐλεγκτικός as an allusion to "die Streitsüchtigkeit des Schüler des Parmenides" (241) shows that he too makes no distinction between *elenchos* and eristic.

77. Another indication of this failure is the Stranger's description of a form of "eristic" that is pursued not for money but for the pleasure it itself provides, to the neglect of the practitioner's own affairs (225d7–10). Not only did Socrates neglect his own affairs in the pursuit of the *elenchos* (see *Apology* 23b7–c1), but the Stranger's word for this neglect, ἀδολεσχία, was commonly applied to what many saw as Socrates' idle loquaciousness (see Aristophanes' *Tagenistai*, fr. 490 Kock). Thus the Stranger implicitly identifies Socrates' method with a form of eristic differing from sophistry only in its impracticality. In wrongly claiming that the sophist is distinguished from the ἀδολέσχης by the fact "daß die Art des διαλέγεσθαι des Sophisten doch einen ernsten Charakter hat, daß es ein Reden ist, dem es auf irgendetwas ankommt" (305)—the only thing the sophist is in fact said to be in earnest about is *money*—Heidegger surprisingly attributes to sophistry that "Sachlichkeit" he earlier denied it. In doing so he unwittingly equates the contrasted Socratic method with "bloßes Bildungsgeschwätz" (304–5).

78. Kenneth Sayre, in "A Maieutic View of Five Late Dialogues," in *Methods of Interpreting Plato and His Dialogues*, ed. James Carl Klagge and Nicholas D. Smith, Oxford Studies in Ancient Philosophy, supp. vol. (Oxford: Clarendon Press, 1992), 221–43, assumes that the Stranger's procedure "is first to enlist Theaetetus as a partner in conversation, which he considers preferable to solitary discourse (217c–d)" (222), that he "pointedly reject[s] the option of a 'long solitary address' . . . in favor of a conversation with a tractable respondent" (227), and that, along with Socrates and Parmenides in other dialogues, he "is quite explicit about declining to apply it [the method] in any other than a conversational context" (238). A cursory glance at 217c–d is sufficient to refute these claims.

by Parmenides. The venerable philosopher is himself as "harsh" (τραχύς) as possible, completely demolishing the young Socrates' theory of forms. This method of cross-examination and refutation is Socrates' ideal (λόγους παγκάλους is how he describes the discussion with Parmenides at 217c5). The Stranger, however, represents a complete rejection of this ideal.

Heidegger's own interpretation of 217c–d is especially revealing of the shortcomings of his approach. Heidegger is so determined to portray in a good light the Stranger's preference for monologue over dialogue that he simply misinterprets what the Stranger says. He characterizes the Stranger's demand for a respondent who will converse in an untroublesome and tractable way (ἀλύπως and εὐηνίως, 217d1) as a demand for someone who "within the argumentation and discussion ... is not influenced by his moods" and is "not stubborn as a mule" ("nicht bockig"), that is, "does not dig in his heels, is not dogmatic [*nicht rechthaberisch ist*], does not approach a discussion with the idea in his head that he is always right, whether or not the things themselves agree" (GA 19, 250, my trans.). On this interpretation, all that the Stranger is requesting is an interlocutor who is not excessively emotional, moody, dogmatic, arrogant, obnoxious, and quarrelsome. This is surely a reasonable demand that rules out no one but a Thrasymachus. But Heidegger's interpretation is clearly not defensible. What the Stranger requests and gets is not simply a serious and well-behaved interlocutor, but rather one who contributes as little as possible to the discussion. Heidegger himself at one point observes that Theaetetus "throughout the whole dialogue ... has not particularly accomplished very much" (515). He therefore recognizes the peculiar character of the Stranger's method: "In this way, a peculiar mixed form of the mode of treating the theme comes into being: indeed a *dialogue, a discussion,* which, however, in part already has the character of a monological treatise; and the reason for this resides in the *difficulty of the subject matter* [*Schwierigkeit der Sache*]" (251). Yet why need discussion of a difficult issue be monological? The Stranger provides no explanation, and Heidegger accepts his justification without a question.[79]

4. Different Effects of the Elenctic Method of Purification and the Stranger's Method

Another important difference between the methods of Socrates and the Stranger is to be found in their effects on the interlocutor. According to the Stranger's own account, the elenctic method, by freeing the interlocutor of ignorant opinions, affords the greatest pleasure and the most enduring benefit

---

79. In the 1922 introduction Heidegger betrays a preference similar to the Stranger's: he claims that the literary form of Aristotle's research, i.e., "Abhandlungen im Stil der thematischen Exposition und Untersuchung," provides the only appropriate basis for the determinate methodological aims of his own interpretation (PIA, 39).

(230c2–3). The Stranger, on the other hand, does not suggest that his own method will produce any pleasure or in any way benefit Theaetetus. Instead, he says to his newly chosen interlocutor: "From now on I must, it seems, direct my speech towards you. If, however, you get fed up with the long task [ἂν δ' ἄρα τι τῷ μήκει πονῶν ἄχθῃ], do not blame me for this, but these friends of yours" (218a7–9). Pleasure? Benefit? No, just a long, burdensome task. The reason is that the goal of this discussion is not to purify Theaetetus of ignorant and contradictory opinions (which was the goal of Socrates' conversation with Theaetetus in the *Theaetetus*). The role of Theaetetus is simply to be the addressee of a long speech. This requires that he stay awake and attentively follow what is being said. If, however, he gets too tired or bored, he can have someone else take his place (218b1–6). The interlocutor is interchangeable.

5. Who Is the Philosopher? Who Is Plato?

The fundamental rifts just noted between Socrates and the Stranger raise many difficult questions. Which method corresponds to Plato's own conception of philosophy or dialectic: Socrates' negative, indirect, and dialogical method of purification or the Stranger's method of division, which, while conclusive and direct, is monological and does not discriminate between bad and good? If both, what is the relation between them, and what exactly is Plato trying to show by juxtaposing them? By reading the dialogue as a treatise and simply identifying Plato with whomever the main speaker happens to be at any given point, Heidegger cannot even raise these questions.

I cannot here embark upon the discussion of the *Sophist* as a whole needed to address all of the above questions adequately.[80] To show, however, the seriousness of the methodological discordance that Heidegger fails to pursue, I conclude with some evidence that Plato meant us to see the limitations of the Stranger's method as a *philosophical* method, that he therefore cannot be simply identified with the Stranger, and that Socrates' silence throughout most of the dialogue is a *critical* silence. If this is the case, then Heidegger, in ignoring the criticisms built into the dialogue form and reading the *Sophist* as a treatise authored by the Stranger = Plato, has been led astray.

6. The Stranger Fails to Meet Socrates' Demand for a Distinction Between the Philosopher and the Sophist

Clearly what leads most interpreters of the *Sophist*, in contradiction to their practice in other dialogues, to identify Plato with the Stranger rather than

---

80. For more discussion, though still far from a complete or adequate interpretation, see my "Plato's Eleatic Stranger: His Master's Voice?" in *Who Speaks for Plato?* 161–81.

with Socrates is that the Stranger speaks much more. What this approach fails to recognize is the extraordinary importance of what Socrates *does* say. It is Socrates, we must recall, who introduces and defines the project that occupies the Stranger in both the *Sophist* and the *Statesman*. It is therefore in terms of the project *as Socrates* defines it that we must judge the Stranger's results. In general, what Socrates requests is an account of the relations between sophist, statesman, and philosopher. But why does this concern him? At the dramatic date of the dialogue, Meletus has just brought against Socrates the charge that will lead to his condemnation and death. Socrates will soon in the *Apology* need to defend the worth of the philosophy he practices. In doing so, he will need to distinguish himself from the sophists before the misrepresentations circulated by Aristophanes' *Clouds*, and he will need to explain his relation to the *polis* and his lack of involvement in politics. In short, the question Socrates raises is not an idle, academic one, but rather one of utmost existential urgency. What is at stake is the worth of the philosophical life as such. That this is Socrates' principal concern is clear in the way he introduces the problem he wants the Stranger to address: "These men—those, that is, who are not counterfeit but genuine philosophers—appear in many different guises, thanks to the ignorance of others, as they visit cities, observing from above the life below, and they seem to some to be of no worth (τοῦ μηδενὸς τίμιοι), and to others to be worth everything (ἄξιοι τοῦ παντός)" (216c4–8). It is this dispute concerning the worth of philosophy that requires us to distinguish it from the different guises in which it appears, in particular, from sophistry and statesmanship. Can the Stranger's method perform this task? Can it distinguish philosophy from sophistry in such a way as to show the greater worth of philosophy?

Here we need to recall what was already seen above: the Stranger's method does not honor (τιμᾷ) one art more than another, even if the two arts are generalship (στρατηγική) and the art of removing lice (φθειριστική). This in itself appears to make the method unfit for meeting Socrates' request. Furthermore, this implication is made as clear as possible by the way in which Plato characterizes the Stranger's hesitation before identifying the elenctic art of purification with sophistry in the fifth definition: the Stranger is made to express the fear that such an identification might grant the sophist too much honor (Μὴ μεῖζον αὐτοῖς προσάπτωμεν γέρας, 231a3). Yet the Stranger admitted only three pages of the Greek text earlier that his method honors all arts equally (τιμᾷ πρὸς τοῦτο ἐξ ἴσου πάσας, 227b2). Is it any wonder, then, that he proceeds to make the identification anyway, that he fails at this crucial point to keep the sophist and the philosopher distinct? The Stranger's value-neutral method cannot distinguish the philosopher from the sophist if this can be done only, as Socrates suggests, by showing the greater worth of the philosopher.

At the beginning of the *Statesman* Socrates expresses indirectly—yet unmistakeably to a reader sensitive to such indirectness—his dissatisfaction with what the Stranger has accomplished. At first Socrates appears pleased with the preceding discussion, since he thanks Theodorus for introducing him to both Theaetetus and the Stranger. When, however, Theodorus proudly replies that Socrates will owe him three times as much thanks after the Stranger has defined the statesman and the philosopher, Socrates, with seemingly incongruous seriousness, reproaches him. "My dear Theodorus, are we to say that we heard our greatest mathematician and geometer say that? . . . Are we to say that we heard you counting as being of equal worth these men who are so distant from one another in honor as to defy any of your mathematical proportions!" (Τῶν ἀνδρῶν ἕκαστον θέντος τῆς ἴσης ἀξίας, οἳ τῇ τιμῇ πλέον ἀλλήλων ἀφεστᾶσιν ἢ κατὰ τὴν ἀναλογίαν τὴν τῆς ὑμετέρας τέχνης, 257b2–4). Note that Socrates's criticism goes beyond Theodorus's casual comment: mathematics itself, despite all its precision and analytical rigor, cannot understand or express the degree to which the philosopher surpasses the sophist in worth. Indeed, such relations of worth lie completely outside the domain of mathematics: it can comprehend or express proportions only in terms of units deemed equal. When two things are characterized by a fundamental disparity of worth—fundamental in the sense that the one is not equal to any amount of the other—there can be no counting or reckoning. To put the point crudely, no number of sophists can equal one philosopher and therefore no mathematical proportion can express their relation. But what Socrates asserts to be true of mathematics is also true of the Stranger's method. According to the Stranger's own admission in both the *Sophist* and the *Statesman,* his method does not honor one thing more than another, it does not make distinctions of worth. Socrates' example of mathematics now illuminates why this is so. Just as mathematics can count only with equal units, so can the method of division divide only like from like or equal from equal. One can divide between two classes only if both belong to a common genus and therefore only if there is a fundamental sameness in both that renders them comparable. We can make a division between land animals and aquatic animals only because both are animals. We can divide between generalship and the art of removing lice only if both are equally, for example, forms of hunting. A division also requires a certain equality between what is divided. One side of the division cannot be "larger," more inclusive, broader or in any way more important than the other if the division is not to be forced or lopsided (see *Statesman,* 262bff.).

If what Socrates claims at the beginning of the *Statesman* is correct, the difference between the sophist and the philosopher has nothing to do with making long or short speeches, demanding or refusing money, or other such obvious traits: instead it is an essential disparity of worth so great that it prevents them from being included within any one genus and thus defies any classificatory division. There is no *essential* sameness uniting the sophist and the philosopher, only a superficial, accidental sameness; there is no equality of worth between them, but a difference of worth to which no proportion can do justice. But then the Stranger's method must fail in the attempt to divide the sophist from the philosopher and thus in the attempt to define either one. Socrates may indeed not say much, but his criticism at 257b2-4, veiled as a criticism of Theodorus, the Stranger's defender, says it all.

The Stranger's sixth and concluding definition of the sophist confirms Socrates' criticism. It is therefore unfortunate that Heidegger's lecture course came to an end before he could discuss it. The characteristics that the Stranger's final divisions ascribe to the sophist are the following: (1) He produces semblances as opposed to likenesses (266d-e). (2) His semblances are produced through his own person (his own voice), rather than through any instrument. This is called "imitation" (μίμησις, 267a). (3) His imitation is based on opinion (δόξα), not knowledge. This is called "opinion-imitation" (δοξομιμητική). (4) He does not naively think that he has knowledge, but strongly suspects that he does not. His imitation is therefore *ironic* (εἰρωνικός, 268a). (5) He does not give long speeches in public before a multitude, but in private and through short questions forces his interlocutor to contradict himself (268b-c). Most of the sophists encountered in Plato's own dialogues do not have all of these characteristics; in fact, it is not clear that *any* of them do. (The closest are the two brothers in the *Euthydemus*, but it is not clear that characteristics 1 and 4 apply to them.) More importantly, however, this definition does not clearly distinguish the sophist from the philosopher. The Stranger recognizes that someone with characteristic 5 could be either a sophist or a σοφός (268b10). What he sees as decisively distinguishing them is characteristic 3: the sophist's lack of knowledge. However, if we take into account Socrates' own profession of ignorance and the distinction in the *Symposium* between σοφία and φιλοσοφία, we see that this characteristic cannot distinguish the sophist from the philosopher. If anyone who refutes others in private without possessing wisdom is a sophist, then Socrates is condemned as a sophist. The Stranger's attribution of even Socratic irony to the sophist only provides further evidence for this condemnation. Nor can the distinction between semblances and likenesses help Socrates: the Stranger repeatedly expresses his uncertainty about which side of the distinction the sophist belongs to (236c-d, 264c), and his final decision is made without any explanation and therefore arbitrarily. Here we see that for the Stranger philosophy is simply wisdom and that therefore ignorance, irony, and the use of images all belong to sophistry. It is this view that explains the Stranger's inability, demonstrated repeatedly in this dialogue, to distinguish the Socratic philosopher from the sophist.[81] Socrates' criticism at the beginning of the *Statesman* informs us of the crucial dividing issue that is completely and necessarily eclipsed in the Stranger's divisions: the issue of worth, the issue of ethics, of how *best* to live, which in the *Gorgias*, for example, is the central issue in distinguishing the sophist from the philosopher.[82] The dialogue's conclusion thus confirms what Socrates suggests: a method incapable of discriminating better from worse cannot reveal what philosophy is.

7. Heidegger's Kinship with the Stranger

But why was Heidegger blind to these indications of the serious limitations of the Stranger's method? One reason is that Heidegger, as a result of reading the *Sophist* through Aristotle, fails to do justice to its dialogical form. The problem with reading a dialogue as a treatise is that one misses the criticisms and limitations with which the very context of the dialogue surrounds what is said. Heidegger is inattentive to the silent, critical presence of Socrates, his reading being guided instead by the presence of Aristotle (to the extent that he actually sees the young Aristotle behind a number of things that are said in the dialogue!).[83] Thus, he sees the *Sophist* as more "wissenschaftlich" (read: more like Aristotle) than the "earlier dialogues" (see 189) and, as seen above, he has no misgivings about the Stranger's elimination of genuine dialogue through the choice of a completely pliant interlocutor.

But there is a deeper and related reason for Heidegger's blindness, one that can be discovered only through the lecture course held one year after the *Sophist* lectures: *Die Grundbegriffe der antiken Philosophie*. As already noted, Heidegger in that course expresses his view that Plato in the later dialogues abandoned the idea of the good and sundered the problem of being from the ethical orientation of Socratic inquiry. With this view in the background, Heidegger would have no reason to be troubled by the inability of the Stranger's method to respond to questions of worth, to distinguish better from worse.

---

81. The Stranger even credits the sophists with the τί ἐστιν question, a question that in Plato's dialogues is unique to Socrates. The sophists, he tells Theaetetus, will not only ask them, "What is an image?" but will not accept examples as a response and will insist on being told that which is common to all images and allows the same word "image" to be applied to all of them (239e–240a). Not only is this claim not borne out by anything the sophists are depicted as doing in the dialogues, but the distinctively Socratic method is thereby equated with sophistry.

82. Aristotle also locates the difference between sophistry and dialectic in a "choice of life" (προαίρεσις τοῦ βίου, *Metaph*. 1004b24–25). Significantly, Heidegger sees the dialectician as choosing nothing more than "Sachlichkeit" (GA 19, 214–16).

83. Heidegger suggests that the young Aristotle is behind the part of the dialogue concerned with the γιγαντομαχία (GA 19, 483–85), though he admits that this cannot be proven and is solely "meine persönliche Überzeugung" (483). For the specific influences he finds, see the next chapter.

Yet Heidegger's thesis goes even further: he sees Plato as abandoning not only Socrates' ethical orientation, but also Socratic *dialectic* with its indirect, maieutic character and its emphasis on the τί ἐστιν question. Thus, Heidegger maintains that Plato in the *Theaetetus* describes Socrates' maieutic method only to abandon it and present his own, distinct method: the method of collection and division.[84] This view explains Heidegger's insensitivity to the disparity between Socratic dialectic and the Stranger's dialectic: believing that the former has been discarded, he can easily identify Plato with the latter.

But the important question is *why* Heidegger subscribed to this interpretation. Not only does he fail to present any detailed arguments in its defense[85] (he himself will have no problem rejecting it only a few years later), but he does not even consistently abide by it: as we have seen, Heidegger still identifies Plato with Socrates at the beginning of the *Sophist* and appeals to the Socratic method to explain how the dialogue can reveal the nature of the philosopher without defining or "capturing" it in the Stranger's divisions. Why, then, does this interpretation appeal to Heidegger? One reason, of course, is that Aristotle is the standard here. Heidegger sees the Stranger's method as approximating, though still falling short of,[86] the level of Aristotelian ontology, an ontology uncontaminated by any practical conception of the good or by the unclarity and tentativeness of Socratic dialectic.[87] But it is only with the question of *why* Aristotle is made the standard here that we arrive at the crucial point: Heidegger finds in both Aristotle and the Stranger, and *not* in Socrates or the earlier Plato, his own conception of what philosophy should be. The reason why he defends, without argument and even at the cost of inconsistency, the view that Plato in the later dialogues abandoned the idea of the good along with the ethical orientation of Socratic dialectic is his belief that this is what Plato *should* have done.

---

84. The following observation on the *Theaetetus* is to be found in Heidegger's own manuscript: "Man wird nicht fehlgehen, wenn *Plato* hier noch einmal *Sokrates* im ganzen schildert, um dann die eigene Methode dagegen durchzuführen" (GA 22, 111). This point is even more explicit in Mörchen's transcript: "Die so dargestellte maieutische Methode wird gerade in diesem und den folgenden Dialogen von Plato abgegeben" (266). The transcript then records the following comment about Socrates' asking of the "τί ἐστιν" question: "Dies ist die bisherige Art des διαλέγεσθαι nach des *Sokrates* Vorbild" (266). The connection between the abandonment of the Socratic conception of dialectic and the abandonment of the idea of the good is made clear in the following aside recorded again in Mörchen's transcript: "(Stillschweigend wird im 'Theätet' von Plato selbst die frühere Methode des Vordringens zu den Ideen und zum ἀγαθόν kritisiert)" (265). Heidegger sees the later dialectic as distinct from the earlier not only in its rejection of the idea of the good, but also in its recognition of multiplicity within Being itself and thus in its focus on exhibiting the relations between different εἴδη of Being, as opposed to simply inquiring after an isolated εἶδος. For a clear statement of this difference, see 282.

85. One thing at issue here is of course the whole "developmentalist" hypothesis which Heidegger appears to accept without question. In his manuscript can be found this note: "*Platonische Fragen:* Echtheit der Dialoge, Feststellung ihrer Abfassungszeit, Chronologie; inhaltliches Problem: Platos philosophische Entwicklung" (GA 22, 94).

86. For Aristotelian critiques of the later dialectical method, see GA 19, 288 and 294.

87. Brumbaugh describes the Stranger as "much more of an Aristotelian than Plato" (107).

My suggestion, in short, is that the most important reason why Heidegger fails to note the criticisms of the Stranger's method embedded in the dialogue is that the Stranger's limitations are Heidegger's own, at least in this lecture course and perhaps beyond. Just as the Stranger's method eclipses the questions of worth, of better and worse, with which Socrates' elenctic purification concerns itself, so is Heidegger's ranking of Aristotelian σοφία above Platonic φρόνησις motivated in part by a desire to disassociate ontology from ethics. Just as the Stranger identifies φιλοσοφία with σοφία, just as he assumes the possibility of *seeing* the forms prior to their articulation (what besides intuition can ground and justify the Stranger's divisions?), so does Heidegger. Just as the Stranger debases Socratic *elenchos* to eristic, so does Heidegger debase dialectic by assigning it a purely secondary role within philosophy. Just as the Socratic *elenchos* makes sudden and mysterious appearances throughout the Stranger's discussion without being recognized for what it is and therefore without being integrated into the Stranger's own conception of philosophy, so do references to a Socratic method appear suddenly at key places in Heidegger's text without being integrated into his conception of dialectic (which he simply identifies with the Stranger's method of "collection and division").[88] Finally, just as the Stranger rejects genuine dialogue in favor of a thinly disguised monologue, so does Heidegger bypass the chance of pursuing a genuinely dialogical interpretation of the *Sophist* in favor of a monological one, that is, one that reads the dialogue as a treatise and hears only one voice, the voice of the author presumably speaking through the main interlocutor. These limitations go "beyond" the *Sophist* lectures if, as suggested above, the dramatic shifts in Heidegger's interpretation of the ἀγαθόν do not represent a fundamental change of position on the relation between ethics and ontology. Furthermore, even in later works the dialogues, though read with more sensitivity to their form, still tend to be read mostly as treatises with little or no attention to overall context.

In the 1922 course on Aristotle's ontology and logic we find an extraordinary passage in which Heidegger makes fully explicit the motivation behind his neglect of the dialogue form and the related insistence on interpreting Plato through Aristotle:

> Precisely when one assumes that Platonic philosophy is scientific philosophy, that it has grown out of scientific investigation, one must characterize

---

88. Stanley Rosen rightly criticizes Heidegger for identifying dialectic with the logical technique of collection and division and thereby ignoring "the playful or ironical dialectic of man": "Therefore he [Heidegger] seems to be quite deaf to the possibility that there is a note of irony in the dialogical speeches about the techniques of division and collection." "Heidegger's Interpretation of Plato," in *Essays in Metaphysics*, ed. Carl G. Vaught (University Park: Pennsylvania State University Press, 1970), 64.

the attempt to arrive at a genuine understanding of this philosophy from the dialogues as in principle a methodologically wrong-headed way of interpretation. This would be possible only if one could remove and isolate the movement of expression that lies in the literary form of the dialogue, with all of the modifications of expression that the dialogue brings to its content as well as to the whole form of life being discussed and the world at issue, and thus free the movement of philosophical investigation itself. (GA 62, 170)

Heidegger could not make more explicit the opposition he sees between scientific philosophy and the dialogue form. An interpretation of Plato's philosophy that is based on a reading of his dialogues as dialogues would be simply wrongheaded if Plato's philosophy is genuinely scientific. And the implication is that this philosophy would not be truly philosophical, would not represent genuine philosophical investigation, if it were not scientific. Furthermore, what Heidegger proceeds to say immediately following the cited passage sets the agenda for the *Sophist* course to be delivered two years later: that is, that the described removal of the literary form of the dialogues is not an impossible undertaking in the case of the *late* dialogues but requires "the clear and concrete step-back from the broad basis of Aristotelian investigation" (170) since, as Heidegger asserts later in the course, Aristotle is the first and last "radical scientific philosopher" (256). There even follows an allusion to the hermeneutical principle, repeatedly invoked in the *Sophist* course, of interpreting the obscure from the perspective of what is more clear. All of this shows that Heidegger's appeal to Aristotle's philosophy rather than to the dialogue form as the guideline of his interpretation of the *Sophist* is quite premeditated and rooted in a particular conception of philosophy as scientific investigation.[89]

D. HEIDEGGER AND DIALOGUE

But is this conception of philosophy as a science from which dialogue must be stripped away as a mere literary form Plato's own? That Plato on the contrary sees philosophy, in the form of dialectic, as taking place in dialogue with others is implied by the passage from the *Seventh Letter* cited above (it makes sense to speak of "questioning and answering without envy" only in the context of two

---

89. Later in the course, in insisting again on the importance of scientific investigation, Heidegger asserts: "Die Philosophie muß aus ihrem Literaturdasein herausgerissen werden" (180). In striking contrast, Heidegger prefaces his reading of Aristotle with the following hermeneutical principle: "Gerade je entscheidener das Absehen auf eine prinzipielle Aneigung einer überlieferten Philosophie geht, um so weniger gleichgültig ist der literarische Ausdruckscharakter der vorgegebenen Quellen" (4).

or more inquirers) and made explicit by an earlier passage: "from frequent dialogue [συνουσία] concerning the thing itself and living together (συζῆν), suddenly, as a light kindled from a leaping flame, [knowledge] comes to be in the soul where it presently nourishes itself" (341c6–d2).⁹⁰ This connection between dialectic and dialogue must be noted in order to see that Heidegger in disassociating philosophy from the one also disassociates it from the other. Thus, Heidegger not only is unwilling, as has been seen, to make anything of the dialogue form of Plato's writings, tending to treat it as accidental to the philosophical content, which could be expressed just as well, if not better, in a treatise, but also refuses to make dialogue central to his conception of philosophy, despite elements in his own thought that could be seen as encouraging this.

Both the opposition and the affinity are evident in the SS 1924 course. In turning here to Aristotle's determination of the being of man, Heidegger on the one hand makes the observation that has been seen to constitute a central motif of both this course and the *Sophist* course: "Existence, the radical fundamental possibility of existing [*Dasein*] is for the Greeks the βίος θεωρητικός: life tarries in pure observation" (GA 18, 44). Yet here Heidegger notes a tension between this and the priority the Greeks also give to hearing: "'Hearing,' ἀκούειν, that which corresponds to speaking, is the fundamental αἴσθησις. In hearing I am in communication with other human beings, insofar as being human means speaking. The explicit emphasis on ἀκούειν is remarkable because otherwise the fundamental possibility of existence for the Greeks is located in θεωρεῖν, in ὁρᾶν. How this is coherent is something we will articulate later" (44). Here we have a recognition of the possibility that the Greeks gave to dialogue a priority at least equal to that which they gave to vision. Hearing what others say is in this case at least as important as seeing something for oneself. The reason is to be found in what Heidegger was already seen to acknowledge above: the centrality of speaking to being human, a relation that in the cited passage seems to be even an identity. The *human* way of getting at the truth is conversation with other human beings and the kind of shared seeing such conversation makes possible, not a vision that one possesses for oneself independently of such conversation. But why, then, does Heidegger not emphasize *this* legacy of the Greeks? Why does he instead, in the *Sophist* course and beyond, give all the emphasis to the priority of seeing and θεωρεῖν?

If Heidegger in the cited passage claims that he will "later" articulate how the two Greek priorities cohere, this "later" appears to be at 104ff. Here Heidegger says that even though seeing discloses the world in the most genuine sense, hearing is still the genuine αἴσθησις because "it is the *perception of*

---

90. For a thorough examination of both the description and practice of dialectic in Plato's dialogues, see my *Dialectic and Dialogue*.

speaking, because it is the *possibility of being with one another* [*Miteinanderseins*]" (104). But oddly and revealingly, what Heidegger proceeds to emphasize is not speaking *with others*, but rather the fundamental ability of man to listen to his own speaking (104–5). "Man is not only a speaker and listener, but he is in himself the kind of being that *listens to itself* [*auf sich hört*]" (104). We seem closer here to the silent voice of conscience described in *Being and Time* than we are to dialogue.[91]

Yet Heidegger does give central importance to being and speaking with others in his discussion of Aristotle's definition of man as an animal possessing λόγος. Heidegger observes that this definition is introduced in the context of arguing that the πόλις exists by nature. The reason, according to Heidegger, is that this definition presupposes and reveals being-with-one-another (*Miteinandersein*), κοινωνία, to be a fundamental way of being for man (46–47), since being-with-one-another is a speaking-with-one-another (*Miteinandersprechendsein*, 47). Heidegger goes so far as to suggest that λέγειν is the ground of κοινωνία (50). The presence of others is not accidental to speaking; rather, "speaking is in itself as such expressing oneself in speech [*Sichaussprechen*], speaking together with other speakers and therefore the ontological [*seinsmäßige*] foundation of κοινωνία" (50; see also 17). *Miteinandersein* and *Sprechendsein*, as Heidegger later specifies, are equally primordial (*gleichursprünglich*): one is not to be deduced from the other (64). All these observations would suggest a position that makes dialogue central not only to philosophy but to human existence as such. But does Heidegger himself develop such a position and pursue its implications? Or is he, as the above discussion already suggests, too captivated by the other Greek legacy, that is, the priority granted to *nous*, *sophia*, and *theoria*?

The problem is that where authentic existence is identified with a choice for a seeing/saying opposed to the ordinary, everyday speaking (saying something of something) that characterizes our being-with-one-another, the latter inevitably gets identified with inauthenticity. Thus, at one point in the course, Heidegger explicitly identifies ordinary, everyday *Miteinandersein* with *das Man*: we are together in saying what "one" says. "The One maintains itself and has its genuine power in language" (64).[92] Heidegger does indeed immediately suggest

---

91. As Taminiaux observes with regard to *Being and Time*: "Bien sûr le *Dasein* est avec d'autres. Le *Mit-Sein* détermine sa condition. Mais il n'est pas essentiellement interpellé par eux, référé à eux, déféré devant eux. En définitive c'est avec lui-même qu'il parle, en écoutant la voix de son for interne" (*Sillages*, 30; see also 259).

92. Similarly, in the 1924 lecture *The Concept of Time* Heidegger, after giving an almost identical account of *Miteinandersein* as *Sprechen* (GA 64, 113), characterizes *Miteinandersein* as follows: "Dasein, bestimmt als Miteinandersein, besagt zugleich: geführt sein von der herrschenden Auslegung, die das Dasein von sich selbst gibt; von dem, was *man* meint, von der Mode, von den Strömungen, von dem, was los ist: die Strömung, die keiner ist, das, was Mode ist: niemand" (120).

that a genuine, authentic *Miteinandersein* can develop from this: "Through a sharper determination of the One you will see that it is at the same time the possibility from which a genuine being-with-one-another in determinate ways grows" (64). But neither here nor elsewhere does Heidegger explain how this genuine *Miteinandersein* would grow and what it would involve. Neither here nor elsewhere does he so much as suggest that such a genuine *Miteinandersein* might be essential to the philosophical life. At one point in the course Heidegger grants that authenticity (for which he uses the Greek ἕξις, for reasons that cannot be discussed here) is possible even in the case of *Miteinandersein* (that such a claim should even need to be made in the interpretation of Aristotle's ethics already reveals a great deal): "There is a ἕξις also with regard to ὁμιλία, συζῆν: *it is being in control of the genuineness of one's relations to others and to oneself*" (264). But here again this is left undeveloped. Instead, the only Aristotelian virtues Heidegger discusses in any detail are courage and truthfulness: the virtues that, at least on Heidegger's interpretation, characterize the solitary life dedicated to science. These are not accidental oversights. When one characterizes the goal of philosophy as Heidegger has been seen to do, that is, as a direct seeing/saying of what something is in and by itself, the kind of conversation in and as which we normally exist with one another cannot but appear to be a distorting obstacle to be opposed and overcome. Gestures toward an authentic *Miteinandersein* must remain no more than gestures where the battle is between everyday conversing with one another and the philosopher's solitary choice of the scientific life *against* this conversation. Any genuine and autonomous realm of ethics or politics simply disappears. Thus, this is what becomes of *Miteinandersein* and *Miteinandersprechen* in the context of Heidegger's description of *Dasein*'s decision for *Wissenschaft*: "Speaking as communication [*Mitteilen*] that moves itself around in interpretedness [*Ausgelegtheit*] is hidden and unintentional distortion [*Verstellen*], as *communication* distorting assertion about . . . i.e., *leading-astray* [*Irre-Führung*]" (358; see also 355–56). It is hard to imagine such an assertion coming from someone who considers dialogue central to the philosophical project; on the contrary, the cited sentence comes at least close to saying that dialogue as such distorts. In short, while Heidegger in 1924 recognizes two priorities in the Greeks, that of seeing and that of hearing, and while Plato's dialectic clearly reconciles both priorities in the way described above, Heidegger appropriates the former at the expense of the latter.[93]

As for later texts, the closest Heidegger ever comes to realizing the potential of grounding a dialogical conception of philosophy on his account of

---

93. Though it is worth noting that Heidegger's *Handschrift* for the SS 1924 course repeatedly uses the word *Hinhören* (in the sense of listening to what Aristotle has to say) to describe the task of the course (see, e.g., 333). Yet this is perhaps why Heidegger insists that what he is doing in the course is *not* philosophy (334) but rather philology (4–5).

Miteinandersein is not in the rather spare account of *Miteinandersein* in *Sein und Zeit*, but rather in the richer account of the WS 1928–29 course *Einleitung in die Philosophie* (GA 27, 83–148). The central thesis of this later account is that *Miteinandersein* is a being-involved-with-(*Sein bei*)-something-common (*Gemeinsames*) and that what we partake of in common is the *truth* or *unconcealedness* of the things to which we relate. In short, *Miteinandersein* is a "sharing in the truth" (*Sichteilen in die Wahrheit*, 92–106). Heidegger accordingly characterizes a special form of *Miteinandersein*, friendship, as growing and resting "in a genuine passion for the matter that is shared [*gemeinsame Sache*]" (147). Yet especially important in the present context is that Heidegger also maintains, conversely, that every *Sein bei* . . . is *Miteinandersein* (118), and thus that truth is of its essence *shared with* . . . , even if one hides the truth from others (127–28), even if others do not exist (138). That Heidegger sees this argument as capable of applying to philosophy becomes clear when later in the course he uses the above language to translate the very passage from the *Seventh Letter* cited above (341c6–d2): the συνουσία and συζῆν which the passage describes as kindling knowledge in the soul are translated/interpreted by Heidegger as "a genuine being-together, *being-with-one-another in the matter itself [bei der Sache selbst]*, which grows out of a *shared concern with the matter*" (221). Yet what is surprising is again that Heidegger does not pursue this conception of philosophy beyond this suggestive translation and that he elsewhere gives little or no emphasis to dialogue as an essential component of philosophy. In an important paper contrasting the Heideggerian and Gadamerian conceptions of truth, Robert J. Dostal, while initially granting that like Gadamer, Heidegger "also makes conversation significant for thought and the experience of truth," points out that the terms *conversation* and *dialogue* are completely absent in *Being and Time*, despite the prominence of these notions in German philosophy at the time, and that the "conversation" that becomes an important theme in Heidegger's later work on Hölderlin is characterized as a listening to, and naming of, the gods.[94] It should be added that

---

94. "The Experience of Truth for Gadamer and Heidegger: Taking Time and Sudden Lightning," in *Hermeneutics and Truth*, ed. Brice R. Wachterhauser (Evanston: Northwestern University Press, 1994), 59–61. Gadamer describes well the monological character of Heidegger's thought when he explains the violence of Heidegger's interpretations of Hölderlin by observing "daß er nur sich, nur das, was seiner Aufgabe entgegenkommt, entgegentönt, was auf seine Frage Antwort verheißt, überhaupt zu hören vermag, als ein wahrhaft von seiner Sache Besessener." "Martin Heidegger 75 Jahre," in *Gesammelte Werke*, vol. 3 (Tübingen: J. C. B. Mohr, 1987), 191; hereafter GW 3. After describing Gadamer as maintaining that "truth is a function of 'dialogue,' not only with the great minds of the past, but also with other human beings with whom we share our lives" (181), Wachterhauser observes: "In Heidegger, by contrast, there is almost no emphasis on dialogue as such. Despite his extensive scholarship, his thought is increasingly a soliloquy on Being and its fate or at best it is a dialogue with other great minds of the past. But there is little or no emphasis on shared inquiry into a common reality or critical questioning of each other" (*Beyond Being*, 182).

Heidegger also makes another kind of dialogue central to his philosophy, that is, dialogue with classic philosophical texts (see note below): as we see from *Phaedrus* 275d–277a and *Protagoras* 347c–348a, however, this is certainly not something that Plato would recognize as genuine dialogue.[95]

Illuminating in this regard is an exchange that took place between Heidegger and Karl Jaspers. In a letter of August 6, 1949, after admitting the difficulties he is having in understanding what Heidegger has written, Jaspers writes: "You debate with yourself [*selber*], even vehemently, even contentiously. But the question of how we are to get out of monologues—and their mere repetition by others—is indeed a vital question of our contemporary philosophizing" (JHBW, 178–79). In a letter of August 12, 1949, Heidegger responds: "What you say about monologues is correct [*trifft*]. However, much would already be won if monologues were allowed to remain what they are: they are not yet strong enough for that" (181). He then quotes Nietzsche: "A hundred profound solitudes together form the city of Venice—that is her magic. An image for the men of the future," and comments: "What is thought here lies outside the alternative between communication and lack of communication" (181). On August 17, Jaspers replies: "What you say about monologues—that we are 'perhaps not yet strong enough' for that—and about solitude—outside the alternative of communication and lack of communication—I believe I understand in the case of works like those of Laotse and Spinoza. . . . For us everything seems to me to depend on the truth that unites us and that has its factual appearance in the deepening and strengthening [*Vertiefung*] of communication" (183). Jaspers then proceeds to warn against the "great temptation" of abandoning "the world, men and friends,—and in exchange for nothing but—if successful—an eternal light, an unrealizable abyss" (184). What I believe Jaspers offers here is a Platonic critique of Heidegger.[96] The position Jaspers defends, and with which he himself would credit Plato (see, for example, his letter of July 10, 1949 [175–76]), is one that sees dialectic/dialogue as essential to philosophy and therefore is precisely the position that Heidegger rejects in favor of an identification of philosophy with a form of *solitary seeing*.

---

95. Heidegger also notoriously shows little interest in the concrete possibilities of *Miteinandersein* and therefore in ethics. Thus even an attempt to defend "a 'dialogical' interpretation of authenticity" (71) must grant that such an interpretation goes well beyond Heidegger's "inadequate treatment of Being-with-Others" and even against his explicit intention. Lawrence Vogel, *The Fragile "We": Ethical Implications of Heidegger's "Being and Time"* (Evanston: Northwestern University Press, 1994), 7, 100–102.

96. For a perceptive and succinct account of the differences between Jaspers and Heidegger, see Rüdiger Safranski, *Martin Heidegger: Between Good and Evil*, trans. Ewald Osers (Cambridge, Mass.: Harvard University Press, 1998), 387–88. For more extensive accounts of their relationship, see Alan M. Olson, ed., *Heidegger and Jaspers* (Philadelphia: Temple University Press, 1994), and Arno Baruzzi, *Philosophieren mit Jaspers und Heidegger* (Würzburg: ERGON Verlag, 1999).

E. CONCLUSION

Central to Heidegger's *Auseinandersetzung* with Plato in the 1920s is thus an opposition to the dialectic and dialogue granted a central place in philosophy by Plato, as well as to what Gadamer would call Plato's "dialectical ethics." This opposition has been seen to presuppose, and be motivated by, a commitment to phenomenology with its central belief in the possibility of some sort of unmediated seeing, an interpretation of this seeing as inherently "theoretical" (even if in the Greek rather than the modern sense), and a determination to see the truth for oneself without the distracting mediation of dialogue. Furthermore, all of these presuppositions have been seen to be at the very least unjustified, if not positively misguided. Yet the story told in this chapter cannot be the whole story. This is because what ultimately motivates Heidegger more than anything else is the question of being. If he opposes dialectic, dialogue, and ethics in Plato in favor of the commitments enumerated above, he does so ultimately for the sake of ontology, that is, in the name of raising the question of being. Specifically, what justifies the opposition is his conviction that the λόγος that Platonic dialectic and dialogue are incapable of "completely twisting out of" blocks access to the question of being by instead assuming a particular conception of being: being as *presence*. To make λόγος the guiding perspective in the interpretation of being is inevitably to reduce being to what-lies-there-before-one as that about which one can make assertions. The present chapter has already argued that Plato's philosophy is not as confined to the perspective of λόγος as Heidegger suggests. But the question that needs to be considered next is whether the perspective of dialectic and dialogue leads Plato to assume an identification of being with constant presence. To answer this question, it is necessary to turn in the next chapter to a part of Heidegger's course on the *Sophist* not yet considered: his reading of the dialogue's "ontological digression."

2

LOGOS AND BEING

The preceding chapter, in focusing on Heidegger's critique of dialectic and his suppression of the dimensions of ethics and dialogue, does not consider Heidegger's treatment of the "ontological digression" of the *Sophist*. The importance of this part of the dialogue for Heidegger is beyond doubt and is confirmed by his citation of a key passage from it at the beginning of *Being and Time*. Yet even here Heidegger's reading of Plato is primarily critical. Specifically, he charges that because in the *Sophist* the method of separation and division is applied not only to objects in the world, such as the angler, but also to being itself and its structures, Plato recognized no distinction between the way of dealing with beings (*Behandlungsart des Seienden*) and the way of dealing with being (*Behandlungsart des Seins*; GA 19, 287).[1] What underlies this charge is Heidegger's conviction, which he seeks to support in the present course, that to address being by way of λόγος and its structure, which is what the method of διαίρεσις does,[2] is inevitably to collapse the distinction between being and beings by identifying being with static presence. Heidegger further suggests that Plato's ideas or forms are a product of this approach

---

1. See 350–52 for the claim that the *Seinscharakter* of the object of dialectic (whether *Seiendes* or *Sein*) is left undetermined. Heidegger also speaks here of a transformation of dialectic from being concerned with objects to being concerned with *Seinsstrukturen* (see also 363). At 249–50, Heidegger insists that both division and collection are *modes of seeing*, that they ultimately rest on the simple seeing or having of the ἄτομον εἶδος. To the extent that this is dialectic, dialectic would indeed be ontic. Yet Heidegger recognizes that dialectic will need to undergo a transformation in the second half of the dialogue if it is to deal with the κοινωνία of the γένη, whereas "up to now we have seen only *one* γένος and, oriented toward that one, a taking apart of the εἴδη" (351; trans. R.S.).

Speaking of the method of diairesis, Wolfgang Wieland writes: "Hier is Platon einer Ordnung im Bereich der Prädikate auf der Spur, die nicht von der Art einer Ordnung ist, wie sie im Bereich identifizierbarer und unterscheidbarer Gegestände besteht." *Platon und die Formen des Wissens*, 2nd ed. (Göttingen: Vandenhoeck and Ruprecht, 1999), 144. But Wieland also suggests that this method brackets the question of the ontological status of the forms. "Denn hier geht es um Strukturgesetzlichkeiten des Ideenbereichs, die man auch dann mit Aussicht auf Erfolg erörtern kann, wenn man die Frage danach, was eine Idee as solche ist, auf sich beruhen läßt" (145).

2. As Heidegger notes, "dieses διαιρεῖν als λέγειν bezeichnet wird" (GA 19, 286).

to being and the confusion it produces (287). It is to a consideration of these charges that the present chapter is devoted.

A. THE TENSIONS IN HEIDEGGER'S CRITIQUE

Before looking at Heidegger's account of why Plato failed to recognize and uphold the ontological difference, we need to note the tension and lack of clarity in Heidegger's characterization of this failure. One of the places in which Heidegger appears to support his thesis is where he charges Plato with the failure to distinguish between three meanings of the word ἕτερον: (1) what is other; (2) being-other-than; (3) otherness (543). (Heidegger here attributes the failure to Plato's treatment of ἕτερον as an empty γένος applicable to every possible thing.) Yet as Heidegger himself points out ten pages later (553), the different meanings of ἕτερον are made clear in the claim at 256c that motion is other (*Anderes*) than the other (*Andersheit*).[3] Likewise, the immediately preceding claim (256a–b) that motion is the same as itself (*Selbiges*) while being other than the same (*Selbigkeit*) appears to make perfectly clear the distinction between the ontical and ontological meanings of ταὐτόν (550–51). Thus, the ambiguity or confusion with regard to the distinction between *an other* and *being-other*, or *the same* and *being-the-same* with which Heidegger charges Plato simply does not exist in the text, as Heidegger himself must recognize.[4]

At one point Heidegger charges Plato with the more general failure to bring out the distinction between categorial content and that to which the categories apply, the distinction that would explain how being can be distinguished from otherness when every being is other (546–47). But Heidegger's precise criticism is once again unclear, since he grants that Plato uses the distinction. "Here, at this point, Plato speaks of a noncoincidence of the categorial content of ὄν and ἕτερον; later, however, he tries to show precisely that every ὄν is ἕτερον" (546). Is not Plato then certainly aware of the distinction? But Heidegger asserts: "This is the remarkable unclarity we still find here in Plato: he indeed operates with this distinction but does not genuinely expose it"

---

3. In only citing and uncritically accepting Heidegger's charge at 543, David Webb misses the at least partial retraction of this charge ten pages later. "Continuity and Difference in Heidegger's *Sophist*," *Southern Journal of Philosophy* 38 (2000): 150–51.

4. Commenting on 255a, Heidegger asserts that Plato in his "earlier position" identified addressing x as y with claiming that y is present in x as an essence. "For example, if I say this chair here is wood, that means, in terms of Plato's earlier position and also in a certain sense still in accord with the current new position: in this something, woodness is present" (540, trans. R.S.). Accordingly, the claim that κίνησις is ἕτερον is taken to mean that movement is otherness. One must wonder from where Heidegger gets his knowledge of Plato's "earlier position." Not only does Plato nowhere commit himself (or rather, his characters) to a characterization of participation as "presence in" (see *Phaedo* 100d5–6), but he certainly nowhere claims that a thing is identical with the form "present in" it.

("er zwar mit diesem Unterschied arbeitet, ihn aber doch nicht eigentlich als solchen herausstellt," 546). But what would it mean here to make the distinction more explicit? To make it the object of explicit thematic statements? As we will see, Heidegger himself suggests that making the distinction into the explicit object of a statement would in fact cover it over by transforming it into an objective relation between two objects. What better way is there, then, to show the distinction than to put it to work in the dialectical inquiry?

It might be thought that Heidegger's charge is that Plato, like all metaphysics after him, assumes the ontological difference without being explicitly aware of it. Yet this is certainly not a charge supported by Heidegger's own interpretation of the *Sophist*. In the Stranger's critique of the telling of stories about being (Μῦθόν τινα ... διηγεῖσθαι, 242c8) by previous philosophers, namely, the pluralists and the monists, Heidegger rightly recognizes the aim of distinguishing the ontological from the ontical in a way that goes beyond even the first step taken by Parmenides in this direction (438–39; also 441, 444–46). On Heidegger's reading, Plato, against both those who maintain a multiplicity of beings and those who say there is one being, argues that there exists a multiplicity within being itself: "Gegenüber dem mehrfachen Seienden handelt es sich jetzt um eine Mehrfachheit im Sein selbst" (444). In this way Plato's critique of Parmenides is not, Heidegger insists, simply a return to the ontic position of the pluralists. Heidegger even goes on to suggest that the question of the meaning of being is the genuinely central concern of the entire dialogue (446–47); and what he writes on these pages (446–49) reads like a first draft of the beginning of *Being and Time*. At this point in the course, Plato's project in the *Sophist* becomes barely distinguishable from Heidegger's own in *Being and Time*.[5] We are thus confronted with these questions: From what in the dialogue is Heidegger attempting to distance himself? What does he see as preventing Plato from fully appropriating his otherwise explicit awareness of the ontological difference?

B. THE GUIDING PERSPECTIVE OF ΛΌΓΟΣ AS UNDERMINING THE ONTIC/ONTOLOGICAL DISTINCTION

At the end of the pages of the course that read like a first draft of *Being and Time*, Heidegger makes explicit what he sees as the limitation to Plato's approach and

---

5. In the second section of *Being and Time* Heidegger even uses the phrase "μῦθόν τινα ... διηγεῖσθαι" to characterize those who fail to distinguish the inquiry into Being from an inquiry into beings; he thus implies that his own critique of the failure to raise the question of Being is a revival of a similar critique by Plato (SZ, 6). It is therefore not surprising that Heidegger in the WS 1931/32 *Vom Wesen der Wahrheit* course should refer to the *Sophist* as "wohl philosophisch der bedeutendste überhaupt" of the dialogues (GA 34, 68).

therefore what he wishes to distance himself from. The limitation, to which Heidegger returns again and again throughout the course, is that for Plato, as for the Greeks in general, the "guiding perspective" ("leitende Hinsicht") is λόγος: "And thus Plato's entire criticism of the traditional and contemporary doctrines of being, as well as his positive discussion of being, move in this λέγειν. Therefore, ontology for Plato is διαλέγεσθαι and dialectic" (449).[6] The problem is that λόγος is characterized by an immediate and neutral *making-present* of that which it is about (see especially *Zusatz* 43, 640). Therefore, to approach being through λόγος is inevitably to equate it with mere presence and thereby to objectify it in a way that covers over the ontological difference. The connection Heidegger sees is made especially clear in the following passage: "*This irruption of λόγος, of the logical in this rigorously Greek sense, in this questioning of ὄν is motivated by the fact that ὄν, the being of beings itself, is primarily interpreted as presence, and λόγος is the primary way in which I make present to myself something,* namely, that about which I speak [*in der ich mir etwas,* nämlich das, worüber ich spreche, *primär vergegenwärtige*]" (GA 19, 225; the translation has been significantly modified). But do we have any choice but to approach the question of being from within λόγος? And does such an approach necessarily condemn one to confinement to λόγος and thereby to a conception of being as *presence*? Is it not possible to approach being from within λόγος in such a way as to expose continually the limitations of λόγος? Heidegger is careful to qualify that while Greek ontology is dominated by λόγος, this is not to say that it is dominated by *logic* (see especially *Zusatz* 41, 638–39). What distinguishes Greek λόγος from logic is that it has not yet been divorced from its function of revealing or disclosing; it has not yet degenerated into the statement or proposition. Heidegger expresses his assessment of Greek ontology with all possible succinctness in the following note entitled τὰ ὄντα as λεγόμενα: "*Limits of Greek ontology: In* λόγος *and its predominance. Compensated: In so far as* ἀποφαίνεσθαι. *Not 'Logic'*" (*Zusatz* 46, 641). But as long as approaching being from the perspective of λόγος is "compensated" by the recognition that λόγος

---

6. See also 438: "Der λόγος ist nämlich die *Zugangsart* der griechischen ontologischen Forschung zum Sein des Seienden"; and 529: "daß der λόγος die Zugangsart zum Seienden ist und daß der λόγος einzig die Möglichkeiten umgrenzt, inerhalb deren etwas über das Seiende und sein Sein zu erfahren ist." Throughout the course Heidegger draws attention to the way in which λόγος guides the discussion. Heidegger, for example, notes that the discussion of non-being at 236e–237a is oriented toward the phenomena of δόξα and λόγος; he adds that these phenomena are not as distinct as might appear since δόξα is for Plato a type of λόγος (407). From 240a1 Heidegger infers that what is at issue in the discussion is the λεγόμενον, which he defines as follows: "Das im λέγειν Sichtbare ist das λεγόμενον, das, *als was* etwas angesprochen wird" (427); on the next page he adds that the discussion of εἴδωλον "gar nicht darum handelt, mit den sinnlichen Augen zu sehen, sondern mit den Augen des νοῦς" (428). For Heidegger, Plato's use of γράμματα as illustrations for the κοινωνία of beings shows that what is spoken, the λεγόμενον, is "gleichsam der Repräsentant des Seienden selbst" (518). See also at 525, where Heidegger claims the fundamental characteristic of dialectic to be that in it τὰ ὄντα are grasped as λεγόμενα. Early in the course (27) Heidegger describes the orientation of the Greeks, and of everyday *Dasein*, as a "Verfallen an das λεγόμενον."

is ἀποφαίνεσθαι, such an approach is presumably not confined to "what is said" but can recognize the extent to which λόγος falls short of the revealing or disclosure which it only serves: as was noted in the preceding chapter, this is precisely the insight that Heidegger must grant Plato when he turns in the present course to a reading of the critique of writing in the *Phaedrus* (GA 19, 340–45). Such an approach from the perspective of λόγος can still recognize the extent to which λόγος in objectifying being distorts how it shows itself. In this case, how is such an approach a limitation or, admitting that it is a limitation from some ideal perspective, how is it a limitation that can be *overcome*?

If what Heidegger is taking issue with here is a λόγος that is absolutized and divorced from that concrete existence[7] in which occurs the disclosure or "intuition" to which λόγος should be subordinated, then this is certainly not the kind of λόγος we encounter in the Platonic dialogues. First, recall Heidegger's own observation, bizarrely presented as a criticism, that Plato *uses* the distinction between categorial content and that to which the categories apply without actually bringing it forth in an explicit manner. But is this not precisely how Plato avoids the objectification of the distinction that would result from making it the object of a λόγος? Plato's dialogues are ἔργον as well as λόγος, and what gets revealed ἔργῳ is precisely what cannot be revealed as the object of a λόγος. Indeed, as was suggested in the preceding chapter, the most significant and striking ἔργον of the dialogue, which Heidegger nevertheless completely ignores, is the *silence* of the soon-to-be-condemned Socrates. This silent presence of Socrates was seen to put question marks around all that is spoken.[8]

1. The Λόγος of Motion

This general point about Plato's dialogues can be illustrated by two examples Heidegger discusses of how a phenomenon is distorted when made an object of λόγος and interpreted according to its structure. The aim of what follows is to show that while in each case the λόγος does indeed cover over the phenomenon, Plato's perspective cannot be identified with the perspective of the λόγος. Plato is perfectly aware of the distorting objectification performed by the λόγος and seeks to counter it by drawing our attention to the performance itself, to the ἔργον.

---

7. This is suggested by the following passages: "in the discussion of ὄν, λόγος as mode of access is now so isolated that, with no regard to the *what*, that which is asked for is simply the saidness and the sayability" (640); "What is the mode of access to beings in ontological questioning? Plato and Aristotle: λόγος—and indeed with a certain explicitness, but only this far, that λόγος remains *the only one*" (638).

8. Monique Dixsaut has argued that the target of the critique of Parmenides, or the parricide, is the naive kind of λόγος that is unconscious of itself and that fails to distinguish itself from what it is about. *Platon et la question de la pensée* (Paris: J. Vrin, 2000), 183. The goal of such a critique is to return λόγος to its movement and danger, its "errance" (184), since for Plato the λόγος is not "cet unique chemin qu'il faut suivre, mais un moyen périlleux de frayer de multiples voies" (188).

The first example concerns motion (κίνησις). According to Heidegger, in claiming that motion and rest (στάσις) rule each other out and do not admit κοινωνία with each other (252d), "Plato" is clearly understanding the relation between them ontically rather than ontologically (512–16). If we consider the being of being-in-motion and the being of being-at-rest, we see that "rest is nothing other than a determinate limit case of motion, an eminent possibility of what is moved with regard to its possible being" (516).[9] This is what Aristotle saw in contrast to Plato, Heidegger asserts. But even if we grant this ontological relation between rest and motion, would it not still be at least misleading to say that motion "shares in" rest or vice versa? As Heidegger himself acknowledges, the topic of investigation here is τὸ λεγόμενον, how motion and rest are expressed in speech. Certainly on the level of predication, motion and rest do exclude each other. We cannot say that "motion is at rest" or that "rest is in motion" without collapsing language into incoherence. This, and apparently this only, is the reason why motion and rest are said at 252d to be incapable of mixing.

But must we then conclude with Heidegger that Plato, precisely because focused on τὸ λεγόμενον, had neither the means nor the possibility of seeing or explaining the being of motion (516) and that he therefore could understand motion and rest only as excluding each other? Later in the course Heidegger must himself acknowledge that the dialogue recognizes the possibility of "a certain ταὐτόν of κίνησις and στάσις" (549). Heidegger explains (551–53) by commenting on the following claim made by the Stranger at 556b6–8: "So if change itself ever somehow had a share [πῃ μεταλάμβανεν] in rest, there would be nothing strange about labeling it resting?" (White trans.) The Stranger has to argue that it would not be strange to say that change is resting because from the perspective of ordinary language, which is the perspective adopted earlier, this would be highly strange. Furthermore, the Stranger must make the qualification that change somehow (πῃ) shares in rest because to say that it shares in rest without qualification would be highly misleading. But what exactly is the connection between motion and rest that the Stranger is hinting at here? Heidegger interprets this passage as referring to the earlier discussion of knowledge and the point made there that the motion of the soul (a motion which the soul *is*, according to the *Symposium*) is directed at what is eternal, unchanging, and thus at rest. In the movement of knowing, what is at rest is somehow present. Heidegger insists, however, that Plato is speaking here only of a relation between what is moved (*Bewegtes*) and what is not moved (*Unbewegtes*) and is therefore far from the Aristotelian demonstration that rest is a type of motion (*Bewegung*) and from the kind of ontological analysis of the

---

9. See also Heidegger's comments on the relation between rest and motion in the SS 1924 course *Grundbegriffe der aristotelischen Philosophie* (GA 18, 314).

being of motion that makes this demonstration possible. "This moved being in its being towards what is unmoved is here simply grasped dialectically-eidetically in the sense of εἴδη" (553). We thus have here an essential part of Heidegger's criticism of the διαίρεσις of forms: such a διαίρεσις treats motion and rest as separate things (the moved and the unmoved) that can then be related to one another in a purely external and opaque manner.[10]

Heidegger's criticism holds to the extent to which motion and rest are made *objects* of dialectic. But as Heidegger's own interpretation suggests, Plato draws our attention to the fact that dialectic is *itself* motion and rest. Heidegger observes that in the critique of the giants' identification of being with body, Plato has recourse, as he often does, to the being we ourselves are (i.e., the soul and its ways of being [246eff.]). If Heidegger adds that Plato here "does not bring to life an explicit questioning [*Fragestellung*] directed at the being of man" (469), then he is blind to the way in which this *Fragestellung* is alive in the dialogue form itself. If κίνησις is in a fundamental way covered up when made an object of λόγος, a λεγόμενον, does not the dialogue continually draw our attention to the κίνησις that we ourselves *are*, the κίνησις that *is* λόγος rather than an *object* of λόγος (see GA 62, 244)? Heidegger himself, in his discussion of the critique of the "friends of the forms," emphasizes the fact that κίνησις enters the dialogue's discussion (see 248e4) through the introduction of the soul and knowledge among beings (487–89; see also 578). He also draws attention to the fact that κίνησις, thus introduced as the motion of the soul, provides the guideline for the whole subsequent ontological discussion. "What is the significance of the fact that κίνησις guides the dialectical analysis?

---

10. In the SS 1924 course Heidegger, after attributing to Aristotle the view that κίνησις is a way of being of what-is-there (*des Daseienden*), describes this view as a critique of Plato, who, Heidegger claims, characterizes what is moved as only participating in κίνησις and treats κίνησις itself as an idea like all the others (GA 18, 288, 385). Yet as Heidegger well knows, κίνησις is introduced into the dialogue through a recognition of the κίνησις intrinsic to knowing and to the very being of the soul. Furthermore, there seems to be a fundamental confusion in Heidegger's critique: Plato's talk of an "idea" of κίνησις is a recognition of the distinction between the being of κίνησις and the κίνησις of a being (Heidegger's own ontological difference!). To make such a distinction is not to make a being's κίνησις into something separate from it. This would be equivalent to saying that because Heidegger makes a distinction between being and beings he must separate being from beings! Heidegger's objection is pursued further at 302–3 when he asserts: "Plato sagt: Der Kasten *hat* Holz; Holz ist eine Idee, also *hat* der Kasten *teil* am Holz" (301); against this Aristotle saw that "Der Kasten ist nicht Kasten und *dazu* Holz, der Stein nicht Stein und *dazu* Bewegung. Der Stein *hat nicht teil* an der Bewegung, die selbst ein Sein ist (Plato), sondern die Bewegung *ist im Daseienden* in dem Sinne, daß es charakterisiert ist als ἐκείνινον: Der Stein ist beweglich wie der Kasten hölzern" (302). But *Bewegung* for Plato is not *a* being! In Heidegger's *Handschrift* we find the following: "Grundbestimmung der κίνησις: kein παρά, kein καθ'αὑτό, kein χωριστόν, nicht ein Seiendes an ihm selbst, eigenständig, sondern *im Bewegenden* und in Bewegung Seienden" (370). This is the source of the confusion: Heidegger accepts the attribution to Plato of the view that the forms are "separate"; thus, if motion is a form it is a separate being. Yet I maintain that Plato would agree with Heidegger when he asserts: "Das Bewegte besteht auch nicht aus Bewegung! Was ist also Bewegung? Kein Seiendes, aber ein *Wie von Sein,* also von da zu bestimmen!" (372).

It means nothing else than that *the dialectical consideration properly focuses on the ψυχή, and specifically on the ψυχή in its basic comportment of λέγειν, and, further, on this λέγειν of the ψυχή qua κίνησις.* ... Κίνησις is nothing arbitrary here but is the apriori title for ψυχή and λόγος, specifically in the sense, even if unclarified, of the μεταξύ" (578–79). Finally, as already noted earlier, Heidegger sees κίνησις and στάσις as brought together in the *Symposium*'s characterization of the soul as desire (ὄρεξις) and in between (μεταξύ) (552). In a note Heidegger even relates this characterization of the soul to his own characterization of the being of *Dasein* as care: "The soul *is* desire (*Care is the being of Dasein!*) *Intentionality—being to*—ψυχή—in the horizon of κίνησις and στάσις, γένεσις—ἀεί, *Heraclitus—Parmenides*" (641).[11] If motion and rest are treated as opposite things when made objects of the inquiry, they are revealed in their essential unity by the very movement of the inquiry, which is also the movement of human existence as such. Heidegger grants that what he claims Aristotle was the first to see—that there is in motion something at rest, namely, the ὑποκείμενον (592)—already showed itself to Plato ("Plato schon vorschwebte"). Is it not, then, precisely in the existential context of the dialogue that this phenomenon shows itself? And is it not this movement of the soul, as ὄρεξις and μεταξύ, that is concretized, without being objectified for λόγος, in the silent Socrates? And is not the Stranger's λόγος revealed to be at odds with itself precisely in seeking to make its own movement into its object? And might it not therefore be with good reason that Plato avoided a more explicit analysis of the being of movement?

As was noted in the preceding chapter, Heidegger himself recognizes what he calls the Socratic disposition of Plato's philosophy, that is, that what is positive is revealed in actually being carried out (enactment!), rather than in being made the explicit theme of a reflection (532; see also 245).[12] The problem is that

---

11. See also GA 19, 368–69. Similarly, in the WS 1931–32 course *Vom Wesen der Wahrheit*, Heidegger, commenting on the use of the word ἐπορέγεται at *Theaetetus* 186a4–5 to characterize the relation between the soul and Being (οὐσία), writes: "Die Seele *ist* dieses Strebnis nach dem Sein" (GA 34, 203). Heidegger calls this "Seinserstrebnis" (203), which he also identifies with ἔρως (216; see also Heidegger's characterization of ἔρως as "der Drang *zum Sein Selbst*" in GA 19 [315] in the context of interpreting the *Phaedrus*). Though Heidegger does not speak here of κίνησις and στάσις, the unity of the two is evident in his claim that what is striven for is in some sense *had* in the striving itself: "das Bestrebte ist im Streben *da*, und gerade im *Nicht*-streben-danach ist es *weg*" (211) and "Das Wonach des Strebens, das Bestrebte als solches, wird *im* Streben gehabt, *als* Bestrebtes *ist* es ein Gehabtes" (211). See also Heidegger's discussion in the SS 1931 course (GA 33, 148–54) of the characterization of the soul as κίνησις and ὄρεξις in Aristotle; Heidegger finds in Aristotle, though in a modified form, the characterization of the soul's movement as ἔρως, which he here calls "eine spezifisch Platonische Weise, die lebendige Art der Bewegung zu sehen" (154).

12. Cf. Gadamer's observation that "it is precisely this that is Socratic in this dialectic: that it carries out, itself, what it sees human existence as." *Plato's Dialectical Ethics: Phenomenological Interpretations Relating to the "Philebus,"* trans. Robert M. Wallace (New Haven: Yale University Press, 1991), 4; *Platos dialektische Ethik* (Hamburg: Felix Meiner, 2000), 6–7.

Heidegger's own reading of the dialogue for the most part does not remain true to this insight. What Heidegger's observation implies is that Plato does *not* reveal what is positive by making it the object of a λόγος. There is in the dialogues a careful balance between making something the object of a λόγος and at the same time revealing how it resists such objectification. Heidegger's response to this delicate balance appears to be to focus on only one side of the balance at any given point and draw attention to its inadequacy: thus Plato is sometimes charged with revealing something in practice without making it the object of an explicit analysis and at other times is charged with collapsing the ontological into the ontic by making it an object of explicit analysis.[13]

2. The Λόγος of Λόγος

The second example to be considered is Heidegger's claim that Plato treats the relation between being and λόγος as like the relation between one being and another being, that is, ontically and not phenomenologically (508). Plato is said to treat the κοινωνία between λόγος and ὄν as not differing from the κοινωνία between one γένος and another. While there appears no evidence for this claim in the passage Heidegger is discussing at this point, 251aff., the

---

13. Following Heidegger, Webb asserts that while "it will be sufficient neither for movement to be treated ontically as a thing, nor for it to remain concealed as an undeveloped theme," this is nevertheless all that dialectic is capable of doing (2000, 154). But this claim is false: dialectic exposes the inadequacy of treating movement as its object by revealing *itself* to be movement. When Webb asserts that "at no point does it [dialectic] reveal movement itself as the *condition* of the belonging together of the different *archai*" (154), this too is false: it is the introduction of movement, in particular the movement of knowing, into the discussion that leads to the characterization of Being as δύναμις, which, in Heidegger's own view, is the condition of the combining of the different γένη. There is no question that the discussion does treat movement as one γένος or εἶδος, both separate from and combining with others (see Webb, "Continuity and Difference," 161), but this is due to what Webb himself calls "the discrepancy between what is to be disclosed and the form of disclosure" (154), a discrepancy to which the dialogue continually draws our attention and which in Plato's view, unlike that of Webb or Heidegger, can never be reduced or overcome. Precisely in juxtaposing the discussion *of* movement with the movement of the discussion itself, the dialogue does, contra Webb, "let movement show (speak) itself from itself" (154). The crucial point is made by Webb himself in a note: "The movement of thinking conceived in this way is in fact reflected more accurately in the movement into which the Platonic dialogue draws its participants, and above all perhaps, its readers. The extent to which the dramatic structure, and textual self-relation problematizes many of the assertions made in the course of the dialogues themselves is well documented" (169n32). But this is precisely what Heidegger misses, and Webb himself oddly makes no use of this insight in the main body of his article. Gadamer's reading of Plato provides an instructive contrast to that of Heidegger and Webb. The influence of Heidegger is very palpable in Gadamer's first book, *Plato's Dialectical Ethics,* and there is a clear echo of Heidegger's critique of Plato in the *Sophist* course when Gadamer charges that in introducing the categories of the limited, the unlimited, and the mixed in the *Philebus,* Plato "shows no conceptual awareness of the purely ontological nature of these characterizations" (*Plato's Dialectical Ethics,* 132; *Platos dialektische Ethik,* 96). Yet Gadamer not only adds the qualification that "Nevertheless, Plato's true opinion here is an ontological one" (133; 96), but also, and more importantly, he acknowledges in his introduction to the book that any conceptualization of what is shown in the dialogues (of the kind undertaken by Aristotle) is necessarily a "flattening" ("Verflachung") that fails to capture something essential (7–8; 9–10).

claim does receive strong confirmation from 260aff. (which clearly picks up from the earlier passage). There λόγος is characterized as a γένος (260a5) and the question asked is whether or not this γένος, like the other γένη (or εἴδη, 260d7), "mixes" (μετέχειν, 260d7–8; κοινωνεῖν, 260e2) with non-being, or, in other words, whether or not non-being "mixes" (μείγνυται, 260b11) with it. In his exposition of this part of the text, Heidegger's criticism takes the form of arguing that while the full phenomenon of λόγος includes three other structures of κοινωνία besides that between name (ὄνομα) and verb (ῥῆμα), "Plato grasps them all together and without differentiation as σύνθεσις and does not explicitly fix them as such" (597; my trans.), though they "are there latently" ("latent vorliegen"). The second κοινωνία is that between λόγος and ὄν. While this second κοινωνία is recognized in Plato's claim that every λόγος is λόγος τινός, a claim that Heidegger describes as a fundamental insight into what Husserl called "intentionality" (598), Heidegger asserts that this insight "is not thoroughly given its true phenomenological value in Plato" ("phänomenologisch nicht durchgängig ausgewertet ist bei Plato," 597), presumably because it is not sharply distinguished from the other types of κοινωνία.[14] The third type of κοινωνία identified by Heidegger is the structural form λόγος has of addressing something *as* something (601). Finally, Heidegger finds a fourth type in another as-structure: the λόγος showing something as the *same* as itself or as other than itself (605): this is the type of κοινωνία that makes truth or falsehood possible. In addition to the general charge that Plato does not differentiate between these four different types of κοινωνία (see the summary of the four structures at 606), Heidegger's main criticism is again that the κοινωνία between λόγος and beings (intentionality) is not distinguished from the κοινωνία between beings themselves, that is, between the different εἴδη or γένη. Thus, Heidegger claims that Plato demonstrates the possibility of falsehood "rein dialektisch," that is by showing that the κοινωνία of the five kinds itself stands in a κοινωνία with λόγος as an ὄν (603).

This criticism is made several times throughout the course. According to what Heidegger claims at 432, Plato sees false speech as an "entwining" (συμπλοκή) of non-being and a being, that is, λόγος, and therefore solves the problem of false speech only "by means of a formal-ontological consideration" (432–33). In commenting on the claim made at 244d3, in criticism of Parmenides, that a word is distinct from what it means, Heidegger asserts that Plato "does not reflect further on the specific structure of the connection of the word with what it means.... He understands this fact purely ontically here: something is together with something" (453). At 461 Heidedgger claims that in

14. Also in the characterization of λέγειν as λέγειν τι, a characterization that runs through the entire discussion, Heidegger sees the phenomenon of "intentionality" (though he remarks that this is a misleading term) (424–25). That the recognition of this intentionality is not a triviality, Heidegger argues, is shown by the trouble it cost Plato to remain true to it (424).

order to comprehend the critique of Parmenides and the last parts of the dialogue, one must recognize that both ὄνομα and λόγος are being treated here as beings, that is, ontically. Specifically, ὄνομα is identified with sound (φθογγή) and λέγειν with utterance (φθέγγεσθαι), an identification that for Heidegger represents a confusion between being-said (*Gesagtsein;* λέγειν qua *Aufdecken*) and being-spoken (*Ausgesprochensein*). On page 476 Heidegger points out that the word κοινωνεῖν first occurs (248a11) as a description of the relation between perception (αἴσθησις) and becoming (γένεσις) and between reasoning (λογισμός) and being (οὐσία), but comments that the phenomenological sense of this κοινωνεῖν (intentionality) "immediately turns over into a completely naive ontical one" (478), that of one thing being with another thing.

One must certainly agree with Heidegger that the text treats the relation between λόγος and τὸ ὄν ontically, as a relation between two beings, and thereby fails to make explicit what is unique and distinctive about this relation as a way of being-in-the-world (in other words, the ontological sense of the relation). But the crucial question is this: Is not the treating of λόγος as a being, and of the relation between λόγος and τὸ ὄν as a relation between two beings, an unavoidable consequence of making λόγος the *object of* a λόγος? And is not Plato fully aware of this? Heidegger himself, as we have seen, grants Plato an awareness of the phenomenon of intentionality. If this phenomenon gets distorted in the text, this seems to be not a result of Plato's lack of awareness, but rather an inevitable result of making the phenomenon the object of a λόγος. To make the relation between λόγος and being into the object of a λόγος is unavoidably to make it an objective relation between two objects. The crucial question is whether there is any way of escaping this circularity of a λόγος of λόγος. Short of escaping λόγος altogether, the possibility that presents itself is that of emphasizing the *performance* of λέγειν as that which resists objectification: λόγος as ἔργον and movement. But this is precisely what the dialogue form is especially suited to doing. And we have again in Socrates someone who embodies λόγος, who is a lover of λόγος, but who here resists joining in the λόγος of λόγος. It is significant in this regard that at the very start of the dialogue Socrates defers to the Stranger as to a god by describing himself as "being bad with λόγοι" ("φαύλους ἡμᾶς ὄντας ἐν τοῖς λόγοις," 216b5), a self-description supported by the discussion Socrates led on the previous day (in the *Theaetetus*), a discussion caught in the circle of seeking a knowledge of knowledge and therefore ending in ἀπορία. In the present dialogue it is the Stranger who, with the divine pretensions of his λόγος, is fully caught in the circle of a λόγος of λόγος. And again we must be careful not simply to identify the Stranger with Plato.

Markus Brach, in a book in large part devoted to Heidegger's *Sophist* lectures, makes clear and explicit the implications of Heidegger's critique in such a way as to expose inadvertently its limitations. In the *Sophist,* Brach writes, "The λόγος becomes a topic in λόγος and thereby hides within itself its event-character [*Ereignischarakter*] as existentiell temporalization of Dasein in speaking about something."[15] But it is precisely on account of this inevitable self-obstructing character of a λόγος of λόγος that Plato chooses to reveal the *Ereignischarakter* dramatically by writing a dialogue. It is therefore erroneous to claim, as Brach does, following Heidegger, that on account of the prior objectification of that about which the λόγος speaks, "the temporal sense of philosophizing itself thereby does not come into view for [Plato] himself,"[16] or that "*Dasein* withdraws from its own fundamental happening [*Grundgeschehen*] while speaking about it. It forgets that it *is* this fundamental happening."[17] The point of the dialogue form is precisely to prevent us from forgetting this *Grundgeschehen* by keeping it constantly in view. In a note for the course Heidegger himself outlines the criticism that Brach develops: "Greek ontology—not only world—*objectivity*—and what is encountered, the immediate, but also the how of reaching the immediate,—and both *in indifference!*" (640). Charging Plato with this indifference between the *what* and the *how,* for example, between the being which λόγος is about and the being of λόγος itself, is the basis for charging Plato with indifference between the ontic and the ontological. Ironically, however, Heidegger can make this charge only by focusing exclusively on what is said in the dialogue while mostly ignoring the *performance* of the dialogue, or the *how.* What is said about saying may distort the being or *how* of saying, but the dialogue itself exposes this limitation by displaying the being of saying *in deed.*

C. HEIDEGGER ON PLATO'S FORMS

The suggestion I am making is that the Platonic dialogue reveals being (the being of motion, the being of λόγος) in performance in such a way as to resist, and expose the limitations of, the objectifications these phenomena inevitably undergo when made the content of a λόγος. But the major hurdle to such a suggestion still needs to be addressed. Does not Plato's characterization of being as εἶδος imply an identification of being with being objectively present?

---

15. "Der λόγος wird Thema im λόγος und verbirgt dadurch in sich selbst seinen Ereignischarakter als existenzieller Zeitigung des Daseins im Sprechen über Etwas." *Heidegger—Platon: Vom Neukantilismus zur existentiellen Interpretation des "Sophistes"* (Würzburg: Königshausen and Neumann, 1996), 382.

16. "Der Zeitigungssinn des Philosophierens selbst kommt ihm [Plato] selbst dabei nicht in den Blick" (390).

17. "Das Dasein entzieht sich seinem Grundgeschehen, indem es über es spricht. Es vergißt, daß es dieses Grundgeschehen ist" (397).

And does not this characterization thus betray a confinement to being as addressed and made present in λέγειν? As the above analysis of Heidegger's critique of the dialogue's treatment of the relation between λόγος and being shows, he sees the particular kind of λόγος carried out in the dialogue, that is, the method of dividing and collecting εἴδη, as collapsing the ontological into the ontic. To treat motion, being, otherness, sameness, and rest as εἴδη is to treat them as things objectively present that are to be related to, and divided from, one another in relations that are themselves objectively present. But while this is indeed what becomes of the εἴδη when made objects of λόγος, is this how Plato understands them?

1. The Question of "Separation"

The view that the Platonic εἴδη are objects or things that possess the characteristics they are supposed to be (that, for example, the form of beauty is a superlatively beautiful thing) is an old one and has usually gone hand in hand with the idea that Plato separated the εἴδη, that is, turned them into things existing in their own world distinct from the world of sensible objects. Heidegger himself (100–103) appears to believe with Aristotle that Plato separated the forms. Not only does he speak of Plato's "doctrine of the χωρισμός of the ideas," but even asserts that "Plato indeed explicitly assigns to the ideas a τόπος, namely the οὐρανός" (101). But this is a baffling assertion. Neither in the *Sophist* nor anywhere else does Plato assign the ideas to the place of the heavens. In the myth of the *Phaedrus*, on the contrary, the ideas are described as existing in a ὑπερουράνιος τόπος: a paradoxical (or "paratopical"!) place that, being *beyond* the heavens, is really *no place*,[18] but which *myth* must envision as a place (247c3).

Furthermore, in no dialogue do we find a "doctrine of the χωρισμός of the ideas": the *Parmenides* is the only dialogue in which the ideas are described as existing χωρίς, but there this view is criticized as resulting in the absurdity of the ideas existing in a world of their own cut off from this world of sensible objects. In the *Sophist*, the "friends of the forms" are perhaps credited with separating being from becoming when their position is described as follows: "In your speech you distinguish as separate becoming and being? [Γένεσιν, τὴν δὲ οὐσίαν χωρίς που διελόμενοι λέγετε]" (248a7–8). However, this may mean only that they *sharply distinguish* between being and becoming without implying the *separate existence* of the forms. Even if "the friends of the forms" are described as separating the forms, however, this position is of course immediately subjected to critique. The "friends of the forms" are not Plato. Heidegger

---

18. Even Aristotle recognizes that the ideas are not literally in any place: see *Physics* 203a6–10 and 209b33–210a2.

himself sees the "friends of the forms" as referring to Megarians, though he also claims, without any evidence, that this is a position to which Plato earlier subscribed (439–40, 479).[19] Whatever the historical identity of the "friends of the forms," Wolfgang Wieland is certainly right to see in the critique of their position a warning "against an overly naive thematization and objectification of the ideas" (1999, 112; see 108–12). Both here and in the *Parmenides* Plato is explicitly distancing himself from a characterization of the forms as another set of things (in addition to the things of the sensible world) existing in a separate world of their own. When Heidegger therefore suggests that Plato himself "promulgates" ("ausgibt") a type of χωρίζειν as "the determination of the method of grasping the ideas," he is, as so often, getting his knowledge of what Plato claims not from the dialogues, but from Aristotle, and this despite his own warning later in the course against attributing to Plato a simplistic distinction between the sensible and the supersensible (580).[20]

2. Εἶδος as What Is Seen?

The separation of the εἴδη is not, however, what Heidegger's account most insists on. What he insists on instead is the identification of εἶδος with what is seen by and present to a pure perceiving: it is this identification that allows Heidegger to see in the characterization of being as εἶδος a collapse of the ontological into the ontic. Heidegger specifically criticizes Plato for failing to distinguish between γένος and εἶδος, where such a distinction would preserve

19. I cannot here argue that a theory of separate forms is not found even in "earlier" dialogues, but this argument, along with an interpretation of the *Parmenides*, can be found in my "Plato's Dialectic of Forms," in *Plato's Forms: Varieties of Interpretation*, ed. William Welton (Lanham, Md.: Lexington Books, 2003), 31–83. Without the doctrine of the χωρισμός, to which he continually appeals without, of course, citing a single Platonic text for support, Walter Patt could not reach the conclusion he does concerning the difference between Heidegger and Plato: "Bei Platon herrscht ein Gegensatz zwischen echtem Seiendem und Unverborgenem einerseits und scheinhaftem Seiendem und Schattenhaftem andererseits. Heidegger sieht dagegen Stufen innerhalb der *einen* umfassenden Unverborgenheit. Damit ist auch klar, daß die Idee im Denken Platons nicht nur das Sein, sondern zudem das eigentliche Seiende darstellt, das vom minderen Seienden durch eine *ontische Differenz* geschieden ist." *Formen des Anti-Platonismus bei Kant, Nietzsche und Heidegger* (Frankfurt am Main: Vittorio Klostermann, 1997), 286. What is "clear" to me is that Plato too sees steps within one all-encompassing disclosedness (since only this view can make sense of the analogies of the *Republic*) and that the dialogues, far from defending a characterization of the ideas as things separated by a gulf from sensible objects, subject this characterization to critique (in the *Sophist* and *Parmenides* most explicitly).

20. As will be seen in chapter 3, in the WS 1931–32 course *Vom Wesen der Wahrheit*, Heidegger is much more circumspect in his treatment of Plato's forms, warning against an objectification of them and insisting that their way of being is left an open question. Yet already in the 1937–38 course *Grundfragen der Philosophie*, Heidegger returns to treating the ideas as present-at-hand objects existing outside of any human perception (GA 45, 85). Patt draws attention to this contradiction (1997, 217–18). What Heidegger appears to miss in the later course and elsewhere is what Wieland so well articulates: "Der höhere Seinsrang der Idee zwingt nicht dazu, die Idee als ein Ding höherer Art anzusetzen. Gerade umgekehrt läßt sich nämlich von Dingen nur dann sinnvoll reden, wenn man von ihnen etwas aussagt und sie damit auf Ideen bezieht" (1999, 143).

to some extent the differentiation between the ontological and the ontical (523–24, 529, 547). According to Heidegger, γένος means "stem, descent, lineage, that from which something originates; i.e., it refers to a being in its being, thus that which a being, as this being, always already was" (524; see also 243, 258); in other words, γένος is the being of a being. On the other hand, "the εἶδος is relative to pure perceiving, νοεῖν; it is what is sighted in pure perception.... γένος is a structural concept pertaining to being itself; εἶδος is a concept referring to the givenness of the being of beings.... εἶδος basically says nothing about the being of beings" (524; translation modified). Heidegger immediately adds, however, that εἶδος does suggest that a being is to be grasped primarily in its *presence*: in a marginal notation he identifies γένος with *Gewesenheit* and εἶδος with *Anwesenheit* (524n3). According to Heidegger, it is because this concept of εἶδος guides his ontological investigation that Plato is unable to overcome certain difficulties in this investigation.

But have we not seen Heidegger make the apparently different claim that it is λόγος that guides Plato's questioning and that creates the problems? These are for Heidegger not different claims, since in his view the approach to being as λεγόμενον leads to the characterization of being as εἶδος. Early in the course, in the discussion of Aristotle that is meant to prepare us for reading the *Sophist*, Heidegger even identifies λόγος and εἶδος: "Λόγος here means λέγειν, pre-presentification [*Vergegenwärtigen*] in speech. The λόγος qua λεγόμενον, however, is the εἶδος. We have here an echo of the Platonic way of speaking and seeing; for an εἶδος is nothing else than an idea" (45). Much later, in reading the *Sophist* itself, Heidegger observes: "Insofar as it is always a matter of an encounter in λέγειν, even as regards the concretion of the factually existing thing here and now, the concrete presence is always an εἶδος" (525). To encounter something by making it present in speech is necessarily to reduce it to its "outward look" or εἶδος. Heidegger can thus at one point characterize λέγειν as "the making present of the visibility of beings themselves and thereby of beings in what they are" (579; my trans.).[21]

The criticism with regard to λόγος has already been addressed, but two points need to be made here with regard to εἶδος: (1) If Plato at least sometimes uses the concept of γένος, is this not sufficient to show that he is not confined to understanding the being of beings only in terms of their presence for a seeing? Perhaps to avoid this conclusion, Heidegger suggests that Plato got the concept of γένος from Aristotle (522). However, even if this unfounded surmise is true, Plato would still have had the concept. (2) That Plato uses the terms εἶδος and γένος "promiscuously" (523) is the sign of philosophical confusion only if one assumes, as Heidegger does, that the two terms can have

---

21. In the SS 1931 course, Heidegger again identifies λόγος and εἶδος (GA 33, 142).

only the meanings suggested by their etymologies. But this seems a ridiculous assumption.[22] From the facts that Plato used the word εἶδος to refer to the being of beings and that this word comes from a verb meaning "to see," can we conclude that he identified the being of beings with "what is seen in a pure perception"?[23] Theodor Peperzak[24] has persuasively argued against such a conclusion, concluding instead that "The synonymy of many expressions with εἶδος and 'ἰδέα' shows that the etymological reference to seeing is not essential to an understanding of these terms" (91–92; cf. Wieland 1999, 132–34). Among the synonyms for εἶδος and ἰδέα that Peperzak has in mind here are αὐτὸ τό . . . , αὐτό, τὸ καθ'αὐτό, ὃ ἔστι, ὡς ἔστι, τὸ ἀληθῶς ὄν, τὸ ὄντως ὄν, and even simply τὸ ὄν. These other terms, which are used at least as frequently as εἶδος and ἰδέα to refer to the so-called forms, of course make no reference to "seeing" or "visibility." Heidegger is reading an entire ontology into the etymology of terms Plato uses rather casually and interchangeably with other etymologically unrelated terms. Peperzak also provides a positive characterization of the forms that differs from Heidegger's and shows what Heidegger's misses: "The idea is neither a thing above or outside the phenomena nor something simply given to our spontaneity. It is not a look, but rather an astonishing secret that urges us to discover and admire its genuine but hidden presence" (91). The only change that should be made to this characterization is to substitute the word "power" for the word "presence": for reasons to be explained below, the ἰδέα should not be seen as static presence, not even hidden presence, but instead as a *power* (δύναμις).[25] That Peperzak recognizes

---

22. Jonathan Barnes has criticized Heidegger on this point, insisting that by the fifth century B.C. the words εἶδος and ἰδέα had lost any semantic connection to the verb ἰδεῖν "et dans les emplois standards de ces deux mots—mots assez fréquents dans le grec ordinaire—on ne sent plus aucune trace de la visibilité, de l'*Aussehen*." "Heidegger spéléologue," *Revue de Métaphysique et de Morale* 95 (1990): 183. After claiming that the ideas are in no sense "visible," Barnes concludes: "Parler de l'évidence' ou de l'*Aussehen* à propos des Idées est tout à fait trompeur" (183). See also Dixsaut's observations on the relative infrequency of a technical usage of the terms εἶδος and ἰδέα in the dialogues (*Platon et la question de la pensée*, 75–78).

23. Heidegger translates ἰδέα τῆς θατέρου at 255e4 as "Sichtbarkeit von Anderssein" (548). And in the claim that non-being must be numbered as an εἶδος (258c3), Heidegger sees the claim that non-being has its own "Sichtbarkeit" (566). An appeal to etymology appears to be the only justification for either the translation or the interpretation. And one must wonder what it can mean to speak of the "visibility" of otherness when otherness is clearly treated in the text as a relation that always points beyond itself. As for the "seeing" metaphor used often in the dialogues to characterize knowledge of the forms, there is no reason to take such a metaphor literally. As Wieland rightly observes, the absence in the dialogues of any appeal to a literal intuition of the forms makes it advisable "in der Metaphorik der Ideenschau nur ein Musterbild für Formen nichtdiskursiver Erkenntnis überhaupt zu sehen" (*Platon und die Formen des Wissens*, 149).

24. "Did Heidegger Understand Plato's Idea of Truth?" in *Platonic Transformations: With and after Hegel, Heidegger, and Levinas* (Lanham, Md.: Rowman and Littlefield, 1997), 89–94.

25. Accepting Heidegger's characterization of the ἰδέα as "look," Patt states the following difference between Heidegger and Plato: "Für Platon ist das Sein als Idee das Unverborgenste, das schlechthin Scheinende im Sinne des Lichtverbreitenden, Leuchtenden. Dagegen ist für Heidegger Seyn Scheinen

this to some extent is suggested by the emphasis he gives to the paradigmatic, commanding, or normative character of the forms or ideas: the ἰδέα of something is not only what it *is*, but also what it *ought to be*. As Peperzak states the point, the ἰδέα is "the union of being (*Sein*) and ought (*Sollen*) before their difference arises" (93). And as Peperzak himself notes, this normative character of the forms is completely lost in Heidegger's reduction of the forms to "looks" (94).[26]

Heidegger himself appears to see beyond such a reduction when he characterizes the μέγιστα γένη as *presuppositions* of discourse, rather than as objects of discourse (538–39).[27] Dialectic, Heidegger insists, does not deduce the γένη, but instead discloses them as already there in what we say: "what is still and already there is uncovered, is looked *to* [*es wird aufgedeckt, nachgesehen, was noch und schon da ist*]" (539; my trans.). But the γένη are in this case disclosed not as objects, but instead as what is presupposed in every addressing of objects. The form or idea of a thing is what must be already disclosed if I am to address that thing as what it is; as such a presupposition, the form or idea is the *being* of the thing addressed and not *another thing*. In other words, the ἰδέα is what makes possible a thing's having a particular "look" and form of address and cannot therefore itself be a "look." To discover the ideas as presuppositions is incompatible with objectifying them.[28] Heidegger himself appears to recognize this when, earlier in the course, he makes the striking claim that if phenomenological research has any kinship with Plato, this lies in Plato's understanding of ὑπόθεσις (451–52), which, Heidegger insists, is not an ontic hypothesis. The Greek ὑπόθεσις is not something we postulate after the fact to explain what we say and do, but rather what already and always underlies what we say and do, whether explicitly or not. It is this kind of ὑπόθεσις that phenomenology seeks to uncover, and it is as this kind of ὑπόθεσις that the ideas or forms must be understood.

If we return to the claim at 539 that a γένος is not deduced, but rather uncovered as "was noch und schon da ist," i.e., as presupposed, as ὑπόθεσις, we find an extremely important marginal gloss by Heidegger on the phrase "was noch und schon da ist": "self-asserting, being in power: δύναμις [*sich geltend macht, an der Macht ist*: δύναμις]." Here we have a recognition of how

---

als Sich-verbergen im Sich-zeigen" (1997, 286). In my view, and I believe Peperzak's, Plato's position is much closer to that attributed here to Heidegger.

26. For further discussion of this normative character of the forms, see also my *Dialectic and Dialogue: Plato's Practice of Philosophical Inquiry* (Evanston: Northwestern University Press, 1998), 212–16; and Rafael Ferber, *Platos Idee des Guten*, 2nd ed. (Sankt Augustin: Academia Verlag Richarz, 1989), 30.

27. Cf. Gadamer on the γένη (sameness and difference, specifically) as the condition of the possibility of dialectic (*Plato's Dialectical Ethics*, 95; *Platos dialektische Ethik*, 69).

28. This is a point on which Wieland rightly insists: see, e.g., *Platon und die Formen des Wissens*, 100.

the forms are discovered and how they should be characterized: not as *present*, as Heidegger otherwise insists, nor as *looks*, but as *sich geltend machend*, as asserting their rights and demanding recognition, as being in power: as δύναμις.

D. BEING AS ΔΥΝΑΜΙΣ

1. Being as Presence

This last point gets at the real heart of the matter. In arguing that Plato approaches being entirely from the perspective of λόγος and that accordingly he identifies being with εἶδος in the sense of what is visible to a pure perceiving, Heidegger's ultimate aim is to show that being for Plato, and for the Greeks generally, is *presence* or, more precisely, *being-made-present-for-use*, that is, *produced* (*Her-gestelltsein*, 269–70).[29] Heidegger makes this aim fully explicit in introducing his discussion of the battle of the gods and giants (γιγαντομαχία περὶ τῆς οὐσίας). He first observes: "The question of the meaning of οὐσία itself is not alive for the Greeks as an ontological theme; instead, they always ask only: which beings genuinely satisfy the meaning of being and which ontological characters result thereby? The meaning of being itself remains unquestioned. This does not imply, however, that the Greeks had no concept of being. For without one the question of what satisfies the meaning of being would be groundless and without direction.... The meaning of being implicitly guiding this ontology is being = presence" (466).[30] Heidegger then proceeds to make clear his intention to "demonstrate, by the success of an actual interpretation of Plato's ensuing discussions, that this sense of being in fact guided the ontological questioning of the Greek—otherwise there is no way to demonstrate the function of this meaning of being in Greek philosophy" (467) Heidegger's interpretation of Plato, however, is in this respect *not* a success.[31] One can indeed grant that what Heidegger says here about the

---

29. While its presuppositions are being challenged here, the thesis that the Greeks interpreted being as being-produced will be taken up more explicitly in the last chapter.

30. See also GA 19, 34, and especially 398: "Sein für die Griechen eben heißt: Anwesend-sein, Gegenwärtig-sein." Heidegger does grant, however, that the positions of the friends of the forms and the giants are not, like the positions criticized earlier, purely ontic, but instead expressly ontological (465).

31. That this same interpretation of Plato's conception of Being pervades Gadamer's *Plato's dialectical Ethics* (see, e.g., 9, 35, 133; *Platos dialektische Ethik*, 10, 27, 96) is a clear sign of Heidegger's influence on the book. Gadamer does try to provide some defense of this interpretation through his critique of Plato's account of the affects in the *Philebus* (161, 169, 172, 190–95; *Platos dialektische Ethik*, 116, 122, 124, 137–40), but for a response see my "Plato's Dialectical Ethics: Or Taking Gadamer at His Word," in *Hermeneutic Philosophy and Plato: Gadamer's Response to the "Philebus,"* ed. Christopher J. Gill and François Renaud (Sankt Augustin: Academia Verlag, forthcoming).

identification of being with presence is true of the naive stories (μῦθοι) about being attributed to the pluralists and monists earlier in the dialogue, as well as probably being true of the positions identified with the giants and the "friends of the forms." But these positions are criticized in the present dialogue precisely for the naivete of their "natural attitude," that is, for their exclusive focus on what beings there are and their failure to reflect on what it means to address any being as being in the first place. Is this not evidence against Heidegger's thesis as a thesis about all Greek philosophy? Specifically, there are two main ways in which Heidegger's interpretation can be shown to fail: (1) Heidegger can maintain his thesis only by subordinating the characterization of being as δύναμις, which emerges from Plato's critique of naive ontology, to the characterization of being as presence; such a subordination, however, is arbitrary and forced; (2) to maintain his thesis that Plato identified being with presence Heidegger must also insist that the discussion of being in the *Sophist* is *not* aporetic, despite the clear evidence in the text to the contrary.[32]

Let us first review how the characterization of being as δύναμις emerges from the battle of the gods and giants. Against the position of the giants, who acknowledge as existing only what can be touched with the hands or seen with the eyes, it is objected that while the soul and justice cannot be seen (ὁρατόν) or touched (ἁπτόν), they must nevertheless exist, since anything capable of suffering (παθεῖν) something (as the soul can become just) or doing (ποιεῖν) something (as justice can affect the soul) must exist. From this objection the following delimitation (ὅρος) of being is inferred: beings are nothing other than the capability to do or to suffer (δύναμις, 247e4; Heidegger translates "Möglichkeit"). While the "friends of the forms" initially must reject this characterization of being on account of their view that being excludes all becoming and motion (248c4–9), they too must ultimately accept it if they are to admit knowledge, life, and soul among beings (248d–249a). Note how in both cases the characterization of being as δύναμις is required to account for the human soul and its ways of being. As has already been noted, not the beings that are the objects of human comportment, but the being of human comportment itself provides the guideline for the whole ontological discussion.

Turning to Heidegger's reading, we see that he makes much of the characterization of being as δύναμις, insisting, against other interpreters, on the central role this characterization plays in the dialogue (see, e.g., 474–75). But is not this characterization of being in tension with the identification of being with presence that Heidegger insists on finding in the Greeks? Capability, even if the capability of being present with something else, is not at all the

---

32. Stanley Rosen has argued that "there is no single, uniform, general doctrine of being in Plato, and certainly no doctrine of being as production or manufacture" ("Remarks on Heidegger's Plato," in HPD, 187), though with no explicit reference to the *Sophist* in this essay.

same as presence. Nevertheless, Heidegger finds a simple way of preserving his thesis concerning Greek ontology: as soon as he encounters in the text the delimitation of being as the δύναμις *of presence*, he quickly inverts it to *the presence of* δύναμις. If one believes that such an inversion requires some justification, one will be disappointed, since none is offered. Instead, Heidegger makes the inversion in language that suggests that no inversion has taken place, that the "presence of δύναμις" is just another way of saying "the δύναμις of presence." The inversion takes place in the following paraphrase Heidegger provides of the characterization of being at 247e: "Δύναμις, as *the possibility of co-presence [Mit-Anwesenheit] with something*, in short, δύναμις κοινωνίας, or in a fuller determination [!], *παρουσία δυνάμεως κοινωνίας, the being-present-at-hand [Vorhandensein] of the possibility of being with one another*" (486; trans. modified). In this shift from being as the δύναμις of παρουσία to being as the παρουσία of δύναμις, a shift not only undefended but even hidden in the word "or," it is hard to see anything but an arbitrary imposition on the text of Heidegger's thesis concerning Greek ontology.[33] What we have in the text is a conception of being not as presence, but rather as the δύναμις that makes presence possible. Does not this conception point beyond presence?[34] If being is the δύναμις of presence, it cannot itself be something present. If beings are nothing but the power or capability of being present, then for a being "to be" cannot mean "to be present." But it is perhaps granting Heidegger too much even to agree that what the text calls a δύναμις *of doing and suffering* is a δύναμις *of co-presence*. The text indeed says that for something like justice, "to

---

33. Günter Figal also draws attention to the questionableness of this move in "Refraining from Dialectic: Heidegger's Interpretation of Plato in the Sophist Lectures (1924/25)," in *Interrogating the Tradition: Hermeneutics and the History of Philosophy*, ed. Charles E. Scott and John Sallis (Albany: State University of New York Press, 2000), 108.

34. In the SS 1931 course on Aristotle's *Metaphysics* Θ, Heidegger insists that the Megarian rejection of the distinction between δύναμις and ἐνέργεια is "gut griechisch" (GA 33, 182) because it rests on a conception of being as presence: their claim is that a capability is present, and therefore is at all, only when it is being enacted. Furthermore, if Heidegger also insists that the Megarian thesis is much stronger than Aristotle recognized it to be, and that Aristotle should have taken it much more seriously, this is because he sees Aristotle as committed to the same conception of Being as presence: "Aristoteles und die Megariker sind sich ganz darüber einig, was Wirklichkeit überhaupt, Vorhandensein von etwas, bedeutet; es bedeutet 'Anwesenheit von etwas'" (179). I argue elsewhere that this cannot stand as an interpretation of Aristotle and appeal to the notion of ἐνέργεια to challenge Heidegger's claim that Aristotle interprets being from the perspective of production (a claim made already in GA 62, especially 250–51): see "Whose Metaphysics of Presence? Heidegger's Interpretation of *Dunamis* and *Energeia* in Aristotle," *Southern Journal of Philosophy* 44, no. 4 (2006): 533–68. Here we should note the striking similarity of Heidegger's strategy in both courses: in each course he insists that Plato's or Aristotle's critique of a naive ontology (that of the "storytellers," in the one case, and that of the Megarians, in the other) does not really overcome the characterization of Being that underlies this naive ontology. For this reason Heidegger can even claim that the Megarians had "the same rank" as Aristotle and Plato, "obwohl sie das Schicksal haben, in der Geschichte vergessen zu sein" (GA 33, 163). This claim illustrates well the kind of leveling entailed by the claim that there is one understanding of Being shared by all Greeks.

be" means "to be capable of being present" in the soul (248a5–10). However, for the soul itself, "to be" means "to be capable of becoming just or unjust, wise or foolish, knowing or ignorant, etc.": it is hard to see how this capability of doing and suffering that defines the soul could be reduced to a capability of *being-present*. Heidegger makes much of the claim at 247a5–8 that whatever can come to be present (παρουσία, παραγίγνεσθαι) in something else *is*. But in the text this is not inverted to the claim that *to be* just means *to be capable of being present* or, in Heidegger's words, that being means "to be capable of presence with something [*im Stande sein zur Anwesenheit bei etwas*]" (470). What we get instead at 247e is the claim that to be means to be capable of *doing or suffering*. Heidegger tries to broaden the meanings of πάσχειν and ποιεῖν, claiming that the former means only "to be determined by an other" (475) and that the latter means "to bring something into being, to help something into being, to genuinely contribute to the being of a being [*das Sein eines Seienden eigentlich mitausmachen*]" (475; trans. modified). This interpretation, however, seems incompatible with the substitution of the word δρᾶν (to do or act) for ποιεῖν at 248c5 (a text that Heidegger cites but does not comment on). How can δρᾶν possibly mean "das Sein eines Seienden eigentlich mitausmachen"?

What Heidegger's interpretation of δύναμις as presence requires for support is at the very least some evidence that Plato treats δύναμις as itself something present for a pure perceiving. But no such evidence is offered. The only implicit justification at 486 for attributing to Plato a conception of being as presence is Heidegger's claim that Plato's characterization of being must reconcile the characterization of being as *resistance* (*Widerständigkeit*), taken from the giants, with the characterization of being, taken from the "friends of the forms," according to which "what exists is that which is present in a pure perceiving" ("seiend ist das, was gegenwärtig ist im reinen Vernhemen"). But Heidegger does not show that this latter characterization of being as presence survives the critique of the "friends of the forms" so as to need to be integrated into the new characterization of being as δύναμις. In fact, the characterization of being as presence cannot survive the critique, for the simple and obvious reason that the "friends of the forms" are forced to acknowledge that at least one thing truly *is* without being present in a pure perceiving: namely, the act of perceiving itself! The conception of being as presence for a pure perceiving is shattered by the recognition that the movement of perception (and motion in general) itself is a being, and this conception must therefore give way before the alternative conception of being as δύναμις.[35] What leads to

---

35. In this case the distinction between Plato's conception of being and Heidegger's cannot be as simple and straightforward as Patt makes it. Referring to Heidegger's own identification of Being in his later writings with a certain sense of *Anwesenheit*, Patt can distinguish Plato's position only by

the characterization of being as δύναμις is precisely the introduction into the ontological discussion of a motion, that is, knowing, that resists the objectifications into which both the giants and the friends of the forms force being.³⁶ When it is argued above that Plato's dialogues can reveal in performance or ἔργῳ a sense of being that resists objectification or "presentification" in a λόγος, this sense of being is precisely δύναμις. Heidegger's arbitrary reduction of δύναμις to *presence* goes hand in hand with his reduction of the dialogue itself to λόγος.³⁷

Later in the course Heidegger argues that Plato, in claiming that what is "other" (ἕτερον) is a "relation-to" (πρός τι), fails to see that the πρός τι is a structure presupposed by both what is other and what is the same (544–45). Heidegger attributes this failure to "the inner limitation of Greek ontology." While he does not here spell out what this limitation is, by this point in the course what is meant is evident: Heidegger is suggesting that it is the Greek

---

attributing to him a conception of Being as "dauernde Gegenwart" and a prioritizing of the temporal dimension of "Gegenwart" (*Formen des Anti-Platonismus*, 224). Yet the evidence of the *Sophist* speaks against both attributions. Patt, following Heidegger himself, appears throughout to identify Plato's position with one like that of the "friends of the forms," e.g., when he asserts that "Die 'Idee' ist für Platon das 'ruhende Sein,' das sich vom Seienden als dem Veränderlichen abhebt" (213). Patt's account of the relation between Heidegger and Plato strangely, and without explanation, avoids any detailed discussion of the *Sophist* lectures (when at 190 he mentions the recently published texts pertinent to Heidegger's 'Auseinandersetzung' with Plato, the *Sophist* lectures, clearly the most pertinent and important of these texts, are not mentioned, though Patt knows them well enough to cite them later a few times in passing).

36. Speaking of the battle between the "gods" and the "giants," Wieland rightly notes: "Gemeinsam ist dem, was jede der beiden Parteien als wahres Sein ansetzt, der Charakter der Gegenständlichkeit. Das gilt gerade auch für die unkörperlichen Ideen der Ideenfreunde. Gerade sie werden von ihren Vertretern als für sich und selbstständig existierende Wesenheiten, als autarke Entitäten behandelt" (*Platon und die Formen des Wissens*, 109).

37. At 519–20 Heidegger again appears to be forcing a conception of being = presence onto the text. In discussing the Birdcage Analogy in the *Theaetetus*, Heidegger draws attention to the distinction made there between κεκτῆσθαι and ἔχειν and interprets the latter as meaning "Gegenwärtig-da-sein." He then suggests that the birds described as flying among all the others in the cage parallel the description in the *Sophist* of beings that are to be found among all other beings in the way that vowels hold all the consonants together. But then Heidegger says the following of these all-pervading beings: "Wenn Sein interpretiert wird als Gegenwärtig-sein, so besagt das: Es sind solche Bestimmungen, die in jedem Seienden immer schon, *im vorhinein*, da sind, also eine ausgezeichnete Gegenwart präsentieren" (520). But how does the present passage support this interpretation of Being? The birds here are precisely *not* present, *not* had, though they are capable of being made present: they are there (possessed) without being present (had). As Heidegger himself seems to see, Being is here understood as δύναμις (519). In his course on Aristotle's *Metaphysics* Θ, Heidegger interprets the dispute between Aristotle and the Megarians as follows: while for the Megarians a δύναμις exists, i.e., *is present*, only in enactment (*Vollzug*), for Aristotle it *is present* in the mode of being *had* (ἔχειν) (GA 33, 189; 219). That Aristotle does not understand the "being had" of a capability as a mode of *being present*, as Heidegger insists ("Diese Gehaltenheit ist seine wirkliche Anwesenheit," 219), is something I argue in "Whose Metaphysics of Presence?" I in any case see no evidence in Plato for equating possession and having with presence. On the other hand, it seems that nothing could count as evidence against Heidegger's thesis that all the Greeks understood Being as presence.

identification of being with presence that prevents Plato from seeing the πρός τι structure in being itself.[38] But here again Heidegger appears more committed to his thesis about the Greek conception of being than he is to a careful reading of the text. The distinction in the text is between beings said *according to themselves* (αὐτὰ καθ' αὑτά) and beings said in relation to *other* things (πρὸς ἄλλα) (255c13-15). Heidegger immediately proceeds to paraphrase this distinction as one between what is disclosed in λόγος "as itself in its simple presence" ("als es selbst in seiner schlichten Anwesenheit") and what is disclosed "in the mode of the πρός τι, with regard to a relation-to" ("in der Weise des πρός τι, im Hinblick auf einen Bezug zu," 544, my trans.). But this paraphrase is an evident distortion of the text and a mere setup for the following objection to "the inner limitation of Greek ontology." The distinction in the text is not one between beings disclosed in pure presence and beings disclosed in relation to something (πρός τι), but rather a distinction between beings disclosed in relation to themselves (καθ' αὑτά) and beings disclosed in relation to something other than themselves. Thus, both kinds of being are characterized by a "relation-to": what is said to characterize "the other" at 255d1 is accordingly not its being πρός τι, but its being πρός ἕτερον. Therefore, Heidegger's assertion that "here, in the *Sophist*, Plato claims the πρός τι only *for* the ἕτερον itself, as a conceptual determination of it" (545) is simply false. It is Heidegger's own arbitrary paraphrase that makes the πρός τι the distinctive characteristic of "the other": what the text makes the distinctive characteristic of "the other" is only the πρός ἕτερον; furthermore, in characterizing beings that are not "other" as being καθ' αὑτά, the text makes clear that they too are characterized by relation.

Heidegger's identification of the same "failure" in a passage of the *Philebus* is, if possible, even more arbitrary. The claim he cites is the following: "these things are not beautiful in relation to something (πρός τι), but are always beautiful in themselves (καθ' αὑτά)" (51c6). But here again the πρός τι has the restricted meaning of "relative to something else": the contrast is between things beautiful in themselves and therefore without qualification and things beautiful only in relation to other things. Thus, when the claim is repeated a few lines later in the text (51d8-9), the phrase πρὸς ἕτερον is substituted for πρός τι. Here again there is no evidence that relation as such is being restricted to only one type of being. On the contrary, the implication is that all being is relation, whether to itself or to something other.

It of course could be objected that Plato nowhere explicitly claims that the πρός τι is a universal structure of all beings. But to this one must make the

---

38. In the SS 1924 course, Heidegger, in discussing the concept of πρός τι in Aristotle, argues that it must be seen as a determination of the being of the world (GA 18, 323-24, 389-90).

following two replies: (1) There is no reason or occasion in the text for Plato to make this explicit ontological claim. We must be careful to avoid the fallacy of assuming that whatever is not explicitly stated in a text is something Plato had not yet thought of at the time of writing the text. (2) To define being as δύναμις κοινωνίας is clearly to make the πρός τι a universal ontological structure. Heidegger himself brings this out clearly in his discussion of the statement of this definition at 248b5–6, which identifies κοινωνεῖν with "a being affected (πάθημα) or an affecting (ποίημα) by way of a certain capacity (ἐκ δυνάμεώς τινος) and resulting from the coming together of beings towards each other (πρὸς ἄλληλα)." Heidegger comments: "Thus we have again *the being with one another, the being related to one another, and the possibility for that. This possibility is nothing else than the meaning of being.* Κοινωνεῖν is simply another version of the πρὸς ἄλληλα, 'to affect one another,' in such a way that being now means, if we insert κοινωνία: δύναμις κοινωνίας, the possibility of being with one another" (478–79). It is as a result of this conception of being that the self-sameness of a kind or form will be interpreted not as some self-identical presence, but rather as its participation in the same (sameness) in relation to itself (διὰ τὴν μέθεξιν ταὐτοῦ πρὸς ἑαυτήν, 256b1). Could the πρός τι character of all being be made any clearer than this? Here we have another case of Heidegger imposing on Plato a conception of being as presence despite the different perspective opened up by the characterization of being as δύναμις, and despite what the text might show to the contrary.[39]

2. Being as Ἀπορία

The problem with Heidegger's reading of Plato, however, is not only his restriction of Plato to a conception of being as presence, but also his restriction of Plato to *any* conception of being. There is a good amount of evidence in the text that even the characterization of being as δύναμις is not considered to be fully adequate or final. That the dialogue allows being to remain an ἀπορία is, however, a view that Heidegger takes great pains to resist: such

---

39. Heidegger will not even credit Plato with the characterization of being as δύναμις, since he maintains that Plato got this definition from Aristotle (GA 19, 484–85) Heidegger gives two reasons for seeing the influence of Aristotle in the discussion, though he admits that this cannot be proven: (1) the incorporation of *somata* into the ontological discussion is, in Heidegger's view, unprecedented for Plato; (2) it is more plausible to see Plato as taking the concept of δύναμις from Aristotle rather than vice versa, because Aristotle's treatment of the concept "presupposes a much more radical ontological meditation"; specifically, Aristotle "sees the phenomenon of movement positively, which Plato never does" (484; see also GA 62, 321). But there is a certain circularity here: unless we assume that Plato is merely following Aristotle's lead in the *Sophist*, we must say that he sees the phenomenon of movement positively here. And is it the case that movement in other dialogues is relegated to non-being? Is Plato's position in other dialogues the same as that ascribed here to the "friends of the forms"? Heidegger simply assumes that these questions are to be answered in the affirmative.

a suggestion, after all, brings the dialogue uncomfortably close to his own position and undermines his thesis that "Greek ontology" is committed to a naive and unproblematized identification of being with presence. Heidegger points out how the Stranger's characterization of being, in the course of critiquing the giants, as συμφυὲς γεγονός, that is, as that which is already there for both the visible and the invisible (247d2), already contains both the notions of συμπλοκή and γένος that will be made explicit later (473). He then takes this as evidence that the conception of being that is about to be introduced (being as δύναμις) is preliminary *only* in the sense that it will later be worked out more fully and not in the sense that it might be given up later (473). This is how Heidegger interprets (474–76) the Stranger's claim at 247e7–248a1 that the characterization of being as δύναμις "might later appear otherwise" (εἰς ὕστερον ἕτερον ἂν φανείη). But can this interpretation stand? Heidegger wants to interpret the Greek here as meaning that this characterization of being will later be handled more thoroughly ("die später eindringender behandelt wird," 474). Obviously, the obstacle to such a reading is the word ἕτερον, which suggests not a more thorough handling of the same characterization, but rather a different characterization. Heidegger can overcome this obstacle only by performing some interpretative somersaults at 476. Appealing to the later identification of non-being with being-ἕτερον, Heidegger claims that the word ἕτερον does not express complete difference, but that instead the claim that every being is ἕτερον means that it is itself *and* something else. From this he infers that "the ἕτερον expresses what something also is as itself." This is apparently supposed to convince us that the phrase in question, εἰς ὕστερον ἕτερον ἂν φανείη, means "might later appear the same, and different only in the sense of being more fully worked out." Such a strained and highly implausible reading of fairly simple Greek hardly requires refutation. Furthermore, there is absolutely no reason to accept Heidegger's insistence that the reference to "progressing a little ahead" at 250a5–6 (ἵνα ἅμα τι καὶ προΐωμεν) means exactly the same as what is said at 247e7 (476, 490). Heidegger's assertion that if we do not accept this suggestion "the whole dialogue becomes a great confusion" (476) only shows how desperately he needs this reading of 247e7.

One can agree with Heidegger's contention that the characterization of being as δύναμις remains behind the subsequent discussion in the *Sophist*. The εἰς ὕστερον can be taken to refer not to some later point in the dialogue, but rather to some discussion outside the dialogue. Its function, like the function of similar qualifications in other dialogues,[40] is to prevent us from taking

---

40. For example, at *Republic* 430c a definition of courage is accepted with the proviso that a better discussion can be undertaken at some other time (αὖθις); at 506e Socrates, having agreed to discuss the "offspring" of the good, defers discussion of the good itself to another time (εἰσαῦθις).

the present inquiry, and the characterization of being that guides it, as final or sufficient. Heidegger, however, needs to take the characterization of being offered here as final[41] in order to interpret its limitations as the inherent limitations of Greek ontology.[42] Furthermore, if the word ἕτερον in the present passage refers ahead to the later characterization of not-being as ἕτερον, as Heidegger suggests, it does so in a way opposite to that suggested by Heidegger: if being will later prove "other," this is so in the sense that it will prove to have otherness, or alterity, at its very core, that it will prove to lack any self-identical presence and thus be incapable of delimitation and definition.[43] In this case, any finality or *euporia* in the discussion of being would be in principle impossible.

Heidegger himself, in commenting on an extremely important text at 250e–251a, writes: "Plato is certainly not so especially convinced of the finality of the inquiry which he carries out here in the *Sophist*,—an important warning for anyone who would want to expound a system of Platonic philosophy!" (498).[44] But is Heidegger always, or even often, heedful of this warning? In the passage at 250e–251a in which Heidegger finds this warning, the Stranger, having come to the conclusion that being is distinct from both motion and rest and therefore falls outside of (ἐκτός, 250d2) both, observes that being has proven as perplexing as non-being (ἐξ ἴσου . . . ἀπορίας μετειλήφατον, 250e6). This equal ἀπορία does create the hope that any clarification of the one will

---

41. Heidegger denies, for example, that the Stranger's description of himself as "proposing" or "suggesting" (προτεινομένων ἡμῶν, 247d5) the characterization of Being as δύναμις in any way implies that this characterization "nur versuchsweise vorgeschlagen wird" (474).

42. At 533 Heidegger insists again that the characterization of Being as δύναμις is nothing preliminary since it is the fundamental presupposition for dialectic. Then he adds: "Of course, what this actually is, and what accordingly is presupposed in the δύναμις κοινωνίας, is something to which Plato gave no further thought. And to question after this was not possible within the horizon of his ontology or Greek ontology as a whole" (533). But, as I am trying to show, this limited horizon, presumably the horizon defined by λόγος and presence, is one into which Heidegger forces Plato, rather than one within which Plato is himself confined.

43. Just as the main speaker of the dialogue is given no name and identified only as a Stranger who, while his γένος is from Elea, is *other* than the disciples of Zeno and Parmenides. At least that is what the most plausible reading of the Greek text suggests. Nestor Cordero has made a very persuasive, and to me absolutely convincing, case for a construction of the Greek at 216a diametrically opposed to the one that has been taken for granted by all modern translations: he reads τὸ μὲν γένος ἐξ Ἐλέας, ἕτερον δὲ τῶν ἀμφὶ Παρμενίδην καὶ Ζήνωνα ἑταίρων. For Cordero's defense of this reading, see Plato, *Le Sophiste*, trans. Nestor Cordero (Paris: Flammarion, 1993), 281–84. This reading finds support in the manuscripts and makes sense of a μὲν . . . δὲ contrast that otherwise appears utterly void of meaning (and accordingly is left untranslated by Bury in the Loeb edition): after informing Socrates that the Stranger is from Elea, why would Theodorus say that *on the other hand* he is a friend of Parmenides and Zeno, and then add that he is nevertheless very much a philosopher? Furthermore, it would be very characteristic of Plato to allude in the very opening of the dialogue to what will later be a major theme of the dialogue: τὸ ἕτερον (as Cordero himself observes at 212).

44. Likewise, in the Stranger's request at 241c8 Heidegger sees a request not to expect too much from the subsequent discussion (433).

also clarify the other. However, at 251a1 the Stranger acknowledges the possibility that we will prove incapable of bringing either into view (ἰδεῖν). Even in this case, the Stranger adds, the discussion will still proceed. How exactly it will proceed depends on how one interprets the unclear Greek at 251a2. The Greek reads: τὸν γοῦν λόγον ὅπῃπερ ἂν οἷοί τε ὦμεν εὐπρεπέστατα διωσόμεθα οὕτως ἀμφοῖν ἅμα. Fowler translates: "We will at any rate push our discussion through between both of them at once as creditably as we can." Heidegger suggests, rather halfheartedly, a different translation/interpretation: "Even if we do not get ὄν and μὴ ὄν into view as such, we shall still try to submit our speaking about them, our mode of talking about them, to a concrete investigation" (498).[45] That Heidegger does not strongly commit himself to this reading is understandable, since it is hard to see how it is to be gotten out of the Greek.[46]

Whatever the correct translation, however, the crucial point is that we have in the present passage a recognition of the possibility that the λόγος will need to proceed *without* being able to bring being and non-being into view, and thus a recognition that a system of philosophy may prove an impossibility. Is not this recognition counterevidence to Heidegger's thesis that Plato identified being with presence for a pure perceiving? The ἀπορία the Stranger describes prevents us from, in the Stranger's words, "securing for ourselves something clear about being" (ἐναργές τι περὶ αὐτοῦ παρ' ἑαυτῷ βεβαιώσασθαι, 250c10). This may indeed be the goal of any λόγος about being, but does not the dialogue here expose again the limitations of any such λόγος? Furthermore, this ἀπορία of being, which is introduced in the dialogue *after* the suggested characterization of being as δύναμις, is at no later point in the dialogue said to be overcome. At 254a we do have the description of the philosopher as residing in the pure light of being, as dwelling near (προσκείμενος) the ἰδέα of being through reasoning (διὰ λογισμῶν).[47] Ironically, however, this philosopher proves as difficult to see clearly (ἰδεῖν μὲν χαλεπὸν ἐναργῶς) as the sophist, though for opposed reasons: in the one case it is the light of being that blinds, while in the other it is the darkness of non-being. Furthermore, the ideal of philosophy described here does not correspond to the philosophy actually

---

45. As Brach suggests (396), Heidegger wishes through such an interpretation to show that the inquiry will move from an examination of being to an examination of λόγος.

46. Robinson, in the latest Oxford edition of the text, suggests reading διακριβωσόμεθα in place of διωσόμεθα, though this reading is not found in any of the manuscripts. This would produce a meaning like the following: "we will at any rate examine precisely our account of both of them as well as we can." On this interpretation, it is hard to see how "precise examination" is something we *fall back on* when we fail to catch sight of being and non-being.

47. Heidegger's reading into 253e5 of the view that philosophy is to be found only in the pure seeing ("reines Sehen") of νοεῖν does not seem warranted by the text (530). Καθαρῶς φιλοσοφεῖν need not be identified with νοεῖν. In any case, such a characterization of philosophy certainly seems in conflict with the philosophy practiced in the dialogue.

carried out in the dialogue. A little later in the text, at 254c6, the Stranger must again admit that "we may not be able to grasp with full clarity [being and non-being]" (μὴ πάσῃ σαφηνείᾳ δυνάμεθα λαβεῖν [τό ὄν καὶ μὴ ὄν])."[48] And never in the dialogue does the Stranger claim that such a clear grasp has been attained.

We do, of course, get a definition of non-being as what is *other* (ἕτερον). This definition, however, captures a rather limited sort of non-being: what is not *x* only in the sense of being some other thing, *y*. According to this sense of non-being, what is not is as much a being as what it negates. But what of a sense of non-being as the contrary of being, that is, as not a being at all? The Stranger says, after defining what is not as what is other: "We've said good-bye long ago to any contrary of *that which is,* and to whether it is or not, and also to whether or not an account can be given of it" (258e7–29a1; White trans.) The ἀπορία of non-being as the *contrary* of being has not been solved, but has simply been let go. Here we get a clearer idea of what was meant at 251a2 by "pushing forward the discussion" without bringing being or non-being clearly into view. And we should recall the exact nature of the ἀπορία confronted at that stage of the dialogue. Though it seems that any being must be either in motion or at rest, being proved to be beyond motion and rest. The source of this ἀπορία is of course that being is not a being; unlike a being that must be at motion or at rest, being encompasses both motion and rest and thereby transcends them. But how do we conceive of what is not a being, of what is not in motion or at rest? This ἀπορία is equal to the one that confronts us in attempting to understand non-being when, instead of identifying it with a being that is other than another being, we try to grasp it as not a being at all, as the contrary of being. The dialogue both forcefully draws our attention to this equal ἀπορία and leaves it unresolved.

That the dialogue allows being and non-being to remain in ἀπορία could of course itself be seen as a limitation, but only if one is convinced of the possibility of giving a precise characterization of being. Is Heidegger himself convinced of such a possibility? Here it is necessary to consider an important text at 453, where Heidegger claims that the whole inquiry of the present dialogue occurs in the *Indifferenz des Ontischen und des Ontologischen* (453; see also 455–60)—a claim that has been shown here to be preposterous. Yet the reason Heidegger gives here, after the suggestion already considered above that Plato understands the relation between a word and what it signifies purely ontically, is that Plato "has not yet elaborated an actually precise concept of being versus beings." The irony, of course, is that Heidegger himself

---

48. Heidegger only paraphrases this loosely by saying that the inquiry will not be able to achieve every possible clarity (he does not say about what), but only what is needed for the present purpose (GA 19, 535).

nowhere elaborates such a precise concept ("wirklich scharfer Begriff"); and Heidegger's own emphasis on the limitations of λόγος makes the possibility of such a concept highly suspect. In any case, Heidegger's own example shows that one does not need such a concept in order to recognize and maintain the ontological difference.

It is significant that when Heidegger finds in the difficult argument at 244b–245a, against the thesis that being is *one*, a lack of clarity with regard to the distinction between being and beings (as well as a lack of clarity with regard to the meaning of the "not") (459), he proceeds to point out that these obscurities have not been clarified to the present day. And it is clearly Plato's intention in this aporetic argument to expose these obscurities, of which he must therefore have been perfectly aware. Heidegger also grants that the subsequent discussions in the dialogue "will, in one direction at least, bring a certain light into the confusion: it sets in motion an essentially more positive grasp of negation which then became of far-reaching significance for Aristotle" (460; trans. modified). And Heidegger must also grant at one point that the arguments of the dialogue are not to be understood as "purely ontical in a sophistical sense" (453). The crucial point, then, is that Plato is drawing our attention to the same ἀπορίαι to which Heidegger draws our attention: he is not blinded to them by a naive ontology that equates being with presence nor by an indifference towards the distinction between the ontological and the ontic. If showing the latter is the aim of Heidegger's interpretation of the latter part of the dialogue, this interpretation must be counted a failure.

E. CONCLUSION: THE RELATION BETWEEN BEING AND ΛΟΓΟΣ

This chapter has attempted to show that Plato, because he recognizes the ontological difference and the inescapable tendency of both language and the "seeing" that guides it to objectify the structures of being, deals with this dilemma by not identifying himself with the speaking voice (the Stranger), by surrounding what is said with a very palpable philosophical silence (Socrates), and by drawing our attention, through the performative aspect of the dialogue, to the limitations of the dialogue's λόγος and thus indirectly to the phenomena themselves. In his detailed reading of the dialogue, Heidegger shows no awareness of these strategies. Instead, for him the limitations of the dialogue's λόγος are Plato's limitations, and not only Plato's but those of Greek ontology, and not only those of Greek ontology, but those of the whole of Western metaphysics. As such they are also for Heidegger limitations to be overcome. But how? What is the alternative to making λόγος the guiding perspective in our interpretation of being? And is any such alternative really necessary? Λόγος is no doubt Plato's guiding perspective, but in such a way that he does not remain "locked" within it (as does the "telling of stories" for which earlier philosophers are criticized): through dialectic (which Heidegger himself recognizes as a *Miteinandersprechen* that goes beyond "telling stories"[443]), and the form of writing best suited to dialectic (dialogue), Plato continually exposes the limits of this perspective from within. Furthermore, we have seen that the understanding of being presupposed by Plato's dialectic is not that understanding of being as static presence with which Heidegger charges the Greeks and which would indeed block any genuine questioning of being and privilege beings as what lies there before us to be spoken about; on the contrary, from the perspective of dialectic, being is understood as power or capability: a conception inherently open-ended and aporetic and so inviting further questioning. But even if there remains some limitation to the perspective of Plato's dialectic, is it possible to get "outside" of this perspective in a way that Plato does not; that is, is it possible to twist completely out of λόγος? This is certainly the implication of Heidegger's critique.

The preceding chapter gave some indication of what Heidegger during this period began to sketch out as an alternative to the guiding perspective of λόγος. Later chapters will provide a detailed and critical discussion of this alternative as it is developed in Heidegger's later work. First, however, it is necessary to turn to the topic that receives scant attention in Heidegger's reading of Plato during the 1920s but that becomes absolutely central to this reading during the 1930s and 1940s: the nature of truth. These two topics are of course not unrelated, since Heidegger's central thesis will be that with Plato truth becomes for the first time a property of λόγος (i.e., the correctness of a λόγος in its correspondence to reality) rather than unconcealment. Thus, despite the many changes that will emerge in the way Heidegger reads Plato's dialogues, and despite the many indications of a growing affinity, a fundamental consistency in his critique of Plato will become evident. The 1940 essay "Plato's Doctrine of Truth" can be seen as simply the most extreme, polemical, and one-sided expression of the critique that is already coming to expression in the 1920s. However, if in what follows the history of Heidegger's reading of truth in Plato will be told in great detail, this is because the many tangents, complications, inconsistencies, and reversals in Heidegger's ongoing interpretation in his courses are much more revealing of what is at stake in his confrontation with Plato and much more philosophically provocative than that dogmatic statement on Plato's doctrine that Heidegger saw fit to publish. The definition of being as δύναμις, the dialogue form, the ethical problematic of the good, dialectic's ability to mediate between λόγος and νοῦς: these are only some of the many aspects of Plato's philosophy that Heidegger's reading must both acknowledge and suppress in order to remain faithful to his critique.

PART 2

HEIDEGGER ON PLATO'S TRUTH AND UNTRUTH IN THE 1930S AND 1940S

Referring to his distinction between truth as unconcealment and truth as correctness, Heidegger in the 1931–32 course *Vom Wesen der Wahrheit*, a course devoted to the interpretation of Plato's Cave Analogy and a part of the *Theaetetus*, asserts that Plato's philosophy "is indeed nothing but a battle between these two conceptions of truth" ("ist ja nichts anderes als Kampf der beiden Wahrheitsbegriffe," GA 34, 46), an assertion that is repeated in the 1933–34 version of the same course (GA 36/37, 124, 127). In the later 1937–38 course *Grundfragen der Philosophie*, a course in which Heidegger originally intended to provide an interpretation of the Cave Analogy but never got around to doing so (see GA 45, 223), Heidegger presumably has the same idea in mind when he asserts : "Each of his [Plato's] dialogues, indeed practically every segment of his dialogues, points either directly or indirectly in the direction of the question of ἀλήθεια" (222). This interpretation of Plato's philosophy as nothing but a battle between truth as unconcealment and truth as correctness is what explains Heidegger's promotion of the Cave Analogy in the *Republic*, in which he sees this battle waged most clearly and explicitly, to the central text of Plato's philosophy, indeed, to a completely self-contained résumé of Plato's thought. Thus, when he claims that the war between the two conceptions of truth can be found in *every* dialogue (GA 36/37, 128), he also claims that the Cave Analogy can be found in every dialogue (124). The Cave Analogy can be ripped out of the *Republic*, Heidegger insists, without this in the least affecting its content or meaning (GA 34, 18). One can thus conclude that there is in Heidegger's reading of Plato in the 1930s a reduction of the Cave

Analogy to the battle between two conceptions of truth, and a reduction of all of Plato's dialogues to the Cave Analogy.

In the 1926 course *Grundbegriffe der antiken Philosophie* (GA 22), and even in the 1929 *Einführung in das akademische Studium* (GA 28, 347–61), both texts in which Heidegger interprets the Cave Analogy, there is no hint of the interpretation of this analogy, much less of Plato's work as a whole, as a battleground between two conceptions of truth. Starting in the 1930s, however, this becomes Heidegger's dominant interpretation of Plato, and this interpretation receives its best-known exposition in the 1940 essay "Platons Lehre von der Wahrheit" (PLW). It is not until the 1960s, with the essay "Das Ende der Philosophie und die Aufgabe des Denkens" (ZSD, 61–80), that Heidegger's interpretation is substantially modified, though not through any rereading of Plato's texts. There he grants that the Greeks always experienced truth (ἀλήθεια) as correctness (ὀρθότης) and therefore concludes that his earlier thesis of a transformation in the essence of truth from unconcealment to correctness is untenable ("unhaltbar") (78). In other words, the battle between unconcealment and correctness is already lost to the derivative correctness well before Plato comes onto the scene. But if this is in some sense a retraction of Heidegger's earlier interpretation of Plato, it is also in another sense its natural outcome. As will be shown below, between the 1931–32 course and the 1940 essay the battle between the two conceptions of truth becomes on Heidegger's reading increasingly uneven: while in the 1931–32 interpretation the dominant conception of truth in Plato is unconcealment, with truth as correctness only beginning to emerge in its dependence on this prior conception of truth, by the 1940 essay it is truth as correctness that Heidegger sees as dominant in Plato, with only faint traces of the more original conception remaining. The conclusion in the 1960s that truth is experienced *only* as correctness in Plato, and even before Plato, is only the next and final step in the direction of Heidegger's critique of Plato as it has developed since the beginning of the 1930s. This is why Heidegger's retraction in the 1960s does not bring with it any rereading of Plato's philosophy.

The task of the next chapter is to assess and chart the development of Heidegger's critique of Plato, namely, the critique that in Plato there is a reduction of truth to mere correctness that blocks any genuine questioning of both the meaning of truth and the meaning of being. Heidegger's certainly questionable reduction of Plato's philosophy to the question of the essence of truth will not be directly challenged here, but it will be seen not to be quite as reductive as it might at first seem. The question of truth is not for Heidegger a mere question of epistemology, and his interpretation of Plato on truth will be seen to be an interpretation of Plato's "ideas" as such and the idea of the good in particular. Indeed, despite Heidegger's insistence on the independence of the Cave Analogy from its context, his interpretation of Plato will be seen to depend primarily on the account of the good in the Sun Analogy. Therefore, Heidegger's reading can be said to engage the whole of Plato's philosophy on the ontological level, though he can still be criticized for excluding as purely derivative and irrelevant to Plato's real philosophy the politics and ethics that in fact comprise the bulk of the *Republic*.[1] The next chapter will follow Heidegger in his exclusive concern for Plato's ontology to show that even here and on his own terms his reading of Plato cannot stand.

Yet the account of Heidegger's interpretation of truth in Plato cannot end with the examination of his evolving interpretation of the Cave and Sun analogies, even though most accounts do end here or, rather, do not go much or at all beyond the published 1940 essay. Yet what is thereby neglected is the other interpretation offered in the 1931–32 course: an interpretation of Plato's *Theaetetus*.[2] This is at least partly because the 1940 essay drops all reference to the *Theaetetus* from its argument. Yet in the 1931–32 course the *Theaetetus* plays an absolutely central role in Heidegger's argument regarding a transformation in the essence of truth. There the Cave Analogy is not taken by itself to show that Plato understood truth as correctness. On the contrary, Heidegger there

---

1. For such a critique see William A. Galston, "Heidegger's Plato: A Critique of *Plato's Doctrine of Truth*," *Philosophical Forum* 13, no. 4 (1982): 371–84; Adriaan T. Peperzak, "Did Heidegger Understand Plato's Idea of Truth?" in *Platonic Transformations: With and after Hegel, Heidegger, and Levinas* (Lanham, Md.: Rowman and Littlefield, 1997), 57–111, especially 72–76, and "Heidegger and Plato's Idea of the Good," in *Reading Heidegger: Commemorations*, ed. John Sallis (Bloomington: Indiana University Press, 1993), 258–85. Both criticize Heidegger for interpreting the philosopher's descent back into the cave, and the danger he encounters there, as representing simply the everyday power of concealment (Galston, "Heidegger's Plato," 375–76; Peperzak, "Heidegger and Plato's Idea of the Good," 270). Peperzak also objects that the context of the *Republic* as a whole, being a discussion of the essence of δικαιοσύνη, runs counter to Heidegger's attempt to deprive the idea of the good of any ethical meaning (275). Gadamer also opposes this aspect of Heidegger's Plato interpretation; for a good description and documentation of this opposition, see Catherine H. Zuckert, *Postmodern Platos* (Chicago: University of Chicago Press, 1996), 72. Yet, counter to what Galston and Peperzak suggest, Heidegger does not always ignore the political context of the *Republic*, since his discussion of the Myth of Er in the *Parmenides* course (1942–43), for example, does take it into account. The problem is that he gives δικαιοσύνη a purely ontological characterization (GA 54, 137) and denies that the πόλις is anything political (142). For further discussion, see Zuckert, *Postmodern Platos*, 50–51, and chapter 5 of the present book. For how Heidegger could nevertheless undertake a political appropriation of the Cave Analogy during his involvement with National Socialism, see my "Heidegger's 1933 Misappropriation of Plato's *Republic*," Προβλήματα: *quaderni di filosofia* 3 (2003): 39–80.

2. Drew Hyland's recent critique of Heidegger's interpretation of Plato, for example, mentions that the 1931–32 course contains a reading of the *Theaetetus*, but then skips any detailed discussion of this reading by turning quickly to the essay on *Plato's Doctrine of Truth*. Hyland, *Questioning Platonism: Continental Interpretations of Plato* (Albany: State University of New York Press, 2004), 53–55. As for what is currently the only volume of essays devoted to Heidegger's reading of Plato (HPD), we find in it no detailed discussion and evaluation of Heidegger's reading of the *Theaetetus*, but only some passing references to this part of the lecture course by Inwood ("Truth and Untruth in Plato and Heidegger," in HPD, 79–81, 89) and a very brief summary by Fritsche ("With Plato into the *Kairos* Before the *Kehre*: On Heidegger's Different Interpretations of Plato," in HPD, 154–55).

asserts the aim of his interpretation of the Cave Analogy to be that of gaining a better understanding of ἀλήθεια as unconcealment and of its intimate connection with the essence of man, as indeed a happening of this essence (117). Where criticism begins is in the context of what Heidegger later claims to be the *decisive* outcome of the interpretation of the Cave Analogy: that reflection on the essence of truth as unconcealment is impossible without reflection on the essence of untruth as concealment, that the question of the essence of truth must transform itself into the question of the essence of untruth (127). As Heidegger asserts, "the question of untruth is *no* detour [*Umweg*], but the only way possible, the direct way to the essence of truth" (128). In this context, Heidegger suggests that, however central an understanding of truth as unconcealment may be to the Cave Analogy, Plato failed to think the essence of concealment and therefore inaugurated a turn away from unconcealment in the conception of truth. But to show this, Heidegger must consider how Plato thought about and understood *untruth*. This is where the turn to a reading of the *Theaetetus* becomes absolutely indispensable, because it is in this dialogue, according to Heidegger, that Plato genuinely walked a part of the way of the question of untruth "for the first and last time in the history of philosophy" (129). Only if Heidegger can show that along this way Plato fails to grasp untruth as concealment, and instead identifies it with mere error in thinking and speaking, can he show that Plato understood truth as mere correctness in speaking and thinking (see 143).

But if this is the case, then why does Heidegger later abandon all reference to the *Theaetetus* in his account of Plato's "doctrine of truth"? Such an abandonment is already underway in the 1933–34 version of the *Vom Wesen der Wahrheit* course, since already there we see the interpretation of the *Theaetetus* drastically cut in comparison to the 1931–32 version. Why then this marginalization and eventual complete disappearance of the *Theaetetus* from the account of Plato's "doctrine of truth"? There are a number of possible answers here, ranging from the purely practical to the philosophical.[3] Chapter 4, however, seeks to show what must have been at least a very important factor: Heidegger's extraordinarily perceptive and careful reading of the *Theaetetus* simply does not support his thesis, so that the thesis must later be made to rest entirely on the Cave Analogy, a shift of the burden of proof already begun in the 1933–34 version of the course. This thesis is forgotten through much of Heidegger's reading of the *Theaetetus* and when it suddenly appears at the very end of the course, without the support of the texts Heidegger discusses,

3. One suggested by Johannes Fritsche, for example, is a turn in Heidegger's thought from "sempiternal existentialia discovered in structural analyses" to "language and its changes in the history of being" ("With Plato into the *Kairos*," 158). But this cannot be the whole story, since it does not explain why the *Theaetetus* would drop out of Heidegger's critical account of "Plato's doctrine of truth."

much less those he does not discuss, it cannot help but look like a *deus ex machina*. What Heidegger uncovers in the *Theaetetus* is a conception of our relation to being and truth that cannot be reduced to any kind of correspondence and therefore resists an interpretation of untruth as incorrectness. But then the argument of chapter 4 is not the purely negative one that Heidegger misinterpreted Plato. The aim instead is to show that Heidegger's engagement with the text of the *Theaetetus*, an engagement that begins already in the 1926 course *Die Grundbegriffe der antiken Philosophie* but is eventually abandoned in favor of the historical construct of Platonism, offers a special opportunity for glimpsing what might have become a genuine dialogue and affinity between Plato and Heidegger. In Heidegger's account of the history of metaphysics as Platonism, the *Theaetetus* interpretation is the discarded trace of a very different reading of Plato.

There is another "marginal" text in Heidegger's reading of Plato, and significantly it too concerns the essence of untruth. In 1942, the year in which "Plato's Doctrine of Truth" was first published, Heidegger, in a course ostensibly devoted to Parmenides, offers a brief and partial reading of the Myth of Er in Book 10 of the *Republic*.[4] What primarily comes to expression in this myth, on Heidegger's reading, is λήθη, concealment. What Heidegger finds in Plato's myth, a myth whose significance was presumably hidden from him in 1931–32 when he asserted the *Theaetetus* to be the first and last time in the history of philosophy that the way of questioning concealment was genuinely taken, goes well beyond what Plato was credited with in 1931–32. While in the 1931–32 course Heidegger interprets the Greek word for untruth, ψεῦδος, as meaning *Verdrehung* and argues that truth is thereby necessarily interpreted as *Nichtverdehen* and *Treffen* (138), in the 1942 course Heidegger interprets ψεῦδος as a concealing that is also a letting appear and accordingly sees this name for untruth as supporting and confirming the understanding of ἀλήθεια as unconcealment (43–48). Furthermore, while in 1931–32 Heidegger asserts that the Greeks interpreted λήθη as a mere not-being-present-at-hand (142), in the Myth of Er he finds a genuine experience and thinking (*An-denken*) of λήθη (190). A reason for these shifts is that in 1942 it is the *Roman* interpretation of truth and untruth that is seen as the decisive step towards the identification of the two with correctness and falsehood. Nevertheless, even in the 1942 course we find repeated the claim that Plato interpreted truth as correspondence, but

---

4. This is another Heideggerian reading of Plato that has been strangely neglected in the literature. The essays collected in HPD ignore it entirely; indeed, it is referred to in the essay by Margolis only to be dismissed with the assertion that "the text of the lecure course from 1942 to 1943, published as *Parmenides*, seems, when *not* read in close accord with the essay on Plato [i.e., 'Plato's Doctrine of Truth'], hardly more than bombast" (124). I invite the reader of chapter 5 below to reach his or her own judgment.

here, as in the case of the interpretation of the *Theaetetus*, this claim is a mere assertion in tension with what is revealed by Heidegger's reading of the text.

The form of these two texts marginal to Heidegger's main interpretation of Platonism is certainly significant: one is a *dialogue* and the other is a *myth*. One can of course claim that all of Plato's works are dialogues, but Heidegger certainly does not read them all in this way. While Heidegger abstracts the Cave Analogy from its dialogical context in the *Republic* and reads the *Sophist* in the 1924–25 course as a treatise, he emphasizes the dialogical character of the *Theaetetus* (see 194, e.g.).[5] As for the Myth of Er, he gives great importance to its character as mythic discourse, insisting that this discourse is a form of *nonmetaphysical* saying (145). What Heidegger's reading of both the *Theaetetus* and the Myth of Er may therefore show is the extent to which a reading of Plato that is attentive to both the dialogical and the mythic discourse in his works resists the metaphysical doctrine (*Lehre*) with which he wishes to identify Plato. In his account of the history of metaphysics as Platonism, Heidegger strangely marginalizes his own readings of the texts that resist such an account. The argument of chapters 4 and 5 is that what gets marginalized here is precisely what should be made central. If Heidegger anywhere genuinely engages Plato's thought, it is not in "Plato's Doctrine of Truth," but in his reading of the texts that problematize and therefore get excluded from this doctrine.

5. Therefore, I cannot agree with Hyland that Heidegger's reading of the *Theaetetus* is as insensitive to the dialogical context as are his other readings (*Questioning Platonism*, 54). Though he indeed interprets only a part of the *Theaetetus*, this chapter will show that in focusing on this turning point he usually has the whole in view, that he sees in the very way the conversation unfolds a paradigm of philosophizing, and that he is almost Straussian in his emphasis on the importance of every detail in the text.

3

FROM THE 1931–32 AND 1933–34 COURSES ON THE
ESSENCE OF TRUTH TO "PLATO'S DOCTRINE OF TRUTH":
HEIDEGGER'S TRANSFORMATION OF PLATO INTO
PLATONISM THROUGH THE INTERPRETATION OF THE
SUN AND CAVE ANALOGIES OF THE *REPUBLIC*

A. THE COURSES ON THE ESSENCE OF TRUTH
FROM WS 1931/32 AND WS 1933/34

1. Truth as the Play of Concealment and Unconcealment in the Cave

In the courses of 1931–32 and 1933–34, Heidegger's interpretation of the Cave Analogy emphasizes the extent to which it is not a static image but a story, the story of prisoners being freed from their bonds, gradually making the difficult ascent out of the cave, and then gradually adjusting their eyes to the light outside the cave. Heidegger's account thus divides the analogy into its different stages and focuses our attention on what is happening at each stage. But what he sees these stages as exhibiting in their progression is a conception of truth not as correctness and not as a property of assertions, but as a "property" of being, specifically, being in its unconcealment. Heidegger can thus claim in 1931–32 that the central unifying theme of the analogy is "the true" (τὸ ἀληθές): "and this has nothing to do with imitation and correctness and correspondence" ("und dabei gibt es nichts von Angleichung und Richtigkeit und Übereinstimmung," GA 34, 30).

Crucial to Heidegger's reading is Socrates' claim that when a prisoner is freed from his chains and forcibly turned around, he will, because blinded by the light of the fire, believe that the shadows he saw on the wall when in his chains are *truer* (ἀληθέστερα) than the things now shown to him, even though the latter are *more being* (μᾶλλον ὄντα) than the former. Heidegger interprets the comparative ἀληθέστερα as meaning "more unconcealed" ("unverborgener," GA 34, 32). Whether or not this is a fully adequate interpretation,[1] it is justified at least to the extent that Socrates only a few lines later repeats what appears to be the same claim about the prisoners who have been turned around, but now in the significantly different form of saying that they will judge what they saw earlier to be "in reality more manifest" ("τῷ ὄντι σαφέστερα," 515e3–4) than what they are shown now: σαφέστερα appears to be simply substituted here for ἀληθέστερα. Furthermore, and this is the crucial point, it is indeed hard to see how ἀληθέστερα could mean "more correct." First, how can correctness admit degrees? Something either is correct or it is not. We can of course be closer to or further from being correct (closer to or further from the truth, as we say), but this does not mean that truth as correctness itself admits of degrees. On the other hand, not only does it make sense to speak of degrees of unconcealment, but the possibility of varying in degree appears as essential to the notion of unconcealment as it is to the notions of light and darkness. Secondly, what the prisoner judges (mistakenly) to be "more true" are not statements but the very things he takes to be (again, mistakenly) "more real": the shadows on the wall. Clearly the prisoner does not see the shadows as "more true" in the sense of "more correct," since not only are the shadows not statements about anything, but from the perspective of the prisoner they are not even *shadows of* anything, but rather the only beings there are.

As Heidegger notes, the comparative "more true" goes hand in hand with the comparative "more being": the degrees of truth are paralleled by degrees of being.[2] As he states the point in 1933–34: "Not only what is true [*das Wahre*] and what is unconcealed [*Unverborgene*] has degrees and levels, but also what is [*das Seiende*]. Something can be more or less *being* [*seiend*]; even a human being can be more or less being [*seiend*]" (GA 36/37, 137–38; see also GA 34, 33). The degrees of truth characterize not statements but degrees of being. The prisoner considers the shadows "more true" because, compared to the bright light of the fire that blinds him, they are much more unconcealed and manifest; but precisely because they are more unconcealed and manifest, they are also for him more real. From the perspective of Socrates or someone who has emerged from the cave, in contrast, the fire and the objects placed before it are, once the eye of one's soul adjusts to them, more manifest *and* more

---

1. I am not persuaded by Michael Inwood's objection that "Plato cannot mean by *alêtheia* what Heidegger means by *Unverborgenheit*. The concepts belong to different problem-contexts. The shadows are *unverborgen*; they are not really *to alêthês*." "Truth and Untruth in Plato and Heidegger," in HPD, 82–83. The analogy appears to require that the shadows be true in some sense and to some extent (that they are not "the true" is obvious and not in contradiction with Heidegger's reading): not only because they are *more true* to the prisoners, but also because they are *less true* in themselves.

2. This assumption of the Cave Analogy is later made explicit by Aristotle: ἕκαστον ὡς ἔχει τοῦ εἶναι, οὕτω καὶ τῆς ἀληθείας (*Metaph*. 993b30–31).

real than the shadows on the wall. Of course the sunlight and the objects illuminated by it outside of the cave are in turn more manifest and more truly being than the artificial light and objects within the cave. It is because the ascent out of the cave is an ascent both from what is less to what is more unconcealed, and from what is less to what is more being, that Heidegger can interpret the Cave Analogy as a whole as exhibiting and putting to work a conception of truth as unconcealment and thus as a characteristic of being itself. Indeed, Heidegger considers unavoidable the conclusion that "what is at issue in the *entire* analogy is predominantly ἀλήθεια" (GA 34, 42), where ἀλήθεια is understood in what Heidegger takes to be the original sense of unconcealment. But in the margin next to the cited claim Heidegger some time later wrote: "yes and no" (42). This is because Heidegger will later, *and only later*, interpret the Cave Analogy as largely eclipsing the original meaning of ἀλήθεια in favor of correctness.

There is another important dimension to Heidegger's account of the Cave Analogy as a history. If on the side of being we have an ascent to an ever-greater degree of unconcealment, on the side of human existence we have an ascent to an ever-greater degree of freedom. These are not two different ascents but rather the same ascent: this means that existing in greater unconcealment is itself greater freedom. After all, the Cave Analogy itself describes the turning of the prisoner toward what is more true and more real as a *freeing* of the prisoner. Thus, Heidegger sees this stage of the analogy as showing that "the happening and existence of unconcealment as such goes hand in hand with the *freeing* of man, more precisely: with the success of this freeing, that is, with genuine *being*-free" (GA 34, 37–38). Heidegger sees his reading as only confirmed by the failure of the first attempt to free the prisoner: in merely being turned around toward a light to which his eyes are not adjusted, the prisoner is not really freed: he wants to return to the shadows on the wall and remain in his bonds because he cannot yet recognize the shadows as shadows nor therefore the bonds as bonds. It is only when the prisoner is dragged out of the cave altogether and made to undergo a gradual habituation (συνήθεια) to the light outside that he is genuinely freed (GA 34, 41–42). In other words, genuine freedom requires a genuine dwelling and existing in what is most true and most real. Therefore, what is at issue in the Cave Analogy for Heidegger is not only the essence of truth but also, and inextricably, the essence of man. Truth as the unconcealment of being is also the disclosing (*Entbergsamkeit*) that sets us free. Thus, Heidegger later in the course asserts: "The question concerning the essence of truth as unconcealment is the question concerning the history of man's essence" (GA 34, 114). In case this interpretation of the Cave Analogy as a history of our essence might appear arbitrary or forced, Heidegger points out that the analogy is introduced by Socrates as analogous to our nature (ἡ ἡμετέρα φύσις) with respect to παιδεία and ἀπαιδευσία: in other words, our nature not as something static, but as something characterized by a history occurring between the poles of παιδεία and ἀπαιδευσία. It is this history that the analogy proceeds to recount.

As Heidegger well recognizes, the Cave Analogy describes not only an ascent out of the cave but also a descent back into the cave. But it is not immediately clear how the account of the descent can fit into Heidegger's interpretation. If the ascent is an ascent from what is less unconcealed to what is most unconcealed as well as from the bonds of a prisoner to the most genuine freedom, then it seems that with the conclusion of the ascent everything there is to say about truth as unconcealment and freedom has already been said. The account of the descent must therefore be turning to a completely different point; if the analogy is essentially concerned with the essence of truth and freedom, then the account of the descent would be nothing but an inessential add-on. But this is precisely what Heidegger denies; on his interpretation, the account of the descent adds something essential to the account of the essence of freedom and truth. Heidegger argues that the descent back into the cave is a necessary stage in the process of becoming free, that it is in fact the completion of this process. "Freedom is neither merely the being-freed *from* the fetters nor also *only* having-become-free *for* the light, but rather genuine being-free is *being-a-liberator* from the darkness" ("*Befreier-sein* aus dem Dunkel," 91). In other words, genuine being-free is a continual *setting-free*, not only of others but presumably also of oneself. Freedom is not a stable possession but a continual struggle. The reason is that truth itself is not a stable possession, as Heidegger proceeds to explain: "In other words: the truth is not a calm possession [*ruhender Besitz*] in the enjoyment of which we come to rest at some particular standpoint in order from there to lecture at the rest of humanity, but rather unconcealment *happens* [*geschieht*] only in the *history* [*Geschichte*] of constant setting-free" (91; see also GA 36/37, 184).

But that both freedom and truth must be continuously conquered presupposes something else: that concealment belongs to the very essence of unconcealment. "Therefore, truth is not so simply unconcealment of beings [*Offenbarkeit von Seiendem*], whereby the previous hiddenness [*Verdecktheit*] would be left behind somewhere, but rather is necessarily and in itself the overcoming of a concealment [*Überwindung einer Verbergung*]; concealment belongs to unconcealement in its very essence [*wesensmäßig*]—*as the valley belongs to the mountain*" (90). In this way, what is at issue in the description of the descent is still truth as unconcealment, but now in its character of a constant overcoming of concealment. As Heidegger states the point in the 1933–34 version of the course, to the essence of truth belongs untruth (187). Truth is therefore a battle: "every standing in the truth is confrontation [*Auseinandersetzung*], a fighting [*Kämpfen*]" (185). In this way Heidegger highlights the elements of struggle, pain, and even mortal danger to be found in Plato's analogy. Whether or not this interpretation of the descent does full justice to Plato's description of it is something to be considered in a later chapter.

2. Truth as "Correctness" in the Cave

What is important in the present context is noting that in Heidegger's interpretation of the Cave Analogy in the 1931–32 and 1933–34 courses the conception of truth at issue in the description of both the ascent and the descent is nothing but truth as unconcealment. What then of the transformation of truth from unconcealment to correctness? The reason why Heidegger turns to a reading of the Cave Analogy is, in his own words, to follow ("nachgehen") this transformation (GA 34, 17). What is therefore surprising is that Heidegger's reading of the Cave Analogy per se does little or even nothing to demonstrate this transformation of the essence of truth. Only in Socrates' claim that the freed prisoner when turned towards what *is more* will see ὀρθότερον (515d) does Heidegger find a conception of truth as correctness. Even here, however, Heidegger insists that, far from replacing or transforming truth as unconcealment, the correctness introduced in this passage is made completely dependent on truth as unconcealment. In the 1931–32 course, Heidegger interprets the use of the word ὀρθότερον here as showing only how truth as correctness is grounded in truth as unconcealment (GA 34, 34–35). In 1933–34 he elaborates: "Emergence of correctness in connection with unconcealment. The *correctness* of seeing and regarding [*Die* Richtigkeit *des Sehens und Besehens*] is grounded in the actual *turning-towards* and *proximity* of being [*in der jeweiligen* Zuwendung *und* Nähe *des Seins*], in the manner and way in which beings are manifest and unconcealed [*offenbar und unverborgen*]. *Truth as correctness is impossible with truth as unconcealment*" (GA 36/37, 138). This grounding is what Heidegger here takes Plato's sentence to express, and not some transformation of the one conception of truth into the other.

One can and should, however, go even further than Heidegger here and say that the word ὀρθότερον is in the cited passage so grounded in unconcealment that it appears to mean no more than "turned towards what is more unconcealed." In other words, the comparative here clearly cannot mean "greater correspondence": the word ὀρθότερον describes not a greater correspondence to the same objects but a turn to a completely different set of objects. The prisoner sees ὀρθότερον not because he now sees the shadows more accurately, but because he has completely turned away from the shadows toward objects that are more real and more unconcealed.[3] Therefore, the

---

3. As Inwood notes, "for Plato the higher being and truth of the object is crucial, whereas it does not matter to the correspondence theory. Plato has in mind the clarity and distinctness of the vision as much as its accuracy" ("Truth and Untruth," 73).

comparative in ὀρθότερον can only mean a relation to a *greater degree of being and unconcealment*. In other words, ὀρθότερον cannot mean "more correct" but only "turned toward what is more unconcealed." But then one must ask if there is a conception of truth as correctness here at all. What is expressed in the comparative ὀρθότερον is a degree of unconcealment and not of correctness. One could interpret "seeing ὀρθότερον" as meaning "seeing more clearly," as long as one specifies that the source of the greater clarity is to be found not in seeing itself (better eyes, for example) but rather in the inherently greater clarity of the objects to which seeing is now turned. To see ὀρθότερον is not to improve one's vision of the same objects, but rather to turn one's vision to completely different objects that are more real and more inherently manifest.

Yet even if Heidegger is wrong to find a conception of truth as correctness expressed in the word ὀρθότερον, the important point in the present context is that even he does not see in the cited passage, in either the course of 1931–32 or the course of 1933–34, a *transformation* of the essence of truth.[4] Even if truth is there understood as correctness, it is made completely derivative of truth as unconcealment. But then again we must ask: where does Heidegger attempt to demonstrate a transformation of the essence of truth in Plato? In the 1931–32 course, Heidegger does make one objection to Plato in his account of the Cave Analogy: after providing his interpretation of the ascent, Heidegger suggests that Plato does not understand unconcealment originally (*ursprünglich*) enough because concealment (as distinct from what is merely false or apparent) is not understood *ursprünglich* enough (93). He does not pursue this objection, however, because he claims that we must first attempt to understand Plato's idea of the good. For this understanding, however, Heidegger must turn to a different analogy: that of the sun.

We thus see that despite the central importance Heidegger grants the Cave Analogy, he can demonstrate the inadequacy of Plato's understanding of truth as unconcealment and the transformation of truth into correctness only by going beyond this analogy. This is why Heidegger has to leave the Cave Analogy altogether in order to establish his thesis. Of course, the analogy of the sun and the analogy of the cave are closely related and Socrates himself draws on the former to explain the latter. Furthermore, Heidegger in 1931–32 declines to focus on the analogies in book 6, claiming to remain instead within the Cave Analogy and to draw in the Sun Analogy only for clarification (GA 34, 98). It

---

4. A marginal notation to the text of WS 1931/32 interprets ὀρθός as follows: "ὀρθός (rectus—Recht): gerade-zu, ohne Umschweife, ohne Umwege, nicht über die Schatten, die Sache selbst" (GA 34, 34). "Seeing more directly" is certainly closer to what Socrates means than is "seeing more correctly." However, even the interpretation of "seeing more directly" is problematic, since the prisoners see the relevant objects *for the first time*; one cannot strictly say that they already saw these objects indirectly through their shadows since they did not, and still do not, recognize these shadows *as* shadows.

is only in this "clarification," however, that any support is given to the thesis of a transformation of the essence of truth, and even this support is in the course of 1931–32 largely implied and tentative. Only as Heidegger turns away from what is recounted in the Cave Analogy to an abstract consideration of the ideas and the idea of the good can he offer support for his thesis of a transformation of truth from unconcealment to correctness.[5] The final outcome of this tendency will be the 1940 essay, in which the story of the ascent and descent is only briefly paraphrased and quickly left behind in favor of a systematic account of Plato's "doctrine of truth."

3. The Sun Analogy

To see where exactly Heidegger is going and to organize and assess the main points of his interpretation accordingly, it will be helpful to begin with a statement of his general thesis, though with the proviso that this thesis is made fully explicit only in the 1940 essay. Heidegger's main argument is that in Plato truth and being are subordinated to (yoked under) the ideas as well as to the knowing/seeing to which the ideas are essentially related. This subordination makes inevitable the transformation of truth into a property of the relation between knowing and the objects known, that is, into correctness. This thesis requires three "reductions" (though such a description of course anticipates the critique to come), which are carried out in the courses of the 1930s: (i) the reduction of ideas to beings present for a seeing; (ii) the reduction of the light of truth to the ideas; (iii) the reduction of the good to both the light of truth and the ideas. What I will argue is that all of these reductions are incompatible with Plato's Sun Analogy and can be pushed through only by means of serious distortions and misinterpretations of this analogy.

(a) The ἰδέα as "What Is Seen in Seeing [das im Sehen Gesichtete]" (GA 36/37, 149, 151) or as "Projected Making-Possible"?

Appealing to the etymology of the word ἰδέα, Heidegger interprets it as the "look" of a being (*Anblick*; GA 34, 51; GA 36/37, 152), or "what is seen" (*gesichtet*; GA 34, 51; GA 36/37, 149, 151). This of course does not mean that the ἰδέα is "seen" in the way a color is seen. When we recognize a table as a table, its tableness or ἰδέα is not something our eyes perceive in its color or texture or shape. Yet Heidegger insists that the ἰδέα of a table is nevertheless a "look" which the table offers to some sort of intellectual vision. What needs to be

---

5. Peperzak makes the significant observation that "if Heidegger had really restricted himself to the cave story (514a1–517a7), he could not have spoken of Plato's 'doctrine of ideas,' since neither *idea* nor *eidos* occurs there even once." Adriaan T. Peperzak, "Did Heidegger Understand Plato's Idea of Truth?" in *Platonic Transformations: With and after Hegel, Heidegger, and Levinas* (Lanham, Md.: Rowman and Littlefield, 1997), 90.

noted here are the two important consequences that this characterization of the ἰδέα has for our understanding of its being:

(1) As a "look" that is "seen," the ἰδέα *is* by *being-present*. This is made clear by Heidegger in the following passage:

> "Idea" is *the view* [*der Anblick*] of *what* something offers itself *as* being [*dessen, als was seiend sich etwas darbietet*]. These views [*Anblicke*] are that in which the individual thing *presents* itself [*sich präsentiert*] as this and that, that in which it is present and *presencing* [*präsent und anwesend ist*]. Presence-at-hand [*Anwesenheit*] is called by the Greeks παρουσία or abbreviated [*verkürzt*], οὐσία, and presence [*Anwesenheit*] means for the Greeks *being*. Something *is*, that means: it is present-at-hand [*anwesend*], or better: it *west an* (as we must say in German), in the present [*Gegenwart*]. (GA 34, 51)

To interpret being as ἰδέα is for Heidegger to interpret being as *presence*, since the ἰδέα is nothing but the "look" in which something presents itself as what it is. The ἰδέα is what makes something present and therefore is itself a being-present. If only what is present at hand can be seen with the eyes, so can the mind's eye only see what is in some sense present-at-hand.

(2) The second consequence is that the ἰδέα can *be* only in and for a seeing. This point is stated with special clarity in the 1933–34 course: "It lies in the essence of the idea that it is always related to a *seeing*. To the idea belongs the reference [*der Bezug*] to a seeing. The characteristic of that which Plato calls idea is no addendum (*Zugabe*); it always belongs to it to be *seen* [*gesichtet*]. That which is seen [*das Gesichtete*] refers always to a seeing. The idea is always seen [*gesichtet*]" (GA 36/37, 171; see also GA 34, 70–72). The ideas are therefore not something outside of seeing to which seeing can sometimes have access. They are not beings that can either be seen or not seen. To define the idea as *das Gesichtete* is to make its very being inseparable from a seeing. The ideas are of course not dependent on seeing in the sense of being produced or invented by seeing. But neither are they independent of seeing if this means that being-seen is accidental to their being. As Heidegger states the point in 1931–32, the ideas are neither subjective nor objective (GA 34, 71). For them to be "looks" is for them always to be seen; they can exist only together with a seeing, though seeing does not produce them. It is in this way that Heidegger can see in Plato's interpretation of being as ἰδέα a promotion of "seeing," and the thinking of which "seeing" is an interpretation, to the ultimate guideline and standard for the interpretation of being and truth.[6]

---

6. Thus also in a 1944 *Übung* led by Heidegger under the title "Skizzen zu Skizzen zu Grundbegriffe des Denkens," it is inferred from the interpretation of the ἰδέα (see 271–80) that "Die platonische Bestimmung des Seins hat also wesentlichen Bezug auf die Sicht" (GA 87, 276).

Yet this characterization of the ἰδέα as something present for a seeing appears to be pushed to the breaking point by other claims Heidegger is led to make about the ἰδέα. First, if the ἰδέα can be characterized as "present" at all, Heidegger must acknowledge that this cannot mean that it is present as an *object* or as something *present-at-hand* (*vorhanden*). As Heidegger himself points out, the ἰδέα is not a being present-at-hand along with other beings; as the *being of* beings it is something *other than* beings. Commenting on the Cave Analogy's characterization of the beings that we encounter in our everyday existence (and thus precisely the beings that are present-at-hand), Heidegger asks: "But is yet something *else* [*anderes*] to be found beyond beings?" (GA 34, 47). This "other" is not other, yet unknown beings (other shadows), but the idea (48). "The idea should be something *other* [*ein* Anderes] than beings [*das Seiende*]" (48). If Heidegger proceeds to identify this "other" with a "look" that "is present," he later insists, immediately after emphasizing the relation of the ἰδέα to seeing, that *what* exactly the ἰδέα is and *how* it is remains an open question: "The ideas are not therefore present at hand [*vorhandenen*] objects hidden somewhere that one could conjure up through some kind of hocus-pocus. Just as little are they something that *subjects* carry around with them, something subjective in the sense that they are made and invented by subjects (humans, as we know them). They are neither things, objective, nor something merely thought up, subjective. *What* they are, *how* they are, indeed, *whether* they at all "are," that remains undecided to this very day" (GA 34, 71; see also GA 36/37, 172). How is this conclusion to be reconciled with the fact that, as we have seen, Heidegger asserts, without the slightest hesitation or sign of doubt, that *what* the ideas are is "looks" and *how* they are is through being-present?

Furthermore, Heidegger later characterizes the being of the ἰδέα in a way that significantly differs from his initial characterization: the ἰδέα is "other" than beings as *what makes them possible*. The being of the ἰδέα is a making-possible. This dimension of the ἰδέα emerges when Heidegger has to explain its relation to the good. The ἰδέα is "good" in the sense that "to *make beings possible* [ermöglichen], is the *essence of the idea*" (GA 36/37, 194). Is this not significantly different from identifying the essence of the idea with a being-seen as the "look" of beings? As for the idea being present, Heidegger now characterizes its being in this way: "The idea as what-makes-possible [*das Ermöglichende*] must be what genuinely sets itself through [*das eigentlich sich Durchsetzende*], what brings to a stand [*In-Stand-setzende*]" (194). As opposed to being merely present, the idea sets itself through and assumes a position in making beings possible. Heidegger in the context of characterizing the ἰδέα as what-makes-possible accordingly appeals to the definition of being in the *Sophist* not as presence, but as δύναμις. The ἰδέα *is* as a power that enables beings to be, both in what they are and how they are. "In the idea we catch sight of *what* each being is and *how* it is, in short: the *being* [*Sein*] of beings"

(GA 34, 52). But in this case it is hard to see how the ἰδέα can have as its way of being being-present in a "look." The way of being of a δύναμις is not a being-present, and it is not something that is "seen," either literally or metaphorically, but rather something that is *exercised*.

Heidegger must indeed greatly modify the metaphor of "seeing" in order to make it correspond to the way of being that characterizes the ἰδέα. If the ἰδέα is a "power," the "seeing" in question here certainly cannot be anything analogous to the passive seeing of an object. As that through which and within which beings are encountered as what and how they are, the ἰδέα is not some ob-ject to be gazed at but rather a pro-ject beyond beings that can be "grasped" only in being carried out through the interpretation of beings. We know the ἰδέα not in contemplation, but in creative, inventive interpretation. Heidegger makes this clear when he asks himself what kind of a "seeing" could possibly be involved here:

> But what kind of a looking [*ein Blicken*] is that? No looking-at [*Anblicken*], in something like the way in which we gape at something at-hand [*ein Vorhandenes angaffen*], not a mere finding [*Vor-finden*] and taking into view [*Aufnehmen in den Blick*], but rather a seeing in the sense of en-visioning [*Er-blickens*], that is to say: to *form* [bilden] for the very first time what is envisioned [*das Erblickte*] (the look [*den Anblick*]) *through* looking and *in* looking,—to form in advance, to pre-form [*vor-bilden*]. This pre-forming envisioning [*vor-bildende Erblicken*] of being, of essence [*des Wesens*], also already *binds itself* [bindet sich] to what is projected in such a projection [*das in solchem Entwurf Entworfene*]. (GA 34, 71)

Thus, if the ἰδέα is a "look" (*Anblick*), it is a strange kind of look in being one that we ourselves "form" or "shape." The "form" is something we "form" not in the sense that we "make it up," not in the sense that it is subjective,[7] but rather

---

7. Heidegger rightly insists that the ideas are neither subjective nor objective, as we have seen, but he still wants to make the ideas into something "human" in a way that certainly goes against Plato's interpretation: "Es gibt keine Wahrheit an sich, sondern Wahrheit ist *Entscheidung* und *Schicksal* des Menschen, ist etwas *Menschliches*" (GA 36/37, 172). Inwood makes much of this contrast: "In Heidegger's view, our looking constitutes what it looks at. There are no objective Ideas independent of our vision of them. But that is not Plato" (90). Yet even the later Heidegger would not characterize truth as a human decision or a destiny. In WS 1931–32, after the sentence "Die Idee ist dem Erblicken wensensmäßig verhaftet und *ist* nichts *außerhalb* dieses Erblickens," Heidegger wrote some time later on the margin: "? ja und nein!" (GA 34, 104). This ambiguous "yes and no" is, I think, much nearer to Plato; or, in other words, the question would never have occurred to Plato. In any case, to ignore the "no" in Heidegger's position and attribute to him the view that "there really is nothing outside the cave unless we put it there," as Inwood does ("Truth and Untruth," 91), is to turn him into Nietzsche (and a crude Nietzsche at that!).

in the sense that it is disclosed to us only through our active participation and involvement in it. If there is "seeing" here, it is an inventive seeing, an en-visioning (*Er-blicken*) that must actively bring out what does not simply offer itself to a look; Heidegger at one point even characterizes the ἰδέα as "*interpretation* [*Auslegung*] of 'being'" (GA 34, 57). In "seeing" the form, there is none of that separation between subject and object that normally characterizes seeing. "Seeing" is here a "projection" (*Entwurf*), not in the sense of some *ex nihilo* creation, but rather in the sense of carrying out a possibility already projected (*Entworfene*). If we put this together with what has been learned about the *being* of an ἰδέα, we can conclude that "seeing" an ἰδέα is the projection of what makes-possible.

But then why insist on the metaphor of "seeing" at all? Other metaphors can certainly convey much better the kind of active participation and inventiveness that characterize knowledge of an ἰδέα. The answer is that Plato, unlike Heidegger, does *not* insist on this metaphor. In a very important passage at *Republic* VI, 490a8, which Heidegger himself cites and translates, the process of coming to know the ἰδέα, the "what it is," is described without any appeal to the metaphor of "seeing": instead, our relation to the ὂν ὄντως is described as ἔρως; and in case we are tempted to reduce this ἔρως to some visual relation to beauty, Plato instead speaks of touching (ἅψασθαι), nearing (πλησιάσας), and mixing (μιγείς). These metaphors of course indicate particularly well that knowledge of the ἰδέα is as far as can be from having the character of disinterested contemplation. Our relation to the ἰδέα is comparable to lovemaking, the offspring of which is as much a reflection of the one parent as of the other; this of course is the central metaphor of the *Symposium*. Yet Heidegger is so determined to make the metaphor of "seeing" dominant that his translation/paraphrase of 490a8ff. in 1931–32 (GA 34, 68) contains the phrase "seeing with this power of the soul [*mit diesem Vermögen der Seele sehend*]," even though the "seeing" metaphor is completely absent from the passage, being replaced by those of touching and lovemaking.

Interestingly, in the 1933–34 version of the course, Heidegger's translation drops the word *sehend* and also specifies that the "power" [*Vermögen*] in question is ἔρως: "With that power whose function it is to grasp what something is, i.e., eros" (GA 36/37, 169). Furthermore, there is another related way in which this later version of the course significantly departs from the earlier version: in the later version, which is preoccupied with the nature of language in a way that the earlier one is not (section 5, "Zur Wahrheit und Sprache" [GA 36/37, 100–117], has no parallel in the earlier version), Heidegger, after asserting that for the Greeks "seeing grasping [*das sehende Erfassen*], θεωρεῖν (from which comes 'theory') assumes a prominent role in their interpretation of man; the eyes, seeing. What is seen [*das Gesichtete*] accordingly possesses a marked priority for the overall interpretation of the world" (157), immediately adds, appealing to Aristotle, that hearing rules Greek existence just as essentially ("so wesentlich wie") as seeing (157). This hearing is a hearing of what is spoken, where "*language* [*die* Sprache] is the fundamental medium of the being-with-one-another [*Miteinandersein*] of human beings" (158). In confirmation of this, we should recall that what Plato often claims to be essential to knowing the ἰδέα is not "vision" but rather the process of *question and answer* that characterizes dialectic (ἐρωτᾶν τε καὶ ἀποκρίνεσθαι ἐπιστημονέστατα, *Rep.* 534d 9–10). Knowledge of the ἰδέα is thus at least as much a hearing as a seeing. As for which in his view has priority for the Greeks, seeing or hearing, Heidegger in 1933–34 says: "But this does not reach a definitive decision" ("Es kommt aber nicht zu einer vollkommenen Entscheidung," 158).

Yet even here Heidegger does not in any way retract the prioritization of seeing in his interpretation of the Greeks. Later in the same course, he appears to forget completely what he said earlier when he asserts, with no qualification whatsoever, that what we have learned from the preceding is that the Greeks gave the "preference" [*Vorzug*] to seeing out of all the senses (197). Heidegger thus continues to make the metaphor of seeing the exclusive guideline to his interpretation of the ἰδέα. To follow Heidegger in this, one must believe that the etymology of the word ἰδέα is more important to its interpretation in Plato than is its actual use by Plato. In other words, one must believe that even when Plato describes our relation to the ἰδέα as one of "touching" and "mixing," he is still compelled by the etymology of the word ἰδέα to understand the relation as primarily one of seeing. Such an interpretation seems preposterous.

Yet, one could object, it is surely significant that in describing our relation to the good, Plato uses visual analogies that make seeing the central and indeed exclusive metaphor for knowing. If, after all, Plato had used the metaphor of lovemaking instead of seeing in the Cave Analogy, this might have made the analogy much more appealing to Glaucon and many contemporary readers! But Heidegger himself, in his SS 1929 *Einführung in das akademische Studium*, provides a perfectly good explanation of why seeing is made the paradigm in the central analogies of the *Republic*: seeing differs from the other senses in requiring a "third genos" besides its object in order to see: light, or what Heidegger calls *Helle* (GA 28, 357). On this account, the metaphor of seeing is used in order to indicate the dependence of knowing on some other principle besides the object known, this other principle being ultimately the good itself. It would have been very difficult, and perhaps even impossible, to illustrate through the metaphor of touching the dependence of both knower and known on some higher principle. But if this is the explanation, then the comparison of the ἰδέα to "something seen" is demanded by the point the analogies wish to make and *not* by Plato's understanding of the ἰδέα as intrinsically "something seen."

The visual metaphor obviously has its use, and is put to very good use in the dialogues, but neither this metaphor nor any other should predetermine our understanding of the being of the ἰδέα. To insist on a translation of ἰδέα as *Anblick* or *Gesichtetes* on the basis of nothing more than etymology, even when this is in tension or even contradiction with what the dialogues reveal about what/how the ἰδέα is and how it is known, seems terribly misguided.[8] Here we must recall Heidegger's own insistence that the way of being of the ideas is left an open question in the dialogues. At one point he even claims that talk of a "theory of ideas" "is simply the most disastrous thing that could have happened to Platonic philosophy" and insists that "when we run across the word ἰδέα in Plato . . . , we should not interpret it with the help of any representation, common or otherwise, of idea and theory of ideas, but must on the contrary always consider that Plato means with the word ἰδέα something that stands in relation to his inmost philosophical questioning, that opens and guides this questioning, and that even *remained* a question for Plato during his entire life" (GA 34, 172–73). But in immediately identifying the ἰδέα with a "look present to a seeing," Heidegger has in fact closed off the question.

In summary, the following aspects of Heidegger's account of the ideas do not sit well with, or at least greatly qualify, his characterization of them as beings fully present for a seeing:

1. They are not *objects* of any kind; the exact character of their being needs to remain open, even, apparently, whether they are beings or being.
2. Accordingly, if the ideas exist for a "seeing" this is not any kind of theoretical intuition of an object but an *en-visioning* (*Er-blicken*) and pre-forming (*Vor-bilden*), i.e., a seeing that is inventive and creative, indeed, a *projection* (*Entwurf*).
3. If Heidegger insists that "idea" means what "is seen," he must in his interpretation grant it the quite different sense of a *power* that *makes possible* (*das Ermöglichende*).[9]

---

8. Jonathan Barnes has in my view successfully discredited Heidegger's etymological argument here: see "Heidegger spéléologue," *Revue de Métaphysique et de Morale* 95 (1990): 183. See also Peperzak, "Did Heidegger Understand Plato's Idea of Truth?" 90–94, as well as Goldschmidt's comment: "L'idée, si l'on écarte sa réduction, naïve, à l'homonymie du sensible (naïveté, il est vrai, qui traîne encore dans des publications 'savantes'), est un concept de structure et de fonction, non de substance." Victor Goldschmidt, *Platonisme et pensée contemporaine* (Paris: J. Vrin, 2000), 260.

9. Heidegger recognizes the tension in his reading when he refers to the following ambiguity in Plato's ideas: "Zwiedeutigkeit: 1. durchlassend, 2. selbst seiend, Gegenstand, Vorhandenes, Oberes— Unteres—Bereiche, Schichten; χωρισμός, Kluft!" (294). But "2." is Heidegger's invention. Or rather, it rests on nothing more than Heidegger's insistence on making the metaphor of seeing and the etymology of ἰδέα all decisive. If there is a genuine ambiguity here, it is one that results from the fact that the ideas, though the being of particular objects, are not ultimate: above them are being itself and the good. But this is precisely what Heidegger fails to see.

4. Heidegger here sees the idea as causing not only *what* a thing is (its "look") but also *how* it is, its existence.

In short, according to these aspects of Heidegger's interpretation, the idea, rather than being itself an object for a seeing, is the *being of* an object that as such exists in a projection that transcends the object. These ways in which Heidegger's interpretation of the ἰδέα is in tension with his reduction of it to something present to a seeing need to be emphasized here because in later texts these dimensions of his interpretation will simply disappear in favor of the reduction. The development of Heidegger's reading of Plato will in general be seen to be one from a richer but conflicted reading to an increasingly simplifying and reductive reading.

(b) Ideas and Light

In the context of interpreting the Cave Analogy, Heidegger himself raises the question of the relation between the metaphor of light that plays such a central role in this analogy and the ideas (GA 34, 46). The characteristics of light that Heidegger proceeds to identify as central to understanding this relation are its transparence (*Durchsichtigkeit*) and perviousness (*Durchlässigkeit*). Heidegger clarifies these characteristics by pointing out that while glass is also transparent and pervious, light, as that which renders glass transparent and pervious, is itself transparent and pervious in a more fundamental sense: it is "the genuine, and in the first place transparent [*Durchsichtige*]" (56). While glass can be made transparent through light, light is itself this transparence. If we can see the trees outside only through the window, we can see through the window only through light. It is therefore primarily the light, and not the glass of the window, that makes the objects outside accessible to our vision. Heidegger concludes: "Light first lets through *for* the look the object as something visible and lets the seeing look through *to* an object to be seen. Light is the letting-through, the pervious [*das Durchlassende*]" (56).

Heidegger then proceeds to make the crucial and, as I will argue, disastrous move of identifying the ideas with light as thus defined: "being [*das Sein*], the idea, is the pervious [*das Durchlassende*]: the *light*. What is the fundamental essence of light, that is the fundamental accomplishment [*Grundleistung*] of the idea" (57). Heidegger's justification for this conclusion is that it is through a thing's idea, in the *light* of this idea, that we see it as what it is. This view is on a certain level indisputable: as we have seen, the idea is what makes beings possible in their being; in this sense, it could be said to allow beings to "appear" in the way light enables visible objects to appear. However, this does not warrant Heidegger's conclusion, and for a simple reason: while the idea might provide the light within which a particular sensible object appears as what it is, the idea cannot provide this light without *itself being illuminated*. It is not the cause of the light of being and truth, nor is itself this light, but is that *through which* this light illumines particular sensible objects. In Heidegger's terms, the idea is not "in the first place transparent" but rather "in the second place transparent [*das in zweiter Linie Durchsichtige*]": or in terms of his example, the ideas are the "glass" through which sensible objects can be seen as they are, but are not the light that enables this glass to be transparent.

This point could not possibly be made clearer by Plato's analogies. In the Cave Analogy, the ideas correspond to the objects outside of the cave *illumined by the light of the sun;* they are *not* themselves this light.[10] Yet Heidegger asserts: "But the light is the image [*Sinnbild*] for the idea. The idea contains and gives being [*enthält und gibt das Sein*]" (GA 34, 60). The first claim is simply wrong, for the reason already stated. When Heidegger later in further describing the outside of the cave identifies the ideas with "the light, the illuminating [*Lichtende*], that which first enables visibility [*Sichtbarkeit erst Ermöglichende*]" (65), he simply ignores the objects visible outside of the cave, objects that can be nothing other than the ideas. The same mistake is repeated in the 1933–34 version of the course (GA 36/37, 153). As for the second claim made on page 60 of the 1931–32 course, it is seriously misleading: the idea may give sensible objects their being, but it is not the ultimate source of being, as the Sun Analogy will be seen to make perfectly clear.

In turning to the Sun Analogy, which will prove absolutely central to his critique of Plato, Heidegger makes exactly the same mistake he makes in interpreting the Cave Analogy: "To the image of light, of brightness [*Helle*], correspond the ideas" (GA 34, 106); a mistake that is again repeated in the 1933–34 version of the course. In this case Heidegger's interpretation is not only implicitly but explicitly contradicted by the text. In two passages Socrates makes clear that what corresponds to the light of the sun in his analogy is not the ideas, but *truth* [ἀλήθεια]: at 508d4–5 Socrates describes truth and being as illuminating the ideas (καταλάμπει ἀλήθειά τε καὶ τὸ ὄν), so that the ideas, rather than being themselves the light, are described as what is illumined by the light of truth and being; at 508e6–509a1 Socrates treats knowledge and truth as the analogues of vision and light. Confronted with these texts, the diagram Heidegger provides of the Sun Analogy (GA 34, 106) must be judged seriously inaccurate: it puts the ἰδέαι in the role of linking knowing (νοεῖν) and what is known (νοούμενον), when clearly they should be put under what is known; being and truth, which *Socrates* makes the link between knowing and what is known, accordingly disappear from Heidegger's diagram altogether. In another diagram found in a *Zusatz* published with the course (GA 34, 326), being and truth are to be found, but in some completely indeterminate role corresponding to no part of the analogy. Ironically, it is Heidegger, rather than Plato, who here does not know what to do with being and truth. We can also begin to see here the irony, not to say absurdity, of Heidegger's critique of Plato: if he can later criticize Plato for subjugating ἀλήθεια to the ideas, this is only because he assigns to the ideas the role Plato assigns to ἀλήθεια!

The mystery is that in none of his interpretations does Heidegger take into account 508d4–5, where truth and being are described as *illuminating* the objects of knowledge, rather than *being illuminated*. This is a crucial line because it keeps distinct the ideas, which, as both being and being true, are knowable, from being and truth themselves; the latter are the light, the former what is known in this light. Thus, this line by itself refutes Heidegger's interpretation. How, then, could Heidegger have ignored it? There is some evidence that he simply misread it. The only place in which Heidegger cites the line, though without any explanation or discussion, is the 1926 course *Die Grundbegriffe der antiken Philosophie*. At one place in his manuscript for the course he simply lists key terms and phrases, sometimes with a translation. In this context he significantly cites the line in question without the genitive οὗ that is its object; then directly underneath the citation he provides what is presumably a translation: "what illumines disclosedness and being [*was beleuchtet die Entdecktheit und das Sein*]" (GA 22, 100). This translation appears to make *Entdecktheit* and *Sein* the objects that are illuminated by the light, rather than themselves the light that illuminates. Could this misreading be the source of Heidegger's failure to see the challenge this passage poses to his interpretation? In any case, not everything rests on this passage: the other passage cited above, 508e6–509a1, by itself makes perfectly clear that truth is the analogue to light.

(c) How the Good Becomes a "Yoke"

Heidegger's diagram of the Sun Analogy for the 1933–34 version of the course (GA 36/37, 196), in contrast to that for the earlier version, not only includes ἀλήθειά τε καὶ τὸ ὄν, but places them right underneath the good. This is not, however, because he now sees them as the "yoke" between knowledge and the ideas, but rather because he wants to characterize both of them as yoked under the idea of the good. Indeed, it is only in the 1933–34 version of the course that Heidegger's critique becomes for the first time explicit: Plato identified the idea of the good with a yoke that yokes being (the understanding of being) and truth (unconcealment) together, but never clarified "how it actually stands with this yoke [*wie es mit diesem Joch eigentlich steht*]" (GA 36/37, 220–21; also 294). According to what Heidegger proceeds to say, this is not merely an oversight, since it is impossible to explain this yoke once what is under it has been assumed to be two things next to each other needing a relation (221). In this way Plato makes inevitable a misinterpretation of what is under the yoke as subject and object and a misinterpretation of truth as the correspondence between the two (correctness).

Heidegger's interpretation and critique make a great deal of the metaphor of a yoke. In Heidegger's notes for the 1933–34 course, we even find the following: "The fundamental fact [*Grundtatbestand*]—the yoke. The achievement and essence of the ἀγαθόν" (290). Someone who is unfamiliar with Plato's text might therefore be surprised to find that this metaphor of a yoke is used only in describing the side of the Sun Analogy concerned with seeing and visibility (508a1) and is not used at all in describing the relations between knowledge, truth, and the good. Furthermore, and most importantly, even if one believes that the analogy justifies the transfer of the metaphor from one side of the analogy to the other, what is compared to a yoke at 508a1 is not the sun, but the light it produces. Therefore, even if one transfers the metaphor to the other side of the analogy, it is not the good that would be compared to a yoke, but rather the "light" it produces, that is, truth. This means that if anything on this side of the analogy can be compared to a yoke, it would be truth as the yoke between knowledge (νοῦς) and what is known (τὰ νοούμενα) (as light [φῶς] is the yoke between sight [ὄψις] and what is seen [τὰ ὁρώμενα]). Heidegger's critique, however, depends on the interpretation that truth is yoked by the good together with being, with the result that it inevitably degenerates from unconcealment into mere correctness. This interpretation is simply a complete misreading of the text, and an absolutely disastrous one, since Heidegger's entire critique depends on the "fundamental fact" that the yoke is the essence and achievement of the good.

Heidegger's interpretation of the yoke in the earlier 1931–32 version of the course starts out on the right track, but soon goes astray. Heidegger recognizes that the yoke between seeing and being-seen is light (GA 34, 102); on the top of page 103 he even appears to recognize that the analogue to light, and therefore the yoke, is ἀλήθεια. But then, by quoting the claim that the idea of the good brings ἀλήθεια to what is known (508e1-2), he starts slipping into equating the yoke with the good. Thus, at 104 we find the claim that "so are unconcealment [*Unverborgenheit*] of beings in their being and apprehension [*Vernehmen*] in *one* yoke"; and by 111–12 there is no other yoke but the good. Already in the SS 1929 course we find the same slip: while Heidegger sees that "light" or *das Helle* is the yoke that yokes seeing and what is seen (GA 28, 357), he goes on to interpret the analogue to light as being the good rather than ἀλήθεια, while ἀλήθεια is identified with what is known (γιγνωσκόμενον) (358). Interestingly, Heidegger's reading of the analogies in the SS 1926 course

10. See Inwood, "Truth and Untruth," 84.

Grundbegriffe der antiken Philosophie, makes no reference to the yoke; the term ζυγόν is not even listed on the pages of Heidegger's manuscript that contain an otherwise exhaustive list of the key Greek terms and phrases in the analogies (GA 22, 100–101). He was clearly at the time far from the later promotion of the yoke to being the very essence of the good.

Heidegger's unfortunate slip in identifying the yoke with the good results in other distortions. In 1931–32 what the good yokes are apparently the ideas, which in their turn are the causes of being and unconcealment and therefore themselves most truly being and unconcealed (GA 34, 104–6). This is a complete inversion of what Socrates says: as already noted, being and truth are themselves the light and yoke that first cause the ideas to be and be known. In 1933–34 we find the suggestion that the good yokes together being and truth (see GA 36/37, 205, 220, 290). Yet if there is anything that is yoked on Socrates' account, it is the power of knowing[11] and what is known, while truth and being, far from needing a yoke, are *one* and as such themselves the yoke. The sameness of being and truth is shown in the fact that Socrates makes both of them the analogues of light: just as things can be seen only when illuminated by the light of the sun, so only those things "on which shines the light of truth and being" (οὗ καταλάμπει ἀλήθειά τε καὶ τὸ ὄν, 508d4–5) can be known by us. In conclusion, it is difficult to avoid the harsh judgment that Heidegger's reading of the Sun Analogy is a complete distortion.

The text does of course make the good the provider (παρέχον, 508e1; παρασχομένη, 517c4) of truth and thus in some sense the master over it (κυρία, 517c4). Yet by erroneously attributing to the good the metaphor of a yoke and then giving the most crudely literal interpretation of this metaphor, so that the yoke and what it yokes are three completely separate "things" related only externally in a relation of subjugation,[12] Heidegger greatly coarsens and oversimplifies the relation between the good and truth and being hinted at in the text. Far from it being the case that being, truth, and knowledge are assumed to be separately existing things next to one another that then need to be externally yoked together in order to be brought into any relation, the Sun Analogy makes clear that truth and being do not exist at all prior to and independently of the

---

11. Heidegger's interpretation is possible at all only through a bizarre identification of τὸ ὄν with the *understanding of* being (*Seinsverständnis*; GA 36/37, 220). Inwood considers this identification very significant and explains it as follows: "The Ideas have switched sides. Ideas are no longer objects of thoughts. They are consituents of our *Seinsverständnis*, our ways of looking at things, not things in their own right" ("Truth and Untruth," 91). Inwood then uses this reading to support his interpretation, criticized in note 7 above, of the fundamental difference between Plato and Heidegger. It should be added here that Inwood's reading clearly assumes a subjective/objective distinction that is entirely unsuited to, and indeed incompatible with, what Heidegger calls *Seinsverständnis*.

12. As Paul Friedländer aptly observes in writing on "Platons Lehre von der Wahrheit," in Heidegger's interpretation "aus dem Joch der Vereinigung wird das Joch der Unterjochung." *Platon,* 3rd ed., vol. 1, *Seinswahrheit und Lebenswirklichkeit* (Berlin: Walter de Gruyter, 1964), 241–42.

good. And this means that the difference itself between knowing and being known, who knows and what is known, does not exist independently of the good. The Good is the source of both the difference and the unity and in this sense the source of the yoke that is truth, rather than being itself this yoke.

One can in a similar way respond to Heidegger's claim that the yoke is not itself brought into question (see especially GA 36/37, 221, 294). If Plato had identified the yoke with the good, then he would thereby have made it something ultimate (though certainly not self-evident). But since he instead identifies the yoke with the being and truth derived from the good, he makes it not something ultimate but rather something to be questioned and explained. In other words, Plato's analogy opens up the space required for questioning being and truth in terms of, or from the perspective of, the good. As for the relation between being and truth, a relation too close to require in Plato's eyes any yoke whatsoever, their common source in the good grounds and enables us to think this relation.

Of a conception of truth as "correctness" there is not so much as a hint in the Sun Analogy. Truth is treated as one with being, rather than as a property of the mind. And even if truth is characterized as a yoke between the mind and what is known, it can no more be understood as correspondence than light can be understood as a correspondence between the eyes and what is seen. Truth is not a yoke in the sense of a correspondence between an already existing power of knowing and an already existing and manifest object of knowledge; it is rather that which first provides the power of knowing and the power of being known and even, in its identity with being, the being of what knows and the being of what is known. If it is a yoke, it is one that first constitutes what it yokes. Perhaps it was precisely in order to avoid any misunderstanding here that Plato, though using the metaphor of the yoke in describing the function of light, where there was no danger of light being taken to be some external object that yokes together from the outside two preexisting and already seeing or visible things, *avoided* the metaphor in describing the function of truth. Unfortunately, Plato's care here was lost on Heidegger.

This is not to say that ἀλήθεια in Plato is nothing but a characteristic of being, that is, its being unconcealed. Obviously, if something can be true in the sense of being unconcealed, my relation to it can also be characterized as "true." "Truth" as synonymous with being and "truth" as a description of our comportment toward being are obviously not exclusive, since the former grounds the latter. Thus, if the word ὀρθότερον at 515d4 does express a distinct sense of truth, it is still one inseparable from the identification of "more true" with "more being" that governs the account of the ascent out of the cave. The gaze of the prisoner here is not more ὀρθότερον because it corresponds better to the beings he sees; the beings he sees at this stage of the ascent are ones he has not seen at all before, except very indirectly through their shadows; furthermore, the gaze of the prisoners facing the wall of the cave corresponds perfectly to the shadows before them, so that there can be no question of this correspondence becoming better. If the prisoner who has been turned around sees ὀρθότερον, this can be only in the sense that the objects he sees now for the first time are more real and more unconcealed. Rather than there being an idea of better or worse correspondence here, more or less correct vision, what is assumed is a complete assimilation of seeing to what is seen, so that the seeing becomes ὀρθότερον as the object seen itself becomes ἀληθέστερον. This assimilation is what the Greeks called ὁμοίωσις, which is not correctness or correspondence, contrary to Heidegger's identification of the two in the courses of the 1930s (see GA 34, 8, 12, 17; GA 36/37, 294–95).

One crucial point may require clarification here: to say that Plato did not understand truth as "correspondence" or "correctness" is not to say that he identified it with "unconcealment" and that he did not know the experience of getting things wrong or being mistaken and thus the experience of being right. What this means instead is that Plato did not see this "getting something right" as the essence of ἀλήθεια but rather as something derivative of it. He did not understand ἀλήθεια as the bridging of some fundamental gap between an independently preexisting subject and an independently preexisting object, but rather as the fundamental absence of such a gap, that is, as the light that must always already be there as soon as there is a knower capable of knowing and an object capable of being known. Heidegger's interpretation of ἀλήθεια as "unconcealment" has the merit of helping us to understand this point by drawing our attention both to the "objective" sense of truth in Plato *and* to the Greek association of truth with a certain kind of manifestness, an association particularly evident in the Cave Analogy.[13] This is not to say, however, that "unconcealment" is a fully adequate, or even the best, interpretation of ἀλήθεια in Plato or the Greeks in general. The argument of the present chapter is only that Plato preserves the questionworthiness of ἀλήθεια and does not reduce it to "correctness."

13. Barnes justifies a categorical rejection of the interpretation of ἀλήθεια as "unconcealment" by asserting that even the "objective sense" of truth, which he acknowledges, has nothing to do with unconcealment: "En premier lieu, être vrai au sens objectif ne s'identifie pas du point de vue sémantique avec être non-caché, être non-voilé. On peut cacher les vraies vaches. Les vraies houris sont toujours voilées. Être vrai, même dans son usage objectif, ne signifie jamais être non-caché. (Être ἀληθής ne signifie jamais être ἀκάλυπτος)" ("Heidegger spéléologue," 192). This is certainly true of our objective sense of truth as used of cows, etc., but misses completely what is distinctive of the Greek conception: as Aristotle explicitly claims, those things that are *most true* (ἀληθέστατα, *Metaph.* 993b28–29) are *by nature most manifest* (τὰ τῇ φύσει φανερώτατα πάντων 993b11) even when, due to the limitations of our own vision, they are hidden or invisible *to us*. This is certainly true of the objects outside Plato's cave: as the analogy itself conveys, these objects are by nature brighter and more manifest than

(d) How the Good Loses Its transcendence

(1) THE GOOD AS "BEYOND BEING"   Yet we are by no means done with Heidegger's interpretation. This is because he still has a way of supporting his critique of Plato while granting all of the above. Heidegger could respond as follows: even if being and truth are distinct from, and prior to, the ideas; even if they, and not the good, are the yoke between the ideas as what is known and the power of knowing, it is still the case that the good is made the *cause* of being and truth *and* that the good is an idea. Therefore, even in being subordinated only to the good, being and truth are still being subordinated to an idea, and thus, since the idea is "what is seen," to a seeing. This subordination of truth to what exists for a seeing and thus to seeing itself is what sets it on the way to becoming mere correctness or correspondence.

Yet, even if we put aside for the moment the objections made above to Heidegger's identification of the idea with "what is seen," his critique is countered by a crucial lesson of the Sun Analogy that has not yet been mentioned: *if the good is the cause of being and truth, it exerts this causality not as itself a being or something true, but as beyond truth and being.* While the good can in some sense be described as being and being unconcealed, while it can even be called an ἰδέα and must be so characterized to the extent that it can itself be known, Socrates yet insists that it is a "cause" of being and truth only insofar as it is itself *beyond* being (ἐπέκεινα τῆς οὐσίας, 509b9). In other words, it does not bring about being as itself a super-being or highest-being, but as beyond being altogether. Accordingly, it is not the source of the ideas through being itself a super-idea or highest-idea, but rather through being altogether beyond the being of the ideas. If we acknowledge this transcendence of the good that Socrates emphasizes, then Heidegger's critique as just outlined loses its foundation. In being subordinated to the good, being and truth are not made subservient to the "seeing" of ideas but rather are opened up to a transcendence that surpasses being itself. Instead of a reduction of being and truth to the ideas, we have in the good an attempt to think beyond being and truth and thus beyond the ideas that they illuminate. It is this lesson of

---

the shadows in the cave, even though the prisoners would be completely unable to see them without a long process of habituation. Thus the claim that the prisoners who are turned around will consider the objects they saw earlier as "more true" (ἡγεῖσθαι . . . ἀληθέστερα, 515d6–7) parallels the claim that they will consider these objects "more manifest" (νομίζειν ταῦτα τῷ ὄντι σαφέστερα, 515e3–4). Jan Szaif, in contrast to Barnes, does not rule out an etymological interpretation of ἀλήθεια as unconcealment within the context of the analogy, but does not see this as the sole interpretation at work there. *Platons Begriff der Wahrheit*, 3rd ed. (Munich: Karl Alber, 1998), 145–52. One of his arguments, however, appears based on a misunderstanding: he suggests that the etymological interpretation would incorrectly identify ἀλήθεια with "being-known" or "knowability" (151); Heidegger at least sees "unconcealment" *as what makes possible* "being-known" or "knowability."

the Sun Analogy that must now be explored and shown to resist Heidegger's reading.

Here again elements of Heidegger's interpretation in the courses of the 1930s can be used against him, since he himself there acknowledges, and even emphasizes, the transcendence of the good. According to Heidegger's reading, the good is "beyond being" in the sense that it is the power that makes possible or enables being and unconcealment. As he states the point in 1931–32, the good is the "*empowering [Ermächtigung]* of both being and unconcealment" (GA 34, 99),[14] it is "the enablement of being as such and unconcealment as such" ("die Ermöglichung von Sein als solchem und Unverborgenheit als solcher," 109). Heidegger in this context draws attention to an extraordinary word choice in the text that most commentators oddly ignore: soon after referring to τὴν τοῦ ἀγαθοῦ ἰδέαν (508e2–3), Socrates refers to τὴν τοῦ ἀγαθοῦ ἕξιν (509a5). This substitution of ἕξις for ἰδέα certainly merits reflection, the kind of reflection that is prevented by the common translation of ἕξις as "nature." Heidegger himself comments as follows: "The ἀγαθόν has the character of ἕξις, of that which *is able [was* vermag], that is, what by itself carries the first and last *power [Macht]*. Only in this perspective of making it possible [*Ermöchlichung*] for being and truth at all to happen can what Plato means by the idea of the good be questioned and sought" (GA 34, 105). That translating the phrase in question as "power or capability of the good" would not be unfaithful to the text is shown by the fact that Socrates goes on to describe the good as surpassing being "in power" (δύναμει, 509b9). The good is a power, as is every other idea to a lesser degree, as has been seen; and it is this that allows the substitution of ἕξις for ἰδέα. Heidegger therefore rightly cites in this context the definition of being as δύναμις in the *Sophist*, emphasizing the seriousness and importance of this definition for Plato (110–11).

In 1933–34 Heidegger likewise recognizes that the good, and accordingly each idea, is to be understood as δύναμις. The following passage is especially clear and significant:

> The ἀγαθόν is not only beyond being, but is *in this very transcendence [in der Jenseitigkeit]* in a direct *relation to being and truth* (ἀλήθεια), namely as that which *empowers [ermächtigt]* both in what they are. In worth and in δύναμις and in power, the good is superior [*überlegen*] to

---

14. Already in the SS 1929 *Einführung in das Akademisches Studium*, Heidegger emphasized the good's making possible of truth and thus of human *Dasein*. "Im ἀγαθόν handelt es sich um die Grundermöchlichung des menschlichen Daseins als Offenbarmachens von Seiendem; also um die Ermöglichung des Wesens der Wahrheit" (361). The good is that for the sake of which *Dasein* can be what it is. It is "die Entscheidung des Daseins zu sich selbst als umwillen dessen das Dasein ist, was es ist" (361). What is in the background here is the interpretation of the good as transcendence found in the *Vom Wesen des Grundes* text written at the same time: see WG, 158–59.

all else; the good is itself still power, the power of empowering [*Macht des Ermächtigens*]. The Good is the highest power, in so far as it provides the power for [*ermächtigt zu*] the ὄντως ὄν and the ἀληθινόν, which are on their side already the most powerful [*das Mächtigste ist*] (GA 36/37, 200; see also 203–4).

Heidegger infers that we cannot know the good by perceiving it as an object, but only by putting ourselves under its power: "Not when I take it (the idea of the good) as an object, but rather when I place myself under the *power* [*mich unter die* Macht *einstelle*] that characterizes the power as power, can it be apprehended [*vernehmbar*]" (200). Thus, of the definition of the good as "empowering of being and unconcealment to their shared essence" (200), Heidegger observes: "This however says nothing when it is only defined and not grasped out of a *comportment* [*Haltung*]" (200).

There can be no question that Heidegger's characterization of the good as a power in these courses does justice to its transcendence, both in placing it genuinely beyond the being and truth it empowers and in distinguishing it from any kind of object that could be known through some sort of passive contemplation, insisting instead that it can be apprehended only in a certain comportment. This is not to say that Heidegger's characterization is fully adequate and beyond reproach: it has already been noted in the first chapter how much such a characterization drains the good of any determinate ethical content.[15] However, what is important in the present context is to note what is illuminating and valuable in Heidegger's interpretation: that it takes very seriously and thinks through the transcendence Socrates attributes to the good. What makes this especially noteworthy is that Heidegger's interpretation will only a few years later completely repudiate this transcendence, with disastrous results for the interpretation of Plato.

Yet the greatest virtue of Heidegger's interpretation of the good in the courses of the early 1930s is that he not only tries to think the transcendence of the good, but also reflects on what this transcendence implies for how we think being and truth. In transcending being and truth, the good opens up the

---

15. Heidegger is certainly going too far in claiming that "ἀγαθόν bedeutet nie einen Inhalt, sondern mehr ein 'Wie,' eine ausgezeichnete Weise des Seins" (202; see also 220), that the ἀγαθόν is "nichts *Inhaltliches*" (290). Galston rightly objects to Heidegger's "determined refusal to see Platonic good as related in any way to the beautiful, pleasurable, or desirable." William A. Galston, "Heidegger's Plato: A Critique of *Plato's Doctrine of Truth*," *Philosophical Forum* 13, no. 4 (1982): 384n24. While Galston agrees with Heidegger that "the Good is not the same as moral virtue," he rightly insists that "it is related to it because moral striving is in some ways a reflection of the philosophic quest" (380). For a similar point, see Peperzak, "Did Heidegger Understand Plato's Idea of Truth?" 94–95, and the question at 96: "Does Heidegger want to banish the thought that the ultimate and most originary has ethical connotations and that it can be loved for itself, without any reference to its possible use?"

space *within which* we can bring them into question and thus genuinely make them a matter for thinking. If there were nothing beyond being and truth, if they were in the strongest sense ultimate and insurpassable, then from what perspective could we think them, with a view to what could we question them, in terms of what could we judge their unity? If the good is the power that *enables* being and truth, it is also what enables the *questioning* of being and truth. Indeed, this questioning is precisely the comportment through which we place ourselves under the power of the good and thus "apprehend" it. In bringing being and truth into question, I experience the good that empowers them; indeed, I in some sense reenact this empowering. As Heidegger states the central point in 1931–32, the good is "what we interrogate [*erfragen*] in asking about being and unconcealment,—that which is at issue in such questioning [*worauf es in solchem Fragen ankommt*], that to which we come back in such questioning. What we question there is what grants [*gewährt*] being and unconcealment" (GA 34, 109). On this reading, the good in its transcendence does not answer the question of being, much less prevent this question from being asked; on the contrary, it is what enables the question of being.

But in this case, the good in its transcendence is what enables philosophy as such. Heidegger in 1931–32 does not hesitate to draw this inference. To the suggestion of some scholars that Plato in later dialogues gave up the idea of the good, Heidegger objects that in this case "He would have had to give up the idea of philosophy altogether!" (GA 34, 110). Heidegger even goes on to argue that while Plato's *Seventh Letter* does not name the good, it clearly intends it in the claim that what is ultimately knowable and therefore questionable is "the truly being" (τὸ ἀληθῶς ὄν, 110). Heidegger does not spell out his argument here, but the context makes it clear enough: the characterization of "the truly being" as what is ultimately knowable and questionable is a reference to the good because without the good truth and being could not be questioned. On Heidegger's reading here, the good in Plato is nothing less than what enables philosophy as the questioning of truth and being. Thus, in the 1927 course *Grundprobleme der Phänomenologie*, Heidegger can say of his own questioning of being: "What we are seeking is the ἐπέκεινα τῆς οὐσίας" (GA 24, 404).

(2) IDEA OF THE GOOD?   But if this is so, how can Heidegger already in the courses of the early 1930s, though much more forcefully and dogmatically in later texts, proceed to argue that in making ἀλήθεια dependent on the good Plato fails to think it and instead inaugurates its reduction to mere correctness? If Heidegger himself characterizes the good in its transcendence as that *without which we could not think or question* ἀλήθεια, then how can he turn around and characterize the good as the *obstacle* that kept Plato from thinking or questioning ἀλήθεια? What makes this possible is Heidegger's ultimate

denial of the transcendence *despite* all that he has been seen to acknowledge above. This denial is prepared by a move in Heidegger's interpretation that is both highest questionable and fatal. In the 1931–32 course, immediately after characterizing the good as what empowers and enables being and truth, Heidegger adds the following decisive, and in my view catastrophic, "but": "But when 'the good,' that is, that which is at issue in the questioning of being and truth, is still itself, and it precisely [*gerade es*], an idea, then what we already said about the idea in general is true of this *highest* idea in the *highest* degree. Idea is what is seen [*das Gesichtete*], the vis*able* [*Sichtbare*], essentially related to a *seeing*" (111). It is by this move, and this move alone, that Heidegger can transform the dependence of ἀλήθεια on the good in Plato into a reduction of ἀλήθεια to a relation between seeing and what is seen.

Yet what Heidegger asserts here is not only far from being persuasive but demonstrably incorrect. It is unpersuasive because it simply does not follow that because the good is called an idea, everything must be true of it that is true of the other ideas, only to a greater degree. It is demonstrably incorrect because while the good may be like the ideas in being δύναμις, as *beyond being* in δύναμις it is radically unlike the ideas. One thing that is true of the ideas is not true at all, in any degree, of the good: it is not being (οὐκ οὐσίας ὄντος, 509b8).[16] This is hardly, one must acknowledge, a trivial or negligible difference. Yet it is precisely this difference that Heidegger is neglecting in the cited passage. His "but" does not simply qualify the transcendence of the good which he has just finished describing, but rather turns away from it entirely. Since what Heidegger says here is the linchpin of his critique, these objections deserve to be developed further.

If the good is the cause of truth and being, the power that enables truth and being, this is precisely what the ideas are *not*. As argued above in critique of Heidegger's related error of identifying the ideas with light in Plato's analogy, the ideas are illuminated by, and therefore dependent on, truth and being; they are not the cause of truth and being. This is why only the good, and *not* the ideas, is said to be beyond being. So if both the good and the ideas are δύναμις, and if this enables the good in some contexts to be called an idea and to be described as "of being" (τοῦ ὄντος, *Rep.* 518c5–d1, 526e5) or even "among beings" (ἐν τοῖς οὖσι, *Rep.* 532c4–7),[17] they are still radically different kinds of

---

16. See Robert J. Dostal on this point: "Beyond Being: Heidegger's Plato," in *Martin Heidegger: Critical Assessments*, vol. 2, ed. Christopher Macann (New York: Routledge, 1992), 68–69. One can only agree with Dostal's conclusion that Heidegger "does not adequately attend to the significant distinctiveness of the Good" (69).

17. Passages such as these have been used to deny the transcendence of the good in Plato: see especially M. Baltes, "Is the Idea of the Good in Plato's *Republic* Beyond?" in *Studies in Plato and the Platonic Tradition: Essays Presented to J. Whittake*, ed. M. Joyal (Hampshire: Aldershot, 1997), 3–23.

power. The idea causes the being and truth of particular objects, but it does not cause being and truth as such and therefore is not beyond being and truth. To use again Heidegger's own example, the idea is like the window that, while certainly making visible what is within a room, is not itself the ultimate source of light. In contrast, the good is the ultimate source of light; it is the cause of being and truth *as such*. Therefore, when Heidegger asks the important question of how the good can still be an idea when it lies beyond the ideas, he gives the wrong answer: "Only and simply this: that the highest idea most originally and genuinely carries out [*waltet*] what is in any case already the *job* [*Amt*] of the idea: *allowing the unconcealment* of beings *to spring forth together-with* [*mit-entspringen lassen*] and, as what is envisioned [*das Erblickte*], *to give the being of beings to be understood* [*das Sein des Seienden zu verstehen geben*] (neither without the other)" (GA 34, 99). It is *not* the job or the power of the ideas to enable the springing-forth of being and unconcealment. If the good were itself simply an idea and known as an idea, we would have to posit another principle from which it derives its light.[18] There must therefore be a radical discontinuity and leap between the power that defines the ideas and that which defines the good.

Given this radical discontinuity, even if the ideas were a being-seen relative to a seeing, the mere transfer of this characteristic of the ideas to the good itself would not be justified: that they share one characteristic—which in this case could simply be that both the good and the ideas are powers—does not justify the conclusion that they share all characteristics. Furthermore, the characterization of the ideas as what is visible for a seeing has been shown to be an inadequate characterization even of the ideas, in that it does not do justice to the characteristic of the ideas Heidegger himself emphasizes: that they are δύναμις. And how immeasurably more inadequate must it be as a characterization of the good, which, on Heidegger's own interpretation, is pure δύναμις graspable only by a submission to its power in and through a certain disposition or bearing (*Haltung*).

But for an excellent rebuttal, see Rafael Ferber, "L'Idea del Bene è o non è transcendente? Ancora su ἐπέκεινα τῆς οὐσίας," in *Platone e la Tradizione Platonica: Studi su filosofia antica*, ed. Mauro Bonsái and Franco Trabattoni (Milan: Cisalpino, 2003), 127–49. Ferber does not deny the contradictions in the text, but rather rightly sees that these contradictions are a *consequence* of the good's transcendence: "A maggior ragione è impossibile parlare senza contraddizione dell'aldilà dell'essere, poiché ogni enunciato vero sull'aldilà presuppone a sua volta l'esistenza di questo aldilà" (145).

18. This is a point excellently made by Peperzak: "If we take seriously Plato's analogies concerning the good, it *cannot* be known as a *noēton*, an *ousia*, a truth, or an idea, for if it were, it would presuppose *another* 'light' and *another* source of 'light' to make it knowable. *The good cannot be an idea in the normal 'platonic' sense of the word.* Is this the reason that Plato prefers to speak of 'the good' instead of 'the idea of the good'? Or does the word 'idea' still have that early, vague meaning that permits analogy, homonymy, or ambiguity?" ("Did Heidegger Understand Plato's Idea of Truth?" 98; see also 106).

Heidegger himself emphasizes the difficulty, if not impossibility, of seeing and saying the good. In 1931–32, Heidegger stresses the difficulty of seeing the good (the μόγις ὁρᾶσθαι at 517c1) and what he describes as the even greater difficulty of *saying* something about it (GA 34, 96). Furthermore, in a perceptive but brief interpretation of the *Seventh Letter*, he finds there the view that "the envisioning [*Erblicken*] succeeds, if at all, only in a questioning, learning disposition [*Haltung*]" (97). This interpretation also emphasizes the discursive character of our access even to what is ultimately unsayable: "However, we can understand what cannot be said [*Unsagbare*] only on the basis of first saying correctly what can be said,—said, that is, in and through the work of philosophizing. Only one who knows how to say correctly what can be said can bring himself before what cannot be said" (97–98). Accordingly, in 1933–34 Heidegger insists that the good is not known through some sudden intuition: "Only the work of philosophy, not some so-called intuition [*Intuition*], leads to that which Plato intends" (GA 36/37, 191). Heidegger grants that the good is "unsagbar" compared to other things that can be learned, but then repeats the point he learned from the *Seventh Letter* in 1931–32: "But the unsayable [*das Unsagbare*] is, strictly speaking, what I run up against [*auf was ich stoße*], when I concern myself, and have concerned myself, with what is in the most genuine sense sayable [*das im höchsten Sinne Sagbare*]" (191). All of these perfectly just observations on how we come to know the good hardly support the characterization of it as *das Gesichtete*. The only justification for such a characterization is (1) etymology and (2) a false inference: the inference that if the good can be called an ἰδέα in *any* sense, it must be an ἰδέα in *every* sense in which any other ἰδέα is an ἰδέα.[19]

It can be concluded that the tension already noted between Heidegger's characterization of the ἰδέα as an object that is seen and his characterization of it as *good* in the sense of *making-possible* reaches the breaking point in his account of the good itself. What is in no way justified is precisely the inference Heidegger needs: that to subordinate in any way ἀλήθεια to τὸ ἀγαθόν is to subordinate it to a seeing and being-seen and thus to transform it into the correspondence between subject and object. If ἀλήθεια undergoes a transformation into correctness, this occurs not in Plato's text, which on the contrary poses numerous obstacles to such a transformation, but in Heidegger's own creative distortion of the text. One thing that can be said to characterize this distortion is a focus on the words Plato uses rather than on *how they are used* in a particular context. Momentous conclusions are derived from the mere designation of the good as an ἰδέα, with no acknowledgment that the meaning of the word and the extent of its application are significantly qualified by the other things said about the

---

19. Peperzak goes so far as to claim that the word ἰδέα "must be understood in an equivocal way" here (ibid., 106), but this is probably going too far.

good in the context. If the good is characterized in one context as not being and in another context as of or in being, Heidegger draws whatever conclusions he wishes from each claim without tracing the difference back to the difference in contexts: specifically, in this case, the difference between seeing the good as a cause of being and truth, in which case it must be considered beyond being, and seeing it as itself something to be known or desired, in which case it must be considered as in some sense belonging to being.[20] Furthermore, the word *yoke* has been seen to acquire in Heidegger's reading a life of its own completely divorced from its context in the text: a feature of Heidegger's interpretation that will become even more pronounced later. What is obscured and distorted in all of these cases is precisely what Plato's analogies are meant to indicate, and *only indicate*: the nature and transcendence of the good.

4. Conclusion of Section A

In charting the development of Heidegger's interpretation, it is important to note that the course of WS 1931/32, even after introducing the Sun Analogy into the Cave Analogy, only hints at the transformation of truth into correctness. At 117, Heidegger informs us that the reason why the interpretation of the Cave Analogy was undertaken was to gain a better understanding of ἀλήθεια as unconcealment and of its intimate connection with the essence of man, as indeed a happening of this essence. There is not a word here about truth as "correctness." Rather than attempting to demonstrate the transformation of truth from unconcealment into correctness on the basis of the analogies of the *Republic*, Heidegger instead has recourse, in the second half of the course, to the *Theaetetus* and the characterization there of untruth as falsehood (ψευδής), a characterization that Heidegger sees as resulting in a corresponding conception of truth as ἀψευδές or correctness (see 137). That this

---

20. Alain Boutot at one point asks the important question "Heidegger devait inévitablement rencontrer, à vrai dire, le problème de la transcendance de l'idée du Bien chez Platon. Platon, en effet, n'essaie-t-il pas par là de penser au-delà de l'οὐσία, au-delà de l'étantité en direction de l'être lui-même? Si tel était le cas, Heidegger ne pourrait plus dire que l'être comme tel est resté impensé chez Platon ni que ce dernier marque vraiment l'avènement de ce qu'il appelle le 'nihilisme,' c'est-à-dire l'avènement de l'histoire de l'oubli de l'être." *Heidegger et Platon: Le problème du nihilisme* (Paris: Presses Universitaires de France, 1987), 159. But Boutot then cites the passages describing the good as somehow within being, passages describing the good in the context of our knowledge and desire and saying nothing explicit about its exact relation to being, as by themselves showing that Plato could not think beyond οὐσία and thereby bring it into question (160): as if these passages could simply *cancel* the *explicit assertion* at 509b9–10 that the good is *not* οὐσία but *beyond* οὐσία! There is no doubt still a paradox and a problem in Plato's conception of the good, one that Peperzak expresses in the following question: "How, then, can it, despite its beyondness, be 'seen' and 'known' *as if* it were a being, a truth, an essence, or a virtue?" ("Did Heidegger Understand Plato's Idea of Truth?" 98). But then the problem is that Heidegger and Boutot suppress the paradox and thus fail to think it through. As Peperzak rightly insists, "In any case we will miss the whole secret of 'the good' if we betray all of Plato's efforts by reducing it to the dimension of essences and their manifestation" (ibid.).

turn to the *Theaetetus* backfires by doing more to undermine than support Heidegger's thesis will be the argument of the next chapter. The version of the course delivered in 1933–34, as we have seen, goes further in the direction of what will become the essay "Platons Lehre von der Wahrheit," arguing, on the basis of the Sun rather than the Cave Analogy, that the failure to question the nature of the yoke yoking together the knowledge possessed by the subject and the truth of the object starts taking us down the road to truth as correctness.[21] It is therefore perhaps not only due to time limitations that the discussion of the *Theaetetus* is greatly curtailed and abbreviated in 1933–34: it is no longer as essential to Heidegger's case. Any reference to the *Theaetetus* will of course disappear completely from the essay on Plato's doctrine of truth. Even the interpretation of the Sun Analogy in the 1933–34 course, however, only suggests an inception of the transformation of truth in Plato. Both courses, furthermore, have been seen to contain insights in their interpretation of Plato that resist the reductions required by the thesis of a transformation of the essence of truth. Unfortunately, what will prove to determine Heidegger's later reading of Plato are not the insights, but rather the serious errors and reductive simplifications that, rather than being corrected, will become only more entrenched and more liberated from the text they distort.

The following diagrams will serve to outline and summarize the ways in which Heidegger must transform the Sun Analogy to defend his thesis.

DIAGRAM OF THE SUN ANALOGY

Sun = τἀγαθόν, ἰδέα = ἕξις τοῦ ἀγαθοῦ, ἐπέκεινα τῆς οὐσίας
beyond
↓
Light (φῶς) as yoke (ζυγόν), sun-like (ἡλιοειδῆ)
= truth and being (ἀλήθειά τε καὶ τὸ ὄν), good-like (ἀγαθοειδῆ)
↙   ↓   ↘

| ὄψις = νοῦς the knower's being and power of knowing = the soul (ψυχή) | seeing = knowledge (good-like) ὄψις = γνῶσις (ἀγαθοειδῆ) | τὰ ὁρώμενα = τὰ νοούμενα the being and being-known of the εἴδη = the being (ὃ ἔστιν) of beings |

21. It is possible that the differences between the 1931–32 and 1933–34 courses are even greater than the texts published in the *Gesamtausgabe* would lead us to believe. As Fritsche observes, Heidegger made additions to his manuscript for the 1931–32 course after the course was delivered and certainly when he redelivered the course in 1933–34 on the basis of the same manuscript (HPD, 171–72n23). Given the editorial practice of the *Gesamtausgabe*, to produce a continuous text out of all of the materials available, there is really no way of telling what in GA 34 was delivered in 1931–32 and what represents a later addition. It is certainly possible that as Heidegger developed Plato's "doctrine of truth" in the context of a "history of being," he went back to his manuscript for the earlier courses and made additions/revisions to bring it into line with this doctrine. Therefore, while the present chapter shows that it is possible to trace a development even from the published texts, the development could have been even more extensive and significant than these texts suggest. Until we have a critical edition of these courses, there is no way to know for certain.

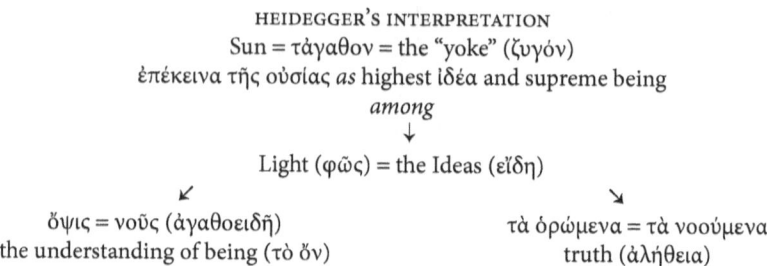

B. PLATO'S TRUTH IN THE *BEITRÄGE* OF 1936–38

1. Truth Under the Yoke Again

A very important stage on the road from the courses of the early 1930s to the essay "Platons Lehre von der Wahrheit" is to be found in the *Beiträge* of 1936–38. Though the discussions of truth in Plato are relatively brief in this text, they are very rich and absolutely decisive for the development of Heidegger's interpretation. Specifically, this text further develops the main points of Heidegger's critique as they began to emerge in the earlier courses while also significantly departing from important aspects of Heidegger's interpretation there, precisely those aspects that have been seen to be in tension with his critique. Furthermore, in the *Beiträge* another philosopher besides Plato makes his influence felt in Heidegger's interpretation of Plato and can probably even be said to guide and determine this interpretation more than anything in Plato's own texts.

We should first consider the important continuity between the *Beiträge* and the earlier courses, a continuity to be found in the perpetuation of a mistake. In the *Beiträge* Heidegger writes: "The relation which Plato already *prepared* [*vorbereitete*] between ψυχή and ἀλήθεια (ὄν) as ζυγόν has since Descartes become with increasing sharpness the subject-object relation" (GA 65, 198). As has been seen, there is in Plato's Sun Analogy no yoke between the soul (ψυχή) and truth (being) (ἀλήθεια [ὄν]) because if anything is the yoke there, it is truth (being) itself. Plato therefore does not in any way prepare the relation that will later become the subject-object relation. Truth (being) is not yoked but is itself the yoke: this means that it is what grounds and makes possible any relation/distinction between knowing subject and known object, rather than being the product of such a distinction; speaking more strictly, it is what grounds the relation between knower and known in such a way that the dichotomy expressed by our terms *subject* and *object* is never allowed to arise. The subject-object relation in Descartes is not an outcome, however distant, of what is to be found in Plato, but rather its complete reversal.

The cited sentence, however, is only an isolated observation in the context of Heidegger's discussion of the relation between thinking and being in Western metaphysics. It is sections 209–11 of the *Beiträge* that deal directly and most thoroughly with Plato's conception of truth. Here we are told again that with Plato "ἀλήθεια is itself forced [*gezwängt*] under the 'yoke'" (332), the yoke of "correctness" (*Richtigkeit*, 333). However, what is highly surprising is that Heidegger here, in contrast to the earlier courses, nevertheless identifies ἀλήθεια with both the light (332) and the yoke (ζυγόν, 333, 335) in Plato's analogy. It is as if he at least partially recognized his earlier mistake and now found himself compelled to acknowledge the relations clearly stated in the text. But if he now must acknowledge that ἀλήθεια is the analogue to light and the yoke, how can he continue to maintain that ἀλήθεια is *yoked under* the yoke of "correctness"? The answer lies in Heidegger's reduction of the light of ἀλήθεια to *both* the *being-seen* or *disclosedness* of beings and their *availability for* (*Zugänglichkeit*) knowing. As thus reduced, ἀλήθεια can no longer itself be the yoke because it must itself be yoked together with knowing; the yoke thus becomes mere correctness (*Richtigkeit*). In other words, though ἀλήθεια starts off as itself the yoke to the extent it is unconcealment, once it becomes only the availability and visibility (*Gesichtetheit*, 33) of beings for knowing, it must itself be yoked under truth as correctness.

But what is the evidence for such a reduction occurring in Plato? What makes it possible for Heidegger to interpret Plato in this way is precisely the mistake he made already in 1931–32: the reduction of "light," and therefore ἀλήθεια, to the visibility of the ideas. This reduction is clear in the following passage: "Therefore, the *brightness* [*die* Helle], that is, the ἰδέα itself as something seen [*Gesichtetes*], is the *yoke*, ζυγόν, though characteristically this is never explicitly said [*nie ausgesprochen*]" (335). The light is thus reduced to the ἰδέα as "something seen," with the result that the ἰδέα must now itself become the yoke. This, as has already been shown, is a serious mistake. Even if the ideas are rightly characterized as nothing more than the visibility of beings (itself questionable), Plato clearly distinguishes this visibility from the light of truth and being that makes it possible. It is significant that Heidegger here must grant that his identification of light with ἰδέα = ζυγόν is never actually said in the text. But for him this silence is "characteristic" ("kennzeichnend"), meaning that it betrays Plato's fundamental thought. We are thus on our way to what in 1940 will become Plato's "unspoken" doctrine of truth. It is as if Heidegger, recognizing now that the doctrine he wishes to attribute to Plato is not to be found in the text, must hand it over to the "unsaid" for safekeeping.[22] Even if one agrees with Heidegger's notorious claim that a thinker's central

---

22. "Die 'Lehre' eines Denkers ist das in seinem Sagen Ungesagte, dem der Mensch ausgesetzt wird, auf daß er dafür sich verschwende" (PLW, 201).

and greatest thought always remains unsaid, the problem is that the "unsaid" doctrine he attributes to Plato does not simply go beyond what is said in the text but directly contradicts it. To maintain that a thinker's greatest thought is to be found in what he leaves unsaid is one thing; to claim that it is to be found in the *opposite* of what he says is quite another.[23]

These sections of the *Beiträge* also show that Heidegger must not only elevate Plato's one-time use of the metaphor of a yoke to a fundamental doctrine, but can identify this yoke with "correctness" only by interpreting it very literally, as something external and subsequent to what it yokes: "The yoke, or truth grasped as a yoke, is the archetype [*Vorform*] for truth as correctness [*Richtigkeit*], insofar as the yoke is grasped and investigated as the *linking* itself [*das* Verknüpfende *selbst*] and not as the ground of the agreement [*der Grund des Übereinkommens gefaßt*]; that is to say, ἀλήθεια is genuinely lost [*geht eigentlich verloren*]" (335). But if instead of basing our interpretation entirely on the metaphor of a yoke taken completely out of context, we base it on a careful reading of the text, it becomes clear that the light of being and truth is the ground that makes possible knowledge and the ideas both individually and in their coming-together; it is not a mere "connection" that brings together preexisting and predisclosed ideas with a preexisting power of knowledge. And the charge that Heidegger takes the metaphor of the yoke completely out of context is very precisely meant: the only context in which Plato uses this metaphor is as a description of light; since Plato clearly does not take light to be a mere link, he clearly does not intend the metaphor to be interpreted this literally. The way in which Heidegger here interprets Plato is comparable to interpreting Heidegger's famous characterization of language as "the house of being" as showing that Heidegger understood language and being as two separate things, with the former only housing the latter as an external container and with the two therefore capable of existing separately, just as the owner of a house can leave his house whenever he wants to.

As in the earlier courses, Heidegger does not in the *Beiträge* go so far as to claim that ἀλήθεια in Plato becomes only correctness. He still acknowledges that ὁμοίωσις is still ἀλήθεια, still rests on the ground of unconcealment. He now adds that ἀλήθεια as such is lost altogether only later in the Roman *rectitudo* (354). This is a crucial qualification because it means that the transformation of truth into mere correctness as opposed to unconcealment occurs well after Plato. This thesis is indeed defended at length in the *Parmenides* course of WS 1942/43 (see especially GA 54, 72–78) and will be examined below in

---

23. And Heidegger presumably would not justify reading into a text the opposite of what it explicitly says. In "Platons Lehre von der Wahrheit" he recognizes the objection that his interpretation "droht in eine gewaltsame Umdeutung auszuarten" (PLW, 216). But as we will see, this is exactly what his interpretation degenerates into.

the chapter dedicated to that course.[24] However, it will be seen that even there Heidegger still understands ὁμοίωσις itself as an *Angleichung* and "adequation" and therefore continues to see in it a fundamental transformation of the earlier essence of truth.

Some of the specific criticisms of Plato's account of ἀλήθεια made in the *Beiträge* can be answered on the basis of the above corrections to Heidegger's interpretation. One such criticism is that "ἀλήθεια remains overall the unconcealment of *beings* [*Unverborgenheit des Seienden*], never that of being [*des Seyns*]" (332). In the Sun Analogy, as we have seen, ἀλήθεια, rather than being treated as a characteristic of beings (e.g., their "visibility"), is identified with being (τὸ ὄν), while both truth and being are distinguished from the ideas they illuminate. It is as the truth of being that ἀλήθεια can cause the disclosedness of the ideas and beings. One can in the same way answer the objection Heidegger states as follows: "the illumination [*das Leuchten*], the brightness [*die Helle*], comes from beings [*vom Seienden her*]. The brightness is seen from the perspective of beings, *insofar as these are* ἰδέα" (335). A fundamental point of Plato's analogy, indeed perhaps the main point, is precisely not to put the origin of the light that illuminates beings in beings themselves nor even in the ideas of beings. And it is precisely because the light does not have its source in beings that Plato must postulate as its origin what is beyond being: the good.

Another criticism is that in being identified with light, ἀλήθεια loses its α-privative character (332); in other words, it becomes, like light itself, something purely positive, something that only discloses without concealing. But in reading so much into the light metaphor taken in isolation, Heidegger appears to forget his own earlier interpretation of the Cave Analogy as a whole. As shown above, that interpretation emphasized the extent to which the analogy showed concealment to belong to the very heart of unconcealment. The story told in the analogy, on Heidegger's reading, shows how truth can occur only in a constant battle with untruth, shows, in other words, that "openness [*Offenbarkeit*] of beings is necessarily in itself the overcoming [*Überwindung*] of a concealment [*Verbergung*]; concealment belongs essentially [*wesensmäßig*] to unconcealment—*as the valley belongs to the mountain*" (GA 34, 90). It is true that Heidegger goes on to suggest that Plato's analogy does not understood unconcealment "originally" (*ursprünglich*) enough because it does not understand concealment (as distinct from what is merely false or apparent) originally enough (GA 34, 93). Significantly, however, and as already noted above, Heidegger must postpone a final judgment on Plato's conception until after a discussion of the idea of the good, to which he now immediately turns (94).

---

24. See Boutot, *Heidegger et Platon*, 207–10.

This is presumably because his claim that Plato did not understand concealment and unconcealment originally enough depends on what his discussion of the idea of the good will try to show: that Plato subjugated and reduced ἀλήθεια to the ideas. Such a reduction of ἀλήθεια to the "visibility" of beings would obviously deprive it of its α-privative character. This reduction, however, has proved to be Heidegger's invention. If Heidegger finds it necessary to turn to the Sun Analogy to support his critique of Plato's conception of truth, this is because the Cave Analogy itself makes clear the property light has of concealing itself in what it illumines and of blinding any attempt to look at it directly, as well as the constant struggle against the greater attraction of darkness that any gradual emergence into the light requires.[25]

The charge Heidegger proceeds to make in the *Beiträge*, that Plato leaves unquestioned "*openness as such* [*die* Offenheit as solche]," is to be answered in the same way as the other criticisms because it is based on the same mistaken assumption: that "ἀλήθεια remains determined by [*festgelegt auf*] accessibility [*Zugänglichkeit*] and demonstrability [*Offenbarkeit* (δηλούμενον)]" (GA 65, 333). Rather than restricting ἀλήθεια to the accessibility and demonstrability of beings, Plato makes it prior to them by grounding it in the good. As neither ultimate nor reduced to the visibility of beings, ἀλήθεια is opened up for questioning. With the good Plato provides a specific direction in which ἀλήθεια can be questioned. Recall that Heidegger himself described this as the function of the good: the good is what we "come back to" in questioning truth and being and therefore what enables such questioning. And yet in the sections of the *Beiträge* focused on Plato's conception of truth, the good is not even mentioned. The reason can be found in how the good is characterized elsewhere in the *Beiträge*, a characterization diametrically opposed to that found in the courses of 1931–32 and 1933–34.

2. The Good Loses Its Transcendence: The ἐπέκεινα Is Demoted to Value (Thanks to Nietzsche)

In the *Beiträge* Heidegger indeed completely reverses his earlier assessment of Plato's characterization of the ἀγαθόν as ἐπέκεινα τῆς οὐσίας. If earlier he saw in the ἀγαθόν as ἐπέκεινα τῆς οὐσίας "what we interrogate [*erfragen*] in asking about being and unconcealment,—that which is at issue in such questioning [*worauf es in solchem Fragen ankommt*], that to which we come back in such questioning" (GA 34, 111), he now sees it as representing "the *denial in*

---

25. Following Heidegger, though not this particular claim in the *Beiträge*, Boutot asserts that the essence of being, which is simultaneously to give itself and hide, disappears with Plato in favor of "la métaphysique de la pleine positivité ontologique, . . . la métaphysique de la pleine lumière" (ibid., 142). One must wonder how any reader of Plato's dialogues could maintain such a thesis.

principle [*grundsätzliche Verleugnung*] of further and more original questioning into beings as a whole, i.e., into being" (211). This reversal is explicit in a note Heidegger made at some point on the margin of his copy of *Vom Wesen des Grundes* next to his claim in that text that the ἀγαθόν is a "ἕξις [*Mächtigkeit*]" that has truth, understanding, and even being in its power: "No! Dasein is not at all grasped [*begriffen*] and not experienced. ἐπέκεινα is also not transcendence, but ἀγαθόν as αἰτία" (GA 9, 160). So why this extraordinary reversal? The answer is to be found in a dramatic change in Heidegger's interpretation of the ἐπέκεινα. As he now interprets it, the good is ἐπέκεινα τῆς οὐσίας not in the sense of genuinely transcending οὐσία, but only in the sense of *adding to οὐσία a relation to man*. The ἀγαθόν, according to Heidegger here, is to be understood as the condition (and thus αἰτία) of human happiness or, more generally, the condition of life (*Bedingung des "Lebens"*). Thus, while Heidegger still understands the ἀγαθόν as what "makes possible," what is "good for" (*tauglich*) something, he no longer interprets it as making possible being and truth, but only as making possible human life. Therefore, to speak of the ἀγαθόν in an ontological context is not to transcend being and thus bring it into question, but rather to relate being to human existence by turning it into a goal, ideal, or "meaning." But in this case, the ἐπέκεινα τῆς οὐσίας, far from giving a direction, a *worauf*, to the questioning of being and truth, completely denies the possibility of such questioning: it takes being as a given, as something obvious and self-evident, and then only relates it to human life by characterizing it as good. In short, to see being as "good" is necessarily to prevent any questioning of being.

What has happened here? What has caused Heidegger to change so drastically his interpretation of the Platonic ἀγαθόν?[26] Is the cause something he has newly discovered in Plato's texts? No. The cause can be stated in one word, or rather one name: Nietzsche. If this influence is not sufficiently clear in Heidegger's characterization of the ἀγαθόν as a "condition of life," it is crystal clear in his characterization of the ἀγαθόν as a step toward value-thinking. If the ἀγαθόν is ἐπέκεινα τῆς οὐσίας only in the sense of relating οὐσία to human life, then it sets us on the one-way and irreversible path toward the reduction of being to a mere value posited by human life for its own self-preservation and self-overcoming. If the transformation of being into a value

---

26. Cf. Boutot's account of the changes in Heidegger's interpretation of the good (ibid., 161–67); however, both Heidegger's courses on the essence of truth from the earlier 1930s and the *Beiträge* were not available to Boutot. See also Jean-François Courtine, *Heidegger et la phénoménologie* (Paris: J. Vrin, 1990), 146–50, and the first chapter of the present book. In the 1938–39 text *Die Überwindung der Metaphysik*, Heidegger explicitly rejects his interpretation of the ἀγαθόν as transcendence in *Vom Wesen des Grundes* in favor of the thesis that the ἀγαθόν is the "destruction" of ἀλήθεια: "Die ungenügende Auslegung des ἐπέκεινα in 'Vom Wesen des Grundes'—im ἀγαθόν die eigentliche Zerstörung der ἀλήθεια" (GA 67, 41; see also 66).

represents the culmination of the oblivion of being, this oblivion begins with Plato's ἀγαθόν. Plato is the precursor of Nietzsche or, more specifically, the great-great-grandfather of Nietzsche's nihilism. Thus, at one point Heidegger can characterize Nietzsche's question about the *value* (*Wert*) of truth as "a genuinely *platonizing* [*platonisierende*] question" (216). The interpretation of being and truth in terms of the ἀγαθόν is a decisive step toward the interpretation of them as values. Heidegger makes no secret of the fact that he is here interpreting Plato through Nietzsche's eyes. At one point he explicitly credits Nietzsche with being the first to see "the key position [*Schlüsselstellung*] of Plato and the importance [*Tragweite*] of Platonism for the history of the West (the emergence of nihilism)" (219).[27]

But what reason is there for accepting this interpretation of Plato as a "proto-Nietzsche," apart from the compelling narrative it produces of the history of metaphysics as nihilism? While the ἀγαθόν in the *Republic* is certainly characterized as a principle of action and decision, there is no suggestion that it is this relation to human existence that makes it ἐπέκεινα τῆς οὐσίας. On the contrary, what is said to make the ἀγαθόν ἐπέκεινα τῆς οὐσίας is its being the source, or the "provider," of being and truth. *This* account of the good's transcendence, however, despite being Plato's own account, is simply ignored in the *Beiträge* discussion in favor of the account inspired by Nietzsche. Plato's account is also presumably preempted by the dogmatic assertion that Plato's questioning concerns only beings and their beingness: "But because the question only concerns beings and their beingness [*Seiendheit*], it can never hit upon being itself [*das Seyn selbst*] under the impulse of being [*von diesem her*]" (210).

In one of the Nietzsche lectures, *Der europäische Nihilismus* (SS 1940; GA 6.2), we find the argument that to characterize being as a condition at all, whether or not a condition of human life, is already to inaugurate the retreat of being before beings, since a condition necessarily retreats before what it conditions, and to proceed on the path toward the understanding of being as a mere value conditioning life. This argument, however, itself rests on distortions of the Sun Analogy, distortions that again amount to ridding the ἀγαθόν of its transcendence. These are the principal moves, all of which are untenable:

(1) After identifying the "third" (*Dritte*) between seeing and visibility with light (φῶς), Heidegger identifies the third between knowing and what is known with the idea of the good (GA 6.2, 200). While Heidegger earlier

---

27. Boutot rightly asks if Heidegger's reading of Plato is not secretly determined by Nietzsche's: "Autrement dit, Heidegger ne verrait-il pas Platon et le platonisme à travers Nietzsche lui-même?" (*Heidegger et Platon*, 290). See Boutot's discussion of the convergences between Heidegger's and Nietzsche's interpretations of Plato (291–98). His conclusion is that "Heidegger, parlant de Platon et du platonisme, est peut-être plus nietzschéen qu'il ne le pense" (300).

made the mistake of making the ideas the analogue to light, now he makes the mistake of making the good the analogue to light. Both are mistakes because, to repeat again the point that must be repeated ad nauseam in confronting Heidegger's reading, the analogue to light is ἀλήθεια, which is not the good but only good-like (ἀγαθοειδῆ, 509a3–4).

(2) The ἐπέκεινα τῆς οὐσίας is effectively eliminated in the following extraordinary sentence, which purports to tell us the only meaning this phrase can possibly have: "This can only mean: if the ἀγαθόν remains in the fundamental character of the ἰδέα, it constitutes the genuine essence of beingness [*das eigentliche Wesen der Seiendheit*]" (201).[28] Note the peculiar reasoning both implicit and explicit here: Because the ἀγαθόν is called an ἰδέα, and because ἰδέα is Plato's interpretation of οὐσία (as Heidegger has just finished arguing, 194), to say that the ἀγαθόν is ἐπέκεινα τῆς οὐσίας can only mean that it is the οὐσία (*das eigentliche Wesen*) of οὐσία. Here we see a feature of Heidegger's reading that has been encountered before: the reference to the ἀγαθόν as an ἰδέα—where ἰδέα is of course interpreted in Heidegger's peculiar way—takes precedence in the interpretation of the ἀγαθόν over anything else that might be said about it. Here Heidegger goes so far as to deduce from nothing but the designation of the ἀγαθόν as ἰδέα the *only meaning* the phrase ἐπέκεινα τῆς οὐσίας can have, even though this is neither the meaning he himself gave the phrase only a few years earlier nor the meaning Socrates gives it. According to Socrates' account, what is meant by the claim that the good is ἐπέκεινα τῆς οὐσίας is that it cannot itself be being (οὐκ οὐσίας ὄντος, 509b8) since it is that through which being comes to beings. But what is the importance of what Socrates says compared to what is left unsaid in the designation of the ἀγαθόν as ἰδέα? In any case, Heidegger cannot cite the phrase οὐκ οὐσίας ὄντος here because his present argument is precisely that the ἀγαθόν is Plato's interpretation *of being* and that therefore Plato understands being as "condition of possibility," since ἀγαθόν means "what makes possible" ("was zu etwas taugt," 201).

(3) Even earlier, as shown above, Heidegger understood the ἀγαθόν as "making-possible," but as making possible being and truth themselves ("die Ermöglichung von Sein als solchem und Unverborgenheit als solcher," GA 34, 109). Now, however, since the good has been identified with being, it can only be what makes *beings* possible ("was das Seiende tauglich macht, Seiendes zu sein," 201).

(4) In this way we have the completion of a move that was already seen to be underway earlier: the making-possible that characterizes the good is completely assimilated to the making-possible that characterizes the ideas.

28. The same interpretation is to be found in the 1938/39 *Die Überwindung der Metaphysik*: there the good is said to transcend οὐσία only in the sense that it "das Wesen der Seiendheit bestimmt" (GA 67, 163).

The ἀγαθόν, like an idea, simply makes it possible for beings to be beings. This is apparently the explanation of another odd misinterpretation of the text: Heidegger asserts that "The idea as such, i.e., the being of beings, contains the character of ἀγαθοειδές, of that which makes suitable for [*tauglich zu*] . . . —namely, makes beings suitable to be beings. Being receives the essential trait [*Wesenszug*] of making possible [*des Ermöglichenden*]" (204). If we look at the text, we see that what Socrates characterizes as ἀγαθοειδές is not at all the ideas, but rather knowledge (ἐπιστήμη) and truth (ἀλήθεια, 508e6–509a3). This is surely significant: what is like the good are not the ideas in their character as the being of beings, but rather that which first enables the ideas to be disclosed as such and known. But Heidegger's reading, here as elsewhere, reduces everything to the ideas. Indeed, Heidegger here appears to go even further in this direction by effectively reducing the ἀγαθόν to the sum total of all the ideas. This is evident in the passage just cited: if the ideas are the being of beings as what makes it possible for beings to be, and if the ἀγαθόν is the being of beings as what makes it possible for beings to be, then the ideas are not only ἀγαθοειδές, but are the ἀγαθόν itself.

(5) If the ἀγαθόν is characterized as "making-possible" (*Ermöglichung*, δύναμις) in the earlier courses, it is now characterized as "that which makes possible" (*Ermöglichendes*, δύνατον, 201). This change sets the stage for Heidegger's claim that the ἀγαθόν = being is, as a condition, necessarily experienced as *a* being, as what is *most a* being (*Seiendste*). This of course opens the way to finding onto-*theology* in Plato. Accordingly, in the *Beiträge* one finds the interpretation of the ἐπέκεινα as God (θεός) and the divine (θεῖον, GA 65, 211).

Heidegger's charge that Plato interpreted being as a condition of possibility *for* beings, and thus as something that must give way to the beings it serves, thus rests on several claims that are simply untenable as interpretations of what is said in the Platonic text. If the ἀγαθόν is a condition of possibility, it is such not as being but as beyond being, and therefore as making possible not beings but being itself. It should be added here, however, that one must be very careful with terms such as *making possible* and, most of all, the term Heidegger introduces in the Nietzsche course, *conditioning* (*Bedingung*). Nothing that can legitimately be translated with these terms is to be found in Plato's text, and with good reason. Though Plato certainly makes the good in some sense "responsible" for (ἀιτία) being and truth, an interpretation of this "responsibility" as a "conditioning" and "making possible" runs the risk of anachronism and of reducing the relations in question here to ontic relations between beings. The ἀγαθόν is not a "thing" that conditions (*bedingt*) other things; neither it nor the ἀλήθεια τε καὶ τὸ ὄν for which it is responsible are things or beings. On the other hand, the ἀγαθόν is not some logical condition of possibility for theoretical entities. What language to use in describing the relation between the ἀγαθόν and truth and being is of course, as Plato well knows, a serious problem, even greater here, presumably, than it is in the case of describing the relation between the ideas and sensible objects. Plato's only solution is to speak in metaphors and similes, to avoid committing himself to one particular description of the relation in question (the existence in the dialogues of many very different ways of characterizing the relation between ideas and sensible objects is notorious), and even to cultivate a certain ambiguity and indirectness. Consider how he characterizes the relation between the ἀγαθόν, being, and what is: "Through the good (ὑπὸ τοῦ ἀγαθοῦ) not only does being-known come to be-with (παρεῖναι) the things that are known, but also to-be and being (τὸ εἶναί τε καὶ τὴν οὐσίαν) come to be-towards (προσεῖναι) them by way of the good (ὑπ' ἐκείνου)" (509b6–8). This passage cannot receive here the careful and detailed analysis it clearly requires. It is safe to say, however, that what is *not* to be found amidst all the variants of being at play in this passage is that "conditioning" that Heidegger wants to make *the* Platonic interpretation of being.

The characterization of the good as an ontic condition also depends on misinterpreting the Socratic analogy that receives the least attention from Heidegger: the Divided Line. In the context of this analogy, Socrates describes dialectic as moving beyond and even destroying "hypotheses" (τὰς ὑποθέσεις ἀναιροῦσα, 533c8) by treating them literally as "what lies under," not in the sense of principles or starting points (οὐκ ἀρχὰς), but rather as springboards or jumping-off points (οἷον ἐπιβάσεις τε καὶ ὁρμάς, 511b4–5). What dialectic thereby arrives at is what is beyond hypotheses and in no way itself an hypothesis: the good as ἀνυπόθετον. It is not necessary to confront the many controversies and ambiguities that plague the interpretation of the Divided Line and the account of dialectic offered there in order to see the extent to which Heidegger must invert what Socrates explicitly says.[29] In order to make the analogy consistent with the interpretation of the good and the ideas discussed above, Heidegger must first interpret the word ὑπόθεσις as meaning "condition." It is not hard to see that this is a complete inversion of the meaning the word receives in the text. On Socrates' account, dialectic understands the hypotheses not as that from which we descend to subordinate things they make possible (this is at best how mathematics understands them, which is why mathematics is not the upper section of the Line), but rather as springboards from which we jump up and which we therefore put beneath us. Rather than being a condition, the hypothesis is an aid and provocation to a way of thinking that transcends it (τῶν ὑποθέσεων ἀνωτέρω ἐκβαίνειν, 511a6–7). The

---

29. For a detailed interpretation of the Divided Line and an evaluation of the major interpretations that have been offered, see my *Dialectic and Dialogue: Plato's Practice of Philosophical Inquiry* (Evanston: Northwestern University Press, 1998), 218–44.

second thing Heidegger must do is even more extreme and more directly in contradiction with both the letter and spirit of Plato's text: since he wishes to reduce the good to being nothing but an ultimate condition of possibility, he must characterize it as being itself a ὑπόθεσις and thus eliminate the very distinction between the ὑποθέσεις and the ἀνυπόθετον. In other words, he must suppress the ἀνυπόθετον in the Divided Line Analogy in the same way in which he suppresses the ἐπέκεινα τῆς οὐσίας in the Sun Analogy. Both the reduction of the ὑπόθεσις to a condition (for the sake of the beings it conditions)[30] and the collapse of the distinction between ὑπόθεσις and ἀνυπόθετον are explicit in the following passage from the *Beiträge*: "Following from this beginning being (beingness) then becomes ὑπόθεσις, or more precisely [*genauer*] the ἀνυπόθετον, in whose light all that is and all that is not comes to presence [*anwest*]. And so being [*das Seyn*] holds sway [*waltet*] for the sake of beings" (229). While Heidegger insists that being is for Plato a presupposition on the basis of which we can turn to beings, Plato's own analogies characterize being as a springboard beyond which dialectic must question. While Heidegger insists that the good is only being understood as an ontic condition of possibility, Plato's own analogies characterize the good as what cannot be laid down as a ground for anything else, but can be approached only through the never-ceasing questioning and "destruction" of all "grounds" (ἀνυπόθετον). The Good as ἀνυπόθετον is not a more ultimate condition or ground, but rather no ground or condition at all. It is instead that which we can catch a glimpse of only in jumping beyond all conditions or grounds in bringing into question any secured starting points. It is indeed an ἀρχή (510b6, 511b6) but in the sense not of ground or condition, but of the ultimate direction of all questioning and thinking.

In both the *Beiträge* and the 1940 Nietzsche lecture, in conclusion, *both* the ἐπέκεινα τῆς οὐσίας and the ἀνυπόθετον are eliminated *as Socrates explains them*. The effect is not only to identify the ἀγαθόν with being but also to make it responsible for a subordination of being to beings by seeing in it the transformation of being into a condition for beings or a condition for human life. The ἀγαθόν is thus seen as blocking the way to any questioning of being and as indeed inaugurating the eclipse of being behind beings. Yet as we have seen, when in the earlier courses Heidegger remains faithful to how the ἐπέκεινα τῆς οὐσίας is explained in the text, he arrives at the opposite conclusion: that the ἀγαθόν opens the space for, and provokes, the fundamental bringing into

---

30. See also the following from the 1944 *Übung*: "Die Idea ist also das Ermöglichende. Plato gebraucht aber nicht das Wort 'das Ermöglichende,' er gebraucht dafür das Wort: 'Hypothesis.' Wörtlich heißt Hypothesis 'das Untergesetzte.' Die Hypothesis ist die Gesamtumriß des Wissens" (GA 87, 287). See also at 263, where the idea as "hypothesis" is explicitly related to Nietzsche's understanding of values as *Bedingungen*.

question of being and truth. Even then, however, this reading was in tension with Heidegger's insistence that the ἀγαθόν is ἰδέα in exactly the same way the other ideas are. Now it is this latter view that is allowed to dominate and to eliminate the other one in tension with it. The reason for this is again Nietzsche. Only by abandoning his earlier, both richer and more faithful interpretation of Plato's ἀγαθόν can Heidegger turn Plato into a proto-Nietzsche and thus into the originator of that metaphysical tradition said to culminate in Nietzsche. There is no question that the kind of thinking in terms of values and cultural goods that Heidegger describes does indeed block all genuine questioning. But to read such thinking back into Plato's idea of the good, even if only to see it prefigured and anticipated there, requires what can only be characterized as an extremely reductive and irresponsible reading of Plato's texts. The resulting narrative of the history of metaphysics is powerful and can provoke important questions. It becomes a danger to thought, however, when it suppresses possibilities that are there in the Platonic texts and proceeds on the basis of such an obstruction to call for a radical leap into a new beginning.

C. PLATO'S DOCTRINE OF TRUTH IN 1940

It is only against the background of the courses on the essence of truth from the first half of the 1930s and Heidegger's reflection on these courses in the *Beiträge* of 1936–38 that we can now fully understand and assess what is taking place in the 1940 essay on "Plato's Doctrine of Truth."[31] Against the earlier courses, one can see the extent to which the later essay eliminates or suppresses those elements of Heidegger's earlier interpretation that were seen to be in tension with the thesis of the subjugation of truth to being-seen and seeing and thus its transformation into correctness; one can also see that the essay can depart from the earlier interpretation in this way only by means of

---

31. Heidegger tells us that it was "zusammengestellt" in 1940 (WM, 477), though it was first published in 1942. Dostal strangely gives 1930/31 as the date the essay was written ("Beyond Being," 61), presumably on the basis of Heidegger's claim that the "Gedankengang" goes back to the 1930–31 (an error for 1931–32) course (WM, 477). Obviously, to say that the path of thinking pursued in an essay goes back to 1930/31 is not to say that it was *written* in 1930/31. Even stranger is the claim by María del Carmen Paredes that "the new development of Heidegger's thought can be traced, as far as the question of truth is concerned, in the years between the lecture of 1930 and its final version published in 1943." "*Amicus Plato magis amica veritas*: Reading Heidegger in Plato's Cave," in HPD, 116. Here the distinction between the lecture course and the later essay is collapsed as much as possible (and the context shows Paredes to be referring to these texts despite the mistaken dates given in both cases). It is especially important to maintain this distinction because, as we will see, it would not have been even possible for the 1940 essay, in its final and published form, to have been written in 1931/32, for two related reasons: it departs on a number of crucial points from the interpretation in the 1931–32 course, and it relies heavily on the intervening interpretation of Nietzsche.

even greater violence to Plato's text, when it considers the text at all. Against the *Beiträge,* one can see the later essay as the culmination of the coarsening and simplification of Plato's position already underway in the *Beiträge;* one can also see the extent of the essay's unacknowledged debt to Nietzsche (though Nietzsche is explicitly present in the last few pages of the essay). In short, against the background that has been described in the present chapter, the 1940 essay must be seen as exaggerating the worst features of Heidegger's interpretation of Plato and eliminating the good, or as, in other words, a kind of self-caricature. This is undoubtedly a very harsh judgment, but whether or not it is justified can be decided only on the basis of the following analysis.

1. The Transformation of the Ascent from One of Greater Unconcealment and Freedom to One of *Bildung*

With regard to the story of liberation recounted in the Cave Analogy, Heidegger's reading in the essay agrees with his earlier reading to the extent of acknowledging that a conception of truth as unconcealment is at work in this story. Thus here, as in the earlier courses, he interprets the descent back into the cave as showing that "truth originally means that which is wrenched free of concealment [*das einer Verborgenheit Abgerungene*]" (PLW 221). Heidegger even goes on to suggest that the Cave Analogy would be impossible without an understanding of truth as unconcealment: "the unconcealment related to what is concealed (distorted and hidden) [*Verborgenes (Verstelltes und Verhülltes)*], and only it, has an essential relation to the image of a cave lying underneath the daylight. Where truth is of another essence and is not unconcealment, or is not at least partially determined by it, there a 'Cave Analogy' has no hold on the imagination [*keinen Anhalt der Veranschaulichung*]" (222). Here Heidegger is simply repeating a central thesis of his earlier courses.

Yet a crucial departure takes place when Heidegger immediately qualifies the cited claim by asserting that despite the experience of truth as unconcealment in the Cave Analogy, "a different essence of truth pushes itself forward into the predominant position [*in den Vorrang*] instead of unconcealment" (222). This is a much stronger assertion than anything found in the earlier courses. There, as we have seen, though Heidegger claims to see some indications of an emerging conception of truth as correctness, the conception of truth as unconcealment remains predominant; furthermore, these indications are not found in the story of the Cave Analogy itself, but in the account of the good provided by the Sun Analogy. Now Heidegger sees the conception of truth as correctness as dominating in the Cave Analogy the conception of truth as unconcealment, which allows him still to acknowledge that the latter remains to some extent present.

This general shift in Heidegger's reading is facilitated by a specific change in his interpretation that allows the sense of truth as correctness to pervade and dominate the very history recounted in the Cave Analogy in a way that it did not before. This change concerns the notion of παιδεία, the very notion that Socrates identifies as what the analogy is supposed to illustrate. In the 1940 essay, Heidegger first characterizes παιδεία in general terms as "this re-accommodation and accommodation [*Um- und Eingewöhnung*] of man's essence to the realm assigned to him at any given time" (214). But then he proceeds to suggest precisely the translation of παιδεία that he had vehemently rejected earlier. In 1931–32 (GA 34, 114) and 1933–34 (GA 36/37, 207, 217), Heidegger refused categorically to translate παιδεία as *Bildung*. Instead, he there identified παιδεία with "the *self-possession* [*Gehaltenheit*] of man, springing from the 'comportment' [*Haltung*] of making one's way and taking a stand [*des sich durchsetzenden Standhaltens*], a comportment in which man amidst beings as a whole takes a hold for his own essence through a free choice [*durch freie Wahl den Halt nimmt für sein eigenes Wesen*],—that, for which and within which he empowers himself in his essence [*sich selbst in sein Wesen ermächtigt*]" (GA 34, 114–15). Given that it belongs to the essence of a human being to exist within the unconcealment of beings as a whole—what Heidegger takes the Cave Analogy to show—παιδεία is explicitly taking a stand within this unconcealment, which requires recognizing it as such, in a way that is decisive for one's essence. This is why Heidegger can proceed to identify παιδεία as thus interpreted with "philosophizing, understood as questioning one's way through to being and unconcealment, i.e., to that which still empowers these themselves" (115). This questioning comportment, made possible by the good as that which, empowering being and truth, opens up the space for the questioning of being and truth, is also what Heidegger has been seen to call *freedom*. Taking a stand within unconcealment as such, a stand that must always be a questioning comportment, is the παιδεία that constitutes freedom. On this interpretation, then, παιδεία is defined by a conception of truth as unconcealment; παιδεία *is* a certain way of existing in unconcealment.

In the 1940 essay, in contrast, the German word Heidegger claims to come closest to what is named by παιδεία ("am ehesten noch, wenngleich nicht völlig, genügt") is none other than *Bildung* (PLW, 215). Here, of course, he does not understand this word in its nineteenth-century meaning, but rather in a meaning derived from its etymology: *Bildung* is a *bilden*, a *forming*, by means of an "anticipatory measuring-up to a paradigmatic look [*vorgreifenden Anmessung an einem maßgebenden Anblick*], which is therefore called the model [*Vor-bild*], 'Bildung' is at the same time an impressing [*Prägung*] and a being-led by an image [*ein Bild*]" (215). Here we can see that the difference between the earlier interpretation of παιδεία and the present one goes far beyond the choice of words: in the earlier interpretation, παιδεία is a stand in unconcealment characterized by a questioning that puts being and truth themselves in question from the perspective of what empowers them. Now παιδεία has become something much more narrow and much less radical: it means being guided by a certain look or "picture" of the world, measuring onself up to this look or "picture" as to a paradigm. If παιδεία was earlier the process of liberation into ever greater unconcealment, it is now a turn to paradigmatic objects and conformity to these objects. Judged against the earlier identification of παιδεία with freedom, παιδεία as *Bildung* is the negation of such freedom, and this because it is the absence of any genuine questioning. To be "cultivated" is not to question, but only to measure up to a paradigm already given and accepted as self-evident.

But why this radical change in Heidegger's interpretation? Why this transformation of παιδεία from a questioning of being and unconcealment into mere conformity to some ideal picture or look? The reason is not hard to see: the current interpretation of παιδεία allows truth as correspondence and correctness to dominate the Cave Analogy in its entirety. The ascent the analogy describes thereby becomes an ascent of increasingly *greater adequation* to some paradigmatic looks, that is, the ideas outside the cave. Heidegger has transformed the παιδεία that the Cave Analogy is meant to illustrate into nothing but the correspondence between a looking (*blicken*) and a look (*Anblick*). That this is Heidegger's strategy is made clear on page 124, where he suggests, with some air of mystery, that the *Bildung* described in the analogy presupposes a fundamental transformation in the essence of truth. How indeed could it *not* presuppose this when Heidegger has already built such a transformation into his interpretation of παιδεία as *Bildung*, an interpretation presented dogmatically, without even a gesture toward evidence or justification? Is it not enough to see Heidegger's strategy in order for its arbitrariness, not to say dishonesty, to condemn it?

It is not until near the end of the essay that we discover another reason for Heidegger's decision to translate παιδεία as *Bildung*: it enables Heidegger to discover in Plato the beginning of "humanism" (233–34). "Humanism," as Heidegger understands it here, means placing man in the center of beings and making man in some sense the measure for what is, with the necessary consequence that neither the truth of being nor the essence of man can be brought into question. *Bildung* takes for granted an interpretation of the being of beings as a "look" (ἰδέα) existing for a human looking and is in this sense humanism. The transformation of truth from the unconcealment of being into a property of human seeing and asserting (correctness) is humanism. The ἀγαθόν as Heidegger interprets it in the *Beiträge*, that is, as adding to οὐσία only a relation to man, thus leaving both οὐσία and the essence of man unquestioned, is humanism. It is this humanism, therefore, that Heidegger is from the start reading into παιδεία by interpreting it as *Bildung*. Here again the contrast with the interpretation in the courses of the 1930s could not be starker. In the 1933–34 course, Heidegger criticizes, with the following words, Jaeger's translation of παιδεία as "Formung des griechischen Menschen," along with the translations *Bildung* and *Erziehung*: "But that is a notion of scholars [*Gelehrtenvorstellung*]; that is not what is at issue here, that is humanistic [*humanistisch*]" (GA 36/37, 207). If Heidegger now accepts the translation *Bildung*, it is precisely because he needs to make παιδεία 'humanistisch.'"[32] If, after all, Plato must be made the beginning of metaphysics, he must also be made the beginning of humanism, since for Heidegger humanism and metaphysics are the same thing.

But apart from Heidegger's need to introduce truth as correctness and humanism into the Cave Analogy, what recommends his interpretation of παιδεία? Apparently nothing in Plato's text; on the contrary, Socrates' description of the ascent seems impossible to square with Heidegger's reading. At 128 Heidegger describes παιδεία as "the continual habituation in the fixing of one's look on the fixed limits of things that stand fixed in their look" ("die stetige Eingewöhnung in das Festmachen des Blickes auf die festen Grenzen der in ihrem Aussehen feststehenden Dinge," 128). Does this correspond to the συνηθεία (516a5) Socrates describes as taking place outside the cave? What Socrates describes is the freed prisoner's gradual adjustment to the light so that increasingly more and brighter objects become visible to him in this light. As was the case also within the cave, he "sees better" only in the sense that *truer objects* gradually become visible to him. Furthermore, each thing that becomes visible does so only as a step toward something else becoming visible; the prisoner does not look at the reflections in the water for their own sake but only on the way to seeing the originals. The entire process of course culminates in seeing the sun itself as the source of all light. But here too Socrates does not describe the prisoner as simply staring at the sun but instead as "reasoning" (συλλογίζοιτο, 516b9; also 517c1). So is there anywhere in the συνηθεία Socrates describes a learning of how to fix one's look fast onto the fixed limits of things standing fast in their look? Clearly not. The habituation has *nothing* to do with learning how to make one's vision correspond as accurately and correctly as possible to fixed objects with fixed limits. There is

---

32. In Heidegger's notes for the 1933–34 course, there is a hint of the direction his reading will take in the future. Claiming again that παιδεία is neither *Bildung* nor *Erziehung* nor *Formung*, he then adds this qualifying observation: "Beachte: und doch in gewisser Weise Recht, *weil bei Platon* ein Anderes beginnt" (GA 36/37, 291). It is this "other" that Heidegger sees as partly justifying the translation *Bildung* that will come to dominate his interpretation later.

only a becoming visible of things previously not visible as one's eyes adjust, *not to the things themselves, but to the light*; there is no question here of seeing the things more or less "correctly."

This is not to say anything that Heidegger did not himself say in the early 1930s. In the 1931–32 course, he characterizes the συνηθεία Socrates describes as a "*slow becoming-familiar [langsames Vertrautwerden]*—not so much with the things, but rather with the illumination [*Leuchten*] and the brightness [*Helle*] itself" (GA 34, 43); and as has already been noted above, he accordingly characterizes the habituation outside the cave as a process of ever greater unconcealment, rather than as some improvement in the accuracy and fixedness of one's looking. On page 227 of the 1940 essay, Heidegger identifies παιδεία with "making man free and firm [*frei und fest*] for the clear constancy of the view of the essence [*die klare Beständigkeit des Wesensblickes*]." This too is not only a major departure from the earlier identification of human freedom with unconcealment, but is also untenable as an interpretation of the text. What is described as taking place outside the cave is not some clear constancy of a look, but a fluid process of ever greater unconcealment culminating in a process of reasoning.

In conclusion, Heidegger's reversal of his own earlier interpretation of παιδεία is not demanded by anything in the text, but only by what he has already determined to be Plato's "doctrine of truth." Of course, if Heidegger later in the essay can support his claim that a conception of truth as correctness dominates Plato's analogy, then this might in retrospect provide some support for his reading of παιδεία. But little support will in fact be provided by Heidegger's later remarks, which is perhaps why he begins with his question-begging interpretation of παιδεία. In any case, it is Plato's text that, as usual, presents the greatest obstacle to Heidegger's reading.

2. The Yoke Becomes All-Powerful

What Heidegger's essay provides as the main argument for the supposed transformation of the essence of truth in Plato is Plato's supposed subordination of truth to the appearance of the idea. This, as we have seen, is essentially the argument Heidegger begins to sketch out, though very vaguely, in the courses of the 1930s. However, the subordination of truth to the idea is made even more calamitous in the essay by a more reductive interpretation of the ἰδέα. While in the earlier courses Heidegger asserted that "to *make beings possible* [*ermöglichen*], is the *essence of the idea*" (GA 36/37, 194), he now asserts that "the essence of the idea lies in the ability to shine and be seen [*Schein- und Sichtsamkeit*]" (PLW 223). In other words, the being and essence of the ideas is no longer understood primarily as δύναμις; their capability or power is fully subordinated to their visibility. Another related shift is that while Heidegger could earlier identify the idea with the essence *and* existence of beings, it is now fully reduced to *what* something is: the ideas are taken as evidence that "for Plato being has its genuine essence in what-being" (223). In this case, to subordinate truth to the idea is to subordinate it to nothing but the look of a thing, *what* a thing *shows itself* as. And Heidegger now makes fully explicit what was suggested in the earlier courses: that to the extent that unconcealment is subordinated to the idea interpreted as a "look," it is subordinated to seeing, made "relative" to seeing (224). In such a subordination truth can be nothing more than a certain adjustment of seeing to the look of the idea, that is, it can be nothing more than a certain "correctness" in seeing, as well as in speaking.

But what is the evidence for this subordination taking place in Plato? In the essay, Heidegger does little more than dogmatically assert the existence of such a subordination. But his assertions can now be seen to depend on the misreading of the Sun Analogy encountered in the earlier courses. The linchpin of his critique is the following crucial claim: "'unconcealment' now means the unconcealed [*das Unverborgene*] always as what is accessible through the shine of the idea [*als das durch die Scheinsamkeit der Idee Zugängliche*]" (224). It is in this way that unconcealment is made relative to seeing and thus correctness. As has been shown above, however, the Sun Analogy maintains the opposite: not that truth is what is made accessible through the idea, but rather that truth, in its sameness with being, that is, as unconcealment, is what shines (καταλάμπει) upon the idea. This analogy gives truth the same priority over the idea, as what is known, that light has over the object it makes visible. It is therefore simply mistaken to claim, as Heidegger does in defending the view that unconcealment is reduced to what is perceived in the perceiving of an ἰδέα, that "the unconcealed [*das Unverborgene*] is from the outset and exclusively conceived as what is perceived in the perceiving [*Vernehmen*] of an ἰδέα, as what is known in knowing [*Erkennen*] (γιγνώσκειν)" (223). It is not that case that the Sun Analogy identifies ἀλήθεια with *what is known* (γιγνωσκόμενον), as Heidegger already mistakenly assumed in the earlier courses; on the contrary, it sharply distinguishes the light of ἀλήθεια from what is known as that which makes it possible for anything to be known or to be at all.[33] What is known is the idea; what makes knowing possible is ἀλήθεια. Therefore, when Heidegger identifies the unsaid doctrine of the Cave Analogy with "the event in which the

---

33. Blake E. Hestir rightly comments, in interpreting 508d4–6, that "if, as the Sun Analogy suggests, Socrates is claiming that sight is analogous to knowledge and light is analogous to truth, it follows that truth is something quite different from knowledg—after all, when the sun provides light to a visible thing like a tree, that doesn't mean that light or illumination becomes the tree. So it cannot be the case that truth is the *same thing* as the epistemic capacity that Socrates identifies as knowledge." "Plato on the Split Personality of Ontological *Alētheia*,"*Apeiron* 37, no. 2 (2004): 122–23.

ἰδέα becomes master [*Herrwerden*] over ἀλήθεια" (227), one must retort that this doctrine is not only "unsaid" in the Cave Analogy, but is contradicted by what is said in the Sun Analogy, which Heidegger's own interpretation appeals to. It is truth, together with being, that Plato makes the master over the idea.[34]

To express with special force the subjugation that truth undergoes in Plato, Heidegger invokes the metaphor of the yoke: a metaphor that by this point has acquired a life of its own, independent of its original context in Plato's text, and has come completely to dominate, indeed to yoke, Heidegger's interpretation. Heidegger asserts: "ἀλήθεια comes under the yoke of the ἰδέα" (228). If one consults the actual use of this metaphor in Plato's text, something Heidegger neither does himself nor encourages his readers to do, then, as we have seen, one arrives at the opposite conclusion. Even if one insists on applying Plato's description of light as a yoke to the relations between truth, being, and the idea—something Plato himself declines to do—then it is ἀλήθεια, as the analogue to light, that becomes the yoke, while the ἰδέα, as the object of knowledge, becomes what *is yoked* under ἀλήθεια.[35] Of course, the good is "above" ἀλήθεια, but not as a yoke—something to which the good is never even implicitly compared—nor in its character as an ἰδέα, but only in its transcendence beyond being itself. Having looked carefully into the workshop of Heidegger's interpretation in the courses of the early1930s, we are in a position to see Heidegger's claim in the 1940 essay that ἀλήθεια is subjugated to the yoke of the ἰδέα for what it truly is: a complete fabrication.

Yet it is on this fabrication that Heidegger's thesis of a transformation in the essence of truth entirely depends. Stating again that in being subjected to the idea, truth is also subjected to seeing and thus transformed into a property of naming and asserting, Heidegger provides the clearest statement of his thesis: "From the priority [*Vorrang*] of the ἰδέα and of ἰδεῖν over ἀλήθεια there springs a transformation [*Wandlung*] of the essence of truth. Truth becomes ὀρθότης, the correctness of perceiving and asserting [*Richtigkeit des Vernehmens und Aussagens*]" (228). If Heidegger is wrong about the priority, then he is wrong about the transformation. In other words, if there is no yoking of truth, there is no transformation of its essence. It is important to note again the extent to which Heidegger's thesis rests not on the Cave Analogy per se but

---

34. Henry G. Wolz made this objection to Heidegger's reading long ago, though more on the basis of a dramatic reading of the dialogues than on the basis of an interpretation of the Sun Analogy: "For while Heidegger there [in the *Allegory of the Cave*] sees *alétheia* under the yoke of the idea, it now appears that the *idea* stands in the service of *alétheia*, helping the truth of things to shine forth in its own light." "Plato's Doctrine of Truth: Orthotes or Aletheia?" *Philosophy and Phenomenological Research* 27, no. 2 (1966): 166.

35. Peperzak recognizes that Heidegger here "wrongly applies the word 'yoke' of 508a1–2 to the *idea*, and attributes another meaning to it, namely that of domination" ("Did Heidegger Understand Plato's Idea of Truth?" 101).

on a misreading of relations expressed in the Sun Analogy and on the overemphasis, to put it mildly, of a metaphor (the yoke) that occurs only there.[36]

As pointed out above, in the earlier courses the only indication of a conception of truth as correctness that Heidegger detected in the text of the Cave Analogy itself was the description of the prisoners as seeing ὀρθότερον when freed from their chains and turned around toward the fire (515d3–4). There, however, he rightly insisted that a conception of truth as unconcealment is still dominant in this passage, since the prisoners see ὀρθότερον only in being turned toward beings that are *more unconcealed*. In sharp contrast, Heidegger's reading of the same passage in the 1940 essay insists: "Everything depends on the ὀρθότης, on the correctness of looking [*Richtigkeit des Blickens*]" (228). Here truth as correctness has become the dominant and even exclusive conception of truth expressed in the word ὀρθότερον. How can Heidegger go against his earlier reading in this way, when the earlier reading is much closer to the text?[37] As argued above, the word ὀρθότερον can in the context mean only "turned to what is *more real and more unconcealed*" and therefore not "seeing [the same things] more correctly." Heidegger can now reduce the truth expressed in the word ὀρθότερον to mere correctness only by the interesting and far from innocent way in which he constructs his text. For what is surprising is that Heidegger does not even cite 515d3–4 when he is paraphrasing and interpreting that stage of the Cave Analogy. Instead, he postpones citing the passage until after he concludes, in the passage from page 136 cited above, that truth has become correctness in Plato. Why this odd way of dealing with the passage? The reason is not hard to see: by citing the passage only after his conclusion that truth has become correctness in Plato, he can offer it as a verbal confirmation of this conclusion without having to interpret it in its context, an interpretation that would, as the earlier courses show, stand in the way of such a conclusion. Whether this strategy is fully conscious or not, it has clearly been very effective.

36. Heidegger does provide the following textual "evidence" for the ambiguity (*Zweideutigkeit*) of the essence of truth in Plato: the characterization of the idea of the good as πάντων ὀρθῶν τε καὶ καλῶν αἰτία parallels, though in a chiasma, the characterization of it as κυρία ἀλήθειαν καὶ νοῦν παρασχομένη, so that νοῦς corresponds to ὀρθά and ἀλήθεια corresponds to καλά; accordingly we see the good here being made the cause both of correctness in thinking and of truth as unconcealment (229). However, I do not think that this forced and arbitrary reading of the text requires more comment than the refutation to which Barnes ("Heidegger spéléologue," 188–89) and Peperzak ("Did Heidegger Understand Plato's Idea of Truth?" 102–3) have already subjected it.

37. Strangely, Hyland, despite his critique of Heidegger's reading, grants Heidegger much more than he should when he writes: "Without question, Plato does have his Socrates use the term 'correctness' (*orthotes*) several times in the Cave Analogy." Drew Hyland, *Questioning Platonism: Continental Interpretations of Plato* (Albany: State University of New York Press, 2004), 61. Several times? I find only one instance. Furthermore, as Heidegger himself points out in the course, *orthotes* does not simply mean, if at all, "correctness."

3. The Good Loses Its ἐπέκεινα

Discussion of the good plays an important role in Heidegger's 1940 interpretation because there can be no doubt that Plato in some sense subordinates truth to the good. But, as has already been seen, in order to see in the subordination of truth to the good its subjugation to the ἰδέα, Heidegger must interpret the good as being an ἰδέα in exactly the same sense that any other ἰδέα is an ἰδέα; on Heidegger's reading, this means that the good must be interpreted as something seen and thereby relative to a seeing. In other words, Heidegger can find in the good support for his thesis only by denying it any real transcendence vis-à-vis the other ideas. He must interpret the good exclusively as the highest being in the hierarchy of being, rather than as beyond being. If in the courses of the 1930s the text requires Heidegger to acknowledge the good's transcendence, it has been seen that by the time of the *Beiträge* he eliminates this troublesome incoherence through a highly peculiar and Nietzschean interpretation of the ἐπέκεινα τῆς οὐσίας. The 1940 essay, however, offers a much simpler remedy: silence. Here, and for the first time in Heidegger's interpretation of the good, the characterization of the good as ἐπέκεινα τῆς οὐσίας is not even mentioned.[38]

This makes the way free for a characterization of the ἀγαθόν as simply a super-idea (224–26): just as the idea, as itself something visible, makes sensible objects visible in what they are, so the good makes the ideas visible as itself something visible. "As ἰδέα the good is something that shines forth [*ein Scheinendes*], as such it is what gives a view [*das Sichtgebende*] and as this it is itself something that can be seen [*ein Sichtiges*] and therefore something that can be known [*Kennbares*]" (224). If the good and the ideas are still characterized here as in essence a making-possible [*Ermöglichen, Tauglichmachen*] (226), they make possible only visibility and only as themselves visible objects. If there was a tension earlier between the characterization of the idea as a "look" and the characterization of it as a "power," the latter characterization is now completely swallowed up by the former. The crucial point here, however, is that this complete reduction of the ideas to mere "looks" goes hand in hand with a complete reduction of the good to the ideas.[39] Now the good does not differ in being or function from any of the other ideas. Significantly, Heidegger himself appears eventually to have recognized the untenability of this characterization of the good as itself something visible: in a marginal note to the above passage, written in a 1947 edition of the text and therefore dating from any time after

---

38. As Dostal rightly observes, "Given the importance of this phrase to the classical tradition and to Heidegger himself, its absence in this essay is quite obtrusive" ("Beyond Being," 69).

39. In the 1938–39 *Die Überwindung der Metaphysik*, Heidegger even characterizes the good as "die eigentliche Idee" (GA 67, 162) and "die Sichtsamkeit" (163).

that date, Heidegger wrote: "Ἀγαθόν is indeed ἰδέα, but no longer presencing and therefore hardly visible [*kaum sichtbar*]" (GA 9, 227).[40] Yet in the main text he has no such doubt and instead concludes that the good is "highest" only in the two senses that "it has the top position in the order of making-possible, and the look up to it [*der Aufblick zu ihr*] is the steepest [*steilste*] and therefore most arduous [*mühevollste*]" (226). As for that little difference Socrates mentions, that while the ideas are being the good "is not being," it is here passed over in silence. This debasement of the good allows Heidegger to persist in the Nietzschen interpretation of the good that was already sketched out in the *Beiträge:* while the good is not yet a value (*Wert*), Heidegger insists on seeing it as the origin of the notion of value, so that Nietzsche's value thinking can be described as just the most extreme and unbridled Platonism (225).

4. Plato Is Transformed into Platonism

The transformation of Plato into Platonism can indeed be seen as a central task of Heidegger's essay. Such a transformation means ignoring Plato's texts in their specificity and inexhaustible suggestiveness, or grossly simplifying and distorting these texts when they must be confronted at all, with the goal of making "Plato" simply the name of a position or doctrine. In Heidegger's reading, "Plato" becomes the name of a position that characterizes the entire history of metaphysics.[41] Plato's unsaid doctrine of truth is the unsaid doctrine of truth that defines metaphysics as such. The lengths to which Heidegger is willing to go in order to follow Nietzsche in making Plato the emblem and poster child for the history of metaphysics are all too evident in the rather embarrassing final pages of the essay.[42] To find in Plato a characterization of philosophy as metaphysics *avant la lettre*, Heidegger interprets the phrase μετ'ἐκεῖνα at 516c3 as meaning "beyond" the shadow-like sensible objects and

---

40. John Sallis asks the important question, "Can one continue, confidently, even coherently, to call τὸ ἀγαθόν an ἰδέα if it is such as to withdraw itself from self-showing, to remain withdrawn from full presence." *Delimitations: Phenomenology and the End of Metaphysics*, 2nd ed. (Bloomington: Indiana University Press, 1995), 181. In another essay he similarly observes, after citing *Rep.* 517b: "Yet how can there be an idea that does not come to be present—and hence visible—considering that the very sense of idea is to be a look presentable by a vision? How can it be that precisely the highest idea, the one whose luminosity all others presuppose, is itself less than fully luminous, scarcely to be seen?" "Plato's Other Beginning," in *Heidegger and the Greeks: Interpretative Essays*, ed. Drew A. Hyland and John Panteleimon Manoussakis (Bloomington: Indiana University Press, 2006), 188.

41. Boutot must grant that Heidegger's later, more negative reading of Plato "est bien plus une lecture du platonisme de Platon que de Platon lui-même" (*Heidegger et Platon*, 248). He also suggests in concluding his book that his title, *Heidegger et Platon*, "est devenu au cours de notre étude sous la contrainte de la chose même qui est en question *Heidegger et le platonisme*" (325).

42. In Heidegger's identification of Plato with a history, we of course again see Nietzsche's influence. Victor Goldschmidt rightly observes of Heidegger's and Nietzsche's critique of Plato: "Il reste que c'est le schème de l'histoire qui, chez les deux interprètes, fournit l'argumentation fondamental

toward the ideas. Unfortunately, even the most cursory glance at the context shows that the phrase, which is a repetition of the phrase μετὰ ταῦτ'at 516b9, must mean "*after* these"[43] and that the "after" refers back not to sensible objects, which are not even under discussion here, since Socrates is describing the region outside the cave, but to the seeing of the sun/good! *After* seeing the sun, Socrates says, the person outside the cave will infer that it is the cause of everything he sees, that is, of the ideas. The most charitable response to Heidegger's reading of this passage is to say no more about it.

Heidegger needs to find in Plato not only the characterization of philosophy as metaphysics, but also its characterization as theology. Heidegger's expedient here is to assert that Plato calls the good, as the highest cause, τὸ θεῖον. The problem is that he does not provide a single textual reference in support, presumably because this too is an "unsaid" doctrine (233).[44] Furthermore, even if Plato were to call the good θεῖον, this would be only that characterization of the ultimate reality as divine that we find already in the Pre-Socratics; there would be no reason to see here the identification of being with a highest being (God) and thus the beginning of "theology."[45] These embarrassing and best-overlooked aspects of Heidegger's reading are noted here not for the sake of abuse, but to illustrate just what is required to transform Plato into Platonism.

The general conclusion of Heidegger's essay is stated thus: "Unconcealment as platonically [*platonisch*] conceived remains yoked [*eingespannt*] in the relation to envisioning [*Erblicken*], perceiving [*Vernehmen*], thinking [*Denken*] and asserting [*Aussagen*]. To follow this relation is to abandon [*preisgeben*] the essence of unconcealment" (235). Since Plato himself did not yoke unconcealment under this relation to thinking and perceiving but instead let it stand over this relation and rule it, "subjecting" it only to a transcendence beyond being, he certainly did not abandon the essence of unconcealment. The central and ruling image in both the sun and cave analogies is light, and

---

de la critique." *Platonisme et pensée contemporaine* (Paris: J. Vrin, 2000), 217. See ibid., 218–46 for a history and critique of this approach. Goldschmidt says in critique of both Nietzsche and Heidegger: "Il soumettent les doctrines à une simplification caricaturale et, pour les rendre comparables, à une déformation systématique" (242). He also argues that no real dialogue is possible on their approach: "Le dialogue qu'on croit instaurer ainsi, peut bien être 'pensant,' mais c'est l'interprète seul qui pense, et l'auteur reste absent, qui pourrait lui donner la réplique" (242); Goldschmidt also writes of Hegel: "Au dialogue, rendu possible dans l'intemporalité d'une pensée *systématique*, se substitue le discours magistral du dernier-né" (236). Heidegger's interpretation of Plato on truth certainly appears to confirm the legitimacy of Goldschmidt's critique and caution.

43. See Barnes, "Heidegger spéléologue," 179.

44. Boutot is faithful to Heidegger's reading, both in asserting that Plato calls the good τὸ θεῖον and in failing to provide a reference (*Heidegger et Platon*, 180).

45. See Peperzak's dismissal of "the epiphet 'godly' or 'divine' (*theion*, not—as Heidegger on p. 141 says—'*to theion, the* divine')" as not very impressive or important "since many outstanding beings, like men, forces, pleasures, mores, laws, etc., are called 'divine'" ("Did Heidegger Understand Plato's Idea of Truth?" 95).

the analogue to this light is not the ideas but truth. It is therefore simply wrong to assert that Plato's "genuine reflection [*eigentliche Besinnung*] concerns the appearing of a look [*Erscheinen des Aussehens*] that is granted by the brightness of the shine [*der Helle des Scheins*]" (223); his reflection concerns the light or brightness of truth itself. He situates truth as unconcealment, and thus provides a context for reflection on it, by placing the ideas below it and the good above it. Only through the confused entangling of the relations Plato clearly articulates can Heidegger reach his momentous conclusion.

5. Summary of the Departures from Heidegger's Earlier Interpretation

The above reading of "Platons Lehre von der Wahrheit," rather than merely repeating what the essay takes from Heidegger's earlier courses and what has therefore already been discussed above, seeks to note the significant differences and departures.[46] It will be useful to summarize these here:

(1) First, a difference not made explicit above: while in the courses Heidegger made the ideas the analogue of light in both the Sun and Cave analogies, here such an identification reaches its culmination in the absence of any reference whatsoever to light as a specific constituent of the analogies. Light, and therefore what is for Plato the analogue of light, namely, truth and being, are so absorbed into the ideas they illuminate as to disappear completely from the discussion. Accordingly, this component of the analogies is simply ignored by Heidegger: outside the cave are only ideas; in the Sun Analogy only ideas are indicated. This of course makes it much easier to claim that Plato in these analogies reflects only on the appearance of a look and not on the light or brightness that grants this appearance.[47]

(2) While in the courses an acknowledgment of the transcendence of the good beyond being was in tension with the attempt to reduce the good to an idea differing only in degree from other ideas, here Heidegger resolves the tension by not even mentioning the transcendence of the good.

(3) The ideas themselves are greatly impoverished. They are made into mere objects that are seen, and all the earlier qualifications that were in tension with such a characterization have largely disappeared.[48]

---

46. The essay is therefore far from being a mere crystallization of the essential results of the course, as Hyland explicitly suggests (*Questioning Platonism*, 55) and as most scholars assume.

47. Therefore, Hyland rightly objects against the essay: "Only the sun (the idea of the Good) shines in the active sense. The other ideas shine only in the sense that the moon (or the other things that are) shines. *It shines in the light of the sun.* The shining (visibility) of the other ideas is a passive shining in the light of the active shining of the idea of the Good" (ibid., 59).

48. This impoverishment is seen to some extent by Enrico Berti: see "Heideggers Auseinandersetzung mit dem Platonisch-Aristotelischen Wahrheitsverständnis," in *Die Frage nach der Wahrheit*, ed. Ewald Richter (Frankfurt am Main: Vittorio Klostermann, 1997), 99–100; "Heidegger and the Platonic Concept of Truth," in HPD, 102–3.

(4) If Heidegger's use of the metaphor of a yoke was never very close to the text, here it appears completely freed from the context in which it appears in the text. It becomes practically a diabolical symbol of metaphysics, subjugating truth and suppressing any reflection on it; the yoke indeed appears to be for Heidegger the embryo of that "machination" that will come to subjugate the earth and man.[49] A reader of Heidegger's essay who did not have a good knowledge of the Greek text of the *Republic* would never guess that the metaphor of a yoke does not occur in the Cave Analogy or even in the account of the relations between the good, truth, and the ideas.

(5) The essay reverses the interpretation of παιδεία given in the courses: instead of a *Gehaltenheit* of man within beings as a whole, it is now only a matter of fixing our vision on the "look" things offer us. Not *halten*, but *bilden* is now the fundamental comportment. By thus interpreting παιδεία as *Bildung*, Heidegger can make the whole analogy a representation of truth as correctness as well as find in Plato the beginning of "humanism."

(6) While in the courses Heidegger did not really attempt to demonstrate within the context of the Cave Analogy, nor even within the context of the Sun Analogy, a transformation in the essence of truth from unconcealment into correctness, using instead the *Theaetetus* to show this, here this transformation is made into the "unsaid doctrine" of the Cave Analogy. Correspondingly, while in the courses the word ὀρθότερον at 515d3–4 was fully subordinated to truth as unconcealment, here Heidegger does not hesitate to find in it a transformation of truth from unconcealment into correctness.[50]

(7) A difference that partly explains (6) is that in the courses Heidegger insisted on remaining close in his interpretation to what is happening within the Cave Analogy, which he there took to be the happening of unconcealment. Here the Cave Analogy is quickly left behind in favor of notions taken from the Sun Analogy or even dogmatic assertions given no textual basis.

(8) What is entirely new in "Platons Lehre von der Wahrheit" is the reduction of Plato's philosophy to onto-theology and humanism and the characterization of the idea of the good as the precursor of modern value-thinking. This of course all comes from the intervening Nietzsche lectures.

One must conclude that the 1940 essay preserves all of the errors of the *Vom Wesen der Wahrheit* courses and none of the positive insights that mitigated these errors. As already suggested, the essay must appear a caricature to anyone who has studied the courses.[51] It must also be said that in comparison with the

---

49. In an extraordinary passage from the 1938/39 *Die Überwindung der Metaphysik*, Heidegger indeed makes the placing of the good above ἀλήθεια the first and most wide-ranging step toward the assembly-line production of long-range bombers (*Fernkampfflugzeugen*, GA 67, 164)!

50. Enrico Berti recognizes this difference, claiming that the later essay says here "das Gegenteil" of what is asserted in the earlier course ("Heideggers Auseinandersetzung," 102; see also HPD, 104).

51. I therefore find simply baffling Joseph Margolis's assertion that "Heidegger's little essay, 'Plato's Doctrine of Truth,' is an astonishing tour de force, surely one of the most brilliant and arresting of all his brief papers, without which, as far as I can see, nearly everything else he has written on the

depth of thinking and engagement with both the texts and the issues that characterize the courses, the essay "Platons Lehre von der Wahrheit" reads as a kind of propaganda pamphlet aiming only at persuading us that Platonism is the beginning of the end. There is hardly any careful reading of the texts: the text of the Cave Analogy is translated but then receives rather cursory commentary (not going much beyond paraphrase), only to be quickly abandoned in favor of a very dogmatic presentation of the thesis regarding the transformation of truth, a presentation that takes most of its terms from another analogy, the Sun Analogy, which itself receives no detailed interpretation.[52] Furthermore, the few attempts at detailed exegesis are, as has been seen, simply embarrassing.

It must also be said that the essay represents the most extreme inversion of what Plato actually seeks to indicate through his analogies. One could therefore arrive at a good interpretation of what Plato's analogies actually indicate by simply inverting everything said in the following passage, taking whatever Heidegger says Plato does not mean to be precisely what Plato means, and taking whatever Heidegger says Plato means to be precisely what Plato does not mean: "Plato conceives of presencing [*Anwesung*] (οὐσία) as ἰδέα. This [the idea] does not however stand under unconcealment so that, serving the unconcealed, it brings it to appearance.[53] Rather, it is on the contrary the shining (self-showing) [*das Scheinen (Sichzeigen)*] that determines what in its essence and in a peculiar reference back to itself [*im einzigen Rückbezug auf es selbst*] is allowed to be called unconcealment. The ἰδέα is not a representative foreground [*ein darstellender Vordergrund*] of ἀλήθεια, but rather the ground that makes it possible (231–32)." The careful reading of the analogies shows to be true the exact opposite of everything Heidegger asserts in this passage.

D. THE END OF TRUTH: THE 1964 RETRACTION

"Platons Lehre von der Wahrheit" essentially represents the end of Heidegger's interpretation of Plato, as if with this essay he had taken care of, or exorcised,

---

question of truth may simply lack a commanding sense of the grounding arguments he champions" ("Heidegger on Truth and Being," in HPD, 124).

52. Even Boutot's very sympathetic reading of "Platons Lehre von der Wahrheit" draws attention to the fact that Heidegger uses the Cave Analogy to show the persistence in Plato of the original conception of truth as unconcealment but must rely on passages outside of this analogy to establish his thesis that there is in Plato a mutation in the essence of truth (*Heidegger et Platon*, 190–91); as I have argued, this is even truer of the earlier courses (which were not available to Boutot). Yet Boutot tries to do for Heidegger what Heidegger doesn't do for himself: his main argument relies on the use of the word ὀρθότερον (515d3–4) in the Cave Analogy (*Heidegger et Platon*, 192). As has been shown, however, this word interpreted in its context—a context Heidegger here avoids—gives no support to a conception of truth as correctness, but quite the opposite.

53. In the 1938/39 *Die Überwindung der Metaphysik*, Heidegger makes the same point thus: "Die Unverborgenheit kommt in die Botmäßigkeit der ἰδέα, diese, im Wesen nur ein Erscheinen des

Plato once and for all. Once we have identified Plato's central doctrine, a doctrine that is moreover "unsaid" in Plato, what further need is there to study his texts?[54] When Plato is mentioned at all after the 1940 essay, it is usually not as the author of the dialogues, but rather as a label for the fundamental position of Western metaphysics, a position identified with the oblivion of being/unconcealment. The next two chapters will examine two readings of Plato, that of the *Theaetetus* and that of the Myth of Er, that *could* have led Heidegger in the direction of a genuine dialogue with Plato but that got suppressed by the official, published interpretation in the essay. Later chapters will consider texts from Heidegger's later years, where there is a brief, though genuine engagement with the Plato of the dialogues and therefore the recognition of a dimension in Plato that cannot be assimilated to Heidegger's standard and "orthodox" interpretation; furthermore, there is Heidegger's acknowledgment, in letters to Hannah Arendt in 1951 and 1954, of the need to "read Plato anew," an exchange to be discussed in a later chapter (AHB, 125, 148). Yet this need is never met by Heidegger, and the passing glimpses at a nonmetaphysical and non-Platonic Plato in his late texts are never allowed to become an overall rereading of Plato. It is as if Heidegger could not overcome his own 1940 essay, as if his relation to Plato was fatally yoked by it.

Yet there is a later text that has been seen by many as nothing short of a complete reversal of Heidegger's thesis in "Platons Lehre von der Wahrheit." Therefore, this text demands consideration here, even in defiance of the generally chronological progression of the current analysis. In "Das Ende der Philosophie und die Aufgabe des Denkens," written in 1964, Heidegger indeed explicitly retracts his earlier thesis of a transformation of the essence of truth in the Greeks, and while Plato is not explicitly mentioned, Heidegger's retraction clearly undermines the thesis regarding Plato in the 1940 essay. However, if we look at why Heidegger retracts this thesis, we see that this retraction is not so much a retraction of his interpretation of Plato as it is a more extreme version of this interpretation, indeed, its ultimate denouement.[55] For

---

ἀληθές, wird zur Ursache der ἀλήθεια" (GA 67, 162). And again the exact opposite is the case: it is precisely as an "appearing" of ἀλήθεια and as therefore dependent on it that the ἰδέα is characterized in the Sun Analogy, especially in the passage Heidegger insists on ignoring (508d4–5).

54. Boutot goes so far as to justify Heidegger's avoidance of interpreting dialogues as a whole by explaining that the dialogues offer only what Plato thought and said, while Heidegger is interested only in what Plato left unsaid and unthought (15)! And if Heidegger privileges those texts furthest removed from the dialogue form, this is because, Boutot assures us, Plato characterized thinking as a dialogue and Heidegger is not interested in what Plato thought (16)! One must wonder if Heideggerianism, which is not to be identified with Heidegger, can go any further, and become any more absurd, than this. Heidegger himself at least recognizes that fully meeting the demand of experiencing and thinking what Plato left unsaid would ideally require "alle 'Gespräche' Platons in ihrem Zusammenhang durchsprechen" (PLW, 201).

55. Dostal rightly observes that Heidegger does not in this essay "or anywhere else recant his description of the traditional metaphysical notion of truth or his attribution of that notion to Plato.

if Heidegger retracts his thesis of a transformation of the essence of truth, if he now believes that truth did not become correctness in Plato, this is not because, finally seeing the errors in his earlier interpretation, he now believes that truth continued to be understood as unconcealment in Plato. On the contrary, he retracts his thesis that truth became correctness in Plato because he now believes that Plato, and the Greeks generally, always thought of truth only as correctness; though they named ἀλήθεια, they thought, and even experienced, only the correctness of representing and saying ("nur als ὀρθότης, als die Richtigkeit des Vorstellens und Aussagens erfahren wurde," 78).[56] Heidegger therefore now refuses even to use the word *truth* (*Wahrheit*) to designate what he is trying to think (76). While earlier he claimed that there was an ambiguity in the word *Wahrheit* between the meanings of unconcealment and correctness, now he takes it to mean only correctness. Therefore, if Heidegger had rewritten his earlier courses and the essay, he could have changed the titles to *Vom Wesen der Richtigkeit* and "Platons Lehre von der Richtigkeit."

This change, however, is only a further step, and indeed the final step, on the path already taken from the courses of the 1930s to the 1940 essay. As has been seen, while the courses find in the Cave Analogy a genuine thinking of unconcealment *along with* correctness, where the former remains predominant, the later essay essentially equates the truth *thought* by Plato with correctness, acknowledging at most a residue experience of unconcealment in the Cave Analogy. What Heidegger does now is simply eliminate the remaining residue. On his present and final reading, the Greeks thought, and even experienced, nothing but correctness. Consequently, Heidegger will no longer allow his own attempt to think unconcealment as *Lichtung* or *Offenheit* to be called by the Greek term *philosophy*. With its confinement to a conception of truth as correctness, philosophy is brought to an end. Philosophy still has a long life ahead of it, but not as thinking: it can live on only as the calculative reasoning of the technicized sciences (63–65). Plato's doctrine of truth, fully reduced now to correctness, has become cybernetics.

Yet if, as argued above, the direction of Heidegger's reading of Plato was already misguided in the 1930s, its culmination in the present essay is a reductio ad absurdum. If what Heidegger in the 1937–38 course *Grundfragen der*

Accordingly, this late concession affects not so much his Plato interpretation as his interpretation of the Pre-Socratics, and his attempt to find there the doctrine of truth as unconcealment" ("Beyond Being," 66–67). What is affected is the distinction Heidegger describes in the following text from the 1938/39 *Die Überwindung der Metaphysik*: "Unterschied des vorplatonischen *Denkens* und der *Philosophie*, die mit Plato beginnt: ἀλήθεια zur ὀρθότης" (GA 67, 36). Now even the "Pre-Platonists" belong to the "philosophy" that is at an end, while "thinking" is a task that belongs entirely to the future.

56. Though Berti does not discuss this essay, his own conclusion is similar to Heidegger's here: "Sowohl bei Platon als auch bei Aristoteles ist die Wahrheit letztlich vor allem Richtigkeit der Definition, die ihrerseits Kenntnis der Ursachen, d.h. Verstehen (ἐπιστήμη) ist" ("Heideggers Auseinandersetzung," 105; also HPD, 106).

Philosophie referred to as "the fact that, as soon as it became a matter of bringing the essence of truth to knowledge, ἀλήθεια became ὁμοίωσις (correctness)" (205) is not a fact at all, there he at least acknowledged that the Greeks experienced truth as unconcealment, indeed claimed this to be indisputable (*unbestreitbar*). Now even this experience is denied.[57] How are we then to explain the experience Plato describes in the Cave Analogy, an analogy that Heidegger himself earlier claimed to be impossible without an understanding of truth as unconcealment? How can the comparative ἀληθέστερον, of which Heidegger makes so much earlier and which is used to describe objects, be interpreted as meaning simply "more correct"? Of course, Heidegger does not return to these texts in the present essay; he does not even mention Plato's name in the context of retracting his thesis of a transformation of the essence of truth. But then, as has been seen, the texts were never decisive for Heidegger's reading: we have here simply the transformation of one "unsaid" doctrine (the transformation of truth into correctness) into another "unsaid" doctrine (truth as always and nothing but correctness). Not returning to the texts, especially that in which the freed prisoner is described as seeing ὀρθότερον because seeing new objects that are more real and unconcealed, enables Heidegger to reduce Greek ὁμοίωσις to nothing but correctness. While even in the *Beiträge* Heidegger recognized that ὁμοίωσις, unlike *rectitudo*, is still ἀλήθεια, that is, still grounded in unconcealment (354), in the present text he

---

57. Though introducing the essay on the "End of Philosophy" as a major departure from Heidegger's earlier interpretation (*Heidegger et Platon*, 211–14), Boutot in conclusion suggests that the rupture may not be as great as at first appears since Heidegger never claimed that the Greeks explicitly thought truth as unconcealment (215). However, Heidegger *did* claim that they genuinely experienced truth as unconcealment, while even that he now denies. Boutot appeals to Jean Beaufret's assertion that "Heidegger n'a jamais dit que les Grecs auraient ressenti (*gefühlt*), éprouvé (*erfahren*) ou pensé (*gedacht*) la vérité comme ἀλήθεια. Bien au contraire." *Parménide: Le Poème*, 2nd ed. (Paris: Presses universitaires de France, 1984), 12n5). But this claim is simply wrong. One could cite a number of passages, but the one already referred to suffices: "Daß die griechischen Denker die Unverborgenheit des Seienden erfuhren, ist unbestreitbar" (GA 45, 204–5). And since Heidegger proceeds to say that this experience of ἀλήθεια was later lost ("verloren," 205), he clearly is not speaking of an experience of ἀλήθεια as correctness, which is all he will grant the Greeks as ever having had in the later essay. Even in "Platons Lehre von der Wahrheit," Heidegger speaks of "der für die Griechen selbstverständlichen Grunderfahrung der ἀλήθεια" and "das im Sinne der ἀλήθεια anfänglich griechisch gedachte Wesen der Wahrheit, die auf Verborgenes (Verstelltes und Verhülltes) bezogene Unverborgenheit" (130). Sallis writes: "One might be tempted, then, to conclude that unconcealment was simply not experienced among the Greeks, and that it was not in any sense named in sayings such as that of Parmenides which spoke of ἀλήθεια. But this is not Heidegger's conclusion. Rather, the fact that ἀλήθεια meant correctness and not unconcealment signifies for him that unconcealment was experienced by the Greeks only as (through, in the perspective of) correctness" (*Delimitations*, 178). Even so, the cited texts show even this to be a significant departure from his earlier position. And when Sallis asks in another essay, with regard to Heidegger's retraction, "Can it be simply a matter of now granting that the Platonic text is ambiguous or two-sided, that both senses of truth are operative there?" ("Plato's Other Beginning," 186), Heidegger's answer in 1964 would clearly be, "No, there is no ambiguity there at all, because there is no transformation there, because only truth as correctness is operative there."

acknowledges no difference between ὁμοίωσις and *rectitudo*. Even with the Romans there was no transformation of the essence of truth, since the Greeks were already Romans.

Why does Heidegger take this final step toward a reduction of Plato's philosophy, and Greek philosophy in general, to a conception of truth as correctness? Is the cause really Paul Friedländer's critique of Heidegger's translation of ἀλήθεια as "un-concealment"?[58] The irony is that Friedländer comes to see as unjustified ("unberechtigt") his earlier opposition to Heidegger on this point (242),[59] opposing Heidegger's thesis of a transformation of the essence of truth not by asserting that the Greeks always thought and experienced ἀλήθεια as correctness but, on the contrary, by insisting that they from the beginning experienced it as having three distinct but related senses: (1) "the unconcealing, disclosing correctness of saying and opining" ("die unverbergende, enthüllende Rightigkeit des Sagens und Meinens"); (2) "the unconcealed, undisclosed reality of what endures, of being" ("die unverborgene, unverhüllte Wirklichkeit des Bestehenden, Seienden");[60] (3) "the unforgetting, non-deceiving correctness, truthfulness of man, of character" (236).[61] Heidegger can therefore be said to reject the thesis of a transformation of the essence of truth for the opposite reason Friedländer does: not because the Greeks always experienced ἀλήθεια as both unconcealment and correctness, but because they always experienced it only as correctness.[62] Furthermore, even if a philological argument can still be made against the etymology

58. As Courtine suggests when he claims that Heidegger here "se range entièrement à l'analyse de Friedländer et prend acte de ses objections. Singulière concession que ne rend pas simplement caduc l'essai de 1942, mais risque de ruiner des pans entiers de la lecture heideggérienne de la philosophie grecque!" (*Heidegger et la phénoménologie*, 153).

59. All he maintains now is that "perhaps" ("vielleicht") ἀλήθεια was not originally ("ursprünglich") a negative and that it is not experienced as a negative to the same extent ("nicht so durchaus") as words such as ἀ-σέβεια and ἀ-σαφής (234–35).

60. Though not entirely wrong, this is an inadequate interpretation of ἀλήθεια in Plato because, as made clear at 239, it identifies this sense of ἀλήθεια with the idea. Ἀλήθεια, as I have insisted, is not the "undisclosed reality" of the idea, but what makes possible this undisclosed reality. And yet at least Friedländer does not reduce Plato's ἀλήθεια to correctness!

61. In the 1958 lecture "Hegel und die Griechen," Heidegger does not see the Homeric texts Friedländer cites as at all counting against the interpretation of ἀλήθεια as "Unverborgenheit" (WM, 437); and Friedländer, at least in the final version of his remarks, would agree.

62. Even Barnes, who unqualifiedly rejects an interpretation of ἀλήθεια as "un-concealment," still insists on a "sens objectif" that cannot be reduced to the "sens propositionnel" of "correctness" ("Heidegger spéléologue," 191–93). For the same insistence, see Hestir, "Plato on the Split Personality of Ontological *Alētheia*." Hestir also rejects Heidegger's etymological interpretation (112n7) but without explaining why and while granting that ἀλήθεια "has various important connotations for Plato" (113n7). Peperzak writes: "But Heidegger conceded too much when in *The End of Philosophy* (p. 77) he wrote that *alētheia* had always had the meaning of correct (*richtig*) or reliable (*zuverlässig*). He forgot the meaning that he himself had listed as the first meaning in his essay *On the Essence of Truth* and that—as we shall see—is the most important one in the text and the context of the parable of the cave: the *Sachwahrheit* or truth of being itself" ("Did Heidegger Understand Plato's Idea of Truth?" 80).

of ἀλήθεια as ἀ-λήθεια, that is, as originally a negative, when has Heidegger ever allowed a philosophical interpretation to be dictated by a philological argument?[63]

There must be a deeper reason for Heidegger's retraction of his earlier thesis. Is not the reason given in the title of the essay? For philosophy to come to an end and a radically new type of thinking to begin, the "truth" that Greek philosophy sought to understand must be distinguished sharply and definitively from what "calls for thinking." Only by identifying the truth of Greek philosophy with correctness can Heidegger maintain that what he seeks to think is something so different that it can no longer be called "truth." Is not Heidegger's reversal then only his new and most extreme strategy for what he has sought perhaps all along, but especially since his reading of Nietzsche: to twist free of Plato once and for all? If the evidence compels him to retract his thesis of a transformation of the essence of truth, he cannot do so by agreeing with Friedländer that Plato, as well as the Greeks before him, thought and experienced ἀλήθεια *both* as correctness and as unconcealment (see 240): this would entangle his own thinking in Plato's and thus prevent the turn to a radical new beginning.

Yet it is a great irony that at the same time that Heidegger brings Plato to an end by confining him to a conception of truth as correctness, his own thinking provides a description of ἀλήθεια that comes extraordinarily close to the one Plato himself gives in the Sun Analogy: "The calm heart of the clearing [*Lichtung*] is the place of stillness [*Ort der Stille*] from out of which there can be such a thing as the possibility of the belonging-together of being and thinking, that is, presence and perceiving [*Anwesenheit und Vernehmen erst gibt*]" (75). As we have seen, Plato's Sun Analogy characterizes ἀλήθεια precisely as this kind of a "third term" that makes possible knowing and the being of the ideas, both in their belonging-together and individually. It is true that while Plato compares ἀλήθεια as thus characterized to light (*Licht*), Heidegger adopts the verbally similar and yet distinct metaphor of a clearing (*Lichtung*). Yet if Heidegger finds the light metaphor inadequate, it is largely because, as we have seen, he wrongly identifies it with the visibility of the ideas and thus with what is unconcealed. The proximity to Plato is perhaps closest when Heidegger proceeds to suggest: "Unconcealment is, as it were, the element in which being as well as thinking and their belonging-together [*Zusammenhangehörigkeit*] are first given" (76). This is exactly what is thought in the Sun and Cave analogies, once the text is freed from Heidegger's distortions and misinterpretations. But in this case it is not time to declare the end of

---

63. In "Hegel und die Griechen," Heidegger asserts that etymology is not what is decisive for the interpretation of ἀλήθεια (WM, 433, 436).

philosophy in favor of some jump into a radically different kind of thinking; it is time instead to come to terms with the thinking already underway at the very commencement of philosophy.

E. CONCLUSION: THE END OF TRUTH?

The aim of the present critique of Heidegger's reading of Plato is not to show that Heidegger was "wrong," but to show the possible directions of thinking, and possible appropriations of Plato, that this reading suppresses. This means, in other words, showing possible ways in which we have not arrived at the end of philosophy but are only still beginning. The following preliminary and necessarily inadequate reflections are offered solely with this aim in view. Subsequent chapters will pursue these reflections further.

In the *Beiträge*, Heidegger makes clear what he himself seeks when he claims that what is necessary for a genuine questioning and understanding of the essence of truth, which he there understands as "the lighting/clearing concealment/sheltering of the There [*die lichtende Verbergung des Da*]" (61; see also 70), is to free truth from all beings: "the truth *freed once and for all from all beings* in every kind of interpretation, whether as φύσις, ἰδέα or perceptum and object, what is known, what is thought" (329). In the next section Heidegger accordingly asserts that any questioning of the relation of truth to something else, including thinking, necessarily conceals its essence. "This relation can first be questioned only when the original essence of ἀλήθεια has already been surrendered [*aufgegeben*] and it has become correctness [*Richtigkeit*]" (330). This claim that any thinking of truth in relation to beings and in relation to thinking necessarily reduces it to mere correctness depends on Heidegger's interpretation of Plato. If Heidegger's interpretation has been shown to be erroneous, and seriously so, this means that the attempt to think truth in this manner is not necessarily condemned to the reduction of truth to correctness and all that follows in the wake of this on Heidegger's account.

In a text from the 1937–38 course already referred to above, Heidegger states his judgment about the Greeks thus: "That the Greek thinkers experienced [*erfuhren*] the unconcealment of beings is undeniable [since they could come to characterize truth as correctness only by grounding it in this unconcealment, as Heidegger argues earlier in the course]. But it is equally indisputable that they did not make unconcealment itself into a question nor would it have been unfolded in its essence and grounded [*noch sie in ihrem Wesen entfaltet und auf den Grund gebracht worden wäre*]" (GA 45, 205). The proof? "The proof [*Beweis*] for this singular occurrence within the great philosophy of Greek thinking is the fact that, as soon as it came to bringing the essence of truth to knowledge, ἀλήθεια became ὁμοίωσις (correctness)" (205). But this so-called fact, as Heidegger exhibits it in "Platons Lehre von der Wahrheit," has been shown to be based on fundamental misreadings and distortions of the text. What then becomes of Heidegger's *Geschichte*? If truth is reduced to *rectitudo* by the Romans, this reduction is neither found in Plato, nor is an inevitable consequence of his understanding of ἀλήθεια; on the contrary, *rectitudo* would in that case be a profound distortion of Plato's ἀλήθεια and incompatible with it.

In the analogies of the *Republic*, Plato thinks ἀλήθεια in relation to knowing, the ideas, and beings, without reducing it to any of them. Plato also thinks truth and being together, making both in their unity the analogue to light. Furthermore, and this is the crucial point here, Plato can be said to "free truth from beings" *both* by making it the cause of beings (in both their being and being known) *and* by locating its own origin in what is beyond being, that is, the good, thereby preventing truth from being reduced to nothing but the cause of the knowability of beings. Can and must truth, in order to be questioned and understood in itself, be freed from beings more than this? This is the question that Heidegger, in confronting Plato rather than a caricature of Plato, would have had to address.

The Sun Analogy can in fact indicate a path of thinking that avoids the exclusive alternative to which Heidegger wants to confine us, the alternative between thinking truth as correctness and thinking an "opening" so completely removed from any relation between being and knowing that it can no longer even be called "truth." This Heideggerian alternative cannot help but seem an insurmountable dilemma. Heidegger himself, in the passages from the "End of Philosophy" cited above, describes *Lichtung* as the site in which there first occur thinking and being in their belonging together: in thus thinking *Lichtung* in its relation to thinking, Heidegger does exactly what in the *Beiträge* he insists must be avoided. And how indeed *can* this be avoided? The alternative between a thinking of truth in relation to beings that thereby reduces it to mere "correctness" and a seemingly impossible thinking of truth without being—what the *Beiträge* characterize as a "*leap [Einsprung]* into the *Wesung* of truth" (GA 65, 338)—this is precisely the fruitless alternative that Plato's thinking of truth appears to avoid once we free it from Heidegger's distortions and reductions.

In a very important part of the 1937–38 course, Heidegger offers an explanation of why the Greeks did not question ἀλήθεια. The Greeks could not make unconcealment itself questionable and questionworthy without betraying their, task of asking what a being [*das Seiende*] is: "For, in order to keep themselves within the question of what a being is, they had to remain in the environment [*Umkreis*] of that which completes this questioning, in the answer ὄν, ἀλήθεια—for only in this way were beings as a whole unconcealed to them in their constancy [*Ständigkeit*], presence [*Anwesenheit*], form [*Gestalt*] and limit [*Grenze*].... To question beyond ἀλήθεια, to bring ἀλήθεια itself into question in the context and in the direction of the initiated question, would mean to destroy [*erschüttern*] the answer and thereby the question" (GA 45, 138). Yet, as we have seen, in the early 1930s Heidegger himself saw Plato's idea of the good as enabling precisely this questioning beyond ἀλήθεια, this bringing of ἀλήθεια itself into question. If he later silently retracts this view, it is only by violently reducing the good and the light of truth to the supposedly static presence of the idea. It is Heidegger's reading that suppresses the dynamism of Plato's analogies, a dynamism that gives expression to an understanding of being as δύναμις. If he can assume in the cited passage that thinking for the Greeks was a preservation of beings in their enduring presence and therefore could not admit any questioning that would render such presence radically unstable, this is because he himself, against what is at play in Plato's texts and even against his own reading of these texts, reduces Greek παιδεία to the fixing of a look on the fixed limits of an object fixed in its presence. What Plato's analogies illustrate, what his dialectic accomplishes, and what the definition of being in the *Sophist* as δύναμις expresses, is in contrast a mediation between stability and instability, rest and motion, along with a corresponding mediation between affirmation and radical questioning.

Later Heidegger formulates in a different way his explanation of why the Greeks supposedly did not question ἀλήθεια: "In order to bring directly into view what lies in a field of vision [*Gesichtskreis*], the field of vision must precisely itself light up [*aufleuchten*] beforehand, in order that it can shine upon [*bescheine*] what stands within it; however, it can and should not itself become what is genuinely looked at [*das eigens Erblickte*]. The field of vision, ἀλήθεια, must in a certain manner be overlooked [*übersehen*]" (GA 45, 147). But this seems to explain too much. Did not the Greeks in this case overlook ἀλήθεια only in the way in which it must always be overlooked as what Heidegger himself calls "lichtende Verbergung"? This necessary overlooking of ἀλήθεια need not be a failure to think it but can be the very opposite: the thinking of ἀλήθεια in relation to what it enables to come to presence and thus as what withdraws in this presence, that is, as anything but correctness. To go beyond this overlooking of ἀλήθεια in the Greeks, Heidegger would need to make ἀλήθεια itself "the genuinely looked at" (*das eigens Erblickte*). But how is this possible? When Heidegger says a little later that "ἀλήθεια remains in the existence of the Greeks the most powerful [*Mächtigste*] and at the same time the most hidden [*das Verborgenste*]" (205), must one not reply: "And so *must* it remain also in our own existence!" To give this reply is *not* to grant that truth thereby remains unthought and inevitably degenerates into mere correctness.

In the *Beiträge*, Heidegger argues that the understanding/projection of truth as "clearing for concealment" ("Lichtung für die Verbergung") differs fundamentally from ἀλήθεια even before the latter is transformed into correctness: it is "an essentially other project than ἀλήθεια, though it belongs precisely in the recollection [*Erinnerung*] of ἀλήθεια and ἀλήθεια belongs to it" (GA 65, 350).[64] The difference is that in the word ἀλήθεια itself "we see that concealment itself [*die Verbergung selbst*] is experienced [*erfahren*] as what is *to be set aside* [*Beseitigende*], what must be taken away (α-)" (350); the result is that neither concealing (*Verbergung*) nor even unconcealing (*Entbergung*) is brought into question since the focus is put exclusively on what is disclosed (*das Unverborgene*). But is this focus avoidable? Perhaps truth at the most fundamental level is to be thought and understood only privatively and thereby indirectly. But there is no reason why such a privative, indirect thinking of truth—a thinking of truth in analogies and in terms of what it enables—is necessarily a reduction of truth to mere correctness. On the contrary, an insistence on the privative and indirect character of the thinking of truth can be precisely what resists such a reduction.

These reflections admittedly only raise questions, but they are precisely the questions suppressed by Heidegger's reading of Plato, or rather, his initial misreading and later nonreading of Plato. The argument of this chapter is not that Plato has an adequate (or inadequate) "doctrine of truth," but rather that he no more has such a doctrine than Heidegger does.[65] On the one hand, it is difficult to deny what Jan Szaif characterizes as a principal result of his exhaustive study of Plato's concept of truth, that the words ἀλήθεια and ἀληθής occur in Plato primarily in connection with assertion and judgment (17, 69). On the other hand, what the present *Auseinandersetzung* with Heidegger's interpretation has shown is that truth in Plato is also and always that unconcealment that is the object, as well as the ground, of all our thinking and desiring and that therefore even in relation to assertion or judgment it is not plausibly identified with either correctness or correspondence. Thus, even Szaif is forced repeatedly to acknowledge the tendency in Plato to treat truth as an *object* rather than as a *property* of assertion (71) or, as he also describes it, "the tendency ... not to assign directly to assertions or cognitions the true or the truth that is known or asserted, but rather to locate the true or the truth on the level of the real objects and their being at which our assertions

---

64. See also "Doch worauf gründet sich die Bestimmung des Wesens der Wahrheit als lichtende Verbergung? Auf einen Anhalt an die ἀλήθεια" (GA 65, 367); and the interpretation of truth as "Lichtung für die Verbergung" is said to occur in a recollection of ἀλήθεια (343–44).

65. Therefore, the most basic objection that can be made against Heidegger's reading is that Plato did not have a "doctrine": see Hyland, *Questioning Platonism*, 55–56. Both Wolz and Hyland (see 63) find, rather than a doctrine or theory, an exhibition of truth in the very drama of the dialogues as a play of concealment and unconcealment.

and cognitions are directed" (39; see also 69).[66] Truth for Plato is indeed both unconcealment and a characteristic of our speaking and seeing, but not in such a way that the latter sense of truth so suppresses and transforms the former as to require an end of philosophy and a new beginning.[67]

What we find in Plato is not so much a doctrine of truth as a resistance to the reduction of truth to any doctrine. After all, is not any "doctrine of truth" already as such a doctrine of truth as correctness because an attempt to make a correct assertion about truth, because an ortho-doxy of truth? What the analogies of the *Republic* instead enable, and in particular the hint at a principle beyond being, is, as Heidegger himself suggests in the 1931–32 course, the *questioning* of being and truth. The good gives us a direction for this questioning. Heidegger's later tacit rejection of this fundamental insight in favor of a characterization of the good as a precursor of the notion of "value," a notion that prevents and stifles questioning, along with his corresponding reduction of Platonic questioning to a Platonic "teaching," are disastrous mistakes: disastrous not only for the understanding of Plato, but also, and much more importantly, for a recognition of the possibilities of thinking that philosophy still holds for us. Whether what Heidegger characterizes as "Plato's unsaid doctrine of truth" is his own invention, is to be attributed to a later period in the history of philosophy, or is not a historical development at all,[68] one thing must be clear: to impose such a doctrine on Plato's texts is not only to ignore

---

66. Szaif sees this tendency, which he comes to label the ontological-epistemological conception of truth, as persisting in Plato's "late work," including the *Theaetetus* and the *Sophist* (*Platons Begriff der Wahrheit*, 514). However, in these two dialogues Szaif also sees emerging an alternative conception of truth that he calls "the logical": "wird jetzt Wahrheit eindeutig und primär als Eigenschaft der Urteils- oder Aussagehandlung verstanden, die, gewissermaßen vor die Wahl gestellt, zu affirmieren oder negieren, dies in Übereinstimmung mit dem vorgegebenen Sein oder Nichtsein zu tun versucht" (519). Szaif's interpretation of the *Theaetetus* and the *Sophist*, to which I have fundamental objections to make, cannot be assessed here. What is important to note in the present context is that Szaif must acknowledge that the ontological conception of truth persists in the "late" dialogues (522–24), specifically the *Timaios* and the *Philebus*, and that there is no attempt there to mediate systematically between the two conceptions, so that "man im übrigen auch nicht gesichert davon sprechen kann, daß bei ihm [Platon] der logische Wahrheitsbegriff jetzt eindeutig die Priorität besitze" (528) and "man eigentlich nicht von *dem* Platonischen Wahrheitsbegriff sprechen . . . sollte" (530).

67. Hyland has begun making this point in his recent book, *Questioning Platonism*, 61–62. See especially his insistence that "the very notion of unhiddenness is incoherent *without* correct looking. The two are not only compatible but necessarily connected" (62). See also Margolis, "Heidegger on Truth and Being," 138; Inwood, *Platons Begriff der Wahrheit*, 74, 77; and Hestir, "Plato on the Split Personality of Ontological *Alētheia*."

68. The reduction of truth to correctness could perhaps be understood as instead an ever-present temptation. This is what Wolz suggests: "WHERE, then, in the history of philosophy, do we locate the emergence of *orthótēs*? Perhaps the tendency toward a rigidity of mind, which is implied in the notion of truth as *Richtigkeit*, always was and always will be with us, whenever men seek to escape the inextricable complexity of moral matters by looking to fixed standards of judgment, and as long as they cannot control their craving for the kind of security which demands certainty in matters of ultimate concern" ("Plato's Doctrine of Truth," 182).

and distort what they say but also, and more importantly, to miss the opportunity and provocation they afford us for genuine reflection on the question of truth and being.

In the 1938–39 text *Besinnung*, Heidegger asserts the following: "*That* unconcealment is presence [*Anwesung*] and that this latter is disclosing [*Entbergung*] and thereby sheltering [*Bergung*] und hiding [*Verbergung*], and *what* has become capable of being experienced [*erfahrbar*] here, this remains outside of Greek thinking" (GA 66, 316). Therefore, he can claim that "the demarcation [*Fassung*] of unconcealment as *openness* [*Offenheit*] of beings" is un-Greek, though thought by way of a return to the Greeks. With the Greeks "neither presence [*Anwesung*] (in its hidden temporal character, hidden *from the very beginning* [*auch anfänglich*]) nor concealment [*Verbergung*] and *openness* [*Offenheit*] is questioned and made worthy of thought [*denk-würdig*]" (GA 66, 316). If this is the case, then Plato was "un-Greek," since the similes of the *Republic* and the good that they serve to hint at, not to mention the dialogues as a whole, are meant to initiate and hold open precisely such questioning. Ironically, it is Heidegger who closes off the questioning in Plato's dialogues. What he would have us believe is Plato's yoke has turned out to be Heidegger's own: a yoke that he has imposed on the truth at work and indicated in Plato's dialogues, a yoke by which he has curbed the questioning of ἀλήθεια alive in these dialogues. Alain Boutot is only drawing out the ultimate implication of Heidegger's reading when, toward the end of his book on Heidegger and Plato, he writes, with an honesty and bluntness one can only admire, the following barbaric sentence: "Platon n'a rien à nous dire sur l'être et sa vérité" (314). Perhaps we are still barbarians who do not know what is "Greek" and what is "un-Greek." Perhaps it is much too early for an "end of philosophy."

4

THE DIALOGUE THAT COULD HAVE BEEN:
HEIDEGGER ON THE *THEAETETUS*

A. THE *THEAETETUS* INTERPRETATION IN *DIE GRUNDBEGRIFFE DER ANTIKEN PHILOSOPHIE* (SS 1926)

Before we turn to the interpretation of the *Theaetetus* in the 1931–32 course *Vom Wesen der Wahrheit,* it will be profitable to consider the earlier interpretation in the 1926 course *Die Grundbegriffe der antiken Philosophie.* The two interpretations are both similar and different in significant ways. One obvious difference is that the 1926 interpretation attempts to read the dialogue in its entirety, skipping only 157b–180c, though admittedly the reading, at least in Heidegger's published notes for the course, is often very sketchy. The 1931–32 reading, in contrast, focuses on 184b–197e and thus approximately one-fifth of the dialogue, citing a line from the *Theaetetus* itself (187e2–3) to justify this narrow focus: "For it is better to work through a little in the right way than to work through much in an inadequate way" (GA 34, 149). One might therefore think that gaps in the later interpretation can be filled in with the earlier interpretation, but while this may sometimes be justified, such a procedure is problematic given the significant differences between the two interpretations.

One central difference is that while the aim of the 1931–32 interpretation is to examine the way in which Plato interprets untruth, this is not at all the aim of the 1926 interpretation. Indeed, while Heidegger's interpretation of Plato in 1926 focuses on the same texts as in 1931–32, the Cave Analogy and the *Theaetetus,* it is for a completely different reason, since what is at issue in the 1926 interpretation is not the essence of truth, much less a transformation in the essence of truth. What explains Heidegger's interest in the *Theaetetus* in 1926 are presumably the things he claims to be distinctive of this dialogue: (1) the idea of *Wissenschaft*; (2) the concrete presentation of the dialogical working out of a problem; (3) a bridge between Plato's earlier position and his later one: the development of the fundamental problem and its method: dialectic (GA 22, 107). While Heidegger's reading in 1931–32 continues to emphasize the second characteristic, the other two said to distinguish the *Theaetetus* in 1926 drop out of the later interpretation altogether.

Far from continuing to see the idea of *Wissenschaft* as central to the *Theaetetus*, Heidegger in 1931–32 insists that the question "What is *episteme*?" is *not* asking "What is *Wissenschaft*?" *Episteme* in the *Theaetetus* does not have "the meaning of scientific-theoretical being-informed of something" (GA 34, 153), but instead means "the *ruling knowing-oneself-around* in something, in dealings with a thing and in this thing itself" (153). It is only with Aristotle, Heidegger now claims, that the concept of *episteme* is narrowed to the extent that it "is in part synonymous with what we call Wissenschaft" (154). The reason for this change in Heidegger's reading of the *Theaetetus* is to be found in his own development. If in 1926 he interprets the *Theaetetus* as being about *Wissenschaft* and interprets Plato's conception of *episteme* through Aristotle's conception—which he at the time takes to be not narrower, but rather clearer and more precise than Plato's—this is because Heidegger is at the time convinced that philosophy can be *Wissenschaft*. This idea that guides Heidegger's thinking through the 1920s is explicitly and definitively rejected in the 1931–32 course: "*philosophia, philosophein* does not mean Wissenschaft (investigation of things in a delimited area and from a limited perspective of questioning), and also not first or fundamental-Wissenschaft, but instead: in questioning oneself holding oneself open for asking after the being and essence of things, being conversant with what is ultimately at issue with regard to beings and being as such. In short, the philosopher is the friend of being" (82). It is for this reason that Heidegger now does not find the idea of *Wissenschaft* in the *Theaetetus*, but rather a much broader conception of *episteme* as "sich verstehen auf etwas . . . sich auskennen in etwas."

In 1926 Heidegger sees the *Theaetetus* as a turning point in Plato's development. This development is seen as having three main and related aspects: (1) the abandonment of the idea of the good as an interpretation of being or, as Heidegger also states the point, the freeing of the problem of being from the idea of the good (GA 22, 113–14); (2) while Plato earlier relegated both κίνησις and δόξα to non-being, he now gives a more positive appraisal of them (115, 124, 273); (3) Socrates' maieutic method and "What is x?" question are abandoned in favor of a new conception of dialectic; if Plato describes this Socratic method at 148e–151d, this is only as a gesture of farewell (111, 265–66). In 1931–32 there is in contrast no talk of Plato's development along any of these lines. That Plato abandoned, or minimized the importance of, the idea of the good in later dialogues starting with the *Theaetetus* is explicitly and vehemently denied (GA 34, 110). As for the second alleged development, it too disappears in 1931–32. One must hope that this is at least in part because the thesis is clearly false: how could one maintain that in the *Meno, Republic,* and *Symposium,* δόξα is relegated to non-being? What perhaps saves Heidegger from this error in 1931–32 is the recognition there of ἔρως as a positive phenomenon and of its intimate relation to δόξα. Finally, there is in the later course no talk of one method being abandoned in favor of another; indeed, there is little talk of method at all. This is at least in part due to the more narrow focus. The part of the text that describes Socrates' maieutic method is not discussed. Also not discussed is the final thesis that *episteme* is δόξα with λόγος: yet it is in this discussion of λόγος that Heidegger in 1926 finds a working out of the problem of dialectic, though the notes for this part of the course are extremely sketchy. The significance of these lacunae in the 1931–32 account will need to be discussed in the context of an analysis of that course. What needs to be noted here is that even apart from the issue of development, the 1926 interpretation makes the problem of dialectic absolutely central, while the 1931–32 interpretation cannot be said to address it at all. In 1926 Heidegger even describes the aim of his reading of the *Theaetetus* as being to work through "the characteristic of the central—and fundamental—problem of Platonic philosophy, ψυχή and dialectic" (GA 22, 112). And here again we come upon a fundamental difference between the two interpretations. In 1931–32 Heidegger also works through the *Theaetetus* as a means of getting at the central and fundamental problem of Platonic philosophy, but there this problem is not ψυχή and dialectic: instead, there Heidegger asserts that Plato's philosophy "is indeed nothing but a battle between the two conceptions of truth" (GA 34, 46), those of truth as unconcealment and truth as correctness. The essence of truth has taken the place of ψυχή and dialectic as the central problem of Plato's philosophy and therefore of the paradigmatic dialogue *Theaetetus*.

These two problems are of course not unrelated. What is ultimately at issue both in the question of the ψυχή and dialectic and in the question of the essence of truth is *the question of being*. Here we arrive at the fundamental continuity between both interpretations. If the 1926 interpretation emphasizes the problem of *Wissenschaft* and dialectic, it at the same time insists that the *Theaetetus* is not a work of epistemology. In asking, "What is ἐπιστήμη?" the dialogue is asking, "What is the nature of our access to being?" and therefore, "What is being?" It therefore cannot consider the identification of ἐπιστήμη with *aisthesis* without considering how being is disclosed to αἴσθησις, i.e., as κίνησις. It also cannot consider the identification of ἐπιστήμη with δόξα without addressing the problem of non-being raised by the phenomenon of false δόξα (GA 22, 112–13). As for λόγος and dialectic, Heidegger insists that the discussion of λόγος in the third definition of ἐπιστήμη "is *ontological*, once again oriented towards the general problem of being, in other words, towards the question concerning the μὴ ὄν, i.e., ἕτερον, in general the πρός τι" (134), and that the problem of dialectic is a "purely ontological problem of grasping the ontological relations which the ideas have among themselves" (280). Therefore, Heidegger insists that the *Theaetetus* is not a work of epistemology, but rather a work of ontology, and ontology in the most legitimate sense if our only way of addressing the question of being is by way of addressing the nature of our access to being: "Perhaps there can in general be no question of being without looking back on our manner of accessing beings, and in the end the explicit question regarding knowledge is nothing other than the more incisive posing of the problem in the direction of the determination of being" (113). There is therefore no "epistemology," Heidegger asserts, in the *Theaetetus* (113).[1] This insistence that the *Theaetetus* is a work of ontology is just as strong in 1931–32, though what does receive extra emphasis there is the extent to which what is in question is *our own being* (GA 34, 157).

This prevailing ontological interest explains an important similarity in what part of the text is given the greatest weight. Already in 1926 Heidegger gives special importance to the text on which he will focus in 1931–32 and which he will there claim to be the text on which the entire history of philosophy depends (GA 34, 182). This is 184–87 (or even more narrowly, 185a8–186c6), where the question of our relation to being is explicitly addressed. Socrates characterizes being as common (*koinon*) to all the senses, that is, as not perceived through a particular sense organ. Since any knowledge must be knowledge of being, and being is not perceived through any of the senses, knowledge cannot be identified with perception. But if the human soul does not grasp being through any of the body's sense organs, it must do so in itself and through itself. In 1926 Heidegger finds in this argument "categories, discovery of the categorial as opposed to the sensible ... the material content of the problem: *sensible* and *categorial intuition*" (GA 22, 123). Thus, what Heidegger finds in this passage is the idea in which he always saw both his greatest debt to Husserl and his major breakthrough to the problem of being: the idea that being is *immediately given to us*, though not in perception. Heidegger in 1931–32 will find the same fundamental discovery in the passage, though there, as will be seen, he will develop this idea much more fully and radically, seeing the relation to being described in the passage as characterized not so much by intuition as by erotic striving.

But while in 1926 Heidegger describes Plato as simply bumping against these phenomena without being able to master them (GA 22, 273), in 1931–32 he gives a much more positive assessment of Plato's grasp of the phenomena.

---

1. See also at 264, 266. "Die Frage 'Was ist Erkenntnis?' soll nicht herausinterpretiert werden. Aber die ruht auf der Frage nach dem Sein" (267). Also Beilage 6. at 192: "'*Theätet*': Was ist Wissen? Zugrunde liegt die Frage nach dem Sein."

It is therefore important to see the reason for the more negative assessment in 1926. The central reason is that on Heidegger's reading the phenomena seen at 184–87 are obstructed and lost in other parts of the dialogue. Specifically, and most importantly, before giving the argument at 184–87 against the thesis *episteme = aisthesis*, Socrates gives another argument: that the postulate of universal and unqualified κίνησις on which this thesis has been based dissolves both the object of perception and perception itself. Heidegger objects: "One easily sees that in this critique the genuine *phenomenon of perception* (intentionality) *is lost*. Perception is discussed in the same way as the perceived being (the moved). The intentional structure of perception is reduced to a present-at-hand causal nexus (*Wirkungszusammenhang*) of what is perceived, the effected one of a coming-together (*ein gewirktes eines Zusammentreffens*)" (120). Thus, while the argument at 184–87 appeals to the intentional structure of our relation to being in order to refute the thesis, the earlier argument ignores this structure altogether. Thus, at 267–68 Heidegger distinguishes between "two fundamental directions of philosophy": (1) one that considers perception, knowledge, etc. according to their intentional structure; (2) one that considers them in an objective naturalistic sense: as a relation between an event in some subject and a physical event. Heidegger then comments: "In the case of *Plato* 1. and 2. are mixed together" (268).

One could of course object that rather than there being any confusion here, Plato offers the argument at 184–87 precisely because he recognizes the inadequacy of what has come before. This indeed appears to be Heidegger's assumption in 1931–32. There he does not make the charge of confusion and does not even discuss the earlier argument concerning universal flux. Furthermore, he sees in the passage at 184–87 not some kind of accidental "bumping against" phenomena, but a real mastery of the phenomena and a turning point in the discussion recognized by Plato as such. This shift in Heidegger's assessment of Plato results from a shift in how Heidegger reads the dialogue. As already noted above, Heidegger in both interpretations emphasizes *how* the questions are raised and addressed in the dialogue, that is, how the dialogue is conducted and progresses. Furthermore, in both cases he sees the motor of the discussion, both what keeps it going and presents it with the setbacks it must continually overcome, as a tension between assumed theories and how the phenomena show themselves. But the crucial difference is that while in 1926 he tends to see Plato as trapped in the assumed theories and prevented by them from truly mastering and seeing the phenomena, in 1931–32 he tends to see the obstructive theories as those of ordinary human understanding (and of Theaetetus in particular, see GA 34, 274), which Plato deliberately presents with the aim of showing their inadequacy and thereby indicating what is required for a genuine grasp of the phenomena.

An especially good illustration of this difference in how Heidegger reads the dialogue can be found in how he interprets the refutation of the thesis that false opinion is *allodoxia*. In 1926 he asserts: "Here 'other than it is' is interpreted as one *in place of* [*statt*] the other. ἕτερον . . . ὡς ἕτερον (189d7), 'the one as another.' In place of, but not as" (GA 22, 129). He then concisely expresses his judgment on the argument in the following sentence: "Theory in front of the phenomenon, though a first step in its direction" (129; see also the *Beilage* at 194: "Theses against phenomena"). Thus, Heidegger proceeds to say that the genuine phenomenon breaks through in the example of mistaking someone I see in the distance for Socrates: "Here the phenomenon is expressly described, the phenomenon of *overlooking* [*Versehens*]: I falsely take someone to be another" (130). But then comes the critique: "But the adequate interpretation is held back by a preconstructed theory" (130). In the *Nachschrift* Heidegger puts the point this way: "Now the positive phenomenon breaks through in Plato, without his taking it seriously" (277).[2] When Heidegger proceeds to explain what exactly in the phenomenon is overlooked, one sees that what is stated at 129 is indeed the problem in his eyes: "It belongs precisely to the *phenomenon* that I think *it is he*. That it in fact is not he is something already covered up in the phenomenon. In the phenomenon of overlooking (*des Versehens*) something is taken to be not something which it is not, but rather what I think that it is. Something unknown plays precisely no role here" (130). And Heidegger insists on this crucial point: "Knowledge is not at all unambiguous, *a being and its being are distinct*" (131). A failure to see this and a dogmatic thesis about λόγος are therefore what, according to Heidegger, lead to the rejection of this interpretation of δόξα. The dogmatic thesis about λόγος is that of Antisthenes as described at 275–76: λόγος as identification, that is, the assertion that A is B as the identification of A with B. Heidegger here asserts that not only is the phenomenon of the "as" not "in view" for Plato ("nicht im Blick"), but that even in Aristotle "it is not yet conceptually grasped" (275). "The phenomenon of the 'as' remains in any case obscure for *Plato* and *Aristotle*. In Plato it is most immediately ἀντί, 'in the place of'" (278).

In 1931–32 the same criticism is made of Socrates' refutation: "Exchange [*Auswechslung*], in short, is not mistake [*Verwechslung*]; the latter is not grasped in its essence by the former" (GA 34, 283). But the assessment of what is going on in the dialogue is completely different. Heidegger here does not protray this assumption, as well as the assumptions guiding the other

---

2. This is made a critique of Greek interpretation as such: "Die *griechische* Interpretation fällt aus dem Phänomen heraus und charakterisiert es durch objektive Resultate, d. h., sie sieht den objektiven Tatbestand, daß das X nicht Sokrates war und daß ich X nicht as X, das es in Wirklichkeit ist, erkannte, in das Phänomen hinein" (130).

arguments against the possibility of false δόξα, that is that something must either be *or* not be, be known *or* not be known, as ones to which Plato is committed or confined. In the 1933–34 version of the course Heidegger concludes his summary of the arguments against false δόξα with the question "What then must give way? The *matter itself* [*Tatbestand*], that which is experienced every day, or fundamental principles that have held sway for hundreds of years?" (GA 36/37, 254). Heidegger then unequivocally asserts that Plato's decision (*Entscheidung*) is for the phenomenon (255). The theories that obstruct the phenomenon he now attributes not to Plato, but to Theaetetus as the representative of ordinary human understanding. After asking why the attempt to explain how false δόξα can believe what is not fails, Heidegger answers: "Obviously, because the phenomenon is not fully seen. And why not? Because Theaetetus is not yet *free* enough to learn to *see*, because in the clarification of the phenomenon he is still too much under the influence of common principles and concepts into which he in anticipation forces the phenomenon and thereby distorts it" (GA 34, 274). It is in this context that Heidegger characterizes Theaetetus as the representative "of sound human understanding that thinks and speaks in Greek" ("griechisch," 274; the addition of "griechisch" here is not obviously necessary or defensible). Therefore, if Plato allows the discussion to be obstructed by assumed theories, it is precisely to expose the inadequacy of these theories and thereby point indirectly to what a proper grasp of the phenomenon would require. If he allows the theories and the phenomena to be at odds with each other in the discussion, this is not because he is undecided between them or confused, but rather because experiencing this tension is a way of coming to see the phenomena. The opinion of ordinary understanding that blocks the phenomenon of *allodoxia* is the view that δόξα has *two* objects, so that it is simply the switching of one for the other; what needs to be seen instead is that δόξα has one object characterized by *Mehrfältigkeit* (283). Heidegger then interprets Plato's Wax and Aviary analogies as at least in part drawing attention to this *Mehrfältigkeit* (309ff.) Therefore, rather than attributing any confusion to Plato here, Heidegger can assert that Plato saw with perfect clarity the fundamental task ("sich ganz klar war"): opening the proper field of vision within which the *question* of the essence of false *doxa* can be placed (290–91).

I suggest that this shift toward a much more sympathetic treatment of Plato's method in 1931–32 is the result of a shift in Heidegger's own conception of philosophy. In the later course, after asserting that the theses guiding the discussion of δόξα must give way before the phenomenon (GA 34, 285), Heidegger immediately adds a crucial qualification not to be found in 1926: that the phenomena are not directly and immediately accessible, that they can be seen only in the light of certain presuppositions. The belief in the possibility of seeing the phenomena without presuppositions is now identified as an error of phenomenology: "It was an error of phenomenology to believe that the phenomena could already be correctly seen through the mere putting aside of presuppositions [*durch bloße Unvoreingenommenheit*]" (286). In the 1933–34 version of the course, he makes the same point that there is no such thing as seeing things "rein" and "unvoreingenommen" (GA 36/37, 256) immediately after claiming that Plato decides for the phenomena. Heidegger in both cases makes clear that he is not claiming we are confined to subjective and inadequate assumptions and thereby cut off from the phenomenon. The difficult but yet possible task is that of developing from the phenomena themselves perspectives that are adequate to them: the question is "if the leading perspective is adequate to the phenomenon itself, if it is derived in advance from its own content or not (or only invented)" (GA 34, 286); or, in the words used in 1933–34, "It is necessary to decide whether the perspective within which I question corresponds to the object or not" (GA 36/37, 256). But how is this possible? If the phenomenon is not accessible independently of certain assumed perspectives, how can I determine whether or not a given perspective is adequate to the phenomenon? Heidegger does not answer this question here. However, the implication appears to be that the answer can be found in how the discussion in the *Theaetetus* proceeds: for this discussion moves towards a more adequate perspective on the phenomenon of δόξα, not through the unmediated intuition Heidegger now declares to be impossible, but rather by way of exposing the inadequacy of the prevailing and common perspectives. To use Plato's own term for what is taking place in the dialogue, the alternative to both unmediated intuition of the phenomenon and confinement to inadequate assumptions and perspectives is *dialectic*. The conviction of such dialectic is precisely that there is no way of getting at the phenomena themselves except by working through, against, and beyond the predominant assumptions and opinions. That Heidegger is now sympathetic toward this dialectic must be a result of his rejection of the "error of phenomenology."

Conversely, if Heidegger is not sympathetic toward Plato's dialectic in 1926, this must be because he is there still committed in some way to the "error of phenomenology." Indeed, as shown in chapter 1, throughout the 1920s Heidegger criticizes dialectic precisely for failing to get at how the phenomena show and give themselves because remaining caught in ordinary opinions and assumptions. Thus, he was seen to claim at one point that phenomenology and dialectic are as incompatible as fire and water (GA 63, 42). It is this kind of assumption that explains Heidegger's impatience with Plato's method in 1926. If Plato in the *Theaetetus* places theories before the phenomena, or approaches the phenomena only by way of theories, this only shows that he is not serious about the phenomena (GA 22, 277). The implication is that Plato should push all theories aside and describe the phenomena directly as they show themselves. In 1931 Heidegger no longer believes in the possibility of such directness and therefore is much more responsive to the indirectness of Plato's method. This goes along with the other shift described above: the abandonment of the view that philosophy can be *Wissenschaft*. This shift also brings a more positive assessment of another feature of Plato's indirectness: the use of images and analogies. According to the 1926 course, Plato resorts to "myths" such as that of the cave only because he has not mastered the problems (GA 22, 102), cannot make clear distinctions (258) and is naive (263). In 1931–32, it is as if Heidegger were arguing against his earlier self when he insists that if Plato speaks in images, this is not because he is still in some unclarity with regard to the matter itself but, on the contrary, because he "is *super clear* (überklar) about the fact that it is not demonstrable and describable. There is something in all genuine philosophy before which all describing and proving forsake one and degenerate into empty busy-work, even if this be the most resplendent science [*so glänzende Wissenschaft*]" (GA 34, 19). Thus, an image or myth is no longer, as in 1926, a failure to attain the higher level of science, but rather a more adequate way than science of accessing what, as ultimate and essential (*Letztes und Wesentliches*), cannot be described or proven. Later in the 1931–32 course, Heidegger explains thus Plato's use of the Wax and Aviary analogies: "We arrive here in the same situation as with the Cave Analogy: Plato stands before a task (clear to him as such, but also new) in the face of which he does not at all dare to deal directly and immediately with the new phenomena or even to master them in an initial attempt" (293). Given Heidegger's rejection of phenomenology's error of believing in the possibility of an immediate and presuppositionless seeing of the phenomena, Plato's procedure here no longer appears as the serious limitation it appeared to be in 1926. And of course, in 1942 Plato's use of a myth to think λήθη will be considered anything but a limitation.

This is not to suggest that in 1931–32 Heidegger simply embraces Plato's dialectic or the results achieved by it. As will be seen, his reading of the *Theaetetus* remains critical. However, fundamental affinities now emerge that greatly complicate Heidegger's attempted *Auseinandersetzung* with Plato. Indeed, it may be the case that Heidegger is closer to Plato in his reading of the *Theaetetus* than he is in his reading of any other Platonic text, the *Sophist* included. We will therefore need to be especially attentive to how Heidegger attempts to distance himself from Plato, that is, to how he transforms Plato into the beginning of metaphysics. This attempt will be seen to involve a partial abandonment of the text of the *Theaetetus*, both in the sense of overlooking crucial parts and dimensions of this text and in the sense of appealing to Platonic "doctrines" not found within it. One can say that while Heidegger's reading of Plato in 1931–32 is more open to the phenomena of the text than in 1926, a new theory not found at all in 1926 now comes to obstruct the phenomena: the theory of the transformation of the essence of truth.

B. THE INTERPRETATION OF THE *THEAETETUS* IN THE *VOM WESEN DER WAHRHEIT* COURSE OF 1931–32 AND 1933–34

1. Being and Truth as Had in Being Striven After

The above contrast with the 1926 interpretation already provides a sense of the aim, assumptions, and style of Heidegger's 1931–32 interpretation. What is required now is a detailed analysis of Heidegger's reading with the aim of seeing both what genuine possibilities in the text it uncovers as well as what it suppresses and imposes. Since interpretation of the *Theaetetus* in the 1933–34 version of the course is seriously curtailed, the analysis will follow the 1931–32 version, referring to the later version only when it offers a significant departure or addition.

As already noted, Heidegger here, as in 1926, insists that the question of the *Theaetetus* is an ontological rather than epistemological one. This perspective is especially evident in how Heidegger interprets the question that is the first to be addressed in the dialogue: is ἐπιστήμη the same as αἴσθησις? Translating αἴσθησις as "perceivedness" (*Wahrgenommenheit*) to emphasize its position "between" the subjective activity of perceiving and the object perceived, he characterizes as follows the question at issue: "The question of whether the *perceivedness* of something is unconcealment (*Unverborgenheit*) leads to the question of whether in αἴσθησις as such, in perceiving comportment [*im wahrnehmenden Verhalten*] as perceiving, there lies enclosed a possible comportment to *beings*" (GA 34, 166). In this way, by making a relation to beings the condition for something counting as ἐπιστήμη, Heidegger transforms the apparently "epistemological" question of the dialogue into an ontological one, though ontological not in the sense of examining being as an "object" independent of us, but rather in the sense of examining being in its relation to us and thus examining our own being.

Heidegger's claim that the question of ἐπιστήμη depends on the question of being and the question of truth is by no means arbitrary but is instead well supported by the text. At 186c-e Socrates presents the following argument for why ἐπιστήμη cannot be the same as αἴσθησις:

1. What does not lay hold of being cannot lay hold of truth (186c7–8).
2. There can be no ἐπιστήμη in what does not lay hold of truth (186c9–10).

3. Αἴσθησις has been shown not to lay hold of being.
4. Therefore, αἴσθησις also cannot lay hold of truth (186e4–5).
5. Therefore, there can be no ἐπιστήμη in αἴσθησις, i.e., ἐπιστήμη and αἴσθησις cannot be the same (186e9–10).

The argument could not be clearer: it is the lack of contact with being and truth (the conjunction is of course significant) that prevents αἴσθησις from being ἐπιστήμη. It is also undeniable that Socrates cannot show that αἴσθησις does not lay hold of being except by way of an account of what our relation to being is. What could be questioned is the extraordinary emphasis Heidegger gives this account and the argument based upon it. He clearly considers this part of the text to be the dialogue's heart and inner core, which is why he begins his detailed reading of the text only here. Indeed, as already noted, Heidegger considers 184–87 not only the ultimate basis of the entire dialogue, but even the ultimate basis of the entire history of Western philosophy! Whether this assessment is justified and whether this emphasis provides the dialogue with its needed center of gravity or throws it out of balance can be determined only by following Heidegger in his reading.

The specific text with which Heidegger begins his reading is Socrates' argument at 184b7–e6 that our ears, eyes, and other sense organs are not that *with which* (ᾧ) we perceive, but rather that *through which* (δι' οὗ) we perceive. This distinction then enables Socrates to find a unifying principle, or what he calls one ἰδέα, behind the multiplicity of different perceptions or sensations. If it were the case that we see with our eyes, hear with our ears, smell with our nose, etc., there would be no connection between seeing, hearing, and smelling but these different sensations would simply lie side by side in us, like soldiers in a bronze horse, to use Socrates' metaphor. On the other hand, if our eyes, ears, and noses are only that *through which* we hear, see, and smell, there can be one principle with which we perceive through these different organs and back toward which all of these different perceptions are "stretched" and "gathered" ("εἰς ... πάντα ταῦτα συντείνει," 184d3–4). Three things are important to note about this unity which Socrates postulates in the diversity of different perceptions: (1) though Socrates says that this unifying principle could be called ψυχή, he does not commit himself to this designation, allowing that it could be called something else (184d3); (2) he refers to it as an ἰδέα, thus treating it not as a "thing" but as a certain form or structure; (3) it unifies by having all things "stretched together" toward it, rather than by "encompassing" all or being "common" to all. One can therefore conclude that Socrates carefully avoids identifying the unity here with any kind of object and instead identifies it with what one could call some kind of structure of relations.

This and more is captured in Heidegger's interpretation, which he summarizes as follows: "We do not perceive colors and sounds and smells because we see or hear or smell, but on the contrary: because our self is in its essence relational [*verhältnishaft*], i.e., holds before and ahead of itself a region of perceptability as such and relates itself to it [*zu diesem sich* verhält], therefore can we in perceiving disperse ourselves within one and the same region and only thereby can we, remaining the same, transpose ourselves now into a seeing—or hearing—, now into a smelling—relation" (176–77). If the sense organ is only that *through which* we perceive, then it is not the ultimate cause of perception. Instead, we must already exist in a relation to what is perceivable, all that is perceivable must already be "stretched" and "gathered" toward us, in order for us then to use a sense organ as that through which actually to perceive this or that perceivable object. The sense organ does not first create the relation to the perceptible object, as it would it if were that *with which* we perceive, but rather as that *through which* we perceive already presupposes this relation.

This conclusion, however, to some extent gets ahead of the text, since it is only with the next move that Socrates makes explicit a relation between the soul and being that precedes and is independent of sensation. Indeed, we will see that the reason why Socrates insists on a unifying principle behind the different perceptions is to show that the soul relates to being *through itself* alone and not through any of the sense organs. It is this part of the argument at185a8–186c6 on which Heidegger claims the whole of Western philosophy rests. Heidegger accordingly interprets this text with great care and in the minutest detail, insisting at one point: "The unprecedented characteristic of every Platonic text is that every 'and,' 'but,' 'perhaps' is placed in its completely determinate and unequivocal spot [*an seinen ganz bestimmten, eindeutigen Platz gesetzt ist*] and is not idle talk [*Geschwätz*]" (191). Heidegger therefore cannot help but express in the strongest terms his admiration for how the discussion is carried out in the *Theaetetus*: "We begin to suspect what a model of genuine, working philosophizing emerges before us" (194). Heidegger's reading of the specific text in question itself proves, in its care and perceptiveness, a model of genuinely philosophical interpretation.

Socrates' initial point in this text is a simple but momentous one. It has been argued that we see something not *with* our eyes but *through* our eyes; we hear something not *with* but *through* our ears. But if we perceive something with regard to *both* what is seen and what is heard, that is, something in some way *common* to both (τὸ κοινόν), *this* we cannot perceive either through our eyes or through our ears. Each organ has its specific object, and therefore what we perceive through one cannot be perceived through the other (184e8–185a2). But what is "common" to what is seen, what is heard, and the specific objects of the other senses? As Socrates points out, I can say equally of what I hear and what I see that "it is" or "it is not." The crucial question then is this: what power, and through what means (ἡ διὰ τίνος δύναμις), can reveal to me (δηλοῖ σοι) the "being" or "not being" common to the objects of different senses (185c4–7)? Socrates also identifies other κοινά, which are summarized by Theaetetus: similarity and dissimilarity, sameness and difference, and number can be "perceived" and said with regard to the objects of different senses in relation to each other (185c9–d1): I can say that what I see is *different from* what I hear and that each is *the same as* itself; I can say that what I see and hear are *two* things and that each is *one* (185a8–b2). But if colors and sounds are perceived through different senses, what enables me to relate the two and perceive *both* together as *being, being the same or different, being one or two*, etc.? Clearly these "common" terms *exceed* what is known through the senses, so that Heidegger describes them here, though only provisionally, as an "excess" (*Mehrbestand*, 186).

Given Socrates' earlier argument, the answer appears obvious: if that *with which* we perceive sounds, colors, etc., *through* the different senses is itself *one* ἰδέα, what Socrates allows to be called the ψυχή, and if therefore the objects of the different senses all together stretch back to (συντείνει) this one ἰδέα, then clearly that which can relate the objects of the different senses to one another and see what is common to them can be nothing but the ψυχή. Yet it is extremely important to see that the answer is not quite this simple. Heidegger in attending to every word of the text rightly insists that Socrates' question is not simply what δύναμις reveals the κοινά, but *through what* (διὰ τίνος) it does so (191). What is never questioned by Socrates is that being, difference, number, etc., just as much as the objects of the senses, must be "perceived" *through* something. What is assumed here is that being, difference, etc. are not simply given to us in some pure immediacy, are not simply "in us," but rather that in some sense we must "get out" to them *by means of* something. Therefore, the answer Theaetetus gives to Socrates' question, the answer that makes Socrates judge him to be beautiful and not ugly at all (185e3–4), is not simply "the ψυχή," since such an answer would not have answered Socrates' specific question. Instead, Theaetetus's beautiful answer is the following: "the soul itself *through itself* (αὐτὴ δι' αὑτῆς) appears to me to examine (ἐπισκοπεῖν) with regard to all things what is common (τὰ κοινά)" (185e1–2). The answer is thus not simply that the soul is what examines τὰ κοινά but that it does so *through itself*.

One might be tempted to understand Theaetetus's answer, as prompted by Socrates' carefully formulated question, as saying in effect that the soul perceives τὰ κοινά *not through anything*. The temptation, in other words, is to take the phrase "through itself" to mean simply "in itself." In this case the suggestion would be that being, difference, sameness, etc., unlike the objects of the senses, are immediately "in" the soul so that the soul does not have to *reach* them *through* anything. A major merit of Heidegger's reading, in contrast, is to insist on preserving the διά. But what does this mean? Just as the soul can see a color only *through* the eyes, so can it "see" being only *through* something. But since this "something" has turned out to be the soul itself, is not the διά thereby effectively eliminated? In the phrase αὐτὴ δι' αὑτῆς, does not the identity of what is on both sides of the διά effectively eliminate the διά, so that the phrase means no more than αὐτή? This conclusion is precisely what Heidegger resists: in the phrase "the soul itself *through* itself," the "through" is not eliminated, but is rather *made internal to the soul itself*. The διά is not outside the soul in some sense organ, but rather characterizes the soul itself. This means that the soul is in itself the way-through-to the κοινά, that the διά is not some relation between the soul and the κοινά, but that the soul is in itself this relation. Put in terms of the language of "stretching" (συντείνει) Socrates used earlier, the soul is *in itself stretched toward* being and the other κοινά. Thus, Heidegger concludes from the cited passage: "It [the soul] is *in itself*, as such, *stretched* [*erstreckt*] out toward the other [*zu Anderem hin*] that can be given to it, and maintains itself constantly and only *in* such a stretch [*Erstreckung*]. As what in its very constitution perceives [*das von Haus aus Vernehmende*], being-a-soul means in itself being-stretched, throughway [*Durchgang*], stretching-oneself towards something [*Sich-erstrecken zu etwas*]" (197). If this conclusion appears to go well beyond the text, it must be noted again that it is a result of refusing to eliminate from the text the phrase δι' αὑτῆς. Furthermore, the suggestion here that the soul is in itself "stretched towards" being will receive strong confirmation in an extraordinary passage that Heidegger, unlike others, refuses to overlook.

Before we turn to that passage, it is necessary to examine another important aspect of Theaetetus's beautiful answer to Socrates' question. Even if we agree that the soul is inherently "stretched out toward," and thus related to, being and the other κοινά, that still does not tell us anything about the nature and character of this relation. *How* exactly does the soul relate itself to the κοινά? The word Theaetetus uses in his answer to describe the relation is ἐπισκοπεῖν: the soul "observes" or "examines" what the objects of the different senses have in common. Here Theaetetus is simply picking up on Socrates' own use of the word ἐπισκέψασθαι (185b5, c1). What Heidegger's interpretation infers from the use of these words is that Plato is characterizing the soul's relation to being as one of *unmediated seeing*: "In the perception [*Vernehmen*] of being, not-being, being-different, etc., the soul is itself *seeing, immediately* [*unmittelbar*] perceiving" (197). This interpretation appears questionable. Even if the word σκοπεῖν has the meaning of "looking" or "contemplating," the prefix ἐπι- appears to distance such looking from a simple immediate seeing; ἐπισκοπεῖν is probably best translated here as "examining" or "investigating." The word Socrates himself uses, ἐπισκέψασθαι, suggests even more strongly such a translation. Furthermore, as Heidegger himself notes, the other verb Socrates uses to describe the soul's relation to the κοινά is διανοεῖν (185a4, a9, b7). This use of ἐπισκοπεῖν and διανοεῖν as synonyms certainly does not support an emphasis on the connotation of "seeing" or "looking" in the former. It is perhaps for this reason that Heidegger earlier insists that διανοεῖν does not mean "thinking" but rather "durchnehmendes Vernehmen" (180–81, 186). Whether or not this insistence is justified can be shown only in the course of reading the rest of the text. What can be said here, however, is that any interpretation of διανοεῖν that gives some weight to the prefix δια-, even an interpretation as "*durchnehmendes* Vernehmen," hardly supports the characterization of the relation in question as an "immediate seeing or perceiving."

Another way in which Heidegger supports his reading is to stress the fact that at 185e6–7 the word ἐπισκοπεῖν is used "equally for the perception of color and sound and, *in the same sense* [*im gleichen Sinne*], for the perception of being, not-being, being-different and the like" (199; my emphasis). But that Socrates in using the word ἐπισκοπεῖν to describe both what the soul does *through itself* and what it does *through the sense organs* is using this word strictly, with the same sense in both cases, rather than loosely, in a way that includes and leaves undistinguished various senses: this is simply Heidegger's assertion. Whether the sense is indeed the same, whether the soul "immediately perceives" being in the way it "immediately perceives" a color, can be decided only by examining what Socrates proceeds to say. And indeed what Socrates immediately proceeds to say will be seen to give the word ἐπισκοπεῖν as it applies to the soul's relation to being a sense radically different from that which it has as applied to the soul's relation to sensible objects.

Before turning to this important passage, however, we need to step away from the text for a moment in order to see what is at work in Heidegger's reading beyond the text itself. Why does Heidegger insist on characterizing the soul's relation to the κοινά as an immediate seeing? The reason is that this is absolutely essential to his thesis regarding the transformation of the essence of truth, a thesis implicitly guiding Heidegger's reading, but not made explicit, as we will see, until the very end of the course. The main building blocks of Heidegger's argument have already emerged from his interpretation of the Cave Analogy: (1) Plato interprets being in its unconcealment (or truth) as ἰδέα and therefore as *what is seen*, since ἰδέα means *Anblick* or *Ansehen*; (2) this interpretation of being and truth makes them relative to *a seeing*; (3) in thus being subordinated to what is seen (the ἰδέα) and therefore to seeing, truth is transformed into the mere "adequation" of seeing to what is seen: truth is seeing *correctly* and untruth (the false) is seeing incorrectly (*Versehen*). That Heidegger wishes to show that such a transformation is taking place in the passage presently under consideration is made clear in a note found with Heidegger's manuscript for the course, and therefore obviously not delivered. The note reads as follows: "This (*Theaetetus* 184 to 187) is the most essential section, the one that carries all with it. Here also is especially clear the turn [*Wendepunkt*] that Greek thinking accomplishes in relation to its beginning [*gegenüber seinem Anfang*] in order to go over into 'metaphysics,' i.e., to ground it on the doctrine of being as ἰδέα and of truth as ὁμοίωσις. Only now does 'philosophy' begin" (327–28). The transformation to which Heidegger refers here comes to be stated with special clarity, as we have seen, in the 1940 essay "Plato's Doctrine of Truth." There Heidegger, claiming that what is at issue in every comportment towards beings for Plato is "the ἰδεῖν of the ἰδέα" and thus the adjusting of one to the other, writes: "As a result of this matching [*Angleichung*] of perceiving [*Vernehmen*] as an ἰδεῖν to the ἰδέα, a ὁμοίωσις occurs, an agreement [*Übereinstimmung*] between knowing and the thing itself. Thus arises, out of the priority of ἰδέα and ἰδεῖν over ἀλήθεια, a transformation in the essence of truth. Truth becomes ὀρθότης, correctness of perceiving [*Vernehmen*] and asserting" (PLW, 228). As already noted above, however, in the 1940 essay there is no mention of the *Theaetetus*. To find the transformation Heidegger describes in the passage of the *Theaetetus* under consideration, as Heidegger in the cited note claims we can, we must be able to see in the characterization there of the soul's relation to being the reduction of this relation to one between a seeing and what is seen, as well as between an asserting and what is asserted. Thus Heidegger's insistence. But that Heidegger's thesis needs this reading of the text should make us all the more vigilant, and especially on the lookout for ways in which the text resists this reading. And we should ask ourselves: why is it that while in 1931–32 Heidegger describes *Theaetetus* 184–87 as the turning point in the transformation of truth and the beginning of metaphysics, he does not cite it in "Plato's Doctrine of Truth" nor in any of his later accounts of the history of metaphysics and the transformation of truth? Does the text ultimately prove resistant to Heidegger's history of metaphysics?

As already noted, an extraordinary text immediately problematizes the identification of the soul's relation to being with any kind of "immediate seeing." At 186a4–5 Theaetetus includes being among the things the soul itself by itself ἐπορέγεται, strives for, stretches itself out towards. What must be noted here is the unquestioned and unremarked substitution of the word ἐπορέγεσθαι for the word ἐπισκοπεῖν used only a few lines earlier and in exactly the same context. For this substitution to be possible, what must be predominantly heard in the word ἐπισκοπεῖν is not "seeing" or "looking" but rather "investigating," "searching," and thus a kind of *striving*. As thus understood, this ἐπισκοπεῖν is certainly quite different from the kind of ἐπισκοπεῖν that characterizes the perception of sensible objects through the sense organs. Heidegger himself does not comment on the substitution as such, but he does give great emphasis to the use of the word ἐπορέγεται and is prompted by it to launch into an extraordinarily extensive and perceptive analysis of the kind of "striving" involved here. Later he will return to a characterization of the relation as a "seeing," but the intervening discussion will have transformed this seeing into a peculiar "seeing-striving" radically unlike the passive and immediate intuition of an object.

That Heidegger should give the emphasis he does to the word ἐπορέγεται is not surprising, given that it provides strong textual confirmation of the interpretation he has been developing. Heidegger has argued that the characterization of the soul as relating to the κοινά itself *through itself* is to be understood as a characterization of the soul as in itself *stretched out toward* the κοινά; now the text says explicitly that the soul ἐπορέγεται, *strives for*, or *stretches itself out toward*, the κοινά. Heidegger draws attention to the middle voice here (203): the striving or stretching is not something "outside" the soul that it merely "does," but rather something that reflects back on it and intimately involves it. What the soul desires, it desires for and in relation to itself; it is *itself* stretched out toward what it desires. Thus, Heidegger concludes: "The soul *is* this striving for being [*Strebnis nach dem Sein*]" (203), or what Heidegger calls "Seinserstrebnis" (203). That Heidegger should speak predominantly of a striving for being rather than a striving for sameness or number has its basis in the text: at 186a2–3, Socrates says of being (οὐσία) that it most of all (μάλιστα, in comparison, presumably, with the other κοινά) follows upon all things ("ἐπὶ πάντων παρέπεται"). Heidegger interprets this passage as giving a clear predominance to being (202–3): because being "most of all" follows upon all things, it is the "striving for being" that is foremost in our relation to all things.[3]

Before proceeding to Heidegger's analysis of this *Seinserstrebnis*, it is important first to counter the possible objection that Heidegger is reading into one word, ἐπορέγεται, something foreign to Plato's thought. As Heidegger himself at one point notes, in speaking of *Seinserstrebnis* he is speaking of nothing other than what Plato himself calls ἔρως (216). Though Heidegger does not cite any particular text, and while the discussion of ἔρως in the *Symposium* might come most immediately to mind, the *Phaedrus* is especially worth citing in this context. While the *Symposium* characterizes our relation to the

---

3. Heidegger takes the παρά in παρέπεται to mean "anwesend" (203). But the word is not πάρεστι but παρέπεται! Here again Heidegger is willfully reducing what is expressed in the text to being = presence.

"form" of beauty as ἔρως, the *Phaedrus* makes clear that while beauty may be the form "most manifest" to the senses and thus most capable of awakening ἔρως (250d7–e1), our relation to all of the forms, and thus to being in general, is ἔρως. Furthermore, Socrates' Great Speech includes the argument that the soul is immortal because a *self-mover* (τὸ αὐτὸ ἑαυτὸ κινοῦν, 245e7–246a1). Socrates proceeds to illustrate the nature of the soul's self-motion with the metaphor of the soul's wings, wings that enable the soul to move up to the "place beyond the heavens" where the "forms" of true being are to be found. This movement toward being represented by the wings and characterizing the soul's innate self-motion is ἔρως; metaphorically, it is through ἔρως that the wings are nourished and given their power, not of *moving the soul* toward being (as if the soul needed to be moved by something distinct from itself), but rather of *being* the soul's own self-motion towards being. Thus, a reading of the *Phaedrus* can only show Heidegger's claim that the soul *is Seinserstrebnis* to be quite faithful to Plato. It can also show why in the *Theaetetus* the word ἐπορέγεται suddenly appears in the context of describing the soul's relation to being.

Let us now turn to Heidegger's important analysis. The first point Heidegger makes, against the possible objection that if the soul is only "striving" for being it cannot "have" it, is that striving does not rule out every kind of having. This is because "what is striven after [*das Bestrebte*] is there [*da*] in the striving, and is *gone* [*weg*] precisely in *not*-striving-after-it" (211). Thus, "the after-what of striving, what is striven after as such, is had *in* striving, *as* striven-after it *is* something had [*ein Gehabtes*]" (211). However, it is nevertheless the case that what is striven after is in some sense *not* had. One should in this context recall Diotima's description of ἔρως: as the child of both *Poros* and *Penia*, it is both a have and a have-not. Heidegger must therefore proceed to distinguish between two kinds of *having*:

(1) "The having at one's disposal of things and goods [*das Verfügen über Dinge und Güter*]." Heidegger characterizes this as an *inauthentic* having in the strict sense that it is a having through which you *lose yourself in what is had, are possessed by what you possess*. In this having, "the apparent freedom of disposing of and using is in essence [*im Grunde*] an enslavement [*Knechtschaft*] to the unchoosability [*Wahllosigkeit*] and contingency [*Zufälligkeit*] of desires [*Bedürfnisse*]" (213). Possessing money, for example, is only an enslavement to the unchosen need I have for money. Heidegger therefore also associates an *inauthentic striving* with this *inauthentic having*: one in which you are possessed by the object of desire and lose yourself in it (214).

(2) Before describing what an *authentic* having would be, Heidegger describes *authentic striving*, that is, striving in which one maintains and preserves onself rather than losing oneself in the object: "What such striving

seeks is not the possession [*Besitz*] of what is striven after, but rather that what is striven after *remain* [*bleibe*] something striven-after [*ein Be-strebtes*], something held in striving [*im Streben Gehaltenes*], so that he who strives [*der Strebende*] should be able to find his way back from it to himself [*von ihm her auf sich zu sich selbst finde*]" (215). Here one should recall Diotima's analysis of the "middle" position of ἔρως between possession and lack and her example of the ἔρως for wisdom, that is, philosophy. To *possess* wisdom is not to strive for it and therefore not to be a philosopher, indeed, not to be human or mortal. But if the philosopher lacks wisdom, it cannot be in the same way the ignorant nonphilosopher lacks wisdom. What, then, is the difference? The ignorant person, not recognizing his lack of wisdom, does not even strive for it, while the philosopher, recognizing the lack, does strive for it (203e4–204b7). But one could object: how can *mere striving* put the philosopher in a position nearer to wisdom, that is, entitle the philosopher to a position *between* ignorance and wisdom and thus above ignorance? A person who desires wisdom does not thereby in the least cease being ignorant, just as someone who desires food does not thereby become any less hungry. But Diotima's point appears to be precisely the point Heidegger explicitly articulates here: in genuinely striving after wisdom, the philosopher "has" this wisdom *as* something striven for, this wisdom is continually *held* in this striving, and in such a way that the philosopher identifies himself with this striving.

But then what is the authentic having that corresponds to this authentic striving? In exactly what sense is wisdom "had" by the philosopher who strives after it? More generally, in what sense is the "object" of ἔρως "had" *in* ἔρως if not in the sense of being *possessed*? Heidegger describes the following two dimensions of authentic having: "1. In striving-for [*Erstreben*] what is striven after is never taken into possession as a thing or the like [*nie wie ein Ding und dergleichen in Besitz genommen*], but rather is kept as striven-after [*als Bestrebtes erhalten*] without being taken [*ungenommen*]. 2. This keeping [*Erhaltung*], however, holds what is striven after back towards he who strives [*hält das Bestrebte auf das Strebende selbst zurück*], so that it might thereby become a measure and law for his comportment towards beings and thus make possible existence from out of the ground of beings as a whole [*aus dem Grunde des Seienden im Ganzen*]" (216). One can summarize by saying that the "having" that characterizes authentic striving is neither a taking nor possessing, but rather a "holding" that both holds *away from us* what is striven *after* and holds it *for us* as what *we* are striving for. Here again Diotima's example is helpful: in striving for wisdom the philosopher does not possess it, but does "hold" it for himself as striven-for in such a way that it can become a measure and a law for how he acts and how he exists. Ironically, it is the very fact that what is striven for is *not* possessed that gives it such normative power over who we are and how we act. It is not what we possess that defines who we are: the possession of money, for example, is something external to me in which I can only lose myself. Instead, it is what we *strive for*, and in this striving *maintain in a continual relation to ourselves*, that defines who we are. This is why Heidegger characterizes only the latter kind of having and striving as "authentic."

The above analysis, it must now be recalled, is meant to explain *Seinserstrebnis*, the soul's striving, stretching-out towards being. What can now be said about this fundamental relation? To characterize the soul's relation to being as ἐπορέγεσθαι is to characterize this relation as not one of possessing or "taking" being, but rather as one of keeping being as something striven-for in such a way that the soul can measure and guide what it says and does *by* being. What exactly this means of course requires much more elucidation. But the first question that needs to be asked is this: if this is the soul's relation to being, then how could this relation possibly be characterized as a "seeing," much less an immediate seeing? If the soul in its striving does not "have" being *as an object*, then in what sense can it be said to *see* being? In Heidegger's terms, if in the soul's striving being is not *genommen*, then how can it be *ver-nommen*? Plato of course often uses the seeing metaphor to characterize the soul's relation to being. But chapter 3 already argued against Heidegger's tendency to overemphasize this metaphor and take it too literally, citing a passage from the *Republic* that describes in terms of ἔρως how we come to know being and uses only metaphors that gravitate around this "erotic" characterization: touching, getting close, intercourse, giving birth, and labor pains; from this description the seeing metaphor is completely absent (490a–b). When one in addition now finds the word ἐπορέγεσθαι being used in the *Theaetetus* to describe the soul's relation to being, how can one persist in claiming that seeing is the predominant, much less exclusive, way in which Plato understands the relation to being?

Yet Heidegger does persist. After his account of striving, he tries to reconcile this striving with his earlier characterization of the soul's relation to being as a seeing by speaking of a "*seeing* striving" (*sehendes* Streben) (223). Yet to make this hybrid at all coherent, Heidegger must give a characterization of seeing that departs significantly from the earlier talk of "immediate perceiving." The passage in which he does so deserves very careful scrutiny:

> Not only looking [*Blicken*] in the sense of mere looking at [*Anblicken*], gaping at something present-at-hand [*Angaffens eines Vorhandenen*], but rather with the character of striving [*Strebenscharakter*]: seeing in the sense of aiming at [*Absehens auf*] . . . , ahead [*voraus*], towards [*hin zu*] . . . , at something [*auf etwas zu*], directed at [*ausgerichtet auf*] . . . ; σκοπός is what is en-visioned [*das Er-blickte*], something at which is

aimed *in advance* [im voraus *abgesehen ist*]: the aim [*Ab-sicht*], the goal (its appraisal [*Schätzung*]). What we *genuinely* "have in view" ["*im Auge haben*"] is precisely that which we normally do *not* look at [*anblikken*], but *only* have in view, and indeed medially: *standard-giving* [*maßgebend*] authoritative for us (for our comportment). (222–23)

Heidegger's earlier point that what is striven for is *had* in striving as a measure and law is here being translated into the language of vision. Yet what needs to be noted is the extent to which this characterization of striving as a "seeing" and of what is striven after as "seen" pushes the metaphor of seeing to its extreme limit, invoking more the ultimate condition of seeing than seeing itself. In striving, the aim is not passively looked at, regarded, observed, or "seen" as if it were an object; instead, the aim is *projected* (en-visioned) and only held "in view" as that which we "see to" in all our comportment toward—and this includes the seeing of—beings; it is, in other words, held "in view" not as something itself viewed but rather as the outer boundary and measure of the view. With regard to our relation to being, this means that the "seeing" that characterizes this relation is not a *looking at* but a *looking to*. Though we do not possess being as an object so as to be able to *look at* it, we do "have" it in our striving in such a way that we can *look to* it as a measure and law for our existing and acting. But even if we can describe the aiming-at-being and having-regard-to-being that characterize *Seinserstrebnis* as *a kind of seeing*, is this the kind of seeing that supports Heidegger's thesis regarding the transformation of truth? Is looking to being as measure and law a matter of *seeing correctly or incorrectly*? Are not instead such looking-to and the unconcealment of being in such looking-to what *make possible* any kind of correspondence and correctness between "seeing" and beings? I can look at beings as beings correctly or incorrectly only on the basis of already looking *to* their being. In other words, any truth as correspondence between perceiving and beings can occur only on the basis of truth as the unconcealment of being that occurs in the striving for being. As we will see, Heidegger himself will articulate in this way the structure implicit in the text.

What gives Heidegger the opportunity to reintroduce the language of "seeing" into the account of the soul's relation to being is the phrase σκοπεῖσθαι τὴν οὐσίαν at 186a11. Yet as Heidegger recognizes, this is immediately followed by the use of the word ἀναλογίζεσθαι to characterize how the soul deals with being. Thus, a little later in the text we find a contrast between the things that affect the soul through the body and "the reasonings about them with respect to their being and advantageousness" (τὰ περὶ τούτων ἀναλογίσματα πρός τε οὐσίαν καὶ ὠφέλειαν, 186c2–3). The same contrast is also then expressed as a distinction between the παθήματα and the συλλογισμός περὶ ἐκείνων, with the claim that only in the latter case is it possible οὐσίας καὶ ἀληθείας ἅψασθαι. It is in this way that Socrates reaches the conclusion already noted above: that it is not through the senses that we "lay hold of" being and truth; that whatever fails to lay hold of being and truth cannot be knowledge (ἐπιστήμη); that therefore perception cannot be knowledge. Three crucial points need to be noted: (1) truth (ἀλήθεια) is not treated here as a property of the seeing/striving relation to being, but is rather identified with being and therefore with what is striven *for*. In other words, there appears to be no conception of truth as correspondence or correctness here. Heidegger himself notes this. In Socrates' suggestion that whatever does not get hold of being cannot get hold of truth (Οἷόν τε οὖν ἀληθείας τυχεῖν, ᾧ μηδὲ οὐσίας, 186c7), Heidegger sees the following: "Unconcealment [*Unverborgenheit*] is in itself unconcealment of beings; indeed, we saw that the word 'unconcealment' in the Greeks even mostly means nothing other than beings themselves in their unconcealment [*das Seiende selbst in seiner Unverborgenheit*]" (241). (2) What Heidegger does not draw attention to is that the relation to both being and truth is throughout the present section described in the language of touching rather than of seeing (ἅψασθαι, τυχεῖν). What is said to be essential to knowledge is not "seeing" being and truth, but rather "laying hold of" and "grasping" being and truth. This language was already noted in the important passage from the *Republic* cited in chapter 3 and again in this chapter. This abandonment of the seeing metaphor in crucial contexts should warn us against making too much of the metaphor when it does occur. Being is for Plato no more "seen" than it is "touched," "mixed with," "desired," etc. (3) The language of seeing also gives way here to a characterization of our relation to being as a kind of thinking and speaking, λογίζεσθαι and λέγειν.

Yet in the introduction of λέγειν here, Heidegger sees, without stating this explicitly in the present context, important confirmation of his thesis regarding a transformation in the essence of truth. In this transformation truth becomes a property of seeing *and speaking*, that is, correctness. Here it is again helpful to look ahead at where Heidegger is going. At the very end of the present course, Heidegger will claim that Plato comes to interpret ψεῦδος as the in-correctness of λόγος, of assertion (*Aussage*), and thus truth as the correctness of assertion (319). It remains to be seen whether the account of false δόξα in the *Theaetetus* provides any support for such a conclusion. Yet is not such support already to be found in the present passage? Does not the characterization of our relation to ἀλήθεια as a λογίζεσθαι and λέγειν inevitably turn it into an object of assertion and thus ultimately into a property of assertion?

Yet Heidegger's own reading of the present passage certainly does not support such a conclusion, since he insists that ἀναλογίζεσθαι and συλλογισμός have nothing to do with "assertion," nor therefore with deducing and inferring, nor therefore with "logic." Heidegger here interprets λέγειν not as an asserting but as a gathering-together, a bringing of one thing in relation to another (223). λογίζεσθαι has accordingly for Heidegger the meaning of bringing one thing together with another in such a way as to reckon with both (224). This meaning is only intensified by the prefixes ἀνα- and συν-: in the first case, going up and down, back and forth, between one thing and another; in the second case, bringing one thing together with another. The context in which the word ἀναλογίζεσθαι is introduced appears to confirm Heidegger's reading: for it is immediately after asserting that being is to be looked to (σκοπεῖσθαι) in "those things most in relation to each other" (ἐν τοῖς μάλιστα πρὸς ἄλληλα, 186a10–11) that Theaetetus describes the soul as ἀναλογιζομένη. Ἀναλογίζεσθαι is a following of the relations between one thing and another, a being-referred by one thing to another. What Heidegger insists on is that in ἀναλογίζεσθαι and συλλογισμός as understood here, the relations in which being is found are not made the explicit object of an assertion or argument, as in an "analogy" or "syllogism"; these relations are instead *reckoned with*. In other words, the "reckoning" that characterizes the λογίζεσθα at issue here is not a calculating, deducing, inferring, and proving, but rather a *reckoning with*. Heidegger states this point clearly in the following passage: "These entire relations of being [*Bezüge des Seins*] are not *grasped* [*erfaßt*] as such and meant and themselves made into objects, but rather they are only there [*da*], insofar as they are reckoned on [*auf sie gerechnet*], are reckoned with [*ihnen Rechnung getragen wird*],—where? In the perceiving [*Wahrnehmen*] and experiencing and handling [*Betreiben*] (and so on) of beings" (224). This account of λογίζεσθα clearly supports, and is indeed necessitated by, the account of *Seinserstrebnis*: in striving after being, just as we cannot look *at* it—since we do not possess it as an object—but can only look *to* it, so we cannot make it the object of an assertion or argument, but can only reckon *with* it in our dealings with beings. Thus, Heidegger can conclude: "ἀναλογίζεσθαι characterizes the way in which what is striven after [*das Erstrebte*] comes into play here" (224). In the striving after being, the relations of being come into play only as something to be reckoned with or on (ἀναλογίσματα).

We can conclude that being, and therefore also truth, is characterized in this part of the *Theaetetus* not as something seen nor as an object of assertion—so that there is strictly speaking no onto-logy here—but rather as what we must look *to* and reckon *with* in advance of any seeing of, making assertions about, or in general dealing with beings. This is the conclusion Heidegger explicitly draws from a reading of 186b2–10. In this passage, after stating that the soul perceives softness and hardness through the sense of touch, Socrates adds: "But as for the being [of what is soft or hard] and *that* they are [ὅτι ἐστόν] and their opposition [ἐναντιοτής] to one another and in turn the being of this opposition, these the soul itself attempts [πειρᾶται] to discriminate [κρίνειν] in rising up to them [ἐπανιοῦσα]⁴ and setting them up against each other [συμβάλλουσα πρὸς ἄλληλα]" (186b6–9). Here again we have a description of the soul as relating, bringing together the κοινά and doing so itself from out of itself, rather than through the senses. What Heidegger finds to be new in this passage is the word κρίνειν: the description of the soul as explicitly discriminating—not "judging," Heidegger rightly insists—the different "characters of being" (*Seinscharaktere*) and their essential relations. Yet as Heidegger points out, being and its relations are not *given* to the soul as explicitly articulated and discriminated: κρίνειν is described as a *task* of the soul, something it *attempts* to do (πειρᾶται). This of course fits into the characterization of the soul's relation to being as a *striving*. Socrates himself emphasizes the word πειρᾶται here when, immediately following the passage in question, he claims that while the things that affect the soul through the body are perceived "by nature" by both human beings and animals, the things reckoned with, the ἀναλογίσματα, develop only with great difficulty, through a long period of time, with much work and education (186c2–5). On Heidegger's interpretation, "what we perceive [*vernehmen*] in going through the senses is there φύσει; that what is perceived [*Vernommene*] is encountered as being (in its being) first unfolds through παιδεία, in the course of the *history* [*Geschichte*] of Dasein (μόγις καὶ ἐν χρόνῳ)" (235). Here again the crucial point needs to be stressed: being and its relations are not "possessed" as the objects of an intuition or assertion, but rather are "had" only in striving, attempting, working, exercise, and training. Thus, later in the text Socrates can characterize the soul's relation to being, a relation that has been characterized earlier as ἐπισκοπεῖν, ἐπορέγεσθαι, and ἀναλογίζεσθαι, as a πραγματεύεσθαι περὶ τὰ ὄντα (187a5), an engaging oneself with beings, an encountering of beings within an activity and practice (in Heidegger's reading, "Sich Bemühen um das Seiende, Sich-umtun im Seienden," 250–51). It is precisely in such a practical dealing with beings that being is "had."

Here we come to Heidegger's important conclusion, based immediately on 186b2–10 but in fact the result of his entire reading: that the striving after being is the ground or condition of our comportment toward beings. Here is the conclusion in Heidegger's own words:

---

4. Ἐπανιοῦσα has been translated in widely divergent ways: e.g., "reviewing" (McDowell), "rising to" (Levitt, Burnyeat), "récapitule" (Narcy). The Levitt/Burnyeat translation seems to be the most justifiable: one should compare the use of ἐπανιέναι in the *Symposium* to describe the ascent from beautiful things to beauty itself. Before I can compare the being of one thing to another, I must ascend to this being from the sensible particular: the movement of comparison presupposes a movement of transcendence. In this way the term ἐπανιοῦσα can be seen as picking up what is expressed earlier by the term ἐπορέγεται. Heidegger's own paraphrase of ἐπανιοῦσα is arguably the most faithful translation: "sie von sich aus hin- und zurückgeht" (228). The soul's ascent to being is a continual back and forth.

> We can in perceiving [*Wahrnehmen*] have before us what is perceived [*Wahrgenommenes*], this and that thing determined so and so (something colored, sounding), only *on the basis of* [auf dem Grunde des] the striving after being [*Erstrebnisses des Seins*]. Only because the soul strives after being [*erstrebt*], can it now in the light of what is striven for [*im Licht des Erstrebten*] have before itself now this and now that given thing as something obtained and had [als ein Erreichtes und Gehabtes vor sich haben], that is, *take*-as-unconcealed, perceive [*wahr*-nehmen]. All having-before-oneself, and having in general, of beings is grounded in the striving after being [*gründet in einem Erstreben des Seins*]. (230–31).

Being and truth are not themselves perceived, looked at, grasped, or obtained; instead, in being striven after they cast the light within which and by which anything can be grasped and perceived. As noted in chapter 3, in the *Republic*, and in the context of the Sun Analogy, Socrates says that the soul obtains knowledge when it turns to *that on which shine truth and being* ("οὗ καταλάμπει ἀλήθειά τε καὶ τὸ ὄν," 508d4–5). Truth and being are here not *what is seen*, but rather *what casts the light* in which and by which something can first come to be seen and the soul can come to see. This is why it is appropriate to characterize being and truth as what is looked to rather than looked at, what is reckoned with rather than reckoned about. What the discussion of the *Theaetetus* has added is the recognition that in order to cast their light, in order to be "had" as the measure and law for what we know and do, being and truth do not need to be possessed as objects, do not need to be themselves transformed into objects seen and grasped, but need to be "had" only as that at which our striving, our ἔρως is directed. They are given "before," "in advance of," any having of beings. If being is what Heidegger called earlier a "Mehrbestand," this is the case only from a perspective that starts with beings; we now see that it is truer to the order of nature to call it a "Vorgabe" (231).

If being as given in striving cannot be treated as an object, neither can *Seinserstrebnis* itself be objectified. The soul's striving after being is not an external relation between two "things"—strictly speaking, one should not speak of a "relation" here at all—that can therefore be objectively described; it is not a thing or a "property" of the soul or an event. Since this striving is not an object of knowledge but rather what first makes knowledge possible, the only way of "knowing" it is to enact it and carry it out. In other words, the only way of knowing the striving after being is to strive after being. Because we overlook or forget that this striving can *be* only in and as striving itself, "we fall into the danger of searching somewhere for the striving after being [*Seinserstrebnis*] as if it were something lying there [*Vorliegendes*], in order to talk about it [*darüber zu reden*] and in this sense to win a concept of it. This danger continually threatens us because *Dasein* constantly falls into believing that the authentic having of something means that what is had is a possession [*das Gehabte ein Besitz ist*] in *the* sense of possession which we explained above" (239). This is a key point for understanding how to read the present dialogue as such. If what Socrates says *indicates* that the soul's relation to being is a striving that looks to, reckons on, works with, etc., this striving is not made here into the object of some kind of scientific treatise because its very nature must resist this. As ὄρεξις and πραγματεία, the soul's relation to being cannot be objectively described, but can only be enacted, that is, in the case of the dialogue, can only be shown *at work* in the discussion carried out by Socrates and Theaetetus. If one asks, "But what exactly is this striving after being?" the "answer" must be: look at what Socrates and Theaetetus are *doing*. And here we may have the cause of both the circularity of the discussion, to which Socrates repeatedly draws our attention, as well as its final *aporia*. In seeking to determine what ἐπιστήμη is, Socrates is seeking, in the language of 186c–e, to determine how we "lay hold" of being and truth. But: (1) Is not the discussion, in striving for being and truth, already "laying hold" of them, so that as Socrates himself points out, he and Theaetetus constantly find themselves employing the language of knowledge in their search for what knowledge is (196d11–e7)? The search must already in some sense "have" what it is searching for, as Heidegger's analysis of striving has shown. (2) If knowledge results from the striving after being, in which striving being and truth cast their light and thus provide the measure for knowledge, can there be any way of "defining" knowledge? How is one to analyze knowledge and build it from the ground up, that is, put it together from its "elements," when knowledge depends on, and is conditioned by, a striving relation to being that cannot itself be defined or analyzed? Is not the final *aporia* necessary? Are we not shown that knowledge cannot be made the object of knowledge, that its nature can be "known" only in its performance or enactment? As Socrates points out, he and Theaetetus are in their search constantly and unavoidably claiming knowledge. If this "circle" brings about the *aporia*, it may also contain the "answer."[5] Though Heidegger does not explicitly draw this conclusion from what he says at 239, we have already noted that he does repeatedly draw attention to the performance of the dialogue and even identifies the "result" with this performance itself. He states this point with special clarity in the 1933–34 version of the course: "The result [*Ergebnis*] is not what stands at the end, but rather the *movement of the questioning itself* [*Gang des Fragens selbst*]" (GA 36/37, 239). "The *enactment* [*Vollzug*] of questioning and of the holding-out [*Aushaltens*] in questioning is that through which the essence of things discloses itself [*sich eröffnet*]; every answer ruins the question" (239).

---

5. I defend such a reading of the dialogue in "Knowledge and Virtue as Dispositions in Plato's *Theaetetus*" (forthcoming).

2. *Doxa* and the Problem of Untruth

The reader might be getting impatient by this point for the same reason Heidegger feared his original auditors were getting impatient. What has become of the question of untruth? (247). Did not Heidegger claim to choose the *Theaetetus* precisely in order to address the problem of untruth? (248). Heidegger responds that the question of untruth explicitly arises in the dialogue only with the second answer to the question, "What is knowledge?" It is the identification of knowledge with δόξα that introduces the problem of *false* δόξα. But then why did Heidegger not begin his reading with this second answer, given that he in any case is not providing a reading of the entire dialogue? (248). Though Heidegger claims that the answer cannot be clear until after his reading is finished, he does provide this response: what is crucial is understanding the context within which, and the ground upon which, the question of untruth first arises for Plato (248). In the context of what questions, we must ask, is the question of the essence of truth posed, is the decisive step toward the problem taken? It must certainly be agreed that the analysis of 185a–186e provides an essential context for understanding Plato's approach to the problem of truth and untruth. Furthermore, there is a sense in which *truth*, if not *untruth*, is explicitly at issue in this part of the text, with the characterization of the "laying hold" of being as a "laying hold" of truth. But there has already been seen to be reason to doubt that the context provided by this text in any way supports a step toward a conception of truth as correctness. If 185a–186e is of crucial importance, it is precisely in showing how far Plato is from reducing truth, or even subordinating it, to correctness. Yet this is exactly the step that Heidegger wants us to see Plato as ultimately taking. This is made clear when Heidegger mysteriously characterizes the decisive step in question as one "that at the same time brings within itself the opportunity [*die Gelegenheit*] for the question immediately to lose its way and sink into a harmlessness, something purely incidental [*Nebensächlichkeit*] and easily irritating, and for untruth [*Unwahrheit*], unloved with perhaps some justification, to come to count as the opposite of truth understood as the characteristic of an assertion [*eines Charakters der Aussage*]" (249). One must wonder how this step toward truth as the mere characteristic of an assertion, and of untruth as its mere opposite, could possibly be taken *from* what is revealed in 185a–186e, except to the extent that any thinking of being and truth, including Heidegger's own, can be leveled to the level of ordinary understanding and thus rendered harmless. For what could be further from a conception of truth as the mere property of an assertion than a conception of truth as "had" in a striving and casting there the light *to* which we must look and *on* which we must reckon "in advance of" perceiving, making assertions about, or in any way dealing with, beings? Indeed, the characterization of truth at 185a–186e not only does not support, but is positively incompatible with, making truth the object of assertions, much less a mere property of assertions.

We have seen that Heidegger characterizes both the ἀναλογίζεσθαι and the συλλογισμός carried out with respect to being as beyond, or rather before, logic. What Plato has in view here, he asserts, is something much more fundamental than logic ("etwas viel Ursprünglicheres," 225). Yet then follows the suggestion that what Plato expresses here will still somehow inevitably lead to the subordination of being and truth to logic. "Indeed, if there is little question here of relating being to logical thinking and the logical formation of thinking (forms of thinking and judgment), it is equally important to note how hereby λόγος is taken back to the ψυχή and man and that in the development of philosophy—in a certain sense already with Aristotle—, from these starting-points [Ansätze] one ultimately arrives at bringing the relation of the soul to being and its forms into an essential relation to ratio, to judgment and to the forms of thinking" (225). What makes the step possible, according to this passage, is taking λόγος back to the soul and man. What does this mean? It cannot mean giving the soul power over λόγος, as if the soul were a subject that uses λόγος like a tool. Λόγος, on Heidegger's own account of 185a–186e, characterizes the soul's striving relation to being, a relation that the soul itself *is*. If this is bringing λόγος back to the soul, it is also a keeping of λόγος out there with being. How is the characterization of λόγος as a reckoning *with* being that *is* the soul the *Ansatz* for a conception of λόγος as the ratiocination and calculation concerned only with beings and constituting no more than a property or power of the soul?

One might here begin to suspect that Heidegger's own reading of this important text undercuts the thesis he otherwise wishes to maintain about Plato. Of course, it still needs to be seen whether or not the discussion of δόξα in the *Theaetetus* adds any support to Heidegger's thesis. Before turning to this discussion, however, we need to consider an extremely important text that was skipped above and that seriously brings into question what can be considered the foundation of Heidegger's reading of Plato and the Greeks: the thesis that the Greeks understood being as *presence*. This thesis, as Heidegger normally interprets it, has two implications: (1) that the Greeks interpreted being from the perspective of time, but did so naively and inexplicitly; (2) that their identification of being with mere presence was the result of an impoverished conception of time. This thesis is closely tied to the thesis regarding the transformation in the essence of truth, in a way that can be sketched briefly and crudely as follows: the understanding of being as presence is what leads to the interpretation of being as the "look" in which a thing presents itself, that is, its ἰδέα; this leads to making being relative to a looking (ἰδεῖν) and accordingly to transforming truth into correctness in this looking. Thus, Heidegger can write in "Platons Lehre von der Wahrheit": "The transformation itself [of truth from the unconcealment of beings to the correctness of looking (*Richtigkeit des Blickens*)] is accomplished in the determination of the being of beings (i.e., in Greek, of the presencing of what is present [*der Anwesung des Anwesenden*]) as ἰδέα" (WM, 231).

In chapter 2 the *Sophist* was seen to bring into question, and indeed render untenable, Heidegger's thesis concerning the Greek conception of being. Now the same can be said of *Theaetetus* 185a–186e. How is an understanding of being as "had" and "unconcealed" in *striving*, as looked *to* without being looked *at*, as reckoned *with* without being reckoned *about*, compatible with an understanding of being as *presence*? Indeed, in the *striving after being*, must not being necessarily reveal itself not only within the horizon of presence, but also within the horizons of past and future, with priority given to the future? Being does not reveal itself here as an object for a looking and therefore not as something present, but rather as "stretched out" in a striving that continually relates past and present to the future. This, one might object, may be very true, but does Plato himself see this? Does he anywhere say this? The remarkable answer is that he does, or rather, that he lets Theaetetus do so. Part of the passage in which the word ἀναλογίζεσθαι first occurs has been considered above, but the most important part has been saved for now. Here Theaetetus claims that being is to be "spotted" in those things most related to each other. This suggestion already moves away from an identification of being with static presence and suggests a much richer relation between being and time. But this is made explicit when Theaetetus describes the soul as "reckoning with" in itself (ἀναλογιζομένη ἐν ἑαυτῇ). But reckoning with what? Being, of course, but more specifically, "what has been and what is present in relation to what will be" (τὰ γεγονότα καὶ τὰ παρόντα πρὸς τὰ μέλλοντα, 186a11–b1). Heidegger is forced to recognize here an explicit recognition of the connection between being and time: here "the relation to being is in itself a reckoning with time" (226), where "time" is *not* understood as "clock-time" (*Uhrzeit*), that is, as a succession of nows. What is seen here at 186a11–b1, Heidegger continues, is completely lost with Aristotle (227). But then the "Greek conception" of being ceases being "Greek" and becomes at best "Aristotelian."[6] In the present passage from the *Theaetetus*, we have neither the naiveté that Heidegger attributes to the Greek conception of being, since the relation between being and time is made quite explicit—that is, reckoning with being is identified with reckoning with time—nor the reduction of being to the dimension

---

6. Though as noted already in chapter 1, I have argued elsewhere that the thesis of being as presence is not even Aristotelian: see my "Whose Metaphysics of Presence? Heidegger's Interpretation of *Energeia* and *Dunamis* in Aristotle," *Southern Journal of Philosophy* 44 (2006): 533–68.

of presence, since instead the priority is clearly given to the future. So what is Heidegger's overall assessment? What Plato hits upon here "lights up only as a first faint twilight [*Dämmerung aufleuchtet*],—only just as quickly (and definitively) to sink back into the night of the blind logic of the understanding that then comes to power and to disappear" (226). The analogy here of course suggests that the insight at 186a11–b1 is only a faint, brief glimmer doomed from the start to be lost. Yet Heidegger's own reading of the context shows that the recognition here of a connection between being and time is not an anomaly but rather perfectly in accord with, and even required by, the characterization of the soul's relation to being, specifically, the suggestion that it is in the soul's striving and relating that it "lays hold of" being. Heidegger's concluding judgment is expressed as follows: "To what extent there is already there in Plato an explicit and original insight into the relation of being to time is something that cannot be objectively determined. It is enough that these relations of the present and past, and indeed with a *prominent* relation to the *future* [*mit einem* hervorragenden *Bezug zur* Zukunft] already come into view here [*in den Blick kommen*]" (227). Is this not indeed enough to discredit the view that Plato understood being exclusively as presence? And is not the entire context of the text Heidegger has been interpreting evidence, if not objective proof, that we do indeed have here an original and explicit insight into the relation between being and time? It should be noted, in anticipation, that in the 1942 course on *Parmenides* Heidegger will acknowledge another dimension of the soul's relation to being, as Plato characterizes it, that again suggests explicit insight into the relation between being and time: *reminiscence* (ἀνάμνησις).

If the discussion in the *Theaetetus* now turns to δόξα, this is because, as Heidegger is at pains to show, δόξα satisfies precisely the requirements αἴσθησις proved incapable of satisfying. Specifically, we have seen that whatever is to satisfy the essence of knowledge as the "having of unconcealment" (ἀληθείας ἅψασθαι) must include both of the following moments: (1) the becoming-manifest or self-showing of something and (2) the "being-relation [*Seinsverhältnis*] to beings, which the soul takes up in itself [*in sich selbst aufnimmt*]" (257). What allows δόξα to satisfy both conditions, according to Heidegger, is that it has two meanings, each corresponding to one of these conditions. Heidegger's excellent analysis of the meaning of δόξα (251–57) shows that its two distinct meanings are the following:

1. The *look* (*Aussehen*) or *appearance* (*Anschein*) of a being;
2. Our relation (*Verhalten*) to this look, our perception of that which shows itself, our "holding it to be the case [*Dafürhalten*] that something is such and such" (256).

That δόξα in Plato has these two distinct meanings is commonly recognized. What Heidegger shows, however, is that both meanings are essential to δόξα being a candidate for knowledge: to rephrase the two conditions listed above, in knowledge there must be a self-showing or manifestness of being (which is precisely lacking in perception) *and* the soul must relate itself to this self-showing *in and through itself* (i.e., not through the sense organs of the body). Δόξα, as expressing both the manifestness and self-showing on the part of being and a comportment of the soul, captures both moments of knowledge and, most importantly, captures them in their unity. As we have seen, being shows itself in the soul's striving after being: it is not the case that the self-showing of being and the soul's comportment toward being are two different things. This is why Heidegger insists that while we can distinguish between two meanings of δόξα, it is crucial to recognize that what the word δόξα expresses is the unity of these two meanings (256). Belief is always a response to what appears and what appears always appears to a believing. If δόξα can have both subjective and objective meanings, this is because what it expresses is neither subjective nor objective but rather in between.

It also important to note something else that is confirmed by the introduction of δόξα. As we have seen, the soul's relation to being has already been characterized in such a way that it cannot possibly be identified with mere seeing or intuition. While the first meaning of δόξα, "look" or "appearance," might by itself encourage a characterization of this relation as a "seeing," the second meaning, from which the first cannot be simply separated, prevents this. This second meaning expresses a believing or opining that the soul undertakes in and through itself, a coming to hold that something is such and such. This meaning thus corresponds well to the characterization of the soul's relation to being as a searching, striving, working, rather than as a mere seeing or intuiting. Here we should recall the comparison made in the *Symposium* between δόξα and ἔρως, a comparison that is really more of an identification: δόξα is between ignorance and wisdom as a *striving for* wisdom and thus as ἔρως. If δόξα can mean "look," the relation to this look on the part of the soul that it expresses in its other meaning is not "seeing" but a searching, striving, and reckoning. In the text of the *Theaetetus*, δοξάζειν—and it is the *verbal* form that occurs first—is introduced (187a8) as the name we give to the soul when it "itself by itself busies and exerts itself with regard to beings" (πραγματεύηται περὶ τὰ ὄντα, 187a5–6). Thus, we can conclude that what δόξα names is as far as can be from a passive seeing or looking: it names a πραγματεία that the soul undertakes through and by itself. Heidegger himself sees this when he comments as follows on the two meanings of δόξα: "In the first meaning what is at issue is the *envisioning* of a look [*das* Erblicken *einer*

Ansicht], the perceiving [*das Vernehmen*] (taking [*Hinnehmen*]) of a look that announces itself [*eines sich kundgebenden Anblickes*], while what is at issue in the second meaning is the *taking-in-hand* [*das* Sich-vornehmen] of the same, the perceiving of something from out of *ourselves* [*Vernehmen einer Sache von* uns *aus*] (and thereby regarding and taking it *as* such and such)" (257). Note how here the soul's relation to being and beings can no longer be simply identified even with the more active and creative seeing Heidegger names "erblicken": in striving after and looking *to* being, the soul does not simply en-vision a "look," but takes beings in hand as such and such.

Heidegger sees the phenomenon of untruth as cutting across both meanings of δόξα: a *look* or *Anblick* can only "*pre*-tend [*vor-geben*] that what is presented [*das Dargestellte*] looks like this [*sehe so aus*]"; a view [*Ansicht*] can "hold or not hold [*stimmen oder nicht stimmen*]" (258). Heidegger claims that what is encountered in both cases is the phenomenon of *distortion* (*Verkehrung*). It is therefore within the realm of δόξα that the Greeks encountered untruth as they understood it: "Untruth is grasped by the Greeks as τὸ ψεῦδος, distortion [*Verkehrung*]" (257). If the discussion of δόξα focuses on the phenomenon of untruth, this is necessary, Heidegger claims, because "δόξα in reality cannot at all be grasped any further unless this phenomenon of distortion is reckoned with" (257). After all, what more can we say about a look or view unless we address the possibility of a distorted look or view?

As noted above, Heidegger's reading of the initial arguments against the possibility of δόξα shows that each is guided by an unquestioned principle that proves inadequate to the phenomenon. The first argument assumes as its *Leitsatz* the exclusive alternative of knowing or not knowing, that is, the impossibility of the same person knowing and not knowing the same thing (188a10–b1). On the basis of such an assumption, it is easy to show that believing falsely is impossible, since one cannot believe that things one knows are other things (ἕτερα) one knows, nor that things one does not know are other things one does not know, nor that things one knows are other things one does not know or vice versa. The second argument also assumes an exclusive alternative, but this time between being and not-being. Again on the basis of this assumption, it is easy to show that false belief is impossible, since such belief must be both about *what is* (i.e., it must have an object) and about *what is not* (since otherwise it would not be false).

Heidegger rightly suggests that these arguments are meant to show us the need of recognizing an *in between* (μεταξύ) between knowledge and ignorance, between being and not-being. What is unacceptable, however, is Heidegger's suggestion that Plato is discovering this μεταξύ only now and only by way of the discussion of false belief. Thus, Heidegger says the following regarding the assumption of the first argument: "This is for the Greeks at the time, and also for Plato in the transition [*und auch Platon noch im Übergang*] something absolutely self-evident [*eine absolute Selbstverständlichkeit*]. That there is an *in-between* [*Zwischen*] between the two, that precisely is first Plato's great *discovery*. The discussion of ψευδὴς δόξα is the one way to this discovery [*der eine Weg dazu*]" (267). Here we have a trace of the developmentalist thesis about Plato that was seen to dominate Heidegger's reading of the dialogue in 1926. Against this thesis it needs to be noted, first, that the recognition of a μεταξύ between knowing and not-knowing, and the identification of δόξα with this μεταξύ, is to be found in Plato well before the *Theaetetus* on any standard chronology of the dialogues; in the *Euthydemus* the exclusive alternative between knowing and not-knowing is exposed as an eristic trick; in the *Symposium*, as already noted, δόξα is, along with ἔρως, explicitly identified with a μεταξύ; in the *Republic* δόξα is again explicitly situated between knowing and not-knowing. Secondly, in none of these cases is the recognition of a μεταξύ the *result* of a discussion of false opinion, since false opinion is not even an explicit subject of discussion. It is therefore at least very misleading to say the following: "We will see that even this alternative (being or not-being), despite securely standing for the Greeks for centuries, is shaken to its foundation [*erschüttert wird*]: that there is an *in-between* [*Zwischen*] between being and not-being, just as there is between knowing and not-knowing. This in-between is the ground for the possibility of the ψεῦδος" (274). It is highly questionable that the exclusive alternative between being and not-being ever stood unshaken for Plato.

There is an indication in the text, which Heidegger himself points to (266), that the present arguments are made possible only by a deliberate putting aside of the already recognized dimension of the μεταξύ. Socrates can maintain his exclusive alternative between knowing or not knowing only by explicitly putting aside the μεταξύ of learning (μανθάνειν) and forgetting (ἐπιλανθάνεσθαι), claiming that they are at present irrelevant to the argument (νῦν γὰρ ἡμῖν πρὸς λόγον ἐστιν οὐδέν, 188a2–4). This of course is anything but irrelevant! One need only recall that in the *Meno*, and specifically in the episode with the slave, δόξα is what results from learning as the recollection of what has been forgotten. Furthermore, as already noted, in both the *Republic* and the *Symposium*, δόξα is explicitly characterized as μεταξύ knowing and not-knowing. In the *Theaetetus* itself, the μεταξύ dismissed as irrelevant at 188a must later be reintroduced into the discussion. At 191a8–b1 Socrates claims that he and Theaetetus should not have agreed that it is impossible for someone to believe falsely that what he knows is something he does not know, since this is possible in a way (πῃ δυνατόν). The phenomena Socrates then appeals to, by means of the Wax Analogy, are none other than learning and forgetting. Before introducing the analogy, Socrates explicitly asks Theaetetus:

"Is it not possible later to learn what one at first does not know?" (191c3–4). In this return of the discussion to the phenomena dismissed earlier in favor of an abstract principle, Heidegger sees the "wonderful composition of the dialogue" (289). It now becomes clear that if the μεταξύ of learning and forgetting was dismissed earlier as irrelevant to the argument, this was only to show the impossibility of accounting for δόξα without appealing to this μεταξύ. If learning and forgetting were irrelevant to the λόγος asserting that one must either know or not know something, it is now this λόγος that has become irrelevant to the phenomena. As Heidegger writes: "So we see that the phenomenon itself demands [*fordert von sich aus*] taking into view such in-between phenomena [*Zwischenphänomene*]" (290). But then it must be emphasized again that the recognition of the μεταξύ has been there throughout Plato's work: if it is momentarily suppressed, this is only to demonstrate its indispensability.

In thus anticipating the Wax Analogy, the present analysis has gotten ahead of itself. After refuting the possibility of false belief by appealing to the exclusive alternatives of knowing or not knowing and being or not being, Socrates suggests a characterization of false belief as "believing-other" (ἀλλοδοξία). Heidegger sees this suggestion as responding in the following ways to the earlier objections: (1) in false belief (ψευδὴς δόξα) *a being* is meant, but one being *in place of* another; (2) a ψευδὴς δόξα has two objects: one instead of the other; (3) the falsehood lies in the fact that something is *missed* [*verfehlt*] (278). Yet Socrates proceeds to refute even this suggestion by pointing to the difficulty of explaining the "exchange" required here: if δοξάζειν is a thinking that the soul carries out in itself, how can the soul exchange one thing it is thinking about for another thing it is thinking about? "Having a belief about both, it is impossible to believe that the one is the other" (Ἄμφω μὲν ἄρα δοξάζοντα ἀδύνατον τό γε ἕτερον ἕτερον δοξάζειν, 190d5–6). And it is of course at least equally impossible to exchange something of which one is thinking with something else of which one has no thought at all (190d8–9). Heidegger's diagnosis of this refutation has already been noted above: he sees Socrates' argument as failing to keep *mistaking* (*Verwechslung*) distinct from *exchanging* (*Auswechslung*). Mistaking Socrates for Theaetetus is not merely a matter of putting one in the place of the other. What is missing here is the "as-structure": not Theaetetus *in place* of Socrates, but Socrates *as* Theaetetus.

Heidegger sees these initial negative arguments as having positive results. In particular, they demonstrate how essential to δόξα are the following moments: the other (ἕτερον), the μεταξύ, and the as-structure. The last moment especially suggests as a positive outcome the characterization of δόξα as λόγος instead of as a kind of seeing. Socrates in the course of discussing the characterization of δόξα as ἀλλοδοξία indeed explicitly characterizes δόξα as a λόγος that the soul speaks silently to itself (190a5–6). Yet Heidegger refuses to see as the positive gain of this discussion that "διανοεῖν (δόξα) is more incisively [*eindringlicher*] worked out as λόγος [*herausgestellt wird*]" (282), since he believes that this is what leads the discussion astray; Heidegger therefore insists that the positive gain is instead the recognition that "the riddle [*das Rätselhafte*] of the phenomena lies in the fact that it has two objects, the one and the other" (282), though the "solution" to the riddle will turn out to be that there is only *one object*, though a "disparate" one. But what must be asked at this point is *why* Heidegger believes that the association of δόξα with λόγος is what will lead the discussion astray. In the cited passage Heidegger provides no explanation, but the crucial explanation is given a couple of pages later: "The demonstration of the λόγος-characteristic in δόξα is of significance insofar as this characteristic will in the later development of the δόξα-concept be the *only one* that is maintained and the original elements that lie in δόξα will disappear behind this characteristic, so that δόξα, as 'opinion,' will come into the proximity of the *assertion* and the genuine phenomenon will be lost" (284). Here emerges clearly the thesis behind Heidegger's reading of the dialogue: in being characterized as λόγος, δόξα will be put on the way toward becoming assertion, with the result that the truth and falsehood of δόξα will become mere correctness and incorrectness in an assertion. Yet it is significant that Heidegger does not claim that δόξα already is assertion in the *Theaetetus*; he claims only that the dialogue puts δόξα on the path to later entering the proximity of assertion. But what does this mean?

Certainly the characterization of δόξα that Socrates offers at 190a identifies it with some kind of assertion. Δόξα, he suggests, is when the soul "arrives at something definite [ὁρίσασα], either by a gradual process or by a sudden leap, when it affirms [φῇ] one thing consistently and without divided counsel [μὴ διστάζῃ]" (190a2-4) He then proceeds to identify δόξα as thus characterized with a silent λόγος (190a5-6). Yet what is especially significant in this passage is the sharp distinction Socrates makes between this δόξα/λόγος and the *thinking* from which it is derived and which it brings to an end. This thinking (διανοεῖν) is a "λόγος which the soul proceeds through (διεξέρχεται) itself by itself (αὐτὴ πρὸς αὐτήν) concerning those things which it examines or looks to (σκοπῇ)" (189e6-7). As Heidegger himself points out, the language here should remind us of the earlier description of the soul as relating itself through itself to being and the other κοινά. There this relation was described as a striving, reckoning with, and looking to.[7] In the present

---

7. Heidegger's discussion of 189e-190a returns to the characterization of the soul's relation to being as ἀναλογίζεσθαι and συλλογισμός (280-81). "Die Aufhellung der ἀλλοδοξία ergibt sich daraus: das Setzen, das Sich-vor-stellen des einen *statt* des anderen erweist sich als ein Sagen des einen *für* das andere. Was die Seele eigentlich *sagt*, wenn sie sich etwas sagt, ist, allgemein genommen, daß sie sagt: ein Sein. . . . In der δόξα liegt immer das Sich-sagen und -vorstellen von Sein" (281).

passage the elements of "reckoning with" and "looking to" are captured in the words λόγος and σκοπεῖν, respectively. But the present passage proceeds to tell us more about the nature of the λόγος through which the soul relates itself to the being it seeks: this λόγος is nothing other than dialectic (διαλέγεσθαι), that is, the soul questioning and answering itself (αὐτὴ ἑαυτὴν ἐρωτῶσα καὶ ἀποκρινομένη) (190a1). Thus, unlike the λόγος that characterizes δόξα, this dialectical λόγος does not at all have the structure of definitely affirming one thing rather than another, that is, it does not have the structure of affirmation, but rather the structure of "divided counsel," of the back-and-forth of question and answer. Thinking is not belief and belief is not thinking. Furthermore, what Socrates says makes perfectly clear which is prior to which: the λόγος of belief is only the final outcome, the sedimentation, as it were, of the prior λόγος that characterizes thinking. This characterization of thinking clearly corresponds to the characterization of the soul's relation to being as a striving: the soul cannot capture being as an object of assertions, but can only seek it and look to it in the give-and-take of question and answer. It is by asking itself questions and responding to these questions that the soul strives after being. As the *Symposium* implies, ἔρως is dialectical.

Two things in particular need to be noted here. First, the λόγος of δόξα involves a certain kind of "seeing" and so is not reducible to assertion. In this context it is significant that Socrates uses the verb δοξάζειν with a direct object. In the sentence already cited above, Socrates literally says: "Believing both [Ἄμφω μὲν ἄρα δοξάζοντα] it is impossible to believe the one the other [ἕτερον ἕτερον δοξάζειν]." *We* must paraphrase the first part of this sentence as "Having a belief *about* both" or "thinking *about* both," but Socrates can say "believing both." Δοξάζειν is here not believing *that x* is such and such, but simply *believing x*. And it is precisely Socrates' insistence on understanding δοξάζειν in this way, his refusal to reduce δοξάζειν to *asserting that,* that creates the problems for the discussion and continues to do so until the very end of the dialogue. Secondly, whatever kind of assertion and intuition characterize δόξα, they are made possible by, and are only the sedimented product of, a very different kind of λόγος and seeing that characterize the soul's relation to being. The λόγος that characterizes the soul's relation to being is not assertion but a process of question and answer that reckons with being; the seeing that characterizes the soul's relation to being is not an intuition of being but a looking-to being in questioning and answering.

The third thing to note is that Socrates in his very presentation of this characterization of the λόγος of δόξα and the λόγος of thinking characterizes himself as only having an idea *without knowing* (ὥς γε μὴ εἰδώς σοι ἀποφαίνομαι, 189e7) and asks Theaetetus what he thinks (190a6–7). Does this not show that Socrates in possessing neither δόξα in the sense of a fixed, unwavering affirmation nor knowledge possesses instead that dialectical λόγος that he has described as characterizing thinking? The questioning and answering that looks to and reckons with the kind of being in question is precisely what characterizes Socrates' relation to being in both this dialogue and others. Socratic dialogue is opening up to another the soul's dialogue with itself by means of the voice. Far from leaving the Socratic method behind, as Heidegger suggested in 1926, the dialogues' characterization of the soul's relation to being seems always to be guided by the paradigm of this method. And again the crucial point to note is that Socrates does not seek the truth of being by making assertions or intuiting phenomena, but rather by making both asserting and seeing serve the process of question and answer.

Why then see in Socrates' characterization of δόξα as λόγος a first step toward a reduction of δόξα to assertion and truth to correctness, as Heidegger clearly does? Not only is λόγος not identified exclusively with assertion in the dialogue, but it is given an alternative, positive, and coherent characterization as dialectic. Furthermore, this characterization encompasses both assertion and intuition by assigning subordinate roles to both and accordingly transforming their natures: intuition ceases to be a *looking at* and becomes a *looking to;* λόγος ceases to be an *assertion that* and becomes a questioning and answering that *reckons with* the matter at hand. Of course, λόγος could always be reduced to mere assertion by being abstracted from the dialectical process and thus disassociated from any striving after and looking to the thing itself. But the dialogue, far from encouraging such a reduction, or preparing the first step towards it, resists it in everything it says and in every move it makes. We thus begin to see how the Heideggerian thesis of a transformation in the essence of truth does not sit well with the text of the *Theaetetus*.

We must therefore be somewhat worried by Heidegger's next move: in turning to the Wax and Aviary analogies, he tells us that he will now turn away from the method of textual exegesis. He will from this point on give "an anticipating [*vorgreifende*], comprehensive presentation [*zusammenfassende Darstellung*] of the foundational task of the main inquiry [*der grundlegenden Aufgabe der Hauptuntersuchung*]" (291), instead, presumably, of going through the text line by line. We of course must initially follow Heidegger's new way of proceeding to see where it takes him, but without losing sight of what Heidegger's "comprehensive presentation" excludes.

Heidegger interprets the Wax Analogy as indicating the possibility of having something before one even when it is absent (*abwesend*). Heidegger himself explains the phenomenon at issue here by means of a distinction between having-present (*Gegenwärtigen*) and bringing to mind (*Vergegenwärtigen*), between, for example, being in front of a ski tower in the Black Forest and bringing the ski tower to mind during a lecture (296–97). This

Vergegenwärtigen cannot be identified with a recollecting or remembering of something forgotten: every remembering is a bringing to mind, but not every bringing to mind is a remembering. Heidegger accordingly insists that what Socrates calls μνημονεύειν "does not mean recollection [*Erinnerung*] nor remembrance [*Gedächtnis*], but being-mindful [*Eingedenk-sein*]" (295). The other important point Heidegger insists on is that Socrates' image is only *an image*. Socrates does not mean to suggest that when I bring to mind something absent what is absent exists as an "imprint" in my mind. In bringing to mind the tower in the Black Forest, I am intending, and existing in a relation to, the tower itself and not some "imprint" or "image" in my head. Socrates' image is only meant to indicate that in bringing-to-mind, the appearance or look of what is absent does not come from the thing itself, since it is absent, but somehow from me. It is only later philosophy that took literally what for Socrates was only an image, postulating the existence of "images" or "imprints" in "our heads" and making these, rather than the things themselves, what we "bring to mind." Heidegger's interpretation has an important consequence: on this interpretation, Socrates, unlike later philosophers, does not identify bringing-to-mind with having-something-present-in-one's-mind, but instead understands it as a relation to what is absent *as absent*. What the Wax Analogy images is the bringing before us of something absent *as absent*, the presence of what is absent in its absence. In other words, the phenomenon indicated by this image is one that defies the opposition between presence and absence. In a very important marginal note Heidegger writes: "being is presence [*Sein ist Anwesenheit*], not-being absence [*Nichtsein Abwesenheit*]; but even what is absent [*Abwesendes*] can *be*!" (295). But is this not precisely what the Wax Analogy attempts to express. and does this not show that Plato does not simply identify being with presence?

Heidegger could respond that his own explanation of the phenomenon goes well beyond what is expressed in Plato's analogy. He indeed prefaces his account of both analogies by suggesting that if Plato resorts here to *Gleichnisse*, this shows that he stands before a task "in the face of which he does not at all dare [*gar nicht wagt*] to deal with the phenomena directly and without mediation [*unmittelbar direkt über die Phänomene zu handeln*] or even to master them in an initial approach [*im ersten Anlauf zu bewältigen*]" (293). This is presumably why Heidegger, in turning to the distinction between *Gegenwärtigen* and *Vergegenwärtigen*, tells us that he is leaving Plato's image to give his own account of the phenomena (296). But three points need to be made here: (1) If Plato resorts to images, this may be on account of what Heidegger himself claimed in rejecting the naiveté of phenomenology: that the phenomenon is not accessible directly and without mediation. Plato is led by the phenomena instead of by a theory, but the only way of getting at the phenomena is by way of theories and images, or more specifically, by way of their simultaneous use and critique. The Wax Analogy can serve its purpose, therefore, only if its limitations are clearly exposed.

(2) And yet Heidegger's most obvious departure from the text is his failure even to mention Socrates' refutation of the Wax Analogy as an account of false belief. Socrates describes a number of cases in which false belief would be impossible according to the Wax Analogy and some cases in which it would be possible, but the general account of false belief that emerges from the analogy or, in Heidegger's terms, from the distinction between *Gegenwärtigen* and *Vergegenwärtigen*, is succinctly stated by Socrates as follows: "False judgment resides, not in our perceptions among themselves nor yet in our thoughts, but in the fitting together of perception and thought [ἐν τῇ συνάψει αἰσθήσεως πρὸς διάνοιαν]" (195c8–d2). More specifically, false belief is the failure to match up the perceptions with the right "marks" in our mind, so that like a bad archer one misses the mark and errs (παραλλάξαι τοῦ σκοποῦ καὶ ἁμαρτεῖν, 194a3–4). Yet even before the succinct statement of this characterization of false belief is given at 195d, Socrates is accusing himself of annoying ignorance (δυσμαθία) and garrulousness (ἀδολεσχία) for having offered this characterization (195c1–2). This is because it is untenable for the obvious reason that many cases of false belief, such as "2 + 2 = 5," make no reference to perception and thus involve no matching up of perceptions to thought. That Heidegger says not a word, here or later in the course, about Socrates' disgusted rejection of this characterization of false belief as a mismatching between perceptions and thoughts or as a "missing of the mark" will prove, as will be seen, of great importance. What needs to be noted here is that if false belief involves the presence of what is absent, this cannot simply mean the presence in thought of what is absent to perception.

(3) As Heidegger himself will proceed to show, the earlier account of the soul's relation to being already opens up a space beyond the opposition between presence and absence and thus a space for false belief.

Though without explaining why the discussion requires this, Heidegger does see that the Aviary Analogy goes beyond the Wax Analogy by in essence repeating the distinction between *Gegenwärtigen* and *Vergegenwärtigen* within *Vergegenwärtigen* itself (306). In other words, just as we can have a bird either in the sense of keeping it in the cage or in the sense of laying hold of it, so there are two senses in which we can have something in mind without perceiving it: we can have it either in the sense of simply retaining it or in the sense of explicitly attending to it. Heidegger then proceeds to draw the important inference from both images: "Now we see: the field of beings, to which we constantly relate ourselves, is not at all exhausted by the region of *those* beings which we have in immediate presence [*in unmittelbarer Gegenwart halten*], but is essentially *wider*. The usual starting point of the theory of knowledge, which asks about an object, a given, is therefore off track [*verkehrt*]" (307). What Plato, according to Heidegger, fundamentally wants to bring out is the "essential twofold possibility [*zwiefache Möglichkeit*] under which every accessible being [*zugängliche Seiende*] stands" (307): having without perceiving, perceiving with the possibility of having (see 307). Furthermore, the Aviary Analogy shows that even the power of having [*das Vermögen des Behaltens*] itself is characterized by a twofold possibility: retaining and bringing explicitly into view (307). Does this not mean that what Plato shows is precisely that the field of being is wider than that of what is present and that the accessibility of beings is characterized by a diversity that cannot be reduced to presence? The analogies make perfectly clear that for Plato a being can be had without being an object either for perception or for the "mind's eye," that, in other words, it can be had while being absent for both perception and thought. That Plato should hold such a view, however, should not surprise any careful reader of the dialogue, since the soul's relation to being has already been characterized as a striving, reckoning with, looking to, and give-and-take of question and answer for which or in which being is not present as an object.[8]

Before we proceed to how Heidegger situates the possibility of false belief within this broader field of beings, it is again important to note what his interpretation passes over in silence. What he leaves out is again nothing less than Socrates' refutation of the account of false belief that emerges from the aviary example, and thus the need for the final part of the dialogue. The account that emerges is as follows: since I can possess a piece of knowledge without laying hold of it, it can happen that in seeking a piece of knowledge I have, I lay hold of the wrong one. For example, in seeking the answer to "6 + 6 = ?" I can mistakenly lay hold of "11" rather than "12." But the objection to which this account is vulnerable is obvious (196c–2): how can I lay hold of the wrong piece of knowledge? If it is something I know, I should be able to recognize it for what it is and not lay hold of it when I am looking for something else. Theaetetus's suggestion that we have pieces of ignorance as well as pieces of knowledge only makes matters worse, since how can we possibly mistake a piece of ignorance for a piece of knowledge (199e)?

With this objection we return, as Socrates explicitly acknowledges (200a–c), to the problem that has plagued the whole discussion: false belief appears both to presuppose, and to be rendered impossible by, a certain kind of knowing. And it is not only false belief that presupposes some sort of knowing, but the very discussion carried out by Socrates and Theaetetus, a discussion that continually

---

8. Yet both analogies fail because in the end they cannot adequately express the dynamic, erotic nature of the soul and of its relation to being: see my "Wax Tablets, Aviaries, or Imaginary Pregnancies? On the Powers in Theaetetus' Soul," *Études platoniciennes* 4 (2007): 273–93.

presupposes and appeals to the knowledge it seeks to define. Socrates explicitly draws attention to this circularity after the refutation of the wax tablet example (196d–197a). Now at 200c–d, after the refutation of the final account of false belief, Socrates suggests that the discussion has been hopelessly circular all along since it was a mistake to attempt to explain false judgment before giving a satisfactory account of knowledge. But can we explain what knowledge is before we know what falsehood is? How do we extricate ourselves from this circle?

Perhaps no extrication from the circle is possible: in other words, perhaps we cannot give an "objective" account of belief and knowledge from a position outside them. If our relation to being is indeed characterized by striving and the dialectical process of question and answer, perhaps all we can do is enter this relation and allow both δόξα and ἐπιστήμη to be enacted within in it. When Socrates proceeds to claim that δόξα and ἐπιστήμη are not the same, the example he appeals to (201a–c) is very revealing. Jurors, Socrates argues, can be persuaded by the lawyers to believe what is true, but because they are not eyewitnesses, they cannot *know* what happened. The jurors can thus have true belief without having knowledge. The distinctive mark of knowledge in this example is direct experience or acquaintance (ἰδόντι μόνον ἔστιν εἰδέναι, 201b8). This fits in with the way in which "knowledge" has been used throughout the dialogue: the "knowing" that false belief has been seen to presuppose is an acquaintance with the things about which it is a false belief; for example, one must "know" both Socrates and Theodorus before one can mistake the one for the other. Furthermore, the "knowledge of knowledge" Socrates has accused Theaetetus and himself of assuming throughout the discussion is the unavoidable use of the word "know" and the corresponding acquaintance with what it means. But is not this "experience" precisely that relation of the soul to being which has been characterized in terms of striving and the give-and-take of question and answer? Is not this relation the "knowing" presupposed by all belief, whether true or false? And is not the only "solution" possible here the explicit taking up of this experience in which we already exist? Here it needs to be noted that the jury example is ambiguous, since in fact Socrates gives *two* reasons for their lack of knowledge: their lack of direct experience and the fact that the clock in the courtroom prevents the kind of *discussion* that alone could teach them the truth of what happened (201b3). Thus, the direct experience that is said here to characterize knowledge is not some immediate intuition, but instead involves the mediation of λόγος in the sense of philosophical discussion or dialectic. If these suggestions are any where close to the mark, then we can see why the concluding discussion of the dialogue, that disassociates the λόγος distinctive of knowledge from both the dialectic of question and answer and the kind of acquaintance with which the jury example identifies knowledge, must fail.

Yet all of this, the refutations, the confessions of circularity, the final failed account of knowledge, is passed over in silence by Heidegger. The implications of this become immediately evident in the account of δόξα Heidegger proceeds to give, again independently of any textual exegesis. Heidegger sees the dialogue as having provided three building blocks from which the essence of δόξα can now be built up. He expresses these and their relations as follows: "For example: what encounters us from a distance, perceived in αἴσθησις; this thing which is present immediately and bodily [*unmittelbar leibhaft Anwesende*] is taken for Theaetetus, this for-which is thereby represented [*vorgestellt*] and brought to mind [*vergegenwärtigt*] (μνημονεύειν) in advance; this thing brought-to-mind [*Vergegenwärtigte*] is asserted of [*zugesprochen*] (λόγος) what presents itself (what encounters us) [*dem Gegenwärtigen (Begegnenden)*]" (311). Heidegger then summarizes as follows the account of δοξάζειν that this analysis yields: "We can now say, going beyond Plato [*hinausgehend über Platon*]: δοξάζειν is a comportment [*ein Verhalten*] which in its unity is *at the same time* [*zumal*] in presencing directed at something that encounters us bodily [*gerichtet ist gegenwärtigend auf etwas leibhaft Begegnendes*] and in bringing-to-mind directed at something represented in advance [*vergegenwärtigend auf ein im voraus Vor-gestelltes*]. In short: this comportment of δόξα is in itself *gabled* [*gegabelt*]" (312). Yet if we keep in mind the text Heidegger has left behind, we must conclude that this account of δόξα not only goes beyond Plato, but goes completely *against* Plato. The text Heidegger appeals to as support for his account of δόξα is Socrates' characterization of it at 195d1–2 as "the joining of perception to thought" (σύναψις αἰσθήσεως πρὸς διάνοιαν, 311). But as seen above, and as Heidegger declines to mention, Socrates dismisses this characterization, even before it is formulated, as a product of his ignorance and garrulousness. The reason is that there are many cases of belief that do not involve the building block of what is bodily present. Even if we were to substitute for Heidegger's distinction between what is bodily present and what is brought-to-mind the distinction made in the Aviary Analogy between what is had in mind and what is the focus of the mind's attention, that distinction too was rejected by Socrates as an account of the possibility of false belief. The one thing that *should* be embraced in Heidegger's account is the reference back to the earlier account of the structure of the soul's relation to being, that is, what Heidegger characterizes as a gable and now explains thus: "The *gable* is the condition of the possibility of truth, but also at the same time the condition of the possibility of untruth; both stand under the same conditions. What is meant by this gable? It is the image of the fundamental constitution [*Grundverfassung*] of human *Dasein*, of its essential structure [*Wesensbaues*]" (314).

But if δόξα is to be situated within this "gable," it is as the product of the striving, searching give-and-take of question and answer and *not* as asserting what is represented of what is perceived. What grounds δόξα is not what is *represented* in advance (*das Vorgestellte*), but rather what is *striven for* in advance (*das Erstrebte*). Δόξα does not assert what is represented of what is perceived, but rather emerges in the give-and-take of question and answer with a look to what is striven for. Heidegger believes that his account of δόξα now makes it possible to characterize ψευδής δόξα as a mis-perceiving or mistaking [*Ver-sehen*]: "This looking-past [*Vorbei-sehen*] in the form of a seeing-as [*Ansehen-als*] ... is a mistaking-oneself [*Sich-versehen*], namely, with regard to what is seen bodily [*leibhaft Gesehenen*], which looks like Theaetetus and also like Socrates" (316). This is different from the looking-away [*Ab-sehen*] in the earlier identification of δόξα with exchanging [*Verwechselung*]: "Insofar as I mistake myself in something [*mich an etwas versehe*], in seeing I overlook it [*sehe ich* an ihm *vorbei*], and *in* this overlooking-it [*An-ihm-vorbei-sehen*] is it precisely *seen*" (317; Heidegger in this context refers to Plato's use of the words παρορᾶν, παρακούειν, παρανοεῖν at 195a). What according to Heidegger makes this *Ver-sehen* possible is again the *Gabelung*. This *Gabelung* shows that the making-present looking-at (*das gegenwärtigend Hinsehen*) "as a seeing of something as something [*als Ansehen von etwas als etwas*] necessarily must always look in a *direction* [*Richtung*], either in one or the other" (317). Though Heidegger's citation of 194b2ff. in support of this interpretation again does not mention that Socrates soon finds inadequate the characterization of false belief he offers there, Heidegger's account is nevertheless convincing or illuminating to the extent that it remains true to the earlier account of the soul's relation to being and the other κοινά. Only because the soul exists in a relation to being as what is striven for does it always look in a certain direction, and only because it always looks in a certain direction can it in δόξα overlook or misperceive what it encounters. However, such a *Ver-sehen* has nothing to do with asserting some pregiven representation of some perceived object; instead, it is a seeking that "has" the being it strives after *only in* this striving and therefore exists in the constant danger of mis-taking what it strives for. What we have here is not the mistaking of a perception with a representation, but rather a striving that misses what it strives for. The discussion carried out in the *Theaetetus* is a perfect example and enactment of this understanding of false belief. Socrates and Theaetetus seek the essence of knowledge, something that they already in their search and striving somehow "have," presuppose, and rely on. Moving in this direction, they encounter something that presents itself as being what they seek, that is, perception. This δόξα in which perception appears as knowledge eventually proves false, but not through some comparison of this representation of knowledge with a perception (obviously no perception can be the criterion for deciding whether or not knowledge is perception), nor through any comparison of it with some other representation, but rather in the give-and-take of question and answer. The "criterion" for truth or falsehood, if we can use that term, is here not some "matching" or correspondence, but rather the dialectical discussion itself. In other words, Socrates does not test the truth of Theaetetus's definitions of knowledge by seeing if they match up with some perception or representation, but rather by submitting them to the process of dialectic. If we place Heidegger's account of false belief into this context, then it certainly has much to recommend it. Within the context of the soul's dialectical striving after being, false belief is that *Ver-sehen* that occurs when the soul mis-takes what it desires to have, or mis-sees what it desires to see, and that can be exposed as false only in the process of this dialectical striving.

Yet even if, despite the *aporia* with which it ends, the *Theaetetus* is suggesting something like this characterization of false belief, how does it support the thesis with which Heidegger approached the dialogue? What Heidegger needs to show is at least the inception of a reduction of false belief to an assertion that incorrectly asserts one thing of another, or that mismatches a certain predicate with a certain subject. But where is there any sign of this in the above account? What Socrates and Theaetetus are striving after is not given as some kind of object to which they can match or mismatch anything. If their δόξα proves false it is only by failing to offer them something they seek, by failing to satisfy their desire. It is false not because it is "incorrect" but because it *does not satisfy*, because it fails to take us as far as we vaguely seek to go. Furthermore, there is no talk in the dialogue of a distinction between subject and predicate and therefore not the remotest indication that truth and falsehood lie in a match or mismatch between the two. In short, we have seen repeatedly how what is explicitly asserted or implied in the dialogue stands against any reduction of the soul's relation to being, and therefore of truth or falsehood in this relation, to assertion and predication. So what has become of Heidegger's thesis? How can he possibly show that we have in this dialogue a transformation of the essence of truth into correctness?

That Heidegger faces a serious problem here is confirmed by the arbitrariness of his next and final move in the course. Heidegger now informs us that we have yet to see how *Plato himself* understood the phenomenon of *Versehen*, thus implying that the account Heidegger has just given is not Plato, though without explaining why this is the case (318). The account Heidegger then proceeds to attribute to Plato is the following: mistaking Theaetetus for Socrates is not simply seeing Theaetetus *as* Socrates, but failing to hit on the right predicate that corresponds to what is seen, that is, Theaetetus. This attribution then of course enables Heidegger to maintain his thesis that truth is here on the way to becoming mere correspondence and correctness. "The not-hitting-on [*Nicht-treffen*] is a missing [*ein Verfehlen*] of the appropriate *predicate*. The not-hitting-on is a missing of the right *direction* [*der rechten Richtung*]: a being-incorrect [*Un-richtig-sein*]. The self-mistaking *looking*-at [*sich-versehende An*-sehen] of what encounters (as Socrates) is an in-correct *speaking*-of [*un-richtiges An*-sprechen] what encounters. Incorrectness in the *predicate* means incorrectness of the *asserting* [*Unrichtigkeit des* Aussagens]. In this way Plato comes to grasp the essence of the ψεῦδος as in-correctness of the λόγος, of the assertion [*Aussage*]" (319). In this way the thesis of a transformation in the essence of truth is upheld.

Of course, a little question remains to be asked: on what basis does Heidegger suddenly and at the very end of the course attribute to Plato a conception of the ψεῦδος as the failure to hit on the right predicate that corresponds to what is seen? The astonishing answer is that Heidegger does little more than assert that this is Plato's view. As we have seen, he already abandoned earlier a careful exegesis of the text, and he does not return to such exegesis here. The only text he cites (319) in support of his interpretation is 194a3, where Socrates compares false belief to a bad archer who misses his target. Yet, as can be learned from the text, though not from Heidegger's loose and very incomplete account of the text, the conception of false belief that underlies the archer example, that is, false belief as a mismatching of perception and thought, is explicitly rejected by Socrates as hopelessly inadequate. Furthermore, we have seen that Socrates' discussion of the aviary example even rejects the characterization of false belief as a mismatching of thoughts with thoughts (ἡ τῶν ἐπιστημῶν μεταλλαγή, 199c10). Therefore, if the dialogue has anything to say about correspondence, it is that false belief cannot be adequately interpreted as a lack of correspondence between two things, whether thoughts or perceptions. Yet Heidegger forces precisely such an interpretation on Plato by ignoring the refutations and citing 194a3 with a complete disregard for its context.

Furthermore, even the account of false belief that emerges from the Wax Tablet Analogy does not support the account of false belief as a failure to hit on the right predicate. To make it do so, Heidegger must misinterpret the phenomena themselves, insisting that in order mistakenly to see Theaetetus as Socrates, I must have both Theaetetus and Socrates "in mind" (*Vergegenwärtigung*) (318–19). Yet this insistence is clearly mistaken: I could "mis-see" the man coming down the road as Socrates precisely because I have no prior acquaintance with Theaetetus and therefore do not know that there exists another person who looks so much like Socrates. This is precisely the kind of example Theaetetus adduces at 191b. If the example is dismissed there as impossible because resulting "in our knowing and not knowing the things which we know," this is before the introduction of the Wax Tablet Analogy and the distinction it makes possible between what is known and what is perceived. After the introduction of this analogy, Socrates implicitly acknowledges the possibility of Theaetetus's example when he lists among the cases in which false belief is possible the following: "The cases in which he may think that things which he knows are some other things which he knows and perceives; *or which he does not know, but perceives*" (ἢ ὧν μὴ οἶδεν, αἰσθάνεται δέ, 192c, Burnyeat's translation). Accordingly, what Socrates later rules out as an occasion for false belief is the case in which I know one and do not know the other, but *perceive neither* (193a8–10). In the case Socrates allows, that is, when in perceiving Theaetetus, whom I do not know, I see him *as* Socrates, whom I do know, my false belief clearly cannot be a matter of failing to hit upon the right predicate (Theaetetus), because in this case I do not at all have this predicate in mind. I am on the lookout for Socrates and therefore see the similar Theaetetus coming towards me from a distance *as* Socrates.

Yet what perhaps most runs counter to the whole thrust of the dialogue is Heidegger's reduction of δόξα to *assertion*, so that δοξάζειν means simply asserting a predicate of a subject. This reduction is clear when Heidegger now insists that we have in Plato "the determination [*Fassung*] of δόξα as *assertion*; i.e., a retreat of the *original* character of the look [*Ansicht*]: of *looking*-at [*An*-sehens]" (319). This claim, like all the other claims in these final pages of the course, not only is a dogmatic assertion completely lacking in support, but runs counter to Heidegger's own initially careful reading of the text. As noted above, even in being identified with λόγος, δόξα does not in any way forsake its complementary, though not necessarily more "original," connotation of appearance and look, and for two main reasons: (1) it is seen as derivative from λόγος in the sense not of assertion but *dialogue*, that is, the give-and-take of question and answer that must always have somehow in view that toward which the questions and answers are directed; (2) δόξα is thereby firmly rooted in the earlier account of the soul's relation to being as a striving after being characterized by both "reckoning-with" and "looking-to." In short, the dialogue offers a very rich positive conception of the ground of δόξα and at the very same time explicitly rejects any attempt to reduce δόξα to mere assertion and correspondence. How perverse and upside down, then, must Heidegger's conclusion appear.

Here it is important to insist on something already suggested above but given no consideration by Heidegger: Socrates' dialogue with Theaetetus is not only *about* the distinction between true and false δόξα, but is itself the act of separating the true from the false. Early in the dialogue Socrates explicitly claims that the greatest accomplishment of his maieutic art is the ability to distinguish the true from the false: "This is the greatest thing in our skill [μέγιστον δὲ τοῦτ' ἔνι τῇ ἡμετέρᾳ τέχνῃ]: that it is able in all possible ways to test [βασανίζειν] whether the mind of a youth gives birth [ἀποτίκτει τοῦ νέου ἡ διάνοια] to a mere semblance and falsehood [εἴδωλον καὶ ψεῦδος] or to something genuine and true [ἢ γόνιμόν τε καὶ ἀληθές]" (150b9–c3). Note the identification here of what is false with semblance and of what is true with what is genuine: we thus have in Socrates' description of the very goal of his method precisely the conception of falsehood and truth that Heidegger claims is abandoned in favor of correctness and incorrectness. But how does Socrates test a δόξα to determine whether it is a false semblance or the true and genuine being sought for? All of Theaetetus's "births" in the dialogue of course prove false. But how do they prove false? Not, clearly, through the matching of what Theaetetus says to some pregiven representation or perception, not through the comparison of his "ignorance-birds" with his "knowledge-birds." Instead, what shows a δόξα to be false is nothing other than dialectic, the give-and-take of question and answer through which the "faultiness," "inadequacy," and "unsatisfactoriness" of a δόξα must eventually emerge. As Socrates suggests in the *Gorgias*, true and genuine is what survives the test of the *elenchos*, while false and fake is what does not (473b). There is no question here of "correspondence" or "matching," because truth and falsehood are not understood here primarily in terms of assertion and predication. Theaetetus's beliefs are false not because they do not hit on the right predicate, but because, when submitted to questioning, they prove to reveal the phenomenon only partially and incompletely.

Of course, this assumes that Socrates and Theaetetus already exist in a relation to that which they seek; otherwise, by looking *to what* or by reckoning *with what* could they come to see a given δόξα as *falling short*? This is the circularity of the discussion to which Socrates draws our attention: he and Theaetetus must continually assume what they seek to know, especially since what they seek to know is the nature of knowledge itself! This circularity cannot be eliminated, since it is the very structure of our relation to being: in striving after being, we must already "have" in this very striving what is striven after. What this circularity means is only that δόξα, in its twofold possibility of being true and being false, must be situated within this striving after being. It is only within this striving, and the dialectic that defines it, that something can both come to appear in a way that is distorted or skewed *and* ultimately come to be recognized as such. The general problem, then, with the explicit accounts of false δόξα in the dialogue is that they abstract it from this striving/dialectical relation to being, abstract it from the very context within which Socrates tests the falseness or genuineness of a δόξα, and treat it as some kind of objective matching or mismatching between two things. Here the circle repeats itself, but now in such a way as to be vicious and absurd: false δόξα must somehow be built out of "pieces of knowledge." It is not the mismatching of pieces of knowledge that constitutes false δόξα, but rather the equally knowing and not-knowing relation to being as enacted in the dialectical striving after being. It should be noted that if the final account of knowledge as δόξα along with λόγος fails, this is because this account oddly abstracts from the knowledge that has been at issue in, and presupposed throughout, the whole discussion: the knowledge at work in the dialectical exchange of question and answer. While earlier δόξα was seen as the result of λόγος in the sense of *dialectic* or, more specifically, the silent exchange of question and answer undertaken by the soul with itself, this sense of λόγος is now completely ignored in favor of purely objectifying and comparatively impoverished conceptions of λόγος: (1) the mere expression of a thought; (2) the enumeration of elements; and (3) the statement of a distinguishing mark. Here, as in other Platonic dialogues, it is essential to consider not only what is said, but also what the performance of the dialogue reveals.[9]

Heidegger's insistence that what he calls the "gable" provides the needed "direction" that first grounds the possibility of both true and false δόξα is completely right. To this extent his account of the crucial characterization of the soul's relation to being and the other κοινά at 184–87 is invaluable for an understanding of what is at issue in the dialogue. Compared to this careful and insightful reading of the text, what are we to make of the dogmatic, arbitrary, and unsupported claims made towards the end of the course? They cannot help but appear as a *deus ex machina* introduced at the last minute to save Heidegger's thesis concerning the transformation of the essence of truth. As we have seen, Heidegger's careful reading of the text, far from supporting this thesis, works against it. Is it any wonder, then, that he must eventually put the text aside and simply assert, with no more support than a metaphor taken completely out of context, that *Plato himself*, despite whatever the dialogue might show, understood the ψεῦδος as a failure to hit upon the right predicate that corresponds with a perception? And is it any wonder that in the 1940 essay purporting to tell us Plato's doctrine of truth, the *Theaetetus* has disappeared altogether? Whatever overall reading of the *Theaetetus* one ultimately adopts, and whether or not one accepts the above suggestions regarding the performative character of the dialogue, there can be no doubt that this dialogue is an obstacle to Heidegger's thesis regarding the transformation of the essence of truth.

An inference Heidegger proceeds to draw from the account of the ψεῦδος he forces on Plato is that Plato was denied insight into the belonging-together of truth and untruth. Since correctness and incorrectness rule each other out,

9. Again see my papers on the *Theaetetus* cited above.

the transformation of truth into correctness and falsehood into incorrectness "blocked the insight that and how untruth *belongs* to the essence of truth" (320). Heidegger then sketches (320–21) the way Plato *could have taken* but did not take. He could have recognized that what is seen in *Ver-sehen* shows itself in such a way that it hides itself and that this "self-concealing [*Sich-verbergen*] in and *through* self-showing [*das Sich-zeigen*] is *seeming* [*das* Scheinen]" (320–21). This seeming could then have been seen as an unconcealment [*Unverborgenheit*] to which concealment [*Verborgenheit*] essentially belongs (321). Yet it is precisely this relation between truth and untruth that cannot push its way through "under the domination [*Vorherrschaft*] of λόγος (the transformation [*Umbildung*] of δόξα into 'opinion' ['*Meinung*'])" (321). But why did Plato force truth and untruth under the domination of λόγος instead of giving the relation between truth and untruth its due? Heidegger comments that Plato *could* have gone the way of seeing how truth and untruth belong together; why he did not do so "is in the end a mystery of the spirit itself [*ein Geheimnis des Geistes selbst*]" (320). Yet by now we should consider the true "mystery of the spirit" to be why Heidegger, against the evidence of the text, insists that Plato did not go the way of thinking truth and untruth together and instead subjected both to the assertion. Socrates, as noted above, explicitly identifies the falsehood he wishes to test in Theaetetus's opinions with semblance as opposed to genuineness. Furthermore, all of the dialogue's attempts to explain false δόξα independently of true δόξα fail, presumably because, according to the above suggestion, we are meant to see both as belonging together in the dialectical striving that characterizes the soul's relation to being. To say that they belong together means that they are so entangled that they can be extricated only through the constant give-and-take of question and answer. Indeed, Socratic dialogue, as continually under the power and threat of semblance, illustrates especially well the belonging-together of truth and untruth. As for the subjugation of truth and untruth to assertion, a subjugation that would block insight into what is shown at work in Socratic dialogue itself, this has been seen to be nothing more than Heidegger's invention. Plato not only *could have* pursued the way Heidegger describes, but *actually did so*. The mystery is why Heidegger refused to see this.

C. CONCLUSION: HEIDEGGER'S ORTHODOXY

With the critique of Plato for failing to think truth and un-truth as belonging together, Heidegger is only returning to the thesis with which he introduced his reading of the *Theaetetus*. There he argues that there is a discrepancy between the Greek conceptions of falsehood and truth, shown by the fact that the Greek word for falsehood (ψεῦδος) and the Greek word for truth (ἀλήθεια) have completely different origins. Ψεῦδος, Heidegger proceeds to argue, does not simply mean "concealment" (*Verborgenheit*) but rather "distortion" (*Verdrehung*) (136; or *Verstellen*), that is, not simply concealing a thing, but presenting it in such a way as to misrepresent it. But then which of the two different phenomena expressed by ἀλήθεια and ψεῦδος, that is, unconcealment and distortion, comes to define the other? Heidegger clearly states his answer and his overriding thesis in the following passage, which, on account of its importance, merits being cited at length:

> In the first place let us firmly maintain this: with the emergence of ψεῦδος (distortion [*die Verdrehung*]) as the opposite [*Gegenbegriff*] of ἀλήθεια, ἀλήθεια as unconcealing [*Entbergen*] takes the orientation for its meaning from ψεύδεσθαι and comes to mean the same as ἀ-ψευδεῖν, transforms itself into the opposite of distorting [*Verdrehen*] (not-distorting). Through this noteworthy juxtaposition, ἀληθεύειν loses its fundamental meaning [*Grundbedeutung*] and becomes uprooted from the fundamental experience itself [*Grunderfahrung selbst*] out of which unconcealment [*die Unverborgenheit*] was understood. In this way ἀλήθεια moves into an opposition to *the kind of* concealing [*Verbergen*] that is a covering-up [*Verdecken*] and distorting [*Verstellen*], and not simply to concealment [*Verborgenheit*] and concealing [*Verbergung*] as such, but rather to distortion [*Verdrehung*], which perhaps has *within* itself the moment of concealment [*Verborgenheit*], but without this moment emerging [*welches aber nicht herauskommt*]. This covering-up [*Verdecken*] (distorting [*Verdrehen*]) is thereby initially in *a position of combating* [*Abwehrstellung gegen*] uncovering [*das Aufdecken*] (making-unconcealed); "uncovering" thus receives the meaning of not-distorting [*nicht-verstellen*], not-hiding [*nicht-verstecken*], *hitting upon* [*treffen*],—which is something other than what came before: simply and for the first time tearing what is concealed [*Verborgenes*] out of its concealment [*der Verborgenheit*]. (138)

But that truth is opposed only to distorting and thus comes to be identified only with "hitting upon" and "getting right" is precisely what Heidegger's reading of the *Theaetetus* fails to show. This is why at the end of the course he can return to the thesis stated on page 138 only by means of dogmatic assertions no longer based on a careful reading of the text. Ψεῦδος in the dialogue of course does not mean only "concealment," since something can be concealed without being untrue. But ψεῦδος does preserve its sense of "semblance" and therefore its connection to concealment, so that it does not demand as its opposite a conception of truth as mere "getting right."

Furthermore, Heidegger's assertion that ψεῦδος provides the orientation for the meaning of ἀλήθεια rather than vice versa is not supported by the dialogue. As we have already noted, Socrates suggests that the attempts to explain false δόξα have failed because false δόξα presupposes some kind of knowledge of what it is about and because therefore they were mistaken to seek to understand ψευδὴς δόξα before ἐπιστήμη (200c7–d2). Is this not equivalent to saying that ψευδὴς δόξα can be understood only on the basis of a prior understanding of ἀληθεύειν? As suggested above, the ἐπιστήμη and thus ἀληθεύειν presupposed by the possibility of ψευδὴς δόξα is precisely that striving that has been shown to characterize the soul's relation to being, a striving *in which* being is unconcealed as what is striven after. What the dialogue indicates very clearly is that ψευδὴς δόξα can be understood only on the basis of that prior unconcealment that makes possible our dialectical and striving relation to being and that one could call ἐπιστήμη. It is Heidegger's interpretation of the dialogue, or rather his relinquishing of the task of interpreting the dialogue, that inverts this priority.

It is important to note that Heidegger does partly qualify the thesis cited above by proceeding to show that the Greeks did recognize a sense of concealment (*Verborgenheit*) more fundamental than the ψεῦδος: what they called λήθη (oblivion). Heidegger argues (139–42) that λήθη does not mean primarily "forgetting" (*Vergessen*) but rather the concealment of beings as a whole that first makes a forgetting possible. Yet Heidegger proceeds to assert that even this phenomenon of λήθη was not grasped with sufficient originality by the Greeks: "Concealment, λήθη, is worn down [*abgeschliffen*] to a mere not-being-present-at-hand [*Nicht-vorhandensein*], being-away [*Wegsein*], absence [*Abwesenheit*]" (142). This reduction is of course a result of the Greek understanding of being: "The meaning of being in the sense of presence [*Anwesenheit*] is the reason why ἀλήθεια (unconcealment) is worn down to mere being-at-hand [*Vorhandensein*] (not-away) and, accordingly, concealment to mere being-away [*Wegsein*]. But this means: the ancient understanding of being thus prevents the commenced fundamental experience of the *concealment* of beings from unfolding itself in its proper depth and *at* its origin" (143). Yet this thesis that being meant presence for the Greeks has been seen to be brought into question repeatedly by what is said and shown in the *Theaetetus*. If being is "had" in the striving itself after being, it cannot be had as something present or at hand. On the contrary, in this striving, being not only cannot manifest itself as an object to be possessed, but must manifest itself as stretched out in the three temporal dimensions of past, present, and future, with priority given not to the present but to the future. Furthermore, the discussion of false belief was seen to presuppose that what we neither perceive nor explicitly attend to need not be simply "away" but can still be *had*; in other words, a being can be *had without being present*. In short, the dialogue repeatedly assumes and explicitly draws our attention to an understanding of, and relation to, being that far surpasses presence. In this case, there is in the dialogue no conception of being that prevents reflection on concealment as concealment and in its relation to unconcealment. Far from reducing concealment to mere absence, the dialogue, in characterizing our relation to being as a striving and "having" that are never a possessing and making-present, makes concealment pervade our relation to being or, in other words, makes every unconcealment of being at the same time a concealment.

The conclusion seems unavoidable: Heidegger's own reading of the *Theaetetus* completely overturns the theses on which this reading is premised. However, this overturning is only implicit, and Heidegger tries to prevent it at the end of the course, even at the cost of completely dogmatic and arbitrary assertions. Yet, as already indicated in the introduction to part 2 of this book, there is another and later text in which Heidegger explicitly revokes the claims that have just been cited: specifically, a text in which he denies that ψεῦδος and ἀλήθεια name completely different phenomena and defends an interpretation of ψεῦδος as concealment; and in which he not only also claims that the Greeks experienced λήθη as the concealment of beings as a whole (and not as mere absence) but also finds *Plato* thematizing precisely this original sense of λήθη. This text is the 1942 course on Parmenides. It is to this text that we must therefore now turn in completing our examination of what could be called the secret history of Heidegger's reading of Plato on truth and untruth: in other words, what gets suppressed and occluded by the official and definitive position in "Platons Lehre von der Wahrheit."

5

THE 1942 INTERPRETATION OF ΛΉΘΗ IN THE
MYTH OF ER (*REPUBLIC* BOOK 10)

A. THE ROMAN VERSUS THE GREEK CONCEPTION OF TRUTH

Before Heidegger in the *Parmenides* course turns to the Myth of Er in Plato's *Republic*, he provides an extensive reflection on the nature of ψεῦδος and ἀλήθεια for the Greeks. Justice cannot be done here to Heidegger's discussion in its entirety; instead attention will be drawn only to those points most relevant to the present context. Relatively early in the course Heidegger raises the problem that the opposite of ἀλήθεια in Greek is not λαθόν, but ψεῦδος. Yet he immediately (GA 54, 39–40) proceeds to warn against drawing from this the hasty conclusion that therefore truth could not have been understood by the Greeks as unconcealment (*Unverborgenheit*). He argues that if the essence of truth is for the Greeks in some way determined by τὸ ψεῦδος as its opposite, "on the other hand, presumably τὸ ψεῦδος, the false, nevertheless in its essence always remains *a form* of what is concealed [*des Verborgenen*] and of concealing [*des Verbergens*]" (33). It is precisely this dimension of concealment that Heidegger's account of τὸ ψεῦδος emphasizes. Taking the modern and Greek-derived word "pseudonym" as a clue and arguing that this word does not mean "*false* name" but rather a name that both conceals *and* reveals the author in a certain way (43–44), Heidegger concludes that ψεῦδος means a concealing that is also a letting-appear. "The ψεῦδος belongs within the essence [*Wesensbereich*] of covering-up [*des Verdeckens*], and thus to a form of concealing [*einer Art des Verbergens*]. The covering-up that pervades the ψεῦδος is, however, always at the same time a revealing [*Enthüllen*] and showing [*Zeigen*] and bringing-to-appearance [*Zum-erscheinen-bringen*]" (45). This account of τὸ ψεῦδος stresses its character as semblance (*Scheinen*), that is, as a concealing that is also an unconcealing and vice versa, in other words, as a peculiar belonging-together of concealment and unconcealment. While such an understanding of τὸ ψεῦδος was seen above to be present to some extent in the *Theaetetus*, Heidegger in 1931–32 insisted that it is precisely such a conception that Plato did not pursue. Furthermore, Heidegger's aim in the present course is to show precisely how to τὸ ψεῦδος *belongs together with* ἀλήθεια understood as unconcealment. From a passage in Homer (*Iliad* 2.348ff.), Heidegger concludes that "Ψεῦδος is a dis-torting concealing [*Verbergen*], 'hiding' [*Verhehlen*] in the narrow sense" (48) and sees this characterization as explaining how ψεῦδος can be the opposite of ἀληθές. Furthermore, he uses a passage from Hesiod to suggest that being ἀψευδές is grounded in being ἀληθές, and thus in unconcealing (48). It seems, therefore, that, rather than, as in 1931–32, interpreting τὸ ψεῦδος as uprooted from its original ground of concealment and thus as uprooting ἀλήθεια from the original experience of unconcealment, Heidegger here stresses the extent to which τὸ ψεῦδος still means concealment and thus remains grounded in ἀλήθεια as unconcealment.

There is a very significant and clear reason for this shift in Heidegger's reading. That reason is the Romans. In contrast to what he claimed in 1931–32, Heidegger now sees the translation of τὸ ψεῦδος as "the *false*" as a Roman interpretation of τὸ ψεῦδος that for the first time and definitively uproots it from the original experience of concealment and semblance. "False" comes from *falsum, fallo*, σφάλλω: bringing to a fall, rendering unstable (*wankend machen*), toppling (57). In understanding untruth from the perspective of making fall, the Romans are understanding it from the perspective of *imperium* (58–60). From this perspective of *imperium* as what stands upright and commands, untruth is experienced as a *trick* that trips up, undermines, makes fall. But in this conception of "the false," any relation to concealment has been lost: something is "false" not because it hides and conceals, but because it trips one up and brings one to a fall, because it defeats and subjects one. Heidegger therefore now sees the decisive transformation of the essence of truth in the move from the Greek ψεῦδος to the Roman *falsum*. "The Greek ψεῦδος as what hides [*das Verhehlende*] and as what from this perspective is also 'deceptive' [*Täuschende*] is now no longer experienced and interpreted from out of concealing [*Verbergen*], but instead from out of tricking [*Hintergehen*]" (61). How complete and radical a transformation this was is made clear by Heidegger's discussion of what the Romans opposed to *falsum*, which was *verum* (69–71). Heidegger attempts to show that *verum* originally meant "closing, covering [*Verschleißung, Bedeckung*]" and thus the opposite of the Greek ἀλήθεια. This is because, Heidegger explains, what is for the Romans the decisive *Wesensbereich* for truth is not concealment (*Verbergung*), but rather *imperium*; therefore, in the covering and closing meant by *verum* the Romans saw not the opposite of truth, but rather a securing (*Sicherung*), self-determination (*Sich-behaupten*), remaining-on-the top (*Obenbleiben*), and thus the opposite of *falsum* (71). *Verum* also becomes here *rectum* understood as what rules (*regere, das Regime*) and what commands (*iustum*, 71). To express the extent of the transformation as succinctly and extremely as possible, one can say the following: concealment for the Romans is power and therefore truth, while unconcealment is vulnerability and therefore falsehood.

This does not mean that Heidegger now abandons his thesis that a transformation in the essence of truth already took place with Plato and Aristotle. Yet the thesis is certainly rendered more ambiguous and harder to defend. Heidegger still claims that the transformation in the essence of ἀλήθεια begins with Plato, but now adds that it takes place "above all [*vor allem*] through the thinking of Aristotle" (72). The location of the transformation primarily in Aristotle seems new and surprising. After all, the influential essay published by the time this course was given is entitled not "Aristoteles Lehre von der Wahrheit" but "Platons Lehre von der Wahrheit." Yet there is a reason for giving central importance to Aristotle here. Heidegger now locates the transformation in the word ὁμοίωσις, indeed even asserts that this word becomes "as it were the authoritative [*maßgebende*] 'representation' of ἀλήθεια" (73); however, only in Aristotle can one find even an implicit association of this word with the conception of truth.[1] In order to locate a transformation of the essence of truth in the word ὁμοίωσις, Heidegger must furthermore interpret this word as meaning "the uncovering [*entbergende*] corresponding [*Entsprechen*] that asserts [*ausspricht*] the unconcealed [*das Unverborgene*]" (72). In this way, and in this way only, can he see the Greek and Roman conceptions of truth as displaying a fundamental kinship despite the great difference already indicated. For what he can now claim to be the same in both cases is an understanding of truth in terms of *correspondence*, even if in the case of the Greeks "this correspondence [*Ensprechung*] still maintains itself and carries itself out fully within the space of the essence [*Wesensraum*] of ἀλήθεια as unconcealment" (72), while in the case of the Romans it ceases to do so. Specifically, Heidegger describes the kinship as follows: "The Greek ὁμοίωσις as uncovering [*entbergende*] correspondence [*Entsprechung*] and the Roman *rectitudo* as measuring-oneself-against [*Sichrichten nach*] . . . both have the character of an approximation [*Angleichung*] of the assertion [*Aussage*] and thinking [*des Denkens*] to the state-of-affairs that lies before and stays put [*an den vorliegenden und feststehenden Sachverhalt*]. Approximation [*Angleichung*] means *adaequatio*" (73). It is only by means of this claim that Heidegger can proceed to make the conception of truth as *adaequatio intellectus ad rem*, the adequation of the intellect to the thing, "metaphysics' concept of truth"

---

1. Friedrich Ast's *Lexicon Platonicum* (Berlin: Herman Barsdorf, 1908) lists only three occurrences in Plato of the word ὁμοίωσις, which Ast translates as *similitudo*: *Epinomis* 990d, *Republic* 454c, and *Theaetetus* 176b. None of these passages have anything to do with truth.

and thus a concept of truth already present in the beginning of metaphysics with Plato. What is lost in the transformation of ὁμοίωσις into *rectitudo* is the essential realm of uncovering (*Entbergung*, 73), but the "adequation" remains the same.

This thesis is merely asserted here, and, like other dogmatic assertions made by Heidegger, it begins to crumble with a little reflection. The following objections can and should be made: (1) This identification of truth with the adequation of the intellect to the thing is nowhere to be found in Plato's *Theaetatus*. Not only are all attempts to identify false belief with some kind of "mismatching" refuted, but the characterization of our relation to being and the other κοινά as a striving, as well as the indication of the different ways in which beings can be had without being present or possessed, render completely absurd the suggestion that truth is a correspondence to some state of affairs that lies before us and stands firm. Furthermore, when Plato does use the word ὁμοίωσις, as he does in the *Theaetetus* itself to describe our relation not to truth but to *god*, the word clearly does not mean "correspondence" but "assimilation" and "becoming-like." It is not a "matching" between two things, but a transformation and appropriation. To claim therefore (171) that Plato transforms the essence of truth into ὁμοίωσις understood as *adaequatio* seems preposterous.

(2) Even in Aristotle an explicit identification of truth with ὁμοίωσις is not to be found. Bonitz finds only one occurrence of the word ὁμοίωσις in Aristotle (περὶ Φυτῶν, 826b34) and in a context that has nothing to do with truth.[2] Of course, there is the famous passage of *De Interpretatione* where Aristotle describes "the affections of the soul" (τὰ παθήματα τῆς ψυχῆς) as "likenesses of the things themselves" (ὁμοιώματα τῶν πραγμάτων, 16a7–8). First, however, it is clear from the context that this ὁμοίωσις is not truth, but rather a prior condition of truth; truth itself is to be found only in combination (σύνθεσις) and differentiation (διαίρεσις). Secondly, Heidegger himself elsewhere, in a course delivered in 1925–26, rightly insists that the ὁμοιώματα at issue in this passage have nothing to do with "some kind of *Angleichung* of a state of the soul to a physical thing—something which is absurd" (GA 21, 167). And what Heidegger is arguing against in the context surrounding his reading of *De Interpretatione* is precisely the attempt to find in Aristotle any conception of truth as *Abbildung* and *Nachbildung* "in the sense of a correspondence that measures itself against something [*im Sinn einer nachmessenden Übereinstimmung*]" (163). In a note Heidegger suggests that "ὁμοίωσις is spoken from out of the perspective of ἀποφαίνεσθαι: a letting-see approximates [*gleicht*

---

2. Hermann Bonitz, *Index Aristotelicus*, vol. 5 of *Aristotelis Opera* (Berlin: Walter de Gruyter, 1961).

sich an] in the only way that makes sense in the case of such a comportment [*in der Weise wie das einzig bei einem solchen Verhalten Sinn hat*]: in νόημα" (GA 21, 167n2). Ὁμοίωσις is here a letting-see, an unconcealing of what is unconcealed. Citing as an illustration of ὁμοίωσις Aristotle's claim at 19a33 that λόγοι are true (ἀληθεῖς) in a way similar to (ὁμοίως) the way in which things (πράγματα) are true, Heidegger translates/interprets: "Λόγοι (namely, the demonstrative [*aufweisende*] letting-be-seen of beings) are unconcealing (*entdeckend*) in the same way beings are, insofar as they are unconcealed [*entdeckt*]" (167n1). Obviously, the conception of truth Heidegger here sees at work in ὁμοίωσις is truth as unconcealment. Thus, the thesis Heidegger is explicitly defending in this 1925–26 course is that "the Aristotelian concept of truth and in general the Greek concept of truth are neither to be oriented towards a copying [*Abbilden*] nor are to be understood at all in the sense of this kind of correspondence [*Übereinstimmung*], but are rather to be oriented in comprehension toward unconcealing and concealing [*im Verständnis auf Entdecken und Verdecken hierauf zu orientieren*]" (162–63). In the face of this earlier characterization of ὁμοίωσις as a letting-be-seen and unconcealing that cannot be understood as a copying and corresponding, it is certainly hard to see how and why Heidegger in 1942 understands Aristotelian ὁμοίωσις as a correspondence that corresponds by way of asserting.

(3) Given the radical transformation that Heidegger himself sees as separating the Roman from the Greek conception of truth, it is a priori implausible that *rectitudo* would preserve the Greek ὁμοίωσις largely unaltered. Indeed, if ὁμοίωσις still maintains itself completely within the realm of unconcealment, then it must be, as Heidegger himself earlier maintained, an *unconcealing* rather than some "dequation" between two things. Truth becomes adequation only when the original experience of unconcealment is lost. It is as if Heidegger, having shifted the major transformation of the essence of truth to the Romans, can preserve his original thesis regarding the transformation of the essence of truth in Plato and Aristotle only by himself Latinizing the Greeks.

But what of the word ὀρθότης? Does not the use of this word in Plato and Aristotle indicate a conception of truth as correctness and thus as correspondence? Heidegger later in the course, in the context of interpreting a line from Pindar, provides an extremely important account of ὀρθότης that in fact appears to distinguish it sharply from "correctness." Heidegger's interpretation needs to be quoted in full:

The way, ὀδός, means ὀρθά. The Greek ὀρθός means "straight ahead" [*"geradeaus"*], along [*längs und entlang*], namely, along the prospect and view [*Durchblick*] on what is unconcealed [*das Unverborgene*]. The fundamental meaning of ὀρθός is not the same as that of the Roman

> *rectum*, of what is oriented toward an above [*des nach oben gerichteten*] because judging, ordering, and "ruling" from above [*weil von oben her richtenden und befehlenden und "regierenden"*]. The Roman *rectitudo* has also obstructed [*verbaut*] the Greek ὀρθότης that belongs to ὁμοίωσις, the essence of which originally allowed access to ἀλήθεια [*ursprünglich in die* ἀλήθεια *eingelassen hat*]. The uncovering likening-oneself to the unconcealed within unconcealment [*entbergende Sichangleichen an das Unverborgene innerhalb der Unverborgenheit*] is a going-along [*ein entlang Gehen*], namely, along the way that leads directly, ὀρθῶς, to the unconcealed. Ὁμοίωσις is ὀρθότης. The ὀρθός as thought by the Greeks has originally nothing in common [*anfänglich nichts gemeinsam*] with the Roman *rectum* and the German *recht*. (120; see also 122)

But if even the Greek ὀρθός does not mean "right" or "correct" but rather "straight ahead to the unconcealed," then how can Heidegger still claim to find in Plato and Aristotle a conception of truth as "correctness" or *Richtigkeit*? With the Romans Heidegger appears to have found a new origin for this conception and thereby to have rendered untenable his claim to find this origin in the Greeks. As Heidegger's account of the original meaning of the word *verum* especially shows, the Roman conception of truth is not a "fulfillment" or inevitable outgrowth of the Greek conception but rather its complete *overturning*. And as the passage just cited makes clear, *rectitudo*, in completely uprooting ὁμοίωσις from the ground of unconcealment, completely transforms and even inverts its nature: ὁμοίωσις goes from being an unconcealing that as such is "like" the unconcealed to being the "correct" correspondence between two things.

By locating the origin of the notions of correctness and incorrectness in the Romans, Heidegger is indeed now able to grant much more to the Greek experience of truth and untruth than he does elsewhere. Now only does he provide, as we have seen, a much richer interpretation of ψεῦδος that stresses its character as concealment, but he also does not now confine the Greeks to even this experience of concealment as ψεῦδος. Instead, he describes different forms of concealing [*Verbergung*] and concealment [*Verborgenheit*] (92–92) in order to show "that unconcealment [*die Unverborgenheit*] has as its 'opposite' not only concealing [*Verbergung*] in the sense of distortion [*Verstellung*] and falsehood, that instead there are ways of concealing [*Weisen der Verbergung*] that not only display another form [*andere Art*], but also carry with them nothing of the specifically 'negative' character of falsehood and distortion [*Verstellung*]" (95). What Heidegger finds "astonishing" is that these ways of concealing [*Verbergung*] are not named by the Greeks, not an account of an oversight, but perhaps because "they are so essential" (95). These different types of concealing need not be described here. What instead requires our attention is Heidegger's claim that the Greeks do name one type of concealing [*Verbergung*] that cannot be identified with distortion [*Verstellung*], that "*is constantly present in Greek existence, but that in its essence is not further considered*, unless the word itself which names this concealing and its sphere already held for the Greeks sufficient revelations" (95). This word is λήθη.

If the Greeks name λήθη, this does not mean that they say much *about* it. Yet Heidegger defends the Greek silence about λήθη as appropriate. After all, would not speaking about this ultimate concealment betray it? Speaking of the Greek silence with regard to λήθη, Heidegger writes: "We too rarely consider that the same Greeks to whom the word and saying were granted in an originary way even for this very reason could be silent in a unique way. For 'being-silent' ["*Schweigen*"] is not mere not-saying. Whoever does not have anything essential to say also cannot be silent" (108). If the Greeks did not express the essential relations between λήθη and ἀλήθεια in the way we must, this is because "the Greeks are very silent when we reflect on what is essential to them [*ihr Wesenhaftes*]. When, however, they do say this, they do so in a way that is at the same time characterized by silence [*in einer zugleich verschweigenden Weise*]" (116). The Greek silence regarding λήθη is not a sign that they did not experience it in a profound and original way, but quite the opposite.

We therefore do not find in this course anything like the suggestion in the 1931–32 course that the Greeks failed to experience λήθη originally by reducing it to mere not-being-present-at-hand and absence, thus making it the mere "other" of truth as reduced to presence-at-hand. On the contrary, in a poem by Pindar Heidegger finds clear evidence "that in Greek existence the reciprocal counter-essencing [*das wechselweise Gegenwesen*] between ἀλήθεια and λήθη is experienced in an original manner [*ursprünglich erfahren ist*]" (129). Heidegger does indeed add that the Greeks did not *think* this relation or its terms, but he explains as follows why this was so:

> In Greek existence neither *ἀλήθεια* nor *λήθη* is ever specifically thought through in its proper essence and in the ground of its essence [*je eigens auf ihr eigenes Wesen und auf ihren Wesensgrund durchdacht*], because, that is, they already, in advance of *all* thinking and composing [*allem Denken und Dichten vorauf*], pervade what is to be thought as the "essence" ["*Wesen*"]. Greek existence thinks and composes [*dichtet*] and "acts ["*handelt*"] *in* the essence of ἀλήθεια and λήθη, but it does not think and compose *about* this essence [*auf dieses Wesen*] and does not "undertake an action ["*handelt*"] with regard to it [*darüber*]. It suffices to Greek existence to be addressed, claimed [*angesprochen*] and encircled [*umfangen*] by ἀλήθεια itself (129).

Thus, if the Greeks did not think *about* ἀλήθεια and λήθη, this is because their thinking was so fully and completely claimed *by* them.³ There is no suggestion here of a failure to think ἀλήθεια and λήθη in the sense of a misunderstanding or superficial understanding of their essence. There is no suggestion here that the Greeks reduced ἀλήθεια and λήθη to mere presence and absence. On the contrary, both their silence and their lack of explicit reflection with regard to ἀλήθεια and λήθη show only how deeply rooted they were in the experience of both. It thus becomes hard to see here a limitation, or at least one that could ever be overcome. This means that it also becomes hard to see here the beginning of a road that will lead inexorably to the eclipse of ἀλήθεια in correctness.

B. SAYING ΛΉΘΗ IN THE MYTH OF ER

It turns out in any case that the Greeks did not refrain entirely from thinking and saying λήθη. Heidegger will in the course focus his attention on a Greek text in which λήθη is not only named, but is also thematized as the subject of a discourse. This discourse, however, does not take the form of a scientific treatise asserting propositions about λήθη: such a form of discourse would be completely inappropriate to what is not an object nor a being standing in unconcealment, but rather withdrawal into concealment. The only appropriate discourse would be one that unconceals in such a way as also to conceal, as to allow what it unconceals its proper concealment; a discourse, in other words, that in its saying maintains silence. This discourse is *myth*. According to Heidegger, "'the mythical'—μῦθος-character [*-hafte*] is the unconcealing and concealing [*Entbergen und Verbergen*] sheltered in the unconcealing-concealing word [*im entbergend-verbergenden Wort*], as which unconcealing and concealing the fundamental essence [*das Grundwesen*] of being itself originally appears" (104). That λήθη should come to word in a myth is therefore certainly not a limitation betraying a primitive and unscientific way of thinking. Myth and λήθη go together, so that an interpretation of saying as

---

3. See also the following passage: "Freilich haben die Griechen über dieses anfänglichere Wesen der ἀλήθεια noch weniger gedacht und gesagt als über das Wesen der λήθη: denn ihnen ist die ἀλήθεια der einfache Anfang alles Wesenden" (199). But Heidegger here suggests that the Greeks did not *need* to do this; only "Wir Späteren" have this need (199). Also: "Das im Wesen der ἀλήθεια Nächste wird deshalb dem Gesetz zufolge, nach dem der Anfang anfängt, *auch von den Griechen notwendig übersehen*. Dies Übersehen kommt nicht aus einer Unachtsamkeit; es ist nicht die Folge einer Versäumnis oder eines Unvermögens, sondern im Gegenteil: Aufgrund ihrer Treue zur erst anfänglichen Erfahrung des sich noch entziehenden Anfangs *übersehen die Griechen das Anfängliche des Anfangs*" (202). But the question is whether this could ever be "seen," whether what is most near and the first beginning is overlooked only "at first" or necessarily "always."

mere assertion necessarily renders the experience of λήθη inaccessible behind a conception of untruth as mere incorrectness.

But where does Heidegger find this myth of λήθη? The answer should shock: not in the early Greek poets, not in the pre-Socratics, but *in Plato*. The strangeness of Heidegger's turning to Plato for the mythic expression of λήθη cannot be sufficiently emphasized. This is strange for two related reasons. First, according to Heidegger we have in Plato the transformation of the essence of truth and untruth from unconcealment and concealment to correctness and incorrectness. This transformation is a move *away from* an understanding of ψεῦδος as concealment and a fortiori from the experience of that concealment more original than ψεῦδος and named by the word λήθη. How very strange, then, that one should have to turn to Plato for an account of λήθη, that one should find in Plato what Heidegger himself characterizes as "a thinking *of* [ein Denken an], not only a thinking 'about' [ein Denken 'über'] λήθη" (190). Secondly, if in Plato truth becomes correctness, this is at least partly because in Plato λόγος becomes assertion. This thesis is stated in the present course with no ambiguity whatsoever. At one point Heidegger suggests three titles for "the hidden essential history of the West": (1) Being and Word (*Sein und Wort*); (2) Being and Ratio; (3) Being and Time (113). Heidegger then justifies locating the beginning of Being and Ratio in Plato by maintaining that with Plato and Aristotle "the word becomes λόγος in the sense of assertion" (113). How strange, then, to find in Plato λόγος in the sense of μῦθος! And how incredibly strange to find in a philosopher who supposedly reduced λόγος to assertion and ψεῦδος to incorrectness a myth devoted precisely to a concealment more fundamental than ψεῦδος itself![4]

How does Heidegger explain this "anomaly"? That myths should be found in Plato's dialogues he explains as follows: "People have already been puzzled about why in general 'myths' sometimes crop up in Plato's dialogues. The ground lies in the fact that Plato's thinking prepares itself for [sich anschickt] giving up the original thinking [das anfängliche Denken] in favor of what is later named 'metaphysics'; that even this beginning metaphysical thinking, however, must at the same time preserve a recollection of the original thinking. Therefore, the saying [die Sage]" (145). Oddly, then, the presence of myths in Plato's dialogues is taken by Heidegger to be only a *confirmation* that a completely different kind of thinking is beginning here; after all, must not traces of

---

4. And in the myth Heidegger finds an *Ent-sprechung* that differs significantly from the *adaequatio* he otherwise seeks to find in Plato. In speaking of the way in which for the Greeks myth ("das Sagenhafte") must "ent-sprechen dem Gotthaften," Heidegger writes: "Dieses Ent-sprechen ist überhaupt das anfängliche Wesen aller Entsprechung (Homologie), das Wort 'Entsprechung' wesentlich wörtlich genommen. Mit der Einsicht in diese Entsprechung, in der ein Spruch, ein Wort, eine Sage dem Sein ent-spricht, d. h. es als das Selbe in einem Gleichen sagend entbirgt, sind nun auch wir in den Stand gesetzt, die noch ausstehende Antwort auf eine früher gestellte Frage zu geben" (169–70).

the earlier thinking be found in such a beginning? In short, the myths in Plato are being treated as some ghostly remnant of an earlier understanding of saying, one that Plato himself is leaving behind in the turn toward metaphysics. If, however, we are not convinced by Heidegger's demonstration elsewhere, as in the 1931–32 course, that we have in Plato the beginning of the reduction of λόγος to assertion and of ἀλήθεια to correctness, then Plato's myths appear in a very different light, as a clear indication that we do not have in Plato the later metaphysical conception of λόγος and truth. In other words, the question is whether the myths represent an archaizing, anomalous, and marginal moment in Plato or whether they form an indispensable part of Plato's central and defining relation to λόγος and truth. Are the myths what Plato is leaving behind or where he wishes to go? That the myths generally do not appear at the beginning of a dialogue but at its conclusion or climatic turning point, and that, far from being fragments of earlier myths, they are extraordinarily elaborate and original, certainly suggest the latter alternative. If the myths are only preserved remnants of an earlier saying, then such remnants comprise a surprisingly large part of Plato's creative output.

It is not only mythical discourse that stands in contrast to a conception of λόγος as assertion: so does the dialogue form as such. If Plato was the first to interpret λόγος as assertion, it is remarkable that he was at such pains to avoid presenting his thought in the form of assertions. Instead of writing treatises in which he could demonstrate the truth of certain assertions, Plato instead wrote dramatic dialogues in which characters, who never include Plato himself, question and respond to each other. What we see put to work in Plato's writings is not λόγος as assertion, but rather λόγος as question and answer, precisely the conception of λόγος we found articulated in the *Theaetetus*. How, then, does Heidegger account for the dialogue form? How else? It too can be nothing but a remnant of an earlier form of saying. Thus, Heidegger writes: "It is as if, before the end of Greek thinking, this thinking itself should wish to show, through its unique way of saying, what an essential rank the word has where man comes immediately into the relation to ἀλήθεια" (131–32). Thus, the dialogue form recalls the original relation to ἀλήθεια and the priority of the word (as opposed to assertion and ratio) this relation makes possible at the very same time that Plato moves philosophy away from both ἀλήθεια and the word. Strangely, Plato's philosophy and the dialogue form thus turn out to be at odds with one another. Yet it is not as if Plato were unaware of the implications of the dialogue form. Heidegger adds to the above the observation that in the *Phaedrus* Plato shows a very clear understanding of the priority the spoken word has over the written word. Heidegger indeed then counters: "But where would Plato's 'dialogues' be if they too had not become written text?" (132). This of course is a legitimate question, but written dialogue is nevertheless *not* λόγος as assertion (*Aussage*); in other words, it still preserves, as much as a written text possibly can, the spoken and living word.

What needs to be noted here is Heidegger's general procedure. First the Platonic myths, now the dialogue form itself: at this rate, Heidegger is in danger of turning the whole of Plato into a mere recollection of an earlier and more originary thinking and saying. Does it not then become time to question the thesis of a "metaphysical Plato" who transforms truth into correctness and λόγος into assertion? Just how much in Plato can be explained away in order to uphold this thesis? If, as we saw in Heidegger's reading of the *Theaetetus*, this "metaphysical Plato" is a mere construction receiving no support from the text, then ultimately it is the dialogues in their entirely that must be explained away. There is the Plato of the dialogues and the metaphysical Plato, and never shall the two meet. Heidegger himself warns against identifying Plato with Platonism. In the context of criticizing not only "Christian" readings of Plato but also Nietzsche's "un-Greek" reading of Plato and the Pre-Socratics, Heidegger comments: "But what lies nearer at hand than the opinion that those interpretations of Plato's philosophy that approach it with the help of a 'Platonism' are the most appropriate? However, this procedure is comparable to wanting to 'explain' the fresh leaf on the tree through the leaf that has fallen on the ground" (139–40). But does not Heidegger himself fall into such an absurd procedure? Is not the metaphysical transformation of truth and λόγος the "dead leaf" with which he tries to interpret Plato? Are not the things Heidegger characterizes as remnants of an earlier thinking and saying, the myths and the dialogue form itself, precisely the living leaves that still hang on the tree? Does he not himself fall into the trap of "Platonizing" Plato? That Heidegger's explicit rejection here of a "Platonizing" interpretation of Plato is not *only* a rejection of the "Christian" or "Neoplatonic" interpretation of Plato is made clear by the following words: "But even there where one remains completely outside the distinction between Christian and pagan, one always thinks Plato's philosophy Platonically in the sense of Platonism. . . . But to want to interpret Plato through any kind of Platonism is the true ruination [*der eigentliche Verderb*]" (144). Yet how can Heidegger's constant appeal to a metaphysical Plato incompatible with what he himself finds in the dialogues escape precisely this charge? How can his tendency to interpret Plato in terms of what *came after* (e.g., the pair "Being and Ratio") not be seen as an interpretation of Plato through Platonism?

Yet it is nevertheless the case that Heidegger's reading of Plato's myth of λήθη is perhaps further from a Platonizing interpretation of Plato than are his interpretations of other texts elsewhere. How, indeed, could it not be? It is therefore time to turn to a necessarily partial and incomplete account of Heidegger's interpretation of the myth. Indeed, Heidegger characterizes his own interpretation as incomplete and partial because the myth "is so far-reaching [*weit gespannt*] and rich, that it for this very reason cannot be represented [*dargestellt*] here" (136). What Heidegger says of Plato's myth is true of his own interpretation; thus the necessary incompleteness of any account of one or the other. The goal of what follows is limited first to outlining the central moments and insights Heidegger identifies in Plato's myth and then to identifying the central dimensions of the myth which Heidegger's interpretation excludes.

Heidegger devotes much time to interpreting the τόπος τις δαιμόνιος to which Er is said to go after his death (614b9–c1). What especially concerns him is the meaning of the word δαιμόνιον. What Heidegger finds expressed in this word is the extra-ordinary (*das Un-geheure*), but in the sense of "the essence and ground of the extra-ordinary" (151). The δαιμόνιον is the extra-ordinary not in the sense that it goes against the ordinary, but rather in the sense that "it everywhere encloses what currently offers itself as the ordinary [*das jeweilig Geheure umgibt*] and everywhere offers itself in everything ordinary [*in alles Geheure sich dargibt*], without, however, being the ordinary" (150). The extra-ordinary as thus understood is not "exceptional," un-natural or super-natural, but rather what is "most natural" in the sense of φύσις (151). Indeed, it seems that on Heidegger's reading the τόπος τις δαιμόνιος could be said to be φύσις itself. If those beings that exist φύσει are "the ordinary," then φύσις is that extra-ordinary out of which the ordinary emerges and within which it is enclosed.

The effect of such a reading is to make the place to which Er goes not some remote "beyond," not some "other world," but rather the extra-ordinary and yet all-pervasive and all-encompassing dimension of this world. The δαιμόνιον, as that extra-ordinary out of which everything "ordinary" arises and in which everything "ordinary" is grounded, is always present. The τόπος τις δαιμόνιος is simply that place in which the δαιμόνιον presents itself specifically *as such*: "A δαιμόνιος τόπος is an 'extraordinary place' [*'ungeheure Ortschaft'*]. That now means: a Where, in whose sites and paths [*dessen Plätze und Gänge*] the extra-ordinary properly shines in [*eigens hereinscheint*] and the essencing of being [*das Wesen des Seins*] essences in an exceptional sense [*in einem ausgezeichnete Sinne west*]" (174). Thus. one can say that what shines forth in the δαιμόνιος τόπος is the extraordinariness or uncanniness of being itself (φύσις). This would explain Heidegger's otherwise surprising interpretation of the Socratic δαιμόνιον: "The Socratic-Platonic talk of the δαιμόνιον as an inner voice only means that its attuning and determining [*Stimmen und Bestimmen*] does not come from outside, that is, not from some present-at-hand being, but rather from out of being itself as invisible and ungraspable [*aus dem unsichtbaren und ungreifbaren Sein selbst*], which is nearer to the essence of man [*Menschenwesen*] than every importunate palpability of beings [*aufdringliche Handgreiflichkeit des Seienden*]" (174). The δαιμόνιον is that through which and in which being in its extra-ordinariness attunes and orders us.

The δαιμόνιος τόπος is therefore also the place where the unconcealing/concealing play of ἀλήθεια especially comes to presence. Thus, Heidegger observes: "We find it hard to get at this simple essence of the δαιμόνιον because we do not experience the essence of ἀλήθεια. For the δαίμονες, the self-showing and indicating [*Sichzeigenden, Weisenden*], are what they are and are as they are *only* in the essential realm [*Wesensbereich*] of unconcealing [*Entbergung*] and of self-unconcealing being itself [*sich entbergenden Seins selbst*]" (151). Heidegger therefore at one point suggests that Parmenides in naming the goddess Ἀλήθεια at the beginning of his poem names precisely the δαιμόνιος τόπος (188). Furthermore, it is on the basis of this essence of ἀλήθεια as unconcealment that Heidegger explains the suitability of mythic discourse to the δαιμόνιον: "The word as the naming of being, the μῦθος, names being in its original looking-in [*Hereinblicken*] and appearing [*Scheinen*]—names τὸ θεῖον, i.e., the gods. Because τὸ θεῖον and τὸ δαιμόνιον (the godly) is the extra-ordinary that looks into unconcealment [*das in die Unverborgenheit Hereinblickende*] and offers itself in the ordinary [*in das Geheure sich dargebende*], for this reason is μῦθος, whose essence is determined by unconcealing [*Entbergung*] as essentially as is the θεῖον and δαιμόνιον, the only adequate form of relating to being in its appearing [*zum erscheinenden Sein*]" (166). It is in ἀλήθεια as unconcealment that both myth, as the unconcealing-concealing word, and the δαιμόνιον, as the looking-in and self-showing extra-ordinary, meet. Ἀλήθεια is the *place* for both. The δαιμόνιος τόπος, in short, is extra-ordinary being in its self-emerging (φύσις) and self-unconcealing (ἀλήθεια).

It is therefore all the more extraordinary that λήθη, the forgetfulness that forgets itself, the complete withdrawal into concealment, should have its home in this δαιμόνιος τόπος. Not only is λήθη opposed to ἀλήθεια, but the myth also makes clear its opposition to φύσις. At 621a3ff. we are told by Er that the plain of λήθη is "empty of trees and of whatever else the earth brings forth [κενὸν δένδρων τε καὶ ὅσα γῆ φύει]." Λήθη does not allow anything to emerge (φύει) from the concealment and sheltering of the earth; as a holding-back and withdrawing it is opposed to the self-emergence named φύσις. Thus, Heidegger writes: "λήθη appears as the counter-essence [*das Gegenwesen*] to φύσις" (176). But this does not mean that λήθη is the mere negation of φύσις and being; it is not *nothing*, as is made clear by its being located within the δαιμόνιος τόπος. As Heidegger asserts, "The 'away' of what is withdrawn itself comes to presence [*west an*] in the prevailing of the withdrawal [*im Wesen des Entzugs*]" (176).

This is not to suggest, however, that λήθη is simply "in" the place of ἀλήθεια, as if it were subordinate to and encompassed by ἀλήθεια. In interpreting the myth's reference to the "field of λήθη," Heidegger insists that λήθη is not in a place, but is itself place. The field or plain is not something external to λήθη; instead λήθη "is the place-like [*Orthafte*] and the Where, so that the withdrawing concealment [*entziehende Verbergung*] no longer occurs somewhere in a field, but much more on its side unfolds itself as the Where for what must belong there" (181). Does not indeed withdrawing concealment shelter and "place" what emerges into unconcealment? Rather than being nothing and nowhere, is not λήθη, precisely as the counter-essence to ἀλήθεια and φύσις, what first makes possible un-concealment and e-merging? Are not, after all, the δαιμόνιος τόπος named Ἀλήθεια and the place of λήθη the *same place* in the myth or, if one prefers, two dimensions of the same place?

What Heidegger indeed sees the myth as saying is not only ἀλήθεια nor only λήθη, but the belonging-together of ἀλήθεια and λήθη, of unconcealment and concealment. Heidegger finds this belonging-together expressed with special clarity at 621a7ff., where we are told that the human souls must drink a certain measure of the water of the river that flows through the plain of λήθη before they can start on the new lives they have chosen. The effect of drinking this water is to forget what has been (621b). The myth does not explain *why* entering into a new life and thus a new mode of unconcealment, that is, a new relation to beings in their being, must be preceded by this oblivion. Heidegger offers the following explanation:

> Every man who measures out upon the earth the journey pregnant with death [*die todesträchtige Fahrt*] is on the earth and in the midst of beings in such a way that on account of this drink a concealing and withdrawing of beings holds sway [*eine Verbergung und ein Entzug des Seienden waltet*], so that beings are only to the extent that at the same time and counter to this concealing and withdrawing [*entgegen dieser Verbergung und dieser Entgängnis*] an unconcealment [*Unverborgenheit*] holds sway [*waltet*], in which the unconcealed [*das Unverborgene*] remains capable of being held and is held [*behaltbar und behalten*]. (178)

If we must drink oblivion and concealment before entering upon life, then the unconcealment that defines life, that unconcealment within which we encounter and relate to beings, must occur against and be won from the prior concealment. That we *drink* the water which induces λήθη means, as Heidegger suggests, that it "enters into the human being and determines him from out of the interior of his essence [*aus dem Innern seines Wesens bestimmt*]" (187). But in this case, ἀ-λήθεια in our relation to being can occur and hold sway only in a constant struggle with λήθη. Standing at the very entrance into human life as its precondition, λήθη is not something that can be simply pushed aside in favor of ἀλήθεια, but always belongs together with it. Indeed, truth could not be experienced as ἀ-λήθεια, un-concealment, unless λήθη, concealment, holds sway from the very beginning. Thus, Heidegger interprets the need for all human beings to drink a measure of the water that flows through the plain of λήθη as showing that "λήθη belongs to the essence of ἀλήθεια" and that "therefore un-concealment itself cannot be simply the mere setting-aside [*Beseitigung*] of concealment" (183). A little later Heidegger gives the following positive characterization of the relation: "λήθη, forgetting [*die Vergessung*] as withdrawing concealment [*die entziehende Verbergung*], is that withdrawal [*Entzug*] through which the essence of ἀλήθεια can alone and always directly be preserved [*behalten*] and so remain unforgotten and unforgettable [*unvergessen und unvergeßlich*]" (189). In other words, un-concealment can be preserved and remain what it is only through concealment.

According to Heidegger in another important aspect of his interpretation, it is because our relation to the being of beings must be a constant saving and preserving of unconcealment against concealment that Plato characterized this relation as ἀνάμνησις (184). "The ἰδέα is the face [*das Gesicht*] with which at any time [*jeweils*] the self-unconcealing being [*das sich entbergende Seiende*] looks at [*ansieht*] human beings. The ἰδέα is the presence of what comes to presence [*die Anwesenheit des Anwesenden*]: the being of beings. But because ἀλήθεια is the overcoming [*die Überwindung*] of λήθη, the unconcealed must be saved [*gerettet*] in unconcealment and sheltered in it [*geborgen*]" (184). This saving of what is unconcealed *from* λήθη and *in* unconcealment is precisely what ἀνάμνησις is. Heidegger therefore resists a "psychological" interpretation of ἀνάμνησις as the psychical act of "remembering" something that has been forgotten. Here it should be recalled that on Plato's account *all* learning, all coming-to-know the ἰδέα of something, is ἀνάμνησις. Not only things that we happen to have forgotten, but the being of anything whatsoever, can be known only in and through ἀνάμνησις. This means that every ἰδέα is concealed in λήθη as soon as we are born and therefore can be known only through being *retrieved and saved* from this λήθη. What is at issue in ἀνάμνησις is not the play of psychological states but the strife and belonging-together of ἀλήθεια and λήθη.

However, Heidegger proceeds to claim that with the transformation of the essence of truth in Plato, that is, the transformation of truth and untruth into properties of human seeing and saying, there is necessarily a move in the direction of a purely psychological interpretation of ἀνάμνησις: "Indeed, with Plato begins, at the same time as the transformation of the essence of ἀλήθεια into ὁμοίωσις, a transformation of λήθη, i.e., here of the ἀνάμνησις that works against it. The event [*Ereignis*] of withdrawing concealing transforms itself into the human comportment of forgetting [*zum menschlichen Verhalten des Vergessen*]. At the same time, what stands *against* λήθη becomes a fetching-back-again [*Wiederzurück-holen*] through man" (185).

As usual, Heidegger gives no evidence for the transformation. He grants only that what Plato says cannot be interpreted *only* from the perspective of that towards which he begins the transformation. Again we have the contrast between the transformation which Heidegger asserts is there and what his own reading of the text shows: in this case, while Plato's text on Heidegger's own reading shows the belonging-together of ἀλήθεια and λήθη in being itself and characterizes our relation to being as ἀνάμνησις in response to this understanding of being, we must believe that the transformation of ἀλήθεια and λήθη into mere "subjective states" begins with Plato. Though Heidegger himself does not cite the account of ἀνάμνησις in the *Phaedrus*,[5] it provides a crucial contrast and supplement to what we are told in the Myth of Er. There, in another extraordinary myth, Socrates again states a condition for entering human life and explicitly maintains that an understanding of learning as ἀνάμνησις necessarily results from this condition. What is striking, however, is that the conditions stated in the two myths appear completely opposed: while in the Myth of Er, what is necessary for souls to enter a human life is drinking the water from the plain of λήθη (πᾶσιν ἀναγκαῖον εἶναι πιεῖν), what the myth in the *Phaedrus* asserts to be necessary is *seeing the truth*: "For a soul that has never seen the truth will never enter this [human] form" (οὐ γὰρ ἥ γε μήποτε ἰδοῦσα τὴν ἀλήθειαν εἰς τόδε ἥξει τὸ σχῆμα, 249b5–6). This contrast is made all the more striking by the fact that what the souls are described as visiting prior to their embodiment in the *Phaedrus* is not τὸ τῆς Λήθης πεδίον but rather τὸ ἀληθείας πεδίον (248b6). How can these two accounts be reconciled? It is precisely the notion of ἀνάμνησις that points to the answer. In the *Phaedrus*, immediately after claiming that every soul must have seen the truth before entering human form, Socrates adds that it is therefore necessary (δεῖ) to recollect (ἀνάμνησις, 249c2). If a soul has necessarily already seen the truth before taking on human form, then its learning of the truth in this life can only take the form of recollection. But there is another side to this that the *Phaedrus* does not mention but that becomes the focus in the Myth of Er: if learning is ἀνάμνησις, this is not only because we have seen the truth, but also because this truth has immediately fallen into oblivion and concealment. The myths of the *Republic* and the *Phaedrus* recount two sides of the human destiny that necessarily go together: we are equally under the power

---

5. Though he does discuss the passage elsewhere, such as in the 1928 course *The Metaphysical Foundations of Logic*, where what Heidegger emphasizes is not the belonging-together of concealment and unconcealment but rather the relation of the understanding of being to time (GA 26, 185–87)

of ἀλήθεια and λήθη, we emerge into this life from both the plain of ἀλήθεια and the plain of λήθη, and this is why our relation to being has the character of continually freeing and saving what is unconcealed from concealment: ἀνάμνησις. We are born in oblivion and in truth. What thus characterizes human existence is the simultaneous concealment and unconcealment of beings.[6] Indeed, reading the myths of the *Phaedrus* and the *Republic* together perhaps shows that τὸ τῆς Λήθης πεδίον and τὸ ἀληθείας πεδίον are not two completely different places, but belong together in and as the same place. As we have seen, Heidegger's interpretation of τὸ τῆς Λήθης πεδίον as found in the δαιμόνιος τόπος effectively turns it into τὸ ἀληθείας πεδίον.

What needs to be stressed here is that Plato characterizes both ἀλήθεια and λήθη as *places* to which the human soul goes and from which it comes. What could be further from a transformation of ἀλήθεια and λήθη into properties of human speaking and saying? Furthermore, a comparison of the myth in the *Phaedrus* with the Myth of Er only further confirms what Heidegger's interpretation finds in the latter on its own: that Plato thought ἀλήθεια and λήθη *together*. That the myth of the *Phaedrus* names τὸ ἀληθείας πεδίον without naming τὸ τῆς Λήθης πεδίον and that the Myth of Er names τὸ τῆς Λήθης πεδίον without naming τὸ ἀληθείας πεδίον only shows that the two are thought so closely together that the naming of one suffices to imply the other. What could be further from a transformation ἀλήθεια and λήθη into the mutually exclusive opposites of correctness and incorrectness? Finally, the characterization of our relation to being as ἀνάμνησις is for Plato demanded by the inextricably intertwined events of concealment and unconcealment that define human existence as such. It is because they exist simultaneously in the plain of unconcealment and the plain of concealment that human beings can have no other relation to being than that of ἀνάμνησις. Furthermore, it needs to be stressed that ἀνάμνησις is therefore the way in which we strive after the being that was both unconcealed and concealed to us; as such, it is not some merely mental capacity or faculty, but *a way of existing*. According to the account of the *Phaedrus*, ἀνάμνησις occurs in falling in love: a love

---

6. Michael Inwood asks: "Would Plato agree that being human means standing in the hidden? In one sense, he would. Everyone begins as a prisoner, and most people remain prisoners for life. In another sense, he would not. Once the philosopher has left the cave and seen the sun (the Idea of the good), nothing is hidden from him" ("Truth and Untruth in Plato and Heidegger," in HPD, 86). But this last claim ignores not only the Myth of Er but even the full implications of the Cave Analogy itself: in particular, Socrates' insistence on the difficulty of seeing the sun and the requirement that the philosopher return to the cave. Inwood therefore sees a contrast between Plato and Heidegger (see also 87) where there is really more agreement. For another interpretation that brings Plato and Heidegger much closer together on this point while still recognizing a difference, see Gregory Fried, "Back to the Cave: A Platonic Rejoinder to Heideggerian Postmodernism," in *Heidegger and the Greeks: Interpretative Essays*, ed. Drew A. Hyland and John Panteleimon Manoussakis (Bloomington: Indiana University Press, 2006), 170.

that completely overwhelms and transforms one's existence.[7] What could be further from a transformation of ἀνάμνησις into a purely subjective state of remembering? Ἀλήθεια and λήθη are the place where being conceals and unconceals itself and ἀνάμνησις is the continual movement of human existence (back) to that place.

Heidegger draws attention to another way in which the Myth of Er illustrates the idea of recollection and thus the belonging-together of concealment and unconcealment. At the end of the myth, Socrates comments on how this μῦθος, the μῦθος of λήθη, was "saved" (ἐσώθη) from λήθη, since Er was prevented from drinking the water of the river. Socrates then adds that this saved μῦθος is precisely what can save us (621b). Er's story is of course itself a "recollection," but peculiarly it is a recollection of λήθη. Such a remembering of forgetfulness, such an unconcealment of concealment, can "save" us, not by eliminating λήθη, but by, in Socrates' words, enabling us to pass through in the proper manner the river flowing through the place of λήθη ("τὸν τῆς Λήθης ποταμὸν εὖ διαβησόμεθα," 621b). On Heidegger's reading, this proper passing-through is what Socrates earlier describes as drinking the proper measure. We have yet to consider what "proper measure" could mean here, but before doing so, we should finally take into consideration the name of the river whose water is to be drunk.

The name of the river is Ἀμέλης (Careless). Why is this the name of the river that runs through the plain of λήθη? Assuming that the river and the plain are distinct, that thus carelessness is not the same as λήθη or concealment, as Heidegger insists (187), then what is the relation between the two? Heidegger comments that the water of the river Ἀμέλης cannot be held in any container because it is "die reine Entgägnis selbst" (pure withdrawal itself). Thus, it is in carelessness that beings withdraw and remain concealed. Carelessness "flows through" concealment as that which entrusts beings to their concealment. But then it is the opposite of carelessness, *care*, that brings beings into unconcealment and preserves them there, that enables us to "recollect" by bringing us back into an unconcealing relation to beings. In other words, the "carelessness" that belongs to the field of λήθη is the opposite of what the *Theaetetus* characterized as the striving after being in its unconcealment, so that the latter can now itself be characterized as care. This care is what Heidegger calls "the μελέτη τῆς ἀληθείας, caring [*Sorge*] about unconcealment, caring that beings be and remain sheltered [*geborgen*] in the unconcealed [*das Unverborgene*] and thereby enduring [*beständig*]" (177). If the water of the river Careless cannot, as

---

7. For how this connection between *anamnesis* and *eros* solves the problems that have traditionally plagued the interpretation of *anamnesis*, see my "How Is the Truth of Beings in the Soul: Interpreting *Anamnesis* in Plato," *Elenchos* 28 (2007): 275–301.

pure withdrawal into concealment, be contained (621a5–6), then it is care that holds, contains, and preserves beings in the unconcealed.

Yet to stop here in one's interpretation would be to miss what is most crucial. The above makes it appear that caring about unconcealment and the carelessness in which being remain concealed are simply opposites. After all, is not carelessness the opposite of care? And yet the myth (621a6–7) describes passing through the plan of concealment and drinking of the water of carelessness as the necessary and indispensable precondition of entering any life, that is, any measure of unconcealment within which we relate to beings as unconcealed. If the myth shows the belonging together of concealment and unconcealment, then so does it also show the belonging together of careless and care. All care for beings remaining and enduring in the unconcealed requires a certain measure of carelessness, that is, a willingness to allow what is unconcealed to remain concealed, to entrust it to its concealment. If beings did not remain concealed, there would be no caring about their being unconcealed but instead a full possession of beings in some sort of intuition. This is indicated by Heidegger when he interprets the "carelessness" (*Sorglosigkeit*) as "not caring about [*Sich-nicht-Sorgen um*] ἀλήθεια, because the prevailing [*das Walten*] of λήθη, of withdrawing concealment [*Verbergung*], itself takes care [*besorgt*]" (177). The withdrawing concealment that is λήθη itself takes care of beings in the sense of preserving and sheltering them for unconcealment. Stated paradoxically, carelessness cares for beings by entrusting them to their concealment, while care is care-less in allowing a certain measure of concealment in what it cares to unconceal. Stated less paradoxically, care is possible only on the basis of a certain measure of carelessness, as recollection is possible only on the basis of forgetting.

It is only now that another peculiar feature of the myth can be understood. While everyone must drink the water of carelessness, we are told that some drink the "right measure" (μέτρον τι) while others drink beyond the right measure (πλέον τοῦ μέτρου, 621a6–b1). Who is being distinguished from whom here, and what exactly is the nature of the distinction? On Heidegger's reading, those who drink the right measure are philosophers, while those who drink beyond the right measure and thus fall into extreme carelessness and forgetfulness are "die Philosophie-losen." The justification in the text for such a reading is the suggestion that those who drink beyond the right measure do so because they lack φρόνησις (621a7), which in turn suggests that φρόνησις is what enables the others to determine what the right measure is. If Heidegger equates the latter with philosophers, that is because he maintains that "Φρόνησις means here the same as 'philosophy,' and this title means having the sight [*Blick*] for what is essential" (178).

Whether or not this is an adequate characterization of what φρόνησις means here for Plato is to be discussed below. The crucial thing to note here is that according to this passage of the myth, φρόνησις, and philosophy as defined by it, makes possible and involves not the complete overcoming of carelessness and forgetfulness, not the overcoming of concealment in a clear and distinct intuition and comprehension of beings, but rather the right measure of carelessness and forgetfulness, that is, the granting of the right measure of concealment to beings. In other words, both the philosopher and the nonphilosopher exist in carelessness, forgetfulness, and concealment: the difference lies only in the *measure*. If φρόνησις were understood as some sort of theoretical intuition or the possession of a body of propositions, then what is said at 621a6–b1 would be meaningless. But the meaning is clear if φρόνησις is instead understood as a caring that in caring for beings to be unconcealed also entrusts them to their concealment, as a constant recollecting of what has been necessarily forgotten. In other words, φρόνησις is the recognition that the truth will always remain inseparable from untruth and that therefore our relation to truth must always have the form of a constant caring and striving. Beings are most concealed to the person who believes them to be completely unconcealed. A Thrasymachus can think he knows exactly what justice is and thus not *care* for it because in drinking the water of carelessness beyond measure he has lost sight of the essence of justice altogether. Having φρόνησις with regard to justice thus means not possessing a definition or theory of justice, but rather acknowledging the concealment of justice in the measure necessary for caring about the unconcealment or truth of justice. Thus, philosophy, as characterized by φρόνησις, is, as Heidegger insists, not a body of knowledge or a set of theories but *a way of existing*: "'Philosophy' is therefore not a mere business thinking carries out with general concepts, a business to which one can either dedicate oneself or not, without in either case anything essential taking place. Philosophy means being addressed by being itself. Philosophy is in itself the fundamental way in which man in the midst of beings comports himself towards them" (179). This comportment is what the *Theaetetus* characterized as a striving after being and truth and what in the Myth of Er is characterized as a caring for truth or unconcealment that is grounded in the carelessness of concealment and forgetting.

A passage Heidegger does not cite or discuss further clarifies this conception of philosophy. Shortly after the passage cited above and in the very last sentence of the dialogue, Socrates recommends that "we always pursue the upward path and in every way practice/care for [ἐπιτηδεύσομεν] justice with φρόνησις" (621c4–6). Here again what φρόνησις provides is not some theory or body of knowledge but the ability to pursue a path: that path that is always underway from the underworld to the upper world, from concealment to unconcealment, from λήθη to recollection. What φρόνησις provides is the ability to *practice* justice, where this necessarily also means caring for the truth of justice. Such a path and practice is available neither to those who have not drunk the water of carelessness, because as gods they would be beyond any path or practice, nor to those who have drunk this water beyond measure, because like the prisoners in the cave they would not even see the path; instead, such a path and practice is available only to those who have drunk carelessness in the right measure, that is, just enough to care about the truth without possessing it.

All of the mentioned features of the Myth of Er thus say, on Heidegger's own reading, the belonging-together of concealment and unconcealment as the place within which human beings dwell and exist. What, then, has become of the supposed transformation of truth and untruth into a correctness and an incorrectness that both exclude each other and are properties of thinking and speaking? Where is there so much as a hint of such a transformation in that concealing saying of concealment that is the Myth of Er? Heidegger sees this "transformation," and thus the loss of the fundamental experience of λήθη, in the central position the myth accords to human existence. Heidegger characterizes the transformation as follows: in Plato's myth, "the necessity of ἀλήθεια and its essential relation to λήθη as its preceding ground is according to the μῦθος interpreted from the perspective of the origin of man's essence and his destiny. This focus [*betonte Blick*] on man is already the sign that the fundamental position of thinking within Greek existence is undergoing a transformation.... λήθη is no longer experienced purely as an event [*rein ereignishaft erfahren*], but rather is thought from the perspective of the behavior [*Verhalten*] of man in the sense of the later 'forgetting'" (192). Therefore, while truth and untruth may not be interpreted as correctness and incorrectness in Plato's myth, the emphasis this myth puts on our relation to truth and untruth already puts truth and untruth on the path toward becoming mere properties of our seeing and speaking.

The first thing to note is that this account of the transformation truth undergoes in Plato is quite different from, and much weaker than, the thesis of "Plato's Doctrine of Truth." It allows that truth in Plato is still interpreted as an unconcealment in which we dwell and to which concealment necessarily belongs: the claim is only that there is an emphasis on the human relation to truth that will eventually result in a reduction of truth to the human, that is, to humanism. Furthermore, interpreted thus, the transformation obviously cannot be said to *begin* with Plato in any meaningful sense. In conclusion, Heidegger himself draws attention to the fact that in a line from Homer (*Iliad* 23.358ff.) ἀλήθεια and ἔπος are named together (193), thereby hinting, without explicitly claiming, that the transformation is already beginning there. Furthermore, one could argue that interpreted thus, the transformation is *still* taking place in Heidegger's own *Being and Time*: a text that seeks to interpret the meaning of being by way of interpreting the being of that being for whom being is an issue, that is, human being or *Dasein*. But in these ways Heidegger's thesis that at some point (when?) truth underwent a transformation, a "catastrophe" in the literal sense, that set it on the road to becoming (inevitably? why?) mere "correctness" becomes increasingly suspect. One must ask if Heidegger, rather than uncovering a historical transformation, is not instead pointing to an inescapable human limitation or, put more positively, human "measure" in the sense described in the Myth of Er. How can we *not* think ἀλήθεια and λήθη "together with" our existing and speaking? And why must doing so result eventually in a reduction of truth to correctness and of λήθη to forgetting?

It is important to note that Heidegger does not identify the emphasis on the human he finds in the Greeks with the subjectivity that defines modern metaphysics. That the Greeks gave the priority to the being-a-self (*Selbstsein*) of man "is immediately seen in the way in which beings as what shine forth unconcealed are brought exclusively into the paradigmatic relation to reason (νοῦς) and to ψυχή, to the essence of 'life'" (206). Even so, Heidegger insists that being-a-self (*Selbstsein*) is not subjectivity (205). But then why must the critique of modern subjectivity be pursued back to the Greeks? Presumably because in Heidegger's view the emphasis on the self in the Greeks is the first step toward modern subjectivity. But is this inevitable? Why must we believe that any interpretation of being and truth in terms of their relation to the essence of being human must inevitably lead to the subjectivity of modern metaphysics?

Heidegger at one point speaks of the "peculiarly swaying character of transition" (207) that characterizes the beginning of metaphysics in the Greeks and that he sees as grounded in the fact that "in the commencing metaphysics appearing (*das Erscheinen*) in the sense of arising and coming forth, but also appearing in the sense of showing itself for a perceiving [*Vernehmen*] and for a 'Soul,' are held fast" (206–7). But the crucial questions are these: is this *Übergangscharakter* an historical event (and if so to be dated how?) or rather the inescapable essence of philosophy as such? And is the later metaphysics of subjectivity the necessary product and culmination of this *Übergang* or its betrayal? These critical questions are to be pursued at the end of the current chapter and in later chapters. First, however, some consideration must finally be given to what Heidegger's interpretation of the Myth of Er leaves out. This consideration is appropriate here because only now are Heidegger's motives apparent. Given his insistence that it is the focus on the human, that is, humanism, that necessarily obstructs the experience and thinking of ἀλήθεια and λήθη in their unity, it should now be no surprise that Heidegger's reading of the myth excludes what is "human-all-too-human" within it, specifically, the ethical choice of how to live and the question of politics.

C. PURGING THE MYTH OF ER: THE ONTOLOGIZING OF ETHICS AND POLITICS

One of the strangest features of Heidegger's interpretation is its complete reduction of the political dimension of the myth to a purely ontological one. Indeed, it is not only the myth that gets "ontologized" but the whole of the *Republic* and, in principle, every dialogue, since Heidegger at one point asserts: "A thinking conversation [*Gespräch*] always speaks of the being of beings" (140). Thus, any dialogue of Plato that did not speak of the being of beings, that was not at its core ontology, would not be "thinking." The way in which the *Republic* in particular is transformed into not only mainly, but even exclusively a work of ontology is evident in Heidegger's explanation of the sense in which Plato's πολιτεία is a "utopia." This must be understood, Heidegger asserts, as "the insight that 'actually' the being of beings is nowhere present at hand among beings, as if it were a part of them. Accordingly, being would also have to be a utopia. But in truth being itself and it alone is the τόπος for all beings, and Plato's *Politeia* is no 'utopia,' but exactly the opposite, namely, the metaphysically determined τόπος *of the essence of the* πόλις. Plato's Politeia is an interiorizing/recalling [*eine Erinnerung*] of the essential [*Wesenhafte*], but not a factical planning" (141). This passage seems at first to say no more than that Plato's πόλις is a utopia only in the sense in which *being* is a utopia, that is, in the sense of being the true *topos*. But then what Heidegger proceeds to say makes clear that the *topos* that is the city is itself "metaphysically determined," and thus to be identified with *being* rather with the kind of planning that defines the organization and constitution of a city. Being and the πόλις are not simply utopias in a similar way, but are the *same* utopia, that is, the same *topos*. This is made explicit in the following passage: "The πόλις is as little some thing 'political' as space is something spatial. The πόλις itself, however, is the pole of πέλειν, the way in which the being of beings in its unconcealing and concealing defines a place for itself [*sich ein Wo verfügt*] in which the history of mankind can remain gathered" (142).[8] Heidegger is essentially

---

8. Likewise, in the 1936–37 Nietzsche lecture, Heidegger's discussion of the critique of art in the *Republic* addresses the dialogue's political context, but only to insist that δίκη is "ein metaphysischer, kein ursprünglich moralischer Begriff" (N2, 194). Though he there admits that Plato's philosophy drags δίκη into "das Zwielicht des Moralischen," he insists that it is therefore all the more necessary to hang on to the metaphysical meaning (194). Most significant for the topic of the present chapter is Heidegger's claim that the goal of the entire dialogue is to show that the ground and determining essence of all political being is to be found in the *theoretical* (193).

identifying the πόλις here with the "da" of *Da-sein*. If Heidegger can interpret even the *Republic* as having nothing to do with politics, if he can turn it into nothing but a reflection on the "there" of being and thus a work of ontology, his incredible claim that the Greeks "are the unpolitical people par excellence" ("das schlechthin unpolitische Volk sind," 142) should not surprise us.

The δαιμόνιος τόπος described in the Myth of Er itself may indeed seem far removed from the world of politics, but it is there that we witness the spectacle of a man who, descending from heaven after having lived a virtuous life, mistakenly chooses a life of the greatest tyranny for want of philosophy (619b–c). The δαιμόνιος τόπος, the plain of truth and concealment, is still the place where ethical decisions are made and the way of life of both an individual and a community is determined. Yet precisely this is suppressed by Heidegger's reading. Indeed, the aspect of the myth which Heidegger most completely overlooks is precisely that in which Socrates claims to see "the whole of the venture and danger [κίνδυνος] for a human being" (618b7–8): the choice of lives and the need to cultivate the kind of knowledge that will enable one to distinguish between a better life and a worse life (618c–619a). Socrates at this point in the text is interrupting Er's narrative to emphasize what he sees as its point and "moral." In this respect, Heidegger's reading must be seen as opposed to Socrates' own, completely ignoring precisely what Socrates most emphasizes.

The myth describes each soul as taking from the δαιμόνιος τόπος a δαίμων that it itself chooses and that guides it throughout its life (617d–e). This confirms to some extent Heidegger's characterization of the δαιμόνιον as outlined above: it is not something beyond "this life" but rather something that encircles and guides this life. However, the δαίμων a soul chooses is explicitly identified in the myth with a specific way of life characterized by specific goods and evils. It is this dimension of the δαιμόνιον that Heidegger consistently suppresses. Revealing in this regard is his interpretation of εὐδαιμονία. Insisting that this word names the relation of being to man ("Bezug des Seins zum Menschen"), Heidegger adds: "Through the Roman-Christian translation in the sense of *beatitudo* (i.e., of the condition of the *beatus*, of the blessed), εὐδαιμονία is admittedly transformed into a mere property of the human soul, into 'happiness.' However, εὐδαιμονία signifies the 'εὐ' holding sway in appropriate measure—appearing [*Erscheinen*] and presencing [*Anwesen*] of the δαιμόνιον" (173). Here it is the Romans and Christians who are made responsible for reducing what originally named a relation to being to a mere property of the human soul. But presumably the Greeks, through their emphasis on the relation of being *to man*, are already delivering εὐδαιμονία over to this destiny. Here it must be objected that while εὐδαιμονία for the Greeks is certainly not merely a property of the soul, neither is it a name for man's relation to being: εὐδαιμονία is the overall success of a particular human life, and the guiding δαίμων is not the voice of being but rather that which accomplishes the particular life a soul has chosen (620d–e). The δαιμόνιος τόπος is not a purely ontological τόπος, but at least equally an ethical and political τόπος. What is decided there is not only the measure of concealment and unconcealment, but also the measure (τὸν μέσον, 619a5) of good and evil in a particular human life always subject to their alteration (μεταβολὴν τῶν κακῶν καὶ τῶν ἀγαθῶν, 619d5–6). In this context it is possible to see just how reductive is Heidegger's characterization of philosophy as cited above. In the myth philosophy is not simply a matter of being addressed by being, or of how one comports oneself towards beings in their midst, but rather that study and inquiry by which one chooses the good life over the bad (618c1–5) and thereby can attain happiness (619b1). According to the dialogue's final sentence cited above, what the φρόνησις we acquire through philosophy enables us to do is pursue the upward path by practicing and caring for justice. Without philosophy, even a virtuous person can make the tragic choice of a terrible life of injustice (619c8). Indeed, what is centrally at issue in the choice of lives is what is at issue in the discussion of the soul and the πόλις in the *Republic* as a whole: justice versus injustice. This is because, as the myth asserts and the dialogue has argued, the worst life is the one that leads the soul to become most unjust, while the best is the one that leads it to become most just (618e1–3). Yet justice and injustice are themselves subjected by Heidegger to a purely ontological interpretation. What is ordered to man in the πόλις, that is, the unconcealing and concealing of beings as a whole, is "assigned as that which is ordained to the essence of man so that this essence is welcomed and ordered into that which is ordained to it [*dieses ihm Zu-wesende*]. Man must order himself [*sich fügen muß*] within it so that his essence is in order [*in den Fügen ist*]. That which is thus ordered to man [*Zu-gefügte*], ordering itself to him [*Sich-zu-fügende*] and ordering him [*ihn Fügende*] is what we name in the one word *Fug*, or in Greek: δίκη" (137). The δίκαιος is accordingly "the orderly [*der Fügsame*]" while the ἄδικος is "the disorderly [*der Ungefüge*]" (137); δικαιοσύνη is "orderliness [*Fügsamkeit*]" (137). Practicing δικαιοσύνη and being δίκαιος is thus a matter of fitting-into, responding-to, and obeying that unconcealing/concealing of beings as whole that constitutes the "there" of one's being, one's πόλις. It is, in other words, a matter of allowing oneself to be addressed by being and responding to this address, obeying this order of being according to which beings as a whole reveal and conceal themselves. Given Heidegger's characterization of philosophy cited above, one can see that δικαιοσύνη on his reading simply *is* philosophy. The philosopher is the "just" person not because philosophy helps him to be "just" but because being "just" is nothing more than responding to the address of being by comporting oneself towards beings in a way appropriate to how they reveal and conceal themselves. How far this conception is from the δικαιοσύνη at issue in the *Republic* is made especially evident by one extraordinary consequence of Heidegger's reading: the relation between "justice" and "injustice" ceases to be one of opposition. As Heidegger observes, given the belonging together of unconcealment and concealment, "Un-fug" or "dis-order" is not the opposite of δίκη as "Fug" or "order": δίκη can itself be ἄ-δικη in withdrawing and concealing itself and thus abandon us to the errancy and dis-obedience of the ἄδικος. On Heidegger's reading, therefore, the life of "justice" and the life of "injustice" are not two different lives but the same, since in-justice is always a possibility of justice and therefore inseparable from it. But in this case Heidegger's reading of the Myth of Er not only ignores that choice of lives which Socrates characterizes as "the only venture and danger for human beings," but renders such a choice utterly meaningless and impossible.[9]

The defense that could be made here of Heidegger is that in thus purging the Myth of Er of all its ethical and political content he is saving it from itself. In other words, what he is purging it of are precisely those "humanistic" elements that ultimately turn Western metaphysics away from the thinking of being. Yet the question that must be asked is whether such a purge is necessary. Is the kind of focus the Greeks grant the human, is the importance they grant the ethical and political, necessarily the first step in an inevitable turn away from the thinking of unconcealment and concealment in their belonging-together? This question cannot be answered without first considering Heidegger's own attempts in later texts to think being without thinking it from the perspective of its relation to our being and beings in general. These attempts, which Heidegger sees as preparing "another beginning," will be the focus of subsequent chapters. What needs to be noted here is that the difference between the "first beginning" among the Greeks and the "other beginning" Heidegger seeks to prepare is not as clear and as black-and-white as it is often depicted to be. What remains to be shown in the present chapter is just how far, according to Heidegger himself in the *Parmenides* course, the Greeks were able to go in thinking truth and being despite their focus on the relation to human being and thus despite the centrality granted to the ethical and political.

---

9. Therefore, though Richard Wolin does not himself refer to Heidegger's reading of the Myth of Er, there is some support there for his argument that in focusing so exclusively on a conception of truth/untruth as unconcealment/concealment and insisting that the two always belong together, Heidegger leaves himself no basis for concrete political judgment that would be capable of distinguishing between good and bad. *The Politics of Being: The Political Thought of Martin Heidegger* (New York: Columbia University Press, 1990), 118–23. A similar objection is made by Karl Jaspers: "Die 'Wahrheit' so erörtert, daß Wahrheit entschwindet. Ist kein Sinn mehr für Wahrheit und Unwahrheit im konkreten Hier und Jetzt von Erkenntnis und Praxis?" *Notizen zu Martin Heidegger,* ed. Hans Saner (Munich: Piper, 1989), 176.

D. THE GREEK EXPERIENCE OF THE OPEN: A SAYING THAT POINTS AND HINTS VERSUS THE "LEAP"

Though what Heidegger opposes to truth as correctness is truth as unconcealment, both in the present course and in later texts Heidegger seeks to think truth beyond its identification with unconcealment. Once one recognizes the belonging-together of concealment and un-concealment, then what becomes most worthy of thought as the essence of truth is the site of this belonging-together, the clearing within which beings reveal and conceal themselves. This is what Heidegger here calls the *open*: "What holds sway in the essence of unconcealment is the *open* [*das* Offene]" (208). One might at this point be tempted to think that while the Greeks indeed understood truth as uncealment, this open within which the event of unconcealing takes place remained inaccessible to them. But on Heidegger's own account matters are not so simple: "Above all it is necessary first to see that the Greeks in general experienced something in the realm of the essence of ἀλήθεια which required them to speak in some way of the open [*irgendwie vom Offenen zu sagen*]. The essential concept of the open is something we never find in the Greeks. On the other hand, in the realm of the essence of truth and of the Greek thinking of being we come across words and names that nevertheless, though vaguely, point toward [*auf das weisen*] what is here named the open" (208). One must of course ask here how such a thing as a "concept" of the open or a definition of its "essence" would even be possible. What if one cannot think the open except as the Greeks did: in names that only hint and point?

One of these words is ἀ-δηλον, in which Heidegger hears "das Un-offenbare" and thus the naming of openness that comes forth (*west*) in unconcealment (212). And yet Heidegger continues: "*The essence of unconcealment gives us a pointer [die Weisung] toward the open and openness. But what is this? Here Greek saying is silent*" (213). Again one must ask: is not this silence appropriate and necessary? What would it mean to say *what* the open *is*? Is anything more than a pointing possible here? After remarking on how disconcerting (*befremdlich*) the open is for ordinary opinion (213), Heidegger again comments on the nature of the Greek experience of the open: "While the Greeks do not explicitly think through and name the open as the essence of ἀλήθεια, they nevertheless experience it constantly in one respect, namely, in the essential form of what is lighted and what lightens [*des Gelichteten und Lichten*], but this in the shining of light that brings clarity [*die Helle*] with it" (214). Heidegger significantly refers to the Cave Analogy in this context. The cited passage of course hints at the argument Heidegger can still make: because the Greeks experienced the open in terms of light and light exists for a seeing, they opened the way to a reduction of truth to a property of seeing. But we seem here far from the claim that such a reduction already takes place in the Cave Analogy or that it is made inevitable by what the analogy expresses. And here it is important to add that the Cave Analogy does not experience the open only in terms of light but also in terms of what Heidegger claims to be "the still hidden essence of the open as the originally self-opening": *freedom*. The ascent described in the Cave Analogy is an ascent not only toward openness in the sense of light but also toward openness in the sense of freedom. The open region outside of the cave is a region of freedom within which the light of the sun shines and beings are unconcealed: it is therefore not reduced to this light and this unconcealment.

If Heidegger now grants the Greeks an experience of the open as what is prior to the unconcealed and seen, he also now finds in them a kind of seeing appropriate to this open and radically distinct from the kind of seeing that is supposed to play a role in the transformation of truth into correctness. Heidegger speaks of a *Blicken* (158), but he gives this word a meaning which, to my knowledge, he nowhere else gives it. *Blicken* is here described as "more original than the presence of things" because it is what first makes presencing (*Anwesen*) possible. It is not the intuiting of an object, not indeed something we do to something else. Instead, it is a being-looked-at in which what is looking gathers itself in this looking and offers its essence. *Blicken* is thus a "gaze" that neither simply looks nor is looked at, but rather reveals and offers itself in gazing at us. "We must in any case understand *das Blicken* here originally and in the Greek manner as the way in which a man encounters us while he looks at us and in looking gathers himself in this self-disclosing arising and thereby offers and lets 'arise' his essence while holding nothing back" (158). We cannot look at the open in the way we would look at an object. To "see" it is to let it encounter and offer itself to us, to "see" it only in how it looks at us, that is, in how it allows our own being and the beings we encounter to show themselves. In this seeing we are thus allowing our own essence to "arise." In this *Blicken* there is no opposition between seeing and being seen, no distinction between subject and object. From this kind of *Blicken* Heidegger proceeds to distinguish the "grasping seeing" (*erfassende Blicken*), which the Greeks also knew but which did not for them have the priority in the interpreting of appearing (159). Yet even this derivative grasping seeing was not for the Greeks some spying-out for some object, but rather "the 'thinking' ['*Vernehmen*'] of beings from out of an original agreement [*Einvernehmen*] with being [*Sein*]" (160). Thus not even thinking beings in their being was for the Greeks themselves primary.

Has not then the thesis of a Greek transformation of truth into correctness in the correspondence between seeing and the object seen become utterly implausible? And has it not become equally untenable to maintain that the

Greeks reduced being to mere presence and thus failed to think being? The open which the Greeks experienced and pointed towards *is* being, according to Heidegger: "the open into which each being is freed as into its freedom, *the open is being itself.* Each unconcealed being is as such sheltered in the open of being, i.e., in the ground-less" (224). The essence of the open therefore reveals itself only to a thinking that attempts to think being: a thinking Heidegger claims to be difficult not because it is complicated but because it is "simple" (222). Heidegger would presumably say that while the Greeks *experienced* the open and a seeing appropriate to the open, they did not *think* it. But then what does this thinking involve? How can it be more than that pointing and indirect naming that the Greeks already practiced? All Heidegger can answer in the present course is that this thinking requires a radical new beginning and a "leap." This leap can be seen as an attempt to leap beyond his affinity with the Greeks and Plato in particular. That such a leap is either necessary or possible is to be challenged in later chapters. What needs to be noted here is that even this idea that thinking requires a leap is something Heidegger finds already in the Greeks.

Where he finds it is in the notion of ἐξαίφνης. The passage in which Heidegger makes the connection between this notion and his idea of a leap is important enough to quote in full:

> The "it is" of beings, being, shows itself, when it shows itself, in each case only "suddenly," or in Greek, ἐξαίφνης, i.e., ἐξαφανής, in the sense that something falls right into the middle of what appears from out of what does not appear. To this essentially unmediated and immediate falling-in [*Ein-fall*] of being in the being which at the same time and in only this way appears as a being corresponds, on the side of man, a comportment [*ein Verhalten*] that suddenly no longer turns towards beings but instead thinks being. To think being always requires a *leap* [*Sprung*], through which we *jump off* [*abspringen*] from the familiar ground of beings, on which each being is most immediately for us, and *into the ground-less*, as which the Free lights itself up [*als welches sich das Freie lichtet*], which we name when we no longer take anything into consideration [*bedenken*] with respect to beings except the "it is." (222–23)

Does this mean that in recognizing the ἐξαίφνης the Greeks took the leap of thinking being? Heidegger certainly sees in the myth's description of the "sudden" (ἐξαπίνης, 621b3) ascent of the souls towards generation and in Er's description of his sudden (ἐξαίφνης, 621b6) awakening to find himself lying on his funeral pyre a recognition that between ἀλήθεια and λήθη "there is no mediation [*nichts Vermittelndes*] and no transition [*Übergang*], because both immediately belong together in their essence. Everywhere that the belonging is an essential one, the transition [*Übergang*] from one to the other remains the 'sudden' ['*Plötzliche*'], what in each case exists only in a 'no time' [*in einem Nu*] and from the moment [*Augenblick*]" (185).¹⁰ Yet the Greek ἐξαίφνης is not the same as Heidegger's "leap"; it is indeed one of the things that Heidegger must leap from. The leap required to think being is a leap beyond the ἐξαίφνης. Why? The passage cited above suggests the answer. The leap Heidegger has in mind is thinking being *without any longer turning toward beings*. To the extent that, as Heidegger claims, the Greeks think being in its relation to beings and to human being in particular, they do not make the leap. If being and truth appear ἐξαίφνης to Greek thought, there is still some *mediation* here, rather than a radical absolute leap. In Plato's *Symposium*, for example, the being and truth of beauty appears ἐξαίφνης (210e4), but only as a result of seeing beautiful things in order and properly (θεώμενος ἐφεξῆς τε καὶ ὀρθῶς τὰ καλά, 210e3). The thinking of being here, however "sudden," is still mediated by a relation to beings and, most importantly, to our own being understood as ἔρως. For this reason, Heidegger's leap, as a leap beyond all mediation, as an attempt to think being immediately without reference to beings, must be a leap more radical and more "sudden" than the Greek ἐξαίφνης.

E. CONCLUSION: LEAPING BEYOND PLATO

The *Auseinandersetzung* between Plato and Heidegger on the question of truth comes down in the end to the necessity and possibility of this leap. The thesis of "Plato's Doctrine of Truth," the thesis of a transformation of truth in Plato from unconcealment to correctness, has been shown to be untenable not from a perspective outside of Heidegger's thought but rather from the perspective of his own perceptive readings of the Cave and Sun analogies, the *Theaetetus* and the Myth of Er. The present chapter has shown how Heidegger's thesis reaches its most extreme breaking point when he is attentive to a myth in Plato and finds expressed there a concealment that conditions truth

---

10. In an unpublished 1930-31 course, Heidegger interpreted the discussion of the notion of the ἐξαίφνης in the third hypothesis of Plato's *Parmenides* as "the most profound point to which occidental metaphysics has ever advanced. It is the most radical advance into the problem of Being and time—an advance which afterwards was not caught up with [*aufgefangen*] but instead intercepted [*abgefangen*] (by Aristotle)." Cited in Jussi Backman, "All of a Sudden: Heidegger and Plato's *Parmenides*," *Epoché* 11, no. 2 [2007]: 398–99. Summarizing Heidegger's interpretation, Backmann writes: "Plato's 'instant' is that peculiar kind of unified presence which mediates between simple *presence* and simple *absence*, between simple static Being and becoming, between identity and otherness, between the One and the Many" (400). Here we can add not only that the ἐξαίφνης also "mediates" between concealment and unconcealment, but that it strictly speaking represents a turn-around without mediation or transition and thus a belonging-together of what is opposed.

and that cannot be identified with incorrectness; a concealment that arguably can be directly expressed only mythically but that is also implicit in the drama of all of Plato's dialogues. Plato experienced and expressed, through an appropriate type of saying and seeing, unconcealment and concealment in their belonging together in the open (being). In his dialogues we find a mediation between being and human being, silence and speech, *mythos* and *logos*, ethics and ontology: a mediation not incompatible with the unpredictability, unmasterability, and suddenness of the ἐξαίφνης. This Plato, irreducible to a doctrine, is much closer to Heidegger but therefore also a much more formidable opponent. Heidegger cannot critique this Plato as transforming truth into correctness or as reducing concealment to falsehood or even as failing to experience the open within which truth and untruth belong together. The only critique left Heidegger is therefore that the very mediations that characterize Plato's thought, the very "ambiguities" that resist the identification of Plato with any doctrine, represent an inexorable march toward an eclipse of being and thus of the belonging-together of concealment and unconcealment, and that therefore the thinking of being demands a "leap" beyond all mediation. If Plato needs a ladder to being and truth, Heidegger is determined to dispense with the ladder, convinced as he is that any ladder must descend and thus forget that to which it ascended.

This is why an assessment of Heidegger's critique of Plato cannot stop here with his explicit interpretations of Plato's dialogues: interpretations that came to an end, and had to come to an end, after the publication of "Plato's Doctrine of Truth." Instead we must confront his own attempts in the late period to think being beyond all "dialectic," since these attempts are the true legacy of his rejection of Plato. Furthermore, given what the present chapter has shown to get suppressed in Heidegger's reading of the Myth of Er, more is at stake here than the "justness" of Heidegger's thinking as a response to the address of being. Does this "justness" require the sacrifice of "justice" in the ethical and political sense? Is the "leap" one beyond the human and the ontic with no possibility of return? Does the attempt to listen to the one tautological voice of being lead to the silencing of the many voices allowed to speak in the Platonic dialogues? These are the questions we must bring to Heidegger's later thought after having read Plato with and against him. They are therefore the questions that the subsequent chapters will begin to address.

PART 3

OPPORTUNITIES FOR A DIALOGUE WITH PLATO IN THE LATE HEIDEGGER

As the concluding part of chapter 3 already showed, once the interpretation of Plato expressed in its most succinct and exaggerated form in the essay "Plato's Doctrine of Truth" is shown to be untenable, the relation between Plato and Heidegger becomes much more complicated and a genuine dialogue between the two all the more imperative. A number of opportunities for such a dialogue have been uncovered, especially in Heidegger's readings of the *Theaetetus* and the Myth of Er, but also in his earliest reading of the Cave Analogy. These opportunities, however, were suppressed by Heidegger himself with the publication of "Plato's Doctrine of Truth." We are thus left to wonder how a genuine dialogue with Plato would have altered the direction and character of Heidegger's later thought. The aim of chapters 6 and 7 is to pursue this dialogue that Heidegger himself failed to pursue. This is not to be done by confronting Heidegger's text with some external "Platonic" perspective and showing the latter to be "better." Instead, the aim is to uncover in Heidegger's texts themselves certain elements that can be characterized as Platonic and to show that Heidegger's attempts to overcome or suppress these elements do not succeed. In other words, the aim is to demonstrate the need and fruitfulness of a genuine dialogue between Plato and Heidegger by critiquing the direction in which Heidegger's thought is led by the refusal of such a dialogue. If one can characterize what follows as a Platonic critique of Heidegger, this is only with the understanding that the goal is not to prove Plato right and Heidegger wrong, but rather to show that Plato cannot and should not be as quickly and categorically dismissed as he has been by both Heidegger and his "children"; that, in other words, even for postmetaphysical and postmodern thought Plato remains an essential contemporary interlocutor.

There is strong evidence that Heidegger himself later recognized the need to enter into a genuine dialogue with Plato by reconsidering from the ground up his earlier reading of Plato, and even that he saw this as necessitated by possible limitations in his own thinking. In a letter to Hannah Arendt dated April 1, 1951, Heidegger writes: "You mention Plato. He is here by me within reach; however, I must first get certain questions straightened out before I can allow myself the pleasure of reading him once again and completely anew [*ihn noch einmal ganz neu zu lesen*]" (AHB, 125). What questions did Heidegger need to straighten out before returning to Plato? And why did he apparently never carry out this aim of reading Plato anew? When in a letter dated October 10, 1954, Heidegger again expresses his desire to read Plato anew, we get an indication of what is drawing him back to Plato: "And I would like to go through my Plato works once again, beginning with the 'Sophist' course of 1924/5, and read Plato anew [*neu lesen*]. In general—I begin right now to see a little more clearly and freely what I have always sought. At the same time language [*das Sagen*] always remains a great hardship [*Mühsal*], which only means that seeing also still gives me difficulty [*noch seine Not hat*]. *Is it still possible to free language from dialectic?* [*Ob es noch gelingt, die Sprache aus der Dialektik herauszulösen?*]" (148; my emphasis). Dialectic apparently remained a topic of discussion between himself and Arendt for some time: in a letter dated August 10, 1967, Heidegger observes: "Unfortunately there was too little time available for our afternoon conversation about language and dialectic" (156).

These exchanges show that it was Plato's dialectic in particular that Heidegger believed he needed to come to terms with. A critique of dialectic was of course central to Heidegger's course on the *Sophist,* and working through this course again would presumably have involved reconsidering this critique. That Heidegger had doubts here well before his letters to Arendt in the 1950s is shown by a conversation Georg Picht reports having had with Heidegger during a walk through the woods shortly after the Second World War. In this conversation Picht expressed his reasons for finding Heidegger's interpretation of the *Republic*'s Cave Analogy unconvincing. In response, Heidegger, after asking a number of probing and challenging questions, remained standing for a while and then said: "One thing I must confess to you: the structure of Plato's thought is completely obscure to me [*die Struktur des platonischen Denkens ist mir vollkommen dunkel*]."[1] Since the "structure of Plato's thought" can be nothing other than dialectic, what Heidegger is admitting here is in essence a failure to come to terms with Plato's dialectic.

Heidegger nevertheless did not reread Plato, did not work through his *Sophist* lectures again, and did not reconsider his critique of dialectic. As will be seen in what follows, he returns in the Zähringen seminar of 1973 to the same critique of dialectic defended in the *Sophist* course and expressed in the

---

1. Günther Neske, ed., *Erinnerung an Martin Heidegger* (Pfullingen: Günther Neske, 1977), 203.

introduction to *Being and Time*. Therefore, the dialogue with Plato that Heidegger himself on occasion considered desirable and even imperative is one that never happened. It is this dialogue that the following chapters attempt to pursue. As Heidegger himself suggests, what is most centrally at issue in this dialogue is the question of whether it is possible to free language from dialectic. In the texts considered in what follows, Heidegger can be seen attempting to do precisely that. To show that this attempt fails, or is at least highly dubious, is to show that the reconsideration of Plato was indeed imperative and that it could have led Heidegger in a very different direction.

6

CALCULATIVE THINKING, MEDITATIVE THINKING, AND THE PRACTICE OF DIALOGUE

The critique of logos, and therefore of logic, that was seen to put Heidegger at odds with Plato's dialectic in the courses of the 1920s becomes even more pronounced during the 1930s and afterwards. One should therefore expect that Heidegger's antipathy to dialectic and dialogue in Plato's works would become even more uncompromising. This expectation is sometimes fulfilled. However, most striking in the later texts are the moments when Heidegger, rather unexpectedly, betrays a greater sympathy not only to dialectic but to the dialogue form: a sympathy apparently due to a recognition that Plato's relation to logos might be after all quite different from that critiqued under the heading of "logic." The goal of the present chapter is to follow both trajectories in the later Heidegger and bring into question their compatibility: the further intensified critique of logos, on the one hand, and the evidence of a greater affinity to dialectic and dialogue, on the other, culminating in Heidegger's own attempt to write dialogues. In this case as in others, Heidegger will be seen to be largely at odds with himself as a result of failing to come to terms with Plato's legacy.

A. HEIDEGGER'S CRITIQUE OF LOGOS IN THE 1930S

In the course *Grundfragen der Philosophie* (WS 1937/38), Heidegger says: "Since the times of *Plato* and *Aristotle* the question of truth is a question of logic. What this entails is that the search for what truth is proceeds on the tracks and in the perspectives laid down by logic's starting point and field of work as well as its presuppositions" (GA 45, 10). Heidegger then suggests that "the field of vision of *all logic* as logic *blocks* (*verstellt*) precisely the view onto the essence of truth [*den Ausblick auf das Wesen der Wahrheit*]" (11). Why is this the case? Logic is the study of λόγος understood as *assertion* (*Aussage*).

To interpret the essence of truth from the perspective of logic is therefore to interpret it as having its proper place in the assertion, as being a property of the assertion: specifically, the assertion's *correspondence* to what is. In other words, interpreted from the perspective of logic, truth becomes correctness. Such a characterization of truth, however, distorts or covers over the essence of truth as *unconcealment*. The correspondence of a λόγος to a thing presupposes the unconcealedness or openness (*Offenheit*) of the thing itself, of the region between the thing and the person making the assertion, and of the person himself both toward the thing and toward other human beings (19): it is therefore in this openness or unconcealment that the original essence of truth is to be found (96–103). The problem, then, with characterizing truth within the perspective of logic as "correctness" is not that this characterization is "incorrect," but rather that it obstructs the more original essence of truth as openness within which correctness is alone possible. To make λόγος one's guiding perspective is thus from the very outset to block access to the genuine essence of truth.

Yet it is not only truth that gets distorted and covered up by logic as the science of the assertion, but also being, since truth and being cannot be thought separately. As Heidegger insists in the 1937–38 course (46–48), one cannot ask the question of the essence of truth without asking the question of the truth of essence. If in asking about the essence of truth, we simply assume that essence here means some general idea or genus common to all particular cases of truth, then we also assume that the essence of truth is to be determined on the basis of some correspondence to particular cases of truth, that is, we already assume that truth is correspondence. In short, the questions of being/essence and truth are inseparable. But then what kind of interpretation of being results from making logic the guiding perspective? If truth is interpreted as correspondence, then being is simultaneously interpreted as what enables something to be *an object for* such correspondence. In other words, a thing must be *present* to a λόγος, and present in a constant and stable way, in order for the λόγος to be able to be *about* it and to *correspond* to it. Being thus comes to be interpreted as what makes something present to a λόγος and thus as *presence*; more specifically, it comes to be interpreted as the presence of an ἰδέα which enables a being to appear as the specific kind of thing about which I can make assertions and therefore as *what-lies-before* (ὑπο-κείμενον). This point is made with special clarity in the 1935 *Einführung in die Metaphysik* course: "Enduringly present [*beständig anwesend*] is that to which we must in advance return with all grasping and producing, the paradigm, the ἰδέα. Enduringly present is that to which we in every λόγος, assertion, must return as to what is always already lying there before [*Vorliegende*], the ὑποκείμενον, *subjectum*" (EM, 147). In the 1937–38 course, Heidegger repeatedly draws attention to what he sees as the Greek identification of being with constant presence, an identification that results in the identification of being with what is constantly present in the plurality of changing things, that is, the common essence or ἰδέα (see, e.g., 61–69 and 74–75). But for an especially clear summary of the relations between this conception of being, the prominence of λόγος, and truth as correctness, we must return to the 1935 course:

> Truth becomes the correctness of the logos. Logos thereby leaves its original retention [*Einbehalt*] in the happening of unconcealment, and indeed in such a way that now a decision is made about truth and thus about beings from the perspective of logos and in reference back to it; but a decision not only about beings but especially and in the first place about being. Logos is now λέγειν τὶ κατά τινος, to say something about something. That about which we speak is what in each case lies at the ground of the *assertion,* what lies before it [*Vorliegende*], ὑποκείμενον (*subjectum*). From the perspective of logos made self-standing as assertion, being presents itself as *this* lying-before [*Vor-liegen*]. (142).

Thus, in making logic and therefore the assertion my guiding perspective, I inevitably put myself within an understanding of truth as correctness and being as constant presence and lying-before. If the characterization of truth as correctness covers over the essence of truth, then the characterization of being as constant presence covers over the truth of essence. Interpreted from the perspective of λόγος, being is not a presenc*ing,* an emerg*ing* into presence, an "essenc*ing*" (*Wesung*), but rather the *result* of such a presencing or emerging, what is constantly present, what is present at hand and available as an object of assertions, and therefore itself a being. As Heidegger observes in a 1934 course entitled *Logik als die Frage nach dem Wesen der Sprache,* to interpret being as what is constantly present throughout change is also to interpret it as the subject of an assertion, as that of which different and changing properties can be asserted, which is why the Greeks use the word ὑποκείμενον (subject) in both a logical and ontological sense: "The Greeks on the one hand determined all being as what is present [*das Anwesende*], while at the same time the proposition [*der Satz*], λόγος, is the original form and the confirmation [*Bewährung*] of this being" (GA 38, 141). In short, the dominance of the λόγος in onto-*logy* reduces truth to an ontic relation between two things, the assertion and its object, and simultaneously reduces being to a being; what is lost or covered over by the priority of the λόγος or logic is that "openness" or "clearing" which is presupposed by the λόγος and in which both truth and being must be located and thought. Paradoxically, the λόγος of being unavoidably blocks genuine access to being. This is why Heidegger in the 1934 course can go so far as to make his aim that of breaking the rule and power of traditional logic from the ground up, of violently shaking up (*erschüttern*) logic as such "from the beginning and from the ground up [*von ihrem Anfang an aus ihrem Grund*]" (GA 38, 8). Any genuine response to the question of being demands destabilizing and even exploding the very foundations of logic.[1]

B. DIALOGUE AS BRINGING TO SPEECH THE UNSAID

Yet, as argued in earlier chapters, Plato's dialectic appears itself to do this exploding by destabilizing the assertion, by preventing it from being the fixed and final word, and by pointing beyond it. The later Heidegger, unlike the earlier, appears to recognize this dimension of Plato's relation to *logos*. Both this recognition and the continuing critique of dialectic seemingly at odds with it receive a particularly forceful expression in a 1957 lecture series entitled *Grundsätze des Denkens* (GA 79). It is therefore this lecture series that needs to be considered here.

After having delivered the famous lecture on the principle of identity which forms a part of this series, Heidegger begins the next lecture with the observation that, as both written and spoken, the preceding day's lecture in a certain sense "lies fixed [*festliegt*]." Presumably as an antidote to this "fixedness," Heidegger offers Socrates' critique of writing in the *Phaedrus* (GA 79, 130–32), which he cites at length, as an afterword to his own lecture. He is thereby applying this critique to his own written words; he is using a Platonic text to distance himself from his own text, and with Plato he is freeing his thought from enslavement to the dead word. This possibility of a Platonic afterword

---

[1]. For an excellent account of Heidegger's treatment of the question "What is logic?" though only covering the period up to the end of the 1920s, see Jean-François Courtine, "Les 'Recherches Logiques' de Martin Heidegger, de la théorie du jugement à la vérité de l'être," in *Heidegger 1919–1929: De l'herméneutique de la facticité à la métaphysique du Dasein*, ed. Jean-François Courtine (Paris: J. Vrin, 1996), 7–31. The question remains central for Heidegger during this period and leads to the "destruction" of logic, both in the sense of returning to its sources and dismantling it. Worth citing here is Courtine's insightful concluding criticism, for its scope goes well beyond the period that is the focus of the article: "Est-ce que la radicalisation de la destruction phénoménologique en ébranlement, voire démolition constitue une réponse à hauteur de la question initiale: *Was ist das, das Logische*? On peut en douter, non seulement en raison des limitations déjà soulignées dans la mise en perspective de l'histoire de la logique, non seulement en raison de traits fondamentaux qui gouvernent encore l'enquête du dernier Heidegger sur le *Wesen der Sprache*—le 'privilege' du mot, l'unité de sa signification, l'importance de l'ἔτυμον . . . , mais aussi et peut-être surtout en raison de difficultés qu'il y a à réduire purement et simplement la 'logistique' au calcul ou à la pensée calculante, jusqu'à en faire, pour le dernier Heidegger, avec la 'cybernétique,' une détermination centrale du 'Gestell' ou du dispositif de l'arraisonnement" (31). It is precisely such a reduction that I wish to resist in the present chapter and the following by defending against Heidegger a certain kind of dialectic and showing it to be at work in Heidegger's own texts.

to a Heideggerian lecture suggests an unprecedented affinity between the two. This is confirmed by Heidegger's reflections on the critique of writing, since these observations are arguably the most insightful he ever made with regard to Plato's thought and writing.

> He, the poetic master of the thinking word [*der dichtende Meister des denkenden Wortes*], indeed speaks here only of writing, but at the same time indicates what repeatedly struck him anew along his entire philosophical path, namely, that what is thought in thinking cannot be stated [*sich nicht aussagen läßt*]. It would be rash, however, to conclude that therefore what is thought cannot be spoken [*unsagbar*]. Instead Plato knew *this*: that the task of thinking is to bring into the vicinity of thought through speech [*durch ein Sagen*] what is unsaid [*das Ungesagte*], and indeed as the matter to be thought [*als die zu denkende Sache*]. Therefore, even in the texts Plato himself wrote we can never directly read what he thought, even though they are written dialogues: dialogues that we only rarely succeed in releasing into the pure movement of collected thinking because we too eagerly and erringly search for a doctrine. (132–33)

This is the closest Heidegger ever came to understanding the philosophical significance of Plato's decision to write dialogues. It is perhaps also the closest he ever came to appreciating the indirect saying that characterizes dialectic as a mediation between what is said and what must remain unsaid. It finally might also be the closest he ever came to recognizing in Plato his own attempt to think and write at the boundary where philosophy and poetry meet. Yet what is startling is that despite all this, Heidegger's critique of Plato remains essentially the same. Dialectic is still rejected as a first step toward the forgetfulness of being that characterizes the modern age and in favor of a fundamental "leap," a *Grund-Satz*, beyond λόγος and its principles (*Grundsätze*). The object of the present analysis is to consider why another opportunity, and perhaps the most promising, for a genuine dialogue between Heidegger and Plato is once again missed.

C. PLATO'S DIALECTIC OR HEGEL'S?

The affinity suggested by the passage cited above is that Heidegger, like Plato, sees what is to be thought as both inexpressible and nevertheless capable of being conveyed to thought by a certain kind of saying. But what kind of saying? Plato's answer would be διαλέγεσθαι, and Heidegger's reference to the movement (*Bewegung*) of thought in the dialogues might suggest a recognition of this. Yet the affinity reaches its breaking point when Heidegger proceeds to state explicitly what he has assumed throughout the present lectures: that dialectic is simply the precursor of the "reckoning" that characterizes modern thought and presumably is therefore completely incapable of bringing us to think *das Ungesagte*: "Both calculative [*rechnende*] and dialectical thinking are in their ground the same [*im Grunde das Selbe*], in that ground, namely, that the principle of sufficient reason [*der Satz von Grund*] names without being able to think its essence" (133). This indeed constitutes a persistent theme of the lectures: dialectic as the source of the modern characterization of thinking as reckoning. But what justifies this connection between dialectic and reckoning?

It must first be noted that when Heidegger speaks of dialectic in this context he clearly has foremost in mind the dialectic of Fichte, Schelling, and Hegel: it is with these three thinkers, he tells us, that thinking was brought into the dimension of dialectic (82). But what about Plato? This dialectical dimension, Heidegger tells us, was "sketched in advance [*vorgezeichnet*]" by him. Yet here, as in the *Sophist* course three decades earlier, Heidegger makes no effort to think through the great differences between Plato's dialectic and Hegel's. Earlier chapters have already noted the way in which Heidegger's critique of dialectic in the courses of the early 1920s encompasses both Hegel and Plato; indeed, the failure to come to terms with the difference between these two versions of dialectic is a consistent feature of this critique. For example, in a passage from the WS 1929-30 course on the *Basic Concepts of Metaphysics*, Heidegger bases his charge that "*all* dialectic in philosophy is only the expression of an embarrassment" (GA 29/30, 276) on a characterization of dialectic as seeking to eliminate or level off the ambiguity that is in fact essential to philosophy: this characterization is clearly aimed at Hegel and has nothing to do with Plato, whose dialectic, as Heidegger himself recognizes, *preserves* ambiguity. Thus, in the lecture course *Was heisst Denken?* delivered in 1951-52, Heidegger cites Plato's dialogues as evidence that "all that is truly thought by an essential thinking remains—and indeed for essential reasons—ambiguous [*mehrdeutig*]. . . . Ambiguity [*die Mehrdeutigkeit*] is . . . the element within which thinking must move itself in order to be rigorous [*streng*]" (WHD, 68). He then asserts that "no dialogue of Plato arrives at a tangible unambiguous result with which sound human understanding could, as it were, begin to do anything [*an-fangen könnte*]. . . . A Platonic dialogue is inexhaustible [*unausschöpfbar*] not only for posterity and the changing interpretations that arise with it, but in itself, according to its very essence. But this remains the sign of the creative [*des Schöpferischen*] that of course inclines only to those who know how to revere [*verehren*]" (69). The difference, therefore, between a dialectic that levels (*ausgleichen*) the multiplicity of meanings essential to thinking and a dialectic given expression in dialogues that preserve this multiplicity in its inexhaustibility could not be greater. Nevertheless, in the cited text Plato is implicitly, and, in the parallel passage from *Sein und Zeit* (SZ, 25), explicitly, saddled with the "embarrassment."

In the course on Hegel's *Phenomenology of Spirit* from WS 1930/31 (GA 32), Heidegger acknowledges that dialectic is "fundamentally different [*grundverschieden*]" for Plato and Hegel (93). Yet even here there is no attempt to think through this difference. Instead, Heidegger insists that in both cases dialectic is characterized by a "Zu-sich-Sprechen": "What is spoken is oriented towards itself" (93). This last phrase is explained by Heidegger's more in-depth account in *Was heisst Denken?* (100–101), according to which dialectic, while recognizing the inadequacy of the subject-predicate structure for expressing philosophical truth, responds to this inadequacy, not by seeking to transcend λόγος, but instead by making λόγος *reflexive*. "As διαλέγεσθαι, λέγειν, assertion [*das Aussagen*], goes for itself back and forth in its own domain, proceeds through it and thus covers it to the end [*geht ihn aus*]" (101). "All dialectic is according to its essence logic" because "even in dialectic thinking is determined according to the assertion [*Aussage*], λόγος" (101). Here Heidegger does not mention Plato and clearly has Hegel in mind. Dialectic for Hegel is a λόγος of λόγος, or a self-movement of λόγος, which does not seek to transcend or "see beyond" the contradictions of λόγος, but rather to show that they constitute a higher unity. Truth is here to be found not beyond λόγος, but in the reflexivity of λόγος, which means, in the reflexive subject. As Heidegger adds in GA 32 immediately after the passage cited above: "The truth of what is spoken lies ultimately in the 'I,' subject, spirit" (93).

Heidegger might be right about Hegel: Hegel's response to the ambiguity of λόγος is, paradoxically, to "absolutize" λόγος, to make it its own object, to keep it within its own domain, in such a way that the very conceptual movement caused by its contradictions and ambiguities generates absolute knowledge. But can any of the above be said of Plato's dialectic? Clearly not. Plato's dialectic responds to the ambiguity of λόγος not by making it "for itself [*für sich*]," but by turning it "against itself [*gegen sich*]," so that in refuting itself it might point to a truth that lies beyond itself. This is why Plato's dialectic is characterized primarily by refutation and *aporia*, while Hegel's has more the character of integration, assimilation, and progression. In the contradictions generated by λόγος, Plato sees not the imminent truth of a higher synthesis, but rather a limitation that must be overcome if the truth is to be *seen*. Since such an overcoming or transcendence can never be complete, knowledge is for Plato necessarily finite. Furthermore, since truth for Plato is not to be found in the subject, he cannot find it in the reflexivity of λόγος. Heidegger appears either oblivious of these differences or unwilling to pay any attention to them.[2]

D. A SAYING BEYOND ASSERTION

But why this indifference toward very different ways of dealing with λόγος? The apparent answer is that, as previous chapters have repeatedly noted, Heidegger's critique of modern "reckoning" is carried out in the name of a kind of intuition beyond λόγος. From the perspective of such intuition, any way of dealing with λόγος, any form of δια-λόγος, is condemned to be a kind of reckoning with beings that is oblivious to their being. Heidegger's privileging of intuition is made clear when he describes as follows what thinking must seek to do if it is to come nearer to what is expressed in the title of the present lectures: "to transform what is written back into what is heard [*Gehörtes*], and what is heard back into what is seen [*Erblicktes*]" (135). As was noted in chapter 1, in the SS 1924 course Heidegger acknowledged that the Greeks privileged not only seeing but also and equally hearing, due to their recognition that being-with-one-another (*Miteinandersein*), as what defines being human, takes the form of speaking. Yet it was also seen that already in that course, and most emphatically later, Heidegger himself privileges seeing over hearing. This could now not be more explicit in the cited passage: to *think*, one must transform what is heard into something seen. As incapable of bringing about this transformation, as remaining confined to what is said and heard, dialectic must in the end fail to *think* and become instead the non-thinking reckoning that characterizes modern science and technology.

Heidegger claims to find this privileging of seeing in Plato himself, in the *idea*. This too repeats a consistent theme in Heidegger's reading of Plato: the etymological interpretation of *idea* and *eidos* as "what is seen" and thus as what exists for a seeing. This interpretation is normally accompanied by the critique that the interpretation of being as *idea* transforms it into an object existing for a subject. What is thereby criticized is not the privileging of intuition per se, but the interpretation of beings as objects for both seeing and speaking and thus as stuff to be reckoned with and calculated. Yet in the

---

2. One should contrast Gadamer's essay "Hegel and the Dialectic of the Ancient Philosopher," which shows with exceptional clarity and subtlety both the kinship and the important differences between Plato and Hegel. In *Hegel's Dialectic: Five Hermeneutical Studies*, trans. P. Christopher Smith (New Haven: Yale University Press, 1976), 5–34; see especially 21–24 for the differences and 24–27 for the kinship.

present lecture course there appears to be a significant shift in Heidegger's interpretation of the Platonic form, one that deprives the usual criticism of its foundation. Though he, as usual, identifies the *idea* or *eidos* with *Ansehen* and *Aussehen*, he adds that these words are not to be interpreted "optically": "The look [*Das Aussehen*] in the sense of the ἰδέα is no fixed vision [*kein starres Gesicht*], but instead the wafting of χάρις, of grace" (135). He even claims that it would not be sufficiently Greek to think *Ansehen* and *Aussehen* from the perspective of the sense of sight, which implies that Heidegger's own interpretation of the ἰδέα in the 1930s and '40s was not sufficiently Greek. Now, as the wafting of grace, the ἰδέα is not to be seen as a fixed object, but rather is to be received by that thinking that is also a thanking. Through this reinterpretation, which unfortunately is not developed, Heidegger can welcome in Plato the privileging of a "seeing" (what is heard must be transformed into what is seen) that is to be interpreted not "optically," but rather as the direct and immediate reception of a gift. What remains objectionable is dialectic, which, in privileging λόγος and thus what is said and heard, blocks this gift and reduces beings to objects to be reckoned with and calculated. This dominance of λόγος presumably also in the ends transform the wafting of grace into that fixed vision that only reflection and speculation can animate. Thus, despite the reinterpretation, Heidegger can still return to his earlier view by claiming at one point that the characterization of thinking as reflection, which reaches its fulfillment in speculative idealism, is "anticipated [*vorgeahnt*]" in Plato's interpretation of being as ἰδέα (139–40).

But exactly what kind of "seeing" does Heidegger himself privilege in his critique of dialectic, and how is this privileging compatible with the important role played by language in Heidegger's thought during this period? The answer is to be found in the fact that Heidegger interprets language as in essence a revealing or unconcealing that makes possible, but cannot be identified with, language in the ordinary sense of the word. He characterizes both thought and language as a type of νοεῖν and does so in a critique of λόγος as understood by modern logic. After identifying our destiny with the characterization of thinking as λόγος, an identification he claims to be by no means obvious, Heidegger describes what he sees as the main event of this destiny: the disappearance of the fundamental character of λόγος as ἀποφάνσις, "the uncovering bringing-to-appearance," in favor of the characterization of logos as λέγειν τι κατά τινος, "asserting something of something" (143–44). In this shift the λέγειν τι κατά τινος is uprooted from the function λόγος has of revealing or exhibiting (its *Darlegungscharakter*) and is treated as a relation in itself, so that λόγος becomes simply the combination of subject and predicate (144). It is with this conception of λόγος, as it comes to characterize modern logic, that, according to Heidegger, "The way is cleared for the development of thinking as reckoning, grounding, and deducing" (144–45). Thinking ceases to be a matter of receiving the gift of a being's self-showing and becomes instead a matter of reliably connecting a predicate to a subject by means of proof, inference, or calculation. Thinking becomes mastery.

The alternative to this is a radically different kind of saying and thus a reinterpretation of λόγος: one that takes it back into the dimension of "uncovering bringing-to-appearance." Thus, after claiming that the type of thinking required to leap into the *Abgrund* must in a certain sense abandon λόγος (159), Heidegger proceeds to claim that this thinking will nevertheless be λόγος in the more fundamental sense of *Sagen,* understood as "the gathering letting-appear" ("das versammelnde Erscheinenlassen," 161). Yet Heidegger almost in the same breath characterizes thinking as νοεῖν: "Thinking is νοεῖν, being aware: projecting and receiving [*vernehmen: vor- und aufnehmen*], that is, gathering [*versammeln*], bringing to appearance that which is present in its presence" (162). This shows clearly that *Sagen* and νοεῖν mean the same for Heidegger: each is a "gathering bringing to appearance" (*versammelnd zum Vorschein bringen*). Thinking is "in itself a saying [*von Hause aus ein Sagen*], presumably the original one that holds sway throughout all forms of saying" (162), but this is to say that it is νοεῖν. The critique of dialectic, then, is the same here as it was in the *Sophist* course three decades earlier: because confined to λόγος as assertion, dialectic must fail the attain νοεῖν and the different kind of saying that characterizes it.

E. PLATO'S DIALOGUES AND HEIDEGGER'S LEAP

A little later in the 1957 lecture series, however, something startling happens that suggests again a greater affinity here between Heidegger and Plato: Heidegger compares the elaborate preparation required for a leap (*Sprung*) into the essence of language (*das Wesen der Sprache*) to the back-and-forth (*Hin und Her*) of speaking and questioning in Plato's dialogues, which he claims to be without result only for those seeking doctrines and unable to hear *das Ungesagte*. "When something is as distorted [*umstellt*] as the essence of language, already the preparation for the jump there must perforce be elaborate [*umständlich*], even more elaborate, if the comparison be allowed, than the most beautiful dialogues of Plato which, in their to and fro, back and forth of saying and questioning, can be shown to arrive at no result, that is, for the person who hunts for assertions and a doctrine, instead of hearing what is unsaid in what the conversations say [*statt im Sagen der Gespräche das Ungesagte zu hören*]" (164). This passage largely restates the affinity expressed in the passage from pages 132–33 cited above. A difference, of course, is also stated:

the preparation for the jump must be more elaborate than what one finds in Plato's dialogues. But what kind of a difference is this? Is it only a difference in degree or a radical difference in kind? The crucial question is indeed this: why does Heidegger not recognize that Plato's dialectic, as the back-and-forth of saying and asking described here, is not a reckoning and a grounding in the modern sense, but rather a preparation for jumping into the *Ab-grund* or hearing *das Ungesagte*? If Plato's dialectic moves about in the realm of assertions, then so does Heidegger's own thought, whether he likes it or not. As Heidegger has been seen to acknowledge, his present lectures consist of assertions fixed by writing. Once this is recognized, one must ask if dialectic does not understand the role of assertions in the way Heidegger himself does: "We can experience the leap only in leaping, not in assertions [*Aussagen*] about it [though that is of course what the present lecture consists of]. Such assertions can only prepare the leap if they speak of that from which it leaps" (151). Is this not the function of assertions in Plato's dialogues: to prepare for a leap into what remains unsaid? Does not Heidegger himself observe in the passage cited above that Plato's dialogues do not provide doctrines, but instead allow to be heard what is unsaid through what is said? In this way the propositions in Plato could be characterized in the same way in which Heidegger characterizes his own propositions, as "a hint towards a saying [*ein Wink in ein Sagen*]," in which "perhaps what is unsaid addresses us without showing itself [*vielleicht Ungesagtes anspricht, ohne sich selbst zu zeigen*]" (176). In this respect Plato's dialectic is much closer to Heidegger than it is to Hegel: its goal is not to turn λόγος within itself in the quest of absolute reflexivity, but rather to allow λόγος to hint at what it cannot capture or express. For Plato dialectic is not a system, but a leap.

If Heidegger appears implicitly to recognize this affinity, then why does he not consider the possibility that thinking is fundamentally and always, rather than simply in its preparatory phases, *dialectical* in the Platonic sense? Instead, Heidegger explicitly rejects this possibility: "Thinking is saying, but not necessarily talking and speaking and writing [*Denken ist sagen, aber nicht notwendig reden und sprechen und schreiben*], thinking is saying, but not necessarily asserting [*aussagen*] in the sense of the λόγος ἀποφαντικός of logic, not necessarily talking-through [*durchsagen*] in the sense of the λέγειν as διαλέγεσθαι of dialectic" (172).

But *why* is thinking not necessarily διαλέγεσθαι, a διαλέγεσθαι capable of making things manifest in a way that no mere reckoning ever could? The reason can only be that thinking is for Heidegger *Sagen* in the sense of νόησις and therefore a leap beyond any kind of asserting, even in the sense of a "talking-through." In this respect we see that, despite the greater sensitivity to what is taking place in Plato's dialogues, nothing has really changed in Heidegger's attitude towards dialectic since the *Sophist* lectures: there is still the same privileging of pure, unmediated νόησις at the expense of διαλέγεσθαι.³ Yet in the 1957 lectures this rejection of Plato's dialectic appears more arbitrary than ever and cries out for a reassessment; as noted in the introduction to part 3, Heidegger's letters to Arendt from the early 1950s indeed acknowledge the need for such a reassessment. But what could have been gained from such a reassessment? The 1957 lectures appear caught in a dilemma between a characterization of thinking as λόγος in the sense of "reckoning" and a characterization of thinking as λόγος in the sense of a *Sagen* that brings things to appearance (νοεῖν). The gulf between the two is so great that only a leap (*Sprung*) can take one from the former to the latter. Plato's dialectic, however, brings into question this dichotomy, in its exclusivity and radicality, because it cannot be identified with either type of thinking. This dialectic is indeed a form of "considering [*Überlegen*]; this means: to reflect on something [*über etwas nachdenken*] and thereby support what is thought [*und so das Gedachte belegen*]" (GA 79, 105), but it is not a form of "reckoning": rather than grounding assertions, it reveals the groundlessness of assertions with the aim of pointing us beyond them to what cannot be grounded. At one point Heidegger observes that the characterization of thinking in terms of grounding or proving (*Begründen*) goes back to the Greek λόγον διδόναι (153): a frequent motif, of course, in Plato's dialectic. Heidegger than asks how thinking as thus understood can have any relation to the *Ab-grund* (153). His answer is that thinking cannot remain a grounding [*Begründen*] and must necessarily reach the *Ab-grund* to the extent that it begins to think its relation to ground and ground itself (154). But is this not precisely what happens in the Platonic dialogue? Rather than a treatise that proceeds to prove or ground assertions while taking for granted the nature of such grounding and of ground as such, the Platonic dialogue continually reflects on the process of grounding and is continually confronted with its failure and thus with the *Ab-grund*. When Heidegger observes that the Greek word for "principle" (*Satz*) is θέσις and that this means "what lies before" (*das Vorliegende*) and thus already *ground* (110–11), what he does not recognize is that for Plato, as already noted in chapter 3, the task of dialectic is to *destroy* such starting points or assumed grounds (τὰς ὑποθέσεις ἀναιροῦσα, *Rep.* 533c8) in the ascent to something that is not a θέσις at all and in this sense a *Grund* that is also an *Ab-grund*: the good as the "un-hypothetical principle" (ἀρχὴ ἀν-υπόθετον, 510b6–7). Plato therefore suggests that the ὑποθέσεις be

---

3. See Jacques Taminiaux, *The Thracian Maid and the Professional Thinker: Arendt and Heidegger*, trans. Michael Gendre (Albany: State University of New York Press, 1997), 188, 197; and Stanley Rosen, *The Question of Being: A Reversal of Heidegger* (New Haven: Yale University Press, 1993), 297–99. Rosen observes that Heidegger's thinking "remains *theoretical* in the literal sense of disregarding or bracketing all considerations other than the meditating of being" (299).

treated not as principles or grounds from which to deduce conclusions, as they are by sciences such as mathematics, but rather as *springboards* (ὁρμάς, 511b5) from which one can leap to that which is not a ὑπόθεσις at all. These passages show how far Plato's dialectic is from a reckoning with assumed and pregiven grounds or principles. As for the λόγον διδόναι that characterizes this dialectic, it not only is always, as Heidegger fails to note, a giving *and receiving* of λόγοι in conversation, but also continually points beyond itself to what cannot be given in any λόγος. This is the way in which Plato's dialectic overcomes the other dichotomy operative in Heidegger's lectures: this dialectic is indeed a form of bringing things to appearance, but it does so only in and through, rather than independently of or prior to, the process of "speaking for and against" that characterizes it. Dialectic can leap into the unsaid *Ab-grund* without ever leaving behind the grounding and conversing from which it leaps.

It is precisely this dialectic that for Gadamer, in contrast to Heidegger, reveals the essence of language: "Now I maintain that what constitutes our genuine experience with the essence of language is that we in thinking see through [*hindurchsehen*] all that is said and even in our speaking with one another 'look at' ['*hinschauen*'] something that is not in the words or in the models and illustrations of the supposed 'facts.' ... In the end this can succeed at all only in dialogue, i.e., in the back and forth of speaking with one another and in the shared contemplation of what is common [*im gemeinsamen Hinsehen auf das Gemeinsame*].[4] One can say that for Gadamer there is no "seeing" without dialogue and no dialogue without "seeing": phenomenology must take the form of dialectic. If Heidegger, in contrast, insists from beginning to end on the opposition between phenomenology and dialectic, this is because he insists on the possibility of a seeing that is in no way whatsoever an asserting and that will thereby fundamentally transform the essence of language. A reassessment of Plato's dialectic, of the kind eventually carried out by Gadamer, would have to question both the need and the possibility of such a radical "new beginning." Dialectic is, in short, neither a reckoning nor a seeing (νόησις), neither a ground nor a leap into the *Abgrund*, but rather a unified process that incorporates elements of both. Heidegger's own comments on page 164 attribute to Plato's dialectic this mediating role, though without explaining it and without being able to see it as anything more than preparatory.

---

4. "Auf dem Rückgang zum Anfang," in GW3, 410. Precisely this contrast between Gadamer and Heidegger is the topic of a paper by Robert Dostal, "The Experience of Truth for Gadamer and Heidegger: Taking Time and Sudden Lightning," in *Hermeneutics and Truth*, ed. Brice R. Wachterhauser (Evanston: Northwestern University Press, 1994).

F. HEIDEGGER AND THE DIALOGUE FORM

Not only dialectic, but the dialogue form as such, toward which Heidegger finally shows some sensitivity in the passages cited above, merited much more consideration and reconsideration by Heidegger. Heidegger could have seen a justification for Plato's choice of the dialogue form in his claim, at one point in the lecture, that the relation between thinking [*Denken*], being [*Sein*], and language [*Sprache*] cannot be an object for us, cannot be something over against us about which we can speak, because we always already exist within this relation (165). What the dialogue form does is exhibit this relation *in deed* without objectifying it as a subject of assertions. And when Heidegger proceeds to suggest that in some sense thinking and being are "grounded" in language (166–67), this too can be seen as justifying a form of writing that refuses to abstract the thinking of being from the context of conversation. Furthermore, if Heidegger is here more sensitive than usual to the form of Plato's dialogues, this is apparently on account of the way in which the Platonic dialogue illustrates what becomes an important theme in Heidegger's lectures: both the kinship and the difference between poetry and thinking. This is already suggested by the striking way in which Heidgger describes Plato in the passage cited above: he is "der dichtende Meister des denkenden Wortes" (the poetic master of the thinking word). Plato as the author of the dialogues thereby reconciles and unites two activities that Heidegger claims to be distinct: *Dichten* and *Denken*. Unfortunately, Heidegger says little about this distinction here, beyond the negative point that it is not to be identified with a distinction between poetry and philosophy: presumably because *Dichten* as the essence of the work of art cannot be restricted to mere poetry and because thinking cannot be identified with philosophy but must even be opposed to it if the latter is understoodd as a systematic body of ultimate principles. The only indication of the relation Heidegger gives is on the preceding page: "Thinking is in essence saying. Dichten is singing [*das Singen*]. Every singing is a saying but not every saying is a singing" (171).

Plato is therefore in the strange position of being a thinker who *sings* (*der dichtende Meister*) what thinking *says* (*des denkenden Wortes*). What can this mean? Presumably that what Plato as *Dichter* composes and brings to view is the very activity of saying that constitutes thinking. He is not a poet of love or of epic adventures, but rather a poet of thinking, which is indeed itself love and epic adventure. Given what Plato himself describes as the ancient battle between philosophy and poetry (*Rep.* 607b6–7), the poetic character of Plato's works has puzzled, or simply been ignored by, most interpreters. Heidegger is in a position to rethink and do justice to the dialogue form because for him the relation between singing and thinking, despite the difference, is much closer than the relation between poetry and philosophy. In interpreting both singing and thinking as a saying/showing, rather than as an emoting versus an asserting, Heidegger is able to recognize their kinship in Plato's dialogues. What is *gedichtet* in a Platonic dialogue says and shows as much as what is *gedacht* and *gesagt*. The kinship of singing and thinking enables what is unsaid to show itself.

Heidegger probably has in mind here not only Plato's practice but his own, since he too wrote dialogues. This is therefore the point at which to consider briefly Heidegger's own dialogues, with the aim of determining the extent to which they do or do not bring him into a closer kinship with Plato. Apparently Heidegger's first attempt at the genre was the series of three dialogues written in 1945 and published only fifty years later under the title *Feldweg-Gespräche* (GA 77),⁵ though less than one-third of the first and by far longest dialogue (at approximately 150 pages) was published in 1959, under the title *Gelassenheit*.⁶ The date certainly demands some reflection. Why would Heidegger turn to the dialogue form at the very end of World War II, as Germany was collapsing around him? One might assume that the dialogue form, in contrast to the solitary and esoteric meditations of the *Beiträge*, presented Heidegger with the opportunity to engage current world events. Yet, though the three dialogues certainly point to, more or less directly, what is taking place around Heidegger as he writes, they also quite deliberately distance themselves from it.

This is most true of the first dialogue, entitled "Ἀγχιβασίη: A Conversation Right on [*selbdritt auf*] a Country Path Between a Scientific Researcher [*einem Forscher*], a Scholar [*einem Gelehrten*], and a Wise Man [*einem Weisen*]." In this lengthy conversation on the essence of thinking, the speakers keep to the country path and keep their distance from "human habitation"

---

5. Oddly, Hyland's section on "Heidegger's Dialogues" completely overlooks this collection and thus a much longer and dramatically richer version of the *Gelassenheit* dialogue he does discuss, as well as the two dialogues with arguably the most complex and vivid dramatic setting. Drew Hyland, *Questioning Platonism: Continental Interpretations of Plato* (Albany: State University of New York Press, 2004), 68–83.

6. "Zur Erörterung der Gelassenheit: Aus einem Feldweggespräch über das Denken," in G as well as in GA 13, 37–74; translated as "Conversation on a Country Path About Thinking," in *Discourse on Thinking*, trans. John M Anderson and E. Hans Freund (New York: Harper and Row: 1966), 58–90. This first published version is quite literally an excerpt, rather than something reworked to be a complete dialogue in its own right. It simply begins on what is page 105 of the longer version (thus a hundred pages into the dialogue!) and reproduces the rest with some minor modifications and the omission of pages 124–38 and 153–56. Hyland is misled by a note that "this discourse was taken from a conversation written down in 1944–45 between a scientist, a scholar, and a teacher" ("Conversation," 58) into thinking that the originally published excerpt is being presented as a dialogue taken from a conversation that actually took place in 1944–45 (*Questioning Platonism*, 73). What is actually meant is that it is excerpted from a dialogue Heidegger wrote in 1944–45: the dialogue now published in GA 77.

(*die menschliche Behausung*), seeing in the approach to human dwellings an end to their conversation (107, 151).[7] Most significant, however, is one point in the discussion where the Scholar mentions the possibility of reflecting on the current time. They have come to the edge of the wood, and night has already descended. They consider turning back, both on the path and in their conversation, by resuming and gathering all that has been said. But then the Scholar suggests another use for the return trip: the opportunity "after the less needful to address what is necessary in the daily and public matters of our time [*nach dem weniger Nötigen auch das Notwendige der täglichen und öffentlichen Anliegen unserer Zeit zu besprechen*]" (73). Yet the Scholar himself immediately adds that he also wants to move forward in the conversation, and his other suggestion is not taken up by the other two. Instead, they decide to proceed into the dark wood, trusting to the light of the stars.

In the second dialogue, entitled "The Teacher Encounters the Tower-Keeper at the Door to the Tower Stairs," Heidegger thinly disguises himself as an interlocutor who lives high up in a tower (!). Furthermore, it is suggested at the very start of the dialogue that what is taking place in the world is best sensed from this height: "He who lives in the height of a tower room senses the trembling of the world sooner and in more widely spreading vibrations" (163). At one point in the discussion the Tower-Keeper points out that any culture critique is meaningless and must be passed by (194), suggesting that if they were led at all into the vicinity of such a critique, it was only on account of the following ever-present danger: "As so often in our conversations, the always too short-sighted effort to stick to reality through a preoccupation with the today" (194).

The third dialogue, entitled "An Evening Conversation in a Russian Prisoner-of-War Camp Between a Younger Man and an Older Man," and thus the one most directly and explicitly associated with the end of World War II, nevertheless makes clear why the world is best seen from a tower. Rather than taking place on a country path, here the conversation takes place in a Russian prison between two German prisoners of war. The fact that Heidegger's two sons were in a Russian prison at the time makes this setting all the more close

---

7. Hyland suggests a connection here to the opposition between calculative and meditative thinking: "The three participants want to engage in a different kind of thinking, 'releasement,' a nonrepresentational 'willing not to will' that leaves behind the willful representational thinking characteristic of the age of technology. To do so, appropriately enough, they walk outside of the town, 'far from human habitation' and the technological culture embodied there. Or is the situation more radical? Is it perhaps that they *must* carry on this conversation away from human habitation, that ensconced within technological culture such 'released' thinking simply has no chance? Is the *Feldweg* on which this dialogue takes place one more Heideggerian indication of the unlikeliness, perhaps the impossibility, that such a thinking as *Gelassenheit* can take place within fully modern, and that means fully technological, culture?" ("Conversation," 78).

to home. And the conversation itself reflects on "the devastation" [*die Verwüstung*] "that has settled over the homeland and its helpless human beings" (206), a devastation that is identified with "evil itself" [*das Böse selbst*] (207). However, the devastation and the evil are immediately distinguished from what is taking place in the world at the time. The devastation, we are told, cannot be identified simply with what is seen and grasped, with all the destruction and the loss of human life (207), and it did not begin "just yesterday." Later in the discussion we are told that the devastation rules in even greater measure ("ja hier sogar im höchsten Maße") the lands that were untouched by the war (216). As for "the evil," it does not mean here "the morally bad" (207); moral superiority therefore cannot even grasp this evil, much less eliminate or weaken it (209). It is even suggested that morality (*die Moral*) and the attempt to bring about a world order (such as the United Nations) are themselves the offspring of "das Böse." The reason is that the true devastation is "abandonment by being" (*die Seinsverlassenheit*), and before such *Seinsverlassenheit*, human action, planning, and judgment count for nothing (215). Thus, this dialogue, like the other two, is devoted to the essence of thinking as not-willing, as *Gelassenheit*, as a pure waiting that waits for nothing (is not an *Erwarten*).

The effect of these observations is to make the specific historical setting of the dialogue irrelevant and not worthy of reflection as such. This meditation on "the devastation" would be equally at home in New York City during the victory parade (and Heidegger's comment on the victory celebrations is that the victors defeated *themselves* long ago, 240). The devastation of Germany as a result of National Socialism and the victory of the Allies are completely irrelevant to what is to be thought here. Thus, in a note written around the same time as the dialogue, Heidegger can comment tersely: "The war at an end, nothing has changed, nothing new, on the contrary" (241). Toward the end of the dialogue there is an emphasis on becoming genuinely German, but this is seen neither as a matter of affirming nationhood nor as a matter of affirming internationalism (the distinction between the national and the international is also dismissed as inessential), but rather as a matter of genuinely *waiting*, since the German people, as the people of thinkers and poets, are the "waiting" people (233–36). Even the setting of the prison is irrelevant, since the dialogue begins with the suggestion, taken up and pursued later, that the prisoners are unfree only with regard to "the objective" (*das Gegenständliche*) but are free in the most genuine sense to the extent that they exist in "the open" (206, 231). In this way, Heidegger uses the dialogue form not to situate the philosophical conversation within a particular concrete place and time, but rather to suggest such a setting only to bid it farewell. Likewise, while there are different interlocutors in these dialogues, they are never different individuals with names, but only general types. Even when the interlocutor is clearly Heidegger, he is presented only as the general type to which Heidegger belongs ("teacher," "inquirer") rather than as the individual living through Germany's devastating defeat in 1945. Specifics of time, place, and character are irrelevant to the matter under discussion.

But then why the choice of the dialogue form at this time? The only indication of an answer is to be found in what we are told about the nature of dialogue (*Gespräch*). A note Heidegger wrote in connection to the first dialogue provides the most succinct expression of the crucial point: "Where else could the unspoken be purely preserved, sheltered than in true conversation?" (159). This is what Heidegger in the passage cited above sees as a virtue of the Platonic dialogues: the ability to bring the unspoken to thought while still allowing it to remain unspoken. This conception of *Gespräch* is further clarified in the three dialogues, which at key points reflect on the nature of conversation. In the third dialogue, after a series of sentences that are presented as all saying the same, and a reference to the Coming (*das Kommen*) which we await (*warten*), we get the following important exchange:

> The Older Man: The suspected [*Das Vermutlich*] is that ahead of which nothing at all can be thought: that which cannot be anticipated in thought [*das Unvordenkliche*].
> The Younger Man: Therefore the saving power [*das Heilende*] too can never be represented in propositions that assert something of it [*in aussagenden Sätzen*].
> The Older Man: But only suspected in the form of a conversation [*nur gesprächsweise vermuten*], as just now happened with us. (231)

Conversation is thus a way of suspecting/expecting what can never be presented in propositions that assert something of it (and thus think of something ahead of it). Thus, in the first dialogue, after observing that certainties can cause "the uncertain" (*das Ungewisse*), the riddle (*das Rätsel*), to lose its truth, the Wise Man observes: "We learn the courage to suspect [*den Mut zum Vermuten*] in the conversation and from out of the conversation [*im Gespräch aus dem Gespräch*]" (84). But then for someone who is wise in the sense of knowing and who therefore does not require "den Mut zum Vermuten," conversation becomes unnecessary. This is why *der Weise* himself, taking up the suggestion of the researcher, acknowledges that the greatest danger a person like himself faces is being called *weise*. He even proceeds to conclude that there is "vermutlich" no wise person. But then does the interlocutor in this dialogue, who is known by no other name than *der Weise*, not exist?[8] *Der Weise* preserves his identity and existence by reinterpreting his name and suggesting that one can be a *Weiser*, "with which word I do not now mean he who knows [*den Wissenden*], but rather he who is capable of pointing [*weisen*] in the direction from which the hints [*die Winke*] come to man; someone who can at the same time indicate [*weisen*] the way, the manner [*die Weise, die Art*] in which the hints are to be pursued" (84–85). For such a *Weiser*, conversation is the natural element, since it is in conversation that the pointing described can take place.

But how then does this conception of conversation relate to Platonic dialogue? At one point in the first dialogue, attention is drawn to the unusual way in which *Gespräch* is being understood. The "Wise Man" maintains that a conversation is not a conversation when it *wills* something nor is it merely a speaking-with-one-another (*Miteinandersprechen*). Instead, a conversation is a conversation only when something comes to language in it. At this point the researcher objects that however much the Wise Man may distinguish *Gespräch* from what is normally thought with the word "dialogue," "it yet belongs to the essence of a conversation to be about something [*über etwas*] and between speakers" (57). The Wise Man is ready to agree with this, but only with these qualifications: that the conversation attends the arrival of that of which it speaks, rather than presuming to know what it is speaking about from the beginning; and that the speakers must be ready to receive from the conversation something that transforms their essence (57). Thus, it is the conversation that wills something with us, if one should speak of "will" here at all. It seems that these qualifications could all be applied to the Platonic dialogue: there Socrates devotes much of the conversation to destroying the presumption that he and the interlocutors know what the conversation is about (*Meno* 80c8–d1); there the conversation certainly has the ability to transform the essence of the interlocutors since it is concerned with this essence as much as with the ostensible topic (*Laches* 187e–188a); finally, there it is the interlocutors who follow the λόγος rather than vice versa (e.g., *Crito* 48c7, *Phaedrus* 274a4, *Protagoras* 361a, *Rep.* 365d2).

What then are the differences between the Heideggerian *Gespräche* and Platonic dialogues? One should already be obvious: the very different relation to the world of everyday opinion and action, a difference that makes the setting of a Platonic dialogue much more concrete and indispensable than that of a Heideggerian dialogue. Yet there is also a very important difference with regard to what comes to language and how in each case. In the passage

---

8. Interestingly, Heidegger changes the name to "Lehrer" in the excerpt published as "Zur Erörterung der Gelassenheit."

just considered, the Wise Man characterizes what comes to language as "the word" (*das Wort*). This hearkens back to an earlier part of the dialogue in which the Wise Man insists that not every answer (*Antwort*) is the answer to a question; an answer can also respond to a "word," indeed is most genuinely an answer when it responds to a word rather than a question: "not every answer is the answer to a question, because the essential answers are perhaps 'only' counter-words to the word [*Gegenworte zum Wort*]" (23), so that, as the researcher infers, "the question is not at all the genuine way to the essential answers" (23). In this context, even the *question* of being is characterized as not knowing where it is going (24)! Not much clarification is provided here with regard to what "word" is meant to indicate, since this would require a clarification of the essence of language. But what is important to note in the present context is that a "word" is not something we create and give meaning to, but rather that within which something offers itself to us and to which we can only respond. As is suggested in the second dialogue, the meaning (*Deutung*) of a word is not its definition, but its ability to show and point to (*deuten, zeigen*, 174). What is said in the conversation is simply responding to the word as this pointing and showing. The dialogues therefore take the form of a series of reflections on and responses to words that offer themselves in the course of the conversation. Thus, if the latter part of the first dialogue is a response to the word *Gelassenheit*, the Wise Man insists that no one is responsible for introducing this word (119–20). The central accomplishment of a great thinker can therefore be identified with a response to one key word, whether this be the word "transcendental" in Kant or the one-word saying of Heraclitus with which the first dialogue ends.

Platonic conversation, in contrast, is, as practiced and described in the dialogues, a give-and-take of questions and answers, a giving and receiving of *logoi*, in which each interlocutor responds to what the other says. The element of such conversation is the assertions the interlocutors make, not isolated words for which no interlocutor is responsible. This in turn explains the central role of grounding, proving, and explaining in a Platonic dialogue. Not only is this mostly absent from the Heideggerian dialogue, but is explicitly excluded at the start of the second dialogue. There the Teacher arrives at the tower with a sense for *the wonderful* (*das Wundersame*) and thus a desire to understand, figure out, and ground. The Tower-Keeper suggests, however, that *das Wundersame* must be let go along with the will to question, unearth (*Ergründen*), and ground [*Begründen*] ("Fragen als der Willen zum Grund") that responds to it (163–65). But in favor of what? The Tower-Keeper speaks here of *das Seltsame* in contrast to *das Wundersame*. But what is one to do with the former if not attempt to explain it and understand it? The response to a question is indeed to explain and prove. The response to the "word," however, is only to listen. Thus, it is suggested at one point in the first dialogue: "So that in speaking, hearing into [*das Hineinhören*] a conversation would be practically more essential than making assertions [*das Aussagen*]" (75).

But this "hearing" is not a matter of listening *to others*, much less attempting to understand what they say. Dialogue for Plato, as for Gadamer, is a matter of hearing what others say so as to arrive at mutual understanding. Because this is not what Heidegger understands by "hearing," he can also characterize the goal of conversation as seeing. At one point in the second dialogue, the Teacher objects that hardly anyone could understand what the Tower-Keeper has just finished saying. The latter responds: "Because there is nothing here to be understood [*zu verstehen gibt*], since everything depends on looking [*das Blicken*]" (173). When the Teacher protests that one can still demand from the words used here a certain clarity (*Deutlichkeit*), the Tower-Keeper offers the characterization of words already cited above: words as "meaning" only in the sense of showing and hinting at, and as "saying" only in the sense of a "showing-hinting-calling letting-appear of what is to be caught sight of [*zeigend-winkend-rufendes Scheinenlassen des zu Erblickenden*]" (174). When the Teacher then infers that "the word and its meaning [*sein Deuten*], saying and its showing [*das Sagen und sein Zeigen*]" are not to be explained (*erklärt*) in terms of anything else, such as a general definition of sign (*Zeichen*) and expression (*Ausdruck*), the Tower-Keeper goes further: "Not only not in terms of anything else, but not to be explained at all, but only to be seen [*sondern überhaupt nicht zu erklären, sondern nur zu erblicken*]" (174). "Seeing" is thus opposed to understanding and explaining as what is alone at issue in the conversation. Likewise, in the first dialogue, when the Scholar claims not to understand what the Wise Man has just said, the latter claims also not to *understand* since understanding is inappropriate here, given that it means "the ability . . . to represent what is offered in such a way that it is, as it were, put under [*gleichsam untergestellt*] what is already known and in this way secured" (112–13). And as we are told a little later, nothing is to be represented or described in this conversation (115). "Seeing" of course is not to be identified here with clearly having in view some object, but must be brought into relation with the other key words here: *divine* (*ahnen*) and *presume* (*vermuten*). When the Teacher at one point says that he does not see the other way of thinking but can only have a presentiment of it (*nur ahnen*), the Tower-Keeper responds: "Having a presentiment [*Ahnen*] bears more fruit than a presumed seeing that is all-too-sure of itself [*das vermeintliche, seiner selbst allzu sichere Sehen*]" (189). If there is still pervasive talk of "seeing" here, this is because what is *geahnt* and *vermutet* is so directly, in and by itself, rather than being described, represented, interpreted, understood, or explained in terms of something else.

G. REDEFINING HERMENEUTICS

This is why the Heideggerian dialogue cannot be identified with "hermeneutics" in the sense of interpretation. In the dialogue that remains to be considered, the 1959 "Gespräch von der Sprache," Heidegger does return to the notion of hermeneutics after a long silence. Indeed, this dialogue, with its concern with the essence of language and its attempt to interpret Japanese words for language without reducing them to the metaphysical representations of the West, seems to be completely engaged with the topic and the task of hermeneutics. Yet this is true only to the extent that hermeneutics is disassociated from interpretation and identified more with what the earlier dialogues characterized as listening to what comes to language. When the topic of Heidegger's use of the term "hermeneutics" comes up, Heidegger claims to have first become familiar with it in his theological studies. When asked, however, to describe the broader meaning which he eventually came to give the term, Heidegger says only the following: "In S. und Z. hermeneutics means neither the teaching of the art of interpretation [*die Lehre von der Auslegungskunst*] nor interpretation itself [*das Auslegen selbst*], but much more the attempt to determine for the first time [*allererst*] the essence of interpretation [*Wesen der Auslegung*] from the hermeneutical [*aus dem Hermeneutischen*]" (GA 12, 93). This explanation of course leaves the word "hermeneutical" itself completely unclarified, as the Japanese interlocutor is quick to point out. At this point the conversation leaves the notion of hermeneutics, but returns to it later. In this later passage Heidegger explains the notion of hermeneutics by returning to the Greek word ἑρμηνεύειν and relating this word to the messenger-god Hermes through what he calls a "play of thinking . . . that is more binding [*verbindlicher*] than the rigor [*Strenge*] of science" (115).[9] In this way Heidegger is able to characterize as "hermeneutical" in the most original sense the bringing of messages or tidings (*das Bringen von Botschaft und Kunde*).

What is significant about this characterization of hermeneutics is its distinguishing of hermeneutics from interpretation. Hermeneutics in the sense Heidegger gives it here is not itself interpretation, but rather the announcing or conveying of what is to be interpreted; it is, in other words, a disclosing prior to interpretation that first gives interpretation something to interpret. It is along these lines that Heidegger interprets Plato's dialogue *Ion*: the rhapsode is a ἑρμηνῆς in interpreting the words of the poet, but the poet is a ἑρμηνῆς in a deeper and prior sense: he is a messenger (*Botschafter*) of the gods, he

---

9. Heidegger invokes here a play of thinking more binding than science because modern philology has questioned the etymological connection the ancients themselves made between ἑρμηνεύειν and the name of the god Hermes: see Jean Grondin, *L'universalité de l'herméneutique* (Paris: Presses universitaires de France, 1993), 10.

directly conveys a message from the gods. Thus, Heidegger can conclude: "From all this it becomes clear that the hermeneutical [*das Hermeneutische*] is not primarily interpretation [*nicht erst das Auslegen*], but already means before that [*vordem schon*] the bringing of messages and tidings" (115).

But what is the relevance of this conception of hermeneutics to Heidegger's own thinking? To the similar question asked by the Japanese interlocutor, Heidegger responds that this conception of hermeneutics can be used to characterize "the phenomenological thinking" ("das phänomenologische Denken") that opened the way to *Sein und Zeit* and that still demands that being itself be brought to appearance ("daß das Sein selbst zum Scheinen kommt," 116). From what Heidegger says here we can see that the "bringing of tidings" with which Heidegger now identifies hermeneutics is the bringing of being to appearance: the message or "botschaft" is "the presencing of what presences [*Anwesen des Anwesenden*], that is, their divergence from out of their convergence [*die Zwiefalt beider aus ihrer Einfalt*]" (116). Hermeneutics is thus transformed from interpretation into a manifestation or announcing of being prior to interpretation. But such a hermeneutics is a fortiori prior to assertion. Hermeneutics is here not an interpretation of being nor the making of assertions about being, but rather a prior bringing of being to appearance. The "bringing of tidings" with which Heidegger now identifies hermeneutics must be understood as the "calling forth" and "showing" of being accomplished by the word, rather than as the making of assertions about being.

Thus, in the one place in Heidegger's post–*Sein und Zeit* texts where he returns to an extended discussion and appropriation of the notion of hermeneutics, he does so only by sharply distinguishing it from interpretation and identifying it with an invoking and manifesting of being that neither interprets nor asserts: a *Kundgeben* that is *not* an *Auslegen*. That this represents a significant departure from the notion of hermeneutics to be found in *Sein und Zeit* is shown by the following passage from that earlier work: "The λόγος of the phenomenology of *Dasein* has the character of ἑρμηνεύειν, through which the genuine meaning of being and the fundamental structures of its own being are *announced to* [*kundgegeben*] the understanding of being belonging to *Dasein* itself. The phenomenology of *Dasein* is *hermeneutics* in the original meaning of the word, according to which it indicates the business of interpretation [*das Geschäft der Auslegung*]" (37). Here, as in the 1959 conversation on language, hermeneutics is identified with a *Kundgeben* of the meaning of being. The significant and obvious difference, however, is that in *Sein und Zeit* this *Kundgeben* of being is identified with interpretation (*Auslegung*), while in the later text it is explicitly distinguished from interpretation. What this change represents is a shift from the interpretation of being to a saying of being that names, invokes, and brings being into appearance prior to and independently of all interpretation and assertion. If the latter is still to be called "hermeneutics," a designation that the later Heidegger for the most part avoids, then this word must be given a sense very different from that which it has in *Sein und Zeit* and in what is normally called "hermeneutics."[10]

The dialogue between the Japanese and the Inquirer itself enacts this new sense of hermeneutics. The dialogue aimed at here is one that leaves what is at issue *unsaid*, and a fortiori, undescribed, undefined and uninterpreted.

> J: It does not seem strange to us Japanese if a dialogue leaves undetermined [*Unbestimmte*] what is genuinely intended, or even brings it back to the shelter of the undeterminable [*Unbestimmbare*].
> I: That belongs, I believe, to every successful dialogue between thinkers. (95; see also 97–98: a conversation turns out well when it brings us nearer to what is unsaid; and 106)

Words themselves, we are told, are not signs or ciphers (111), which of course as such would call for interpretation, but rather *hints* that *gesture* in a certain direction. Such hints do not assert anything that could be interpreted but only get us to look in a certain direction. And the goal of a dialogue that allows words to be "hints" in this sense is the "simple and free vision" ("einfachen freien Blick") appealed to at 126, in the context of describing the task of pursuing more originally what the Greeks thought in the word *phainesthai* (125). Thus, toward the end of the dialogue, when the Inquirer introduces "saying" as another word for language (and thus as itself a hint that gestures towards the essence of language), he adds that to "say" probably means the same as to "show" "in the sense of: let appear and let shine, but in the manner of hinting [*in der Weise des Winkens*]" (137). But in this case language and the hermeneutic relation [to the two-fold of presence and present beings] are the "same" (116) as the announcing and letting appear of the two-fold of presence and present beings. The hermeneutic relation, like language itself, is opposed to expression (*Ausdruck*) (122–23), that is, to letting one thing *stand for* another, to taking one thing *as* another. It does not express being as something, but announces it in such a way that it itself can appear. This hermeneutical relation, as a "relation" to the twofold of being and beings, is what determines the essence of man. Man is he who bears the message which "the twofold's unconcealment speaks to him" ("die Entbergung der Zwiefalt zuspricht," 128). Note

---

10. Grondin strangely writes of the 1959 conversation on language that "Heidegger n'a jamais été aussi près de la tradition herméneutique qu'ici" (ibid., 155). But he can claim this only because he completely overlooks the sharp distinction Heidegger makes here between hermeneutics and interpretation. That Heidegger should characterize hermeneutics in terms of "hearing a message" does not by itself make his view traditional: all depends on how "hearing" and "message" are understood here.

that what speaks here is not another person, not any statement or assertion, but unconcealment itself. The proper response to such a "saying"/"showing" is not interpretation, but rather hearing and bearing the message: a hearing that is also a seeing.

Yet it is important to note that the above are not to be understood as assertions made about language and hermeneutics, though this summary must give that impression. The dialogue is not *about* language but rather *from* language (143): it responds to the essence of language in such a way as itself to instantiate this essence that it is supposedly about. The dialogue can characterize language as a hinting/showing that bears the message of the twofold only because it is itself a hinting/showing that bears the message of the essence of language. And indeed it is best suited to do so *as dialogue*. Toward the end of the dialogue the Inquirer suggests that "a corresponding saying of language [*ein entsprechendes Sagen von der Sprache*]" (which is not an account *of* language) can only take the form of a *Gespräch*. This is presumably because a dialogue can *say* the essence of language in such a way as to leave it *unsaid*, that is, in such a way as to avoid making it an object of assertions and interpretations. Therefore, we will not get at the essence of language by distilling from the dialogue some of the things said about language (as is done above), but only from following the train of the conversation in such a way that we let it gesture towards this language. In this respect the Heideggerian dialogue cannot be transformed into a treatise without loss. In this respect it is "poetry," if "the genuinely poetic" ("*das eigentlich Dichtende*") is "the welling-up of the message of the twofold's unconcealment" (135). The dialogue enables the twofold's unconcealment to "well up" precisely to the extent that, like poetry and unlike a treatise, it refuses to objectify it in the form of assertions. This welling-up is identified with "graciousness" (the Greek χάρις), and it is presumably this graciousness that must be "mastered" by the poetic master of the thinking word.

But here we return to the question: how does dialogue as thus understood, how does in particular the dialogue between the Japanese and the Inquirer, differ from a Platonic dialogue? The differences again are striking. While in the latter the interlocutors focus on explaining, interpreting, defending and testing each other's words (λόγον διδόναι καὶ δέξασθαι), in the former the focus is on allowing words to gesture toward something that can be brought into view without being said. This results in another divergence: while in a Platonic dialogue the emphasis is on difference and confrontation, with agreement and mutual understanding sought in and through such difference, in a Heideggerian dialogue all the interlocutors come to say the same because they are all responding to the "same" that shows itself. Instead of the conflict of interpretations, there is the bearing of the same message. This is seen in a peculiar feature of Heidegger's dialogues: in precisely the two dialogues in which the interlocutors are most sharply contrasted with regard to their perspectives, these interlocutors are by the end completing each other's sentences and thus quite literally saying the same. This is the case in the dialogue between *dem Forscher, der Gelehrten,* and *dem Weisen* (see 156–57), whose perspectives are sharply opposed through most of the dialogue, even to the point of caricature. This is also the case in the dialogue between the Japanese and the Inquirer, even though the dialogue emphasizes the abyss between the Japanese language and the language of the dialogue as well as the impossibility of translating key Japanese words without significant loss. But even if interpretation cannot bridge the two "houses of being" represented by the Japanese and the German Inquirer, they can both gesture in their distinct ways toward the same and thus end up saying the same.[11] If hermeneutics were nothing but interpretation, each interlocutor would be caught in the hermeneutic circle and thus would not be able to say the same as the other. But Heidegger here rejects talk of the "hermeneutic circle" (142) because, as the announcing and bearing of a message, hermeneutics is open to and receptive of that "same" that lies outside of any circle.

But if dialogue finds its essence in saying the same, a saying that is silent in asserting nothing but only showing/hinting, then does not conversation between particular people in a particular context become accidental to dialogue and thus dispensable? This conclusion not only seems unavoidable but is confirmed by Heidegger's own practice. Despite the claims quoted above regarding the indispensability of *Gespräch,* the fact is that the dialogue form was for Heidegger a fleeting experiment from which he quickly returned to the preferred format of the lecture or essay. The explanation is that, paradoxically,

---

11. Hyland appears to see in this feature of Heidegger's dialogues nothing more than the priority that the Platonic dialogues themselves grant to the matter itself over the egos of the interlocutors (*Questioning Platonism,* 71, 81–82). But there is much more behind this feature, and, contra what Hyland maintains (189n47), I can think of no place in the Platonic dialogues where, beyond the occasional anticipation by one interlocutor of what the other is going to say (a common occurrence in any conversation), the dialogue becomes for a whole stretch a monologue in which the different voices become just one voice (except for the end of the *Gorgias,* but Plato is certainly not presenting Socrates' monologue in the face of Callicles' refusal to converse as the ideal of genuine dialogue!) It is worth noting in this context that while the dialogue between the Japanese and the Inquirer is supposedly based on an actual conversation Heidegger had with Tezuka Tomio, Reinhard May has shown, on the basis of Tezuka's own account of the conversation, that "with the exception of a very few passages in Heidegger's text, there is nothing approaching even an approximate reproduction of the conversation he actually had with Tezuka. There is hardly any 'authenticity' to the 'Conversation' whatsoever." *Heidegger's Hidden Sources,* trans. Graham Parks (New York: Routledge, 1996), 13. One can infer from May's account that what Heidegger leaves out from the original conversation is anything that might distinguish Tezuka's perspective from his own: see, e.g., pages 18–19 on the "inaccuracy" of Heidegger's account of *iki* and *kotoba.* As May observes, "It is easy to see that the 'Conversation' can be read in large part as a monologue" (15).

the *Gespräch* that Heidegger considers essential is not *dialogue* in the Platonic sense of conversing-with-one-another, but rather a silent hinting/showing that announces what, in contrast to all differences of view and perspective, is the "same." Thus, as was observed in chapter 1, *Gespräch* in Heidegger tends to be more *Gespräch* with the gods than with other human beings. A peculiar feature of the drama of the dialogue between the Teacher and the Tower-Keeper is that both of them are walking toward an encounter with a mysterious "guest": mysterious not only because he is the unnamed origin of the "picture" (*Bild*) in the tower that has inspired the dialogue (a picture whose content itself remains completely mysterious), but also because the Tower-Keeper at one point suggests identifying the guest with "the guest pure and simple [*der Gast schlechthin*]" (180). When they finally encounter the guest at the end of the dialogue, the Teacher suggests breaking off the conversation on account of the guest, but the guest insists on continuing the conversation with him, since he is not new to it but is rather on the same path. A possible interpretation of this strange and rather obscure element of the dialogue is that Heideggerian dialogue, as the hermeneutic bearing of a message, is the welcoming of "der Gast schlechthin," of what arrives from without and must be welcomed and made at home. Specifically, the guest appears around the bend at the precise moment that the Tower-Keeper observes that the task of thinking provenance (*Herkunft*) as neither ground (*Grund*) nor abyss (*Abgrund*) (200–201) is a presumption (*Zumutung*) into which we cannot force anyone, but which we must simply *let come to us* (201). Dialogue is a silent, nonwilling, *gelassen* awaiting of what comes. But such "dialogue" can take the form of the solitary and fragmentary meditations that comprise the *Beiträge* or of the self-deconstructing lecture to be considered in the next chapter. Conversation between people of varying characters and perspectives, the giving and receiving of λόγοι, a concrete context rooting the discussion in a concrete problem and decision: these things of which Plato was "poetic master" are not essential to Heideggerian dialogue because they are not for Heidegger essential to thinking. This is not to say that Heidegger's dialogues do not to an extent have these elements of a Platonic dialogue: the crucial point instead is that Heidegger makes these features of the dialogue form inessential at the same time that he employs them.

The difference between Heidegger's understanding of *Gespräch* and Plato's itself becomes an issue in the conversation between the Japanese and the Inquirer. After hearing what the Inquirer has suggested about *Gespräch*, the Japanese remarks that this *Gespräch* is of such a very peculiar sort that we could no longer call every speaking-with-one-another (*Miteinanderreden*) a *Gespräch* (143). The Inquirer responds that this is true if we hear this name in such a way that it names "the gathering around the essence of language [*die*

Versammlung auf das Wesen der Sprache]." It is at this point that the Japanese suggests that in this case the Platonic dialogues would not be *Gespräche*. All that has been said above justifies this suggestion that the Platonic dialogues are not "dialogues" in Heidegger's sense. Yet it is therefore all the more startling that the Inquirer, that is, Heidegger, does not immediately agree but rather replies that he would like to leave the question open ("Ich möchte die Frage offenlassen . . . "). Why? What room is there for doubt and hesitation? All we are told in what follows is that the kind of *Gespräch* is determined by that from where ("von woher") the speakers are addressed ("angesprochen") and that the "woher" that makes a *Gespräch* of a genuine kind ("eigentliche") is "the essence of language as the saying [*das Wesen der Sprache als die Sage*]." But then how could a Platonic dialogue possibly count as a genuine conversation according to this criterion? For the answer, we must return to the 1957 *Grundsätze des Denkens* lectures. There Heidegger asserts, in a passage already quoted, that "Plato knew *this:* that the task of thinking is to bring into the vicinity of thought through speech [*durch ein Sagen*] what is unsaid [*das Ungesagte*], and indeed as the matter to be thought [*als die zu denkende Sache*]." What *could* make a Platonic dialogue a genuine *Gespräch* is thus its ability to put into practice a kind of saying that brings what is unsaid into view for thinking while yet leaving it unsaid. A Platonic dialogue could in this way also be a *Gespräch von der Sprache,* that is, a dialogue that is addressed by and responds to the essence of language as saying. But why is this only an "open question" for Heidegger? The answer must be that he sees much in the Platonic dialogue that is in conflict with its genuineness. If its genuineness lies in a silent saying/showing, then this is obstructed by the focus on λόγοι, that is, on the interpreting and questioning of what the interlocutors say, by the interlocutors' subjectivity and idiosyncracy (in contrast to Heidegger's interlocutors, who are always only generic types), by a detailed setting that pushes to the fore practical questions of how to act and how to live. In other words, there is for Heidegger in a Platonic dialogue a kernel of genuine conversation buried in a great deal of dross. In Plato, the "poetic master" and the "thinker" are at odds (though Heidegger would presumably deny that poetry has anything to do with the features of the Platonic dialogue just described).

Yet the crucial question arises here again: is not Heidegger imposing a false dichotomy on the Platonic dialogue and thereby failing to learn from its unity? If the Platonic dialogue can hint at what remains unsaid in and through the giving and receiving of λόγοι, in and through the process of questioning, proving, and refuting, then is dialectic as opposed to the kind of saying Heidegger aims at as he believes? And can it be identified with even the "anticipation" of the reckoning and calculating that characterizes the age of technology? Is the Platonic dialogue a silent saying obscured by calculating and reckoning, or is it a unique kind of λόγος that is neither the one nor the other? Is it a form of asserting that hints at what lies beyond assertion? Does it bring to appearance the twofold of being and beings only to obscure it through the focus on the practical and the ethical, or does it show a way in which ethics and ontology belong together? These are the possibilities Heidegger fails to consider in not attending more to the Platonic dialogue in its uniqueness and unity. Instead he quickly leaves it behind in favor of the opposition between modern dialectic and a radically new kind of saying. Instead he writes dialogues that seek to leave dialogue behind in a unanimous saying of the same and that identify their own practical dramatic setting with an "evil" (the will!) to be left behind. In a significant passage of the first dialogue of the *Feldweg-Gespräche* collection, *der Forscher* objects that the conversation is again stuck "in the thicket of dialectical explanations [*dem Gestrüpp dialektischer Erörterungen*]." To which *der Weise* surprisingly responds: "What is dialectical may play a role here. But we should hardly be contemptuous of it from the outset as if dialectic were the work of the devil" (59). This response is surprising because, as the present study has repeatedly shown, Heidegger *does* tend to see dialectic as the work of the devil in contrast to the nonasserting (assertive) seeing/saying to which he aspires.

H. BACK TO THE BEGINNING WITH DIALECTIC AND DIALOGUE

What Heidegger stood to gain from a reassessment of dialectic and dialogue in Plato is therefore clear: such a reassessment would have challenged him to see in that "speaking through with others" Plato calls "dialogue" more than mere reckoning, grounding, and valuing, and would have made him reconsider his confidence in the possibility of a "pure seeing" (νόησις), or of what he also characterizes as a *Sagen*, that transcends discourse. Such a reconsideration might also have transformed Heidegger's relationship to traditional metaphysics. In the 1957 lectures Heidegger describes, in words that parallel those used in the dialogue on language, the kind of thinking that is now needed as one whose language "suits the essence of saying and the saying of essence" ("entspricht dem Wesen der Sage und der Sage des Wesens") and thus makes no use of even transformed metaphysical terms, but instead listens back into ("zurückhört") "the unexhausted word-treasury of our language" ("den unverbrauchten Wortschatz unserer Sprache," 175). But why not instead a thinking that deals with the metaphysical terms, as well as the words of our common language, *dialectically* in the Platonic, rather than Hegelian, way? Why not make, or at least prepare, the jump through the *Hin und Her* of question and answer rather than through the attempt to retrieve the ancient and original meanings of our words? Karl Jaspers suggested precisely this alternative to Heidegger at one point in their correspondence; furthermore, he explicitly identified this alternative with Plato. Objecting to Heidegger's failure to distinguish between Plato and Platonism, Jaspers wrote:

> What you call the "twisting free" [*Herausdrehen*] from Platonism is clear to me if you thereby mean the Theory of Ideas and its later transformation into conceptual realism [*Begriffsrealismus*] and its antitheses. Plato himself, for whom something like a "Theory of Ideas" was for a time a means of playing his captivating game, a means that he then gave up and transformed into the new game of that obscure number theory: this Plato seems to me still unequaled in what is essential, i.e., in the seriousness that all of these games served. If the second half of the *Parmenides* were played anew with contemporary means (and not neoplatonically), all bad metaphysics would certainly be overcome and the space would be cleared for hearing in its purity the language of being. (July 10, 1949; JHBW, 175–76)

What Jaspers suggests, in short, is that we can free ourselves to hear *die Sprache des Seins* only by playing dialectically with metaphysical concepts in the way Plato does in the second half of his *Parmenides* (and, to some extent, in all his dialogues). We cannot transcend metaphysics by abandoning it in favor of an altogether different way of seeing and speaking; but we can transcend it by continually exposing its limitations in the dialectical manner of Plato, rather than absolutizing it in the dialectical manner of Hegel. A similar suggestion is made by Gadamer when, against the idea of a distinct "language of metaphysics," he observes: "There is in speaking always the possibility of suspending [*aufheben*] its objectifying tendency.... But suspending [*Aufheben*] means: making use of [*in Brauch nehmen*]."[12] As for Jaspers's suggestion, it is surprising, not to say shocking, that Heidegger in his next letter makes no response to it, even though he addresses most of the other points in Jaspers's letter.

In the later text "The End of Philosophy and the Task of Thinking," Heidegger himself appeared to recognize the alternative that has been seen at issue in his confrontation with Plato: "For it is not yet decided in what way that which needs no proof in order to become accessible to thinking is to be experienced. Is it dialectical mediation, or originarily giving intuition, or neither of the

---

12. "Die Sprache der Metaphysik," in *Gesammelte Werke*, vol. 3 (Tübingen: J. C. B. Mohr, 1987), 237. For more references and discussion, see François Renaud, *Die Resokratisierung Platons: Die Platonische Hermeneutik Hans-Georg Gadamers* (Sankt Augustin: Academia, 1999), 30–34; and Brice R. Wachterhauser, *Beyond Being: Gadamer's Post-Platonic Hermeneutical Ontology* (Evanston: Northwestern University Press, 1999), 170–72.

two?"[13] Yet in another closely parallel text from 1965, "Zur Frage nach der Bestimmung der Sache des Denkens," Heidegger, after asking this question again in almost the same words, proceeds to suggest that both alternatives must be rejected because both fail to recognize the finitude of thought: "Is not the claim to it [dialectical mediation], despite the appearance to the contrary, precisely an absolute one and a failure to recognize the actual finitude of thinking? ... Is not the appeal to such an intuition the same claim to an absolute knowledge?" (GA 16, 633). If, like Heidegger, one can think only of Hegel here, then the answer to both questions must be "Yes." If one thinks of Plato, however, as Heidegger once again fails to do, then the answer must be "No." Plato's dialectic absolutizes neither conceptual mediation nor intuition; on the contrary, by continually opposing the one to the other, it exposes the finitude of each. By revealing our inability to say all that we see as well as our inability to see with perfect clarity all that we say, dialectic exposes the limitations of both our seeing and our saying. Heidegger is the one who, in dismissing dialectic, is continually in danger of presuming too much for language and intuition.[14]

It is therefore not surprising to find Heidegger in the last seminar at Zähringen (1973) explicitly returning to his negative assessment of dialectic almost fifty years earlier in *Sein und Zeit* and in the context of characterizing thinking in terms that clearly suggest νόησις. After commenting on some fragments of Parmenides, including the apparent tautology in the first line of fragment 6 (ἔστι γὰρ εἶναι), Heidegger characterizes the thinking with which he is concerned as "tautological thinking" and identifies this thinking with "the original meaning of phenomenology." Indeed, Heidegger characterizes this tautological thinking he finds in Parmenides in terms of "seeing": "a self-grounding upon that which allows itself to be *seen* by the *look* [*was sich dem Blick hat sehen lassen*]"; "to arrive at the point of grasping in *the look* the being-present:presencing [*dahin zu gelangen, das* Anwesend:Anwesen *in* den Blick

---

13. David Farrell Krell, ed., *Basic Writings*, rev. ed. (San Francisco: Harper, 1993), 449. A similar open question is to be found in the 1955 lecture "Was ist da—die Philosophie?" In speaking of the need to enter into a conversation with the great philosophers of the past, Heidegger says: "Dieses mineinander-Durchsprechen dessen, was immer wieder als das Selbe die Philosophen eigens angeht, ist das Sprechen, das λέγειν im Sinne des διαλέγεσθαι, das Sprechen als Dialog. *Ob der Dialog notwendig eine Dialektik ist und wann, dies lassen wir offen*" (WP, 31, my emphasis). What Heidegger means here by "Dialektik" is unclear; he may again have mainly Hegel in mind. In any case, as in the "End of Philosophy" essay, Heidegger probably does not leave the question open, and, as has been seen, Heidegger's own dialogues are in important ways *not* dialectical.

14. Commenting on the passage from "The End of Philosophy and the Task of Thinking," Dostal identifies the crucial oversight: Heidegger considers only the options of *either* intuition *or* dialectical mediation or *neither*, but not the option of *both*, which is the option that both Plato and Gadamer would affirm ("Experience of Truth," 66). And while Dostal, without having the recently published 1965 lecture, rightly guesses that Heidegger's answer is "neither," he also recognizes that Heidegger's own characterization of thinking is closer to intuition than to dialectical mediation (65–66).

zu fassen]" (VS, 137, my emphases).¹⁵ When Jean Beaufret then asks Heidegger how he presently understands the relation between Parmenides and Heraclitus, Heidegger gives the following remarkable reply: "From a merely historical perspective Heraclitus represents the first step in the direction of dialectic. From this perspective Parmenides is more profound and more essential (if it is correct that dialectic, as 'S. u. Z.' says, is 'a genuine philosophical embarrassment'). In this regard one must recognize that tautology is the only possible way of thinking what dialectic can only cover up" (138). Though Heidegger proceeds to acknowledge the possibility of reading Heraclitus from the perspective of Parmenidean tautology,¹⁶ the important thing to note here is the following: despite the existence of strong incentives for Heidegger to reappraise his rejection of dialectic in *Sein und Zeit*, he remains committed to this rejection to the very end because he remains committed to a characterization of thinking as a tautological (and thus monological) thinking-saying-seeing ('νόησις') that as such transcends any and all dialectic. The charge here is further clarified in the "Colloquium on Dialectic," where Heidegger, again in the context of explaining and justifying his characterization of dialectic in *Being and Time* as a "philosophical embarrassment," maintains that what dialectic covers over is the *auto* of thinking and being expressed by Parmenides in fragment 8, line 34: "The concealment of the relation of the genuine essence of thinking to the essence of being is the embarrassment of dialectic. Identity as inseparable being-together, the αὐτό, is the embarrassment" (22). This identity is an embarrassment to dialectic because it is precisely what dialectic covers up and fails to think. Dialectic can think only mediation and difference, not the identity of the self-same. Furthermore, and more importantly, thinking as dialectic, i.e., as moving in the back and forth of assertions, betrays *in deed* its identity with the being of beings. In turning being into something about which it makes assertions, it sets itself over against being, as opposed to a saying that in asserting nothing about being enables it to come to appearance. Dialectic is in this sense the original sin that expels thinking from the paradise of phenomenology.

This last point is made especially clear in the 1955 lecture, "Was ist das—die Philosophie?" After characterizing philosophy as a "striving" (*eros*) for the "wise" (σοφόν), and thus as "*underway* [*unterwegs*] to the being of beings"— an obviously Platonic characterization—Heidegger insists that both Parmenides and Heraclitus were not philosophers but thinkers *greater* than that

---

15. Heidegger's paraphrase of Χρὴ τὸ λέγειν τε νοεῖν in the first line of fragment six clearly in some sense identifies λέγειν with νοεῖν: "Nötig ist das Sagen (das sich-zeigen-lassen) und das Vernehmen (das sich mit ihm vollzieht)" (136).

16. In the Le Thor seminar of 1966, Heidegger attempts to bring Heraclitus and Parmenides together and insists that dialectic is *not yet* to be found in Heraclitus (VS, 14–18).

in the sense that they were still in "concord" [*Einklang*] with the σοφόν and thus presumably did not need to strive for it (*WP,* 23–25). Here again we hear echoes of Heidegger's critique of dialectic in the 1924–25 *Sophist* course. As a striving only underway to the being of beings, dialectic is incapable of achieving that "concord" with the being of beings that is the mark of genuine σοφία. Indeed, it is so in disaccord with the being of beings that it must ultimately, in the form of reckoning, express its oblivion.

I. CONCLUSION: DIALECTIC VERSUS SOPHIA AGAIN

The picture that emerges from this chapter is a puzzling one: despite the heightened sensitivity and sympathy toward the dialogue form, despite what are at least moments of uncertainty with regard to dialectic, Heidegger's fundamental hostility to both dialectic and dialogue remains unchanged from what it was during the 1920s. We find in the texts considered here many opportunities for reconsideration, both of his interpretation of Plato and accordingly of the direction of his own thinking and writing, but all are allowed to pass. If we ask why, we perhaps find the answer not only in the inspiring myth of an original concord with being before the Fall brought about by the dominance of λόγος as assertion, but most importantly in the persistent belief that regaining this concord is possible and even the central task of thinking. But is it? And why accept this dichotomy between a concord with the being of beings and the discord or oblivion that characterizes reckoning, with the result that these must be assigned to different periods in the history of being? These are the questions we must ask in confronting Heidegger with Plato since, in ways suggested above, the striving that characterizes dialectic is both concord *and* discord; as the child of both Plenty (*Poros*) and Poverty (*Penia*), *eros dialektikos* is both a have and a have-not: it both has and does not have the σοφόν (so that, in Heidegger's words, it is a *Weiser* rather than a *Weise*). Is more than this possible for us mortals, and is it not dangerous hubris to think so? These questions will be pursued in the next chapter through an examination of the way in which Heidegger in another late lecture, "Zeit und Sein," continually falls back into what can only be called "dialectic" in his attempt to think being "as" *Ereignis*.[17] Thus, once again a certain unelective affinity with Plato will show itself along with the real cause of discord.

---

17. For a defense of a similar thesis in the case of another important Heideggerian text, see my "And the Rest Is *Sigetik*: Silencing Logic and Dialectic in Heidegger's *Beiträge zur Philosophie*," *Research in Phenomenology* 38, no. 3 (2008): 358–91.

7

DIALECTIC AND PHENOMENOLOGY IN "ZEIT UND SEIN":
A PIVOTAL CHAPTER IN HEIDEGGER'S
CONFRONTATION WITH PLATO

The lecture "Zeit und Sein" (ZSD, 1–60) is an extraordinary text in a number of ways. Far from being a mere completion of the first part of *Sein und Zeit*—the third section of which was entitled "Zeit und Sein" but left unwritten—it is in an important sense a reversal of *Sein und Zeit*: instead of thinking being through an analysis of *Dasein* and within the "horizon" of time, it attempts to think being and time directly and together as *Ereignis*. To make such an attempt within the confines of a lecture is obviously extremely risky, not to say foolhardy. Heidegger must indeed begin the lecture by renouncing all claim to being immediately understood (1) and must conclude it by casting it aside in an extraordinary gesture of self-repudiation. The fact of this lecture, its *performance*, indeed demands our attention and reflection at least as much as its content does, if form and content can even be distinguished here. But another extraordinary feature of this extraordinary text is that it has been published with its own commentary in the form of a protocol of a seminar with Heidegger. This seminar not only continues the thinking of being carried out in the lecture "Zeit und Sein," but also reflects on what kind of a thinking and *saying* this is. It is to this question that the first part of this chapter is devoted, with the aim of showing what exactly Heidegger offers as an alternative to the "dialectic" he has dismissed as a "philosophical embarrassment." But the seminar also draws attention to an extremely surprising feature of "Zeit und Sein" that few readers or auditors of the lecture would otherwise have noticed: a certain affinity between the thinking carried out there *and Plato*. Since the later Heidegger tends to define his own thinking in stark opposition to "Platonism," this hint at a hidden affinity between Heidegger and Plato is of great importance. Exploring and developing this affinity, instead of somehow making Heidegger a Platonist or Plato a Heideggerian, will uncover where the fundamental difference between them truly lies and therefore where a fruitful

Auseinandersetzung is to be engaged. This is the aim of the second part of the present chapter. This second part will prove a continuation of the first part since both the affinity and difference between Heidegger and Plato will be found in *how* they go about thinking being. This contrast, which ultimately concerns the very nature of philosophical thinking, will be seen to provide a much more fruitful and difficult *Auseinandersetzung* than the usual opposition between a Platonism that forgets being and an Anti-Platonism that can think being only through a radical new beginning. It will therefore also provide a fitting conclusion to the present study.

A. FROM DIALECTIC AND HERMENEUTICS TO PHENOMENOLOGY

1. The Tautological Saying of *Ereignis*

According to Heidegger's own characterization, the lecture entitled "Zeit und Sein" is nothing other than an attempt to say *Ereignis:* more specifically, its sole aim ("die einzige Absicht") is to bring being "as" *Ereignis* into view ("das Sein selbst als das Ereignis in den Blick zu bringen," 22). Heidegger further explains what it means to say or bring into view being "as" *Ereignis* when he identifies this with thinking being *without beings* and therefore without any "looking back" on metaphysics (25). Being is not to be thought here in relation to beings, whether as the ground of beings or as beyond beings or even as different from beings: the "ontological difference" must itself be overcome. Nor is being to be thought, as in *Sein und Zeit*, in relation to that being which in its very being is concerned with its being, that is, *Dasein*. No being is to serve here as the guiding perspective, the starting point or basis for thinking being. Therefore, being is to be thought here without any reference to metaphysics, and this means without any critique or "overcoming" of metaphysics. Many of Heidegger's own earlier texts, including *Sein und Zeit*, raise the question of being only through a critique of metaphysics for neglecting this question in favor of a focus on beings; they think being only by way of a "destruction" of the metaphysical doctrines about beings as a whole that both presuppose and also occlude the truth of being. What Heidegger wishes to abandon here is precisely this detour through a destruction of metaphysics, a detour that necessarily thinks being in relation to metaphysics' account of beings as beings. To think being "as" *Ereignis* we must leave off overcoming metaphysics and leave metaphysics to itself: "Darum gilt es, vom Überwinden abzulassen und die Metaphysik sich selbst zu überlassen" (25).

In the seminar, Heidegger clarifies that thinking being without beings does not mean ignoring the relation between being and beings or treating this relation as inessential. What it means instead is thinking being without regard to its derivation from beings or grounding in beings: "das Sein ohne die Rücksicht auf eine Begründung des Seins aus dem Seienden denken" (35). To think being without beings is not to think being *for the sake of* beings ("umwillen des Seienden," 36). To think being metaphysically as what is beyond or before beings as their cause or a priori condition is to infer being from beings as their necessary presupposition and to think being only for the sake of beings as what makes them possible. To think being without beings is to stop thinking metaphysically. But what is then the problem with thinking being by way of a destruction of metaphysics? Surely, a thinking that destroys metaphysics is not thinking metaphysically. Heidegger's point, however, appears to be that even a critique of the conception of being as the a priori condition of beings still thinks being on the basis of beings, even if only negatively as *not* simply the a priori condition of beings. Paradoxically, even to critique metaphysics' subordination of being to beings as their condition of possibility is to participate in this subordination by thinking being only on the basis of beings. Even the attempt at "overcoming" metaphysics thus remains within its horizon, while what is needed is a complete shift of horizons.

So we must think being "as" *Ereignis* instead of thinking being with beings. But how is this possible? How do we think *Ereignis* itself? Heidegger makes it clear that we cannot say anything *of* or *about Ereignis*. We cannot make it the subject of any assertion or proposition: "the subject-matter however refuses to be said in the form of an assertion [*der Sach-verhalt jedoch verwehrt, von ihm in der Weise einer Aussage zu sagen*]" (20). The very grammar of language is here an obstacle (18–20). To assert anything of *Ereignis* is to turn it into a "subject" of which things are predicated, to turn it into some present-at-hand thing which possesses certain properties. Thus, in attempting to think being by way of the assertion, we inevitably turn it into a being. The assertions "Das Ereignis gibt Sein" and "Das Ereignis gibt Zeit," while in a certain sense "correct," are nevertheless, Heidegger maintains, untrue (*unwahr*) because they conceal and distort (*verbirgt*) the matter itself: "for inadvertently we have represented it as something present [*als etwas Anwesendes vorgestellt*], while we seek, however, to think presence as such [*die Anwesenheit als solche zu denken*]" (20). What is asserted in these assertions inevitably distorts and falsifies what we are attempting to think in them. The thinking of being "as" *Ereignis* therefore cannot take the form of an assertion; in other words, it cannot be a λόγος nor therefore "logical."

Toward the end of the lecture, Heidegger maintains that it is not even possible to say that "Das Ereignis ist" or that "Es gibt das Ereignis" (24). These assertions turn *Ereignis* into something *that is* or *is given*, while what we must think in *Ereignis* is this *be-ing* (verbal) or *giving* itself. What these assertions turn into a predicate, *being* and *giving,* should instead be the subject, though strictly speaking they cannot even be made the subject without being turned into *what is* or *what gives.* As Heidegger maintains, these assertions completely invert the matter itself, treating the river as prior to its source. If even as simple an assertion as "*Ereignis* is" cannot be made here, then obviously there can be no question of thinking *Ereignis* by proving or deducing certain claims about it. If *Ereignis* cannot be the object of an assertion, how can it be made the object of a deduction? Thus, Heidegger says: "Therefore representing-grounding thinking [*das vorstellend-begründende Denken*] cor-responds [*entspricht*] to *Ereignis* as little as does a saying that only asserts [*nur aussagende Sagen*]" (24).

But at this point a painfully obvious question becomes unavoidable: if being "as" *Ereignis* not only cannot be the object of any arguments or deductions but cannot even be the object of the simplest and most basic assertions, then how can one present a lecture on *das Ereignis?* The answer is that, strictly speaking, one cannot. A lecture on *Ereignis* is an impossibility and an absurdity. This is why Heidegger's own lecture ends in the remarkable way it does: by literally dismissing and casting itself aside. These are Heidegger's concluding, or rather self-destructing words: "Even the saying of *Ereignis* in the form of a lecture [*das Sagen vom Ereignis in der Weise eines Vortrags*] remains an obstacle [*Hindernis*] of this kind [i.e., one that needs continually to be overcome]. It has spoken only in propositions [*Aussagesätzen*]" (25). Note that Heidegger here characterizes the lecture not simply as deficient or inadequate, not simply as falling short of the truth of *Ereignis,* but as *an obstacle* to this truth. This is because the lecture necessarily speaks in assertions and, as we have seen, assertions not only fail to express the truth, but positively distort and invert the truth. In the attempt to think *Ereignis, all assertions are untrue.* This means that Heidegger's own lecture, while perhaps "correct"—but of what worth is mere "correctness" when it comes to thinking the "truth" of being?— is also untrue and therefore an obstacle that any attempt to think being "as" *Ereignis* must overcome. But even Heidegger's talk of "overcoming" seems problematic here. If even Heidegger's own lecture remains an obstacle, this is presumably because, in speaking only in assertions, it remains metaphysical. The very structure of the assertion privileges beings over being. But if Heidegger has claimed that even the overcoming of metaphysics stands in the way of thinking being without beings and must therefore be abandoned, is not the attempt to overcome the obstacle of Heidegger's own lecture itself an obstacle to thinking being? In order to think being without beings, would it not be best to leave Heidegger's lecture to itself and forget it as soon as possible?

But in favor of what exactly? If even the assertions in Heidegger's lecture are an obstacle to thinking being, then what form can this thinking take? If it cannot take the form of asserting and predicating, must it not give up altogether the attempt to *say* being "as" *Ereignis* and instead *become silent*? Heidegger does believe that a certain kind of "saying" is still possible here, though it is a saying that, in *asserting nothing*, is also a kind of silence.[1] This is a saying that, instead of asserting something of something else, only says the same of the same: in other words, it is what Heidegger himself was seen in the previous chapter to call a "tautology."[2] Thus, toward the end of the lecture "Zeit und Sein" Heidegger characterizes as follows what remains to be said: "What remains to be said? Only this: das Ereignis ereignet. Thereby we say the same of the same with respect to the same [*Damit sagen wir vom Selben her auf das Selbe zu das Selbe*]" (24). If we cannot say that "*Ereignis is*" nor that "*es gibt* Ereignis" because these assertions are predicating of *Ereignis* "being" and "giving" as if they were something distinct from it, all we can say is that "Ereignis ereignet." Generally, the only way of not asserting something of something else while still saying something is to make what is asserted and that of which it is asserted the same.

Yet even here we need to be careful. "Das Ereignis ereignet" clearly has the form of an ordinary assertion. If we understand it as an assertion, however, we take "ereignen" to be a property of *Ereignis*, something *Ereignis does*, and therefore something distinct from *Ereignis* itself. We therefore must not understand "Das Ereignis ereignet" as an assertion at all; we must not understand it as asserting "ereignen" of "Ereignis." We must instead understand it as saying "Ereignis Ereignis." In other words, we must understand it as saying *Ereignis* without saying anything at all *about Ereignis*. Thus, in the seminar on "Zeit und Sein" the possibility is considered that the sentences "Es gibt Sein" and "Es gibt Zeit" are not assertions (*Aussagen*) at all (43). Indeed, these sentences are not asserting anything of being or time: they are not saying that being or time is something that is "given." How does saying "Es gibt Sein," after all, differ from simply saying "Sein," though perhaps with a special emphasis? How does saying "Ereignis ereignet" differ from simply saying "Ereignis"? This is indeed why Heidegger elsewhere characterizes the saying he opposes to asserting as a *naming*. Thus, in the 1969 seminar at Le Thor we find the insistence on a fundamental distinction between speaking in the sense of "pure naming" ("reine Nennen") and speaking in the sense of asserting something of something (GA 15, 328), with the claim, directed against the modern interpretation of all language from the perspective of the assertion, that only "pure naming" ("reine Nennung") allows the "pure phenomenon"

---

1. What Heidegger in the *Beiträge* calls *Sigetik*: see my "And the Rest Is *Sigetik*: Silencing Logic and Dialectic in Heidegger's *Beiträge zur Philosophie*," *Research in Phenomenology* 38, no. 3 (2008): 358–91.
2. In the 1973 Zähringen seminar: see VS, 137. See also the *Zollikoner Seminare*, where Heidegger invokes the name of Socrates as someone who "said the same of the same" and who "was the greatest thinker of the West insofar as he did not write anything" (ZS, 30).

("reines Phänomen") to come to presence. Later in the same seminar Heidegger asserts that the Greek interpretation of language is "unpoetic" because it interprets *Sagen* as *Aussagen* (λέγειν τι κατὰ τινός; GA 15, 336). What would constitute a "poetic" interpretation, on the other hand, would be the interpretation of *Sagen* as a *naming* that, rather than being an implied assertion (i.e., as the characterization of something as something) is instead a "calling-forth" (*Rufen*): this interpretation Heidegger finds in Hölderlin (336). It is precisely to this poetic conception of saying as naming that Heidegger must appeal in the attempt to say being or *Ereignis* without asserting anything of it. Thus, Heidegger in the *Beiträge* can claim that "every saying of being keeps itself in words and namings" (GA 65, 83), words and namings which, thought from the perspective of everyday opining about beings, are inevitably misinterpreted as "assertion of being [*Ausspruch des Seyns*]."

Yet *can* the saying of being keep itself in words and namings? We have seen that Heidegger's own lecture on "Zeit und Sein" moves entirely within assertions. And how is this avoidable without collapsing the distinction between thinking and poetry which Heidegger still wishes to preserve?[3] Furthermore, as the passage cited above shows, even the words and namings within which the saying of being moves can be misinterpreted. Must not the saying of being, then, be a continual effort of interpretation and as such still move within the asserting of something of something? In other words, the thinking of being cannot simply "name" *Ereignis* and *Sein* and *Zeit*, but must interpret them *as* something or another. How is this possible without making assertions about them?

2. A Saying Beyond Hermeneutics

There is in "Zeit und Sein," however, a clear movement away from characterizing the saying of being as a hermeneutics, and therefore also a movement

---

3. In *Besinnung*, Heidegger writes that because philosophy *says* being and therefore "is only as word in the word" ("deshalb nur als Wort im Wort ist"), and because its word does not signify ("bedeutet") or indicate ("bezeichnet"), it would like immediately to find some way of going over to *Dichtung* as a help in time of need ("Nothilfe") and as a vessel ("Gefäß") (GA 66, 51). But Heidegger asserts here that there is an essential difference between philosophy and *Dichtung* that prevents philosophy from merely taking refuge in the latter. Heidegger does not fully articulate this difference, but he does claim that while philosophy is not a "science," its question of being is characterized by a "cold daring" ("kalte Kühnheit") and its knowledge is "image-less" ("bildlos," 51). This latter claim seems questionable, give Heidegger's own use of images. A later text, the 1941 "Winke," attempts to explain this seeming discrepancy. Though the "Winke" Heidegger writes in this text look like poems, he insists that they are not, concluding: "Das Sagen des Denkens ist im Unterschied zum Wort der Dichtung bildlos. Und wo ein Bild zu sein scheint, ist es weder das Gedichtete einer Dichtung noch das Anschauliche eines 'Sinnes,' sondern nur der Notanker der gewagten, aber nicht geglückten Bildlosigkeit" (DE, 33). But the question is whether the "Bildlosigkeit" of thinking ever succeeds and whether the "Notanker" Heidegger describes is not precisely the "Nothilfe" of poetry. See also *Das Wesen der Sprache* for "die zarte, aber helle Differenz" between thinking and poetry (GA 12, 184–85).

away from the central role accorded interpretation and hermeneutics in *Sein und Zeit*. The preceding chapter already noted such a movement in the 1959 dialogue "Aus einem Gespräch von der Sprache." In the seminar on "Zeit und Sein," and in explicit contrast to the characterization of thinking as understanding (*Verstehen*) and interpretation (*Auslegen*) in *Sein und Zeit*, the following question is raised: "It remains questionable whether interpretation [*Auslegung*] can at all be the distinctive characteristic [*das Kennzeichende*] of thinking, when it is a matter of truly taking up the question of being [*die Seinsfrage*]" (38). Given what the lecture "Zeit und Sein" has been seen to maintain, it seems impossible not to infer a negative answer: interpretation *cannot* be what characterizes the thinking of being that responds to the question of being. How can the tautological thinking/saying of "Ereignis ereignet" have the character of interpretation? What we have here is not the interpretation of *Ereignis as* anything, but rather a saying that, in saying only the same of the same, only names and invokes *Ereignis*. In saying "Ereignis ereignet" we are not "projecting" *Ereignis* onto anything else, we are not understanding it in terms of anything else. Thus, the saying of being or *Ereignis* as characterized in "Zeit und Sein" appears to transcend not only the "as" of assertion but also the "as" of interpretation or, in the language of *Sein und Zeit*, not only the "apophantical 'as'" but also the "hermeneutical 'as'" (SZ, 158).

This abandonment of hermeneutics must be seen as closely linked to the abandonment of the "overcoming" or "destruction" of metaphysics. In the 1922 *Phänomenologischen Interpretationen zu Aristoteles*, Heidegger asserted that "Hermeneutics performs its task [*bewerkstelligt ihre Aufgabe*] only by way of destruction [*nur auf dem Wege der Destruktion*]" (PIA, 34), and the task of "destruction" continued to be assigned a central role in *Sein und Zeit*.[4] Only by way of a "destruction" of the implicit interpretation of being in the metaphysical tradition can an explicit interpretation of being or, in 1922, of "factical life," be carried out. To think being by way of a destruction of metaphysics is necessarily to think being by way of interpreting it. But if Heidegger in "Zeit und Sein" leaves metaphysics to itself, he also disassociates the thinking of being from the task of interpretation: the thinking of being simultaneously ceases to be both destruction and hermeneutics.[5]

    4. Thus, Jean Grondin can write of the period up to and preceding *Sein und Zeit* that "Die eigentliche Methode der hermeneutischen Phänomenologie bleibt also die der Destruktion." *Von Heidegger zu Gadamer: Unterwegs zur Hermeneutik* (Darmstadt: Wissenschaftliche Buchgesellschaft, 2001), 70.
    5. Oddly, Jean Grondin insists that the later Heidegger remains committed to the hermeneutical project "dessus" his defiance of the assertion and his appeal to "silence" and despite his abandonment of the term "hermeneutics" to describe his project. *L'universalité de l'herméneutique* (Paris: Presses universitaires de France, 1993), 151–56. He can do so only by ignoring Heidegger's abandonment of the project of "overcoming" metaphysics in the lecture "Zeit und Sein," as well as by missing the way in which Heidegger's characterization of hermeneutics in the 1959 *Unterwegs zur Sprache* disassociates it from interpretation (see above).

This claim might appear inconsistent with Heidegger's characterization of the aim of the lecture as that of bringing into view being *as Ereignis*. To see being as *Ereignis* is presumably to *interpret* being as *Ereignis*, so that Heidegger's attempt in the lecture to think being as *Ereignis* turns out to be hermeneutics after all. However, if this chapter has put the word "as" in the phrase "being 'as' *Ereignis*" in quotation marks, this is because Heidegger makes clear that the word *as* cannot be given its usual meaning here. The word *as* in "being *as Ereignis*" does not mean what it means in phrases such as "being *as* ἰδέα" or "being *as actualitas*" or "being *as* will": these phrases express interpretations of being, and the word *as* that is used in them is therefore the hermeneutical *as* of interpretation. In contrast, the phrase "being *as Ereignis*" does *not* mean "being *interpreted as Ereignis*," it does not express an *interpretation* of being to be opposed to other interpretations (22). But then what does this *as* mean if it is not the hermeneutical *as*? Heidegger must give it a completely peculiar meaning: "In the phrase: 'being as *Ereignis*' the 'as' now means: being, letting-come-to-presence [*Anwesenlassen*] sent [*geschickt*] in Ereignen" (22). "being *as Ereignis*" thus means something like "being *dispatched into* the 'happening' of *Ereignis*." What is important for the present purpose is to see that the *as* has been rid of any distinctly hermeneutical sense. Indeed, if the thinking of being "in" *Ereignis* must now take place without "looking back" to metaphysics in the attempt to "overcome" its interpretation of being, this is because this thinking is no longer at all concerned with *interpreting* being. Indeed, Heidegger goes so far as to say that since *Ereignis* is not another interpretation of being, with the thinking of *Ereignis* the "history" (in the sense of the "dispensations") of being *comes to an end* (44). Instead of receiving a new interpretation that constitutes a new stage in its history, "being disappears [*verschwindet*] in *Ereignis*" (22, 46). What therefore disappears in being's disappearance into *Ereignis* is not only any subject of assertions, but also any object of interpretation.

But how can we "say" being without asserting anything of it and without interpreting it? The only possibility that remains here is that of a "pure naming" that calls or invokes. Here again we must return to our original questions: Can the thinking of being keep itself within namings? Whatever it may aspire to, can the thinking of being ever escape or transcend assertion and interpretation? And if not, do we not need a characterization of the thinking of being that, rather than identifying it with a tautological naming, does justice to and acknowledges its constant and ineluctable struggle with the limits of assertion and interpretation?

3. Can the Saying of Being Escape a Negative Dialectic?

Besides and even against what Heidegger maintains regarding the saying of being, we have the fact of the lecture "Zeit und Sein." Besides and even against

Heidegger's concluding dismissal of the lecture as a hindrance, we have the delivery of the lecture and the presumed need Heidegger felt to deliver it. Besides and even against Heidegger's insistence that the very grammatical form of the assertion distorts what is at issue in the thinking of being and is thereby *untrue*, we have Heidegger's repeated and even painful struggle to express the truth of being in sentences that undeniably have the form of assertions. Here it needs to be added that the obstacle Heidegger confronts in attempting to say being and *Ereignis* in the lecture is not only the logical and grammatical form of his language, but even the individual words used. In the passage cited above, Heidegger attempts to get beyond the hermeneutical *as* by interpreting the phrase "being *as Ereignis*" as meaning—note how this attempt to get beyond interpretation occurs through an interpretation!—"Sein, Anwesenlassen geschickt im Ereignen." But in the seminar it is acknowledged that the verb *schicken*, meaning "to send" or "dispatch" and substituted here for the word *as*, is, as a verb or *Zeitwort* that expresses action *in time*, completely inappropriate for expressing something that is not in time at all ("nichts Zeitliches ist"), namely time and being themselves! (51). This is a problem not only with the verb *schicken*, but with all of the verbs that play an absolutely central role in Heidegger's attempt to say being and/as/in *Ereignis*, such as *reichen* (reaching out) and *geben* (giving). In short, Heidegger must resort to words with an unavoidable temporal and ontic meaning in the attempt to say the *Ereignis* of time and being themselves. Being is distorted and falsified not only by having something asserted *of* it, but also by *what* is asserted of it.

In an extremely important passage from the seminar protocol, we get an indication that Heidegger recognized that even the thinking of *Ereignis* cannot dispense with what are called there "ontic models" and must continually *work against them*. "The necessity for thinking to use models is tied to language [*hängt mit der Sprache zusammen*]. The language of thinking can proceed only from natural language. This natural language, however, is in its essence [*im Grunde*] historically metaphysical [*geschichtlich-metaphysisch*]. An interpretedness [*Ausgelegtheit*]—in the form of the self-evident [*des Selbstverständlichen*]—is thus already given in it [*in ihr vorgegeben*]. From this perspective, the only possibility for thinking is to search for models in order to deconstruct [*abzuarbeiten*] them and in this way accomplish the transition to the speculative" (54). Since thinking cannot invent a completely new language, it can draw its means of expression from nowhere other than the language which we speak ordinarily and every day; the language of philosophy is not an artificial language, but rather the natural language. This language, however, is not neutral but is rather always and already a certain interpretation of the world. Furthermore, this interpretation, far from being the immediate result of how the things themselves show themselves, is historically conditioned. Specifically, even our ordinary language is an avatar of the entire metaphysical tradition: any simple statement we utter brings with it a metaphysics of substance and property. The use of a verb, as we have seen in the above examples, carries with it a certain conception of time and of actions as occurring in and throughout time. Any use of such language, therefore, to say not beings occurring in time, but being and time themselves, must continually work against and undo the language it is using.

A little later we find the following passage: "The talk of ontic models [*ontischen Modellen*] presupposes that language has an ontic character in principle [*prinzipiell ontischen Charakter hat*], so that any thinking that can show only by way of the word [*nur über das Wort ausweisen kann*] what it wants to say ontologically would find itself in the situation of having to use ontic models for this purpose" (54–55). The sentence already discussed above provides a perfect example of what is being said here: "Sein, Anwesenlassen geschickt im Ereignen." This sentence names two things, *Sein* and *Ereignen*, which it then brings into a relation through an action occurring in time (*schicken*) as well as through a location in space: the one occurs "in" (*im*) the other. In this way what the sentence expresses as an assertion or proposition is something purely ontic, while what Heidegger is trying to express here is something beyond beings as well as beyond both time understood as temporal succession and space understood as location. Here the use of ontic models to express an ontological truth is unavoidable: to express the "relation" between being and *Ereignis*, which of course is not a relation at all, Heidegger must resort to the model of "sending," which, as an action, is something ontic and temporal. And any model employed here would be unavoidably ontic. As already noted, even to speak simply of a "relation" between being and *Ereignis* is to employ an ontic model; even to say that "being *is Ereignis*" is to employ an ontic model, since to say that being *is x* is to turn it into *a being*. If an appeal to ontic models is thus unavoidable, any attempt to say being can do so only by way of working against the models it finds itself compelled to employ.

But a form of thinking that can get at what it wishes to express only negatively by working against the forms of expression it is forced to employ could certainly with justice be called *dialectical*. The way to being appears here to be that of negation, rather than that of some simple and direct naming. At one point in the seminar on "Zeit und Sein" it is even granted that Heidegger's way of thinking could be compared to a *negative theology*. "The manner in which this thinking proceeds [*die Art des Vorgehens dieses Denkens*] could therefore be seen as analogous to the method of a negative theology. This would also show itself in the fact that, and the way in which, the ontic models given in language [*die in der Sprache gegebenen ontischen Modellen*] are deconstructed [*abgearbeitet*] and destroyed [*zerstört*]" (51). The concluding gesture of Heidegger's lecture certainly reinforces this analogy: the lecture ends, as we have seen, by repudiating itself as a hindrance to the truth it is trying to express. In this gesture we clearly have a dismantling and even destruction of the ontic models to which the lecture, moving as it does in the medium of assertions, must inevitably have recourse. It is also significant in this context that when Heidegger asks what can be said of *Ereignis* itself, what he proceeds to answer is only that *Ereignis withdraws,* that to it as such belongs withdrawal (*Entzug*) and disappropriation or disowning (*Enteignis,* 23). In other words, if we can at all go beyond the tautology "Ereignis ereignet," it is only by negating even this tautology and saying "Ereignis *enteignet.*" To say *Ereignis* is ultimately to say its *absence.* Here again the analogy with negative theology is very strong indeed.

4. Phenomenology Comes to the Rescue

If Heidegger's lecture lives from negation and is thoroughly dialectical in the way described above, Heidegger nevertheless, as has been repeatedly noted in the present study, adamantly refuses both here and elsewhere to characterize the saying or thinking of being as in any way dialectical. Thus, early in the lecture Heidegger, in the context of describing the way in which being and time mutually determine each other, dismisses dialectic in a passage that was not delivered orally: "For cases such as these philosophy knows a way out [*Ausweg*]. One lets the contradictions stand, even sharpens them and attempts to bring together into a comprehensive unity [*in einer umfassenden Einheit*] the self-contradicting [*das Sich-Widersprechende*] and mutually exclusive [*Auseinanderfallende*]. One calls this procedure dialectic" (3–4). This identification of dialectic with some totalizing synthesis seems, however, a rather crude caricature that at most has a grain of truth as a description of *Hegelian* dialectic. Dialectic can expose the limits of competing assertions and "ontic models" not as a means to a higher synthesis, but rather as an indirect and negative indication of a truth that these assertions and models can never express. As we have seen, dialectic in this more humble sense seems operative in Heidegger's own text. But then why does Heidegger not acknowledge this dialectical character of his own thinking of being instead of dismissing dialectic at the outset by means of a simplistic caricature?

The answer is that, whatever he may actually *achieve* in this lecture or in other texts, Heidegger is committed to the possibility of a more direct saying that transcends the indirectness and negativity of dialectic. This is made clear when the passages concerning ontic models cited above are immediately followed by a "but": "But even ignoring the fact that language is not only ontic but from the outset ontic-ontological, one can ask whether there could not be a language of thinking that speaks what is *simple* in language [*das* Einfache *der Sprache*] in such a way that the language of thinking would make visible [*sichtbar*] precisely the limitations [*die Begrenztheit*] of metaphysical language. But one cannot talk about this [*Darüber aber kann man nicht reden*]. What decides [this possibility] is whether such a saying [*Sagen*] succeeds or not [*glückt oder nicht*]" (55). That language is both ontical *and* ontological must certainly be granted, but a saying that wishes to isolate the ontological dimension must still in this case continually work against the predominant and most immediately expressed ontic dimension. But the possibility Heidegger is contemplating here is that of a saying that says *the simple* and does so directly. What Heidegger has in mind is clearly what has been called above "tautology": saying the same of the same. Such a saying of the same, because it does not *assert* anything *of* anything, can dispense with the ontic models embedded in assertions and therefore with the constant negation and dismantling of these models. As already noted in the preceding chapter, it is precisely this "tautology" that Heidegger opposes to dialectic in his last seminar at Zähringen. After recognizing genuine tautological thinking in Parmenides' ἔστι γὰρ εἶναι and citing his own dismissal of dialectic as a "genuine philosophical embarrassment" decades earlier in *Sein und Zeit,* Heidegger says: "In this regard one must recognize that tautology is the only possible way of thinking what dialectic can only cover up" (VS, 138). Dialectic covers up being because it remains in the medium of assertions, however negatively it might deal with these assertions. What Heidegger seeks in contrast is a completely different kind of saying: one that like Parmenides' ἔστι γὰρ εἶναι does not assert anything of being, does not judge, conceptualize, or interpret it, but rather brings it to appearance by simply invoking and announcing it.

But is such a saying a genuine possibility? In the cited passage Heidegger claims that this question cannot be answered through any kind of discussion or argument; all we can do is see whether or not the attempt to say being in this direct and dialectically unmediated way *succeeds.* But have not the above reflections shown that at least in the lecture "Zeit und Sein" this saying does *not* succeed, to the extent that what we find in this text instead is a self-dismantling dialectic? And if it does not succeed here in what Heidegger himself characterizes as an attempt to say and think *Ereignis,* then what confidence can there be that it will ever succeed? Furthermore, if Heidegger is genuinely leaving open the question of the success of this saying, then why does he here and everywhere dismiss dialectic so quickly, superficially, and categorically?

To understand fully Heidegger's commitment to a direct, tautological saying of being, it is essential to recognize that such a saying is for Heidegger a *seeing.* Here we need finally to note explicitly what must have already struck us: that Heidegger initially describes the aim of the lecture not as saying or thinking being "as" *Ereignis,* but rather as bringing being "as" *Ereignis into view* ("in den Blick zu bringen"). Thus, the aim of the lecture is explicitly identified with a certain "vision" of being. Accordingly, in the seminar on "Zeit und Sein," the difficulty of hearing or reading this lecture can be identified with a difficulty *in seeing*: "The difficulty of hearing or reading the lecture goes along, in a peculiar way, with the simplicity of the matter [*der Einfachheit der Sache*] under discussion. Therefore, what is important before all else is to arrive at *the simplicity of the look* [*die* Einfachheit des Blickes]" (41; my emphasis). Furthermore, while Heidegger originally identified hermeneutics with "Destruktion," as we have seen, the only mention of "Destruktion" in the lecture "Zeit und Sein," a mention that was not in the orally delivered version of the lecture, makes clear that it is only preliminary to a more complete vision: "Only the dismantling of these obstructions [*Abbau dieser Verdeckungen*]—this is what 'Destruktion' means—provides thinking with a preliminary look into [*einen vorläufigen Einblick in*] that which then discloses itself [*sich enthüllt*] as the sending-of-being [*Seins-Geschick*]" (9). The dismantling or "destruction" of the different interpretations of being that cover it over is only a means toward arriving at a "look" into what reveals itself as the "sending-history" of being; that this look is itself characterized as "preliminary" suggests the possibility of an *Einblick* that is not purely preliminary.[6]

This emphasis on seeing should not be surprising, since the only way in which Heidegger can distinguish the saying of being from asserting or interpreting is by rooting it in some sort of seeing or intuition. Heidegger indeed identifies this saying with naming and tautology, but in order for the latter to be a genuine alternative to assertion and interpretation, it must be capable somehow of bringing what is named or said *directly into view*. The only way in which naming or tautology can summon up or announce being without interpreting it or asserting anything of it is by *letting it be seen*. Naming for Heidegger is not the expression of a meaning nor some kind of hidden description, but rather a bringing to appearance and into the light. Thus, in the text from the 1969 seminar in Le Thor cited above, Heidegger describes "pure naming" as bringing the "pure phenomenon" to presence. This point is also clearly made in Heidegger's description of naming in the 1951 essay on Λόγος in Heraclitus: "Naming (ὄνομα), as thought from the perspective of λέγειν [here interpreted as *lesen*, gathering] is no expression of a meaning [*kein Ausdrücken einer Wortbedeutung*], but a letting-lie-before in the light [*ein vor-liegen-Lassen in dem Licht*] within which something comes to stand through having a name" (GA 7, 228).

6. Thinking is indeed described at 38 as having the characteristic of "Vorläufigkeit," but Heidegger here is at pains to get away from the ordinary meaning of "Vorläufigkeit" and to stress the deeper meaning according to which "dieses Denken jeweil—und zwar in der Weise des Schrittes zurück—vorausläuft."

It is therefore not surprising that while Heidegger would certainly not call his method of proceeding in the lecture *dialectical*, and while he has also been seen to have good reason not to call it *hermeneutical*, he allows it to be called, according to the seminar protocol, *phenomenological* (48). After a reference to the motto "Zu den Sachen selbst," we read: "And it is in this sense that it can be said of Heidegger that he preserves the genuine phenomenology. Indeed, this question of being [*Seinsfrage*] would not have been possible without the fundamental attitude of phenomenology [*die phänomenologische Grundhaltung*]" (48). This is a very important admission and a true one. Without the fundamental phenomenological attitude, that is, without the commitment to an unmediated relation to the things themselves, to the possibility of the phenomena directly showing themselves, the kind of saying of being that Heidegger attempts in response to the question of being, one that bypasses assertion and interpretation in a naming of the same as the same, would be an impossibility. What Heidegger calls "naming" and "tautology" is ultimately that immediate "seeing" of the things themselves to which phenomenology is committed. Thus, in the Zähringen seminar of 1973 Heidegger can identify tautological thinking with "the original meaning of phenomenology" (*Vier Seminare*, 137), just as here he can identify his attempt at a tautological saying of *Ereignis* with "the genuine phenomenology." It should also be recalled that when Heidegger is asked by his Japanese interlocutor in the conversation on language why he gives the word *hermeneutical* the meaning of "das Bringen von Botschaft und Kunde," Heidegger replies that he does so in order to characterize with its help "phenomenological thinking."[7]

The question that now becomes unavoidable should be obvious: *how exactly is a phenomenology of Ereignis possible*? What does *Ereignis* give us to "see"? How is a direct naming of *Ereignis*, with its assumption of some kind of direct access, possible? How can being be *brought into view* "as" *Ereignis*? Clearly, the language of "seeing" and "bringing into view" cannot here refer to anything like the intuition of an object, since being as *Ereignis* is not any kind of object. But then what can this language mean and what is its justification? To grasp the full extent of the difficulty here, we need to recall that if Heidegger's aim in the lecture is to bring being as *Ereignis* into view (22), the seminar tells us that as soon as we succeed in bringing into view being as *Ereignis, it disappears!* "As being as *Ereignis* comes into view [*in den Blick kommt*], it disappears [*verschwindet*] as being" (46). Thus, the saying of being

---

7. See also Heidegger's extraordinary claim in the *Zollikoner Seminare* that phenomenology is more of a "science" than the sciences if one understands "science" according to its root meaning of "seeing": "Die Phänomenologie ist eine wissenschaftlichere Wissenschaft als die Naturwissenschaften, insbesondere wenn man Wissenschaft im Sinne des ursprünglichen Wissens im Sinne des sanskritischen Wortes 'wit' sehen faßt" (ZS, 265).

that brings being into view not only cannot interpret it or make assertions of it: it cannot even see it! But then what is the point of describing this saying as bringing being "into view"? And why speak of phenomenology at all where there is nothing to be seen, or where the phenomenon vanishes as soon as it is seen?

The paradox here is perfectly captured in a phrase Heidegger uses in the 1973 Zähringen seminar to characterize his position as a "phenomenology of the inapparent" ("Phänomenologie des Unscheinbaren").[8] What does this apparently self-contradictory designation mean? How can there be a phenomenology of what does not show itself, a phenomenology of what is not a phenomenon? The phrase can in fact be interpreted in two ways, the first of which rids it of its paradox and makes it rather innocuous. For "phenomenology of the inapparent" could mean "phenomenology of what is *initially and for the most part* inapparent." In this sense, the phenomenology of *Sein und Zeit* is already a "phenomenology of the inapparent," since there we are told that the proper phenomenon of phenomenology is "what at first and for the most part [*zunächst und zumeist*] precisely does *not* show itself [*sich nicht zeigt*]" (*Sein und Zeit*, 35). Here there is no paradox, since making manifest what is *initially and for the most part* hidden is not only a possible task of phenomenology, but apparently the only meaningful one.[9] If this is all Heidegger means by the phrase "phenomenology of the inapparent" in the 1973 seminar as well as, implicitly, in the 1962 lecture, then we are faced again with the critical questions raised above: how can being as *Ereignis* possibly be made "apparent" or brought into view? Given that it is not at all a being, nor in 1962 even a meaning that can be the object of interpretation, how can being as *Ereignis* be thought and said phenomenologically?

But there is obviously another possible interpretation of Heidegger's 1973 phrase: it could mean the phenomenology of what is *never* apparent, of what is *always unscheinbar*. This is the interpretation suggested by the admission

---

8. "Die Phänomenologie ist eine Phänomenologie des Unscheinbaren" (VS, 137).

9. Gérard Guest's paper "Aux confins de l'inapparent (L'extreme phénoménólogie de Heidegger)," in *Phénoménologie: Un siècle de philosophie*, ed. Pascal Dupond and Laurent Cournarie (Paris: Ellipses, 2002), 99–127, which has the merit of drawing to our attention the importance of the notion of a "phenomenology of the inapparent," suffers from a failure to distinguish clearly between the two possible interpretations of this phrase I distinguish here. Instead, his discussion tends to lean toward the first interpretation, on which the phrase is nowhere near as "paradoxical" or "extreme" as he claims. See, for example, 107–8, and the claim at 112: "Car l'*'inapparent' apparaît* ici ne devoir être autre que le mode extrême du '*phénomène*' par excellence: à savoir cela même '*qui dans son inapparaître rend possible à ce qui apparaît d'y paraître*'" (112). There is no reason why being, which initially does not itself appear in making beings appear, cannot itself eventually be made to appear: this, after all, appears to be the goal of the phenomenology of *Being and Time*. See also Guest's reference to "le 'fait' extrême et singulier, et de prime abord [my emphasis] '*inappairaissant*'" (125). In short, he appears often to give "the inapparent" the weak interpretation of "the initially inapparent" while making claims about the paradoxical character of Heidegger's phrase that appear to require a stronger interpretation.

that being as *Ereignis* disappears as soon as it is brought into view. But on this interpretation, the phrase is not only a paradox, but an excruciating one. How can a phenomenology of what is *never* a phenomenon avoid self-destructing? Or if a "phenomenology of the inapparent" in this sense is viable at all, must it not be in the form of dialectic? In this case, the "phenomenology of the inapparent" would be a continually self-deconstructing attempt to bring into view what can never be brought into view but where the always inapparent could nevertheless be indicated in the very process of self-deconstruction. The "phenomenology of the inapparent" would be a contradiction, but a productive one in which the very tension generated by the contradiction could indirectly point to what is never available for a direct seeing or saying.

This dialectical "phenomenology of the inapparent" certainly best describes what has been seen to be Heidegger's *practice* in the lecture "Zeit und Sein." But it has also been seen that Heidegger would reject this description. What he appears to defend "in theory" is the first sense of "phenomenology of the inapparent," according to which it is the bringing into view of what is only initially and for the most part inapparent. Perhaps the key conviction here is what Heidegger in the 1973 seminar claims to have learned from Husserl's notion of categorial intuition (*Vier Seminare*, 116), that being can be *given* and thereby directly and "intuitively" accessed despite whatever might initially cover it up; the conviction, in other words, that being is given in such a way that it can be brought into view once the interpretations that initially conceal it have been "destroyed."[10] Yet a phenomenology in this sense not only does not seem to describe Heidegger's practice, but also seems indefensible, especially if, as Heidegger suggests, its only possible defense is success in practice. It may be that Heidegger leaves the phrase "phenomenology of the inapparent" ambiguous precisely in order to be able to practice dialectic while insisting on and aspiring to something else which this very practice undermines. In any case, no other conclusion to this analysis seems possible than the critique expressed with beautiful clarity and succinctness by Merleau-Ponty: Heidegger "seeks out a direct expression of being while showing on the other hand that it does not admit of direct expression."[11]

B. THE *AUSEINANDERSETZUNG* WITH PLATO

What does the above critique have to do with Heidegger's interpretation of Plato? To the extent that it is a critique of Heidegger's dismissal of dialectic,

---

10. See Guest, "Aux confins de l'inapparent," 109–11.

11. Heidegger "cherche une expression directe de l'être dont il montre par ailleurs qu'il n'est pas susceptible d'expression direct." *Notes de cours, 1959–1961* (Paris: Gallimard, 1996), 148.

it must of course stand in some relation to the ancient philosopher for whom philosophy was nothing more nor less than dialectic. As earlier chapters have already shown, the critique of dialectic indeed plays a central role in Heidegger's opposition to Plato, from the 1924–25 course on the *Sophist* to the 1973 seminar in Zähringen. But what gives the lecture and seminar on "Zeit und Sein" special significance in this history is that here the other differences by which Heidegger earlier tries to distance himself from Plato appear to be either abandoned or greatly minimized, with the result that the disagreement regarding the dialectical character of philosophy appears to remain as the only fundamental difference. Specifically, Heidegger here retracts his earlier view that Plato interpreted the relation between being and beings from the perspective of ποίησις and thus understood being as being-produced (*Hergestelltsein*). That Plato instead used the metaphor of light to characterize the relation between being and beings is explicitly acknowledged to bring Plato into a certain kinship with Heidegger. Another related change is Heidegger's characterization of being as *Anwesen*, a change that at least greatly qualifies his earlier critique of Plato for identifying being with *Anwesenheit*, especially since Heidegger no longer appears to see the Greeks as identifying *Anwesenheit* with some static and purely present presence. In short, Heidegger here appears to grant a greater kinship between himself and Plato than he does anywhere else. This makes the one critique he makes of Plato here all the more telling. This critique, which is directed against the *Phaedo*, will be seen to concern not the identification of being with *Anwesenheit*, but rather the approach to thinking this identification. The difference in approach here will turn out to be precisely a difference between phenomenology and dialectic, or, in the words of the *Phaedo*, between looking directly at the eclipsed sun and taking refuge in λόγοι. In bringing Heidegger and Plato into the closest proximity, "Zeit und Sein"—both the lecture in which this relation is implicit and the seminar in which it is made an explicit issue—reveals with special sharpness the fundamental difference that divides them, a difference that concerns nothing less than the question "What is philosophy?"

1. A New Kinship with Plato

What needs to be considered first is the evidence for a new kinship between Heidegger and Plato. As already noted, the question regarding the relation between being and ποίησις reveals one dimension of this kinship. At one point in the seminar Aristotle is said to have interpreted the being of beings, that is, the coming to presence of what presences (*Anwesen des Anwesenden*), as ποίησις (49). This interpretation of being as *pro-duction* is then said to lead in a direct line to the interpretation of beings as *created* by a supreme being and subsequently to the interpretation of beings as *posited* by a transcendental consciousness. This movement from presencing (*Anwesen*) as production to presencing as creation to presencing as position is in outline the history of the whole of metaphysics. As chapter 2 showed, Heidegger's view that the Greeks interpreted being in terms of production goes back a long way, even antedating his "turn" to a meditation on the history of being. A basic thesis running through the 1924 course on Aristotle's basic concepts, for example, is that the Greeks understood being as *Hergestelltsein* (GA 18, 214, 272, 355, 381). In the course on Plato's *Sophist* from 1924–25, Heidegger stressed the "fundamental connection [*Zusammenhang*] between the meaning of οὐσία and that of ποίησις" (GA 19, 271), concluding that for the Greeks, "being means being-pro-duced [*Sein heißt also Her-gestelltsein*]" (270). Of course, since Heidegger in these passages speaks of the Greeks in general and in the one case bases his thesis on a Platonic dialogue, he is there speaking not only of Aristotle's conception of being, but also of Plato's. That Heidegger does not exclude Plato from this supposedly Greek interpretation of being is most glaringly evident in his bizarre interpretation, discussed in chapter 1, of Plato's "idea of the good" in the 1927 *Basic Problems of Phenomenology* course. On the basis of Plato's description of the idea of the good as the cause not only of knowledge but also of being, Heidegger concludes that the idea of the good is the *producer* of beings: "The ἰδέα ἀγαθοῦ is nothing other than the δημιουργός, the producer [*Hersteller*] and nothing more [*schlechthin*]" (GA 24, 405). This initially baffling interpretation of course makes perfect sense under the assumption that the Greeks understood being as production. Finally, in the *Beiträge* Heidegger, after describing how "the θέσει ὄν and ποιούμενον" become "what now provides thinking interpretation with the comprehensible [*das Verständliche*] and determines even the comprehensibility [*Verständlichkeit*] of beingness," adds the following: "Therefore, τέχνη as the fundamental character of knowledge, i.e., of the fundamental relation to beings as such, stands in the background *and already with Plato is especially pushing itself into the foreground [alsbald bei Plato besonders sich vordrängend]*" (GA 65, 184; my emphasis). Later in the same text Heidegger argues that, while the interpretation of the relation between being and beings in terms of causality (*Ursachemäßige*) and the transcendental condition cannot be read into the Greeks, it is nevertheless "anticipated [*vorgezeichnet*] and demanded [*gefordert*]" by the Greek interpretation of being insofar as "beingness [*Seiendheit*] (ἰδέα) is the genuinely produced [*Hergestellte*] (ποιούμενον) and *therefore* that which constitutes and makes beings [*das Seiende Aus-machende und Machende*]" (478). Thus, if in Heidegger's view at this time the interpretation of our relation to beings in terms of τέχνη is especially predominant in Plato, that is because Plato in interpreting being as ἰδέα is interpreting being from the perspective of production.

This background makes what happens in the "Zeit und Sein" seminar all the more striking. After Aristotle is said to have interpreted being as ποίησις, and after the central role which this interpretation has played in the history of metaphysics is briefly indicated, Plato is explicitly excluded from this interpretation. "In contrast, it was established [wurde geltend gemacht] that, although in his late works—especially in the *Laws*—the productive character of νοῦς already comes increasingly to the forefront, the defining relation between presencing [*Anwesen*] and what presences [*Anwesendem*] is in Plato not understood as ποίησις" (49). This claim must be seen as representing a major revision to Heidegger's account of the history of metaphysics in earlier texts. If the interpretation of being in terms of ποίησις plays a central role in the metaphysics that culminates in modern technology, then this metaphysics can no longer be called "Platonism," but must instead, if it is to be labeled with the name of any philosopher, be called "Aristotelianism."

But what is the support offered for this shift in the interpretation of Plato? We are told that when Plato uses the dative to express the relation between beautiful things and Beauty itself, that is, when he says that beautiful things are beautiful *by* or *with* the beautiful, the being-with or being-by expressed here cannot be identified with any kind of ποίησις. Beauty itself does not *produce* beautiful things, its relation to them being instead characterized as a "being-with" them: παρουσία. "In τῷ καλῷ τὰ καλὰ καλά [by the beautiful the beautiful beautiful] only παρουσία, the being-with of the καλόν with the καλά, is expressed, without it being the case that this being-with is given the meaning of the productive [*des Poietischen*] with regard to what presences [*des Anwesenden*]" (49). The text clearly referred to here, though not mentioned by name in the seminar protocol, is Plato's *Phaedo*. In this dialogue Socrates is found adamantly defending the thesis that "all beautiful things are beautiful through/by/with the beautiful [τῷ καλῷ πάντα τὰ καλὰ καλά]. For this seems to me to be the most secure response [ἀσφαλέστατον] I can give either to myself or another; I do not think that holding on to this I could ever fail [πεσεῖν], but it is safe [ἀσφαλές] for me and for anyone else to respond that beautiful things become beautiful through/by/with the beautiful" (100d7–e3). Here Socrates not only does not characterize the relation in terms of ποίησις, but also is unwilling to let go of his thesis in favor of *any* other because it is the one that appears to him most secure and reliable. Indeed, how could anyone deny that "the beautiful are beautiful by the beautiful" without rendering language itself incoherent? On the other hand, the above translation of the dative τῷ καλῷ as "through/by/with the beautiful" is meant to indicate how ambiguous and indeterminate Socrates' thesis leaves the relation between beauty and what is beautiful. Heidegger will be seen to make precisely this indeterminacy the object of his critique. Before turning to this critique, however, it is first necessary to explore some of the possibilities for a certain kinship between Heidegger and Plato that are opened up by this revision in Heidegger's interpretation of Plato.

Shortly after the passages cited above, we read in the seminar protocol the passing suggestion that a certain closeness to Heidegger ("eine Nähe zu Heidegger") is "without a doubt" ("zweifellos") to be found in the fact that Plato "sought to grasp the relation of presencing to what presences [*den Bezug des Anwesens zum Anwesenden*] in the metaphor of light [*Lichtmetapher*]— that is, not as ποιήσις, making [*Machen*] and so on, but as light" (49). What exactly is the nature of the kinship acknowledged here? The purely negative side of the kinship is evident: neither Plato nor Heidegger interprets the relation between presencing and what presences, being and beings, as production. But there is also the suggestion that the paradigm Plato chooses in the place of ποιήσις, namely, that of *light*, might reveal a more positive kinship with Heidegger. This positive kinship is indeed articulated in the immediately following sentences, the first of which reads: "The letting-come-to-presence [*Anwesenlassen*] thought by Heidegger is, we are told, a *bringing-into-the-open* [*ein ins-Offene-Bringen*]" (49). Is there not a clear affinity between this characterization of being as letting beings come to presence, or bringing them into the open, and Plato's use of the metaphor of light to characterize being, most famously when he compares the good, understood as the source of all being, to the sun (507b–509b)? The good makes beings manifest as beings, thereby at the same time letting them *be*. The good is the cause of the being-known of beings and of their being (509b). In other words, it provides the *light* of ἀλήθεια in which they can first come into presence and *be*.[12] This metaphor of light or *Licht* can literally be heard in the following sentences from Heidegger's lecture: "Time-space [*Zeit-Raum*] now names the open (*das Offene*) that lights/clears [*lichtet*] itself in the reaching-out-to-each-other [*Einander-sich-reichen*] of arriving [*Ankunft*], have-been [*Gewesenheit*] and presence [*Gegenwart*]" (14–15); this "lighting/clearing reaching-out-to-each-other" [*lichtende Einander-sich-reichen*] brings about the lighting/clearing of the opening [*die Lichtung des Offenen*]" (15).

Corresponding to the metaphor of *Licht*, which, in however transformed a shape, enters into Heidegger's description here, Heidegger also throughout the lecture uses, as has already been noted, the metaphor of seeing to describe

---

12. In his interpretation of the Sun Analogy and the Cave Analogy in the 1926 course *Die Grundbegriffe der antiken Philosophie*, Heidegger equates the metaphor of light with *Seinsverständnis*: "Seinsverständnis. Das Licht muß leuchten, obzwar nicht notwendig ist, daß das Licht selbst schon gesehen oder auch nur darum gewußt wird.... Licht ist da, Dasein lebt im Seinsverständnis, ohne daß es darum weiß.... Seinsverständnis: Sehenkönnen des Lichtes, das Seiendes als Seiendes beleuchtet" (GA 22, 103–4).

the thinking that thinks this *Lichtung* in the heart of *Ereignis*.[13] The goal of the lecture, he tells us, is to bring being "as" *Ereignis* "in den Blick" (22). But especially revealing in this context is the following sentence near the end of the lecture: "Indeed, what 'Ereignis' says has now become visible [*erblickbar*] in a look through [*Durchblick*] being itself and time itself, in a look into [*Einblick*] the bestowal of being and the reaching out [*Reichen*] of time-space [*Zeit-Raum*]" 24). This use of the metaphor of seeing or vision of course itself echoes Plato's use of the same metaphor to characterize the knowing made possible by the good: just as the sun not only makes things visible but also gives us the power to see, so the light of truth emanating from the good not only makes the forms, or what the being of each thing is, knowable, but also brings about the power to know. The knowledge that depends on the good is the *analogon* to the seeing that depends on the sun (508d). This affinity between Heidegger and Plato is clearly recognized in the seminar protocol when it continues to assert of Heidegger's thinking of *Anwesenlassen* as *ins-Offene-Bringen*: "Here therefore is made explicit [*ausdrücklich*] what is Greek [*das Griechische*], light and shining-forth [*das Licht und das Scheinen*]" (50). In Heidegger's thinking of presencing as bringing-into-the-open, an "open" that itself occurs as a "lighting" [*Lichtung*], something genuinely Greek, and one can say especially Platonic, comes to expression. Like Plato, Heidegger does not think the unconcealment (*Entbergen*) that characterizes being or letting-come-to-presence according to the model of production or ποιήσις, but rather according to the image of "light" and "manifestness." The recognition of such an affinity represents a significant revision when contrasted with Heidegger's attempt in the 1931 course *On the Essence of Truth*, as discussed in chapter 3, to reduce "light" in Plato's analogies to the work and effect of the forms.

Of course, to speak of affinity here is not to speak of identity or even similarity. Though the word *Licht* can certainly be heard in Heidegger's words *lichten* and *Lichtung*, Heidegger does not understand these words primarily in terms of light. Instead, he emphasizes the image of a clearing or opening in a wood. Even the English words *light* and *clear*, though often referring to visibility, can have this other sense, as when we say an area is "lightly" populated

13. Therefore, Alain Boutot appears unjustified in making the following contrast between Plato and Heidegger: "En récusant cette conception traditionnelle de l'être comme présence constante, et en pensant l'être comme '*das Ereignis*,' comme le 'Il y a,' comme l'avènement de la présence elle-même, Heidegger récuse du même coup l'interprétation traditionnelle de la pensée et de la connaissance comme vision ou contemplation. Avant la vue de l'être, il y a en effet l'écoute et l'attention portée à la venue et à l'avènement de l'être lui-même." *Heidegger et Platon: Le problème du nihilisme* (Paris: Presses universitaires de France, 1987), 124. In addition to the passages cited in the text, one can also cite the following, which shows that Heidegger does not give hearing priority over seeing: "Sobald wir die Sache *vor den Augen* [my emphasis] und im Herzen das Gehör auf das Wort haben, glückt das Denken" (ED, 9).

or that a path is "clear." It is precisely this sense of openness and clearing that Heidegger wants us to hear in the word *Lichtung*.[14] Of course, since it is precisely in a clearing or opening that something can become visible, it is not entirely wrong to hear *light* in *Lichtung*.[15] What Heidegger insists on in the essay "The End of Philosophy and the Task of Thinking" is that *Lichtung* be understood as something prior to light. Thus, he writes: "No look [*Aussehen*] without light—this Plato already knew. But there can be no light and no clarity [*Helle*] without the clearing [*die Lichtung*]. Even darkness [*das Dunkel*] requires it. . . . Nevertheless, the clearing [*Lichtung*] holding forth [*waltende*] in being, in presence [*Anwesenheit*], remains unthought as such in philosophy" ("Ende der Philosophie," 74). Thus, with the word *Lichtung* Heidegger is trying to think what the Greeks left unthought in the metaphor of light, what is *presupposed* by this metaphor as that in which it is grounded. *Lichtung* is

14. "Das Ende der Philosophie und die Aufgabe des Denkens," in ZSD, 72.

15. A transition from the Greek *Licht* to Heidegger's *Lichtung* is to be found in the *Vom Wesen der Wahrheit* course, in both its 1931–32 and 1933–34 versions (GA 34, 59; GA 36/37, 160). In interpreting the metaphor of light in the Cave Analogy, Heidegger observes that "light" is not only *was leuchtet*, but also what frees up, permits passage, *lichtet*. Already here he is using the illustration of *Waldlichtung*. It is the connection between *Licht* and *lichten* that enables Heidegger in these courses to make the connection between *Licht* and freedom. In a section from the slightly later *Besinnung* entitled "Wahrheit als Lichtung," the two meanings of "light" and "clearing"are still thought together: "Lichtung ereignet das Lichte und mahnt an das Licht und sein Leuchten, die Verstrahlung der Helle" (GA 66, 109). See also the following passage from the much later 1953/54 text "Aus einem Gespräch von der Sprache," in which Heidegger explains how his thinking is both Greek and not Greek: "Wenn das Anwesen selbst als Erscheinen gedacht ist, dann waltet im Anwesen das Hervorkommen ins Lichte im Sinne der Unverborgenheit. Diese ereignet sich im Entbergen als einem Lichten. Dieses Lichten selbst bleibt jedoch als Ereignis nach jeder Hinsicht ungedacht. Sich auf das Denken dieses Ungedachten einlassen, heißt: dem griechisch Gedachten usprünglicher nachgehen, es in seiner Wesensherkunft erblicken. Dieser Blick ist auf seine Weise griechisch und ist hinsichtlich des Erblickten doch nicht mehr, nie mehr griechisch" (GA 12, 127). Here the *Lichten* identified with *Ereignis* still appears to preserve a relation to the meaning of "light" and thus its Greek provenance. It is only in even later texts that Heidegger insists on keeping *Licht* and *Lichtung* completely distinct: "Lichtung hat nichts zu tun mit Licht, sondern kommt von 'leicht' . . . Licht setzt Lichtung voraus. Helle kann nur da sein, wo gelichtet worden ist, wo etwas frei ist für das Licht. Das Verdunkeln, das Wegnehmen von Licht, tastet die Lichtung nicht an. Lichtung ist Voraussetzung, daß es hell und dunkel werden kann, das Freie, Offene" (ZS, 16); "Die Anwesenheit des Anwesenden hat als solche keinen Bezug zum Licht im Sinne der Helle. Aber Anwesenheit ist angewiesen auf das Licht im Sinne der Lichtung." "Zur Frage nach der Bestimmung der Sache des Denkens," in GA 16, 629. But the claim that *Lichtung* has nothing to do with, or bears no relation to, the *Licht* that presupposes it appears an overstatement intended to prevent any kind of identification between the two. It is also worth noting that in the *Zollikoner Seminare*, after some discussion of *Lichtung* and *das Offene*, Heidegger indicates the difficulty of understanding what is at issue here by citing both Aristotle and Plato on the difficulty of seeing into the light. Citing Aristotle's claim that "As the eyes of bats are to the light of day [τὸ φέγγος τὸ μεθ'ἡμέραν], so is the vision [νοῦς] of our souls to those things that are by nature most manifest [φανερώτατα] of all" (*Metaph.* 993b9–11), Heidegger comments: "Das ist eben *das Sein*. Das sehen wir am schwersten. Oder Plato sagt: Wenn der Mensch versucht, in das Licht zu sehen, so wird er geblendet" (20). The text Heidegger is referring to in the last sentence is presumably the passage from the *Phaedo* to be discussed below (99d–e). Heidegger concludes this session of the seminar by insisting that we have not even begun to understand the Greeks (20).

therefore not so much a rejection or abandonment of the metaphor of *Licht* as an appropriation of what this metaphor leaves unthought. The word *Lichtung* might have appealed to Heidegger precisely because, while it cannot be identified with light and points to a much more originary dimension, it still preserves in its very sound, unlike *Offenheit*, some link to *Licht*.

Yet the difference between Heidegger and Plato does not appear as great as Heidegger would have us believe in the essay proclaiming the "end of philosophy." Heidegger would have us believe that Plato, with his interpretation of being as εἶδος, remained on the level of what the metaphor of light expresses and did not penetrate to the clearing or opening without which there would be no light. But here it is necessary to repeat a point insisted on in chapter 3, that Plato in the analogy of the sun does not compare the good to light, but rather to the source or principle of light. *Truth (ἀλήθεια) and being are the light* that illuminates the εἴδη (καταλάμπει ἀλήθειά τε καὶ τὸ ὄν, 508d5),[16] in which the εἴδη first become εἴδη, that is, in which they first come to be *manifest* and come *to be*. Yet Plato insists on keeping the good itself distinct from the light of ἀλήθεια and τὸ ὄν: it is the source and origin of this light and thus of the εἴδη, but as such it must be distinct from and beyond this light.[17] Ἀλήθεια is like the good (ἀγαθοειδής), but is not the good (509a1–5); being is not the good, but the good is beyond being (ἐπέκεινα τῆς οὐσίας, 509b9). It is this feature of the analogy that led Heidegger at one point, as noted in chapter 3, to interpret the good as *Dasein*'s transcendence (WG, 158). This interpretation is untenable, but it is untenable for much the same reason that it would be untenable as an interpretation of Heidegger's *Lichtung*: the priority it grants to human-being. On the other hand, equally untenable is Heidegger's later attempt, as documented in chapter 3, to eliminate the good's transcendence altogether by reducing it to an εἶδος and thereby identifying it with what is illuminated or seen. This reading interprets the subordination of ἀλήθεια to the good as its subordination to a "look" for a knower and thus as the degradation of its essence into mere correctness. Against such an interpretation, chapter 3 insisted on what the text makes clear enough: the relation between ἀλήθεια and the good is a relation between, respectively, the light

---

16. See also 508e6 to 509a1, where ἐπιστήμη and ἀλήθεια are made analogous to ὄψις and φῶς.

17. After noting that Levinas appropriates Plato's idea of the good in his own manner when he interprets "le mouvement platonicien" in such a way that "il ne conduit plus au soleil, mais à l'au-delà même de la lumière et de l'être, de la lumière *de* l'être," Derrida suggests in a very important parenthesis that this reading may not in fact be unfaithful to Plato: "(Mais le soleil platonicien, déjà, n'éclairait-t-il pas le soleil visible et l'ex-cedance ne se jouait-elle pas dans la méta-phore de ces deux soleils? Le Bien n'était-il pas la source—nécessairement nocturne—de toute lumière? Lumière (au-delà) de la lumière. Le cœur de la lumière est noir, on l'a souvent remarqué. Puis le soleil de Platon n'éclaire pas seulement: il engendre. Le bien est le père du soleil visible qui donne aux êtres la 'génèse, l'accroissement et la nourriture,' *République*, 508a–509b)." "Violence et métaphysique," in *L'écriture et la différence* (Paris: Éditions du Seuil, 1967), 127–28.

that illuminates the εἴδη (unconcealment!), on the one hand, and that which enables this light or unconcealment, on the other; it is therefore a complete distortion to interpret the relation as one between, respectively, correctness and some visible "look" under which this correctness is "yoked."[18] Might it not therefore be the case that it is precisely with the notion of *Lichtung*, in its double reference to light and to the opening in which and through which light is first possible, that Heidegger finally has a "metaphor" that enables him to do justice to and express what Plato is trying to express in the idea of the good? Instead of further distancing him from Plato, the metaphor of *Lichtung* might open up the space in which a greater affinity with Plato can play itself out.[19]

If Heidegger resists exploring this affinity, it is because, as should be overwhelmingly evident by now, he never stops seeing in Plato's interpretation of being as εἶδος an identification of being with what is seen, with what shows itself to a seeing. Such an identification clearly reduces being to *what is*, to a being, and blocks any thinking of being as the opening or clearing within which something first comes into appearance. Thus, in "The End of Philosophy and the Task of Thinking," Heidegger writes: "The fundamental word of [Plato's] thinking, that is, of the presentation [*Darstellung*] of the being of beings, reads [*lautet*] εἶδος, ἰδέα: the look [*das Aussehen*] within which beings show themselves as such" (74). To identify being with "the look" of a being is both to occlude that which first enables such a look to arise and to initiate the forgetting of the difference between being and beings. Yet it has already been shown in chapter 3 how the idea of the good resists such an interpretation of Plato: the good may be an ἰδέα (517c1, 534c1) as something that can be known, but rather than being merely the look or appearance of a being, it is that which first *grants* and enables such a look or appearance; if it can itself in some sense be known or "seen," then only barely (μόγις ὁρᾶσθαι, 517c1), since it is itself neither knowing nor being known, but rather that which grants knowing and of being known. Since it also and simultaneously grants the *being* of knowing and what is known, Socrates can, as noted above, describe it as not only beyond the light of truth, but even beyond *being* "in dignity and power" (ἐπέκεινα τῆς

---

18. "Die ἀλήθεια kommt unter das Joch der ἰδέα" (PLW, 228).

19. Speaking of Heidegger's retraction of his interpretation of Plato's ἐπέκεινα as transcendence, Jean-François Courtine has asked the right question, namely, "si la nécessité où se trouve Heidegger de renoncer à identifier, en raison d'une autre détermination de l'être-là, la transcendance de l'être-là et l'ἐπέκεινα de l'ἀγαθόν, la vérité transcendantale et l'ἀλήθεια de l'allégorie de la Caverne, le conduit fatalement à mettre en évidence un virage, une mutation platonicienne dans l'essence grecque de la vérité, ou bien si au contraire la pensée de Platon, et singulièrement cette 'allégorie,' n'aurait pas pu, à meilleur droit que pour l'ontologie fondamentale, donner lieu à un nouvel investissement ou surinvestissement, à une autre lecture 'généreuse' de la pensée de Platon, en direction peut-être de la *Lichtung* ou du 'il y a' (*es gibt*)." *Heidegger et la phénoménologie* (Paris: Vrin, 1990), 150. Courtine, however, does not see that the text "Zeit und Sein" opens up, though without pursuing, precisely the possibility of such a "generous" reading.

οὐσίας πρεσβείᾳ καὶ δυνάμει, 509b9–10). The good is beyond being and truth because it is what *enables* both. So if there is some kind of identification here of being with εἶδος, in the sense of the "look" or "appearance" of beings, it is only with the qualification that being as thus interpreted is not ultimate or originary, but derives from a source or origin beyond it. That the word ἰδέα is used to designate this "good" beyond truth and being also suggests that the words εἶδος and ἰδέα are much more flexible and ambiguous in meaning than Heidegger's insistence on translating them as *Aussehen* would allow. Furthermore, Heidegger's claim that εἶδος and ἰδέα are the fundamental words of Plato's thinking must at the very least be qualified by the observation that these are not the only words Plato uses to designate being, nor even the words used most often, and that the other words he uses make absolutely no reference to seeing or visibility: for example, αὐτὸ τό . . . , αὐτό, τὸ καθ'αὑτό, ὅ ἔστι, ὡς ἔστι, τὸ ἀληθῶς ὄν, τὸ ὄντως ὄν, and even simply τὸ ὄν. How central can the interpretation of being as *Aussehen* be in Plato's thinking when he uses the words εἶδος and ἰδέα interchangeably with other words or expressions that do not at all convey the sense of *Aussehen* and when he attempts to think in the ἰδέα of the good that which first grants εἴδη their intelligibility and being?[20]

Here we can return to the seminar on "Zeit und Sein" because what is said there itself renders untenable the restriction of Plato's conception of being to εἶδος interpreted as *Aussehen*. At one point in the seminar, shortly after the passage on Plato discussed above, an important distinction ("wichtiger Unterschied") is made between the disclosing (*Entbergen*) that belongs to ποίησις and the disclosing meant by Heidegger himself. The distinction is explained thus: "While the first refers itself to εἶδος—for this is what is brought out [*herausgestellt*], disclosed [*entborgen*] in ποίησις—the disclosing thought by Heidegger refers itself to the whole of beings [*das ganze Seiende*]" (50). This connection between εἶδος and ποίησις is a central focus in the *Basic Problems of Phenomenology* course (GA 24, 149–58), where Heidegger argues at length that in producing something I am guided by what the thing is to "look like," by an anticipated awareness of the "look" of what is to be produced. The being of a thing disclosed in production is thus being in the sense of "look" (εἶδος). Therefore, in interpreting disclosing (*Enbergen*) and letting-come-to-presence (*Anwesenlassen*) as ποίησις, I restrict this disclosing and coming-to-presence to the look (*Aussehen*) of a thing. Heidegger can accordingly argue in the *Basic Problems of Phenomenology* course that it was the orientation toward productive comportment that led the Greeks to understand being as εἶδος.

---

20. Thus, what must be questioned is precisely the following assertion: "Nicht daß überhaupt die φύσις als ἰδέα gekennzeichnet wurde, sondern daß die ἰδέα als *die einzige und maßgebende Auslegung des Seins* [my emphasis] aufkommt, bleibt das Entscheidende" (EM, 139). A detailed argument against Heidegger's reduction of the Platonic εἶδος to "what is seen" has been pursued in previous chapters.

This thesis is also stated with particular clarity in the 1937–38 *Grundfragen der Philosophie* course: "As the grasping [*Fassen*] of beings, the recognition of them in their unconcealment, develops into τέχνη, the looks [*Anblicke*] of beings that are brought into view [*in den Blick*] in such grasping, the 'ideas,' become inevitably more and more what alone is decisive [*allein Maßgebenden*]" (GA 45, 180–81). Heidegger in his course even holds the perspective of τέχνη responsible for the transformation of truth into correctness: "The grasping [*Fassen*] becomes a being acquainted with [*Sichauskennen in*] the ideas, and that demands the constant approximation [*Angleichung*] to these ideas.... Now even ἀλήθεια is inquired into, but now from the perspective of τέχνη, so that ἀλήθεια is transformed into *correctness* [*Richtigkeit*] of representing and proceeding [*des Vorstellens und Vorgehens*]" (181). In short, the perspective of ποίησις grants predominance to the εἶδος, and this predominance in turn leads to the transformation of truth into what corresponds to the εἶδος, that is, into correctness in seeing and representing.

In contrast, Heidegger does not restrict disclosing to the εἶδος or "look" but rather refers it to all that is. Specifically, what is disclosed in the presencing (*Anwesen*) thought by Heidegger is not only *what* a being is (its εἶδος and essence) but also *that* it is (its "existence"); more accurately, the kind of disclosing thought by Heidegger precedes the distinction between essence and existence, while ποίησις is confined to such a distinction as one between the abiding εἶδος to which the producer "looks" and its particular and contingent realization in the product. Furthermore, because this disclosing discloses more than a "look" to which our seeing can correspond, it does not reduce truth to any kind of correctness but allows it to be thought as the unconcealment within which a look can first appear.

Earlier Heidegger would have found in this distinction between two kinds of *Entbergen* a way of sharply and clearly distancing himself from Plato. But now this is no longer possible. Since in the seminar of "Zeit und Sein," in contrast to the *Basic Problems of Phenomenology* and the *Grundfragen der Philosophie* courses, Plato is said not to have ποίησις as his model in interpreting the relation between *Anwesen* and *Anwesendes*, any justification for confining his interpretation of being to εἶδος in the sense of the "look" of a being is eliminated. Given the distinction between the disclosing that belongs to ποίησις and the disclosing thought by Heidegger, Plato must be placed on Heidegger's side of the distinction. This affinity between Plato and Heidegger, though implicitly acknowledged here, is not explored. Such an exploration would necessarily have led Heidegger either to see in Plato a conception of being that goes beyond εἶδος or to give Plato's εἶδος a much richer sense than that of *Aussehen* or look.

An ideal text for such an exploration would have been the discussion of εἶδος and ἰδέα in book 10 of Plato's *Republic*. The relation to being and truth Socrates initially describes there is the following: the carpenter in producing a bed looks to its ἰδέα (πρὸς τὴν ἰδέαν βλέπων, 596b7) and copies it in the particular bed he is producing; the artist who produces a painting of the bed in contrast does not look to the ἰδέα at all but only at the particular bed which he copies (598a1–4), thus producing only a copy of a copy. The artist accordingly has no knowledge (598d45, 599a2, 601b10) and is three times removed from being, here identified with φύσις (597e3–4), and truth (ἀλήθεια, 597e7). This account clearly remains entirely within the paradigm of ποίησις. Yet it is therefore all the more significant that Socrates a little later in the discussion (601c–602b) alters his model to the extent of now denying even the producer *knowledge*, insisting instead that he has nothing but "true belief" (601e7, 602a4–5). But then who possesses knowledge of the εἶδος? According to Socrates, not the person who produces the bed, but the person who *uses* it (ὁ δὲ χρώμενος [ἕξει] ἐπιστήμην, 602a1). It is in *use* and not in *production* that the εἶδος, which is also the good, beauty, and correctness of each thing (601d4–5), is known.

I suggest that in this revision of the production model, in this prioritizing of use over production as the model for our relation to truth and being,[21] we see emerge a sense of εἶδος that transcends the sense to which Heidegger normally confines it. The εἶδος to which the producer "looks" in making the bed is what Heidegger would call the bed's *Aussehen*, where this means not only its sensible appearance, but also its intelligible form, the structure that all beds share no matter how different they might appear to the senses. But according to Socrates, this relation to the εἶδος as to a sensible and intelligible "look" is a superficial one that merits no other name than δόξα. But how else can the εἶδος disclose itself? What is the difference between how it discloses itself to the producer and how it discloses itself to the user? In actually using the bed, the user experiences the εἶδος not as a "look," whether sensible or intelligible, but rather as a function, ability, or power. The εἶδος of a bed that I can know only in using it is the bed's ability to provide me with a good night's sleep or its ability to support my body comfortably when in an inclined position. This εἶδος I know in using a bed is thus not only *what* it is but also *how* it

---

21. The priority of the user's art to the producer's art is asserted not only in book 10 of the *Republic*, but also in the *Cratylus* 390b–d and the *Euthydemus* 290b–d. These last two texts make especially clear the central importance of the user's art in Plato as a model for philosophical knowledge by characterizing dialectic and the political art, respectively, as forms of this user's art. For discussion of these texts and of the model of use in Plato, see my *Dialectic and Dialogue: Plato's Practice of Philosophical Inquiry* (Evanston: Northwestern University Press, 1998), 67–68, 87–89, 94, 100–101, 114–15, 140–42, 144, 218.

is, not only some abstract and universal "form" common to all beds, but also how this particular bed *performs* and *acts*. In other words, use, unlike production, makes no sharp distinction between essence and existence, so that the εἶδος known in use cannot be put on one side of this distinction. That Socrates should claim that the εἶδος is *known* only in use suggests that what the εἶδος truly is is the function or power that manifests itself in use; εἶδος might etymologically mean "look," and this might be how it appears to the producer, but such an understanding of εἶδος is nothing but opinion or δόξα. And that this conception of εἶδος as power is not confined to book 10 of the *Republic* should be evident by this point; earlier chapters, especially chapter 2, have shown the central role δύναμις plays in Plato's conception of being and of the good.

This notion of εἶδος is one that can also be found in Aristotle, most clearly, for example, when he claims that a dead man, though having the "look" and "shape" of a man, is not a man and thus does not genuinely have the εἶδος of a man:[22] a dead man has the "look" of a man, not only in the sense of having the physical appearance of a man but also in the sense of having the defining structure of a man; however, it lacks the εἶδος of a man because it does not have the function or ability of a man. Yet what needs to be stressed here is the importance of finding in Plato an understanding of εἶδος that transcends the model of ποίησις and that introduces a sense of disclosing not confined to the "look" of beings. When Heidegger finally disassociates Plato from the model of ποίησις in the seminar on "Zeit und Sein," the way is opened, though not taken, toward this richer conception of εἶδος and the possibility it offers of a new affinity with Heidegger's thought.

The final indication to be considered here of an increased affinity between Heidegger and Plato in the period surrounding the event called "Zeit und Sein" concerns precisely their conceptions of being. The principal target of Heidegger's earlier critique of Plato, and of the Greeks in general, was not the identification of being with εἶδος, but the understanding of being presupposed by this identification: being as *presence (Anwesenheit)*.[23] It is because the Greeks understood being as presence that they made εἶδος, as that "look" in which beings present themselves, the fundamental word in the determination of being.[24] While Heidegger never claimed that the interpretation of

---

22. Καὶ ὁ τεθνεὼς ἔχει τὴν αὐτὴν τοῦ σχήματι μορφήν, ἀλλ' ὅμως οὐκ ἔστιν ἄνθρωπος (De part. an. A 1, 640 b34ff.). Heidegger in citing this passage in the 1924 course on Aristotle must acknowledge that "zum εἶδος gehört also auch die δύναμις und das ἔργον" (GA 18, 230).

23. "Etwas west an. Es steht in sich und stellt sich so dar. Es ist. 'Sein' besagt im Grunde für die Griechen Anwesenheit" (EM, 46).

24. "Das Wort ἰδέα meint das Gesichtete am Sichtbaren, den Anblick, den etwas darbietet. Was dargeboten wird, ist das jeweilige Aussehen, εἶδος dessen, was begegnet. Das Aussehen eines Dinges ist das, worin es sich uns, wie wir sagen, präsentiert, sich vor-stellt und als solches vor uns steht, worin und als was es an-west, d. h. im griechischen Sinne *ist*.... Im Aussehen steht das Anwesende, das

being as *Anwesenheit* was "incorrect," he did see it as blocking any genuine reflection on the meaning of being. Specifically, while the word *Anwesenheit* clearly expressed both being and time in their unity, it also stood in the way of thinking this unity by reducing being to only one dimension of time, the present, and then interpreting time itself from the perspective of this interpretation of being as presence-at-hand: it is thus that time comes to be understood as something present-at-hand made up of present-at-hand moments following each other in succession.[25] Yet Heidegger in his later thought, and most clearly in the lecture "Zeit und Sein", himself appropriates the identification of being with *Anwesenheit* that he earlier attributed to the Greeks. Thus, in the lecture we read: "being means: presencing [*Anwesen*], letting-come-to-presence [*Anwesen-lassen*]: presence [*Anwesenheit*]" (10).

Of course, *Anwesen* does not mean for Heidegger the "present" as opposed to past or future; it does not mean *das Jetzt* or *die Gegenwart*. Thus, Heidegger at one point observes: "Not every presence [*Anwesen*] is necessarily the present [*Gegenwart*], a most strange matter [*eine seltsame Sache*]" (14). In other words, not just the present, but also the past and the future *anwesen*. It is impossible to translate *anwesen* here because its meaning is precisely what is at issue. If even the past and the future can *anwesen*, then clearly *Anwesen* cannot mean coming-to-be-now-present-at-hand (*vorhanden*). But then can we not easily distinguish Heidegger's identification of being with *Anwesenheit* from the apparently similar identification by the Greeks by saying that while the Greeks understood *Anwesenheit* as the being-at-hand [*Vorhandenheit*] and constancy [*Beständigkeit*] of a self-same "now," Heidegger has a much richer conception of *Anwesenheit* expressed precisely in the title "Zeit und Sein"?

That a conception of being as static presence cannot be attributed to the Plato who wrote the *Sophist* has been shown in chapter 2; and I have elsewhere challenged the attribution of such a conception to Aristotle.[26] What stands in the way of such an attribution in both cases is the central importance both Greek philosophers accorded the notions of *dunamis* and/or *energeia*. But in "Zeit und Sein" Heidegger himself appears to retreat from the view that the Greeks identified being with static presence. With reference to Parmenides' saying ἔστι γὰρ εἶναι, Heidegger maintains that while the word ἔστι could be translated simply as "it is," we should hear in the emphasis (*Betonung*) the word receives in Parmenides' saying "what the Greeks at the time [*damals*]

Seiende, in seinem Was und Wie an. Es ist ver-nommen und genommen, ist im Besitz eines Hinnehmens, ist dessen Habe, ist verfügbares Anwesen von Anwesendem: οὐσία. So kann denn οὐσία beides bedeuten: Anwesen eines Anwesenden *und* dies Anwesende im Was seines Aussehens" (EM, 138).

25. See ibid., 157.
26. See my "Whose Metaphysics of Presence? Heidegger's Interpretation of *Dunamis* and *Energeia* in Aristotle," *Southern Journal of Philosophy* 44, no. 4 (2006): 533–68.

already thought [*dachten*] in the emphasized ἔστι and what we can parphrase with 'it is capable' [*Es vermag*]" (8). Earlier Heidegger would have claimed that the Greeks understood in the ἔστι, whether emphasized or not, something like "is present-at-hand [*vorhanden*]."[27] Now, however, he appears to grant the Greeks a very different understanding of being: not being as *Vorhandenheit* but being as *Vermögen*, as capability or power. Furthermore, he proceeds to identify this understanding of being with his own attempt to think the *Es gibt*, the "it gives" of being: "To be capable of being [*Sein vermögen*] means: the eventuating and giving of being [*Sein ergeben und geben*]. In the ἔστι is hidden the *Es gibt*" (8). If, therefore, the Greeks thought "capability" in the word ἔστι, then their understanding of *Anwesen*, far from reducing it to some static and enduring present, was not so far from the presencing, giving and "eventing" that Heidegger thinks in *Anwesen*.

Yet as soon as this affinity emerges, Heidegger is quick to point to what is lacking in the Greeks: "At the same time the meaning of this being-capable [*Vermögen*] remained, both at the time and later, just as unthought [*ungedacht*] as the 'it' ['*Es*'] that is capable of being [*das Sein vermag*]" (8). Thus, according to Heidegger, even if the Greeks thought "is capable" in the emphasized ἔστι, they gave no thought to the meaning of capability as such, nor therefore to the meaning of being as such. Yet Heidegger here appears to forget that at least one Greek philosopher made the interpretation of being as capability explicit and to this extent at least *thought* it. This is the same philosopher who has been seen to claim that the good surpasses being *in capability* (δυνάμει), a claim that implies an understanding of both being and the good in terms of capability. What is implied here is made explicit by Plato in a text that, as we saw in chapter 2, Heidegger commented on almost forty years prior to giving the lecture "Zeit und Sein": the *Sophist*, 247d8-e4. There we read: "I say that whatever has any kind of natural [πεφυκὸς] capability [δύναμις] either to do [ποεῖν] something towards anything else or to suffer [παθεῖν] even the smallest affection from the most insignificant thing, and even if only once, every such thing really is [ὄντως εἶναι]. I therefore establish this demarcation: that beings [τὰ ὄντα] are nothing other than capability [δύναμις]." This is as clear a statement as one could desire that the word ἔστι in the most emphatic sense means *es vermag* and that being in the most emphatic sense (ὄντως εἶναι) means *Vermögen*. Furthermore, this characterization of being is in the *Sophist* explicitly offered as a challenge to an understanding of being as εἶδος in the narrow sense of static, immobile presence: an understanding attributed to "friends of the forms" (τῶν εἰδῶν φίλοι, 248a4-5) and quickly refuted. These "friends

---

27. In the 1926 course *Die Grundbegriffe der antiken Philosophie*, Heidegger finds in Parmenides only a conception of being as "constant presence" ("ständige Anwesenheit") (GA 22, 67–68).

of the forms" insist that δύναμις, whether that of doing or suffering, does not accord with [ἁρμόττειν] οὐσία (248b8–9). They are quickly refuted by being shown that in speaking of knowing the forms they are themselves introducing δύναμις into being, both in the sense of the capability of doing (knowing) and in the sense of the capability of being affected (being-known).[28]

Finally, the observations made above show that the characterization of being as δύναμις is not an anomaly in Plato; in other words, that Plato is not outside of the *Sophist* himself a "friend of the forms," where "friends of the forms" are precisely those so enamored of stable and static "looks" as to be incapable of getting beyond them in their understanding of being. If in the *Republic* Plato can include the good within τὸ ὄν (518c5–d1, 526e5, 532c4–7) despite its being beyond the οὐσία of the forms, this is because, in being *more capable* than the forms, it is, like the forms themselves, capability, and capability is the meaning of τὸ ὄν. That the οὐσία of the good is the δύναμις of the good is made fully explicit in the *Philebus* (64e5).[29] If again in the *Republic* Socrates can claim that a thing's εἶδος is known in its use, this is because what can be known only in using a thing is precisely its δύναμις. In case it is thought that this understanding of οὐσία as δύναμις is confined to Plato's "middle" and "late" dialogues, two other texts are worth citing: (1) in the *Laches*, the question initially asked in the form "What is courage?" (τί ἐστιν ἀνδρεία, 190e-3) is later formulated, "What kind of capability is it?" (τίς οὖσα δύναμις, 192b6), with no suggestion that the question has changed; (2) in the *Protagoras*, Socrates asks whether the names of the different virtues all refer to one thing or whether each name refers to a thing with its own οὐσία and δύναμις, where the "and" could easily be taken to be explicative (349b4–5). In short, Plato not only thinks *vermag* in ἔστι but explicitly says it and makes it central to the ontological discussions in the dialogues.

In 1924–25, when Heidegger submits Plato's *Sophist* to a very thorough reading, he cannot see in the characterization of being as δύναμις any possible

---

28. Incredibly, Boutot, in defending Heidegger's critique of Plato for identifying being with constant presence, simply ignores the definition of being as δύναμις in the *Sophist*: "La question de l'être reste dans le *Sophiste* à l'état de question" (*Heidegger et Platon*, 39). Furthermore, he simply identifies Plato with the position of the friends of the forms, despite the fact that this position is refuted in the dialogue: "Cette élimination du mot 'être' du langage mobiliste [the argument of this whole part of the dialogue is that κίνησις must be included in being!] trahit, tout comme l'argumentation des 'Amis de formes' dans le *Sophiste* [which is refuted!], la signification véritable de l'être chez Platon: être veut dire au fond pour lui être permanent, être subsistant" (58). When Boutot wrote his book, Heidegger's lecture course on the *Sophist* was not yet published, but Boutot presumably did have the text of the *Sophist* itself.

29. As was already seen in chapter 3, Heidegger himself, in both versions of the *Vom Wesen der Wahrheit* course presented in WS 1931/32 and WS 1933/34, understands the idea of the good as δύναμις (*Ermächtigung, Macht*) and bases this interpretation on Plato's characterization of being itself as δύναμις (GA 34, 110–11; GA 36/37, 200, 203–4).

affinity with his own attempt to think the meaning of being; though he credits the *Sophist* with asking the question "What is being?" and thus cites it on the very first page of *Sein und Zeit*, he cannot see in the notion of δύναμις a provocative though admittedly provisional invoking and opening up of the meaning of being. The reason is that, judging from the results of his interpretation, Heidegger is at this point in time determined to push through his thesis that the Greeks reduced being to presence-at-hand at whatever violence to the text. Heidegger is deaf to whatever in the *Sophist* resists such a reduction and thus to whatever opens up a genuine possibility of thinking being without reducing it to the presence-at-hand that characterizes beings.

Here it is worth repeating and summarizing my critique of the extraordinary sentence from the *Sophist* course in which Heidegger interprets the definition of being at 247d–e. This sentence reads: "being itself then means for Plato, if he wants to make both positions [i.e., that of the gods and giants] understandable: δύναμις, as *the possibility* [*Möglichkeit*] *of co-presence* [*Mit-Anwesenheit*] *with something*, in short, δύναμις κοινωνίας, or in a fuller determination [!]: παρουσία δυνάμεως κοινωνίας, *the being-present* [*Vorhandensein*] *of the possibility of being with one another*" (GA 19, 486). This sentence makes clear how Heidegger's interpretation seeks to reduce the determination of being as δύναμις to a determination of being as presence-at-hand. This interpretation, however, is clearly untenable for the following three reasons:

(1) The characterization of δύναμις at 247d–e as a δύναμις of *doing* and *being affected* shows that it must be interpreted not as "possibility" [*Möglichkeit*], but as a *positive capability* or *power*, indeed, as *Vermögen*. Furthermore, δύναμις is not at 247d–e a capability of merely being present-with, but rather a capability of *acting* and *being-acted* upon.

(2) To the extent that παρουσία is at issue here, its meaning must be that of *being-with* in the sense of κοινωνία and not that of *being-present-at-hand*; in other words, it must mean *Beisein* and not *Vorhandensein*.

(3) The most serious problem, and the one that betrays Heidegger's determination to push through his thesis at whatever violence to the text, is his inversion of the "δύναμις of presence" (or co-presence) into "the presence of δύναμις," under the pretense that the latter is only a "fuller determination" of the former. The two phrases are in fact radically different, and the difference is one between what the text says and what Heidegger needs it to say. The text defines being as δύναμις and thus makes δύναμις prior to any kind of being-present. The text does not define being as being-present and then conclude that δύναμις is a being because it is present. Instead, the text defines being as δύναμις and concludes that anything that is *capable* thereby *is*. In short, being is not the *being-present* of δύναμις, but rather the δύναμις of acting and being-acted-upon or, if one insists, of being-present-with something else.

But Heidegger has already decided that Plato, being a Greek, must understand being as meaning "being-present" and that therefore whatever the text says must be interpreted accordingly. Thus, even if the text defines being as δύναμις and asserts that δύναμις is what makes a being "really be" (ὄντως εἶναι), it must really, or in a "fuller determination," mean the exact opposite: that it is an identification of what "really is" with what "is present-at-hand" that enables δύναμις to be insofar as it is present-at-hand. In short, it is not being as δύναμις that is really meant, but rather δύναμις as being = presence-at-hand. Surely it is not unjustified to claim that in having to resort to such an inversion, Heidegger's thesis about the Greek conception of being completely discredits itself.

The only reason, however, for repeating here this critique of Heidegger's 1924 interpretation of the determination of being in the *Sophist* is to make evident the following: if Heidegger had been asked to interpret this text again during the seminar on "Zeit und Sein," he would have had to offer a completely different interpretation, indeed, one that completely repudiated his earlier reading. This is because none of the moves criticized above can any longer be made in the context of "Zeit und Sein." Against (1), the 1962 lecture credits the Greeks, as we have seen, with an understanding of being as *Vermögen*, that is, power or capability. Against (2), Heidegger in 1962 no longer identifies παρουσία with *Vorhandensein*; in the discussion of παρουσία in Plato examined above, it is explicitly interpreted as meaning "Beisein." Finally, against (3), Heidegger is no longer sufficiently committed to the thesis that the Greeks understood being as presence-at-hand to be able to justify even in his own eyes the arbitrary inversion of the determination of being as δύναμις that he performed in 1924. This means, in sum, that a reading of the *Sophist* in 1962 would have made Heidegger recognize a much greater affinity with Plato than he was able to recognize in 1924: he would have seen Plato explicitly thinking being as *Vermögen* and thus thinking beyond the "look" of beings and the "light" in which this "look" appears and toward what first enables both the "look" and the "light." This again is not to say that such a reading would have made profound differences disappear, but only that it would have revealed an affinity deep and rich enough to enable a genuine and productive *Auseinandersetzung*, an *Auseinandersetzung* that in fact never took place. There is evidence that Heidegger himself recognized this possibility. Recall what he wrote to Hannah Arendt in the letter dated October 10, 1954: "And I would like to go through my Plato works once again, beginning with the 'Sophist' course of 1924/5, and read Plato anew [*neu lesen*]." Heidegger apparently never carried out his intention, perhaps because the undertaking would have been enormous. A rethinking of the *Sophist* course in particular would have required indeed nothing less than a complete rereading of Plato.

2. What Really Separates Heidegger and Plato?

If there is indeed in 1962 a greater affinity between Heidegger and Plato, why does Heidegger not explore this affinity any further? What still opposes him to Plato in such a way as to prevent a genuine dialogue with Plato? In the seminar on "Zeit und Sein," one basic objection to Plato is expressed. After Plato is said to have understood the relation between *Anwesen* and *Anwesendes* not as ποίησις but as παρουσία, he is subjected to the following critique: "Nowhere does [Plato] explicitly work out [*nirgends ist bei ihm ausgearbeitet*] what this genuine παρουσία is, nowhere does he explicitly [*ausdrücklich*] say what παρουσία accomplishes in relation to the ὄντα" (49). Note that the objection is not that Plato thought being in terms of παρουσία:[30] as we have seen, Heidegger no longer appears to equate παρουσία with "constant presence-at-hand" and has come himself to think of being as *Anwesenheit*. The criticism is that while Heidegger aims to think and say precisely this παρουσία/*Anwesenheit*, Plato leaves it unthought and unarticulated. The passage from the *Phaedo* implicitly referred to here and discussed above certainly seems to confirm this criticism. As has already been noted, the dative in the phrase τῷ καλῷ τὰ καλὰ καλά is highly ambiguous: beautiful things are beautiful *with* the beautiful, or *by* the beautiful, or *through* the beautiful? The exact nature of the relation here between beautiful beings and the being of the beautiful is left very indeterminate. And is this not, as Heidegger suggests, a failing? Even if the failing must be imputed to the self-withdrawal of being itself and not to any negligence on Plato's part, is it not still the case that here, at the beginning of metaphysics, something essential is left unthought and unsaid?

But if we turn again to the discussion in the *Phaedo*, we encounter something that must be, from the perspective of Heidegger's critique, highly surprising: not only a confirmation of the failure to think the relation between being and beings—in this case, between being-beautiful and beautiful beings—but *an explicit avowal of this failure*. This is how Socrates, in a passage that immediately precedes the one discussed earlier in this chapter, introduces the notion of παρουσία into his account of the relation between Beauty itself and the many beautiful things:

> I no longer understand nor can I recognize those other clever reasons [αἰτίας τὰς σοφάς]; but if anyone gives me as the reason why a given thing is beautiful either its having a blooming colour, or its shape, or something else like that, I dismiss those other things—because all others confuse

---

30. In contrast, it is precisely Plato's appeal to the notion of παρουσία that is criticized in the *Vom Wesen der menschlichen Freiheit* course of 1930 (GA 31, 65).

me—but in a plain [ἁπλῶς], artless [ἀτέχνως], and possibly simple-minded [εὐήθως] way, I hold this close to myself: nothing else makes it beautiful except that beautiful itself, whether by its presence [παρουσία] or communion [κοινωνία] or whatever the manner and nature of the relation may be; as I don't go so far as to affirm that, but only that it is by the beautiful [τῷ καλῷ] that all beautiful things are beautiful. (100c10–d8; Gallop trans.)

Here Socrates not only refuses to explain the meaning of παρουσία, but will not even commit himself to the word: perhaps the relation between being-beautiful and beautiful beings is better expressed by the word κοινωνία or by some other word. Furthermore, Socrates' refusal here is also Plato's refusal: if we look at Plato's dialogues as a whole, we find the relation between beings and their being expressed with sometimes one of these words, sometimes the other, and sometimes another word not mentioned here, while in no case is the particular word chosen defended or explained. Thus, the relation is described as παρουσία at *Euthydemus* (301a3–4) and as κοινωνία (communion) at *Republic* 476a7. Elsewhere in the *Phaedo*, the word used to express the relation is none of the two Socrates mentions at 100c–d, but rather μετέχειν or μεταλαμβάνειν (participation) (100c5–6, 102b2); this is also the term chosen at *Symposium* 211b2, and *Republic* 476d1–3. Finally, the relation is characterized in yet another totally different way in the *Phaedo* itself (74e3–4), as one of μίμησις (imitation); this is also the characterization to be found at *Symposium* 212a4–5, *Phaedrus* 250a6ff., and *Timaeus* 48e–49a, and in the central similes of the *Republic*. This list suffices to show that Socrates is very serious in asserting that when it comes to the relation between beauty itself and beautiful things, or between any other way of being and beings, he will commit himself to neither a specific explanation nor even a name. He instead will affirm nothing but the ambiguous dative: that beautiful things are beautiful by/through/with the beautiful itself.[31]

It thus appears that we have in the *Phaedo* an even greater confirmation of Heidegger's critique than could have been imagined. What could be more *thoughtless*, what could be more revealing of the forgetfulness of being at the heart of metaphysics, than this blatant refusal to attempt to think and say the relation between being and beings? Instead of thinking the "with" in "being with beings," Plato in the most confusing and confused manner mixes this up with talk of "beings participating in being" or "beings imitating being"; and all this within the same dialogue! But here again the passage cited above holds a

---

31. See my "Plato's Dialectic of Forms," in *Plato's Forms: Varieties of Interpretation*, ed. William Welton (Lanham, Md.: Lexington Books, 2003),

surprise: Socrates himself goes out of his way to indicate the limitations of his approach. He himself characterizes as "plain," "artless," and "simple-minded" his insistence on saying only that beautiful things are beautiful "by" the beautiful. There is on Socrates' own admission some kind of failure of thinking here. But then why does Socrates acquiesce in this simple-mindedness? Why doesn't he persist in thinking the relation between being and beings, despite the "confusion" and disorientation this might cause? To find the answer to this question, we need to move backwards in this text and determine why this "artless" account of the relation between beautiful things and the beautiful itself was introduced in the first place.

What precedes this account is nothing less than a little autobiography in which Socrates explains his failed attempts at discovering precisely the kind of "sophisticated explanations" that he has now come to renounce.[32] Socrates as a young man first turned to natural science and its method of explaining. The predominant characteristic of this method that emerges from Socrates' account is not only the appeal to material causes and thus purely materialistic explanation, but also the attempt to explain the being of beings in terms of *other beings*. In Heidegger's terms, what characterizes the natural science Socrates describes is purely *ontic* explanation: one man is explained to be taller than another by/through *a head* (96d9–e1); ten is said to be greater than eight by/through *two units* (96e2–3). Socrates soon saw, however, the inadequacy of this kind of ontic explanation: *a head* no more explains *being-tall* than it explains the opposite, *being-small*; two units no more explain *being-greater* than they explain *being-less*. This is why Socrates refuses at 100c–d to identify what makes beautiful things beautiful with a particular thing such as a color or shape: if I claim that the color blue in a painting is what makes it beautiful, I will soon be refuted through the discovery of a terribly ugly painting with the same color blue or of a beautiful painting without a trace of blue in it.

This kind of ontic explanation that characterizes natural science, however, is not the only kind of "sophisticated" explanation Socrates explores. Soon after becoming disillusioned with natural science, he heard someone read out of a book by Anaxagoras the claim that "mind" (νοῦς) is the cause of all things (97b8–c2). Upon hearing this, Socrates thought he had finally found the kind of explanation he was looking for. It may seem at this point that Socrates sought simply to substitute one kind of ontic cause for another, namely, the mental cause of νοῦς for the physical causes tried out earlier. What is striking about Socrates' account, however, is that the cause he describes himself as having looked for in Anaxagoras is not νοῦς, but a totally different kind of cause suggested to Socrates by the central role Anaxagoras seemed to grant

---

32. See my *Dialectic and Dialogue*, chap. 7, for a more detailed analysis of this part of the *Phaedo*.

νοῦς. If νοῦς governs the cosmos, Socrates reasoned, then the ultimate explanation of why things are as they are is not νοῦς itself, but that by which νοῦς is itself governed: *the good*. Socrates therefore describes as follows the kind of explanation he hoped to find: "If one should wish to discover the cause [αἰτία] of each thing, of how it comes to be, ceases to be, and is, what needs to be discovered about it is how it is best [βέλτιστον] for it to be or to do or suffer anything else [πάσχειν ἢ ποιεῖν]. From this reasoning it follows that a human being should search for, with regard to both himself and anything else, nothing other than the most excellent [ἄριστον] and the best" (97c6–d4). It first needs to be noted that this is not an *ontic* explanation of any kind, but a purely *ontological* one: why beings *are* or become or cease to be is explained not by reference to a being—not even νοῦς—but by reference to how it is best for them to be. The good is not a being, nor even being, but what explains the being of beings. The other thing to note is the obvious parallel with the status granted the good in the *Republic*. The passage from the *Phaedo* could even be seen as a partial explanation of what is only asserted in the *Republic*: the good causes being in the sense that a being is how it is because it is best for it to be that way. Finally, one can even detect here, especially given the striking reference to πάσχειν ἢ ποιεῖν, the assumption of an understanding of both the good and being as δύναμις or capability: if a being is capable of doing or suffering something, it is because it is best for it to do or suffer this; its capability, what "empowers" it, is the good.[33]

The exact relation between being and the good of course remains here puzzling and unclear. This is why Socrates was not content with his surmises but quickly bought Anaxagoras's book in order that from it he "might know as quickly as possible the best and the worst" (ἵν' ὡς τάχιστα εἰδείην τὸ βέλτιστον καὶ τὸ χεῖρον, 98b5–6). Unfortunately, he discovered only the worst: it turned out that Anaxagoras made no appeal whatsoever to the good, instead using νοῦς merely as an initial cause of motion and then explaining everything thereafter in the purely materialistic and ontic manner that Socrates had already tried out and rejected. Socrates as a result found himself in a strange situation: recognizing the inadequacy of the ontic explanations of natural science, he was also unable to explain being itself in terms of the good. It is important to note that Socrates' situation is no less aporetic in the *Republic*: though he does there introduce the good as the cause or ultimate principle of being, he never explains *how* the good is a cause of being nor even what the good itself "is." Indeed, he explicitly claims to have no knowledge of this. He has, he claims, only *opinion* with regard to the good and not

33. Thus, A. Diès cites this part of the *Phaedo* as evidence for the prevalence in Plato of the identification of οὐσία or φύσις with the δύναμις to act and be acted on. *Définition de l'être et nature des idées dans le "Sophiste" de Platon* (Paris: J. Vrin, 1981), 21–29.

knowledge (506b–d); furthermore, he refuses to express even his full opinion, since it is nothing but an opinion. At 505a5–6 Socrates claims that "we," that is, "we human beings," have no knowledge of the good, and proceeds to demonstrate this by refuting both the vulgar identification of the good with pleasure and the more sophisticated identification of the good with knowledge. A little later at 505e1–2 we are told that *every* soul is in a state of *aporia* with regard to the good. It is on account of this universal *aporia* which Socrates himself shares that his account of the good must completely confine itself to images, analogies, or similes. The analogy of the sun, which is the one that addresses the good most directly, tells us nothing about what the good is nor about how exactly it functions as a principle. How does the good cause truth and being? Well, in a way analogous to the way in which the sun causes light and makes things grow.

In the *Phaedo*, Socrates' strategy is similar: unsatisfied with the explanation of being in terms of beings and unable to know the good as the cause of being, Socrates has recourse to images. But the images to which he has recourse in the *Phaedo* are not simply images in the narrow sense of similes and analogies, but rather the broadest and most pervasive kind of image: language itself. Indeed, Socrates describes his recourse to images not as a simple expedient, but as a fundamental change in orientation, a "turn" (*Kehre!*): "After this, said Socrates, when I had worn myself out in examining beings [τὰ ὄντα σκοπῶν], it seemed to me that I should be careful not to suffer what is suffered by those who look at and contemplate the sun in eclipse. For some of them ruin their eyes if they do not look at a mere image [εἰκών] of the eclipsed sun in water or some other such medium" (99d4–e1). Here Socrates describes his turn from the direct examination of beings to images in what is itself an image! The eclipsed sun that can blind us when contemplated directly is presumably the good. But here the good is *in eclipse*: having proven unable to know the good, Socrates in his inquiries has been able to look directly only at particular beings in which the good must remain hidden. It is the direct examination of these beings in which the good is eclipsed, however, that poses the greatest threat of making one ultimately blind to the truth of beings.

But to what kinds of images can we turn to examine indirectly the truth of beings? Here again Socrates describes the images to which he turned in an image: reflections in water and other similar mediums. But Socrates goes on to tell us exactly what kind of images he has in mind: "I imagined, then, this kind of thing happening to me and feared that I might blind my soul completely in looking at things [πράγματα] with my eyes and trying with each of my senses to lay hold of them. It seemed to me necessary to take refuge in propositions [εἰς τοὺς λόγους καταφυγόντα] and examine in them the truth of beings [τῶν ὄντων τὴν ἀλήθειαν]" (99e1–6). Therefore, as people avoid being blinded by looking at an eclipse of the sun in reflections, Socrates will avoid being blinded by examining the truth of being—which is the good in eclipse, the good hidden in being—not in the beings themselves as he encounters them through his senses, but in what *is said* about them, in λόγοι.

But Socrates is quick to prevent a possible and natural misinterpretation of his analogy: in comparing the turn from beings to λόγοι to the turn from looking directly at the eclipsed sun to looking at it in reflections, Socrates might seem to be suggesting that the turn from beings to λόγοι is a turn from reality to a mere image of reality. But this is exactly what Socrates does *not* want to suggest: "But perhaps my analogy is not quite accurate, for I do not at all agree that someone who examines beings in propositions is examining them in images any more than someone who examines them in things [ἔργα]" (99e6–100a3). Socrates certainly does not want to suggest that the natural scientist who examines beings directly is closer to the truth of beings than is the philosopher who examines the truth of beings in λόγοι. He does not want to suggest that the λόγοι in which he is taking refuge are any more of an image than the things themselves. But why not? Is not a λόγος obviously further removed from the truth of beings than are beings themselves and therefore more of an image? For example, the λόγος "This painting is beautiful" is clearly an image of the beautiful painting itself; therefore, it is clearly further removed from the beauty of this painting than is the painting itself. The turn from beings to λόγοι is therefore a turn towards mere images and thus a turn away from the truth. How can Socrates deny that this is the case?

He can do so because his disappointment with natural science has taught him that a focus on the beings themselves only leaves one in perplexity regarding their truth. In looking at a beautiful painting, what one sees is not the truth of its beauty but rather colors and shapes that cannot be identified with this beauty and that therefore only confuse and perplex anyone seeking to understand the painting's beauty. This is not to say that the painting's colors and shapes have nothing to do with its beauty: certainly, the beauty of that particular painting to some extent manifests itself in those colors and shapes. Because, however, beauty cannot be *reduced* to those colors and shapes, a mere focus on the latter can hide and distract one from it. Beauty is manifest in a painting in the way that the sun is manifest in an eclipse: visible, certainly, but also hidden in a way that blinds anyone who looks directly at it. In the λόγος "This painting is beautiful," on the other hand, beauty is referred to and is present without the distracting and obstructing presence of particular beautiful things. Expressing the painting's beauty in a λόγος universalizes it and abstracts it from the specific properties of this specific painting. In examining such a λόγος and other λόγοι, I am actually closer to the being of the beautiful than I would be in looking at a particular beautiful painting. It may be the case that a λόγος about a particular thing is in some sense the image of that thing, but what Socrates seeks to understand is not beings but the *truth of* beings, and with respect to that truth a λόγος is certainly not more of an image than the thing itself is; on the contrary, beings only blind us to their truth, while it is in λόγοι that this truth can first emerge as such and be examined.

Of course, if the truth of beings could be examined directly and in itself, that is, independently of both beings *and* λόγοι—an examination that would require a knowledge of the good as the principle beyond being—that would clearly be the optimal course, the "first sailing." It is only in relation to that unattainable understanding of being in terms of the good, and not in relation to natural science, that Socrates' flight into λόγοι represents a "second sailing" (δεύτερος πλοῦς, 99d1): it is because we do not have a knowledge of the good to inflate our sails and speed our course that we must resort to the much slower and more laborious alternative of using the oars of λόγοι to move ahead. The voyage described in Socrates' autobiography can therefore be characterized in this way: we start with the ontic examination of the truth of beings in beings themselves, we rise up to the prospect of an ontological examination of being in terms of the good, and we descend to an examination of the truth of beings in λόγοι, where this final stage is still superior to where we began, since the truth of beings, or the being of beings, is more manifest in λόγοι than it is in beings themselves. In summation, the alternative to seeking the truth of beings in beings is not the inevitably blinding attempt to seek it in being itself, but rather seeking it in λόγοι. In modern terms, what we have here is Socrates' abandonment of both ontic science and phenomenological ontology in favor of dialectic.

But what does Socrates' flight into λόγοι have to do with the explanation he goes on to give of why beautiful things are beautiful and his refusal to give any other explanation? Socrates clearly sees his explanation that "the beautiful is beautiful by the beautiful" as a result of his turn to λόγοι. But what is the connection? First, it is important to note the following: like Socrates' flight into λόγοι, saying that "the beautiful are beautiful by the beautiful" or that "the tall are tall by the tall" is an alternative both to an ontic explanation of being by reference to a being (e.g., a color, a shape, or a head) *and* to an ontological explanation that would ground being in the good. Furthermore, the explanation that "the beautiful are beautiful by the beautiful" is itself a flight into λόγοι in a way that can now be clarified. The λόγος "This painting is beautiful" assumes that there is such a thing as beauty itself—otherwise it could not predicate beauty of this and other things—and that this beauty itself is somehow *with* the painting. However, the λόγος expresses neither what the being of beauty itself is nor the exact nature of its being-with beautiful things. Thus, in refusing to say more than that "the beautiful are beautiful by the beautiful," Socrates is indeed taking flight into λόγοι by refusing to say anything more about the truth of beautiful things than what is manifest in λόγοι. However, we must again be careful not to understand the *flight* here too negatively. The truth or being of the beautiful is more manifest in the λόγος "the beautiful are beautiful by the beautiful" than it is in a color or a shape. On the other hand, to "see" the being of the beautiful, or of anything else, only as it is reflected in λόγοι is clearly "simple" and "artless" when compared to an explanation of being-beautiful that would trace it back to its source in the good. The latter explanation, however, is something Socrates has been unable to discover, either from someone else or on his own.

Yet is this inability only a temporary and contingent one? Is the flight into λόγοι only a temporary expedient or an ineluctable destiny? We have seen that the *Republic* does not give us much basis for being confident about the possibility of attaining knowledge of the good and that Socrates himself does not claim such knowledge. However, the question has to be asked here specifically with regard to Socrates' refusal to say anything more about the relation between beauty and beautiful things than that the latter are beautiful "by" the former. Is this only a temporary abstention, or is it necessary? For the answer we need to turn to a part of Socrates' fictional biography that is skipped in the *Phaedo* but presented in the *Parmenides*. In that dialogue, the very young and naive Socrates tries to do, in response to Parmenides' questioning, precisely what the much older Socrates of the *Phaedo* refuses to do: explain the exact nature of the relation between beings and their being (the "form"). All of the characterizations of this relation offered in Plato's dialogues without defense or consistency and listed above are essayed by the young Socrates, and each one is quickly refuted.[34]

An interpretation of the *Parmenides* is obviously beyond the scope of the present chapter, but it should not be too controversial to say that all of Socrates'

---

34. Παρουσία and κοινωνία are not offered as distinct proposals, but these are of course very vague terms, and the specific proposals discussed could be seen as interpretations of them. In the *Euthydemus* Socrates does suggest παρουσία to describe the relation between beauty and beautiful things, but the eristic Dionysodorus quickly shows the ambiguity of this word when he refutes Socrates by asking him if he becomes a cow when a cow is "present with" him (300e–301a). Heidegger discusses this passage in the lecture course *Vom Wesen der menschlichen Freiheit* and rightly sees Plato as indicating there "daß es gar nicht so selbstverständlich ist mit dieser παρουσία, der Seiendheit eines Seienden, eines seienden Dinges" (GA 31, 64). Unfortunately, Heidegger also thinks that Socrates' decision to characterize the relation between Beauty and beautiful things as παρουσία is evidence that Plato understood being as presence. This claim is untenable for two simple reasons: (1) παρουσία is only one of many words used in the dialogues to characterize this relation, and in the passage from the *Phaedo* discussed above Socrates refuses to commit himself to any; (2) in the *Euthydemus* passage both Socrates and Dionysodorus clearly understand παρουσία as meaning not "presence" but rather "being by or with." For further elaboration of these criticisms, see Boutot, *Heidegger et Platon*, 60–63.

attempted explanations exhibit the same basic deficiency: in attempting to give an account or λόγος of the relation between beings and their being, they all inevitably put being on a level with beings, that is, treat it as another being alongside beings. To say that beings "participate" in being is to open oneself up to the unanswerable because absurd question, Does each being partake of a part of being or of the whole of being (130e–131e)? To characterize the relation between being and beings as one of sharing the same being is obviously to turn being into *a being* and thus create the need for introducing a second "being" which being and beings share, which second "being" will itself need to relate to the first "being" and beings through sharing the same "being," and so on *ad infinitum* (first version of "third man" argument," 132a–b). To describe the relation as one of imitation is to make being and beings "like" each other; but this turns being into *a being* that is like beings; a second "being" must then be introduced as that with respect to which being and beings are like one other; but this second "being" must itself be like the first "being" and beings, and so on *ad infinitum* (second version of the "third man" argument," 132c–133a). Even to characterize being as a "thought" is to turn it into a thing that all beings have, with the absurd result that all beings have thought, that is, think (132b–c). Finally, even the insistence on the complete separation between being and beings turns being into a being existing on its own in a separate world (133b–134e). It thus seems that any account of the relation between being and beings, any relation that can be directly expressed in a λόγος, inevitably objectifies being in a way that results in absurdity and self-contradiction.

Parmenides concludes his refutation of the young Socrates, however, by insisting that without the assumption of both the distinction and some sort of "relation" between beings and their being, that is, without the assumption that there are "forms" or "ideas" *of* beings, thought and discourse would be impossible: "But if, on the other hand, . . . someone with all the present difficulties and others of the same sort in view should not allow that there are forms of beings [εἴδη τῶν ὄντων] nor mark off a form for each one, such a person will have nowhere to turn his thought [διάνοια], since he will not allow that there is for each of the beings an idea [ἰδέα] that remains always the same, and he will in this way utterly destroy the power of discourse/dialectic [τὴν τοῦ διαλέγεσθαι δύναμιν]" (135b5–c2). Thus, the conclusion appears to be that while the "difference/togetherness" of being and beings is presupposed by discourse, it cannot be made an *object* of discourse without profound distortion. In this case, Socrates' flight into λόγοι in the *Phaedo* seems inevitable. To say that "the beautiful are beautiful by the beautiful" is to say only how the being of beings manifests itself in the λόγοι that presuppose it: as both *distinct from* and *with* beings. What Socrates cannot do is make this being-with of being and beings the *object* of a λόγος by giving an account of it. From the lesson Parmenides gave him he has learned not to insist on a particular account, or even name, for the being-with of being and beings.

It is here, I suggest, that is to be found a fundamental difference between Plato and Heidegger. But it is first important to note further similarities. If Socrates cannot answer the question "What is παρουσία?" neither can Heidegger answer the question "What is *Ereignis*?" (see 20–21). And when Heidegger insists that we cannot say even "Ereignis ist" or "Es gibt Ereignis," but only "Ereignis ereignet," is this not very similar in spirit and motivation to Socrates' decision to say only that "the beautiful are beautiful by/through/with the beautiful" while refusing to commit himself to any other designation of the relation here? Finally, if Plato continually resorts to images in expressing the being of beings—images that include not only "light" but also "participation" and "imitation" and "sharing," etc.—so does Heidegger: as the reference to the indispensability of "ontic models" in the seminar on "Zeit und Sein" appears to acknowledge not only *Lichtung* but even the verbs central to Heidegger's account of being "as" *Ereignis,* such as *reaching out* (*reichen*), *sending* (*schicken*), and *giving* (*geben*), are all images, as much so, indeed, as the words *participation* and *imitation* in Plato.

But these similarities between Plato and Heidegger only bring the difference into greater relief. This difference can now be expressed as follows: while neither Plato nor Heidegger looks for the truth of beings in beings themselves, Plato turns to λόγοι and how the truth of being manifests itself therein, whereas Heidegger insists on attempting to see and say being directly in a way that bypasses both beings and λόγοι. In terms of Socrates' image, Heidegger insists on looking directly at the sun of being in eclipse (withdrawal, *Entzug*); he wants to bring being "as" *Ereignis* "into view." Plato, on the other hand, believes that such an attempt can result only in blindness and therefore confines himself to "seeing" the truth of beings *indirectly* as reflected in λόγοι. Thus, Plato's "failure" to address directly the question "What is παρουσία?" is not the result of some inevitable "forgetting" of being at the commencement of metaphysics, but *a conscious choice*. The opposition between Plato and Heidegger is not an opposition between the nihilistic forgetting of being, on the one hand, and the attempt finally to think being in a new beginning—though this of course is how Heidegger wants us to understand it—but rather an opposition between two different approaches to thinking being. If Plato is to be criticized for something, it is not for forgetting being but for taking flight into λόγοι; but before we can make such a criticism we must be convinced that Heidegger's attempt to transcend λόγοι in a direct seeing/saying of being is not blindness. The observations made in the first part of this chapter certainly do not support such a conviction.

Indicative of the difference being suggested here is the following question raised in the seminar on "Zeit und Sein" immediately after the acknowledgment of a certain kinship between Plato and Heidegger in their use of the metaphor of light: "It remains to be asked, however, what the metaphorical reference to light would like to say, but *cannot yet* say" (50; my emphasis). This question is closely tied to the criticism that Plato does not explicitly say ("ausdrücklich sagt," 49) what παρουσία is or accomplishes. Here the objection is formulated in the following terms: Plato's use of the metaphor of light would like to say what παρουσία is, but *cannot yet* say this. The obvious response, however, is that a metaphor can never directly say what it as a metaphor can only indirectly hint at. Plato's metaphors are not trying to say what the being of beings is, but are instead a recognition of the impossibility of saying this. Heidegger, on the other hand, even when compelled to resort to images, still insists on trying to say directly what these images can only very imperfectly hint at. The difference is not that Plato's metaphor of light fails to say the truth of beings while Heidegger's metaphor of *Lichtung* succeeds; the difference can instead be said to be Plato's greater recognition of the inescapable deficiency and indirectness that characterizes any metaphor.

But cannot Plato's "flight" into λόγοι and images be criticized as a resignation of thinking? Do not λόγοι and images distort the truth of beings at least as much as they reveal it? How can the truth of beings genuinely be *thought* without a critique of λόγοι and images and the attempt to go beyond them? Here the above description of the difference between Heidegger and Plato needs to be qualified in an important way: Plato is as aware as Heidegger of the need to transcend somehow λόγοι and images in thinking the truth of being. The difference is that for Plato we can transcend λόγοι and images not through some kind of unmediated seeing nor through some radically different kind of "saying," but only dialectically. In other words, for Plato we can catch sight of something beyond λόγος only through a certain way of "going through" (διά), or dealing with, λόγοι, and a way that is primarily negative and destructive.

This difference between Heidegger and Plato is perhaps most clear in a text in which Plato makes the metaphor of light central: the *Seventh Letter*. Here the possibility of any direct expression of being is ruled out because any λόγος that attempts to express being will necessarily place before it some qualification, some property, some attribute which is not being. This critique of λόγοι is expressed in the following two important passages:

> Furthermore, the four [i.e., words, images, definitions, and knowledge] make manifest no less the *qualities* of a thing (τὸ ποῖόν τι) than its *being* (τὸ ὄν) due to the weakness of language (τὸ τῶν λόγων ἀσθενές). (342e2–343a1)

Many more reasons can be given to show how each of the four is unclear, but the greatest is the one we mentioned a little before: given that the being of an object and its qualities are two different things and that what the soul seeks to know is not the qualities (τὸ ποῖόν τι) but the "what" (τὸ τί), each of the four offers the soul, both in words and in deeds, what it does not seek, so that what is said or shown by each of the four is easily refuted by the senses. As a result they fill practically everyone with perplexity (ἀπορία) and confusion. (343b6–c5)

The point here applies to the attempt to express any kind of being, such as the being of beauty or the being of justice, but let us take as our example here being as such, the being of beings: how can I express being in a λόγος? I can say, "This tree *is*"; yet here being is expressed as a quality of the tree, as a ποῖόν τι and not as being. I can say, "being is knowable"; but here I am only *qualifying* being, expressing how it is qualified, and not saying what it is, not expressing the being of being. Even if my λόγος is simply "being is," it is expressing being as something that has being as a property, rather than expressing being itself; and the same weakness is to be found in claims such as "Beauty is beautiful," "Justice is just," etc. In short, the "weakness of λόγοι" is essentially the predicative structure of λόγοι: in asserting something of something else, a λόγος can only qualify this something else, but cannot express its inherent being; it can express what something *is like* (ποῖόν τι) in asserting other things of it, but cannot express what it *is* (τὸ τί). An assertion, in other words, precisely because it can only assert something *of* x, cannot express the being of x, or what x is (whether this be beauty or justice or being itself), but can only presuppose this as given.[35]

This weakness of λόγοι is precisely the weakness with which we see Heidegger continually struggling in "Zeit und Sein." It is what leads Heidegger to reject the assertion, and therefore logic, as the paradigm for thinking being. In the 1924 course on the *Sophist*, Heidegger states precisely the point Plato is making in the letter, though his very brief and superficial discussion of the letter in that course (GA 19, 346–47) does not enable him to see that this is in fact Plato's own point: "Insofar as a λόγος addresses something as something, it is fundamentally unsuited to grasping that which according to its meaning can no longer be addressed as something else, but is to be grasped only in itself" (206). In the lecture "Zeit und Sein," he draws attention to the inadequacy of the subject-predicate structure of the assertion when it comes to expressing the "being" or "giving" of being and time (18–19). Here, then, we

---

35. For a defense of this reading of the philosophical digression in the *Seventh Letter*, see my *Dialectic and Dialogue*, chap. 9; and "Nonpropositional Knowledge in Plato," *Apeiron* 31 (1998): 243–53.

find another important affinity between Plato and Heidegger: both argue that the assertion *as such* is incapable of expressing or saying being. Despite what Heidegger often claims, Plato no more understands the being of beings from the perspective of the assertion, and thus logic, than he understands it from the perspective of ποίησις.

But the reason for stressing this affinity between Plato and Heidegger is again to see better the crucial difference. Heidegger's response to the "weakness of λόγοι" is, as has been seen, to insist that sentences such as "Es gibt Sein" or "Sein ist" are, despite appearances ("entgegen allem Anschein," 19), *not* assertions or λόγοι. They are instead a radically different kind of saying, one that *names* without asserting. It is clear that Plato would not accept this move. First, he would insist that the above claims *are* assertions and that one cannot simply pretend they are not: the "appearance" that is "spited" here is nothing other than the meaning these assertions unavoidably convey. Even if I say only "Ereignis ereignet," I am still asserting something of *Ereignis*, am making some claim about it, whether I want to or not. All one can do is recognize the weakness of such assertions and work against it. Furthermore, it is explicitly argued in the letter that naming no more expresses, or gives one direct access to, the being of a thing than does the assertion. According to the passages cited above, the "weakness of λόγοι" afflicts each of the only means we have for arriving at knowledge of the being of something, of which the "name" is one, along with the image, the definition, and knowledge itself. How the weakness should afflict the definition, which *is* a λόγος, or knowledge, which depends on λόγοι, is not hard to see. As for the image, it clearly can only qualify something in a certain way or express certain properties it has; for example, if I compare being to light, I am saying only that it has an analogous property or function, without expressing what this is. Thus, we have here the point made above against Heidegger's claim that the metaphor of light can *not yet* say what it wants to say: a metaphor can *never* say what the being of something is.

How the "weakness of λόγοι" should afflict the "name," however, is harder to see and not explicitly spelled out in the letter. But an important argument in the *Sophist* does give at least one explanation: a "name," according to that argument, cannot signify (δηλοῖ) being (οὐσίαν ὄντος οὐδὲ μὴ ὄντος) and be true or false except as combined with a verb in a λόγος (262b9–c7). Simply to name is not to *say* (λέγειν) anything (262d5). The Stranger therefore asserts: "Never will a λόγος come to be out of mere names spoken in succession" (262a9–10). In short, the "weakness of λόγοι" for Plato afflicts naming itself because he does not believe that naming can be divorced from the λόγος and be made to express being on its own. Even if I just say "Ereignis," as long as I am meaning and signifying something, there is a hidden assertion in my naming. This is indeed why Heidegger says "Ereignis ereignet" rather than simply "Ereignis."

The letter itself describes a weakness specific to the name: that it does not naturally belong to the thing named and therefore is not stable (βέβαιον); nothing prevents what is now called "round" from being called "straight" and vice versa. This is not to say that the essence of straightness and the essence of roundness are themselves conventional, but only that their names are. Heidegger's belief in the possibility of a direct naming of being, in contrast, assumes that being is somehow present or manifest in the name itself; the name is not a conventional sign for being, but naturally belongs to, or is appropriated by, being as its own presencing. This assumption is made explicit in an extraordinary claim to be found in the 1938–39 text *Besinnung*: writing of philosophy, Heidegger asserts that "its word [*ihr Wort*] never merely signifies or indicates [*bedeutet oder bezeichnet*] what is to be said, but in saying is Beyng itself [*im Sagen das Seyn selbst ist*]" (GA 66, 51). The contrast with Plato's understanding of words, even those of philosophy, could not be sharper. But then what exactly does Heidegger mean? By the word "word" in the above claim he presumably cannot mean the particular configuration of sounds belonging to a particular language. He presumably would agree with Plato that *that* is conventional and could be substituted with another configuration of sounds. "Word" here is presumably a naming distinct from and presupposed by the specific set of letters it uses. This conception of "word" is clearly expressed in the 1933–34 version of the *Vom Wesen der Wahrheit* course: "The word is not itself formed [*geprägt*] as word-sound [*Wortlaut*], but rather the formation of the word [*Wortprägung*] springs from the prior and original formation of the opening-up of beings [*Aufschließens des Seienden*]" (GA 36/37, 113). But then the Platonic objection would be that such a naming still cannot occur independently of the use of a specific word in a specific language and therefore cannot help being "infected" by the instability and conventionality that afflicts such a word. As was suggested above, Heidegger may identify the "word" here with a certain "seeing"; but then the question is how such a "seeing," unmediated by a particular deficient word in a particular language, is possible.

The opposition here between Plato and Heidegger can be summarized by citing the following passage from the *Beiträge* in which Heidegger insists on the possibility of precisely what Plato argues to be impossible in the *Seventh Letter*: the thinking of Beyng, Heidegger claims, "does not assert anything about beyng [*nicht über das Seyn aussagt*], but says [*sagt*] it in a saying [*in einem Sagen*] that belongs [*gehört*] to what is addressed [*Er-sagten*] and dismisses from it [*von sich weist*] all objectification [*alle Vergegenständlichung*] and all distortion [*Umfälschung*] into something circumstantial [*Zuständliches*] (or 'fleeting' [*'Fließendes'*]), because otherwise the field of re-presenting [*die*

Ebene des Vor-stellens] would be immediately entered into and the uncommonness of beyng [*die Ungewöhnlichkeit des Seyns*] would be denied" (GA 65, 472). Against such a claim, Plato maintains that no saying can escape the "weakness of λόγοι" by not asserting anything about what it addresses; that no saying "belongs" to what is addressed but is alienated from it by the conventional means it must employ; that every saying objectifies what it is about; that every saying distorts being into something circumstantial and fleeting or, in Plato's words, expresses τὸ ποῖόν τι in the place of τὸ τί. But all of these objections can be condensed into one claim: that λόγος cannot be dispensed with, left behind, or overcome. This point is made as forcefully as possible in the *Sophist*: "Deprived of λόγος, which is the most important thing, we would be deprived of philosophy" (260a6–7). This of course is simply a reaffirmation of what the *Phaedo* calls the "flight" into λόγοι.

But how can Plato make such a claim, how can he call λόγος "the most important thing" ("τὸ μέγιστον"), when in the *Seventh Letter* he himself draws attention to its fundamental weakness, which is its inability to express being? Plato affirms both the indispensability and the debilitating weakness of λόγοι. But does this not create a terrible dilemma? Must we not in this case renounce all inquiry into what something *is*, all inquiry into *being*? This would be the case only if we were confined to the content of λόγοι and could not use and deal with them in such a way as to gain indirectly some insight into what escapes this content. What Plato goes on to maintain in the *Seventh Letter* is that there *is* such a way of dealing with λόγοι, a way, a μέθοδος, he describes in the following passage that culminates the letter's "philosophical digression": "Only barely [μόγις], when the [three], i.e., names, definitions, as well as appearances and perceptions, are rubbed against each other [τριβόμενα πρὸς ἄλληλα], each of them being refuted through well-meaning [non-adversarial] refutations [ἐν εὐμενέσιν ἐλέγχοις ἐλεγχόμενα] in a process of question and answer without envy, will wisdom [φρόνησις] along with insight [νοῦς] commence to cast its light in an effort at the very limits of human possibility (344b3–c1)." Insight (νοῦς) is clearly asserted to be possible here, even if only as a "limit" possibility, and the context shows that the object of such insight can be nothing other than "true being" (ἀληθῶς ὄν, 342b1). But the only means listed here for attaining such insight are precisely the means described earlier in the letter as expressing or offering not τὸ ὄν but τὸ ποῖόν τι. There is thus a glaring discrepancy between the means and the outcome.

This is precisely why, however, the cited passage gives all the emphasis to the *process*: it is not names, definitions, and images themselves that spark insight into true being, but rather the "rubbing together" and even refutation of these means in the give-and-take of question and answer. What is meant here? Clearly what is depicted in so many of Plato's dialogues: a specific definition of virtue, for example, is questioned by being "rubbed against" a certain claim about virtue acknowledged to be true or against a certain recognized example or "image" of virtue; this can then result in a new definition that is submitted to the same process or in a questioning of the offered example or proposition. Notoriously, this process as carried out in a Socratic discussion, even when carried out with unsparing aggressiveness and thoroughness, always results in *aporia,* at least when judged according to the high standard of success in expressing the true being or "what-it-is" of the topic under discussion. As has been noted by some interpreters, the *Seventh Letter* explains why a Socratic discussion *must* be aporetic: no λόγος can express the true being of a thing, and yet such a λόγος is precisely what the discussion claims to seek.[36] But the above passage from the *Seventh Letter* also shows why such necessarily aporetic discussions are still pursued: the very process of exposing the limitations of λόγοι by opposing them to ("rubbing against") each other in the give-and-take of question and answer can spark insight into the "true being" these λόγοι must in themselves fail to express. Though I need only "rub" one λόγος against other λόγοι to expose its limitations, in thus coming to see its deficiencies I also to some extent come to see that being with respect to which it is deficient. A revealing example of this process in the case of perceptions is to be found in the *Phaedo* (74d9–e5): in coming to see that two seemingly equal sticks fall short of being perfectly equal, I must have some insight into what equality itself is.

The "insight" or νοῦς attained in rubbing λόγοι together, however, can never free itself from this process in which alone it takes place and become something independent and free-standing. What the letter describes is a transcending of λόγοι that can never leave λόγοι behind. Another name for this is *dialectic.* In dialectic insight into "true being" is attained *negatively* and *indirectly,* that is, in the opposing and refuting of λόγοι and thus only *by way of* λόγοι. λόγοι here are neither "dismissed" in favor of some "translogical" seeing or saying nor made the unquestioned guideline for the interpretation of being, as in logic: instead, dialectic proceeds through λόγοι in such a way as to expose their limits and thus enable us, barely and at the very limit of human possibility, to see *through* them—through their cracks, as it were—the being they fail to express, where this seeing "through λόγοι" must not be confused with seeing "without λόγοι."

Given what is shown in the first part of this chapter, it should be evident that Heidegger's lecture "Zeit und Sein" is itself a perfect example of what Plato is describing in the *Seventh Letter.* This lecture is arguably a negative,

---

36. See Rafael Ferber, *Die Unwissenheit des Philosophen oder Warum hat Plato die 'ungeschriebene Lehre' nicht geschrieben?* (Sankt Augustin: Academia Verlag, 1991), 47. I myself have defended this conclusion in *Dialectic and Dialogue,* 262.

destructive, and indirect thinking of being that must in the end cast itself aside. It can use images or "ontic models" only by making us continually aware of their serious inadequacy, which lies in their expression of qualities (extension in space, e.g.) completely incompatible with what Heidegger is trying to say by their means. Every statement made in the lecture must be immediately undermined as a statement. At the end, the lecture as a whole, because consisting of nothing but propositions, must be characterized as an actual hindrance to the thinking of being. One can strengthen the parallel here by suggesting that even the text of the *Seventh Letter* itself, with its propositions and its imagery of rubbing sticks together to ignite the flame of insight, is something that must be refuted if it is to indicate the truth. Indeed, in the *Phaedrus* we are told that to deserve the name of philosopher a writer must have the ability to undergo a refutation concerning what he has written about (εἰς ἔλεγχον ἰὼν) and himself show how poor or bad what he has written is (τὰ γεγραμμένα φαῦλα ἀποδεῖξαι, 278c5–7).

Yet, as has also been seen, if Heidegger's practice in the lecture illustrates well the negative dialectic described in the *Seventh Letter*, what he claims to be doing, or aims to do, is something quite different. He insists on the possibility of a seeing and saying that transcend λόγοι and images altogether. From Plato's perspective, such a pretense is only an obstacle to the genuine, if modest, insight dialectic is capable of offering. The only humanly possible alternative to the flight into λόγοι is the blindness caused by trying to see being directly, even, or rather especially, in its eclipse. Against such a temptation, Plato insists in the letter on the same point he insists on in the *Phaedo* and the *Sophist*: "Anyone who does not lay hold of the four of these means [i.e., names, images, λόγοι, and ἐπιστήμη] *in some way* [ἁμῶς γέ πως], will never fully partake of knowledge of the fifth [i.e., 'true being']" (342d8–e2). The key for Plato of course lies in the "some way." In quickly dismissing dialectic as he does, Heidegger does not reflect sufficiently, or perhaps not at all, on this ἁμῶς γέ πως. His reaction to the deficiency of the four "means" or, in general, the weakness of λόγοι, is to seek some way of not having to lay hold of them. But in the lecture "Zeit und Sein" and elsewhere he of course cannot avoid laying hold of them. This is why Heidegger could have gained much from a genuine *Auseinandersetzung* with the argument of the *Seventh Letter*, an argument Plato claims to have given many times before and that he thinks merits frequent repeating (342a5–6).

C. CONCLUSION

Despite the above observations, it needs to be emphasized in conclusion that the aim of this chapter, as of the book as a whole, is not to prove Plato "right" and Heidegger "wrong." It is indeed the case that critical questions have been raised regarding Heidegger's project. It is also the case that the project of dialectic has been defended against Heidegger's hasty and impatient dismissal. However, this by no means settles the issue. Indeed, it is doubtful that what is at issue here, namely, the nature of philosophy itself, can ever be "settled." The aim of this chapter, as of the book, is instead to create an opening for a genuine *Auseinandersetzung* between Heidegger and Plato and to situate it within this opening. Heidegger for the most part closed off the possibility of such an *Auseinandersetzung* by paying little attention to Plato's dialogues and dialectic, by turning Plato into something called "Platonism" by means of extremely broad and simplistic interpretative strokes, and by ultimately making the name "Plato" a label for the extreme *other* of his own thought.[37] The lecture and seminar "Zeit und Sein" provide a rare though very small opening for a genuine *Auseinandersetzung* by momentarily freeing Plato's thought from that huge construct called the "history of metaphysics," allowing it to stand on its own and thereby allowing the fleeting emergence of genuine and profound affinities between Plato and Heidegger.

The present chapter has sought greatly to expand this small opening by pursuing what is indicated through it. If both Plato and Heidegger reject ποίησις as a model for the interpretation of being, if they both consider the metaphor of light a better though still inadequate model, and if they both see being as a "dynamic," "eventful" presencing, as opposed to a static present, then the kinship between them becomes very strong indeed. Preceding chapters have already pointed in the direction of such a kinship. The first chapter showed how Heidegger himself brings into question the standpoint from which he chooses to critique Plato's dialectic. The second chapter showed how Heidegger's attempt to force upon Plato a conception of being as static presence is undermined not only by the text of the *Sophist* but by aspects of Heidegger's own reading of this text: a reading that emphasizes the characterization of beings in terms of *dunamis*. Chapters 3 through 5 used Heidegger's own courses from the thirties and forties to undermine what he chose to represent publically, in his only work on Plato published during his lifetime, as "Plato's Doctrine of Truth." Specifically, these chapters showed that Plato by no means subjugated the light of truth to the "look" of the idea nor therefore transformed truth into correctness in corresponding to such a look; they also showed that Plato, on Heidegger's own account, did not fail to think untruth in the sense of a fundamental concealment against which alone truth can be

37. Boutot thus claims that "avec Platon, Heidegger se trouve confronté en quelque sorte à l'autre de lui-même. Platon fait sombrer dans l'oubli ce que lui-même cherche à sauver de l'oubli, c'est-à-dire la vérité de l'être; Platon fait entrer la pensée dans le champ de la métaphysique, alors qu lui-même cherche à l'en dégager" (*Heidegger et Platon*, 14).

thought as unconcealment. Finally, chapter 5 showed a greater affinity, though still limited and even suppressed, on the part of the later Heidegger towards dialectic and dialogue, as evidenced both by his explicit reflections in works and letters from this period and by his decision to write dialogues.

But the point of bringing Plato and Heidegger closer together in this way is to reveal where the true and deeper differences lie: differences that are only covered up by the usual simplistic opposition between the two encouraged by Heidegger himself. If Heidegger's thought cannot help but show a certain affinity with Plato's dialectic, he still remains committed throughout his life to the possibility of some sort of immediate phenomenological intuition that bypasses or overcomes the play of *logoi* against *logoi* that is dialectic; he therefore never ceases to experience dialectic as a "philosophical embarrassment." If there is in Plato a close relationship between ethics and ontology—as demonstrated by the idea of the good, the ideal of philosopher-kings, and the lack of a sharp distinction between *phronesis* and *sophia*—there is in Heidegger instead a reduction of the ethical to the ontological and thus a refusal to grant ethics the centrality and the autonomy as a subject of philosophical reflection that it arguably has in Plato's dialogues (if one could speak of a reduction in Plato, it would arguably go the other way: from ontology to ethics). This leads Heidegger to ignore the dialogical situation in Plato's works, which is always an ethical one. Furthermore, if both Plato and Heidegger understand truth as some sort of unconcealment wrested from a fundamental concealment in which we exist, Heidegger insists on opposing this understanding to a conception of truth as the correctness of assertions in corresponding to the way things are and maintains that the latter must necessarily eclipse the former, whereas Plato's dialogues arguably bring into question both the opposition and the thesis of some historical transformation that leads ineluctably to the "forgetting" of being and truth. The two conceptions of truth (if one can even speak of just two conceptions in Plato) arguably require each other and are therefore inseparable, rather than being in a battle in which one must eventually give way to the other. If one finds in Plato not only an experience of truth as unconcealment but also, in distinction from Heidegger, a process of argumentatively critiquing and defending theses with the goal of "getting it right," it is a question whether this is a failing and not rather a strength. If, finally, both Plato and Heidegger wrote dialogues and perceived both the affinity and the gulf between philosophy and poetry, it remains the case that Heidegger's thought, in contrast to Plato's, is fundamentally and inherently monological. If even the dialogues Heidegger wrote are disguised monologues, as argued in chapter 5, this is because Heidegger seems incapable of seeing in dialogue of the sort one finds in Plato anything but "idle talk" in comparison to the serious task of seeing the phenomena for oneself. To debate, to oppose one perspective to another genuinely different perspective, is for Heidegger to cut oneself off from the thing itself. This of course assumes that one has some sort of immediate access to the thing itself independently of the exchange of *logoi*. This has been seen to be the assumption behind not only Heidegger's antipathy to dialogue but also his antipathy to dialectic. We thus arrive here at a fundamental difference considered in the first chapter and revisited in the present chapter: while Plato considered necessary what the *Phaedo* calls a "flight into *logoi*," Heidegger always refused such a flight, insisting on the possibility of directly seeing the sun, even if in eclipse.

In conclusion, while Heidegger tried to make the opposition between Plato and himself one between the forgetting of being and the thinking of being, the opposition is rather between two approaches to thinking being, where one can be called "dialectical/dialogical" and the other "phenomenological/tautological," though these terms cannot fully capture all of the specific differences cited above and developed in the course of this book. If Heidegger did not pursue the kinship with Plato that is allowed to peek through "Zeit und Sein" and the other texts considered in the present study, this may be because it is much easier to argue against the forgetting of being than it is to argue against an alternative way of thinking being. Even, or especially, in the case of Plato, Heidegger resisted genuine dialogue. Such a dialogue is of course no easy matter. There is no easy or guaranteed way to bring into dialogue two fundamentally different conceptions of philosophy, especially when one of them does not see dialogue as central to doing philosophy. If Heidegger did not in later years pursue the need he himself perceived of reading Plato anew, this was not due to laziness but rather to the immensity of the task. Yet the task, to which the present study hopes to have contributed, of pursuing this incomplete, or even uncommenced, dialogue between Plato and Heidegger is indispensable, not only, or even mainly, because of the light it can shed on the thought of both philosophers, but because of the reflection it demands on what we are doing and pursuing when we philosophize. And without constant self-questioning, as both Plato and Heidegger saw very well, philosophy ceases to live.

WORKS CITED

Ast, Friedrich. *Lexicon Platonicum*. Berlin: Herman Barsdorf, 1908.
Backman, Jussi. "All of a Sudden: Heidegger and Plato's *Parmenides*." *Epoché* 11, no. 2 (2007): 393–408.
Baltes, M. "Is the Idea of the Good in Plato's *Republic* Beyond Being?" In *Studies in Plato and the Platonic Tradition: Essays Presented to John Whittaker*, edited by Mark Joyal, 3–23. Aldershot: Ashgate, 1997.
Barnes, Jonathan. "Heidegger spéléologue." *Revue de Métaphysique et de Morale* 95 (1990): 173–95.
Baruzzi, Arno. *Philosophieren mit Jaspers und Heidegger*. Würzburg: ERGON Verlag, 1999.
Beaufret, Jean. *Parménide: Le Poème*. 2nd ed. Paris: Presses universitaires de France, 1984.
Bernasconi, Robert. "Heidegger's Destruction of φρόνησις." In "Spindel Conference 1989: Heidegger and Praxis," edited by Thomas J. Nenon. *Southern Journal of Philosophy* 28, supp. (1989): 127–48.
Berti, Enrico. "Heidegger and the Platonic Concept of Truth." In HPD, 96–107.
———. "Heideggers Auseinandersetzung mit dem Platonisch-Aristotelischen Wahrheitsverständnis." In *Die Frage nach der Wahrheit*, edited by Ewald Richter, 89–105. Frankfurt am Main: Vittorio Klostermann, 1997.
Bonitz, Hermann. *Index Aristotelicus*. Vol. 5 of *Aristotelis Opera*. Berlin: Walter de Gruyter, 1961.
Boutot, Alain. *Heidegger et Platon: Le problème du nihilisme*. Paris: Presses Universitaires de France, 1987.
Brach, Markus. *Heidegger—Platon: Vom Neukantilismus zur existentiellen Interpretation des "Sophistes."* Würzburg: Königshausen und Neumann, 1996.
Brogan, Walter. "Plato's Dialectical Soul: Heidegger on Plato's Ambiguous Relationship to Rhetoric." *Research in Phenomenology* 27 (1997): 3–15.
———. "A Response to Robert Bernasconi's 'Heidegger's Destruction of φρόνησις.'" In "Spindel Conference 1989: Heidegger and Praxis," edited by Thomas J. Nenon. *Southern Journal of Philosophy* 28, supp. (1989): 149–54.
Brumbaugh, Robert S. "Diction and Dialectic: A Note on the *Sophist*." In *Platonic Studies of Greek Philosophy: Form, Arts, Gadgets, and Hemlock*, 103–11. Albany: SUNY Press, 1989.
Courtine, Jean-François. *Heidegger et la phénoménologie*. Paris: J. Vrin, 1990.
———. "Les 'Recherches Logiques' de Martin Heidegger, de la théorie du jugement à la vérité de l'être." In *Heidegger 1919–1929: De l'herméneutique de la facticité à la métaphysique du Dasein*, edited by Jean-François Courtine, 7–31. Paris: J. Vrin, 1996.
Derrida, Jacques. "Violence et métaphysique." In *L'écriture et la différence*, 117–228. Paris: Éditions du Seuil, 1967.
Diès, A. *Définition de l'être et nature des idées dans le "Sophiste" de Platon*. Paris: J. Vrin, 1981.
Dixsaut, Monique. *Platon et la question de la pensée: Étude Platoniciennes*. Paris: J. Vrin, 2000.
Dostal, Robert J. "Beyond Being: Heidegger's Plato." In *Martin Heidegger: Critical Assessments*, vol. 2, edited by Christopher E. Macann, 61–89. New York: Routledge, 1992.

———. "The Experience of Truth for Gadamer and Heidegger: Taking Time and Sudden Lightning." In *Hermeneutics and Truth*, edited by Brice Wachterhauser, 47–67. Evanston: Northwestern University Press, 1994.

———. "Gadamer's Continuous Challenge: Heidegger's Plato Interpretation." In *The Philosophy of Hans-Georg Gadamer*, edited by Lewis Edwin Hahn, 289–307. Chicago: Open Court, 1997.

Ferber, Rafael. "L'Idea del Bene è o non è transcendente? Ancora su ἐπέκεινα τῆς οὐσίας." In *Platone e la Tradizione Platonica: Studi su filosofia antica*, edited by Mauro Bonazzi and Franco Trabattoni, 127–49. Milan: Cisalpino, 2003.

———. *Platos Idee des Guten*. 2nd ed. Sankt Augustin: Academia Verlag Richarz, 1989.

———. *Die Unwissenheit des Philosophen oder Warum hat Plato die "ungeschriebene Lehre" nicht geschrieben?* Sankt Augustin: Academia Verlag, 1991.

Figal, Günter. "Refraining from Dialectic: Heidegger's Interpretation of Plato in the *Sophist* Lectures (1924/25)." In *Interrogating the Tradition: Hermeneutics and the History of Philosophy*, edited by Charles E. Scott and John Sallis, 95–109. Albany: State University of New York Press, 2000.

Fried, Gregory. "Back to the Cave: A Platonic Rejoinder to Heideggerian Postmodernism." In *Heidegger and the Greeks: Interpretative Essays*, edited by Drew A. Hyland and John Panteleimon Manoussakis, 157–76. Bloomington: Indiana University Press, 2006.

Friedländer, Paul. *Platon*. 3rd ed. Vol. 1, *Seinswahrheit und Lebenswirklichkeit*. Berlin: Walter de Gruyter, 1964.

Fritsche, Johannes. "With Plato into the *Kairos* Before the *Kehre*: On Heidegger's Different Interpretations of Plato." In HPD, 140–77.

Gadamer, H. G. *Aristoteles: Nikomachische Ethik VI*. Frankfurt am Main: Vittorio Klostermann, 1998.

———. "Hegel and the Dialectic of the Ancient Philosopher." In *Hegel's Dialectic: Five Hermeneutical Studies*, translated by P. Christopher Smith, 5–34. New Haven: Yale University Press, 1976.

———. "Heideggers 'theologische' Jugendschrift." In PIA, 76–86; originally published in *Dilthey-Jahrbuch für Philosophie und Geschichte der Geisteswissenschaften* 6 (1989): 228–34.

———. "Martin Heidegger 75 Jahre." In *Gesammelte Werke*, vol. 3. Tübingen: J. C. B. Mohr, 1987.

———. *Philosophical Apprenticeships*. Translated by R. Sullivan. Cambridge, Mass.: MIT Press, 1985.

———. *Plato's Dialectical Ethics: Phenomenological Interpretations Relating to the* Philebus. Translated by Robert M. Wallace. New Haven: Yale University Press, 1991.

———. *Platos dialektische Ethik*. Hamburg: Felix Meiner, 2000.

———. "Die Sprache der Metaphysik." In *Gesammelte Werke*, vol. 3 , 229–37. Tübingen: J. C. B. Mohr, 1987.

Galston, William A. "Heidegger's Plato: A Critique of *Plato's Doctrine of Truth*." *Philosophical Forum* 13, no. 4 (1982): 371–84.

Goldschmidt, Victor. *Platonisme et pensée contemporaine*. Paris: J. Vrin, 2000.

Gonzalez, Francisco J. "And the Rest is *Sigetik*: Silencing Logic and Dialectic in Heidegger's *Beiträge zur Philosophie*." *Research in Phenomenology* 38, no. 3 (2008): 358–91.

———. "Beyond or Beneath Good and Evil? Heidegger's Purification of Aristotle's Ethics." In *Heidegger and the Greeks: Interpretative Essays*, edited by Drew A. Hyland and John Panteleimon Manoussakis, 127–56. Bloomington: Indiana University Press, 2006.

———. "Confronting Heidegger on Logos and Being in Plato's *Sophist*." In *Platon und Aristoteles—sub ratione veritatis: Festschrift für Wolfgang Wieland zum 70. Geburtstag*, edited by Gregor Damschen, Rainer Enskat, and Alejandro G. Vigo, 102–33. Göttingen: Vandenhoeck and Ruprecht, 2003.
———. *Dialectic and Dialogue: Plato's Practice of Philosophical Inquiry*. Evanston: Northwestern University Press, 1998.
———. "Dialectic as 'Philosophical Embarrassment': Heidegger's Critique of Plato's Method." *Journal of the History of Philosophy* 40, no. 3 (2002): 361–89.
———. "Heidegger on a Few Pages of Plato's *Theaetetus*." *Epoché* 11, no. 2 (2007): 371–92.
———. "Heidegger's 1933 Misappropriation of Plato's *Republic*." Προβλήματα: *Quaderni di filosofia* 3 (2003): 39–80.
———. "History of an Embarrassment: Heidegger's Critique of Platonic Dialectic." *Journal of the History of Philosophy* 40, no. 3 (2002): 361–89.
———. "How Is the Truth of Beings in the Soul: Interpreting *Anamnesis* in Plato." *Elenchos* 28 (2007): 275–301.
———. "Nonpropositional Knowledge in Plato." *Apeiron* 31 (1998): 235–84.
———. "On the Way to *Sophia*: Heidegger on Plato's Dialectic, Ethics, and *Sophist*." *Research in Phenomenology* 27 (1997): 16–60.
———. "Plato's Dialectical Ethics: Or Taking Gadamer at his Word." In *Hermeneutic Philosophy and Plato: Gadamer's Response to the "Philebus,"* edited by Christopher J. Gill and François Renaud. Sankt Augustin: Academia Verlag, forthcoming.
———. "Plato's Dialectic of Forms." In *Plato's Forms: Varieties of Interpretation*, edited by William Welton, 31–83. Lanham, Md.: Lexington Books, 2003.
———. "Plato's Eleatic Stranger: His Master's Voice?" In Press, *Who Speaks for Plato?* 161–81.
———. "Plato's Question of Truth (Versus Heidegger's Doctrines)." *Proceedings of the Boston Area Colloquium in Ancient Philosophy* 23 (2007): 83–111.
———. "Wax Tablets, Aviaries, or Imaginary Pregnancies? On the Powers in Theaetetus' Soul." *Études platoniciennes* 4 (2007): 273–93.
———. "Whose Metaphysics of Presence? Heidegger's Interpretation of *Dunamis* and *Energeia* in Aristotle." *Southern Journal of Philosophy* 44, no. 4 (2006): 533–68.
———. "Why Heidegger's Hermeneutics Is Not a 'Diahermeneutics.'" *Philosophy Today* 45 (SPEP Supplement 2001): 138–52.
Grondin, Jean. *L'universalité de l'herméneutique*. Paris: Presses universitaires de France, 1993.
———. *Von Heidegger zu Gadamer: Unterwegs zur Hermeneutik*. Darmstadt: Wissenschaftliche Buchgesellschaft, 2001.
Guest, Gérard. "Aux confins de l'inapparent (L'extreme phénoménologie de Heidegger)." In *Phénoménologie: Un siècle de philosophie*, edited by Pascal Dupond and Laurent Cournarie, 99–127. Paris: Ellipses, 2002.
Hestir, Blake E. "Plato on the Split Personality of Ontological *Alētheia*." *Apeiron* 37, no. 2 (2004): 109–50.
Hodge, Joanna. *Heidegger and Ethics*. New York: Routledge, 1995.
Hyland, Drew A. *Questioning Platonism: Continental Interpretations of Plato*. Albany: State University of New York Press, 2004.
Inwood, Michael. "Truth and Untruth in Plato and Heidegger." In HPD, 72–95.
Jaspers, Karl. *Notizen zu Martin Heidegger*. Edited by Hans Saner. Munich: Piper, 1989.
Kisiel, Theodore. "From Intuition to Understanding: On Heidegger's Transposition of Husserlian Phenomenology." *Études Phénoménologiques* 22 (1995): 31–50.
———. *The Genesis of Heidegger's "Being and Time."* Berkeley and Los Angeles: University of California Press, 1993.

Klein, Jacob. *Plato's Trilogy: "Theaetetus," the "Sophist," and the "Statesman."* Chicago: University of Chicago Press, 1977.
Margolis, Joseph. "Heidegger on Truth and Being." In HPD, 121–39.
May, Reinhard. *Heidegger's Hidden Sources.* Translated by Graham Parks. New York: Routledge, 1996.
Merleau-Ponty, Maurice. *Notes de cours, 1959–1961.* Paris: Gallimard, 1996.
Neske, Günther, ed. *Erinnerung an Martin Heidegger.* Pfullingen: Günther Neske, 1977.
Olson, Alan M. *Heidegger and Jaspers.* Philadelphia: Temple University Press, 1994.
Paredes, Maria del Carmen. "*Amicus Plato magis amica veritas:* Reading Heidegger in Plato's Cave." In HPD, 108–20.
Partenie, Catalin. "Imprint: Heidegger's Interpretation of Platonic Dialectic in the *Sophist* Lectures (1924–25)." In HPD, 42–71.
Patt, Walter. *Formen des Anti-Platonismus bei Kant, Nietzsche und Heidegger.* Frankfurt am Main: Vittorio Klostermann, 1997.
Peperzak, Adriaan T. "Did Heidegger Understand Plato's Idea of Truth?" In *Platonic Transformations: With and After Hegel, Heidegger, and Levinas,* 57–111. Lanham, Md.: Rowman and Littlefield, 1997.
———."Heidegger and Plato's Idea of the Good." In *Reading Heidegger: Commemorations,* edited by John Sallis, 258–85. Bloomington: Indiana University Press, 1993.
Plato. *Le Sophiste.* Translated by Nestor Cordero. Paris: Flammarion, 1993.
Pöggeler, Otto. "Ein Streit um Platon: Heidegger und Gadamer." In *Platon in der Abendländischen Geistesgeschichte: Neue Forschungen zum Platonismus,* edited by T. Kobusch and T. Mojsisch, 241–54. Darmstadt: Wissenschaftliche Buchgesellschaft, 1997.
Press, Gerald A., ed. *Who Speaks for Plato? Studies in Platonic Anonymity.* Lanham, Md.: Rowman and Littlefied, 2000.
Renaud, François. *Die Resokratisierung Platons: Die Platonische Hermeneutik Hans-Georg Gadamers.* Sankt Augustin: Academia, 1999.
Riedel, Manfred. "Hermeneutik und Gesprächsdialektik: Gadamers Auseinandersetzung mit Heidegger." In *Hören auf die Sprache,* 96–130. Frankfurt am Main: Suhrkamp, 1990.
Rorty, Richard. "The Reification of Language." In *The Cambridge Companion to Heidegger,* edited by Charles Guignon, 337–57.Cambridge: Cambridge University Press, 1993.
Rosen, Stanley. "Heidegger's Interpretation of Plato." In *Essays in Metaphysics,* edited by Carl G. Vaught. University Park: Penn State Press, 1970.
———. *The Question of Being: A Reversal of Heidegger.* New Haven: Yale University Press, 1993.
———. "Remarks on Heidegger's Plato." In HPD, 178–91.
Ross, W. D. *Aristotle's Metaphysics.* Vol. 1. Oxford: Clarendon Press, 1958.
Safranski, Rüdiger. *Martin Heidegger: Between Good and Evil.* Trans. Ewald Osers. Cambridge: Harvard University Press, 1998.
Sallis, John. *Delimitations: Phenomenology and the End of Metaphysics.* 2nd ed. Bloomington: Indiana University Press, 1995.
———. "Plato's Other Beginning." In *Heidegger and the Greeks: Interpretative Essays,* edited by Drew A. Hyland and John Panteleimon Manoussakis, 177–90. Bloomington: Indiana University Press, 2006.
Sayre, Kenneth. "A Maieutic View of Five Late Dialogues." In *Methods of Interpreting Plato and His Dialogues,* edited by James Carl Klagge and Nicholas D. Smith, 221–43. Oxford Studies in Ancient Philosophy, supp. vol. Oxford: Clarendon Press, 1992.

Shorey, Paul. "The Idea of the Good in Plato's *Republic:* A Study in the Logic of Speculative Ethics." In *Selected Papers*, vol. 2, 28–79. New York: Garland, 1980.
Stemmer, Peter. *Platons Dialektik: Die Früheren und Mittleren Dialoge*. Berlin: Walter de Gruyter, 1992.
Szaif, Jan. *Platons Begriff der Wahrheit*. 3rd ed. Munich: Karl Alber, 1998.
Taminiaux, Jacques. *Heidegger and the Project of Fundamental Ontology*. Translated by Michael Gendre. Albany: State University of New York Press, 1991.
———. "The Husserlian Heritage in Heidegger's Notion of the Self." In *Reading Heidegger from the Start: Essays in His Earliest Thought*, edited by Theodore Kisiel and John van Buren, 269–90. Albany: State University of New York Press, 1994.
———. "Nothingness and the Professional Thinker: Arendt Versus Heidegger." In *The Ancients and the Moderns*, edited by Reginald Lilly, 196–210. Bloomington: Indiana University Press, 1996.
———. "Plato's Legacy in Heidegger's Two Readings of *Antigone*." In HPD, 22–41.
———. *Sillages phénoménologiques: Auditeurs et lecteurs de Heidegger*. Brussels: OUSIA, 2002.
———. *The Thracian Maid and the Professional Thinker: Arendt and Heidegger*. Translated by Michael Gendre. Albany: State University of New York Press, 1997.
Van Buren, John. *The Young Heidegger: Rumor of the Hidden King*. Bloomington: Indiana University Press, 1994.
Vogel, Lawrence. *The Fragile "We": Ethical Implications of Heidegger's "Being and Time."* Evanston: Northwestern University Press, 1994.
Volpi, Franco. "Dasein as *Praxis:* The Heideggerian Assimilation and the Radicalization of the Practical Philosophy of Aristotle." In *Martin Heidegger: Critical Assessments*, vol. 2, edited by Christopher Macann, 90–129. New York: Routledge, 1992.
Wachterhauser, Brice R. *Beyond Being: Gadamer's Post-Platonic Hermeneutical Ontology*. Evanston: Northwestern University Press, 1999.
Webb, David. "Continuity and Difference in Heidegger's *Sophist*." *Southern Journal of Philosophy* 38 (2000): 145–69.
Wieland, Wolfgang. *Platon und die Formen des Wissens*. 2nd ed. Göttingen: Vandenhoeck and Ruprecht, 1999
Wolin, Richard. *The Politics of Being: The Political Thought of Martin Heidegger*. New York: Columbia University Press, 1990.
Wolz, Henry G. *Plato and Heidegger: In Search of Selfhood*. Lewisburg: Bucknell University Press, 1981.
———. "Plato's Doctrine of Truth: Orthotes or Aletheia?" *Philosophy and Phenomenological Research* 27, no. 2 (1966): 157–82.
Zuckert, Catherine. *Postmodern Platos*. Chicago: University of Chicago Press, 1996.

INDEX

ἀνάμνησις (recollection), 202, 205, 239–42
adaequatio. See truth
ἀγαθόν, τό. See good, Plato's idea of the
ἀλήθεια, etymology of, 139, 165 n. 59, 165 n. 62, 166, 170, 222, 225, 231, 238–41. See also truth
Anschauung (intuition). See also categorical intuition; en-visioning; νοῦς; seeing
  and Ausdruck (expression), 12, 16, 26
  and circumspection, 17
  and dialectic, 23 n. 25
  as source of knowledge, 14
  and Verstehen (understanding), 15 n. 13
Arendt, Hannah, 162, 258, 341
Aristotle, 7, 9–11
  being as being-produced, 309
  clearer than Plato, 10–11
  De Anima, 24 n. 27
  εἶδος, understanding of, 320
  De Interpretatione, 228–29
  Metaphysics, 30 n. 33, 38, 43–44, 46, 48, 89 n. 34, 91 n. 37, 314 n. 15
  Nicomachean Ethics, 29, 38, 39 n. 50, 46–47
  Physics, 46, 82 n. 18
  present behind Plato's Sophist, 60, 84, 93 n. 39

Backman, J., 254 n. 10
Baltes, M., 131 n. 18
Barnes, J., 2 n. 1, 85 n. 22, 119 n. 8, 126 n. 13, 155 n. 36, 158 n. 43, 165 n. 62
Beaufret, J., 164 n. 57
being. See also δύναμις; ontological difference; presence
  as admitting degrees, 108
  as aporetic, 93–98
  as "common," 185
  as Hergestelltsein (being-produced), 41 n. 58, 87, 88 n. 32, 89 n. 34, 309–10, 317–18
  as "other," 95
  πρός τι structure of, 91–93
  as φύσις, 236–37
  question of (Seinsfrage), 40, 69, 72, 279, 299, 306
being-in-the-world, 24–25, 80
belief. See δόξα
Bernasconi, R., 36 n. 48, 37 n. 49
Berti, E., 159 n. 48, 160 n. 50, 163 n. 56
Boutot, A., 4, 134 n. 20, 139 n. 24, 140 n. 25, 141 n. 26, 142 n. 27, 157 n. 41, 158 n. 44, 162 n. 54, 164 n. 57, 172, 313 n. 13, 343 n. 37
Brach, M., 5, 80–81, 96 n. 45

Brogan, W., 28 n. 30, 42
Brumbaugh, R. S., 61 n. 87

care, Dasein as, 40, 43, 77, 242–43
categorial intuition, 176, 308
categories, 71–74, 176
collection and division, method of
  as collapsing distinction between being and beings, 70, 76, 78 n. 13, 82, 97
  as mode of seeing, 70 n. 1
  as value-neutral, 53, 55, 57–58, 62
concealment. See λήθη and untruth
Cordero, N., 95 n. 43
Correctness. See ὀρθότης and truth
Courtine, J.-F., 141 n. 26, 165 n. 58, 263 n. 1, 316 n. 19

δαιμόνιον, Socratic, 236
Derrida, Jacques, 1, 315 n. 7
Destruktion, Heideggerian, 45, 294, 295, 299, 301–3, 305, 308
developmentalist hypothesis (as interpretation of Plato), 61 n. 85, 174
dialectic, 8, 29. See also collection and division; dialogue; elenchus; Socratic method
  and calculative thinking, 265
  as criterion of truth, 216–19
  and dialogue, 290 n. 13
  and eristic, 53, 54 n. 76
  as "fantastical," 20
  as logic, 266–67
  λόγος and νοῦς, as mediation between, 24, 27, 50, 99, 266–67, 340–41
  and metaphysics, 288–89
  as motion and rest, 76
  as negation, 302
  νοεῖν, relation to, 22–23
  as ontology for Plato, 73
  and phenomenology, 10–14, 180, 272, 291, 303–4, 308, 332
  as "philosophical embarrassment," 10, 19, 266, 291, 304, 344
  φρόνησις and σοφία, as mediation between, 49–50
  and rhetoric, 47 n. 69
  and sophistry, 22–23, 54 n. 77, 60 n. 82, 98
  as soul's self-questioning and answering, 208–9, 220
  as underway, 9, 24, 47, 49, 291–93
  and the unsaid, 264, 270, 277, 283, 287
  as way of knowing the idea, 118, 213

dialogue. *See also* dialectic; dialogue form; Socratic method
  and Heidegger's conception of philosophy, 67, 272, 344–45
  as listening to the gods, 67
  and monologue, 54–55
  and soul's dialogue with itself, 209
  with the tradition, 68, 290 n. 13
  and truth/untruth, 221
dialogue form
  difference between Platonic and Heideggerian, 278–80, 284–87
  versus the treatise, 56, 60, 62, 81, 99, 106, 184, 198, 206, 220, 234–35, 263–64, 265–66, 269–71, 273–74, 276–77, 284
δίκη (justice), Heidegger's interpretation of, 249–50
Divided Line, Plato's, 145–46
Dixsaut, M., 30 n. 33, 74 n. 8, 85 n. 22
Δόξα/δοξάζειν. *See also* false belief
  and assertion, 218–19
  direct object of, 208
  as "gabled," 214–15
  as "inbetween," 205
  and knowledge, 319–20
  as λόγος, 206–7, 218
  meanings of, 202–3
  and thinking, 208
Dostal, R. J., 36 n. 46, 67, 131 n. 16, 147 n. 31, 156 n. 38, 162–63 n. 55, 272 n. 4, 290 n. 14
δύναμις
  as definition of being, 32, 78 n. 13, 88–91, 99, 115, 128, 169, 322–25, 329
  the Platonic good as, 128–29, 132, 144, 323 n. 29
  the Platonic ideas as, 85, 115, 132, 319–20. *See also* Ideas

εἴδη. *See* Ideas, Platonic
Elenchos, 219
  and eristic, 53–54, 54 n. 77, 62
  as purification, 53
En-visioning (*Er-blicken*), 116–17, 193, 203–4
ἐπιστήμη. *See also* knowledge
  meaning of for Aristotle, 30 n. 31, 174
  meaning of for Plato, 174
ἐπορέγεσθαι, 188–92. *See also* striving
ἔργον
  versus λόγος, 74, 80–81, 91, 198, 220
ἔρως, 9, 35, 77 n. 11, 117, 175, 189–92, 197, 203, 205, 208, 241–42, 254, 291–92. *See also* striving
ethics
  as metontology, 35–36 n. 46
  and ontology, 35, 46, 48, 50 n. 71, 62, 102–3, 249–50, 288, 344

evil
  as not a moral notion, 276, 288

false belief, 204–21. *See also* falsehood; ψεῦδος; untruth
  as "believing other," 206
  versus incorrect assertion, 216–17
  as mismatch between perceptions and thoughts, 211
  as presupposing some kind of knowing, 212, 223
  and semblance, 219
falsehood. *See also* false belief; ψεῦδος; untruth
  as ἀλλοδοξία, 178–79
  as interpretation of untruth, 105
  as κοινωνία, 79
  as Roman interpretation of ψεῦδος, 226–27
Ferber, R., 132 n. 17, 341 n. 36
Figal, G., 19 n. 20, 22 n. 24, 23 n. 26, 36 n. 47, 89 n. 33
freedom, 109–10, 149, 252, 276, 314 n. 15
Fried, G., 241 n. 6
Friedländer, P., 124 n. 12, 165–66
Fritsche, J., 103 n. 2, 104 n. 3, 135 n. 21

Gadamer, H.-G., 5, 11, 39–40, 67 n. 94, 68, 77 n. 12, 78 n. 13, 86 n. 27, 87 n. 31, 267 n. 2, 272, 280, 289
Galston, W. A., 103 n. 1, 129 n. 15
Goldschmidt, V., 119 n. 8, 157–58 n. 42
good, Plato's idea of the, 312–13. *See also* δύναμις.
  abandoned by Plato in later dialogues, 31–32, 60, 130, 174
  as ἀνυπόθετον, 145–46
  aporia regarding, 329–30
  as beyond being, 33–34, 35 n. 43, 127–30, 134, 140–43, 156, 315, 316–17
  as enabling question of being, 130
  as misinterpretation of being, 31–32, 35
  not moral or ethical concept, 33, 129 n. 15
  ontological interpretation of, 30, 44 n. 66
  as unsayable, 133
  as value, 31 n. 36, 33 n. 38, 34, 141, 157, 171
  as "yoke," 122–25, 154, 316
Grondin, J., 281, 283, 299 nn. 4–5
Guest, G., 307 n. 9

having, authentic versus inauthentic, 190–92
hearing, versus seeing as philosophical paradigm
  for the Greeks, 64, 118, 267
  for Heidegger, 280, 284, 313 n. 13
Hegel, 13, 158 n. 42
  his dialectic versus Plato's, 13, 265–67, 288, 290, 303

Heraclitus, 77, 279, 291, 305
Hermeneutics, 281–83, 285, 298–300, 306
Hestir, B. E., 153 n. 33, 165 n. 62, 171 n. 67
Hodge, J., 50 n. 71
ὁμοίωσις, 126, 138–39, 164–65, 168, 188, 227–29
humanism, 43, 150–51, 245–46, 250
ὑποθέσεις, 86, 145–46, 271–72
Husserl, Edmund, 12, 26, 79, 176, 308,
   Heidegger's critique of, 14–19
Hyland, D., 5–6, 103 n. 2, 106 n. 5, 155 n. 37, 159
   nn. 46–47, 170 n. 65, 171 n. 67, 274 nn. 5–6,
   275 n. 7, 285 n. 11

ideas (εἴδη), Platonic, 43 n. 63, 70, 76, 102, 310
   as δυνάμεις (powers), 85–87, 115, 132, 319–20
   εἶδος versus γένος, 83–84
   etymological interpretation of as "looks,"
      84–86, 113–20, 131, 152–53, 267–68, 316–20
   as ἕξις, 128
   as formal structures, 183, 319
   as making-possible, 115
   normative character of, 86
   as presuppositions of discourse, 334
   as projects, 116–17
   separation of, 76 n. 10, 82–83, 119 n. 9, 334
   not subjective nor objective, 115
   no theory of, 119, 335
   as ὑπόθεσις, 86, 146 n. 30
   as "yoke," 137
images
   Plato's use of, 181, 210–11, 335–36
   Heidegger's use of, 335–36
intentionality, 77, 79–80, 177
intuition. *See* Anschauung
Inwood, M., 103 n. 2, 108 n. 1, 111 n. 3, 116 n. 7,
   123 n. 10, 124 n. 11, 171 n. 67, 241 n. 6
irony, 19 n. 19, 59, 62 n. 88

Jaspers, 250 n. 9, 289
   on philosophy as conversation, 68
justice. *See* δίκη

κίνησις. *See* motion
Kisiel, T., 14–18, 39 n. 50, 40 n. 56, 42 n. 60
κοινωνία
   different forms of, 78–80
   between motion and rest, 75–76
   as relation between ideas (forms) and particulars, 327
knowledge. *See also* ἐπιστήμη
   as acquaintance, 213
   conditions of, 202–3
   as dialectical, 220
   distinct from immediate perceiving, 176, 187, 194

as finite, 266, 290
as indefinable, 198
kindled by living together and dialogue, 64, 67
of knowledge, 80, 198, 212–13, 219
as laying hold of being and truth, 194
versus opinion, 59, 213, 329–30
and φρόνησις, 29–30, 244
relation to *praxis*, 30 n. 32, 31
and seeing metaphor, 85 n. 23, 117, 194
and striving for being, 197
as τέχνη, 30 n. 32, 310
traditional conception of, 14, 17
as user's art, 319

language. *See* λόγος, λέγειν
λόγος, λέγειν
   as ἀναλογίζεσθαι, 194–95
   as ἀποφαίνεσθαι, 73–74, 268, 283
   as-structure of, 206
   as being-with-others, 65, 267
   as concealing (idle talk), 8, 21–22
   as defining human existence, 23–25, 64–65
   as διαίρεσις, 70
   different senses of, 220, 234
   as fundamentally ontic, 302–3
   and Greek ontology, 73, 262
   Greek "unpoetic" interpretation of, 298
   as ὁρισμός, 26
   as intentional, 79
   as λέγειν τι κατά τινος, 24, 26–28, 79, 262, 268, 298
   and logic, 73, 194–95, 200, 260–63, 268–69
   as (mis)interpretation of being, 73, 261–63, 295
   as mythic discourse, 233–34
   naming versus asserting, 297–98, 305, 338–39
   versus νοεῖν, 268–69
   as reflecting truth of beings, 331–32
   weakness of, 21, 27–28, 336–40
   written versus spoken, 21, 234–35, 263–64, 297 n. 2
λήθη, 231–46. *See also* untruth
   as belonging together with ἀλήθεια, 238–42, 253–54
   counter-essence to φύσις, 237
   distinct from ψεῦδος, 223
   as experienced by the Greeks, 231
   as forgetting, 245–46
   and μῦθος, 232–33, 237
Lichtung (clearing), 18 n. 18, 166, 168, 312–16, 314 n. 15, 335–36. *See also* Open, the

Marburg School, 12
Margolis, J., 105 n. 4, 160 n. 51, 171 n. 67

May, R., 285 n. 11
Megarians, 83, 89 n. 34, 91 n. 37
Merleau-Ponty, M., 308
metaphysics, 157–58, 188, 227, 233, 235, 245–46, 288, 294–95, 301–3, 309–11, 343. *See also* onto-theology
μεταξύ (the inbetween), 77, 204–6
Miteinandersein
    authentic versus inauthentic, 65–66
    and ethics, 68 n. 95
    as *Miteinandersprechendsein*, 65, 118, 267
    as sharing of the truth, 67
motion (κίνησις), 75–77, 90–91, 93 n. 39
    Plato's conception of, 27 n. 29, 174
    the soul as, 75, 76 n. 10, 77 n. 11
    and the thesis that knowledge is perception, 177
myth (in Plato), 19 n. 19, 72, 82, 88, 105–6, 181, 232–34, 237, 255. *See also* images, Plato's use of

Natorp, P., 12
Nietzsche, F., 34 n. 42, 68, 116 n. 7, 141–42, 146 n. 30, 147–48, 157, 235
non-being
    as εἶδος, 85 n. 23
    and false-belief, 175
    as "other," 97
νοῦς. *See also* Anschauung; en-visioning; seeing
    versus διανοεῖσθαι, 24–25
    impure in humans, 23–24
    possibility of, 340–41
    not "theoretical," 37 n. 49
    as transcending λόγος, 27
    two types of, 24–27

ontological difference, 72, 97–98, 294, 301–3. *See also* being
onto-theology, 144, 158, 160, 195
Open, the, 140, 168, 172, 251–53, 261, 276, 312–13. *See also* Lichtung
ὀρθότης, 111–12, 125–26, 155, 164, 188, 229–30. *See also* truth, as correctness

παιδεία, 110, 149–52, 169, 196
Paredes, Maria de Carmen, 147 n. 31
Parmenides, 51 n. 72, 54–55, 72, 77, 79–80, 237, 290–92, 304, 321, 322 n. 27
Partenie, C. and T. Rockmore, 5, 103 n. 2, 105 n. 4
participation (of particulars in the Platonic ideas). *See also* ideas, Platonic
    different characterizations of in Plato, 327
    as image, 335
    impossibility of defining, 27 n. 29, 334

    as "presence in," 71 n. 4, 311, 333 n. 34
Patt, W., 83 nn. 19–20, 85 n. 25, 90–91 n. 35
Peperzak, A. T., 33 n. 39, 85–86, 103 n. 1, 113 n. 5, 119 n. 8, 129 n. 15, 132 n. 18, 133 n. 19, 134 n. 20, 154 n. 35, 155 n. 36, 158 n. 45, 165 n. 62
phenomenology. *See also* categorical intuition; dialectic, and phenomenology; Husserl; seeing, priority of for Heidegger
    as descriptive, 15
    error of, 180, 210
    and givenness (immediacy), 16
    and hermeneutics, 282
    of the inapparent, 307–8
    lacking standpoints, 12, 26
    as objectifying, 18
    and the question of being, 306
    as science, 306 n. 7
    as "tautology," 290–91, 306–8
    and understanding, 14–15
    as *Wesenschau*, 16
philosophy. *See also* science, philosophy as
    as dialogue versus monologue, 66–68
    and ethics, 249
    and life, 15 n. 12
    versus mathematics, 58
    as φρόνησις, 243–45
    and politics, 249–50
    as purification, 53
    versus sophistry, 58–60
    versus thinking, 290–91
Plato
    Apology, 54 n. 77, 57
    Crito, 278
    Euthydemus, 327, 333 n. 34
    Gorgias, 60, 219
    Ion, 281–82
    Laches, 278, 323
    Laws, 311
    Meno, 205, 278
    Parmenides, 54–55, 82–83, 254 n. 10, 333–34
    Phaedo, 309, 311, 314 n. 15, 326–33, 341
    Phaedrus, 20–21, 68, 74, 77 n. 11, 82, 189–90, 234, 240–42, 278, 327, 342
    Philebus, 323
    Protagoras, 68, 278, 323
    Republic, 31–32, 49, 94 n. 40, 107–61, 205, 236–50, 278, 319, 323, 327, 329–30
    Seventh Letter, 21, 27–28, 63–64, 67, 133, 336–42
    Statesman, 53, 58–59
    Symposium, 9, 59, 75, 77, 117, 189, 196 n. 4, 203, 205, 208, 254, 327
    Theaetetus, 22, 31, 32 n. 37, 56, 61, 77 n. 11, 80, 91 n. 37, 103–5, 173–224
    Timaeus, 32, 327

Platonism, 2–3, 13, 34 n. 42, 105–6, 142, 157–58, 161, 235, 289, 311, 343
φρόνησις, 29, 35–47, 243–45, 249, 340
politics
    Heidegger's, 35 n. 44, 66, 103 n. 1, 250 n. 9
    as ontology, 247–48
    Socrates', 57
πόλις, 65, 103 n. 1
    as nothing "political," 247–48
πρᾶξις, 28–32, 35–36, 40–49
    ontologized, 45–46
presence, 18
    Greek conception of being as, 41 n. 58, 49, 69, 70, 87–93, 95, 99, 114, 189 n. 3, 200–202, 210, 211–12, 223, 231, 253, 261–62, 309, 320–22, 325
    Heideggerian conception of being as, 321
    metaphysics of, 2
ψεῦδος. *See also* false belief; falsehood; untruth
    between being and not-being, 205
    as "distortion," 204, 222
    as form of concealment that unconceals, 225–26
    as "the false," 226
    as incorrectness, 217
    as semblance, 219
ψυχή. *See* soul

questioning
    as more disclosive than answers, 198
    as inessential, 279
    philosophy as, 149, 174

recollection. *See* ἀνάμνησις
reminiscence. *See* ἀνάμνησις
Renaud, F., 289 n. 12
Riedel, M., 28 n. 30
Romans (on truth), 105, 138, 165, 168, 226–30, 248
Rorty, R., 42 n. 62
Rosen, S., 4, 19 n. 19, 28 n. 30, 62 n. 88, 88 n. 32, 271 n. 3
Ross, W. D., 44 n. 65

Sallis, J., 157 n. 40, 164 n. 57
Sayre, K., 54 n. 78
seeing. *See also* Anschauung; en-visioning; νοῦς
    as *Blicken*, 252, 280
    as curiosity, 17 n. 16
    as divining and presuming, 280
    as metaphor in Plato, 117–18, 192, 194, 313, priority of for the Greeks, 16 n. 16, 118, 252
    priority of for Heidegger, 18, 68, 267–68, 272, 280, 284, 288, 304–6, 313 n. 13
    as projection, 117

science (*Wissenschaft*)
    as authentic existence, 39
    as destiny of the German people, 41
    versus dialogue, 66
    as ὕβρις, 49
    philosophy as, 17–18, 29, 42 n. 60, 43, 47, 50, 50 n. 70, 61–62, 174, 181, 306 n. 7
    versus φρόνησις, 41
Shorey, P., 34
silence, as form of saying, 137, 231, 251, 264, 297. *See also* λόγος
Socrates, 54 n. 77
    as greatest thinker of the West, 297 n. 2
    as Plato's mouthpiece, 51–52
    as saying the same of the same, 297 n. 2
Socratic method. *See also* elenchus; dialectic; dialogue
    abandoned by Plato in the late dialogues, 61, 174, 209
    as indirect and reflexive, 51, 77, 80
    as maieutic, 61, 174
    as productive negation, 52–53
    and the τι ἐστι question, 60 n. 81, 61 n. 84
σοφία. *See also* θεωρία
    as being of *Dasein*, 38
    and φρόνησις, 29–32, 35, 38, 39 n. 50, 40–47
    whether human possibility, 48–49
    as movement of life, 40
    versus φιλοσοφία, 59
    as prerogative of the gods, 9
    relation to the eternal, 37–38, 48
    thinking as, 50 n. 71
soul (ψυχή), 175
    as being-capable, 90
    as desire, 77
    as form or structure, 183
    as "inbetween" (μεταξύ), 77
    as motion, 75
    as relational in itself, 186, 200
    as self-mover, 190
    as a striving, 192, 196, 200, 203, 207
striving. *See also* ἐπορέγεσθαι *and* ἔρως
    authentic versus inauthentic, 190–92
    as explanation of possibility of falsehood, 215–16, 219
    as type of seeing, 192–93
Szaif, J., 127 n. 13, 170–71, 171 n. 66

Taminiaux, J., 18–19, 45, 65 n. 91, 271 n. 3
tautological thinking, 290, 297. *See also* λόγος
    versus dialectic, 291, 304
    as phenomenology, 305–6
θεωρία (θεωρεῖν), 10–11, 14, 117. *See also* σοφία
    authentic form of life, 38–41, 43–44, 64
    as authentic πρᾶξις, 43

θεωρία (cont'd)
   and politics, 247 n. 8
   not theoretical, 37–38, 43 n. 64
   versus thinking, 50 n. 71
theory (the theoretical)
   Heidegger's critique of, 13, 14 n. 10, 15 n. 12, 36–37, 177–79
   and the practical, 28, 30, 43
thinking. *See also* dialectic
   versus belief (δόξα), 208
   versus dialectic, 270
   versus interpretation, 299
   as leap, 253–54, 269–72
   versus philosophy, 163, 166–67, 273
   versus poetry, 273–74, 298, 298 n. 3
   as reckoning versus *Sagen*, 271
time (temporality), 81
   and being, 200–202, 223, 293, 301, 321
   and the ἐξαίφνης, 253–54, 254 n. 10
   as time-space, 312–13
truth (ἀλήθεια). *See also* ἀλήθεια *and* ὁμοίωσις
   as *adaequatio*, 227–28
   Aristotle's conception of, 228–29
   as correctness, 111–12, 154–55, 163, 188, 194, 241–42, 245–46, 261–62, 318
   criterion of, 216, 219
   degrees of, 108
   no "doctrine" of in Plato, 170–71
   as "the genuine," 219
   Heideggerian versus Gadamerian conception of, 67
   as κοινωνία, 79
   as "light," 121–22, 124, 143, 197, 315
   Plato's philosophy as battle between two conceptions of, 101–2, 175
   propositional versus intuitional, 14, 16
   Roman conception of, 226–30
   as shared, 67
   and subject/object distinction, 136
   as unconcealment, 107–9, 125–26, 126 n. 13, 148, 194, 237, 295–96, 315–16
   and untruth/concealment (inseparable from), 110, 139, 169–70
   as yoke, 138, 153–54

unconcealment. *See* truth
untruth. *See also* false belief; falsehood; ψεῦδος
   as distortion (*Verkehrung*), 105, 204
   as essential for understanding nature of truth, 104, 139, 220–21, 238–39, 253–54
   as falsehood, 134
   as incorrectness, 188
   as semblance, 222

Van Buren, J., 40 n. 56, 41–42 n. 60
Volgel, L., 68 n. 96
Volpi, F., 42 n. 61, 45 n. 67

Wachterhauser, B. R., 67 n. 94, 289 n. 12
Web, D., 21–22 n. 23, 23 n. 26, 27 n. 29, 71 n. 3, 78 n. 13
Wieland, W., 70 n. 1, 83, 85 n. 23, 86 n. 28, 91 n. 36
Winken (hinting, pointing), 270, 278, 280, 298 n. 3
   versus signs or ciphers, 283
Wissenschaft. *See* science
Wolin, R., 250 n. 9
Wolz, Henry G., 4, 154 n. 34, 170 n. 65, 171 n. 68

www.ingramcontent.com/pod-product-compliance
Lightning Source LLC
Chambersburg PA
CBHW032127010526
44111CB00033B/151